PAPA BEAR

THE LIFE AND LEGACY

OF

GEORGE HALAS

JEFF DAVIS

McGraw·Hill

New York   Chicago   San Francisco   Lisbon   London   Madrid   Mexico City
Milan   New Delhi   San Juan   Seoul   Singapore   Sydney   Toronto

The *McGraw·Hill* Companies

Library of Congress Cataloging-in-Publication Data

Davis, Jeff, 1941–
 Papa Bear : the life and legacy of George Halas / by Jeff Davis.
  p. cm.
 Includes index.
 ISBN 0-07-142206-4
 1. Halas, George Stanley, 1895–1983. 2. Chicago Bears (Football team). 3. Sports
team owners—United States—Biography. I. Title.

 GV939.H26D38 2005
 338.4'7796'092—dc22   2004019990

2 3 4 5 6 7 8 9 0 FGR/FGR 3 2 1 0 9 8 7 6 5 4

ISBN 0-07-142206-4

McGraw-Hill books are available at special quantity discounts to use as premiums and sales
promotions, or for use in corporate training programs. For more information, please write to the
Director of Special Sales, Professional Publishing, McGraw-Hill, Two Penn Plaza, New York, NY
10121-2298. Or contact your local bookstore.

This book is printed on acid-free paper.

CONTENTS

5232

FOREWORD

Gale Sayers

George Halas and I enjoyed an almost father-son relationship. When I first met him in late 1964, I respected him, number one, because he was 69 years old. I earned more respect for him in Chicago's very cold autumns and winters of '65, '66, and '67. You had these 21-year-old kids saying, "Coach, I got a cold. I gotta go inside."

He was the first one on the field and the last one off. That's why I respected him. I would run through a wall for George Halas. That's the way I felt about his being out there at 69, 70, 71 years of age and those kids complaining, "I'm hurting." He was hurting every bit as much, if not more, from a hip so bad he would have to stop coaching and undergo one of the first hip replacements in medical history.

After my second year, I got a Corvette. We played Green Bay in Milwaukee in the preseason and won the ball game. I zoomed back home to Chicago. I must have passed George Halas on the way. He called me the next day. "Gale, my boy," he said (he always said "my boy"), "I think you should get rid of that Corvette." I did what he said.

It's little things like that. In '67 or '68, I was growing a moustache. "Gale," he said, "I know people are growing beards today. I don't think you look good in one." I cut it off. I think that built our relationship. I was talking to his secretary one day. "Gale, you know what?" she said. "George Halas gave you this little bonus for many different things, because of your skills and everything, but he really appreciates your cutting off your moustache."

Things like that, little bitty things like that, all drew us closer and closer. He was just a great man. He founded the National Football League and brought it through the Depression and everything else. Just a great man.

He always said, "Gale, you're a great athlete, but this is not a career; it's a stopping-off place. You play one year, two years. If you're lucky, you play five."

The average life of a football player is three and a half years today. "Gale, this is a short-term proposition," Halas said. "What you need to do is prepare to play, but you also need to prepare just as hard to quit."

When I was elected to the Hall of Fame in 1977, I asked Coach Halas if he would present me. "My boy, I'll be very happy to do it for you." That's exactly what he said. There were no hesitations whatsoever.

Then, in his presentation, he said, "Gale Sayers. His like will not be seen again." He had tears in his eyes, and he admitted it. I said, "I love George Halas."

When I talk about George Halas on speaking tours, I always say that. I thought that way about him. He made me a better person. He made a young man a better man just by talking to him, offering his advice. I always listened to him. I will always remember him. I appreciate him.

PREFACE

I cannot recall the first time I heard the name "George Halas." I do know that he was a familiar name in our household by 1948, when I saw my first Chicago Bears telecast at age seven on the family's brand-new 12-inch RCA. It was a heavy, tube-filled rectangular box and it emitted a high-pitched whistle when the off-on switch was activated, continuing to hum well after my dad, Charlie, or older brother, Bill, adjusted the horizontal and vertical buttons. I do know that the crosstown Cardinals won that game 24–21. I was hooked, not only on television, but on football.

Dad had a friend in Ralph Brizzolara, a fellow golfer at Glen Oak Country Club in Glen Ellyn, Illinois, where we lived. Not only was he an important industrialist, but he happened to be George Halas's best friend and secretary of the Chicago Bears. In 1950, Mr. Brizzolara convinced Dad to buy a half dozen season tickets for his business needs. So, Dad took me to my first Bears game at Wrigley Field in 1951 to see the long-gone New York Yanks.

When we entered the ballpark through the right-field gate by the "353" sign, it looked like an outsized theatrical backstage. Behind me, the ivy on the outfield wall was rusting into winter dormancy. Ahead lay the latticed iron framework of the huge bleachers that Mr. Brizzolara had designed, set up on the same grounds that were home to the Cubs in baseball season. We came to the front and started climbing. Up, up, and up we went, finally stopping at row 40. Dad's seats were on the 45 and the view was magnificent. As much as I loved the result, a 24–21 Bears' win, I could not take my eyes off of the man in the dark suit and fedora on the Bears sideline who paced like a Bear, tugging at his hat brim and growling through cupped hands at the men in striped shirts at calls he didn't like. He was owner-coach George Halas.

Halas looked the part, exuding the special quality that great men possess and normal mortals do not—charisma. Halas, of course, grew older but through the years retained that exuberance and magnetism on the sideline as he urged his massive monsters in navy blue helmets and jerseys, and white pants, to commit mayhem on their unfortunate opponents.

I met Halas in 1973. Johnny Morris, the superb pass catcher for the 1963 champions, who became a leading Chicago sportscaster, brought me to NBC from the ABC station that spring. When things slowed down, or after hours, Johnny regaled me with Halas tales: how he negotiated, how he coached, and how he swore. Halas had been a navyman in two world wars, but no sailor every possessed a saltier vocabulary. Not only did Johnny quote the coach verbatim, he did it in dialect! Those sessions left me holding my sides in laughter, but in absolute respect for the man. Someday, I vowed to myself, when the time is right, I'm going to write about George Halas—the real Halas.

I got to know Halas in subsequent years, interview him, and commiserate with him when his only son, George Jr., "Mugs," died unexpectedly in 1979. I watched with awe a year later as the defiant 85-ycar-old reassumed control of his club, assuring one and all as he did that "there's not a senile bone in this body." Halas set a course toward what became the team's ninth championship season in 1985, one he would not witness, when they won Super Bowl XX.

Thanks to the recollections of those who knew the man—players, associates, friends, writers—I have done my best to solve the puzzle of the remarkable George Halas, who over the summer of 1920 at age 25 organized what became the Chicago Bears and the National Football League. Moving ahead, never taking a backward step, he was the league's majordomo until he drew his last breath on October 31, 1983. This is the Papa Bear, warts and all, in words mostly fair, sometimes foul, the father of his sport—professional football.

ACKNOWLEDGMENTS

The dedicated work and efforts of many fine individuals have made *Papa Bear* possible. It began in late 2001 when a close friend, writer Peter Gent, told me that I needed to call a friend of his in New York who was a literary agent and could help me. When Pete Gent, who played basketball at Michigan State and football with the Dallas Cowboys the way he writes—smart, all out, and edgy—gives such advice, I act. Pronto.

Paul Bresnick, then at the Carlisle Group, became my literary agent, tutor, and guide in the art and craft of creating a proposal that he shopped to publishing houses. Paul diligently found the right publisher for *Papa Bear* at McGraw-Hill Trade and with it my "coach" in New York for nearly two years, a combination Halas-Lombardi-and-great-friend, Mark Weinstein. Mark's sharp eye for detail, dialogue, and story line and, most important, his encouragement, guided me through the end of the writing process. Julia Anderson Bauer and her editorial team in Chicago deftly and professionally handled the fine-tuning and production details up to the printing and binding process.

I thank each and every individual who agreed to talk on the record about George Halas, a man many feared in life but always held in utmost respect. His former players were exceptional, from the late George Connor, the first one I interviewed, to Doug Buffone, the last man who played for Papa Bear. I am grateful to all.

Chuck Mather, who joined Halas and the Bears in 1958, was a constant source of details, pictures, and valuable suggestions. Chuck has become a wonderful friend whose knowledge I treasure greatly.

Bill Jauss was my sounding board. He heard me read aloud every word I wrote and was a wonderful first filter on many subjects, as well as an outstanding interview. That also goes for Bill's wife, Kenmar—my pal Kenny, whose encouragement helped me through many long days at the keyboard.

Bill Gleason provided special help, a spur or two, incredible leads—especially when it came to Chicago's rich and colorful newspaper history—and scores of delightful stories about Halas, Charlie Bidwill, and the Bears' rivalry with the Cardinals.

Cooper Rollow was a wonderful help and is the leading journalist of his time concerning the relationship of Halas and Vince Lombardi.

The indefatigable Eddie Stone, by any account, not just mine, is the greatest football beat reporter that Chicago or any other city has ever seen. Period. Halas knew that truth.

Chet Coppock has been a friend for 35 years and a colleague for many of them. His personal recollections of the Old Man and memories of Wrigley Field, the tickets, and all fleshed out the outline and colored in the palette in rich detail. Chet is a pal, and I treasure our time together, as well as our almost daily phone calls to discuss the Bears and everything else under the sun.

Charles Brizzolara has been a superb friend from the start of the project. His warm encouragement and memories of his father, Ralph, and George Halas carried us through to the end.

I cannot thank Ann Kakasek enough for letting me use the ledgers of her father, Jim McMillen, concerning his financial dealings with Halas, which saved the franchise for Papa Bear in the Depression.

I thank longtime friend Patrick McCaskey, who, as always, was cheerful, pleasant, and good-humored in our amiable dealings. Pat provided most of the pictures from the team's files and other materials, which included his memoir of his grandfather.

No one can beat Jerry Vainisi. He simply is the greatest. If you need confirmation, start with Mike Ditka and hundreds of former Bears.

Last, and most important, I truly appreciate the loving and understanding support provided by my wife, Kris; our kids, Elisabeth Case and Erik; our son-in law, Dan; and our grandsons, Willy and Charlie. They are my inspiration.

KICKOFF

Halas Lives!

*O*n September 29, 2003, the Bears that George Halas conceived, built, and nurtured with loving adoration with every fiber of his being as long as he lived returned to a thoroughly redesigned and rebuilt space-age Soldier Field. The architects plopped it down inside the outer walls and now-shrunken-looking columns that delineated the landmark on Chicago's lakefront.

The Bears had left town in 2002 like Napoleon's Grand Army, conquering heroes and reborn Monsters of the Midway on a mission to pick up momentum from 2001's 13–3 playoff season and go for it all. They bivouacked in corn country at Memorial Stadium on the campus of Halas's alma mater, the University of Illinois in Champaign-Urbana.

Instead, the Bears, coached by Michael McCaskey's second choice, Dick Jauron, were as trapped in Champaign as Napoleon was in Moscow in 1812 when they endured beating after embarrassing beating. At one point, they endured a team-record 8-game losing streak within the framework of a 4–12 campaign. By season's end, they were glad to beat a retreat home to the City of Big Shoulders.

It was a downtrodden bunch, already soundly thumped twice, that came out for the grand opening on September 29, 2003. Unlike the proud, defiant, tough clubs that George Halas cast in his image, the team that his heirs, the McCaskeys, put on display was dull, drab, somewhat polite, and generally lousy.

The McCaskeys were able to accomplish one thing the Old Man never could pull off, though. They were able to make over their ugly, inadequate, amenity-less dump of a home since 1971, Soldier Field, into a 21st-century showplace. Indeed, the change was a Cinderella-like rags-to-riches one that transformed the place into as spectator-friendly a venue as existed in pro football.

If the Papa Bear somehow could return, he would emerge from the tunnel after leaving the plush dressing room to trod across a perfect field with its variety of splendid grasses and grin in delight. He would assume his familiar stance by the team's bench the way he did at Wrigley Field for decades, arms folded, or perhaps hands on hips. Then he would reach up with both hands, tug down his fedora, reset his glasses on his nose, look over the marvelous site, and then, through cupped hands against the din, tell anyone within earshot that he'd as soon trade the whole damn works for the one thing that mattered besides the money he was coining by the truckloads. A victory.

Victory to George Halas was elemental, the best thing in the world, better than a half hour or so of intimacy with a woman, better than getting stiff with the boys over a few drinks. "Look," he explained in 1977 to writer Frank Deford, "the others last a few minutes. To win a game in the National Football league. That lasts a whole week!" (A savoring pause.) "Whatta thrill!"

Then again, he was George Halas, the founder who built a mighty and dreaded professional football team that won more games than any other, whose name connoted passionate anger to the point of savage fear, the *Chicago Bears!* And he founded the National Football League itself in that same year, 1920, that he organized his team in Decatur, Illinois, under the sponsorship of the A. E. Staley Corn Products Company, makers of starch and other farm products.

Problem was, his McCaskey heirs did not understand—indeed, could not possibly comprehend—what their grandpa had done. They had no notion what he accomplished before they were born and was still attaining and achieving during their formative years. All they knew about him when they were 11 little kids crammed into a small suburban house was that he was their grandpa, Mommy's dad, and he never came home until midnight or so because he was busy owning and coaching the most important football team in the world. It was always that way as, one by one, they arrived at adulthood. After all, Grandpa's business wasn't theirs to own in the first place.

Their uncle Mugs was the crown prince, and nobody dared to question that fact. It was a way of life. Mommy had rights, of course, and Grandpa always saw to it that her McCaskey branch was honored. Halas gave his horse-playing son-in-law, Ed, the father of the brood, a job and a salary. He did not let him get his hands on hard-earned dividends he knew the man would piss away on the ponies. Ed and Virginia lived in their house in Arlington Heights for 30 years but did not install air-conditioning although they had the money. Ed, however, still wasted it at the racetrack, as Halas knew he would.

The kids of course had family duties, especially on autumn Sundays. They dressed up and went to the games, where they cheered until hoarse and felt elation only in victory, while they suffered defeats in shame. That was expected, understand it or not.

Grandpa and Grandma Minnie, when she was alive, Uncle Mugs, Aunt Terry, and cousins Christine and Steve came over for Thanksgiving and Christmas dinner. When they went their separate ways later in the evening, life returned to whatever normality could exist in a household where everyone tripped over each other in the tight confines.

Everything changed on a Sunday morning in December 1979. Uncle Mugs died unexpectedly at home, and their family, by that sheer matter of fate, was richer and more powerful than they could have imagined. If only on paper. But they were rich, and someday each of them—11 McCaskeys and Mugs Halas's son and daughter—would own the team. That would come years later. In 2003, Mommy, Virginia Halas McCaskey, still owned the team and, as the daughter of George Halas himself, intended to keep it that way and in the family.

The massive construction project had begun with demolition of the old stands on the night of January 19, 2002, literally within minutes of the Bears' 33–19 playoff loss to the Philadelphia Eagles. The remodeling project came in on time but ran $49 million over the budgeted $606 million.

Of that $655 million, $406 million came from the taxpayers of Illinois. The state floated bonds buttressed by Chicago and state hotel taxes already in use for the White Sox. The new playground with all the bells, whistles, and creature comforts for its witnesses and participants was only the latest in a series of publicly funded playpens built across America for the glorification of professional sport. For the new Soldier Field, the Bears anted up $100 million of their own money, mostly from expensive personal-seat license fees. Another $100 million was manna from heaven in a no-brainer of a 15-year loan from the National Football League, forgiven on issuance, that was good as long as the owning McCaskey family controlled the franchise.

Good news to the McCaskeys. Bad news to fans who had clamored for years for them to sell. The McCaskeys never understood that the $100 franchise fee their grandfather would have paid back in Canton at the charter meeting at the Hupmobile dealership, had anyone there had such cash in pocket, was the start-up for a colossal industry. He nurtured that industry through its infancy and carried it on his back through the Depression, World War II, and two interleague wars afterward to make it bigger than baseball. The price of success and victory was paid through unending work and impossible hours at the office. All they had to do was wait for him to die.

Of course, all bets on the family's selling the team were long shots at best. Yet, should investors be willing and able to assume and pay off the NFL's $100 million note for the privilege of gaining the league's premier charter franchise, who could say what might transpire? That moment, for certain, would not come as long as Virginia lived. The franchise's owner and daughter of the Papa Bear had long made known her intentions to cling tight to her father's legacy as estate trustee for her 11 children and the son and daughter of her late brother, George Jr., known as Mugs.

The prospects remain fascinating to contemplate. Should the team fetch, say $900 million, the children, as owners of 80 percent of the franchise, would stand to collect in the neighborhood of $50–55 million each. For doing exactly nothing but cashing in on their grandfather's legacy. To Virginia and the little McCaskeys, there was a Santa Claus, and his name was Grandpa, as in Papa Bear, as in George Stanley Halas.

As of 2003, many of the kids, none now under the age of 40, said they preferred to hold on to the club. Of course, they would say that in full awareness that their mother was quite alive and in robust health. For public purposes, they had to maintain that stance. Someday, as happens to almost every family business, money would talk. For the foreseeable future, though, frustrated Bears fans could anticipate the worst, more losing seasons. That "worst" had been the norm for Bears followers under age 30 as long as they could remember.

On the weekend of the reopening, the McCaskeys and the alumni who came in for the grand opening clearly recalled the last franchise glory years, the 1980s when Mike Ditka prowled the sidelines and dominated every television newscast with his pungent honesty. Many of those men present played under Ditka. Many of the older ones were his teammates in Coach Halas's last championship season, 1963. A scattered few, namely Ed Sprinkle and George Blanda, played for Halas when he still took out a note each off-season at American National Bank to keep the team afloat until season ticket orders came in. Sprinkle and Blanda were around during the birth of television. Black-and-white TV.

The oldest alum on hand was 89-year-old Chuck Mather, the last living Halas assistant. Mather was still active in his insurance brokerage, playing golf regularly, and relaxing with a noon-hour Canadian Club bracer or two before lunch. Living Hall of Famers who played for Halas—Blanda, Dick Butkus, Stan Jones, and Gale Sayers—attended the gala dinner, fellowship, and game. They were joined at the game by Dan Hampton, the newest Hall of Fame inductee, who spoke to the Soldier Field crowd at halftime. Ditka, who had returned to the fold as commentator during preseason games but remained at arm's length in many other ways, gave a videotaped greeting to the fans on the stadium message board, but he did not attend the functions. He was the most conspicuous absentee other than his close friend, Halas's last general manager, Jerry Vainisi. Vainisi, who was not an invited guest, did use his season tickets on game night.

Mike Singletary flew in from Baltimore, where he had begun his long-deferred coaching career working with Ravens linebackers, to join his fellow Bears alumni on the field. Had the McCaskeys let Singletary near a microphone, it is conceivable the crowd would have yelled for him to come home, run the team, and restore the glory. As embarrassing as that would have been to the incumbent coach, Jauron, it would have been doubly so to the McCaskeys, who had abided losing for so many years.

The McCaskeys saw what happened when Ditka's taped image appeared on the two huge stadium telescreens. As soon as he said, "Welcome back," the crowd erupted in a roar, prompted by memories of the player most in Halas's image and the young man he'd designated his coaching heir at the end of his remarkable life. When they saw the image of Halas himself up on those huge screens in 60-year-old black-and-white footage, a buzz ran through the crowd.

The Bears' opponents for this opener, an "ABC Monday Night" telecast, were their ancient rivals and Halas's favorite opponent since he and Earl "Curly" Lambeau agreed to meet in 1921, the Green Bay Packers. While the Soldier Field project was carried out in the brassiness of Chicago, the Packers had executed a less ostentatious but equally stunning renovation of Lambeau Field, a $295 million job in its own right, to bring capacity to 72,000 and turn the place into a year-round Wisconsin museum worthy of Canton or Cooperstown.

Lest anyone wonder who built their place, the Packers commissioned a pair of 14-foot-tall statues of their founder, Curly Lambeau, who led them to six titles in his 29-year reign from 1921 to 1949, and the even greater Vince Lombardi. His five titles in 7 years in the '60s are the standard of excellence in the sport.

The two men were Halas's greatest rivals in his 40 years of coaching. Both men paid him the respect he was due as the founder and champion of the league, as well as champion of their little hometown when everyone else wanted the league to abandon it. Green Bay's fans and broadcasters reflect the way they feel about Lambeau and Lombardi. The two will never be ignored, nor forgotten, there.

When it came to Halas's family, that full-hearted warmth that Wisconsinites exuded over Lambeau and Lombardi would not hold true in Chicago for George Halas. There was some talk about a statue that may or may not be fashioned in the future. Its makeup, let alone when it would be displayed or where it would be situated, was another matter. As appropriate as a statue would be, the McCaskeys had operated with the hollow sincerity of a young man giving his best girl the corsage the day after the prom.

Moreover, in all the pregame festivities that weekend, not once, not at the alumni dinner, not in Soldier Field, did the McCaskeys, from Virginia on down, grant public mention to the name of their patron, George Halas. Unlike Canton, Ohio, where the address of the Pro Football Hall of Fame is 2121 George Halas Drive NW, in honor of the league founder, his McCaskey family in Chicago, who knew how he felt about their own father, pointedly cut him out of the program.

Instead, they honored Ed, their father, who died on April 8, 2003, with a video at the dinner and a pregame moment of silence. On the back of their helmets, the Bears wore an orange shamrock decal with the initials *EWM* stenciled in blue inside the cloverleaves. The staunchly Catholic McCaskeys inadvertently created a decal that represents the Northern Irish Protestant "Orangemen" who have warred with the "Green Irish" Catholics for generations. That gaffe just might have made Halas laugh. Halas, after all, did give Ed a job in the organization, but only after the passing of the one person he never crossed: Virginia's mother, his wife, Min.

While the McCaskeys made it clear by their lack of action how they felt about George Halas, perhaps it takes a rival warrior to fully appreciate the greatness of such a man. "I loved him. I really did. He cussed me out. I really admired him," said Paul Hornung, the unquestioned symbol of Packers dominance in the era of Halas's great coaching rival, Vince Lombardi.

As much as Hornung loved Lombardi, his champion and mentor, he was wise enough to acknowledge the master. "Halas is the greatest name in the history of this game. He's number one on top. No question. He is the father of professional football."

George Halas may have owned a football team and started its league, but the thing he loved the most was coaching that team, driving men to more victories, 324, than anyone else in his lifetime, a feat Don Shula would finally match and surpass a decade after the Papa Bear's death.

Those who covered him through the years knew that the only thing that mattered was his Bears and how they fared in that day's battle whatever the weather. Many of his greatest triumphs had come in near-impossible conditions—driving rain, snow, and bitter, numbing cold. "Halas didn't alibi, but he was much better when they lost," recalled sportswriter Bill Jauss, at 72 an irrepressible veteran of three Chicago newspapers—the thriving *Tribune* and two gone but never forgotten afternoon treasures, the incisive *Daily News* and Hecht and MacArthur's raucous model for *The Front Page*, the *American*. Jauss sat in on many a postgame session in the old Wrigley Field pressroom, the Pink Poodle, where Halas held forth.

"He would go into explanations about how this play didn't work and why," Jauss said on a still autumn morning 36 years after Halas last prowled the sidelines. Ironically, this was a "George Halas weather" day itself—clear sky, sunlight dancing lightly off the early autumn leaves—in a near-empty park in Wilmette 10 miles north of the Bears' old Wrigley Field stomping grounds. The occasional squeaky wheel of a commuter train punctuated the sylvan serenity as it lurched out of the nearby elevated station beginning its journey toward Wrigley Field and ultimately the Loop.

"It was like a sermon," Jauss recalled. "Nobody said anything. Tom Fitzpatrick, the Pulitzer Prize winner who recently passed, used to say, 'When the bird sings, shut up. Let him sing.' We'd shut up and listen to Halas. He was very informative in the Pink Poodle." Jauss spoke in the voice of a man who had heard the music thousands of times in hundreds of locker rooms and still loved that melody as much as the accompanying lyrics of sport.

Bill Gleason, a South Sider who favored the archenemy Cardinals and bedeviled Halas from his press box perch with the *American* until

Halas ran the Big Red out of town in 1959, was another reporter who relished time in the Pink Poodle combat zone when Halas held court. "Charlie Chamberlain, the Associated Press sports writer, would have enough and pipe up, 'George, why don't you quit this bullshit?' 'Fuck you, Chamberlain,' Halas would scream back. And they'd curse each other for a little while." Gleason still chuckles at the memory of that colorful, contentious cacophony.

No reporter riled Halas as much as Ed Stone, Gleason's colleague at the *American*, who, like Gleason, had the gall to cover the team like a reporter, not a cheerleader. "Halas ran a silent conspiracy," Stone recalled. "When it came to the operation of the team, its maneuvers and personnel, he did everything in secrecy." As long as Halas lived, he and Stone had an abrasive relationship. In 1963, Halas pulled strings to have him removed from the Bears' beat, a banishment that lasted until the 1967 season.

Jauss, Gleason, Stone, and all the others who covered the Old Man through the years knew full well that George Halas was not called the Papa Bear because he was lovable and cuddly. He was the original grizzly, a flesh-and-blood *Ursus horribilis*: surly, snarly, sinister, and smart. Sentiment, to George Halas, was for softies. And George Halas was a hard man, a true godfather who saw fit to run his team, his league, and his family in his own image.

Telling other men what to do and where to go was something George Halas did as well as any commander who ever led forces into combat. So identified with Chicago and the Bears was Halas that people tended to forget who he really was, if indeed they knew at all. That man standing alone on the sidelines drawing all eyes to his being like a Patton or Bradley was the single individual responsible for making pro football America's secular religion.

What Halas did and the way he did it changed everything from the way American families worship to the way they observe holidays. He worked night and day year after year to make football, his game, America's national pastime. He lived to see it happen. He was smart enough to let others take credit for much of the work he did.

Had there been no George Halas, there would be no National Football League. Because there was a Halas, because he ran the league brilliantly for a half century, and because everyone in the council of power listened to him, Halas's NFL became the richest and most powerful sports organization on Earth.

Chicagoans awoke on Sunday, October 30, 1983, to a perfect day for football. Bears football. More sunny than cloudy, this day a slight nip hung in the dampish light wind that wafted lazily off Lake Michigan toward the old Soldier Field, where the Bears would play the Detroit Lions at noon. Longtime fans had a name for it: George Halas weather. As far as the public presumed, the Old Man, now 88 and expected to live forever, would watch on television and take copious notes to hash over that night with his coaching protégé, Mike Ditka.

The 64th edition of Chicago Bears football was young, mistake-prone, and struggling with just two wins in its first six games. The losses in this, his second season after coming home, were nearly driving Ditka crazy. Two of those defeats were especially bitter, and the pot bubbled over a month earlier in Baltimore, after the Bears lost their second straight sudden-death game, this, 22–19, to the inferior Colts. Ditka took out his postgame frustrations on an unyielding steel locker and broke his right hand.

Reporters who'd recoiled at the sight and sound of Iron Mike's display had been certain the young coach would face the wrath of Halas when he got home. But, in his news conference the next day, Ditka flashed a newfound humor that would serve him well in the years ahead, when he referred to himself as "Lefty."

Ditka, the ferocious steelworker's son from Aliquippa, Pennsylvania, outside Pittsburgh, had been a winner all his life from high school, through an all-American career at Pitt, and during a dozen slam-bang seasons as pro football's first tight end.

Ditka burst into stardom upon his 1961 arrival. He was Rookie of the Year and ran off a string of four consecutive All-Pro years to earn a spot in the Halas pantheon of Hall of Famers with such men as Red Grange, Bronko Nagurski, Sid Luckman, George McAfee, Bill George, George Connor, Doug Atkins, Dick Butkus, and Gale Sayers.

Ditka was certain he had blown it all in 1966 when he mouthed off in public, accusing Halas of nursing nickels like manhole covers.

That remark forced Halas's hand, and he exiled the player most in his image, the ultimate Bear, to Philadelphia. Ditka finally gained redemption a stop later in Dallas with the Cowboys. He never really fit there, though. Even Tom Landry called him a Bear.

Finally, when the Bears job opened up after the 1981 season, Ditka wrote to Halas and, to the surprise of the sporting press who were sure Halas had lapsed into senility, got hired. "There were times when he went out of his way to really aggravate the shit out of you," Ditka said two decades later. "He knew he was doing it, but you know what, that was his way of doing things, and who am I to say it was wrong? It's like you'd ask him, 'Coach, why do we practice on Sunday?' He'd look you right in the eye and say, 'You know why we practice on Sunday?' 'No.' 'Because we practice on Sunday.' That's exactly what the hell he'd say. That's the way it was. I loved that man."

Through 1982, George Halas seemed to be indestructible, the highest-profile active octogenarian business leader in America, the unquestioned lord and master of his Chicago Bears. Halas lived by a motto that he had framed and kept in his office: "Never go to bed a loser." Many were convinced, and not just facetiously, that he had entered into a pact with the devil to live forever.

For years, Halas followed a strict regimen. He rose from bed by 6:30 A.M. for a half hour of exercises. After a shower, he fixed a breakfast of grapefruit, bran flakes, a banana to gain the benefits of potassium, coffee, and a pastry. At 8:30, Max Swiatek would pick him up for the 20-minute drive to the office in the CNA Building on the eastern edge of the Loop. At the office by 9:00 A.M., he went over the financial statements with controller Jerry Vainisi and checked the latest market quotes, the only reading matter that truly interested him. At noon, he broke for lunch at his desk, consisting of soup and crackers or a fruit plate and a leafy salad.

After lunch, the Papa Bear closed his office door and took a mid-afternoon nap before he finished his work. Promptly at 6:00, Swiatek told Vainisi the boss was ready, and they joined him for glasses of liebfraumilch and reminiscences. Halas and Swiatek left the office precisely at 6:50 P.M. to arrive 10 minutes later at the Tavern Club at 333 North Michigan a mile away, where Halas met for dinner with his inner circle, men such as federal judge Abe Marovitz; his nephew, Illinois state senator Bill Marovitz; Hall of Famers Sid Luckman and George Connor; businessman Mike Notaro; or Kup, *Sun-Times* columnist Irv Kupcinet. He dined on veal, chicken, or fish along with salad. "It cleans out the pipes," the league founder said. In season, he watched "Monday Night Football" and took notes before finishing the day with another set of exercises and then hitting bed around 11:00. Halas kept a notepad and pencil handy at the bedstead in case he woke up and had an idea he needed to transcribe.

The Papa Bear enjoyed excellent health until the spring of 1982. The only time he'd ever missed work was in 1968 when he flew to England after his retirement for the then-revolutionary hip replacement operation. He needed to repair a 49-year-old injury he incurred in a slide during a spring training game in his brief baseball career with the New York Yankees.

In the spring of 1982, Halas no longer felt quite right. He had lost that quality he called "the old zipperoo." He saw a doctor, who ordered an operation. They opened him up and told him he had pancreatic cancer. Death could come within weeks, or he might last for months, even years.

On January 26, 1983, news crossed the wires in late morning that Paul "Bear" Bryant, the winningest coach in college football history, died in Birmingham, Alabama. Bryant's 323rd victory came in his last game, the Liberty Bowl—ironically, against Illinois, Halas's alma mater. That left him 1 win short of Halas.

At the NBC station, WMAQ-TV, sportscaster Chet Coppock and his producer dispatched weekend man Mark Giangreco and a news crew to the Bears' Loop offices for Halas's reaction. No one in football was more qualified to make that evaluation. And no one took more pride in his own accomplishments. Halas kept them waiting in the corridor all afternoon.

Shortly before 5:00, Giangreco heard a noise in the back hall and saw Swiatek open the rear door to the boss's sanctum. The cameraman turned on his light and raced with Giangreco toward the elevator to head off Halas before he escaped. Trapped, Halas stopped and reluctantly spoke. "Let's go," he growled as the cameraman hastily focused his lens.

"What can you say about the passing of Bear Bryant?" Giangreco asked.

"His record. He had a great record. That's it," Halas snapped as the elevator door closed shut. It was the final public utterance George Halas would ever make.

A few days after his benediction for Coach Bryant, Halas took his annual vacation trip to the Biltmore in Phoenix. When he returned home in late March, he checked into a hospital in absolute secrecy. The doctors told him that nothing had changed. For the first time, he realized this was one opponent he might not beat. He went home, to return in July for abdominal surgery. The doctors took a look and realized there was nothing more to do for the patient than wait for the inevitable. "Take me home," the Old Man ordered his daughter, who quietly spirited him away to the Edgewater Beach Apartments at the top of Lake Shore Drive, where he kept in touch with the office.

Virginia and his secretary, Ruth Hughes, came each day at the end to keep him company as his life ebbed away. His trusted young and energetic operational team, general manager Jerry Vainisi and coach Mike Ditka, visited frequently. In late October, the weakened Old Man presented his boy, Ditka, with a bottle of Dom Perignon accompanied by a note: "Don't open until we win the Super Bowl." Ditka took the champagne home and stowed it away in a safe but accessible place.

The Halas inner circle veiled the truth of his illness in a shroud of secrecy worthy of the Manhattan Project. Vainisi was keeper of the flame. He said, "I knew probably for a year and a half before he died that he had pancreatic cancer. He had been sick, certainly for at least a year."

Just 42 in 1983, Vainisi had been with Halas since 1972 when he took a pay cut from an accounting job at Arthur Andersen for the opportunity to join the Bears as controller and house counsel. Vainisi, a Chicago native, was no stranger to the NFL. His older brother Jack had run the Green Bay Packers for Vince Lombardi until he died unexpectedly in 1960 from a heart attack at age 33. Jerry became Halas's trusted everyman and protégé. Halas appreciated his business sense so much that he stripped son-in-law Ed McCaskey of the title of treasurer, a position he held in name if not in duties, and awarded it to Vainisi, who had done all the financial work anyway along with his other duties as office administrator, team counsel, and personal attorney for the coach and his family.

Late in the summer of 1983, Halas promoted Vainisi to executive vice president and general manager, replacing Jim Finks. "He would call me to his apartment at least weekly," Vainisi said. "I would bring checks for him to sign, not only because he wanted to sign all the checks; he had to sign them."

Halas's absence was noted for the first time in late summer when several television stations ran 20-year retrospectives on the 1963 champions, '63 being the year of the Bears' last title. He had not been available for interviews, which he never would refuse when healthy. Not when it came to his beloved Bears.

The NBC sports team realized something out of the ordinary was at work. Like most reporters, Coppock and his producer both knew Halas professionally. They also knew the way the franchise conducted its Byzantine operations. But no other print or broadcast reporter had Coppock's personal knowledge of Halas away from football.

Charles Coppock, Chet's father, was a volunteer on the chain gang in the 1929 season when he met Halas. They struck up a friendship, and through the years, Charlie Coppock became the Bears' largest single season ticket holder, with 176 seats. The elder Coppock and his wife, Dotty, hosted frequent gatherings for drinks, dinner, card games, and strong fellowship with the likes of the Papa Bear, Red Grange, WGN announcer Jack Brickhouse, George Connor, and Halas's longtime assistant Luke Johnsos. Conversation more often than not focused on the Bears and pro football. The senior Coppock and Johnsos were so close that they formed a partnership in a packaging business.

Chet was just 12 years old when Halas dropped by the Coppocks' home in suburban Northfield one off-season afternoon in 1960. He never forgot the words between his dad and the coach. "I've waited all these years to make some real money, and now it's here, Charlie.

We've finally caught baseball, and we're going to leave it in the dust. Mark my words," the Papa Bear said. "Everything's in place."

Charlie Coppock died in 1975, leaving the ticket rights to Chet, who still would control 34 seats into the 21st century. A year earlier, in 1974, Chet was hired as public-address announcer for Bears home games at Soldier Field the same week he got his first significant break, a sportscasting job in Indianapolis.

Coppock continued to make the back-and-forth trip to Chicago to work the PA at Bears games, missing only once when a blizzard closed Interstate 65, which links Indianapolis to the Windy City. When he moved back to Chicago to join NBC in 1981, Coppock dropped the PA job, but he held on to those precious tickets.

"Chet, I just know something's wrong with the Old Man," the NBC producer said one late-summer afternoon before the start of the '83 season. "I ran into Rudy Custer [Halas's longtime business manager] at lunchtime the other day when Doug Atkins was in town to tape our '63 retrospective. When I asked Rudy about Halas, he danced around it. Think about it. When was the last time you saw the Coach or his car in Lake Forest, or anywhere else?"

A few seconds passed. "You're absolutely right," Coppock said. He agreed to run his sources and reported back a few days later: "My sources won't say exactly what's wrong, but they strongly suggest we get something ready. Soon."

Newspapers routinely prepare ready-to-run obituaries on major figures, especially presidents, famed entertainers, and other notables. After they got caught short and had to scramble when President Kennedy was assassinated in 1963, the large television news operations did the same thing.

The producer put together a two-part Halas obituary, and Chet added his personal reminiscence concerning a man he'd known all his life. It was finished just before Labor Day. Just in case.

Now, on this day in the aforementioned "George Halas weather," genuine anger was in the air as the two hated and hateful rivals warmed up. Upstairs in the Soldier Field press box before the game, everyone was talking about Don Pierson's advancer in the Sunday *Chicago Tribune*. A four-column headline, "Bears-Lions: A series of broken bones," provided blunt testimony to the carnage that lay ahead. Coach Ditka had fired the latest broadside in the contentious rivalry two weeks before when he ordered special-teamer Dave Duerson to chase after Lions kicker Eddie Murray on a kickoff with 1:18 left and the Lions holding a safe 31–17 lead.

"Lay the bastard out," Ditka demanded in the manner of his mentor. Duerson, of course, obeyed orders. Murray later complained that the Bears were notorious for such tactics.

George Halas would have loved it, noted one of the veteran reporters. "He would have laughed out loud," the scribe said, and others nodded in agreement. Going after quarterbacks, getting even, "unintentionally" laying someone out, all that was part of the game, the way the winningest coach in history taught it. Especially so in big games.

Nobody got into chasing Lions more than the legendary Dick Butkus. In one season finale in the early '70s, Butkus called three time-outs in the final seconds when the Bears were hopelessly beaten just so he could deliver that many more forearm shivers to the jaw of his avowed enemy, Detroit center Ed Flanagan.

The single game that still roils aging former Detroit players and their partisans was the regular-season windup at Wrigley Field on December 16, 1956. The Western Division title was on the line. The Lions, who had routed the Bears 42-to-10 two weeks before to take the division lead, held a half-game lead at 9–2 over the 8–2–1 Bears. Chicago fans screamed for Lions blood, and uniformed cops from both cities guarded the player benches. Halas, who'd turned over coaching duties the previous winter to longtime assistant Paddy Driscoll, still called the shots from the press box.

In the second quarter, Detroit was leading 7–3 and driving for another score deep in Bears country. Bobby Layne, the great Lions quarterback who had haunted Halas since he'd reluctantly traded him seven years before in a money-saving move, flipped a pitchout to his left to halfback Gene Gedman and dropped his hands to his sides to watch the play. Onrushing Bears defensive left end Ed "Country" Meadows blindsided Layne and coldcocked him to the ground.

Two Lions helped the addled Layne from the field to the bench, where he sat with a concussion. The Bears swarmed over Layne's lesser replacement, Harry Gilmer, and took a 10-to-7 lead moments later on a Rick Casares 68-yard sweep. They pulled away to win 38-to-21 as the game ended in an all-sides brawl.

After the game, an irate Lions owner Edward Anderson and coach Buddy Parker both called Meadows a hatchet man. Then, as they cited a direct violation of the NFL protocol that Halas himself had enacted decades earlier, Anderson and Parker claimed Meadows carried out a Halas order to get Layne. Still unloading, Anderson complained that Halas and his ally, Washington Redskins owner George Preston Marshall, ran the league. Anderson said he would file an official protest against both Meadows and Halas.

At his table in the Pink Poodle that gray afternoon, Halas nursed a postgame whiskey and fired back. Calling Anderson and Parker ridiculous, he sharpened his focus and fangs on the Lions' owner. "They gave us a physical beating two weeks ago up in Detroit. Bill McColl took 17 stitches on his face," Halas said as he took a sip. He was just warming up. "Did you see a penalty flag against Meadows? Hell no. It was a clean, hard hit."

By now, the reporters would have been led to believe that the Lions somehow had knocked Layne out of the game, instead of Meadows and the Bears. "Anderson's a damn liar," Halas exclaimed.

End of story, especially when Halas's pal Bert Bell, the commissioner, came out the next day and not only quashed the protest but also rapped both Anderson and Parker for criticizing the Founder.

Halas, Ditka knew, would have savored Pierson's article and laughed out loud. Halas firmly believed that bad blood between teams was the best way to bring out the fans and sell a sport he knew was nothing more than controlled warfare in a confined madhouse.

Halas was 26 in 1921 and Warren Harding the president when the team won its first championship. Lyndon Johnson had been president for barely a month after young Jack Kennedy was assassinated in 1963 when the 68-year-old Halas led the Bears to their eighth title more than a decade after he had been written off as an anachronistic old grouch. Halas topped off that title-winning parlay when the pro football writers named him Coach of the Year, an honor he won again in 1965 at age 70. So much for being stuck in the past.

Because he was a bear of a man, cunning, and elusive, George Halas had survived 63 years in the professional football forest, out-hitting and outsmarting the other guy. Halas knew all about football spies. He was first to do it. Late in Halas's tenure, he conducted a secret practice at Wrigley Field. Ray Sons, then of the late *Chicago Daily News*, wrote about it. The next day, Halas took Sons aside. "Ray," he said, "Wrigley Field is our home. What you did when you printed that story was walk in our house and shit on the living room carpet." "Yes," Sons would say years later, "he was foul-mouthed, but he was a holy man."

Halas may have been a holy man at times, but on the football field, the Old Man was a holy terror. Long-retired players recall his epi-thets almost by rote, especially when an official blew a call. Through cupped hands in a voice able to cut through the loudest crowd like a wound-up jet engine before takeoff, Halas would scream, "You missed that one, you fucking cunt! You stink!" One day, after a sim-ilar Halas outburst, another official dropped his flag and promptly marched off 15 yards. "How do I smell from here?" the man in the striped shirt replied.

He never mellowed either. In his retirement news conference on May 27, 1968, Halas said he had to quit because his hip was so painful that he no longer could chase after the officials and tell them what he thought of their calls.

Ask any former player whose ears and nape still turn red at the thought of being on the receiving end of a Halas diatribe, either one-on-one in his office or huddled with sweating teammates at halftime after a bad first half. "That was fuckin' horseshit, you cocksuckers!" Only, when Halas spoke those words in his native West Side–Bohemian dialect, they were filtered through the loose-fitting plate that replaced the original teeth someone knocked out in the leather-helmet era when face masks were something people wore in the Span-ish flu epidemic of 1918. That same phrase always came out "Dat was fuckin' HOARSE-shit, you CACK-suckers!"

The laughter always comes in the retelling. No one dared chuckle in his presence when harangued. It was much more than paychecks that he held over his players' heads, fighting them for every cent in often-demeaning negotiations. It was the grip a great coach who's been through it all so many times seizes and asserts over the collective psyche of an athletic unit. It is the utter surety of purpose a man like that exudes that holds large men captive. In an aura of fear mixed with reverence, it's the absolute conviction that the great man's presence will assure success.

No old Bears or their fans were laughing this October day in Soldier Field. The Lions intercepted two Vince Evans passes in the first quarter, marched to the end zone twice to take a 14-to-0 lead, and never looked back. The Bears committed a dozen penalties and at least twice as many more mistakes from fumbles to missed assignments. Late in the game, Ditka benched Evans for second-year quarterback Jim McMahon while fewer than 10,000 fans, most of them liquored up to the boiling point, stuck around to the final gun. Many in that mob gathered by the tunnel at the northwest corner of the field leading to the locker room to boo their heroes as they filed out. Others tossed paper cups—some empty, others filled with beer. As Ditka left amid an escort of off-duty cops, someone fired a beer. One of the bodyguards deflected it, but Ditka caught a splash or two of suds on his face that ran onto his sweater.

The locker room could provide refuge from all that, and the hot showers could wash off the blood, sweat, and beer, but nothing could cleanse the smell of utter defeat. This was abject despair, the frustration of suffering at the nadir of the long decline of the once proudest franchise in sport now at bottom, helpless as a warship run aground in a nasty sea.

Fortunately for all concerned on the Chicago side, George Halas would never know what happened that awful afternoon. He was lying in a coma in his bed at home in the Edgewater Beach Apartments on the Far North Side. The end was a matter of hours, perhaps a day, away. His loyal former star and confidant Sid Luckman, secretary Ruth Hughes, close friend Mike Notaro, the physician, and his only surviving child, his daughter and designated heir Virginia Halas

McCaskey, maintained the vigil as the breathing turned heavy and labored. The ring of secrecy held fast.

He had been dying since summer, but unlike with Lombardi, or Babe Ruth decades before, there would be no death watches, no banner headlines, no anticipatory stories, no reporter stand-ups beside television trucks with upraised dishes clogging the street outside his apartment building, no crowds gathering. George Halas did not conduct business that way. Never. Especially now. A gentle rain began to fall in Chicago late Sunday night.

By 7:00 the next night, October 31, Halloween, most trick-or-treaters in metropolitan Chicago had returned to their homes toting bags filled with candy. A chill was in the air. The balmy days of Indian summer were history. Winter seemed imminent.

Jim Dooley, whom Papa Bear anointed as his successor in 1968, had barely arrived at home when the phone rang. "Come out and be with the coach," said Ruth Hughes at the other end.

Dooley reached the Edgewater Beach Apartments shortly before 8:00. He entered unit 1802 to meet his friend and patron, Halas's unquestioned favorite player and a man he held in the near-equal esteem as his late son, Sid Luckman. Luckman had boosted Dooley all along, from when he was a player and top draft choice in 1952 out of Miami, to his work as an assistant and as the Papa Bear's coaching successor.

"I went in to see Halas," Dooley said. "He was having a hard time breathing and didn't know who I was at the time. 'It's Dooley,' I said before I gave him a kiss on the forehead. 'Hold tough, Coach. We love you.' Virginia was the only other one in there at that moment. As I went back to the elevator with Ruth, she said, 'I think he'll make it until tomorrow. He wants to die on All Saints' Day.'"

Within minutes of Dooley's departure, Dr. Neal Stone emerged from the master bedroom, noted the time, 8:27 P.M., with a nurse, and began to pack his bag. Inside, pro football's patriarch lay dead. One by one, the inner-circle members went to Virginia, who sat by his side holding his now lifeless hand as she did to his last breath moments before, to extend their sincere condolences.

Luckman left first and placed a prearranged phone call to the sports office at the NBC television studios downtown. It was the first call out of the Halas residence following the coach's death, ahead of the one to the funeral home. The producer answered and heard, "This is Sid Luckman."

He motioned to Coppock to pick up the extension at another desk. "Coach Halas, er, the coach, the coach passed away in his sleep a few minutes ago," Luckman continued. "It was totally peaceful. He's gone. You are the first to know."

The next order of business was to get the word out ahead of Howard Cosell and "Monday Night Football." "Can you join us here at the station, Sid?" Chet asked in hasty necessity. "We'd be honored if you could talk about Coach Halas on the 10 o'clock newscast." Luckman answered, "Absolutely."

The television newsroom and everything else in the station kicked into gear as WMAQ-NBC broke into the network with a bulletin to tell the rest of the world that the founder of the Bears and the National Football League had died peacefully at home.

Back at the Halas co-op, Virginia remained alone with her father's body, praying as she clutched the gnarled hand that had squeezed thousands of others in the confident, viselike handshake that always said, "My word is my bond." Patiently, and with Halas-like determination, she managed to entwine a rosary among his stiffening fingers. When it was done, she rose and left his side as the new owner of the Chicago Bears.

News of George Halas's passing led every newscast in his hometown that night and bumped the usual network shows on all stations to a later start. The story and his picture appeared on the front page of both downtown papers, *Tribune* and *Sun-Times*. Both dailies ran extensive special Halas sections leading up to the Thursday funeral.

It should have been page one in every city that had an NFL franchise and in most others that did not, but too many younger out-of-town editors missed the import of the man's passing. Even America's newspaper of record, the *New York Times*, tucked it deep inside. Under the appropriate headline "George Halas, Football Pioneer, Dies," the *Times* ran a boilerplate Joseph Durso obituary well inside the paper in the B section. Durso observed that Halas made millions not only in football but also in real estate, oil, and sporting goods, "even to the breeding of Shetland ponies."

The two younger men Halas chose to run the team in a race to beat life's final gun, coach Mike Ditka and general manager Jerry Vainisi, deeply felt the loss. Both men knew they must carry his legacy through what likely would be a difficult transition.

"I always felt that I had become the surrogate son, that in his mind, I had replaced Mugs," Vainisi said. "He always made me feel that way. That's the relationship we had."

"I happened to get a second chance, as a coach," Ditka said of the man who ignored his critics and went with his heart in 1982. "Even though it was for a couple of years, that was the biggest disappointment to me—that he wasn't alive to see what happened in '85."

Mindful of the man's common touch and express desires, the immediate family listed his passing, wake, and funeral service arrangements in the agate-type obituaries with those of the others who died that day. When he died in 1970, Halas's steadfast friend and coaching foe, Vince Lombardi, was accorded a solemn high requiem mass at New York's St. Patrick's Cathedral, a virtual state funeral celebrated by Terrence Cardinal Cooke.

Halas had ordered Virginia to make it simple and keep it in the Far North Side neighborhood where he had lived in two places since the Depression. They held the wake the night of All Souls' Day, November 2, at the Birren and Son funeral home on North Clark, a mile away from his apartment. People came from everywhere to pay their respects: former players, businessmen, neighbors, and ordinary Joes and Janes from the immediate neighborhood, downtown, and the suburbs. Many never knew him personally, just by familiarity and the sense he was one of them.

Others came from afar, none more eloquent in his recollections than Hall of Famer George "One Play" McAfee, Halas's great star from his dynasty of the '40s, who flew to Chicago from his home in Durham, North Carolina. "I felt I had to come," McAfee told *Sun-Times* columnist Ray Sons. "George was such a good friend from the time he signed me. He was a tough guy. He stood for no nonsense. But he was fair. He just wanted to win so badly."

McAfee's feelings mirrored those of one of Halas's first Hall of Fame players, Harold "Red" Grange. In an interview the previous June at his Florida home, the Galloping Ghost, no longer traveling, offered a singular description of the quality that best defined Halas. "Guts," Grange said. "There wasn't a man on a football field he was afraid of, and that's what made him such a good coach. George was like God to me. He was one of the best friends I had in life."

Another Halas favorite was Hall of Famer George Connor. Connor was first to learn that the figurative locks were already being changed at Halas Hall, when he walked over to a stoic Virginia after he had paid his respects at the Papa Bear's bier. "Virginia," he told her, "he was a hell of a guy and a good friend of ours." "Yes, he was," Virginia said as she grabbed Connor's arm. She added, "Now, listen, when this is all over, I want to get together with you. He's got a lot of bummers on his list for the Bear Alumni Party. I want to straighten it out."

Connor walked out of that funeral home having seen the Halas in the usually reserved daughter. "She is tough," he told himself. He lit a cigar out on the sidewalk and walked to his car.

Later that evening, National Football League commissioner Pete Rozelle and his wife, Carrie, led the NFL delegation to the funeral home. The group included owners from every team and Gene Upshaw, head of the NFL Players' Association, which Halas had opposed for so many years in its early existence. In 1962, his Bears were the last team to join. Five years later, the NFLPA elected Halas's offensive cocaptain, Mike Pyle, president.

People were still coming to the funeral home by twos and threes or alone. Two veteran newsmen walked outside after paying their respects to the shrunken figure lying serenely in his coffin. "That cancer really ravaged him," one said to the other.

"Yeah. Hey, did you catch that little smile? It's like he knew the ultimate secret."

"God probably told him he'd be the first person in history to take it with him."

"The secret?"

"No, the money, of course." The two men laughed, got in their car, and drove back downtown to work on the late newscast.

The funeral service was held the following morning at St. Ita's, the small parish church a half mile down Clark from the funeral home. A crew of Andy Frain ushers, the security service Halas had employed for decades, handled an overflow audience that overwhelmed the 1,200-seat capacity of the church.

Rozelle led the NFL mourners. The Steelers' Art Rooney, Halas's close friend and fellow participant in a no-longer-allowed lend-lease arrangement that amounted to a major-league finishing school, came in from Pittsburgh. Wellington Mara, the surviving son of Giants founder Tim Mara, came from New York. Lamar Hunt, owner of the Kansas City Chiefs, flew in from his Dallas home. Hunt and Halas forged the NFL-AFL merger in 1966. Max Winter, who owed the existence of his Vikings to Halas, flew in from the Twin Cities. Browns owner Art Modell, who followed the Halas model in negotiating the league's huge television contracts, came from Cleveland. Al Davis, of the Raiders, the only owner to compare in secretiveness and cunning to Halas and, like Halas, a savvy former coach, flew in from the West Coast.

Ditka postponed practice until late afternoon so the team could attend as a unit. Several former players from the Chicago area also attended, most prominent among them, Luckman, Connor, and Sayers.

Six of Virginia and Ed McCaskey's sons, led by Michael, the eldest, served as pallbearers. Michael was a management consultant in Boston and professor at the Harvard Business School. Each man wore the Bears colors: navy blue suit, crisp white dress shirt, orange and blue striped necktie, navy blue stockings, and black oxfords.

Reverend Charles Banet, president of St. Joseph's College in Rensselaer, Indiana, where the Bears trained from 1944 through 1974 and to which the coach donated funds to build a dormitory, Halas Hall, delivered the eulogy. In a direct remark to Virginia, Father Banet said, "He achieved a certain and enviable kind of immortality. He is the founder of the most exciting, in my opinion, national pastime, professional football."

Halas had acquired an image of stinginess and miserliness and, as many said, delighted in it. For certain, he was a tough negotiator. But, as Father Banet said, when it came to people in financial trouble, "he so generously and anonymously aided them in their times of need."

At that remark, a knowing titter broke out in scattered sections of the packed church, especially where most of the reporters were seated. They knew how furious the Old Man would have been when Father Banet or anyone else so foolishly revealed that flinty, old George Halas actually had a soft heart.

Here was a man who helped many a former player or his wife in need, picked up the funeral costs for a young Loyola University assistant basketball coach who left a wife and children, and took care of Brian Piccolo's considerable medical bills during his fatal illness. All without anyone else's hearing about it. One player who appreciated that generosity was Ralph Kurek, a special-teams captain from 1965 through 1970 before he began a 31-year advertising career at DDB Needham, where he managed the Anheuser-Busch account.

"When I went in my second year to negotiate my contract, we were arguing over $500," Kurek recalled. "I wanted a $2,000 raise; he offered me $1,500. So, we agreed on the $250 difference. I was buying a house, and I needed a down payment. I was hoping to get a lead on a bank, some interim financing where I could get a good rate. He asked all the qualifying questions: location, neighborhood, bedrooms, et cetera. 'How much do you need?'

" 'I need $7,000, Coach.'

"He called in [his secretary] Jean Doyle and said, 'Jean, cut a check for $7,000.' I was thinking, 'I just arm-wrestled this guy for $500 and we split the difference.'

" 'Wait a minute, Coach. All I want to do is find out what bank I should go to.'

" 'Don't worry about it, kid.'

" 'What kind of interest will I have to pay?'

" 'Don't worry about it, kid; it won't cost you a cent. You're a good kid. I'll take it out of your salary the next two years.' I thought to myself, 'What a guy!' "

An 85-car procession escorted the Papa Bear's hearse to St. Adalbert's cemetery, in Niles, a half hour away. He was interred in the family mausoleum there. "When I was following Halas's casket to the mausoleum, I was reminded how Halas always suspected the Packers of spying on him," Ray Sons recalled at the Ring Lardner Dinner in late 2002. "He held practice before the team could get into Wrigley Field at a field next to this cemetery, St. Adalbert's. He always feared the spies were running through the tombstones, checking on his practices. He 'knew' it was so when they lined up to stop several special plays he had put in for the game. That was my thought of him heading to a final resting place by what had been that practice field. It made me smile."

The succession was not immediately set. Vainisi took charge, ordering the equipment managers to sew black mourning bands on the left sleeves of the team jerseys. He also had them sew orange footballs over the heart, bearing the initials *GSH* in blue.

The players wore the GSH football patches that Sunday against the Los Angeles Rams in a half-filled Anaheim Stadium. Mistakes, especially in the final two minutes of each half, and the 134 rushing yards of superb Rams rookie Eric Dickerson buried the Bears 21-to-14. Ditka, who had more-than-ample reason to flash his famous temper, instead saw hope in the play of his team, especially permanent quarterback starter Jim McMahon and the electric Walter Payton. In a postgame comment reminiscent of Coach Halas after a close-but-no-cigar 23–14 loss at Green Bay in 1965 when Gale Sayers, making his first start, displayed his obvious greatness, Ditka said, "If we continue to play hard, good things will happen."

After that defeat, the Bears finished strong. They won five of their last six games—among them, victories over San Francisco, Minnesota, and Green Bay—to finish with an 8-and-8 record. It was their first .500 team since the 1979 playoff season. Few realized at the time, especially the cynics who'd seen so much abject defeat, that the charter franchise was about to rise from hibernation with a mighty roar.

Virginia stunned team insiders a few days later when she announced that Michael, her oldest child, would succeed his grandfather to become the third president in team history. In 1984, at Vainisi's urging, Michael ordered the initials *GSH* woven in white into the orange stripes on the navy blue left jersey sleeve, home and road, in permanent tribute to the founder.

For road games, McCaskey brought back navy blue pants with orange and white stripes down the sides. They were to be worn with white stockings trimmed in blue with orange stripes and the white-based road jersey. The last time the Bears had appeared in that uniform was December 8, 1940, the day they won the title at Washington by the most famous score in football history, 73–0.

Michael enjoyed a triumphal homecoming that had seemed almost impossible as recently as the previous summer. Sources say the McCaskeys and Jim Finks had made two runs at Halas on Michael's behalf. The first came in February 1983 when Ed, Virginia, and Finks, who was still general manager, went to Halas and asked him to let Michael join the club as assistant general manager to learn the ropes.

The McCaskeys wanted to fulfill Mugs's promise to Finks that he would succeed Halas as president on his death to run the club for a year afterward in transition. Then Michael would be elevated to president. Halas, who thought his grandson lacked the toughness to run the club, rebuffed them. As unfair as it may have been to Michael, in many ways the eldest grandson paid the price for his grandfather's enmity toward the senior McCaskey.

In August, according to the sources, Virginia, Ed, and Finks made another run at the Old Man, this time at his apartment. Again, he rebuffed them.

The Papa Bear knew he had a dilemma. As a Bohemian, he felt he had to pass on the family business to his children regardless of his feelings about their capabilities, or lack of same. Thus, he admitted to Virginia, the president of the club must be a family member, not an outsider.

When it came to the actual management of the club, Halas told Virginia, "I already have my men in place to run the team." They were his nonfamily operational duo, Jerry Vainisi and Mike Ditka.

The sources do say that before he lapsed into a coma, among his final utterances were three words. "Anybody but Michael."

FIRST QUARTER

1895-1932

ONE

LEARNING
THE ROPES

$\mathcal{J}$eannie Morris met Halas in 1959 as the young wife of Bears star receiver Johnny Morris. She later covered him as a newspaper columnist and television reporter, felt his wrath when she ran stories he didn't like, and was on the receiving end of his subsequent attempts to make nice. "You can draw a lot of conclusions by what he accomplished and the sort of bodies he left on the road," she said, "but you can't really know him. He came up in a hardscrabble way. Like a lot of people who did that, his possessions, including his football players, were important for him to control and to husband: his money, his resources, his family. He was someone who needed to control all that and did effectively."

Many other critics have tried to capsulize Halas. They always come up short. One, the late Bill Furlong, described Halas as having "all the warmth of breaking bones."

Says Mike Pyle, offensive cocaptain with Mike Ditka on the Papa Bear's last title team, "George Halas was an ambitious, and very shrewd, individual. Crude and shrewd." Pyle disputes the comparison between the Father of Professional Football and the Father of his Country: "Shrewd people can't do it all truthfully, can they? Halas was shrewd."

By his own admission, Halas never read literature, much less Shakespeare, but Shakespearean scholar Harold Bloom's characterization of Henry V as "shrewdly brutal as he was brutally shrewd" fits the Old Man to a T.

Money was the driving force from the beginning. There wasn't much to begin with when George Stanley Halas was born in Chicago on February 2, 1895, Groundhog Day. He was the eighth and last child of Bohemian immigrants Frank J. Halas and Barbara Poledna Halas, and the fourth to survive. He learned the ropes from his older brothers, Frank Jr. and Walter.

By the time he was 24 in 1919, he surpassed both boys in every way, including athletically and, certainly, in business acumen. Because he was Bohemian and they were family, he always took care of them. He made "Uncle Frank," as the players fondly called him, the Bears' traveling secretary and gave Walter a scouting job even though his reports, especially in later years, were judged by other coaches to be pedestrian at best. Neither man interfered in George's operation of the Bears, let alone had any voice in policy or strategy.

The Halases lived in Pilsen, named for their home area in that sector of Bohemia, now part of the Czech Republic. Now the heart of Chicago's burgeoning Mexican American community, Pilsen is situated in the middle of the Lower West Side, nearly three miles southwest of the Loop, and stretches to the western city limits. Although the Bohemians left decades ago, Pilsen still looks much the same as it did at the turn of the 20th century when George Halas was a boy. The institutions that anchored the community, its many Catholic churches and the large Peter Cooper Elementary School which Halas attended, remain in generally good repair. However, the brewery that provided income for the Halas family and other tavern owners is gone, as is the family home at 18th Place and Wood Street.

When George was born, Chicago still radiated in the afterglow of the wildly successful World's Columbian Exposition of 1893. It was the fastest-growing city in the country, with more than a million residents, second only to New York. By 1900, Chicago's population would surpass 1,700,000, with plenty of room to keep growing.

A typical newcomer in 1895 was Lars Rockne, a Lutheran from Voss, Norway. Rockne came over in 1893 to display his handcrafted coaches at the fair and decided to settle in the Scandinavian community in Logan Square, a neighborhood on the Northwest Side, with his wife and six children. The Rocknes' son Knute, born in 1888, was destined for a different type of coaching business, after he majored in chemistry and played end for a small Catholic school in northern Indiana, Notre Dame.

Years later, Fighting Irish coach Knute Rockne would hire Walter Halas as an assistant coach and, before that, in the war year of 1918, would play George and his Great Lakes teammates to a tie in their only face-to-face meeting on a football field.

Frank and Barbara Halas constructed a family based on hard work and thrift, on business over warmth and affection, qualities their youngest son carried through life. Frank was a tailor, and Barbara made buttonholes for him. "Halas buttonholes," the author writes in *Halas by Halas*, "taught me that a person must pay attention to the smallest details and joy comes with any task well done."

Early on, Frank Sr. suffered a stroke and subsequently sold the tailor shop and moved the family two blocks away to a place he had built on the west side of Wood Street facing 18th Place, where George was born. The senior Halas opened a grocery on the ground floor and rented out rooms upstairs as he socked away as much as possible. All his sons helped with the many chores that had to be performed. George Halas knew what it meant to shovel coal, stoke furnaces, sweep out buildings, shovel snow.

Life was harsh, but Frank and Barbara imparted strong, clear values and expectations to their children for a lifetime. Loyalty. Church. Education. Work. Thrift. Loyalty was a paramount element—loyalty to family, to friends, to community, to the workplace—and it would be repaid in kind.

Regular worship was essential. The family attended mass at nearby St. Vita's Church at 18th Place and Paulina and, on special occasions, would cross 18th Street to the larger St. Adalbert's. George Halas regularly attended mass all his life, whether at St. Ita's near the Edgewater Beach Apartments or, on Saturday nights, at Old St. Mary's around the corner from the Bears' last downtown offices at 55 East Jackson.

Barbara stressed to her children that the key to advancement in this new land was to become American in every way, especially language. Thus she sent all her children to the public school across the street from St. Vita, Peter Cooper School, for a secular education. George started first grade at Peter Cooper in 1901. By no means a "goody-goody," George nevertheless took an immediate liking to math and to school itself, boasting at age 84 in his memoir that he never missed a day of school in his life, except in college when he was traveling with an athletic team. As much as he liked math, Halas admitted that he never liked literature. Not as a boy. Certainly never as a man. To the end, he preferred numbers, the sort found in a ledger, or the stock market quotes in the financial section of the newspaper.

Young George Halas worked after school, as did his older brothers and sister, Lil, helping their mother in the grocery before it was converted to a saloon. "Father paid me 50 cents a week, but made it clear that most of it should be put into a savings account for university," Halas wrote.

George had a newspaper route, rising each morning at 5:30 to fold the papers and make the deliveries on foot. "I became frugal," Halas proudly wrote. "By being careful with money, I have been able to accomplish things I consider important." Life in that environment hardened Halas. "I think people like that do not tend to share themselves as human beings," Jeannie Morris said.

He needed an outlet, and he found it in the games boys play, athletic competition. He became a Cubs fan by age 10, spending as many summer afternoons as possible at the Cubs' home field, West Side Park. In that first decade of the 20th century, the Cubs were baseball's premier team, and thanks to New York writer Franklin P. Adams (F.P.A.), an ex-Chicagoan turned Giants fan, the Cubs' double-play combination, Tinker to Evers to Chance, became the most publicized trio in American sport with this poem published in the *New York Daily Mail* in 1908:

These are the saddest of possible words—
Tinker to Evers to Chance.
Trio of Bear Cubs, fleeter than birds—
Tinker to Evers to Chance.
Ruthlessly pricking our gonfalon bubble,
Making a Giant hit into a double,
Words that are weighty with nothing but trouble:
"Tinker to Evers to Chance."

Lacking spending cash, Halas knew that to see his heroes in action, he had to use his wits to get inside the ballpark. His parents wouldn't help. Neither would his brothers. So, George found a classmate named John Dubek who loved baseball almost as much as he, and he began to develop the guile and street smarts he would employ the rest of his life.

To reach West Side Park, at Wood and Polk, the boys had to walk a mile and a half—no casual, laugh-filled lark. Trouble lurked virtually every step of the way, most prominently in the persona of "the notorious 14th Street Gang," who blocked unfettered passage.

When he met the "14th Streeters," Halas was not about to retreat in shame. So, he devised his first of hundreds of game plans. "I would take a sock at the nearest punk and both of us would run," wrote Halas. "I believe that's how I developed the speed that, later, was to be helpful in all sports." Those encounters with the "punks" and the ethnic slurs that kids flung at each other—"Bohunk," "Polack," "Mick," "Wop," "Sheeny"—also served to hone the language he would employ on athletic fields and sidelines during his career.

Once they had sworn, slugged, and sped through the danger zone at 14th Street, the boys dashed the final six blocks to the pass gate and turned on the charm like the waifs they were. "Mr. Chance," young George would coo, "I hope you win today. I wish I could see the game." Or, he might say, "I hope you hit a homer today, Mr. Chance."

When Chance was too busy for them, the boys would peer through a knothole in the outfield fence to see the action. On better days, the Peerless Leader, as Chance was called, would heed George's heartfelt appeal. "Come along, kids," Chance would say as he led them through the pass gate.

The lessons George Halas learned in those early years of the 20th century often came the hard way. One Sunday afternoon after a family feast of Bohemian duck with all the trimmings, which George recalled as "marvelous, crisp, and succulent," he decided to take the big step into adulthood: he would try smoking. He grabbed some tissue paper from the bathroom, reached into the garbage can in back and pulled out some corn silk, rolled a "cigarette," lit it, took a few drags, and soon wished he was dead. "Up came the duck. Up came the apple stuffing, the potato dumplings, the sauerkraut. I was finished with cigarettes forever."

A few weeks later, he tried a chaw of tobacco, with similar dire results after he swallowed the juice. Years later, he forbade smoking in the locker room, let alone in his presence.

The kid also tried his hand at shooting craps in the back alley. Young George and his buddies rolled for pennies, with a 10 cent limit. When his father caught George gambling a fourth time, he hustled the boy inside. After an emphatic lecture on the evils of dice, Mr. Halas "reinforced those words with a switch. He drove home every blow effectively." Halas never forgot that paternal lesson.

In 1909, weighing all of 110 pounds, the 14-year-old Halas enrolled at Crane Tech, at Jackson Boulevard and Oakley, two and a half miles west and north of home. "Crane Tech was one of the four technical high schools in the city at the time," said Chicago attorney Charles Brizzolara. Charles's father, Ralph, a second-semester enrollee at Crane, grew up near Oak Park on West Jackson Boulevard. "My father was a half year behind George. They both got an engineering education there."

The school offered courses in carpentry and foundry work, but Halas, who would study engineering in college, prepared for his future by augmenting the technical curriculum with courses in mathematics, physics, English, and history.

With two active older brothers, George took an intense interest in sports. The wiry boy went out for football, track, and indoor baseball, actually softball played in arenas. He had to succeed, for to quit would have invited the wrath of his brothers.

George had just finished football season in his sophomore year when Frank Sr. died unexpectedly on Christmas Eve, 1910. Under terms of his will, Halas wrote, "if Mother remarried, the estate would have been divided among the children." Barbara Halas took over as head of the family, took charge of the finances, and used the money to further her sons' educations. She did not remarry.

Mrs. Halas also gave George his first practical lesson in negotiation. When the city wanted to create a park in 1911 for the community, her properties stood in the heart of the development. They came to her, and Mrs. Halas held out for a good price. The eight-acre park was named for five-term mayor Carter Harrison Sr., who was assassinated on the last day of the Columbian Exposition.

With her money from the city, Mrs. Halas bought a three-story, half-block-long building at 23rd Place and Washtenaw, just west of Pilsen. In this neighborhood, Bohemians were part of a mix that included Poles, Irish, and, by nearby Douglas Park, a large Jewish community. This was the first time Halas had lived with other nationalities.

Mrs. Halas rented out six apartments, designated one for Frank and his young wife, Mamie, and retained another for herself, Walter, and George. She also rented out ground-floor space for a corner saloon. She now attended mass at St. Markus Church, conveniently located one block west at California and 23rd Street. Most important, Halas recalls, "Mother raised my salary, dramatically, to 75 cents a week. She admonished me to save for college."

Late in the indoor-baseball season of 1910–11, George was pitching for Crane Tech against West Side rival Harrison when a shrill girl's voice kept yelling, "Ham and Eggs! Ham and Eggs! Ham can't catch and Eggs can't pitch."

"Ham" was George's battery mate, catcher Jack Hamm. So, George, of course, was "Eggs." The shrill voice belonged to Harrison student Wilhelmina Bushing, who lived at Western near 22nd Street, just out of the Pilsen neighborhood.

"I had to admit she was pretty," wrote Halas of that initial moment of infatuation. He made it his business to get acquainted with the "spirited" girl he always called Min. They saw each other at ice cream socials and the like. Min and George had many obstacles to clear, background and family in the forefront, as she was a German Lutheran and he, of course, the Bohemian Catholic. Love, and ultimately marriage, was far away in the future.

George was finishing his senior year at Crane in 1913 when Frank Jr. took him down a peg. Frank told him he was not ready for college, that he needed to work a year and put on more weight so he could play college football. Barbara concurred, saying, "You will work for a year, then go to Illinois."

Frank told George that night that he had the speed to excel and, with more meat on his frame, would succeed. That pep talk was the reassurance George needed. He was hired at Western Electric's massive Hawthorne Works in nearby Cicero, which made all the telephones and equipment for the Bell system.

"Most everybody worked at Western Electric, just about everybody on the West Side," Charles Brizzolara said. "Everybody" included Charles's father as well as Minnie Bushing. "I made it a point to pass by Min's desk frequently and pause for a few words," Halas wrote in *Halas by Halas*, his quaintly modest prose invoking an enduring memory.

Putting his Crane Tech math skills to work, Halas was designated a timekeeper in the payroll department. "I learned to keep meticulous records," Halas wrote. For the rest of his life, Halas would stay close to the countinghouse.

With 15,000 employees working in a hundred buildings, the Hawthorne Works was a small city unto itself, the utmost in corporate paternalism. Hawthorne had its own power plant, hospital, laundry, greenhouse, brass band, annual beauty pageant, and, to Halas's delight, company baseball team.

The energetic Halas spent every spare moment on one ball field or another playing for Western Electric's team and a semipro unit in Logan Park on Chicago's Northwest Side. By September, he was eager to trade in his baseball flannels and spikes for pads, cleats, jersey, and moleskins in the orange and blue colors of the University of Illinois.

In the waning days of that 1914 summer, as the nations of Europe, including his ancestral homeland of Bohemia, stumbled toward the bloodiest and most brutal war yet waged, 19-year-old George Halas arrived at the Illinois Central's Champaign station filled with optimism, bearing a well-packed suitcase and, thanks to his mother, a decent amount of money, $30.

He registered for classes in civil engineering and went through fraternity rush, where, under Walter's sponsorship, he pledged TEKE, Tau Kappa Epsilon. He then reported to freshman football coach Ralph Jones.

The "beefed-up," 140-pound Halas, by his own admission, did not impress Jones at his high school position, tackle, "but he did put me at relief halfback." For Halas, the position of "relief halfback" was a face-saving way of saying he was a benchwarmer for a freshman team that earned its Class of '19 numerals in heavy scrimmages against a Fighting Illini varsity that won the mythical national championship for head coach Bob Zuppke, two years removed from Oak Park High, due west of Chicago.

Zuppke, "the Dutchman," was a coaching hero for Halas to emulate in the manner of his business model, Alexander Graham Bell. To young Halas, Robert C. Zuppke was the master, "a tremendous coach. He was a careful teacher. He knew how to get the best out of young men. He was an innovator." Zuppke's base offense was the model that Halas, Jones, and Clark Shaughnessy would refine and modernize two decades later: the T formation.

Halas so respected freshman coach Jones that he and his partner, Ed "Dutch" Sternaman, would hire him in the Depression to coach the Bears while they fought for control of the club. In fact, Halas so loved everything about Illinois and the meaning of its fight song, "Illinois Loyalty," that he adopted the school colors of orange and blue for the Bears, darkening the blue to the navy hue to honor his military service.

George played freshman basketball that winter. In the spring, he joined the freshman baseball team. The switch-hitting outfielder impressed athletic director and varsity baseball coach George Huff, who invited him to join the varsity the next year.

George returned to his summer job at Western Electric, where he rejoined his pals Ralph Brizzolara and Charlie Pechous and starred for the company ball team. Minnie Bushing, though, was away much of the summer, touring Europe with a Swedish choral group. The highlight for Min and her group was a performance for the king of Sweden. Love was not yet in the air. With Min gone, Halas played the field, rationalizing that with her, there was nothing "exclusive, nor promising, about our relationship."

While Minnie was away, George had a date with fate that he happily was able to break. For several days, he, Ralph Brizzolara, and hundreds of their fellow Western Electric workers had eagerly anticipated the annual midsummer company outing and picnic at the Indiana Dunes, across Lake Michigan, and they had tickets in hand. "The company teams scheduled a doubleheader," Halas wrote in his memoir.

Ralph Brizzolara and his brother arrived ahead of George and Charlie at the dock on the south bank of the Chicago River by the Clark Street bridge to board the lake steamer *Eastland*. When it came time to shove off, neither of Ralph's friends had arrived. "Father did not see them pierside," Charles Brizzolara recalled. So, they boarded ship, fortunately too late to climb to the topside observation deck, which was teeming with most of the 2,572 Western Electric employees and family members aboard.

As the *Eastland* cast off, happy passengers waved to friends and passersby on shore, but within moments, the top-heavy ship listed, righted itself, and, as the joyous laughter turned to panicked screams, heeled over slowly onto her side to settle on the muddy river bottom as 844 persons died in the worst inland marine disaster in American history. The Brizzolara brothers were among the fortunate ones who got off in time. "My father was pulled through a porthole," said Charles Brizzolara. But, where was Halas?

A grateful Papa Bear gives lifesaving credit to brother Frank, who, he wrote, grabbed him near the front door as he was leaving to catch a streetcar for the Loop and said, "Come on, Kid, I'll weigh you."

Hallas continues, "I never won an argument with Frank, so off came the clothes. I stepped on the scale. I couldn't believe its report— 163!" Then Frank sent George off. " 'Hit a homer,' he shouted as I ran out the door," Halas recalls with pleasure.

Charles Brizzolara, who grew up listening to his father's version, offers another take. "George just overslept."

Whichever version is true, the best friends, Ralph and George, survived. Halas did arrive at the Chicago River in time to see the *Eastland* on its side, a sight he called "appalling." He did not know until Monday morning if Ralph was safe. When Ralph reported to work at Western Electric, he related the details of his harrowing escape.

Halas also was unaware that one of Chicago's seven newspapers had included his name on the list of the dead and missing *Eastland* passengers, confirmation in print that he had a ticket for the ill-fated ship. Then, after dinner that Monday night, the front doorbell rang at 23rd Place and Washtenaw. The callers were two TEKEs from Illinois named Elmer Stumpf and Walter Straub, who had come by to console Mrs. Halas for her loss. "I'll never forget the looks on their faces when I opened the door," Halas told George Vass decades later. When the relieved boys left, Mrs. Halas told George to say a rosary, which he happily did.

That September, Halas, now 6' even and 170 pounds, reported for fall practice and tried out for halfback. He played with unquestioned desire but was no match for larger players who threw him around at will until Coach Zuppke said, "Get the kid out of there before he gets killed."

Zuppke moved Halas to right end, where he remained. Although a scrub that season, he impressed everyone on the staff with his desire and innate tackling ability, a quality that set him apart from most of his teammates. Late that fall, during a scrimmage, when a varsity player intercepted a pass, Halas chased him for 60 yards. "I dived for him and brought him down on the three," he said. "His heel came up, breaking my jaw." After the season, an appreciative Zuppke told him he would start as a junior in 1916.

That spring, Halas hit .350 and played all three outfield positions as the Illini won the conference baseball title. As for football, Zuppke named Halas the starter at right end, but he never played a down. In an early-fall practice scrimmage, he was hurt again. This time it was a leg injury, and both the trainer and player believed it was nothing more than a muscle bruise. When Halas came out for practice the next day, limping, Coach Zuppke yelled at him: "Halas! Stop loafing! Get in there and hit!"

"I blew up," Halas wrote. "My temper is always near the surface," a trait hundreds of former Bears vividly recall decades after wincing at that distinctive voice and its cutting invective. Then, Halas recalled, he removed his helmet and threw it at Zuppke, complaining that he had an injured leg.

"Leave the field!" Zuppke snapped. The Illini trainer sent Halas to the campus infirmary, where an x-ray revealed the leg was broken. Within five days, in a cast and on crutches, Halas got what turned out to be the break of his life. After classes, he watched practices from the sidelines and observed Zuppke at work. Zuppke, who admired the injured player's spunk, put him in charge of the supply room, a job that paid Halas $300 for the rest of the semester. Flashing his business sense, Halas hired another student to run the supply room, paid him $150, pocketed the rest, and, with ample free time, worked on his engineering courses.

In late October in that 1916 season, Zup told Halas he would travel with the team to play undefeated Minnesota. Edwin Pope writes in *Football's Greatest Coaches* that Ring Lardner predicted in his *Chicago Tribune* column that the Gophers, fresh off a 67–0 rout of Iowa, would beat Illinois by 49 points.

Zuppke scrimmaged his team five times that week. When they arrived in Minneapolis, Zuppke surprised everyone with a Friday-night feast. On Saturday morning, the coach warned the team that Minnesota opened every game with the same three backs running the same three plays in order. "Tackle them in that order," he commanded before they took the field for the pregame warm-up.

"Then by prearranged signal, as Minnesota trotted on the field past the Illini," Pope writes, "halfback Dutch Sternaman called loudly to Zuppke, 'They're not so big!' "

" 'No!' Zuppke roared back in direct earshot of the Gophers. 'And the whole bunch together couldn't add two and two.' "

Taking it all in as he stood on the sidelines on crutches was Zuppke's injured end, George Halas, who reported, "I knew how well

Zup prepared a team for a game like that one, but to see it all unfold the way he planned it . . . well, you almost couldn't believe it."

To further rattle Minnesota, Zuppke ordered a squib kickoff. The ball jumped and skittered to the 5, where Minnesota fell on it. On their first offensive play, Zuppke's men came out in a trick formation, with players spread all over the field. Then the Illini slashed through the confounded Gophers to pull off the biggest upset to date in Big Ten history with a 14–9 win. When the exhilarated Halas heard the final gun, "I threw my crutches into the air."

After Christmas, Ralph Jones, also the basketball coach, dropped in on Halas at the TEKE house and ordered him to come out for the team, reminding the lad that he had proved he was ready to go when he tossed his crutches away at Minnesota.

When they played Wisconsin for the Big Ten title, Halas sank a long two-handed set shot at the buzzer to give Illinois the title. He then was named captain for the 1917–18 basketball season. Said Halas, "Jones taught me finesse," another fundamental that he would stress to counter pure brute force.

That spring, Walter Halas's pitching and George's hitting led the Illini to the Western Conference baseball title. The New York Yankees told George they wanted to sign him.

In June, Walter earned his engineering degree to become the first Halas to graduate from college, and George returned for another summer at Western Electric. When he wasn't playing ball, George frequently double-dated with Ralph Brizzolara. George and Min were now serious, as were Ralph and Florence Hurley. Each couple rightly assumed their friends would marry. When George left for his senior year at Illinois, Ralph left Western Electric for a better-paying engineering job at the American Conveyor Belt Company.

By the fall of 1917, the United States had jumped full into the Great War. This was "the war to end all wars," and General John J. Pershing's American Expeditionary Force, the doughboys, were training before they shipped out to go "Over There." Eligible young men who didn't enlist were being scooped up in the draft by the thousands. With war talk swirling around them, the 1917 Illinois football team played a full schedule, going 5–2–1.

At the annual football banquet, Zuppke told his players, "Just when I teach you fellows how to play football, you graduate, and I lose you. Football is the only sport that ends a man's career when it should be beginning."

"His words were to govern the rest of my life," Halas wrote with the benefit of six decades' hindsight. Halas always did believe he would be somebody, but at the moment he thought his destiny was to play big-league baseball.

The beat of the war drums grew thunderous by Christmas 1917, and Halas and his friends all felt the squeeze. Aware that his draft number would come up on his birthday, Halas acted. Throughout college, Halas had planned ahead, taking extra courses, to leave himself just six hours short of graduation after the fall semester so he cold devote extra time to basketball in the winter and baseball in the spring of 1918.

Instead, as soon as Halas finished his fall exams in January, he successfully petitioned the university to waive his final six hours. Basketball coach Jones was upset with his captain for walking out, but Halas did not bend. Armed with his civil engineering degree, he went home, enlisted in the Navy, and was ordered to report to Great Lakes Naval Training Center, near Waukegan, Illinois, for officers' training.

At Great Lakes, Halas formed fast and lasting friendships with several men who would play vital roles in his career. Most prominent were John "Paddy" Driscoll, the homegrown Northwestern University all-American halfback from Evanston; Michigan State all-American center Charlie Bachman; Bachman's Michigan State teammate tackle Hugh Blacklock; and halfback Jimmy Conzelman, from Washington University in St. Louis.

Halas and his athletic classmates were commissioned as ensigns in late spring, but instead of hunting for German submarines in the Atlantic, they were assigned to Special Services. They would play ball for Great Lakes.

When Halas and Driscoll finished the baseball season in late summer, they reported to officers' training school head Lieutenant W. C. McReavy, who doubled as football coach. The shrewd Halas saw that

McReavy was overloaded with work turning out "90-day wonders," new officers, and had no time to coach. So, he volunteered himself, Driscoll, and Bachman as tri-coaches. For appearances' sake, the lieutenant attended games, while they ran the team. McReavy is listed as coach in the official Tournament of Roses history.

Halas and his cronies had assembled the best service team in the Midwest. They opened with a 10–0 win at Iowa and followed with a scoreless tie against Northwestern. Then, Halas faced Zuppke, his mentor, and demonstrated vividly that he had taken the master's 1917 farewell speech to heart as the Sailors beat Illinois 7–0. Knute Rockne's first Notre Dame team was next in early November. The game ended in a 7–7 tie.

Great Lakes put everything together against Purdue, routing the Boilermakers 27–0. That set up a battle for Eastern supremacy with unbeaten Rutgers. Rutgers, led by all-America end and Phi Beta Kappa scholar Paul Robeson, scored first. Then Driscoll went on a tear. He scored 35 points on five touchdown runs and as many drop-kicks for conversions as Great Lakes beat Rutgers 54-to-4. Halas wrote that Robeson told him after the game that he was finished with football and would devote his life to the singing and acting career that would bring him fame as the greatest baritone of his time. In his memoir, Halas is careful not to mention Robeson's controversial politics that took him to the Soviet Union for years, nor does he mention color concerning Robeson.

The Sailors played their final regular-season game at Annapolis, beating Navy 7–6. By that time, the armistice had ended World War I and the pressure was on from the home front to bring home the boys. But Halas, Driscoll, and their mates had one more obligation before they mustered out, a New Year's Day date in the Rose Bowl with the Marines from Mare Island, California.

"That was the only game I ever starred in," Halas mused five decades later to George Vass. Indeed, he was named "Player of the Game." He caught a touchdown pass from Driscoll and, with Great Lakes leading 17–0, ran back an interception 77 yards to the Mare Island 3. "I should have scored," Halas wrote, still upset with himself. "After I took up coaching, I told the carriers that when they reach the 3-yard line, they should dive across the goal. Anyone who can't dive 3 yards should play Parcheesi."

That was mere prelude to a play that left Halas seething for the next 62 years. When Great Lakes failed to punch in the touchdown, Driscoll threw a pass intended for Halas in the end zone. The ball was low, and referee Walter Eckersall ruled it incomplete, saying Halas had trapped it. "He cheated me out of a touchdown. And Walter came from Chicago! I should have expected a little more civic cooperation," Halas persists, validating charges many Bears opponents made through the years that Halas controlled the league and officials to his benefit.

Halas had more to say about officials. "Later when victory meant the Bears ate well, I concerned myself with official decisions. Since that New Year's Day in the Rose Bowl, I have always tried to assist officials to make correct calls. Over the years I have achieved some success in this pursuit."

Halas and his teammates returned to Chicago for a short leave and then headed back to Great Lakes for eventual separation. When he left for home, Driscoll told Halas he planned to play semiprofessional football in the fall. While he waited for his own separation, Halas kept busy the next two months playing basketball and serving as base recreation officer. He was discharged in early March.

When he got home, Halas, who'd suffered a broken jaw and leg at Illinois, promised his mother he was through with football. He packed his civilian clothes into a suitcase and caught a train for Jacksonville, Florida, to report to manager Miller Huggins at the training camp of the New York Yankees.

TWO

DESTINY BECKONS

*N*o man ever took more pride in his "cup of coffee" in major-league baseball, nor talked about it more, than did George Halas. That it came in 1919 with the team that rivaled his prewar Monsters of the Midway as symbols of athletic excellence, the New York Yankees, made it all the more special.

The Old Man had the time of his life in pinstripes. When he arrived at the Yanks' Jacksonville camp, Halas, at 24, was considerably older than most of the other prospects. With a civil engineering degree from the University of Illinois, he also was far better educated than all but a handful of big-league ballplayers.

Manager Miller Huggins was giving him an all-or-nothing chance. Huggins, Halas wrote, seemed to be impressed with his speed. Halas was a decent fielder with a good arm. His big test (and most vivid memory) came in an exhibition against the Brooklyn Dodgers, when the switch-hitting outfielder faced aging left-hander Rube Marquardt. Marquardt, whose best pitch was the curve, was not about to show his best stuff against a rookie in a spring tune-up. So, he fired a fat fastball. Halas, batting right-handed, lined it to deep left center field. Seeing the ball still rolling as he rounded second, Halas roared into third in a slide so hard that he jammed his right hip. He stayed in the game, scored after a fly ball, and played through the pain that, coupled with an inability to hit the curve, ended his career by September.

On the way, he encountered many of the game's great early stars. Memorable moments were few and quite inglorious. Halas hit two long fouls one day off Washington Senators charter Hall of Famer Walter Johnson. Then, says Halas, "he threw a curve. I struck out."

Halas did prove to be as fine a bench jockey as he would become a ref baiter on NFL sidelines. The Yankees were at home in the Polo Grounds, which they shared with the Giants then, and were playing Detroit when Ty Cobb, the Tiger in sharpened spikes, came to bat. A couple of Yankees veterans goaded Halas to give the Georgia Peach the business, the way he used to bait the 14th Street Gang on the way to Cubs games. "How foolish I was!" Halas exclaims. "I shouted nonsense at him, using some gutter terms [one can only imagine]."

The furious Cobb dropped his bat, approached Halas, and snarled: "Punk. I'll see you after the game. Don't forget, punk!" Halas promised to be there. Halas came to his senses in the clubhouse and took his time getting dressed. He emerged, and there was Tyrus Raymond Cobb himself. Instead of a poke, though, Cobb extended his hand. "I like your spirit, kid," he said, "but don't overdo it."

Halas wrote that he and Cobb walked back to the Tigers' hotel in midtown Manhattan, and the great player gave the young man sage advice: "Direct your energy positively. Don't waste yourself being negative." The two men struck up a friendship. After World War II, when the Bears played in Los Angeles, Cobb made a point of calling on Halas.

The Yankees were in Cleveland when Halas no longer could stand the pain throbbing in his injured hip. On an off day, he took a trolley down to Youngstown to visit a former steelworker he knew, a character named Bonesetter Reese who now made his living as an unlicensed chiropractor. Halas had visited Reese twice before for successful treatments on his elbow and ankle when he was playing ball for George Huff at Illinois. This time Reese dug his fingers into Halas's side and explained that he twisted his thigh in that training camp slide. He gave his leg a jerk and pulled it back into alignment. With that, Halas was ready to go, faster than ever.

The Yankees' next stop was Chicago and a series with baseball's best team, the White Sox, eight of whom would dump the World Series that October to the Cincinnati Reds. A year later, the eight "Black Sox" would be banished for life from baseball. On this day, White Sox ace Eddie Cicotte, one of the "Eight Men Out," was pitching. Halas took two called strikes and then swung and missed. Three pitches, three strikes, and out. It was George Halas's last major-league at bat.

After the game, Halas was about to head home for a family dinner when Miller Huggins called him into his office. He told the young man he had to send him down to St. Paul in the American Association. As difficult as it was for Halas to hear the bad news, he was grateful for the grace and consideration Huggins had shown. He finished the season at St. Paul and then went home.

For the record, George Halas appeared in a dozen regular-season games for the 1919 Yankees, just six in right field. The right-handed-throwing switch-hitter batted .091 on two hits, both singles, in 22 at bats. He struck out eight times and scored no runs.

One more myth cries out for correction. Halas told George Vass that after Reese treated his hip injury, "it was too late." Halas explained, "A fellow named Babe Ruth was playing the outfield in my place." Not so. Through 1918, the Babe had been the best pitcher in baseball, leading the Boston Red Sox to their last world championship against the Cubs. In 1919, the Babe was still with Boston and, in his first full year as an everyday player, was staging baseball's first great power display as he hit a record 29 home runs. In the off-season, cash-starved Boston owner Harry Frazee sent him to New York and fame with the Yankees to change the game forever.

Halas did not lose his job in the 1920 spring training. He simply did not report. He had other things to do.

When Halas returned home in September, he put his degree to work designing bridges for the Chicago, Burlington, and Quincy Railroad for $55 a week. "A railroad job is safe," his mother said, reminding him of his vow to quit football.

Halas hated the drudgery but knew he could not ignore his vow. He just could not bank, let alone douse, his competitive fire. Professional football in one form or another had existed in small-town Pennsylvania, Ohio, New York, and even Indiana since 1895, but never in a successful, organized league. Players generally got paid by passing the hat, and it wasn't much.

Halas was still playing baseball for St. Paul back in July when five men gathered in Canton, Ohio, at Ralph Hay's Hupmobile agency to make a serious attempt at forming a league. Hay, who owned the Canton Bulldogs, played host to representatives from the Akron Pros, Columbus Panhandles, Dayton Triangles, and Rochester Jeffersons. Each man agreed to put up $25 to form the first American Professional Football Association.

To bestow prestige on the league, they made Hay's partner, the great Jim Thorpe, league president. In lieu of extra pay, Hay printed Thorpe's figurehead title on the Bulldogs' stationery.

Hay's league had no schedule and played many games against non-league independents. They kept no records, delivered news by word of mouth, and, as before, paid the players after passing the hat through the crowd. Rosters were meaningless as players jumped from team to team each game for more money. Many played college football on Saturdays and then worked under aliases for pay on Sunday, their off day.

One of the first people Halas called after he returned home and joined the Burlington was his Navy buddy Paddy Driscoll. Driscoll told him that he and several of their Great Lakes teammates were playing for the Hammond Pros, an independent semipro team across the Illinois-Indiana state line. Halas then called the team's owner, Dr. Alva A. Young, who offered him $100 a game.

Even at the moral cost of breaking that vow to his mother, Halas accepted. He signed on for the six-game schedule, as much for the chance to play football again as the extra money. The Pros lost a brutal slugfest to Jim Thorpe's Canton Bulldogs in the regular season. In a postseason game, the Pros won and claimed the nonexistent championship of the outlaw league.

For George Halas, season's end meant a return to the mundane life of bridge designer for the CB&Q. By midwinter, he says, he reached a realization: "My real love was football."

A month after his 25th birthday on February 2, 1920, Halas was toiling at his drawing board in the Burlington offices when the phone rang. The caller was a man named George Chamberlain, who said he was general superintendent for the A. E. Staley Corn Products Company of Decatur, 172 miles away in downstate Illinois. Chamberlain invited Halas to stop by after work to see him at the Sherman House in the Loop.

At their meeting that evening, Chamberlain minced no words. He said Mr. Staley, his boss, strongly believed in sports. Staley, Chamberlain said, could prove that the company's successful baseball team, which was managed by former major-league pitching star Iron Man Joe McGinnity, increased sales for Staley's cornstarch, and Staley was convinced that sports improved company morale.

He said Halas came highly recommended from people at the University of Illinois. Staley wanted Halas for his engineering ability, playing skills in both baseball and football, and, most important, the ability he demonstrated at Great Lakes to organize and coach a football team. Chamberlain asked if Halas would move to Decatur, the processing center for the central Illinois corn and soybean belt. Halas's only knowledge of Decatur concerned the local college, James Millikin University, which turned out decent teams.

Halas saw his opening. He asked Chamberlain: Can I recruit players who made their names in college, at Great Lakes, and on semipro teams? Can I offer the players steady, year-round work and a chance to share in gate receipts? Can we practice daily? Can we practice on company time? Chamberlain agreed without hesitation to each condition.

Halas reported for work on March 20, 1920, started putting together a football team, and made some cornstarch on the side. Now that he had the backing, he would make the most of it.

The term *networking* was decades away, but Halas did exactly that. Armed with an extensive contact list that contained names gleaned from Illinois, Great Lakes, and even that brief six-game hitch in 1919 at Hammond, Halas lured prospects with promises of full-time pay from Staley while they played football for a share of the gate. This, Halas explained, was a chance to learn a business and make more money and have more fun at it than anything else they could try. He harvested a bumper crop of football talent off the prairie.

He started close to home, landing several of his Illini teammates, including guards Burt Ingwerson and Ross Petty, plus halfback Ed "Dutch" Sternaman, one of the heroes of the 1916 Minnesota upset. From Decatur, he signed reserve quarterback and aspiring baseball player Charley Dressen, an egotistical bantam who would manage the 1952 and '53 National League champion Brooklyn Dodgers, immortalized in Roger Kahn's masterpiece, *The Boys of Summer*.

In August, Halas hit the road on pro football's first recruiting trip and returned with Wisconsin all-America tackle Ralph Scott; Guy Chamberlain, the "giant" Nebraska end at 6'3", 220 pounds; two Great Lakes teammates, tackle Hugh Blacklock, from Michigan State, and halfback Jimmy Conzelman, whom he would face across the field years later on the Chicago Cardinals sideline.

Halas stopped in Chicago long enough to eat a couple of home-cooked meals, see Minnie, and land three former Notre Damers who had played with him in Hammond. The biggest catch on that trip was the man who would anchor his line for the next 13 seasons, center George "the Brute" Trafton. Trafton became available when Rockne kicked him out of school after learning Trafton used an alias to play for Hammond in 1919.

No sooner had Staley put the boys to work in the mill than Halas pulled them out for a daily two-hour practice to drill them in Zuppke's T formation. This was not the modern T set where the quarterback stands in direct contact with the center to take a hand-to-hand snap. The 1920 quarterback stood a short distance behind the center, ahead of a fullback, positioned between a left and right halfback. The line was set up with foot touching foot. The backs occasionally would shift to enable a direct snap to either the left half (tailback) or fullback.

Halas's daily practices paid off in a unit that was smartly drilled, well conditioned, and ready to play brutal games in cumbersome equipment, leather helmets optional, and without face masks, a dentist's delight. All Halas needed was competition in the form of a league and a schedule. After trying to set up games and haggling over playing dates and sites, he nearly threw up his hands. And that was before they argued over money.

Aware of the 1919 fiasco and unwilling to lose his players one at a time to higher bidders, the hard-nosed Halas reasoned that football needed a real league with a set schedule. Just like baseball. He wrote to Ralph Hay in Canton and asked him to let the Staley Starchmakers of Decatur participate in a meeting of the American Professional Football Association.

Halas was the catalyst. Hay held a preliminary meeting with several nearby operators. They agreed on a basic outline for a league that included a hands-off policy on other teams' players during the season and, to appease the colleges, no signing of players during the season until they had completed college eligibility. Hay set a September 17 general meeting at his auto agency.

Halas would stretch, if not break, both hands-off rules in later years, landing Hall of Fame lineman Ed Healey from Rock Island in 1922, as payment in lieu of gate receipts, and college football's greatest star, Red Grange, in 1925. But first was that matter of getting organized.

Staley engineer Morgan O'Brien accompanied Halas on the train to Canton. Halas did most of the talking when he and representatives of 11 other teams sat down on the running boards of the Hupmobiles, Jordans, and Marmons in Hay's showroom. "We all agreed on the need for a league. In two hours we created the American Professional Football Association," Halas wrote.

Just two of the charter teams remain: Halas's Decatur Staleys, the Starchmakers, who became the Bears, and the Chicago Cardinals, who flew off to St. Louis in 1960, then migrated again in 1988 to Arizona's Valley of the Sun. Each team agreed to put up $100 in cash. "That was a good one," Halas told Vass years later. "No money changed hands."

Because Jim Thorpe was the biggest name in sports, the new franchise holders, at the urging of Columbus promoter and Panhandles owner Joe Carr, unanimously agreed to reelect Thorpe president. After the election, Halas and O'Brien caught the train for Decatur to get down to work.

THREE

FROM
TANK TOWNS
TO THAT
TODDLIN' TOWN

A triumphant George Halas reported to A. E. Staley on Monday morning, September 20, 1920, the first day of autumn, bearing league membership, a schedule, and acres of optimism. Halas was in business to win, whatever it took, foul or fair. Nothing else mattered, nor counted. Except that which he could count. Money.

Halas's Starchmakers were the best-conditioned team in the new league and smartest at knowing and breaking the rules—without getting caught, of course. He taught them to hit first and hardest using everything but brass knuckles, with an assortment that included, and was not limited to, tripping, kneeing, elbowing, slugging, gouging, biting, and, most important, the art of holding. The easiest ruse of all.

The only officials in those days were the referee, umpire, and head linesman. Halas was aware that they could not keep track of the entire field, a truism that holds today even with seven officials and cameras everywhere watching play. "I [held] a bigger opponent when the umpire wasn't looking," Halas wrote.

The Staleys opened for business in Decatur on October 3, 1920, beating the nonleague Moline Tractors 20–0, but only 1,500 locals cared enough to come out to see a start-up operation on the sporting frontier.

Baseball was the national pastime, and it was unraveling day by day in a series of sickening gambling revelations. Within days of the APFA charter meeting in Canton, all hell was breaking loose up north in Chicago. Word filtered through the closed doors of a Cook County grand jury investigation that a gambler testified under oath that the White Sox had fixed the 1919 World Series to lose to the Cincinnati Reds. When eight players—seven of them key players, one a bench-warmer—were indicted, White Sox owner Charles Comiskey suspended them. Most prominent were arguably baseball's greatest pure hitter, Shoeless Joe Jackson, and third baseman George "Buck" Weaver, who maintained their innocence until they died, plus the game's top pitcher, Eddie Cicotte, whose confession cracked the case.

To save their sport, the owners, who had always resisted authority, went to Chicago-based federal judge Kenesaw Mountain Landis and asked him to become commissioner. Landis, a political conservative and racist, extracted supreme powers to run the game as he saw fit. He grabbed control in early 1921 in a sweeping move.

When the eight White Sox players were found innocent in a friendly Chicago court, Landis ignored the verdict and barred them from the game for life. Period. The balance of power then shifted from Chicago and the Midwest to New York and the novalike luminescence of a single athlete. George Herman "Babe" Ruth was far more than Halas's "successor" in right field. He was the most prominent among a galaxy of stars who would transform the Yankees from New York's third team behind the Giants and Brooklyn Dodgers into sport's greatest dynasty.

Ironically, the Black Sox scandal and the smashing New York debut of Babe Ruth may have been the best thing that ever happened to the fledgling American Professional Football Association. Being stuck in a cluster of tank towns and playing for peanuts before small crowds gave the league the time and space to work through its considerable problems out of the limelight.

The charter meeting in Canton did not give the league sufficient lead time to draw up a round-robin schedule and set up proper travel arrangements. APFA teams played games against 33 nonleague teams that 1920 season. Eastern teams stayed close to home in Ohio and western New York while the Western teams confined most of their contests—league and otherwise—to Illinois and other nearby locales.

Thorpe remained a great player, but he lacked the leadership and business skills to run a complicated league. Worse, he was at war with himself, battling alcohol. Fortunately, the rudderless association had 25-year-old George Halas. Worldly beyond his years, he was a tough, shrewd visionary who would set the league on a correct course to someday overtake baseball, and he possessed the patience to see it through as long as it would take. For generations, if need be.

The Staleys won all five of their October games and embarked on a six-game grind in November, all but one on the road. The stretch began at Rock Island in a bone-breaking bloodbath on November 7. The Staleys' 7–0 win in the first game created so much rancor that Halas quartered the team across the Mississippi River in Davenport, Iowa. Most of that anger was directed at George Trafton, who broke the leg of Rock Island star halfback Fred Chicken when he threw him into a fence by the sideline. Trafton barely escaped a bottle- and rock-throwing crowd when a passing motorist gave him a ride to safety.

After the second battle of Rock Island, a scoreless tie, Trafton was left standing as the crowed screamed for his scalp. Halas retreated to the box office, grabbed his cut of the gate, $3,000, and entrusted it to Trafton for safekeeping. The team hurried to catch a train for Decatur, and when they got aboard, Halas went to Trafton, extended his hand, and took the money. As Richard Whittingham writes in *The Chicago Bears*, Halas explained, "I knew if trouble came, I'd be running for [the money]. Trafton would be running for his life."

Halas's crucible came on the Friday-night train trip from Chicago to Minneapolis in mid-November. He knew his team was travel-weary and beaten down from the hard-fought games and short turnarounds. Sometime after lights out, the swaying rhythm and steady clackety-clack from the rails below the Pullman car gave way to the din of shouting and cursing men that jarred Halas awake. He got dressed and got going. As he approached the source, he immediately recognized the familiar calls to action from his childhood on Chicago's West Side and recognized the voices as those of his own men.

"C'mon, Little Joe! Eighter from Decatur! Seven come eleven!" It was a dice game, and he felt the fever as he heard the clatter of cubes and the cheering or groaning with every roll coming from behind a curtain separating a washroom from the corridor. Halas entered to see several of his older players crouched on the floor. Money was changing hands fast with every pass.

What to do? This was the same man whose father years before whaled the tar out of him for shooting craps in the back alley, the same man whose stated policy was "No gambling!" The shrewd young coach did know that his future as boss and leader was on the line as those damn little dice caromed off bulkheads and wobbled to dead stops to reveal their combinations: snake eyes (two) meant defeat; Little Joe (four) was the hard and tricky point; eighter from Decatur was the easier-to-make point; boxcars (double sixes) were lethal. Then there was the tantalizingly expensive seven come eleven, which was good, or seven alone at the end of a streak—that meant craps, which was awful.

Halas could have told them to break it up and go to bed or, worse, order them to study the game plan. Either way, he sensed, the players would have laughed him off the train. So, he joined in and in short time was down $12. "When midnight came," Halas wrote, "I said: 'All right, let's go to bed.' Off to bed went those old-timers." The $12 Halas lost by joining them at that critical moment was a minor investment for the lifelong lesson he gained in handling men: don't pull in the rope until you know they want you to pull it and appreciate it when you do.

As much as Halas understood that penalties were endemic to a rough sport such as football, he drew the line at betting on one's team to win or, the ultimate sin of betting, to lose. "No gambler has ever approached me," Halas wrote in his memoirs. "Perhaps the word got around that it would be wasting their time."

Joe Carr, the man who served as league president from 1921 until his death in 1939, tending to administrative matters while Halas made the big plans and set the course, took a more severe public approach to gambling. *New York Times* writer Arthur Daley held the Panglossian view that Carr was so opposed to gambling that he didn't want to hear of any owner's betting as little as a cigar on a game. In truth, when Carr realized in 1925 that his National Football League was ready for the big time and needed a New York team, he didn't blink when a bookmaker and horseplayer named Tim Mara came up with the $500 franchise fee. The same held in 1933 when another racetrack sharpie named Arthur Rooney cashed in a huge parlay bet worth several hundred thousand dollars after a great day at Saratoga to buy the new Pittsburgh Pirates franchise. Through the years, quite a few other league owners have been notorious gamblers. Try Carroll Rosenbloom, Eddie DeBartolo Jr., and Leonard Tose for openers.

The National Football League was built on gambling, as in risk taking, not mere wagering, and nobody took more risks to make the league work without betting the proceeds than George Halas. As one former player put it, "The paternalistic father who tells his boys to watch out for sex [and every other temptation] is a guy who's done it all himself. Halas was all-knowing." And so he was when it came to gambling.

When he drew up the schedule, the key date for him was November 25, Thanksgiving Day at Cubs' Park, on the North Side, against the Chicago Tigers. In late November, Halas heard that the Tigers were hemorrhaging money, barely able to make huge rental payments to the Cubs, and would fold after the season.

When the Staleys took the field and Halas saw the size of the crowd his unbeaten Starchmakers had attracted—8,000 spectators had showed—he knew this ballpark on the North Side of Chicago was exactly where he belonged. The Staleys didn't disappoint the big crowd, beating the Tigers 6–0.

Thanks to an 11th-hour deal that Halas made with the Cardinals before the team left Decatur for Chicago, Halas barely had time to enjoy Thanksgiving dinner. He had to get the team ready for yet another game. Halas had agreed with Cardinals owner Chris O'Brien to play the Sunday after Thanksgiving if the Staleys beat the Tigers.

Ostensibly, this contest was being staged for the benefit of Chicago fans. In reality, Halas used this game to bring his fledgling league into the big time. It was the start of a contentious rivalry that would become far nastier and more personal than the Bears and Green Bay Packers.

They played on Sunday, November 28, at Normal Park at 61st and Racine before 5,000 fans who braved the cold to see just how good the unbeaten Staleys were. They saw Decatur take a 6–0 lead early and hold on until late in the fourth quarter. That's when accounts diverge.

According to George Vass's account, Lenny Sachs, of the Cardinals, picked up a fumble near the sideline and ran it in from 20 yards out to tie the game. In *The Chicago Bears*, Dick Whittingham reports that an unnamed Cardinals receiver caught a pass by the sideline and, as he was about to be tackled, cut behind the crowd, using them for interference as he scored. The referee, Whittingham writes, fearing the frenzied crowd if he called the play back, let it stand, a decision the writer calls "among the most questionable in NFL history."

For certain, Halas's pal Paddy Driscoll drop-kicked the extra point to ice the 7–6 victory, ending the Staleys' unbeaten streak. As Joe Ziemba notes in *When Football Was Football*, since each team had lost just once to a league team, Halas and O'Brien quickly agreed to a rematch to settle something they called "Midwest honors." It was slated as a home game for the Staleys, but instead of playing in Decatur, Halas paid a call on Cubs president William Veeck—one part courtesy, nine parts business.

In 1913, Charles Weeghman had bought a full city block at the corner of Clark and Addison streets, situated within Waveland Avenue at the north end and Sheffield Avenue on the east side. Weeghman hired architect Zachary Taylor Davis to create a veritable baseball cathedral for his new Federal League entry, the Whales, on this property once home to a seminary. Davis, who designed Comiskey Park for the White Sox in 1909, fashioned a single-deck, 14,000-seat masterpiece with magnificent sight lines. Weeghman Park cost $250,000 and opened in time for the 1914 Federal League season.

When the Federal League disbanded after the 1915 season, Weeghman made his move. Aware that West Side Park, Halas's boyhood hangout, would be razed to make way for the new Cook County Hospital, Weeghman bought the Cubs from the Taft family of Cincinnati and moved the team into his ballpark for the 1916 season. The Cubs won the 1918 pennant, but Weeghman Park's capacity at 14,000 was so small that the team had to play its World Series home games against Boston at Comiskey Park. It was obvious that somebody with deeper pockets needed to step in and take control.

That somebody was chewing gum magnate William Wrigley Jr. He bought the club and ballpark in 1920, renamed the place Cubs' Park, and hired former newspaper columnist William L. Veeck Sr. to run everything as team president. Backed with Wrigley's considerable fortune, Veeck built the upper deck after the 1926 season and rededicated the ballpark as Wrigley Field. The current bleachers were built in 1937. Thanks to Bill Veeck Jr., who planted the ivy himself, the brick outfield walls were covered with the famous vines. While baseball capacity increased to 37,000-plus, Halas found a way to squeeze in more than 50,000 for Bears games.

Those days were far off in the future as Halas in 1920 cut a deal with Veeck Sr. to rent the ballpark for the rematch with the Cardinals. Word traveled fast, and not only was Halas's insightful decision rewarded with the largest attendance for a professional football game to that date as 11,000 fans crowded Cubs' Park, but it was also the prelude to what would become an amiable half-century relationship with the Cubs.

The crowd saw the Staleys dominate play and win the mythical "Western championship" 10–0 in a field-position battle. After the Cardinals rematch, Halas contacted the "Eastern champion" Akron Pros to stage a title game, to be played the following Sunday, December 12, again at Cubs' Park. The Pros had gone 8–0–3 in contrast to the Staleys' 10–1–1 mark.

In direct violation of the league rules he helped write the previous September, Halas signed Paddy Driscoll and a still unknown ringer named "Fletcher" for the showdown. Driscoll, at $300 a game, was the highest-paid player in the league and presumably got his price and a bit extra to play for his old Navy buddy against Akron and the Pros' great black star, the former Brown University all-American and native Chicagoan Fritz Pollard.

Driscoll's appearance with the Staleys turned out to be a cameo role. He returned to the Cardinals in 1921 as player-coach and remained with them until 1926 when Halas finally landed him for keeps. He would stay with the Bears until his death in 1968, after serving a two-year term as nominal head coach in 1956 and '57 under Halas's watchful eye and meddling hand.

The 12,000 fans who packed Cubs' Park witnessed nothing resembling championship football as neither Driscoll nor Pollard could make headway on the half-frozen, slippery field. The game ended in a scoreless tie. And the season ended in a wash.

Halas claimed the world championship, but nobody else in what passed for league authority listened. Because the schedule was an uncoordinated jumble with a surfeit of nonleague teams, and records were not kept, the National Football League does not recognize a 1920 champion. The Ohioans who controlled the APFA out of Canton awarded the Akron Pros a title on grounds they finished the season unbeaten, with three ties, to the Staleys' lone defeat against the Cardinals and two ties. Halas seethed about that "lost title" for the rest of his life.

Halas did honor a vital promise to his players. He gave each man a cut of the season's gate receipts, about $1,600 a man. "I, as coach, player, and manager, was voted an extra share. My take was $2,322.77," Halas, ever the businessman, proudly reported.

At the beginning of 1921, everything was still running smoothly at the Staley Starchworks. Mr. Staley was certain that his young coach and team had helped sales and the company's image. Halas had become engaged to Min, and they were planning to get married that year. By late spring, though, the economy hit the skids and Staley's sales declined.

Halas, busy playing baseball for the company team and preparing for the football season, took time out in early spring to deal with a matter that led to league stabilization. It had become obvious to Halas and his fellow owners that Jim Thorpe had to go. In an April 30 meeting at Canton, they voted to replace him with a man experienced in running minor leagues in baseball as well as a football team. He was Joe Carr, of Columbus, president of the Panhandles.

Carr, born October 22, 1880, was not yet 20 when he organized a baseball team among employees of the Pennsylvania Railroad's Panhandle Division. He was working then as assistant sports editor for the *Ohio State Journal*, and the ball club gave him something to write about and promote. By 1904, the Pennsy wanted a football team. Carr did the work and called them the Columbus Panhandles. Carr left newspapering a short time later to take on another collateral duty as president of the Ohio State Baseball League.

Behind the scenes, George Halas already was pulling the strings as he would for decades. Furious about the league's refusal to honor the 1920 title, Halas led the pro-Carr insurgency the following April. Once elected, Carr, doubtless at Halas's urging, agreed to keep official records and be the arbiter of disputes, especially those involving league standings, a factor that would come into play at the end of that same season.

In a meeting that August, the league admitted several new members, the most prominent being the community-owned Green Bay Packers from northern Wisconsin, coached by a young Notre Dame dropout named Earl "Curly" Lambeau.

By summer's end, it was as plain to Staley as the color of the red ink in his ledgers that the 25 men he was carrying on the payroll represented an expense he could not afford, Halas included. Staley was paying them regular-season wages plus compensating them for two extra hours a day to practice football, over and beyond work, and that simply was not good business.

Before the season opened, Staley met with Halas. "George, I know you like football better than starch," Staley said. That, Papa Bear reported in *Halas by Halas*, left him "flabbergasted." A few seconds later, Staley said, "Why don't you take the team to Chicago? I think football will go over big there." According to George Vass, Halas was about to ask for cash when Staley executed a preemptive strike: "I'll give you $5,000 to get you started. All I ask is you continue to call the team the Staleys for one season."

They shook hands on the agreement, which included Staley ads in the game programs and a Staley demand that the team conduct itself on and off the field to the credit of his company. With the money in hand, Halas contested nothing, not even Staley's hypocritical morals clause. Staley drew up the one-page document, and both men signed it on Thursday, October 6, 1921.

Halas had four days to rent a playing field in Chicago, find a place for his players to stay, and get the team ready for a Monday-night opener in Decatur against Rock Island. He turned over the team to his friend and former Illinois teammate Ed "Dutch" Sternaman, called William Veeck to discuss a rental arrangement at Cubs' Park, and ran to the station to catch a train for Chicago to meet with him.

They wasted no time. Halas wanted to practice and play his home games at the ballpark. Veeck wanted 15 percent of the gate plus the concessions, not a fixed-rate rental. Halas, who feared a fixed rent, was all too happy to agree. He asked for sales from the programs at a dime a copy. "Done," Veeck said.

"I left the park a happy man," Halas wrote. "This verbal agreement stood firm for fifty years. It was a pleasure to do business with people like the Veecks and Wrigleys."

Halas left the ballpark and headed a mile north to one of the many residential apartment-hotels in the congested Uptown community. He rented 10 rooms that cost $2 a week for each player. Then he caught the night train for Decatur. The next day, when he told the team about the move, only one player, John "Jake" Mintun, a Decatur native, stayed behind. He became night superintendent at the Staley mill. After the meeting, Halas telephoned Min in Chicago to tell her that everything was set. He was coming back home with his true love, his team.

For their season opener and final game in Decatur, the Staleys defeated Rock Island 14–10 before 3,600 fans on Monday, October 10. It was the last league game the team would play in central Illinois until 2002, when the Bears played their entire home schedule at Illinois Memorial Stadium in Champaign while Soldier Field was rebuilt. The Staleys caught the train to Chicago after the game and reported for practice at Cubs' Park at 9:00 the next morning. Sharp. There was work to be done.

As the players reported for practice at Cubs' Park, they noticed that something else was new to the operation. George Halas no longer was alone. On the train ride back to Decatur after his whirlwind trip to Chicago to negotiate the lease with Veeck and secure quarters for his players, Halas realized that he needed more than Staley's $5,000 seed money to survive. He needed a partner to defray the many costs involved.

His natural choice in 1921 and confirmed in his memoirs was Paddy Driscoll, but that was out of the question. By brazenly grabbing a share of the Chicago territory for himself, Halas already had stepped on the tocs of Cardinals owner Chris O'Brien. The choice of Chicago or Driscoll was a cinch. Halas took the city and kept his hands off the Cardinals' meal ticket.

Halas turned to his second option. He and Ed "Dutch" Sternaman had been teammates since their Illinois days and had always got along well. With Sternaman still playing, Halas figured, they wouldn't have to hire an extra man. Sternaman, Halas felt, was a good businessman as well and would bring some money to the operation. Each man agreed to take just $100 a game if the money was in the bank, and they shook hands on an agreement to become 50-50 partners. "Had I made it 51-49," Halas wrote, "I would have saved myself a lot of heartaches and difficulties." How right he was!

As much as he had to scramble, Halas always saw the big picture. Blessed with an innate sense of showmanship and an eye for talent, Halas thought like an impresario from the beginning. Chicago was the league's largest city, and he needed a marquee star. He sent after the biggest name in college football.

Charles "Chic" Harley put Ohio State football on the map. After his birth in Chicago, Harley's family moved to Columbus, where he starred at East High School and then enrolled at Ohio State at the same time the school joined the Western Conference to make it the Big Ten. In three seasons, Harley scored 23 touchdowns as the Buckeyes won 21 games, lost just 1, and tied another.

Harley was named to the authoritative Walter Camp all-America team as a sophomore in 1916 and repeated in 1917. After service as an Army Air Corps aviator in the war year 1918, he returned to finish his Ohio State career with another all-America season in 1919. So great was Harley that when Ohio State opened its magnificent Ohio Stadium in 1922, people called it the House That Harley Built.

Harley was blessed with boyish good looks and exceptional athletic skills, and Halas and Sternaman knew his value. Chic came with an agent, however, his brother Bill, and for one of the few times in his life, George Halas did not hold the aces. The Harleys in good faith promised to deliver Chic's superb Buckeye teammates fullback Pete Stinchcomb and guard John "Tarzan" Taylor. Then came the catch. They demanded one-third of the team, a full and equal partnership with Halas and Sternaman.

Thanks to a signed letter of agreement, the Harley brothers briefly held that partnership. The deal collapsed nine games into the season when, in a physical exam Halas and Sternaman demanded for the partnership, doctors discovered that Harley was infected with syphilis. This was before the penicillin cure was discovered, and the disgusted Halas and Sternaman canceled the deal.

In 1922, an undaunted Bill Harley appeared at a league meeting, flashed that letter of agreement, and claimed ownership of the team, but Halas and Sternamen prevailed in an eight-to-two vote. The Harleys then filed suit, but Albert Austrian of Mayer, Meyer, Austrian, and Platt, the lawyer William Veeck recommended, defeated the Harleys' challenge in court on every point. Austrian had represented the White Sox during the gambling scandal.

Chic Harley was through. His mind ravaged by syphilis, he never played another professional game. He spent the rest of his life from 1938 until he died in 1974 at the Veterans Administration Hospital in Danville, Illinois. Six Ohio State players, led by two-time Heisman Trophy winner Archie Griffin, acted as pallbearers at Harley's burial service in Columbus.

The Staleys' grand opening in Chicago on October 16 was an artistic and financial success as 8,000 fans came to Cubs' Park to see the new kids in town outbattle the Rochester Jeffersons 16-to-3. Five weeks later, on November 27, 1921, Curly Lambeau marched the Green Bay Packers into Chicago. "We won 20–0 [Halas scored one of the three Chicago touchdowns] and began what was to be our longest rivalry, and for me, the happiest series of games," wrote Halas.

The teams did not meet in 1922, and the Bears won their only matchups in 1923 and 1924. When they began the annual home-and-home series in 1925, with each team winning at home, the series was under way in earnest, two annual skirmishes for civic and state pride. It became the NFL's most storied rivalry, a colorful, rollicking, hard-fought, insult-filled, ego-driven battle between two teams and between their hard-drinking, boisterous fans and proud cities. Nothing could be more wonderful.

"Halas and Lambeau made it a point never to shake hands after a game," said Lee Remmel, who has seen every Bears-Packers game since 1944 as a fan, sportswriter, and, for decades, Packers publicist. "That suggested something to me right there. It did say something about the nature of the rivalry. About their relationship, I can't say there was any enmity."

Yet, the rivalry founders retained a special bond to the end. "When Curly died in 1965, Halas came up and was one of the pallbearers," said retired *Green Bay Press-Gazette* sports editor Art Daley. "The Packers and Bears are partners in this league's history. I think all football players appreciate a certain amount of tradition. They get it when these two play."

The Staleys lost just once in 1921, 7–6 to the Buffalo All-Americans on Thanksgiving Day. They beat Buffalo 10–7 in the rematch 10 days later, shut out the Canton Bulldogs 10–0 on December 11, and finished the season when the Cardinals played them to a scoreless tie, to finish at 9–1–1, a half game ahead of Buffalo, who played one more game, which ended in a tie and gave them a 9–1–2 record. It was a most satisfactory conclusion to the brief but eventful history of the Staleys, especially for the founder. "The League proclaimed us World Champions" were the only words he needed to say about that 1921 campaign.

Although they won the most league games during the next decade, they would not win another title until 1932, but they were able to make a go of it from the beginning, however modest it might be.

"Wonder of wonders. We paid all our bills and still had $7 in the bank," Halas wrote. "But the players had to seek jobs to see them through to next fall, and Dutch and I had to find a way to finance the new season."

With their obligation to the A. E. Staley Company complete, Halas and Sternaman decided to give their team a new name for the 1922 season. As a lifelong Cubs fan and being a tenant of the team, Halas wanted a name that fit the city and his own personality. Since football players are larger and nastier than baseball players, Halas figured, why not "Bears." Bears it was, and Bears it is.

On January 28, 1922, Sternaman and Halas reincorporated the team as the Chicago Bears Football Club with capital stock of $15,000. Each man put up $2,500 and made another joint contribution of $2,500 to give the team $7,500 in working capital. They locked the remaining $7,500 in stock certificates in a safe.

The name "John L. Driscoll, 816 Foster St., Evanston, Illinois" appears on the original incorporation papers with Halas and Sternaman as a minority partner. The moment league president Carr saw that document, he ordered Halas and Sternaman to stop tampering with Driscoll and ruled that Paddy belonged to the Cardinals as player and head coach.

That spring, Carr pulled the Packers franchise from Lambeau on grounds he illegally hired college players under assumed names and returned the $50 franchise fee to the Acme Packing Company, successors to the founding Indian Packing Company. A chastised Lambeau saved up $50 to buy his share of the team back, got $250 from other local backers, and then rode with a friend to the June 24 league meeting in Canton with the money, which Carr accepted.

The Packers nearly went under again after the 1922 season but were saved by going public. A nonprofit public corporation set up by the publisher of the *Green Bay Press-Gazette* put $5,000 in a local bank and relieved Lambeau of ownership duties so he could coach and manage the team, and get moving on a legend. Financial problems continued to dog the franchise for decades until, in 1956, the Packers made it for keeps, thanks to the supreme efforts of their most earnest opponent but most ardent supporter, George Halas, who led the drive to build the new City Stadium.

One other important order of business was settled in that same league meeting that spring. Halas never had liked the name American Professional Football Association. To Halas, the word *association* had a minor-league, second-class sound to it. "We were first class," he wrote. "I proposed we change our name to *National Football League*. My fellow members agreed."

The 1922 Bears went 9-and-3 in defense of their NFL title, finishing second to the unbeaten and twice-tied Canton Bulldogs, coached by original Staleys player Guy Chamberlain. Halas made the first trade in NFL history that year. Only a week after Rock Island tackle Ed Healey took a failed swing at Halas for his constant holding, Halas grabbed him in lieu of payment of a $100 debt for owed gate receipts. Then, he gladly raised Healey's salary to $100 from the $75 he earned with the Independents and the two became lifelong friends. Healey was inducted into the Hall of Fame in 1964.

When word of Healey's death reached Halas in the press box on December 19, 1978, during the Bears' 14–0 victory over the Packers, he called PA announcer Chet Coppock and ordered him to announce it by saying, "We regretfully must inform you that Ed Healey, the *greatest* offensive tackle in Bears history, passed away today at his home in South Bend, Indiana." Healey's lofty designation certainly would be arguable, but for Halas, no latter-day athlete could ever know what it meant to play for just $100 a game.

The Bears finished second in 1923, again to the Bulldogs, and second for a third straight year in 1924, to Chamberlain and his Cleveland Bulldogs transplants from Canton.

Like the Bears, every other team in the young league struggled at the gate. To pay the bills and feed their families, Halas sold cars on the side and Sternaman ran a gas station. Halas still sought that breakthrough in the form of a marquee player. He knew exactly who that man was.

He saw him in the flesh in 1924 on a rainy early-November afternoon at Illinois Memorial Stadium, romping through the Iowa Hawkeyes 36–0. His name was Grange. Red Grange.

FOUR

THE FIRST
SUPERSTAR

*B*y the start of the 1925 season, George Halas had to scrimp, save, and scheme to keep the Bears afloat. Moreover, he had four mouths to feed: his own, a wife, and two small children. On February 18, 1922, Ralph Brizzolara had stood up as his best man as George married Min Bushing in the rectory at Old St. Mary's Church just south of the Loop.

The family soon began to grow. "I was stunned when our first child arrived on January 5, 1923," Halas relates. "A girl!" So sure were he and Min that they would have George Jr., that they didn't have a girl's name picked out, and on her birth certificate, they left the name line blank. Halas wrote that years later when she applied for a passport, his daughter discovered that her name, "Virginia Marion," was inserted in pencil. Under occupation, Halas had entered "civil engineer," not "football owner, coach, manager, and player."

In 1923, after all, he could not be certain they would make it. Maybe his mother was right about the instability of a career in football. The proof lies on the letterhead. Not only did the partners hold outside jobs, but also, as the stationery from that year shows, they ran the team from their apartments, Halas at 4356 West Washington

Boulevard, Sternaman at 3818 North Sheffield, two blocks north of the ballpark.

The second child, son George Halas Jr., was born November 4, 1925. "He was a wonderful sight," Halas wrote. As Min held the newborn in her arms, he bent over and said, "Hiya, Mugs!" It was the only name anyone ever called George Halas Jr. for the rest of his life.

It remained a happy time for the Halases as Ralph Brizzolara and Florence Hurley got married in November 1925, two months after Mugs's birth, at Blessed Sacrament Church on the West Side. "George was my father's best man, and vice versa," Charles Brizzolara recalled. "George was my sister's godfather. My father was Mugs's godfather. The families were always close. George and my father were best friends."

Halas knew he had to do something to make his Bears and his National Football League something other than a Sunday-afternoon sideshow. Babe Ruth had restored trust in baseball, and college football was king in the fall, especially in the Midwest, where fans flocked in record numbers to huge new concrete-and-steel stadiums.

In his own backyard, Halas was fighting a losing battle for attention and the entertainment dollar against four strong schools. Amos Alonzo Stagg's University of Chicago Maroons had been a power since 1892. Northwestern, in Evanston, fielded perennially strong teams and was building an attractive 50,000-seat stadium. Thanks to Grantland Rice and a clever student publicist named George Strickler, Knute Rockne and Notre Dame over in South Bend were the first to claim the title America's Team. Downstate, Halas's alma mater, Illinois, had the biggest star the game had ever seen, a fellow named Harold "Red" Grange.

The Chicago Bears and their moribund league were no match for the slick, well-financed colleges. Somehow, Halas knew, he had to get out the word that not only could he offer an outstanding product, but also, he had the best product of all. He needed publicity to put fannies in the seats at the ballpark.

Chicago journalism in 1925 thrived in a golden age of its own, thanks in large part to the antics portrayed in *The Front Page*. The delightfully cheeky play by onetime local reporters Ben Hecht and Charles MacArthur became a smash hit with their depiction of a raucous Roaring '20s Chicago newsroom and its assortment of conniving editors and fast-talking, scoop-seeking scribes. Seven papers competed in various ways for readers, and the games people played on the field were no less entertaining than the ones they played in the various sports departments.

In the madcap milieu that passed for Chicago journalism, it would have been easy, if not reasonable, for Halas to throw up his hands and walk away from it. Bill Jauss heard it fisthand: "I started in 1956 at the *Daily News*, and some of the old-timers like Howie Roberts and John P. Carmichael recalled how Halas used to come into the newspaper office himself carrying copy that he had written, advances on his Sunday games. 'Give us a few paragraphs. I'd appreciate it.'" Jauss said Halas would hand out a stack of passes as well. "And the passes often went unused."

In his memoir, Halas admitted how much it hurt, when he made his weekly rounds, to see unused passes lying on reporters' desks. When he and Sternaman decided a professional could do a better job, they paid a *Chicago Post* reporter $25 a game to become the NFL's first public relations man.

Throughout his life, Halas had a knack for finding the right person in time of greatest need. Hustling all those press releases finally paid off one Monday morning when Halas opened the *Tribune* to see a one-inch banner headline over the Bears game story. He immediately visited the paper to personally thank its 24-year-old sports editor, Don Maxwell.

Maxwell in turn told Halas the *Tribune* was grateful to the Bears for putting life into what would have been a dull Monday edition. "When I gave the Bears the banner, I wasn't doing it do help them. I was doing it to help the *Tribune!*" Maxwell said. Maxwell served as sports editor until 1930 and then began an impressive climb to the top of the corporate level as editor, where he remained until his 1969 retirement. He died in 1974.

"Halas considered the *Tribune* to be in his pocket," says retired *Trib* sports editor Cooper Rollow. "The *Tribune* was his favorite paper for several reasons. Number one, it was and is a great newspaper. Number two, Halas thought he could have his way and get maximum publicity in the *Tribune*."

When Maxwell became city editor, he told his successor, Arch Ward, that professional football was a major sport that deserved major coverage. Ward and his successors continued that policy that would earn the *Tribune* citations from the National Football Foundation and the Pro Football Hall of Fame for its contributions to the game.

Maxwell's belief in the Bears and pro football was only the start to what became one of Halas's most enduring friendships, one that Rollow observed through the years. "He and Maxwell were very dear, close friends. They went to dinner together, and they did things together with their very close circle of friends. It was a true friendship but, in addition, helped Halas a heck of a lot and, in a sense, helped Maxwell and the *Tribune*. Remember that those were the days before big-time television."

Television would not emerge for another two decades. In 1925, the hot new medium was radio, and the hot new station was the *Tribune*'s WGN, but the newspaper was the driving force behind the empire, and Don Maxwell cemented his position with Halas forever in the pursuit of Harold "Red" Grange. Before the phenomenal Grange finished his college career at Illinois, Grantland Rice and other press box poets in the post–World War I "golden age of sport" elevated the young man from the prairie to the pantheon of athletic heroism as a peer of Babe Ruth, Bobby Jones, and Jack Dempsey. In summer breaks, Grange kept himself in shape and made enough money to pay for school as he delivered 75-pound ice blocks to residents of his hometown, Wheaton, 29 miles west of Chicago's Loop. An enterprising reporter dubbed the 5'10", 175-pound redhead "the Wheaton Iceman," and it stuck.

Not to be outdone, Rice, already esteemed as the leading sportswriter of that era, thought up an even better name that endured, "the Galloping Ghost." That came the week after Grange destroyed Michigan on October 18, 1924, in perhaps the single greatest performance in football history, to dedicate Illinois Memorial Stadium.

Rice, ironically, was not an eyewitness to that game. He was a thousand miles away sitting in the Polo Grounds press box, where he covered Notre Dame's 13–7 victory over Army and batted out the best-known lead of that golden age:

> *Outlined against a blue-gray October sky, the Four Horsemen rode again. In dramatic lore they were known as Famine, Pestilence, Destruction, and Death. These are only aliases. Their real names are Stuhldreher, Miller, Crowley, and Layden.*

Corralling a Ghost was a much harder task back in Champaign for Michigan's embattled Wolverines, who never could get a clear shot at the Redhead. The largest crowd to see a game in the Midwest to that time, 67,000, squeezed into the stadium while 20,000 more were stranded outside. Those who saw the game or heard the broadcast on WGN discussed it for years afterward.

Grange took the opening kickoff and weaved his way 95 yards to a touchdown. He followed that with a 67-yard end run and cutback for touchdown number two, ran 56 yards for his third score, and added number four on a 45-yard sweep to make it 27–0 Illini. Moments later, Illini coach Bob Zuppke sent in a substitute for the exhausted Grange. Drained by 88-degree Indian summer heat, his brilliant runs, and emotion, Grange removed his helmet, revealing a shock of bright red hair, and trotted to the bench to the roar of the entire stadium. He had gained 363 all-purpose yards in just 12 minutes of play.

Grange sat out the second quarter and returned in the second half. In the third quarter, he ran for a fifth score, his shortest touchdown run of the day, a 12-yarder, as he gained 402 yards for the afternoon. In the fourth quarter, he passed for the sixth Illinois touchdown to complete the 39–14 rout.

Grange played his final college game on Saturday, November 20, 1925, leading Illinois to a 14–9 victory over Ohio State before 85,500 fans at Ohio Stadium, the second-largest crowd in college football history to that time. Pro football was regarded as a low-rent sport played by outlaws and renegades, and coaches such as Michigan's Fielding H. Yost and Grange's own coach at Illinois, Bob Zuppke, helped foster that belief. Thus, many of the fans who went to the game in Columbus were certain it was the last chance to see Red run.

They were mistaken. Delivery would come the next day. Grange was not signed per se, but a man representing him had locked up a secret deal with George Halas a full 10 days before. It had been a cloak-and-dagger operation for a good month.

The deal took root in late October, according to Halas, when a Chicagoan named Frank Zambreno stopped by the team's new Loop offices at 111 West Washington. Zambreno informed Halas that Champaign businessman Charles C. Pyle planned to ask Grange if he could become his manager. Halas nodded when Zambreno asked him if he wanted Grange to play for the Bears if Pyle could persuade him to turn professional.

Grange was oblivious to the machinations. Pyle set the trap at the start of November when he saw Grange enter his Virginia Theater. In a ghostwritten autobiography appropriately titled *The Galloping Ghost*, Grange said Pyle sent an usher to invite him to meet his boss in his office after the show. The naive Grange was no match for the glib Pyle, seated behind his large desk and wearing an expensive three-piece suit, spats over shoes shined to a high gloss, and a neatly trimmed moustache. To the end of his life, in public Grange would call Pyle one of the finest men he ever met. He would say otherwise to close friends.

Pyle immediately handed the Redhead free passes good for the rest of the school year to the Virginia and his other Champaign movie house, the Park Theater. Grange said it was the first gift of any kind he ever received at Illinois.

Pyle was standing in the lobby of the Virginia a week later when Grange entered the theater. He led the football player straight to his office, asked him to take a seat, and popped the question that defined the future of pro football. "How would you like to make a hundred thousand dollars, or even a million?"

Grange agreed on the spot, a decision he said he never regretted. The next day, November 9, Pyle was ensconced in Halas's office deciding the future of the biggest star that football had yet seen. Halas sized up Pyle and knew he was in combat with a sharp, tough operator. "He was suave. I felt I was in the presence of a born promoter," the Papa Bear wrote.

They quickly agreed that Grange would join the Bears immediately after the finale at Ohio State and would play the Bears' final two regular-season games, the first on Thanksgiving with the Cardinals. Pyle then laid out the tour schedule. First, he said, the Bears and Grange should head east to play in New York, Washington, and other cities. After Christmas, they would go to Florida and then proceed along the southern rim of the country, to finish up on the West Coast.

Halas asked about arrangements. "I'll make them," Pyle said. "Pyle had been around," Halas wrote, having sensed that in comparison with this operator, "I was just a country boy." Halas also had a feeling that the talks had moved too easily, confirmed when each man insisted that his side get two-thirds of the take.

The real negotiations, regarding money, lasted through the afternoon and into the night. They kept talking and arguing, but they stayed at it. Finally, the next afternoon, 26 hours after they started, Pyle and Halas shook on the agreement. They would split the earnings 50-50. Halas and Sternaman would supply the Bears and pick up tour costs. Pyle would supply Grange and the crowds. They also agreed that no contract existed. Thus, should anyone ask, they would be telling the truth when they denied that Grange had signed with the Bears.

Grange's future was topic A on sports pages across America the week before the Ohio State–Illinois finale. The secret seeped out of the East when Pyle went there to make arrangements, but the storm center was in Chicago, where Halas and his new close friend, sports editor Don Maxwell, deftly fanned the flames of speculation beneath banner headlines.

On Wednesday, November 18, 1925, under the banner " 'I'll Not Sign Until Saturday'—Grange," Maxwell wrote in a copyrighted article that Red rushed home from Champaign to see his father. In an unsigned inside sidebar, the *Tribune* reported that Lyle Grange was opposed to his son's turning professional. Grange later called that report "hogwash." Grange himself raised a furor in central Illinois when he stormed out of the *Champaign News-Gazette* offices after he denied signing with Halas and the Bears.

Also in that Wednesday's *Tribune* edition, under the head "Rumor That Grange Will Sign with Chicago Bears Persists," the paper all but told its readers that Grange was a Bear. Halas obviously had told Maxwell the details of Grange's deal: the agreement with his still unnamed manager, a tour, then films, all of which happened.

"Zuppke Hides and Defends Grange" was Thursday's *Trib* banner. It was obvious he was going, but not quite gone.

Grange was the entire story by the weekend. On Friday, he insisted he had not signed with the Bears but hinted he would after the game. On Saturday morning, the *Tribune* headline over the pregame advancer read "Grange's Finish Overshadows Ohio Battle."

The brouhaha ended quietly with Grange sewing up Illinois's 14–9 victory over Ohio State as he ended his play-for-no-pay days with a 25-yard touchdown run.

The next day, Grange got off the train in Chicago and checked into the Morrison Hotel. First he signed a contract with his manager, C. C. (now called "Cash and Carry" in newspaper stories across the country) Pyle. That afternoon, with Pyle by his side, Grange signed the agreement Pyle and Halas had hammered out on November 10.

Grange indicated he might return to Illinois to finish his schooling. He did not, leaving the campus so fast that he left an unpaid bill with his fraternity, Zeta Psi, still unmet into the 21st century. Zuppke was so furious with his pupil that they did not speak for years.

In return for the services of the Galloping Ghost, the Bears agreed to pay Grange the unheard-of sum of $100,000. It was more money than the president of the United States made. And he had to earn it in a way no other athlete ever had before or since.

Pyle had obligated Grange and his new Bears teammates to the most debilitating schedule and regimen in the history of sports. He played his first game with the Bears just five days later before a standing-room crowd of 36,000 jammed into the still single-decked Cubs' Park on Thanksgiving Day, November 26, against the crosstown Chicago Cardinals.

"I've often wondered what Halas thought when he saw that crowd," said Chet Coppock, who knew both Halas and Grange as family friends from childhood. "Part of Halas had to be thrilled by the sheer numbers and noise. His other part must have been furious that Grange and Pyle were getting half the gate!"

Before they went home to their turkey dinners, the largest crowd in pro-football history witnessed a 0–0 tie. Grange managed 92 total yards, but Big Red star Paddy Driscoll punted away from the Redhead all day. And that was only the beginning.

Grange and the Bears hit the road, playing 10 games in the next 17 days on a circuit that wound from Chicago to St. Louis to Philadelphia and the biggest game yet, the Polo Grounds, storied home of the New York baseball and new football Giants.

This game gave pro football legitimacy and, in the process, saved the Giants franchise from failing in America's largest and most important city, and Red Grange was solely responsible. The New York papers gave the game such hype that an estimated 73,000 fans stuffed every corner of the Polo Grounds after they literally broke down the gates to get inside. They got what they came for when Grange ran back an interception for a 30-yard touchdown in the fourth quarter to highlight a 19–7 Bears victory.

While his teammates caught a train to Washington for a Tuesday exhibition, Grange and Pyle stayed behind in a New York hotel to rake in the loot. In a single day, they walked away with a then fantastic $35,000 in certified checks for Grange's endorsements on a line of sweaters, shoes, caps, a doll, and a soft drink. Because Grange did not smoke, he turned aside a cigarette company's offer.

Grange also pocketed a $50,000 check for the Giants game. Then he joined his teammates in Washington. A highlight was a trip to the White House where they met nonfan President Calvin Coolidge. As Grange recalled it, they were introduced as "George Halas, Red Grange, and the Chicago Bears." To which the president, whose preferred form of exercise was fishing after a long nap, replied, "Glad to meet you young gentlemen. I've always enjoyed animal acts!"

By that time, the tour had gained a national press following. In that pretelevision era of pack coverage, New York–based syndicates assigned the top writers of the day, Damon Runyon, Westbrook Pegler, and future baseball commissioner Ford Frick, to follow every move Grange made on and off the field and then write about it. And so it went from city to city.

The heavy schedule took its toll. Several Bears, including Grange, got hurt. In Boston, the Providence Steamrollers beat the Bears 9–6 after Grange injured his left arm. In midweek, at Pittsburgh, after Grange broke a blood vessel in his already injured left arm, they lost to an all-star team 21–0. By the time the Bears arrived in Detroit, a blood clot had formed in Grange's arm, and the host Panthers shut out the Bears 9–0. Because Grange could not play, the Panthers had to refund $9,000 to angry fans who had paid to see the Ghost. The eastern segment of the tour ended in Chicago on December 13 in a rematch with the Giants. With Grange still injured and sidelined, the Giants evened the score, beating the Bears 9–0.

Grange was as healed as he could possibly be when the second part of the tour, nine more games, began eight days later. The Bears arrived in south Florida before Christmas in the midst of the great land boom, where lots and money changed hands as fast as the tides. They beat an all-star team 7–0 in Miami on Christmas Day and then caught a train to Tampa. On New Year's Day, Grange ran for a 70-yard touchdown to seal a 17–3 Chicago win against a Tampa Cardinals team that featured Jim Thorpe, at 41, well past his prime.

Grange and the Bears had no time to enjoy the New Year as they suited up the next day in Jacksonville for a 19–6 victory over another all-star aggregation. That night, they and the trailing press corps boarded their train and headed for New Orleans, where, on January 10, after an eight-day layoff, they won their fourth game since Christmas, 14–0. Grange gained 136 yards on 16 carries and scored a touchdown. After the game, they entrained for the 1,800-mile journey to Los Angeles.

On Saturday, January 16, the largest-ever crowd in the West, 75,000, packed Los Angeles Memorial Coliseum to see the Bears beat the hometown Tigers 17–7. Grange sent them home happy, scoring both Chicago touchdowns. A day later, he scored again as the Bears beat an all-star team at a San Diego high school stadium 14–0. Back in Los Angeles, the city council of suburban Glendale unanimously approved a resolution to name a new thoroughfare Grange Street.

A week later, the San Francisco Tigers handed the Bears their only loss on the second tour, winning 14–7. In Portland the following Saturday, January 30, the Bears routed a pickup team 60–3 as Grange scored two more times. They came back a day later in Seattle, beating the Washington All-Stars 34–0. Grange wrapped up the tour with two more touchdowns, gaining 98 yards on nine carries.

After the game, Pyle handed Grange another $50,000 check. With the money he drew weekly, plus two $50,000 checks, Grange had earned $125,000 for playing two months of football. He made another $85,000 in endorsements and a movie deal, for a total of $210,000. Adjusting for inflation, in 2004 dollars, Red Grange earned the equivalent of $5 million!

In 19 games, the Chicago Bears drew 400,000 fans, virtually all of whom came to see Grange. More important, from that 1925–26 tour, professional football came of age. Ironically, Red Grange had climbed the athletic mountain and never would be as good a player again.

In late winter, Illinois athletic director George Huff and coach Bob Zuppke called on Halas and told him the Grange affair had widened the breach between the colleges and pros. Halas then took a rule change to Joe Carr and the league stating that no college player could turn professional until his class had graduated.

In late spring, Pyle pressed Halas and Sternaman to give Grange a one-third share in the Bears. Citing the record-breaking attendance figures from the tour, Pyle argued that only Grange's presence would ensure box office prosperity for the team. Halas and Sternaman turned him down. No man, not even Grange, was worth it, especially when a slicker such as Pyle pulled the strings.

A chagrined Pyle tried to get a second National Football League franchise in New York built around Grange that he would call the Yankees. Giants owner Tim Mara, however, refused to relinquish his territorial rights. So, Pyle declared war on the NFL, setting up his own nine-team American Football League, with Grange and the Yankees the main attraction. The Chicago entry, playing in Comiskey Park, was named the Bulls.

The new league was awash in red ink from opening day on, but Grange prospered in 1926. He made a silent film, *One Minute to Play*, a football story, at the Joseph P. Kennedy–controlled RKO Studios and encored with another silent, *The Racing Romeo.*

The AFL folded, but Pyle talked Grange's Yankees into joining the NFL for the 1927 season after he agreed not to play at Yankee Stadium on dates when Mara's Giants were home across the Harlem River at the Polo Grounds.

In the fourth game of the season, the Bears were leading the Yankees 12–0 at Wrigley Field in the final minute of play when Grange went up for a pass by the sideline. He collided with George Trafton, and they fell together. As the cleat on Grange's right shoe caught in the turf, Trafton landed on top of him, severely twisting Red's right knee.

Grange sat out for a month, and the Yankees' gate receipts plummeted. A frantic Pyle urged his meal ticket to get back in there. The foolish Grange played until he could not stand up. In that era before modern surgical and rehabilitation techniques, the brilliant moves that made him the most talked-about football player in history disappeared forever. Red's longtime broadcast partner George Connor recalled Grange's dismay: "C. C. Pyle had [promoted] marathons, walkathons, dance-athons. He blew all the money. Red never forgot that." Pyle died on February 3, 1939. He was 47.

Through with Pyle, Grange sat out the 1928 season, and the Yanks folded in short order. Grange, meanwhile, went on a theatrical tour and ended up back in Wheaton. In 1929, certain he was washed up as a football player, he went west to make one of the first talkies, again for Kennedy. It was a 12-chapter serial called *The Galloping Ghost.*

The plot called for Red to foil a gang who operated a cap company as a front for illegal activities, among them an attempt to fix a football game. The story was replete with auto and motorcycle chases, plunges off cliffs, a midair plane-to-plane jump, and plenty of fistfights as Red saved the day.

When he performed his own stunts, Grange realized he had enough left to play football, but he had no place to go. Frank Zambreno, now his theatrical booking agent, approached Halas. Reluctant at first to forgive the great star, Halas realized that on a professional basis, he needed the Redhead as much as Grange needed him. And he liked Grange. They worked out their differences and buried the hatchet to their mutual benefit. After Pyle tapped out, Grange lost a huge chunk in the stock-market crash that fall. He was broke, but he also knew that playing for Halas and the Bears would help him with business ventures in Chicago.

In return, George Halas regained a man who made himself the most complete player in the league. No longer the flashing, slashing, dashing runner of Illinois fame, he became a superb blocker, tough straight-ahead runner, receiver, occasional passer, decoy, and, in that era of two-way play, the NFL's best defensive back.

Late in his career, Grange was the central figure in two of the most important plays in early league history. In the second week of December 1932, Chicago was buried under a heavy snowfall and sustained Arctic blast so intense that Wrigley Field became an unplayable, concrete-hard block of ice. Halas persuaded the league to schedule its first indoor playoff game at Chicago Stadium pairing the Bears against the Portsmouth Spartans. Playing on a less-than-regulation field, just 80 yards long, both teams agreed to two ground rules changes that would become a permanent part of the rules. When play stopped by the sideline, instead of putting the ball in play there, as had been the rule, the officials now spotted it near the middle of the field, creating the hash mark. They set the goalposts on the goal line, a move that Halas wanted in order to encourage field goal kicking and scoring.

A league rule stipulated that all passes had to take place at least five yards behind the line of scrimmage. Late in the game after Portsmouth had stopped Bears fullback Bronko Nagurski three times at the goal line, the Bears ad-libbed a play that literally changed the game and broke a scoreless tie. Grange recalled the play in a 1978 interview with WGN's Wally Phillips on his 75th birthday: "I was in the end zone. Somebody knocked me down. I was lying on the dirt when Bronk saw me and made a jump pass. It wasn't a play, really. He hit me with the ball, and that was the only touchdown of the game."

Portsmouth complained that Nagurski had thrown that pass within the mandated five-yard barrier, but the referee awarded the Bears a touchdown that led to a 9–0 win and the title. In the off-season, Halas, to be safe forever, rammed through a rules change to allow passing anywhere behind the scrimmage line.

Grange retired from football in 1935 to enter business in Chicago, where he eventually opened a lucrative insurance brokerage. By 1940, he was announcing college football games on radio, and finally, with the arrival of television, he moved into the new medium in 1947 when Halas televised Bears home games. Those broadcasts and hosting the "Chicago Bears Quarterback Club" shows on Tuesdays gave Red Grange a new fame and plenty of work in a career that lasted through the 1963 season as play-by-play announcer for the Bears nearly four decades after he gained his eternal fame at Illinois.

Not everyone approved of his broadcasting style. Grange had a high-pitched voice and spoke with little inflection. He also drove English teachers crazy with colloquialisms. He might say "purty near" instead of "close." Another was his ear-wrenching misuse of the plural verb, as in "Green Bay are on the 25." All his sins against the mother tongue were excused, though, especially when one of his favorite Bears such as fullback Rick Casares blasted through the line and carried defenders a few extra yards. That's when Grange would blurt out, "Look at that big guy go!"

Yet, as George Connor, his longtime sidekick on Bears telecasts, attests, Grange was always haunted by the memory of Pyle's nose-dive. "Red was a lobby sitter," recalled Connor in 2002. "We'd go out of town, and CBS didn't give us much expense money, but Red didn't let go of any of it. He'd sit in the lobby and wait around until somebody invited him to dinner, and they'd go out."

After his retirement to Indian Lake Estates, Florida, where he and his wife, Margaret (also known affectionately as "Mugs"), built a home in 1954, Grange came back north twice, the last time in 1978 to Wheaton, the other in 1974 to the University of Illinois to mark the golden anniversary of the dedication of Illinois Memorial Stadium. On Friday, October 17, after addressing the football team at practice, the 71-year-old Grange held court at a full-scale press conference in the Varsity Room under the stadium, at a podium near the trophy case that held his famed "77" jersey.

Standing tall under hot lights before a battery of television cameras and radio mikes, he cut loose. As the television and radio reporters got their material, one, two, three reels in, the cameras turned off. Soon, the tape recorders clicked off. The reporters, who had been taking notes, set down their pens and pads and watched.

Grange never stopped talking, spellbinding his younger audience, none of whom had seen him play, with his tales and observations. "There's been no new plays in football since my coach Bob Zuppke thought them up." Or, "If they played both ways like we did, we'd throw over a gimpy-kneed quarterback all day long." After one hour straight, he said thank you and left the podium. Before he walked out of the room, a representative of the Jim Beam Distillery presented Grange with a specially made porcelain bottle of its best blend. It came in a one-of-a-kind container, a hand-painted figure of a football player wearing an orange helmet, moleskin pants, and a blue jersey with the number 77 on back, similar to the jersey in the school's trophy case.

"I suppose George will let me share this with him," Grange said of his former boss, the Papa Bear, who introduced him at a banquet that night. Grange spoke for one more hour. And he did not repeat a single story from his afternoon session. After the banquet, the two men retired to Grange's suite and killed that bottle of Beam.

The next afternoon, on Red Grange Day, 55,000 fans stood and cheered wildly as Old Number 77, wearing sunglasses to defray the glare and effects from the night before, took one last walk alongside the playing field where, a half century before, he had the greatest day any football player ever enjoyed. At halftime, he walked onto the gridiron, took a microphone, and issued a valedictory to his school, state, and sport. "I want to thank you for giving me the privilege to play for the greatest fans in the world," he said. The crowd returned the thanks with one final roar to the individual who, more than any other person, popularized the game of professional football.

Red Grange died in 1991, just short of his 88th birthday.

FIVE

THE LAST ROAR
OF THE '20S

By the 1929 New Year, George Halas was riding the crest of America's unprecedented prosperity. The money he made on the Red Grange tour was hard at work in various investments from the stock market to pro basketball to real estate.

Early in 1929, he repaired the bitter breach with his college coach Bob Zuppke over taking Grange off the Illinois campus in 1925 as, best of all, he made peace with Grange himself and brought him back to the Bears at a bargain wage. At the dawn of this new year, Halas had no idea that by 1930, he and the rest of America would be hanging on by their fingernails after getting cleaned out in the greatest financial collapse in world history.

Back in '26, he opened an account with Paine Webber, and like most every other stock market investor, he took his broker's advice— he spread his money around and, to maximize his value, bought on margin. His portfolio blossomed.

With a friend named Howard Kraft, Halas plunged into real estate speculation at flank speed. Halas and Kraft Realty's first project targeted the largely Bohemian community in Cicero, an area he knew from his time at Western Electric. They bought a four-block, 60-acre parcel there. It ran from 35th south to 39th (now renamed Pershing Road in honor of the World War I hero of heroes) between Austin Boulevard to the west and Central Avenue on the east. The land was within walking distance of Charlie Bidwill's Hawthorne and Sportsman's racetrack complex and short streetcar rides away from the many factories on Chicago's Far West Side. Lots in Austin Boulevard Manor, as they called the development, went on the market for $1,100 each.

In early 1927, Halas got word, most likely from Don Maxwell at the *Tribune*, who got his intelligence from his boss, the owner and publisher Colonel Robert Rutherford McCormick, about a potential real estate bonanza. The First National Bank of Antioch in the Chain O'Lakes resort area just south of the Illinois-Wisconsin border was executor for a huge, buildable piece of heavily wooded property along Petite Lake in nearby Lake Villa. The William Deering family, who owned the land, earned their fortune making farm equipment. The family cashed in big when they sold Deering Harvester to the McCormicks, who in turn formed the International Harvester agribusiness colossus.

Halas confirmed the report with the bank president, C. K. Anderson, and went to work. Halas and Kraft bought the Deering property, subdivided it into attractive, lake-accessible lots, and built a golf course. In the summer of 1927, they found extra money when they rented the Deering mansion and its substantial adjacent grounds to heavyweight boxing champion Gene Tunney for a training camp. Tunney, his entourage, and the national sporting press settled in for a summer of workouts in preparation for his 10-round rematch with former champion Jack Dempsey on September 22 at Soldier Field.

Ever the operator, Halas had the phone company install pay phones so the reporters could file with their home offices. One booth was reserved for the champ. "Every night Tunney would spend hours at a phone dropping in quarters and talking to a girl," Halas remarked in his memoir. "I presume it was the rich young lady he married the next year after the fight." Halas was correct. Her name was Polly Lauder, heiress to a steel fortune. One of their children, John Varick Tunney, served as U.S. senator from California in the '70s.

It was the largest gate in boxing history as 104,943 fans squeezed into every corner of Soldier Field, paying a total of $2,550,658 and gaining the privilege to say they were there for a bout that gained notoriety for the "long count" in the seventh round. After a futile six-round chase, a furious Dempsey finally caught Tunney near the ropes and slugged the champion to the canvas with a five-punch barrage that left him seated with his left arm draped over the middle strand of rope. Dempsey stood over Tunney, and as long as he did, referee Dave Barry refused to start the knockdown count.

When Dempsey finally moved to a neutral corner, Barry began counting. The delay, estimated at 14 seconds by boxing historian Nat Fleischer, gave Tunney the time to regain his senses. Up at the count of "nine," he beat a hasty retreat as Dempsey flailed wildly in a futile chase until the bell sounded. Tunney then easily boxed his way to win the unanimous decision and earn a million-dollar cut for a half hour's work.

Up in Antioch, Halas's banker friend C. K. Anderson, elated with the publicity that Tunney generated for the Petite Lake development and his bank, told Halas, "Anytime I or the bank can be of service, let me know." "What a lifesaving promise that turned out to be," wrote Halas a half century later.

In the winter of 1925–26, Halas sank money into a team in Joe Carr's new American Basketball League. He named his club the Bruins, signed New Yorker John "Honey" Russell as player-coach, and watched the team struggle. The Bruins played their home games at the Illinois National Guard Armory on Broadway on the North Side, won seldom, and barely broke even. When Halas's fellow owner and friend George Preston Marshall folded his Washington Palace Five halfway through the 1927–28 season after losing $65,000 in the venture, Halas should have followed suit.

Instead, he moved the team into the cavernous Chicago Stadium at an exorbitant 50 percent rental fee, lost his shirt when nobody came, and got out as that forerunner of the National Basketball Association disbanded after the 1930–31 season.

Halas was far more concerned with his battle for control of the Bears with partner Ed "Dutch" Sternaman. They had fought for years, beginning in 1926 after Grange left. Soon after, Ed's popular and talented brother Joey quit the Bears to join forces with C. C. Pyle to run a Chicago American Football League entry, the Bulls. The aggressive Joey Sternaman stole the Comiskey Park lease from the Cardinals and then went after their star, Paddy Driscoll. Alarm bells went off in Halas's head. He called Cardinals owner Chris O'Brien and made the trade for Driscoll. Then, Halas outbid Joey Sternaman and made his friend Driscoll the NFL's highest-paid player, at $10,000.

The simmering Halas–Ed Sternaman difference erupted in a battle over the schedule. From the beginning of league play in 1920, the Bears always had met the Cardinals twice each season. This year, 1926, Sternaman wanted to schedule the Cardinals on Thanksgiving and leave October 17 an open date. When Halas learned that Grange's Yankees were going to play Joey's Bulls in Comiskey Park on that same day, he exploded.

To Halas, Dutch Sternaman was betraying the Bears to help his brother. When Halas won the scheduling battle at the league meeting, Sternaman threatened to sell. "How I wish I had bought him out at once," Halas wrote. The relationship had spoiled.

Driscoll's success salved the wounds between Halas and the Sternamans when Paddy led the Bears to a superb 12–1–3 record. It was not quite enough to beat out the Frankford Yellow Jackets, who went 14–1–2, for Guy Chamberlain's fourth coaching title since 1922. As exciting as the title chase had been, NFL attendance, with Grange in the other league, plummeted in Chicago and everywhere else. The Bears cleared only $989 in profits.

Now double-decked, Wrigley Field could accommodate 40,000 fans for football, but the Bears came close to filling the ballpark just once over the next decade, when they drew 30,000 for Grange's 1927 return with the New York Yankees. Most of the crowds fell well below 10,000, and the team lost $3,500 in 1927. The Bears fell out of the hunt in 1928, with just seven wins. Despite the national prosperity that fueled a landslide election for Republican Herbert Hoover over Democrat Al Smith, the NFL was hurting. Fewer fans came to the games, as the Bears held their losses to $563, a loss that foreshadowed the economic future.

Prospects seemed promising, though, for the 1929 Bears. Driscoll, now 34, told Halas and Sternaman he would retire after the season, but that blow was offset by the happy return of Grange, who was joined by his younger brother Gardie, an end on Illinois's 1927 national champions. Gardie would stay with the Bears through the 1931 season.

Halas also signed a talented end from Northwestern named Luke Johnsos, who would become one of the most significant figures in franchise history. A Halas man all the way, Johnsos would play on two championship teams in eight seasons and then remain as an assistant for 30 more years. Johnsos would play an important role in the development of six championship teams and would co-coach the 1943 champions with Hunk Anderson.

Since their arrival in Chicago with the Staleys, Halas and Sternaman had established distinct personas. Halas wore the public face as team spokesman. Sternaman operated behind the scenes. As coaches, Halas, an end, handled line play, teaching his linemen all the tricks—legal and, especially, otherwise—while Sternaman ran the backfield. Both men were strong-willed, stubborn, and positive in their approaches.

The stock market crashed on October 24, 1929, Black Thursday. But after a Friday rally, the Bears took it to the Minneapolis Red Jackets 27–0. The Wall Street bears dumped everything the following Tuesday, October 29. A record 16 million shares changed hands. Business writer Frederick Lewis Allen called it "the Great Liquidation," a catastrophe that wiped out millionaires by the scores and virtually every small investor in America, Halas included.

When the market collapsed, Halas's Paine Webber broker simply pulled the plug on the Papa Bear's portfolio at a huge loss. Halas and Kraft Realty went belly-up, and with it, the firm's developments. They weren't alone; virtually all residential and commercial construction ceased abruptly. It would stay that way well into the mid-1930s. Halas absorbed the body blow and vowed to get everything back and be thrifty above all else.

At first, Sternaman fared better after the crash. He had put his money into an apartment building and gas station, not stocks. He felt safe, but not even real estate was safe in this climate.

Disaster descended on Wrigley Field as well when the New York Giants visited the Sunday after the Great Liquidation. Midway through the first quarter, Grange banged his right elbow hard on the ground while making a tackle. He felt a stinging sensation in the arm as he left the field with trainer Andy Lotshaw and team physician Dr. John Davis.

"Doc Davis took me out of the game, and we went upstairs," said Red in his 1978 interview with WGN's Wally Phillips. "He said, 'We better put it in. We should take you to the hospital and knock you out and do it.' He pulled my shoulder up and snapped it back in. I never had anything hurt me so in my life."

The Giants went on to beat the Grange-less Bears 26–14. Worse, the bickering between Halas and Sternaman turned into open arguments in front of the players. When one would send in a play, the other would countermand it. The defeats piled up.

To keep the Cardinals afloat in 1929, Halas persuaded a Bears fan named Dr. David Jones to buy out O'Brien. Halas so wanted to keep the Cardinals going that he offered to absorb 40 percent of any losses, an offer he never had to redeem. The Bears, however, bottomed out on Thanksgiving Day when a thick, wet snowfall covered the Comiskey Park field.

The Cardinals' great fullback Ernie Nevers ran at will for a record six touchdowns and kicked four extra points, for a still unequaled 40 points, all the scoring, as the Big Red won 40–6. It would stand as the worst defeat in team history until 1955 when the Bears' championship dreams were snowed under 53–14 in another Thanksgiving weekend visit to the Cardinals' nest.

The season ended in a nine-game winless stretch—eight losses and a scoreless tie with the Frankford Yellow Jackets on the last home date of the season. A corporal's guard of 2,123 fans turned out, and the team could not meet its guarantee. The Bears lost $1,082.92 for 1929 and would have slid deeper into the red had it not been for program sales. It also marked the end of Halas's playing career. After the season ended, Halas and Sternaman did the only sensible thing: they agreed to step aside and hire a man they both respected as a coach, unifier, and teacher.

Ralph Jones had coached both men at Illinois before he left the university to serve as athletic director at Lake Forest Academy, a private school 33 miles north of the Loop. While other teams ran either Rockne's Notre Dame box or the single wing, Halas and Sternaman stuck with the same model T they learned at Illinois under Zuppke, only occasionally shifting into the single wing. When Halas and Sternaman interviewed him, Jones promised to deliver a championship within three years. He did it with a thoroughly overhauled T formation.

Jones spaced the linemen and backs to give them operating room and a chance to do more than just run straight ahead. He lined up the quarterback behind the center, placing his right hand on the center's crotch and the left hand below to take a direct snap. That technique permitted the center to keep his head up and also be an effective blocker instead of a head-down snapper.

Jones literally created the quarterback position, making the player a ball handler and passer. More important, as he called the signals, the quarterback for the first time could see and "read" defensive sets and become a real field general, a term Jones encouraged and used. Once he took the snap, the quarterback pivoted to either make a handoff or pitch the ball to another back. In contrast to the directness and brute power of single-wing football, the new T formation was quick-hitting and deceptive, and, for linemen, finesse became as important as strength.

Jones then installed the spice that gave the T a new life: the man in motion. He was taking advantage of a basic football rule that one back may run laterally before the snap. Doing so enabled the Bear to establish a wide running game, help with passing, and, with that deception, aid the inside running game. The man who made the motion work was the still dangerous Red Grange. Grange might start from his left halfback position and run across the formation from left to right before the snap. If left uncovered, he was open to take either a pitchout or a pass. To further confuse the defense, he might take a step to his right and reverse left.

As the Bears began to win, the new Jones T concepts took root. Yet, this still was not the be-all and end-all, for nobody else was willing to put in the time and effort to copy it. Not yet. But Jones's initial changes blazed the trail for Clark Shaughnessy and Halas to establish the Bears dynasty of the '40s.

With Halas and Sternaman out of the mix, Jones was able to exert his own brand of leadership and gain the respect of the players. And, thanks to Halas's eye for talent and his powers of persuasion, Jones gained an extraordinary weapon, a fullback and defensive tackle of extraordinary size, stamina, and density, who could do anything on a football field.

Of all the men who played the game, a mere handful have had the unique natural gifts and intelligence to play any position at the highest performance level and change the game. That short list includes such modern-day Hall of Famers as Jim Brown, Lawrence Taylor, Walter Payton, Marcus Allen, and Bobby Bell.

Halas was able to find and sign more than his share of those special athletes: Grange, Clyde "Bulldog" Turner, George Connor, Rick Casares, Harlon Hill, Dick Butkus, and Gale Sayers among them.

Halas always insisted that Bronko Nagurski was the best of all. Like his fellow Minnesotan of myth, Paul Bunyan, Nagurski was larger than life, a Herculean figure unto himself, pro football's equivalent of Babe Ruth.

When George Halas visited the University of Minnesota campus in early 1930, he saw in Nagurski a farm boy who never lifted a weight in his life, who stood 6'2" and carried 230 pounds on a concrete slab–like frame. Nagurski had a naturally developed 22-inch neck and could not find a ready-made shirt he could button at the collar. His hands were so big that his ring finger, at size 19 and a half, is the largest ever measured for the Pro Football Hall of Fame ring by the L. G. Balfour Company.

Scores of stories, fact or fancy, concerning Nagurski's strength, abound. It's the myth du jour that the Nagurski legend began when Minnesota coach Clarence "Doc" Spears was hunting for prospects in the northern tundra near the Canadian border when he happened upon a young farm boy plowing a field and asked for directions, and the lad picked up the plow and pointed with it. "That boy could have been an all-American at all 11 positions," Coach Spears later said of Bronko Nagurski.

As it was, the *New York Sun*'s 1929 all-America team listed just 10 men for the 11 positions. Minnesota's Nagurski filled both the tackle and fullback slots. After they scrimmaged when Nagurski joined the Bears in 1930, someone asked Grange what it was like trying to bring down the big man wearing number 3. Grange answered, "When you hit him at the ankles, it's like an electric shock. If you hit him above the ankles, you're likely to get killed!"

How mighty was Nagurski? Grange never varied in his answer, the one he gave in 1978 to WGN's Phillips: "Wally, when anybody asks me who was the greatest football player I ever saw, I don't even hesitate. It was Nagurski. I had some folks ask me the other day, 'How good was he?' You have to compare. Bronk played both ways, 60 minutes. On defense, he was equal to Dick Butkus in Butkus's prime. On offense, he was faster and equal to Larry Csonka. Put the two together and you got Nagurski."

He was also an accurate passer. Nagurski's fake plunge and jump pass to Grange that may or may not have been thrown within a five-yard limit behind the line of scrimmage won the 1932 title in Chicago Stadium. After seeing Nagurski execute that play, both Halas and George Preston Marshall, his friend from their basketball days, took note.

Marshall, who owned the Palace Laundry chain in Washington, D.C., got into football when he persuaded four investors to help him start a team in Boston in 1932 and play at Braves Field. In a name tie-in akin to the Cubs and Bears, Marshall called his team the Redskins. When the Redskins lost $40,000 that first season, Marshall's investors dropped out, but he refused to quit. Marshall had the money to stick with it, he knew what football fans wanted, and he was a promotional wizard who envisioned a better game that would result from commonsense rules changes.

Watching the game from the stands in 1930–32, Halas gained a perspective that he never had from the sidelines. When he talked to Marshall, both men agreed that the game was mired in a conservative rut with little to no scoring, and it was bogged down by tie after tie, which skewed the standings. The champion Bears, for instance, opened the 1932 season with three scoreless ties and would finish with six ties, against seven victories and one loss. Overtime would not be adopted until 1974.

When Halas convened the rules committee meeting in February 1933, he and Marshall set a five-item agenda on the table. First, they pushed through the "Nagurski" passing rule to create the constant threat of passing anywhere on the field and give the game needed unpredictability.

Then, Halas asked the committee to make the hash marks a permanent feature of the field. In the Bears-Portsmouth game, the less-than-regulation indoor field was small and narrow. They had to erect plywood sheets in front of the seating area to protect the players on pileups at the sidelines. In order to facilitate play and make it less of a rugbylike scrum, the officials walked the ball to marks on the center of the field to give the players room to work. It worked so well that, starting in 1933, on any play that ended within 5 yards of the sideline, the ball would be moved to a marker, the hash mark, 10 yards inside the sideline. That eliminated time- and down-wasting setup plays to reestablish operating field position.

That change worked so well that the colleges followed suit a year later, a fact Marshall and Halas delightedly exploited as innovators of change. Through the years, the hash marks advanced inward to the present 70 feet 9 inches—23 and a half yards. They now are directly aligned with the goalposts to enable easier field goal kicking. Another victory for common sense.

Marshall took the floor. Telling his fellow owners that more scoring was in order, he proposed moving the goalposts from the end line to the goal line. An enthusiastic Halas jumped aboard, and the rule sailed through with ease.

They relaxed the substitution rules to let players return to the game more easily, and they passed another rule to allow the coach and quarterback to talk to each other on the field during time-outs.

Marshall, the newcomer, also saw something that Halas, Carr, Lambeau, Mara, and the others had overlooked. They all knew that scheduling was haphazard, and basing a championship on winning percentage was a lousy way to settle such an important issue. But they didn't know what to do about it.

Why not split the league into two divisions, Eastern and Western, with uniform scheduling, urged Marshall. Doing so would create rivalries that in turn would stir fan interest and increase attendance in a meaningful schedule where every single game counted. Then, after the regular season, each division champion would meet in a play-off for the league championship. The owners looked at each other, realizing the showman had showed them the way, and when Halas took the floor and seconded the motion, Marshall's motion carried unanimously.

The Eastern teams were Marshall's Boston Redskins, which he would move to Washington in 1937; the Brooklyn Dodgers; the New York Giants; and two expansion teams that paid $2,500 franchise fees, the Philadelphia Eagles, owned by Bert Bell and Lud Wray, and the Pittsburgh Pirates, owned by Art Rooney, who won his franchise fee at the racetrack.

The Western Division teams were the Chicago teams, the Bears and Cardinals; the Green Bay Packers; the Portsmouth Spartans, who would move to Detroit in 1934; and the expansion Cincinnati Reds, who would fold after the 1934 season. As Arthur Daley wrote, "It gave pro ball a purpose it never had before and was perhaps the most important reform ever made."

A few months later, Halas, again with Marshall's backing, got the owners to change the shape of the football from a balloonlike oval better fit for dropkicking to a slimmer, longer model more suited for passing, easier to carry, and still kickable.

Spalding manufactured the league ball through 1940, when Halas persuaded the league to transfer the contract to Chicago-based Wilson Sporting Goods. Halas made sure the new ball was named "the Duke," the nickname of Wellington Mara, son of Giants founder Tim Mara. According to Jerry Vainisi, he passed up the naming rights for the profits: the Old Man owned the royalties to 'the Duke' through his sporting goods outlet, May and Halas.

Thus, Vainisi noted, Halas earned a royalty for every ball used in NFL play. That found-money arrangement lasted until the 1970 merger, when the AFL ball replaced "the Duke" and Pete Rozelle and the league thus took control of the property from Halas.

By this time, many other owners felt that Halas was making the rules to take advantage of his strengths. That certainly was true when it came to the passing and hash marks rules. Both opened the field and favored Nagurski. Halas made certain the kicking rule worked in his favor as well, when, at Nagurski's urging, he signed Minnesota fullback Jack Manders, a kicker so consistent for his era that he earned the nickname "Automatic Jack."

Yet, as much as those changes aided Halas and the Bears, they spurred the other owners to get off their duffs to compete with Halas. The net result, with Marshall's division plan, created a more open, better brand of football and, best of all, put pro football on par with the colleges at last.

As he was caught up with rewriting the rules, Halas also was scrambling to hang on to the franchise. Every other club was walking the line, and after the 1931 season, the league was down by a third from 1929's even dozen as a mere eight teams answered the opening bell.

The league also was all-white. After the 1933 rules meeting, Marshall urged his fellow owners to take up one more item. Saying that "nigrahs" were bad for business and that so many white people were out of work in the Depression, he got his fellow owners, Halas included, to ban black players from the game. That disgraceful policy lasted until the Los Angeles Rams signed Jackie Robinson's great prewar UCLA teammates Kenny Washington and Woodrow Strode in 1946. Paul Brown had already smashed down the race barrier with his Cleveland Browns of the All-American Football Conference in '46 with Marion Motley and Bill Willis.

Marshall's Washington Redskins were the last NFL team to integrate when they traded the rights to 1961 Heisman Trophy winner Ernie Davis to the Cleveland Browns for running back Bobby Mitchell. Mitchell, an Illinois star of the mid-'50s in the same backfield with Ray Nitschke and San Francisco 49ers star Abe Woodson, was moved to wide receiver by 'Skins coach Bill McPeak, where he became a Hall of Famer. After he retired, Mitchell became the Redskins' personnel director, helping the team win three Super Bowls.

SIX

PARTNERS ON THE ROCKS

Early in the summer of 1931, Halas learned that Ed Sternaman was flat-out busted, unable to make either the mortgage payment on his apartment building or his gas station note. Charles Brizzolara picks up the narrative: "George and Sternaman had an arrangement where, if one wanted out, the other had first right of refusal to buy him out. That's what George did."

The newspapers gave the sale perfunctory treatment. It did not rate a *Tribune* byline, only: "Ed Sternaman, former University of Illinois football player, who, with George Halas, has been associated with the Chicago Bears professional football team since the club was organized ten years ago as the Staleys of Decatur, Ill., has sold his interest in the North Side team."

The two men haggled for several intense days until they agreed on $38,000 as the value of Sternaman's 50 percent share of the Bears' stock. Halas agreed to put down $25,000 and come up with the rest on two payments over the next calendar year.

The trick in this Depression economy was to find money when many people couldn't find work, let alone eat. "He did it by borrowing from my father and some others," Charles Brizzolara said. Ralph

Brizzolara sold some stock before the crash and loaned his best friend $5,000, "a lot of money then," Charles Brizzolara said. Coming up with that chunk of money was no small feat in the summer of '31, when unemployment had surpassed 8 million and was shooting toward 14 million by 1933.

Halas continued to chase what money there was, not only to buy out Sternaman but also to keep the club alive. He found another ally in Jim McMillen, who, like Halas before him, starred for Bob Zuppke at Illinois and, like Halas, graduated with a degree in civil engineering. A rangy guard, the 6'1", 215-pound McMillen was captain of the unbeaten 1923 Fighting Illini, clearing the way for sophomore Red Grange in his brilliant all-American debut. He joined the Bears in 1924 and played through '29, when he retired. Instead of taking the Papa Bear's $100 a game to smash the guy across from him in the mouth, McMillen turned to professional wrestling, where he cashed in as one of the top three or four pro wrestlers in America.

Professional wrestling was making its first wildly popular run then, packing arenas such as Madison Square Garden. Not only did the promoters pay well, but also, and most important when times got tough, they paid in cash. A vital clue to the way Halas maneuvered money was stored away for decades in the Antioch, Illinois, home of McMillen's daughter Ann Kakasek. In a May 2003 phone conversation, she remarked that she recently found his account ledger. "Dad kept a record of everything," Ann said. She left the phone to retrieve the book; on her return, she read enough to set off alarms. "Here's his dealings with George Halas, real estate investments they were involved in, and Dad's wrestling earnings and expenses." Then came the clincher, "Why don't you come out and take a look?" The McMillen ledger entries tell a story of devotion, absolute trust, and loyalty to the Papa Bear. They are a Halas Rosetta stone.

McMillen began his business relationship with Halas in 1926 as one of the first investors in the Halas and Kraft Realty Cicero Development. He put down $220 on a $1,100 lot, held it for a year, sold it for a $200 profit, and bought two more lots from Halas, who not only would not let McMillen put money down but gave him a $161 commission check to boot.

On December 15, 1931, when banks were closing in clusters, McMillen had the cash on hand to pay off the property in full. It came to $2,144.76 (including that commission). Property taxes on the vacant lots for the next 24 years averaged slightly more than $20 a year. McMillen held that land until 1955, when he sold it for just $1,000, taking a loss of $1,144.76.

Wrestling was one of the few businesses anywhere that paid in cash, and McMillen cashed in big, banking most of it back home in suburban Chicago. In 1931 alone, with 106 bouts, he took in $40,113 through wrestling the likes of Jim Londos, Strangler Ed Lewis, and Babe Didrickson's future husband, George Zaharias.

By 1931, McMillen was ranked at the top of the "rasslin' racket," as noted in a *Chicago Tribune* story: "Jim was a teammate of the famous Red Grange. . . . When they left college, Grange was the big noise. . . . Today, Jim is famous and wealthy, while Grange is beginning to fade from memory."

His biggest paydays, all cash, came in two championship bouts with Londos in Madison Square Garden, both defeats. On January 26, 1931, he earned $4,660 for 55 minutes. The following February, McMillen took home $5,000 after losing to Londos in 49 grueling minutes in what the old-timers called a "shooting match," straight wrestling, no show-business tricks. They got away with that because they were the best in the game.

McMillen had so much faith in his former coach that on May 14, 1931, when the cash-desperate Halas came calling, McMillen willingly paid $5,000 for 17 and a half acres that the defunct Halas and Kraft Realty company held in Cicero.

Then, a month later, on June 24, 1931, after Halas made his buyout deal with Sternaman, McMillen invested $5,000 more in the Bears. In return for that money, which Halas needed to pay Sternaman, Halas awarded McMillen nine and three-eighths shares, one-sixteenth of the total team stock. He was elected to a title he held until 1960, vice president. During that time, the name J. W. McMillen and his title was always second in line below that of George S. Halas, President–Head Coach, on the club directory and letterhead.

When Halas and the Bears bottomed out after the 1932 season, McMillen came through again to cover a $1,000 loss and repay his vendors. McMillen advanced Halas $200 on January 30 and $300 on February 18.

From 1935 on, Halas still pleaded poverty in contract negotiations with his players. The dividend payments to his investors indicate otherwise. On December 21, 1934, Halas refunded McMillen the $500 to cover the 1932 loss. The first dividend for $1,000 arrived on March 2, 1935. The team declared a regular $1,000 dividend on March 14, 1936, and added two more holiday bonuses in late December totaling $1,500. Dividends kept rolling in throughout the '30s, pushed to the $2,000 level throughout the '40s, and held steady around $1,000 in the '50s.

By the end of June 1931, the Papa Bear's mother, Barbara, joined Brizzolara and McMillen as $5,000 investors. Halas wrote that George Trafton's mother came through with $20,000. Mrs. Trafton not only saved the Bears for Halas but also just may have saved the National Football League. Had Halas failed, it is distinctly possible that the league would have crumbled. The Trafton payment, Halas wrote, gave him enough to meet the first payment to Sternaman and pay seriously due bills. He needed more, though, to give him a small operating cushion and to finish the buyout.

Halas turned to another close friend, Charles Bidwill. Charlie Bidwill owned the Bentley-Murray printing company, the Sportsman's Park racetrack, and neighboring Hawthorne Race Course and believed early on in Halas, sharing his faith in pro football's viability. "Charlie had the charm and personality," recalled Bill Gleason.

Most important, Charlie Bidwill had the money. He came through with $5,000. "By some magic, he got it from a bank that was already closed," Halas wrote. Halas was able to make that $25,000 first installment on July 3, 1931, and have $15,000 on hand to pay the bills. He had enough left to make the second payment, $6,000, on January 25, 1932.

That's when Halas at last did something he should have done months before. He read the fine print in the agreement with Sternaman. He nearly got sick when he learned that he must make the final payment on time, July 31, 1932, or lose everything—the money and the Bears—to Sternaman. As scarce as currency had been the prior summer, there was none to be found in 1932. Yet, he knew one thing for certain. He had to make it. No doubt about it.

By July, most of the banks in America were out of business, and the banks that remained open would not make loans. Halas had just $2,000 on hand by July 31 but was able to talk Sternaman into an extension. Then Sternaman tightened the screws. His lawyer wrote a letter warning that the Bears' stock would be put up for public auction on August 9 if Halas did not get the money by that noon. Halas tried everywhere, still without hope, let alone success.

Halas did not write that one of the people he contacted at that critical moment was his friend Jim McMillen, who had just moved to Antioch. Perhaps he never knew that McMillen learned in conversation at the bank with C. K. Anderson that they had a mutual friend in George Halas. McMillen told Anderson that Halas was in deep trouble and so were his investors, himself included.

Then, Halas wrote, the phone rang in his offices at 111 West Washington at 11:00 A.M. August 9. It was C. K. Anderson. "I understand you need $5,000 right now," Anderson said. Halas told Anderson that he would lose his Bears if he didn't get it by noon. Anderson told Halas to go to the office he maintained at Randolph and LaSalle a block away from the Bears' headquarters. A check would be waiting. Halas wrote that he made the final payment at Chicago Title and Trust at 11:50 A.M. with 10 minutes to spare.

If George Vass's account written eight years earlier than *Halas by Halas* is true, Halas may have negotiated an even tighter escape. The deadline, according to Vass, was 4:00 P.M., not noon, and Halas missed that deadline. He finally got his hands on the check shortly after 6:00 P.M. and hustled it over to Sternaman.

Whichever story is accurate, it is indisputable that the Bears belonged to George Halas from that moment on. "George kept control. He had more than 50 percent of the stock," Charles Brizzolara said in the summer of 2002. All the investors sat on a board of directors, with Halas as chairman, McMillen as vice president, Bidwill as secretary, and Brizzolara, Barbara Halas, and Trafton's mother as members. They knew they had something going, but never in their wildest dreams could they imagine that by 2004 the Bears would be worth $900 million. Each of those $5,000 investments would be worth upward of $56 million.

Years later, Mrs. Trafton thought Halas should appoint her son George as his successor. When she called the question at a board meeting, Frank Halas, voting their mother's shares, sided with the Papa Bear and McMillen. The somewhat peeved woman sold back her stock to Halas, who wrote that he paid her $40,000 for it. "He gave Trafton's stock, share for share, to Mugs and Virginia," Charles Brizzolara said.

In 1954, when McMillen told Halas he needed money to pay college tuition for his two children, the Papa Bear offered $25,000 for the stock. McMillen balked. Finally, Halas wrote, "we settled on $40,000," a true bargain given the way the team's valuation began to increase in subsequent years. On July 4, 1954, Halas paid McMillen $25,000 to transfer his nine and three-eighths shares to Virginia McCaskey to put her on even footing with Mugs as minority shareholders to their father and the Brizzolaras, each of whom now held 8⅓ percent of the stock. As part of that sale, Halas agreed to pay McMillen $2,500 a year for six years to meet the $40,000 agreement, and McMillen retained his vice presidency.

McMillen told his daughter Ann that he would not have sold out to Halas had he known how big the television money would become. Halas apparently never told his friend and investor that he and the Bears already got into television in 1947. Then again, like so much else in Halas's life, business was transacted on a need-to-know basis. The friendship between the two men never wavered.

Jim McMillen invested well throughout his life, buying much of the land outside Antioch for future development besides his winners with Halas. He served two terms as village mayor as well. McMillen began treatment for cancer in early 1983. One day, Ann Kakasek's son-in-law called the Bears' offices and asked to speak to George

Halas. Halas, who was engaged in his own final battle with cancer, answered the phone as he always did when there. He had no idea that his old friend was ill and promised to do what he could. Flowers arrived in McMillen's room at Lake Forest Hospital that same day. "George Halas had flowers sent every single month until the time he died," Ann Kakasek said. "And Virginia then sent them the last three months. That was very classy." Jim McMillen died on January 28, 1984. He was 81.

Charlie Bidwill's term as secretary lasted into 1933, but he remained a Bears fan even after he bought the team's crosstown rivals. That deal transpired in the summer of 1933, when Halas and Cardinals owner Dr. Dave Jones joined Bidwill on his yacht for an evening cruise on Lake Michigan. After a couple of drinks, Bidwill asked Jones if he wanted to sell the team. When the Cardinals' owner said it would take $50,000, Bidwill reached into his pocket and peeled off $2,000 in cash and paid the balance two days later.

By present-day league rules, Bidwill had a conflict-of-interest situation. He would have to divest himself of his interest in the Bears. No problem by 1933 standards. He held on to it. "Charlie owned the Cardinals, plus parts of the Detroit Lions and Bears simultaneously," Bill Gleason said. "That was what the league was like. All those guys, the pioneers of the league, were racetrack gamblers or bookies, like Art Rooney and the Maras." Moreover, Gleason noted, none of the franchises was worth a small fraction of its 21st-century value, despite Halas's 1933 claim in a newspaper interview that the Bears were worth $500,000.

In 1936, Halas somehow persuaded Bidwill to sign the so-called Madison Street agreement. Each team would operate on its side of the city's east-west baseline, Bears to the north, Cardinals to the south. Years after Bidwill's death, Halas invoked that piece of paper when the Cardinals sought to move their games up to Northwestern's Dyche Stadium in Evanston. That refusal to grant a waiver drove the Cardinals out of town.

The Brizzolara family remained the only outside shareholders until the McCaskeys bought them out several years after Halas's death. Until his death in 1972, Ralph Brizzolara stood by Halas as his closest friend and business confidant. After Bidwill bought the Cardinals, Brizzolara took a more active role in the Bears operation as club secretary. During World War II when Halas served Admiral Nimitz in the Pacific, Ralph ran both the Bears and, as executive vice president, American Steel Foundry.

By the end of the 1932 season, after the buyout, Halas was in such dire financial shape that he had to give IOUs to keep the team afloat. One of the players was Joe Savoldi, a fullback he signed in the 1930 season after he was expelled from Notre Dame for being married. Signing Savoldi, a clear-cut violation of the Grange rule Halas had endorsed so avidly after the Grange tour, cost Halas a $1,000 fine from commissioner Joe Carr. Carr and the league did not accept IOUs.

The memory nagged at Halas for the rest of his life. "The only time I ever had to give out IOUs was in fact 1932, which was a Depression year," Halas recalled in his 1978 appearance with Red Grange on WGN's "Wally Phillips Show." "We lost $18,000, and I couldn't get a dime out of the bank."

"I've often said I wish George Halas gave me an IOU and owed me a million dollars because I know I would get it," the loyal Grange said in that same three-way interview. "He never, never reneged on a thing of that type."

"As you remember, I gave you an IOU for a thousand," Halas said to Grange. "I also gave IOUs to Bronko Nagurski, Jack Manders, and Ralph Jones, our coach. You know, I paid them back the next year."

Attendance fell precipitously with winter's early arrival in late November. The Bears were overdrawn at their bank by nearly $1,200 and owed nearly $12,000 more in unpaid bills and IOUs.

In quest of their fourth straight title in 1932, the Packers visited snowbound Wrigley Field on December 11 with a 10–2–1 record against Chicago's awkward 5–1–6 mark. The corporal's guard of 5,000 who braved the Arcticlike conditions saw Nagurski break open a scoreless game in the fourth quarter when he powered over tackle, cut to the sideline, smashed aside the final Green Bay defender with a stiff arm, and scored. The Bears added a safety for the 9–0 victory.

That set up the playoff against the Portsmouth Spartans the following week, but in the euphoria of victory, Halas had to tell Green Bay's general manager, Lee Joannes, that the storm had cut down his gate so badly that "I've run out of chalk," meaning he could not make the $2,500 guarantee. He gave Joannes $1,000 cash and an IOU for $1,500.

He told Joannes to take the $1,500 out of the guarantee when they played their next game in 1933 at Green Bay. "I marked the note paid," Joannes said. "But Halas will never get it back. I put it in our Hall of Fame." Joannes said Halas more than repaid Green Bay in 1956 when he led the bond drive to build New City Stadium, now called Lambeau Field.

Chicago's bitter weather nearly did in Halas for good. The already frightful conditions for the Packers game turned even worse during the week before the championship game as an Arctic deep freeze settled over Chicago. The wet, six-inch snow that covered Wrigley Field during the previous game turned to solid ice as daily highs that week barely reached zero. The Thursday-morning low, four below zero, did it for Halas.

Certain that nobody in his right mind would go to Wrigley Field and, most important, in need of the money he would get from a larger crowd in the Stadium, he made a deal. The game would be played Sunday night in Chicago Stadium, an arena that could hold more than 15,000 for a football game on a scaled-down field. The Bears had played a charity game there in 1930 with the Cardinals. "The ceiling is high enough for regulation punts," wrote the *Tribune*'s Wilfrid Smith.

The stadium crew had to scramble to get the venue ready for football. A circus had just completed its stay, and the crew missed a few animal droppings when they raked the dirt. They hastily erected plywood boards along what would be the sidelines and put down chalked hash marks.

When Nagurski connected with Grange for the game's only touchdown on their controversial jump pass and the Bears added a late safety to beat Portsmouth 9–0, the team wasn't the only winner. A delighted Halas accepted gate receipts at just over $15,000. That covered the rent, the Spartans' guarantee, and the Bears' winning shares and gave him leeway for the off-season.

Early in the off-season, Ralph Jones accepted a job as head football coach at tiny Lake Forest College. Whether Halas pushed Jones out is unclear, but it is no secret that he wanted to get back into coaching. Also, the price was right. He did not have to pay himself to coach, a job that, he told the press after Jones left, he would take on for "this year only." Of course, George added, he would defend the 1932 title using Ralph's remodeled T formation with man in motion.

And, as both Grange and Halas told Wally Phillips in 1978, Papa Bear did make good on all those IOUs.

1933-1945

SEVEN

THE BIG BREAKOUT

*H*alas had a lifelong affair with money, for he knew that with money came power. Few men have wielded both as astutely. "George Halas was a very smart man—not just a football coach; he was a very clever businessman," said Charles Brizzolara.

Before he turned 40, Halas was a man who, as a fresh kid, conned a starch manufacturer into backing his football team and unlikely league; took that man's money and moved his team to the big city, where they survived by his wits; wrote his own press releases to get coverage; passed the hat to make the payroll; outsmarted a slick promoter to land the biggest star the game had ever seen in Red Grange; turned his back on both of them when they wanted to take over his team; closed the circle when he welcomed back the prodigal Grange with open arms to forge a friendship that gave both men prestige even as he underpaid Grange; waited patiently until his partner Edward Sternaman showed his weakness and then sprang to grab the brass ring when he himself was broke; audaciously paid for the team with borrowed money; and had the moxie to run every facet of the operation as sole proprietor and win big in the process.

When it came to understanding the human condition, George Halas the Bear was more of a fox. Whether it was shooting craps with the neighborhood kids in the back alley or, when he was pushing 70, dealing with difficult "kids" such as Rick Casares, Doug Atkins, and Mike Ditka, no one was as cunning. He certainly had reached his peak at age 38 in 1933 as league pioneer and, for the second time, head coach.

Halas held all the cards: sole control of his Bears and, most important, as victor in the Sternaman showdown, proprietary claim on the team's history. Henceforth in the team media guide, he granted his former partner nothing more than agate-type mention on the all-time "honor roll" as a former player and two notations in the chronological history. Otherwise, Edward "Dutch" Sternaman became a nonperson. From that moment on, the Bears were George Halas. George Halas was the Bears.

Thanks to the Bears' new corporate setup, the only long-term debt Halas carried was the $5,000 loan from C. K. Anderson's First National Bank of Antioch. He also expanded his outside interests, many of them deals in oil wells and small investments with Charles Brizzolara's father, Ralph. "They talked a lot about finances and the football team, about what they could and could not, or should not, do," the younger Brizzolara said. "They talked about dividends, payouts, and other financial matters."

Halas may have paid the piper in his 1929 experiences on and off the field, but he never looked askance at a bargain. By keeping his ears open in 1932 when the rest of the country was struggling against the Depression, Halas bagged a cornucopia of moneymakers. It started when one of his game program advertisers, laundry operator William Hauk, alerted Halas about a failing competitor. With Jim McMillen's help, Halas bought the company, renamed it White Bear Laundry, and hired Hauk to manage it.

McMillen paid $457.50 for stock in the White Bear Laundry. Then, on September 12, 1932, McMillen came through with a $1,010 loan to Halas and Hauk for the White Bear. Halas secured that loan with a $1,000 judgment note for two years at 6 percent. Halas repaid the note over the next 10 years. On March 20, 1942, McMillen received a $2,200 payment that doubled the value of the note.

White Bear turned out to be a propitious move as Hauk brought in his son and daughter-in-law, Rita, to help. Of Rita, Halas wrote, "Much later [after Min's death] she became very dear to me."

"George also had the May and Halas wholesale jewelry business and the retail sporting goods store, the George S. Halas Company," Charles Brizzolara said, referring in the second instance to the bankrupt mail-order operation that Halas resurrected. The slogan on Halas's uniforms was "A Bear for Wear," recalls Bill Jauss, who wore a Halas-made uniform in his Northwestern playing days circa 1950. The Wildcats were just one of many clients the George S. Halas Company outfitted.

Halas housed May and Halas and the sporting goods operation under one roof, under the care of Max Swiatek. Swiatek, an aspiring baseball player, was helping the Wrigley Field grounds crew get the ballpark ready for the football season the day he met Halas. Halas took a liking to the enthusiastic young man and hired him to be his chief order taker, order filler, and jack-of-all-trades at May and Halas and for the team itself.

Max remained with the Old Man for the rest of Halas's life in various capacities long after May and Halas folded—as equipment manager, personal driver, and gofer. Even when he was well into his 80s, Max could be found every game day zealously guarding the locker room door. He came to work in the mail room on a regular basis until nearly the end before his death at age 90 in November 2001.

Throughout his life, Halas kept close watch on the markets, seeking winning deals. "He had oil investments, but he would pick and choose them. He did most of the later ones with Bud Adams," Jerry Vainisi said, regarding Halas's search for gushers with the owner of the former Houston Oilers, now Tennessee Titans, and heir to the Phillips Oil fortune. "Adams would send him prospectuses and then call me: 'Please tell Coach he can't pick and choose oil wells. Once you're in, you go for every one.'" Adams explained to Vainisi that seven out of ten may be a miss, but the three wells that hit would more than offset exploration losses on the other seven. Halas, Adams said, "wants the three that hit and nothing to do with the losers."

To Halas, the oil wells and everything else, of course, were subordinate to the Bears. Now reasonably solvent, the team moved to better office space in 1934 at 37 South Wabash on the 10th floor, where they would remain until 1947.

After three years away from the sidelines, Halas, in 1933, decided he needed to reacquaint himself with his players and do some real coaching again. He contacted former Bear and close friend Heartley "Hunk" Anderson, head coach at Notre Dame, and asked a favor. He wanted to take his team to the campus and run the first full-scale training camp in pro football history. That would be fine, Hunk said.

Day after day, under the hot Hoosier sun, Halas and his two assistants, Laurie Walquist and player-coach Red Grange, stressed the fundamentals. The players ran through the maze of ropes to develop footwork. They hit the blocking sled to develop technique and unified starts. They hit the tackling dummy. They ran wind sprints until they nearly dropped. Then they ran some more. Most important, they hit each other, scrimmaging by the hour. When they broke camp, the Bears were the NFL's best-conditioned team.

Anderson did not fare as well at Notre Dame. His 1933 Irish went 3–5–1 and scored only 32 points the entire season, including a 12–7 win over Army at Yankee Stadium in the finale. Hunk's fate had been sealed the previous week when USC shut out the Irish 19–0, the third straight defeat for an Anderson-coached team against Howard Jones's Trojans. Anderson would rejoin the Bears in 1940 and earn Halas's praise as "the greatest defensive coach who ever lived."

Halas now had the money to cover the bills and the expensive training camp. He also had Ralph Jones's 1932 championship plays in hand to guide quarterback Carl Brumbaugh; a large, hostile line led by bookend tackles and future Hall of Famers George Musso, a rookie from Millikin University, in Decatur, and Roy "Link" Lyman; Nagurski, the best player in the game; and Bill Hewitt, the lightning-quick end from Michigan. Hewitt, a smallish, 5'9", tightly strung 190-pounder, was fresh off an All-Pro rookie season.

Hewitt was so great a player that when Halas retired his first set of uniform numbers in 1949, the three honorees were Grange, 77; Nagurski, 3; and Hewitt, 56. Halas liked Hewitt so much that he didn't even mind a 1944 article, "Don't Send My Boy to Halas," that ghostwriter Red Smith wrote for Hewitt for the *Saturday Evening Post*.

Hewitt did not criticize Halas in that story as much as the game itself, for the false expectations it brought young athletes. Hewitt wrote, "We didn't envy the few who made big money. The guy we envied was the white-collar worker with 50 dollars a week and a future." Hewitt stressed that he loved playing football, to his own detriment. But Hewitt also was the first player to reveal the truth about contract negotiations.

As Rick Casares explained, the league was still handling negotiations in his heyday in the '50s and '60s the same way Hewitt had to cope with the Papa Bear. "There was an unwritten law among the pros, which was so asinine and stupid, that you never discussed your contract with a teammate or anybody else in the league," Casares said in 2003. "We were all in the dark. We didn't know what the hell each other was getting. Halas told everybody he was the highest-paid guy on the team. When I tell people that when I left the Halases, I was making $25,000, they fall out. In 10 years with the Bears, the most that I got was $25,000!"

Bill Hewitt would have turned handsprings for that much money when he was playing his way into the Pro Football Hall of Fame. Since college scouting was virtually unknown then, it's likely Halas heard about Hewitt from Don Maxwell through one of his *Tribune* sportswriters. The *Trib* began its sponsorship of the Big Ten Silver Football for the league's most valuable player in 1924, when Red Grange won it. Future president Gerald Ford played center on the freshman team when Hewitt was Michigan's MVP in 1931. Halas figured Hewitt was worth at least a three-cent stamp, so he mailed a contract offer in early May 1932 to the Hewitt family home in Bay City.

Hewitt could scarcely believe Halas's offer: $100 a game! Football had been anything but fun at Michigan, but if Hewitt picked up any knowledge in his economics classes, he learned something about value. He knew that few if any jobs were to be had anywhere in the depressed economy, especially for someone who, a semester later, would just be getting his degree. He also knew he could earn a decent wage playing football. So, he answered Halas. Like any smart Michigan man, he asked for $10 more a game than Halas offered. Over 1932's 13-game schedule, Hewitt calculated, he would earn a splendid $1,430.

To Hewitt's amazement, Halas agreed to the young man's terms and enclosed a round-trip train ticket to Chicago. Everything went smoothly until Hewitt asked Halas for a written guarantee that he would not be cut during the season. Hewitt walked out of that bargaining session with his no-cut clause, but in return for Halas's signature, he had to give back that extra $10 a game. Yet, all was not lost. The Bears won the 1932 title, and the winner's share raised Hewitt's take to $1,750.

When the players reported for the '32 season, Halas assigned Hewitt number 56, and Ralph Jones installed him at first-string left end ahead of Red Grange's brother Gardie, who did not make the 22-man roster. Hewitt, in turn, told Halas and Jones he would not wear a helmet, because it hindered his play. The helmetless Hewitt became an instant favorite with the coaches and his teammates, who affectionately called him "Stinky" because there was no other plausible reason why opponents could or would not get near him.

Halas loved Stinky Hewitt from the start for his speed, pass-catching ability, and refusal to give up on a play. When the Bears lined up on defense, Hewitt was so quick off the ball that everyone thought he was offside. Indeed, Green Bay fans called him something stronger than "Stinky."

"Offside Hewitt!" was a familiar cry from the City Stadium stands. In his *Saturday Evening Post* article, Hewitt revealed that he lined up a yard or two behind the line of scrimmage and took off at the snap, shooting past his opponent into the backfield before the man had time to react. If Hewitt was picked up, the tackle next to him, Link Lyman, carried out both assignments, his and Hewitt's. Decades later, Tom Landry, of Dallas, would take credit for Hewitt's innovation. Landry called it the flex.

As they lined up for the 1933 season kickoff in Green Bay's City Stadium, the Bears and Packers both had scores to settle. The Pack wanted revenge for that 9–0 loss in the snow at Wrigley Field in the final 1932 regular-season game, which cost them a fourth straight title and set up the Bears' championship game and victory over Portsmouth. The Bears had more than a title defense at stake. Until 1928, they held an 8–1–2 lead in the Packers series. Then it was the Packers' turn. Starting in '28, the teams played each other three times a season, and Green Bay quickly caught up. Heading into the 1933 opener, the series was deadlocked after 25 games at 11 wins apiece, with three ties.

From the opening kickoff, this one was all Packers. Green Bay's exceptional fullback, Clarke Hinkle, established the tone when he collided with Nagurski and knocked him out of the game with a smashed nose. One observer compared it to a head-on collision between two locomotives. Worse, for Halas and the Bears, the Packers led 7–0 and, in the words of a *Green Bay Press-Gazette* reporter, "were rubbing it in."

With three minutes to go, Green Bay's Roger Grove lined up for a field goal. "With unerring accuracy, the ball plunked into my tummy. Our ball," wrote Hewitt, who recovered on Chicago's 35.

Three plays later, Brumbaugh called an end-around option pass play for Hewitt. In a 1967 *Tribune* series written under the George S. Halas byline by George Strickler, the coach noted that the team practiced it the day before in Chicago, and Hewitt overthrew his intended target, Luke Johnsos, so badly that the ball hit the clubhouse wall. This time, as Halas wrote, as they broke the huddle, Brumbaugh whispered to Hewitt, "Clubhouse special."

"I shut my eyes and threw it as far as I could," Hewitt wrote. "That noble character Luke Johnsos snatched it out of the air and ran for a touchdown." Then, Automatic Jack Manders tied it with an extra point.

The Bears held the Packers to no gain from their own 20 on the next series. With one minute to play, Hewitt broke through, blocked Arnie Herber's punt with his chest, and chased the ball down to the 1, where he picked it up in stride to score. The 14–7 win started the Bears on their way to the title game and put them ahead in the Packers series, where they have remained ever since.

The Bears followed with five more wins, among them, a 14–10 victory over the Giants at home and a 10–7 triumph over the Packers on October 22, also at Wrigley Field. To quote a latter-day Green Bay hero, Paul Hornung, in a beer ad, it was a matter of "Practice! Practice! Practice!" Unlike with Hornung, who practiced for more pleasurable pursuits, under Halas it really was practice, practice, and more practice—at football.

During most of the '30s, many players held regular jobs and could not work out with the team until Saturdays. Nagurski, for one, hit the road during the week, earning decent money as a pro wrestler. Others held such jobs as bricklayer, carpenter, and gas station attendant. Halas adjusted to the hard times with one exception. Packers Week!

Packers Week! These were the most important games on the schedule for both teams. When the Packers were scheduled to visit Wrigley Field, Halas ordered the players to go on leave from their jobs so they could drill all week. The only way he could retain their loyalty was to make up their lost pay. So, he took out short-term loans at American National Bank, where the Bears did their business. To minimize interest, he would sign a note on Friday or Saturday for, say, $6,000 against anticipated gate receipts of $10,000 in that non-TV era when ticket prices were scaled in cents. After the game, Halas would pay the players their game salaries plus the missed outside wages. Then he would count the gate receipts, repay the short-term note plus interest at American National on Monday morning, and put the rest in the treasury.

The team hit a lull in an early-November cluster of road games when the Bears lost to the Boston Redskins 10–0, tied Bert Bell's new Philadelphia Eagles 3–3, and were shut out by the Giants 3–0 at the Polo Grounds. They swept their last four games, beating the Packers 7–6 on December 10 at Wrigley Field in the finale. It was the last time they were scheduled to face each other three times in the same season.

They had a week to prepare for the Eastern Division champion New York Giants to determine the first true National Football League champion. The Bears had the home field advantage and would enjoy another edge. Before the season, Halas hired a cameraman to film every play of every Bears game, more for the coaches to evaluate the team than to scout opponents. When they got the processed reels back on Monday morning, Halas and his assistants Grange and Walquist screened the films, took notes, and did their best to establish tendencies, discover flaws in their opponents for future reference, and grade their own players. Watching film was a superb supplement to Walter Halas's scouting reports. That information enabled Halas, Grange, and Walquist to put together the game's first "battle plans," or game plans. In time, everyone in the league followed Halas's lead.

The National Football League's first official championship game was played on December 17, 1933, before Chicago's largest crowd of the season. The *Tribune* reported that 21,000 fans came to Wrigley Field, against the official league figure of 26,000.

The Giants wore blue jerseys with red trim and white numerals, red pants, and blue helmets. The Bears came out in white jerseys with blue piping, orange pants, and 20 orange helmets for the 22-man roster. Two of Halas's best—Hewitt, of course, and tackle George Musso—disdained headgear. Halas and Giants coach Steve Owen attacked each other like riverboat gamblers.

"Marshall your adjectives," wrote the *Tribune*'s Wilfrid Smith in his game story the next morning. "Bring out all the superlatives and shuffle them as you would a jigsaw puzzle. All will fit in a description of this championship game." Smith's prose notwithstanding, it may have been the finest football game, college or professional, ever played to that date. It ended in the wildest assortment of finishing plays ever performed in any championship game.

The Bears were trailing 14–9 in the third quarter when Chicago's George Corbett faked a punt. He passed to quarterback Carl Brumbaugh, who took off on a 67-yard dash to the 8. Then Nagurski executed the identical play that won the indoor title game the year before. He faked a plunge and threw a jump pass to rookie Bill Karr in the end zone for the Bears' first touchdown as they took a 16-to-14 lead.

Harry Newman led New York back with a series of passes to the Bears' 8 as the third quarter ended. On the first play of the fourth quarter, the Giants reached deep into their bag of tricks and came up with a flea-flicker. Ken Strong ran to his left and fired a lateral back to Newman and kept running. Newman hit the wide-open Strong in the end zone just before he fell into the first-base dugout. The Giants led 21–16.

The Giants then snuffed two Chicago threats before the Bears got the ball back with just over four minutes left after Strong's pop-up punt fell dead at the New York 47. After Nagurski smashed to the 33 for a first down, the Giants called time. A minute remained. Quarterback Carl Brumbaugh had waited all day for the moment to call a timing play that Hewitt dreamed up earlier in the season. It's now known as the "hook and ladder," but the Bears called it the "Stinky Special."

They worked it to perfection. From the single wing, Nagurski took a direct snap from center Ookie Miller and fired over the middle on a hook pattern to Hewitt at the 19. Hewitt immediately flipped a lateral to the trailing Karr. As Strong zeroed in on Karr, right halfback Gene Ronzani cut him down at the ankles, and Karr scored the go-ahead touchdown. Instead of the Bears' substituting Manders for the point after, Brumbaugh kicked it himself, to give the Bears a 23–21 lead.

After the kickoff, the Giants had time for one more play. Newman, who passed for 201 yards, threw downfield to Dale Burnett. Grange, the deep man for Chicago, sized up the play in a split second. Seeing the Giants' great center Mel Hein in a dead sprint after Burnett to take a lateral, Grange wrapped his arms around Burnett, pinned the man's arms to his body, and wrestled him down as the final gun went off. The Bears were the first modern champions of the National Football League, thanks to what Halas always called the greatest defensive play he ever saw.

They also had turned the corner as a business. Halas, now sole owner, was able to charge $2.20 for box seats and $1 in the bleachers; the team averaged close to 20,000 fans a game, and he paid all the bills.

Among the more interested parties keeping a close eye on the Bears were the folks at Tribune Tower—Halas's pal Don Maxwell, now city editor, and his replacement as sports editor, Arch Ward.

When Maxwell was promoted in 1930, the well-connected Ward became sports editor. Ward, a native of Dubuque, Iowa, was Knute Rockne's first publicist at Notre Dame in 1920, George Gipp's last year. He joined the *Tribune* as a sportswriter in 1925 and took over the section's lead column, "In the Wake of the News."

Ward realized early in his reign as sports editor that he preferred promoting to grinding out a column. He came up with such events as boxing's Golden Gloves, the All-Star baseball game in 1933 to coincide with the Century of Progress World's Fair in Chicago, and, in the summer of 1934, a game to kick off the football season. It would pit an all-star roster of graduating college seniors against the champions of the National Football League, who happened to be the Chicago Bears. Unlike baseball, which rotated the host cities for its All-Star contest, home for the College All-Star game would be otherwise-unused Soldier Field. All benefits would go to Chicago Tribune Charities.

Halas agreed to the game but put little effort into it. Defending a title was more important. So, before 79,472 fans on August 30, the All-Stars and Bears played to a scoreless tie, a result that Ward and his *Tribune* minions claimed as proof positive that the college boys could stay with the pros. The game would last for 42 seasons until the pros called it quits after winning with monotonous regularity. Another, and more practical, reason for them to get out was the fear of injury to high-priced rookies.

Thanks to Don Maxwell, Arch Ward and Halas had formed a beautiful friendship. Though not as ardent a Halas supporter as Maxwell, Ward saw the value in the man and his sport. For his part, Halas thought so much of Ward that he twice tried to get him to accept the job as commissioner, once after the death of Joe Carr in 1939 and again in 1941. When Ward turned him down the second time, Halas pushed for Elmer Layden and persuaded him to step down as coach at Notre Dame. Layden resigned on February 4, 1941, and set up shop in Chicago, just the way Halas wanted it. To keep him in line.

EIGHT

OF RUBBER SHOES AND THE MADMAN OF THE MIDWAY

*R*ed Grange should have retired after his brilliant title-saving tackle in the 1933 title game. Instead, like so many other athletes who can't bear to hang it up, he went for one more in '34. The unsentimental Halas gave the Galloping Ghost a seat on the bench so he could watch the brilliant 210-pound rookie halfback from Tennessee, Beattie Feathers, who was so good that Halas virtually ditched the T formation and returned to the single wing. His '34 Bears had the best running game the league had ever seen.

With Bronko Nagurski clearing the way when he wasn't banging out 586 yards, Feathers gained 1,004 yards on 119 carries. His 8.44 yards per attempt remained the league standard 70 years later. The Bears set a league rushing-yardage record that year that lasted for decades, 2,847. It lasted as a team record until the Walter Payton–Matt Suhey tandem broke it in 1984.

The Bears stormed through the 1934 league schedule, winning all 13 games, for the Western Division title and a championship rematch with the Giants in the Polo Grounds. Feathers, by then, was gone. He was knocked out for the season in the 11th game with a dislocated shoulder in a 17–6 win over the Cardinals at Wrigley Field.

The Bears took an 18-game winning streak into the Polo Grounds to defend their title against the Giants, who had mucked their way through a mediocre Eastern Division with a lackluster 8–5 mark. That included two losses to the Bears, 27–7 on November 4 at Wrigley Field and 10–9 two weeks later at the Polo Grounds before a season-high sellout crowd of 55,000.

In his 1967 *Tribune* series, Halas recalled a wild sequence that began at the start of the fourth quarter in that second match. With the Bears trailing 9–0, Automatic Jack Manders had just had a long run called back, and the Bears were pinned at their own 1-yard line when Feathers lined up to punt from the end zone. As he extended his hands to take the snap, the umpire blew his whistle and yelled, "Penalty!"

"What for?" asked Feathers.

"Because Halas just called me a . . . ," the umpire explained as he marched the ball half the distance to the goal line, 18 inches. Halas admitted the official had quoted him "with amazing accuracy," likely one of his two favorite epithets. Feathers then punted the Bears out of danger.

Three minutes remained when Feathers scored from 12 yards out behind Nagurski's devastating block on New York end Ray Flaherty to cut the deficit to 9–7. With 30 seconds left, Manders kicked a 23-yard field goal for the 10–9 win.

An elated Halas told his boys the curfew was off and invited them to a party at a New York night spot—his treat. Around midnight, the manager asked the coach how everything was. Halas told him it was wonderful but, out of curiosity, asked how large a tab they had run up. "About eight-hundred dollars," the manager replied.

"Eight-hundred dollars!" Halas leapt to his feet. "That's enough! Shut off the drinks! These men are athletes!"

Few teams have been as heavily favored in a championship game as were those Bears, especially with the Giants' star passer, quarterback Harry Newman, out with an injury. Yet, signs of their vulnerability were rife. First was that, statistically, beating an opponent three times in the same year is one of the most difficult tasks in the National Football League. Second, the Giants had nearly caught the Bears hibernating in that 10–9 loss on November 18. Third, and most significant, was the equalizer. Weather.

New York had been inundated with weeklong rains that left the Polo Grounds ankle deep in mud and standing water. Then, a Saturday-night nor'easter lowered the game-time temperature on Sunday, December 9, to nine degrees above zero and pared a predicted sellout to just over 35,000. Those eyewitnesses saw the most unusual championship game ever staged, one decided on footwear.

The Giants emerged from their toasty clubhouse in deep center field before noon for the pregame workout, and they promptly fell on their collective keisters. The rain and precipitous temperature drop had turned most the of the Polo Grounds' gridiron into a rock-hard sheet of ice that more resembled a skating rink than a football field.

When he slipped and fell trying to grab a pass in the warm-up, end Ray Flaherty got up and remarked to coach Steve Owen that he once played in similar conditions when he was in college at Gonzaga. Flaherty told Owen that the team switched to rubber-soled basketball-type shoes to gain traction.

Owen, who was having enough trouble thinking of ways to stifle Nagurski, especially in recalling how he'd mauled Flaherty a month earlier, turned to his trainer, Gus Mauch, for help. Mauch, also the trainer at Manhattan College, ran into the clubhouse, called the school, spoke to a watchman, described the situation, and told him he was sending clubhouse attendant Abe Cohen with a large gunnysack to pick up as many rubber-soled basketball shoes as he could carry. Just before kickoff, Cohen caught the subway for the 85-block ride to Riverdale in the Bronx, north of Manhattan Island.

Both teams suffered. Their hands were numb, and their bodies ached from taking the constant falls on the rock-hard surface. The Giants marched down the field early in the game before Gene Ronzani intercepted an Ed Danowski pass in the end zone. Moments later, the Giants blocked a punt and took a 3–0 lead on Ken Strong's 38-yard field goal.

When they switched sides between quarters, the Bears operated in the sunny end heading toward center field. Nagurski powered in for a touchdown to give Chicago a 7–3 lead. On the next possession, Nagurski powered as close as the 9, but the Giants held at the goal line, and Manders knocked in a 7-yard chip shot to make it 10–3 Chicago.

Cohen arrived at the school late in the first half. What happened next has long been disputed. In his memoir, Halas claims the Giants' clubhouse attendant was nothing more than a common burglar. "During the first half," he wrote, "a Giants emissary broke into the lockers at Manahattan College and took nine pairs of tennis shoes, all he could find."

In *Championship: The Complete NFL Title Story*, longtime *Newark Ledger-Star* writer Jerry Izenberg, an admitted Giants follower from childhood, tells it from the opposite side. "History infers that Abe Cohen had to smash a window to get into the Manhattan gymnasium. It is a good story, but not true." Izenberg claims the watchman Mauch reached awaited Cohen's arrival and took him to a locker room, where Cohen loaded as many basketball shoes as possible into the sack—at least nine pairs, per Halas, perhaps more.

Meanwhile, back at the Polo Grounds, the Bears stubbed their near-frozen toes in a series of missed opportunities in the second quarter. Nagurski pounced on a fumble at the New York 6. He ran it in for an apparent touchdown, but a teammate was offside. After the penalty, the usually reliable Manders registered his first missed field goal attempt in memory, and the Giants dodged the bullet. Halas blew a gasket. When the Bears got the ball back again, Nagurski reached the end zone for a third time only to have the play waved off by a 15-yard holding penalty. The now rattled Manders missed his second straight field goal attempt. Instead of having a 24–3 edge, the Bears had pushed the Giants around the field only to settle for a 10–3 halftime lead.

When the teams returned for the third quarter, the mercury had dipped to zero, and the western, or first base, end of the field lay in deep shadow and now was a sheet of ice. Halas recalled that Giants kicker Ken Strong was wearing "tennis" shoes to open the second half. He says Strong's kicked squirted out of bounds. "We laughed. He kicked again. The ball sailed into the end zone. We stopped laughing."

That part of Halas's story is amusing but fanciful—no other Giant, Strong included, was wearing sneakers. Not yet. He has the time sequence wrong. Cohen was still carrying his bag of shoes on the subway at the start of the second half. The Bears operated at the sunny end in the third quarter, but all they could manage was a Manders field goal to take a 13–3 lead into the fourth quarter. The Bears now had to defend the treacherous shaded end.

"I wish I could forget the fourth quarter," Halas wrote in 1979, still agonized 44 years later by the bitter memory he could have averted had he outfitted the Bears in mere gym shoes—sneakers. With 10 minutes to go, both teams were nearly frozen in place in a Keystone Kops–like comedy of skids and pratfalls. Then Abe Cohen arrived on the sideline, toting his huge shoe bag like one of Santa's elves.

George Allen writes in *Pro and College Football's 50 Greatest Games* that Owen signaled for a time-out and motioned his team to the sidelines. The players rifled through Abe's sack to find basketball shoes that fit and laced them up. Halas, Allen wrote, screamed at the officials, but they replied correctly that the Giants were acting within the rules.

The Giants returned to the field and realized they had traction while Chicago did not. "I shouted to step on their feet. That didn't work either," recalled Halas. Danowski, the erstwhile backup quarterback, suddenly was flawless. Operating in the shadows from the Bears' 35, Danowski threw to now sure-footed Ike Frankian at the goal line for an easy score when Chicago defender Carl Brumbaugh slipped and fell as he tried for the interception. Strong's point after cut the deficit to 13–10.

On the next series, the Giants stopped the slipping-and-sliding Nagurski and forced a punt. On their next play from scrimmage, Strong padded through the still-slipping Bears defenders like a big cat for a 41-yard touchdown. He added the extra point, the Giants now owned a 17–13 lead. Plenty of time remained, but the Bears were dead. "We were helpless," Nagurski recalled in *Halas by Halas*. "We had to mince about."

Strong scored again, and Danowski ran one in for the coup de grâce. The Giants had reeled off 27 points in the final 10 minutes to win the championship 30–13. In New York and most everywhere else, the remarkable contest is remembered forever in three words. *The Sneakers Game*. All George Halas would call it for the rest of his life was "that goddamn rubber shoes game."

Ken Strong told writer Bob Curran years later that the Bears didn't even need sneakers and should have won—Halas just had to make a basic adjustment at the break. "The Bears started the game with new cleats made of the synthetic Bakelite," Strong said. "By the end of the first half, they were nubs. That made a difference. If they had [screwed on] new cleats for the second half, they would have walloped us."

Halas never answered Strong's critique. Bears players through the Halas years griped about the "old equipment" they were forced to use. Halas made them wear threadbare jerseys and pants, patched and repatched dozens of times, over ancient, clunky shoulder pads down to thoroughly worn footwear. Dick Butkus discussed it in his ghosted autobiography, and, as Bill Jauss remembers, it certainly was so in the late '50s: "Some of the cleats [the actual football shoes] were old. One of the Bears, I can't remember which, told me that Bronko Nagurski's name was on one pair. The reasoning went, it will still wear. The frugal Old Man hung on to those shoes."

Football cleats are like golf cleats, easy to change in a hurry. Just screw the old one off and screw in the new one. New cleats should have been mandatory for the Bears' travel kit in 1934. The same man who splurged on his boys in a New York bistro after the 10–9 regular-season win over the Giants could have saved himself all that grief by dropping a few bucks on the most basic football gear, cleats. Instead, he let his hardheaded frugality call the tune at the most inopportune moment. Not the first time he would do so, nor the last.

Then there was that matter of sneakers. "I swore that no Bear would ever go to another game without two pairs of tennis shoes in his bag," wrote Halas. Ironically, the same thing would happen to the

Bears when they met the Giants for the 1956 title at Yankee Stadium, with identical results when they left their gym shoes in Chicago.

Footwear often made the difference in late-season matchups between the two teams. Halas finally did get it right in that department for the 1963 title contest at frozen Wrigley Field against another Giants team.

After the 1934 sneakers/rubber shoes game, the Bears went on a six-game postseason exhibition tour, losing only to the Cardinals, 13–7. They wrapped up the tour on January 27, 1935, at Gilmore Stadium in Hollywood, where they gained hollow revenge in a 21–0 shutout over the Giants. With time for one more play and the ball at the Bears' 20, Halas sent in a play to spring Red Grange and send him out in a blaze of glory. "My feet got heavier and heavier. I finally got pulled down on their 39 by a 230-pound lineman," Grange said. He walked off the field, ending the pro game's first great era.

Bill Hewitt went home to Bay City, Michigan, with $3,400 in earnings for the 13 regular-season games, the championship game in New York, and 13 more exhibitions, an average of $126 a game, with high hopes of making more of the same in 1935 and winning a title as well.

Although they were not defending champions, the Bears broke training camp at St. John's Academy in Delafield, Wisconsin, to open the 1935 exhibition campaign with a 5–0 victory over the College All-Stars at Soldier Field. The All-Stars employed three noteworthy names. Their starting center was future president Gerry Ford, from Michigan. Quarterback Irv Kupcinet joined the Philadelphia Eagles after the game and played two games. After the season, he reported to the sports editor at the *Chicago Times* to begin a newspaper career as a sportswriter. In 1943, Kup began the gossip column that ran until his death in late 2003. The leading All-Star was Green Bay–bound Don Hutson, the end from Alabama, hero of the Crimson Tide's 29–13 Rose Bowl win over Stanford.

The regular season opened at City Stadium in Green Bay, and Hutson chalked up his first of many claims to charter membership in the Pro Football Hall of Fame. The Packers had the ball at their own 17, and Arnie Herber threw far downfield. Hutson put on several moves to get open, make the catch in stride, and sprint away from the Bears defenders. It was the game's only score in a 7–0 Packers victory, their first over the Bears since 1932.

In the rematch at Wrigley Field six weeks later, Johnny Sisk put the Bears up 14–3 on a 55-yard run with three minutes to go. Many of the Packers fans in the crowd of 29,389 left for downtown to catch the Chicago and North Western's northbound milk run to Wisconsin. Had they stuck around, they would have witnessed one of the wildest and most improbable finishes in the long history of the series.

After the kickoff, Halas ordered the Bears to drop back into an early version of the prevent defense. Herber hit Hutson in the flat, and Hutson proceeded to zig, zag, and sprint to a 68-yard touchdown. No sooner had Bears quarterback Bernie Masterson lost a fumble on the next possession than Herber nailed Hutson in the end zone for the 17–14 Green Bay win. After that one, Halas said, "We just concede Hutson two touchdowns and try to stop the other guys."

An injured Nagurski was able to play in just five games, and it became obvious that the 1935 Bears were misfiring on too many cylinders. They finished with a 6–4–2 mark as Dutch Clark led the Detroit Lions to their first championship in their second year after leaving Portsmouth, Ohio, in their rearview mirrors.

The big news of 1935 came before the season when Philadelphia owner Bert Bell proposed a draft of the best collegiate players. It would be held with the teams choosing in reverse order of their standings—worst, first, and so on. "I thought the proposal sound. It made sense," wrote Halas in his memoir.

The two teams that had the most to lose were the dominant Bears and Giants. But when Tim Mara agreed with Halas that the league would benefit, the proposal passed unanimously. Halas admitted that the ulterior motive of the draft may have been to stifle salaries. In fact, it evened competition, which increased attendance, which, in turn, increased salaries.

Bert Bell's Eagles used the initial draft selection on the University of Chicago's Jay Berwanger, first winner of the Downtown Athletic Club Trophy, renamed for John W. Heisman after his death in 1936.

Halas easily landed the bonanza of the draft with two future Hall of Famers in the first and last rounds and picked up another future mainstay, halfback Ray Nolting, a quick, undrafted free agent, from the University of Cincinnati.

Without the benefit of present-day scouting operations that scour the nation, Halas had to rely on tips from his network of players and coaches. On the strong recommendations of Carl Brumbaugh and West Virginia alum Bill Karr, Halas took West Virginia's 6'4", 245-pound left tackle Jumbo Joe Stydahar. Stydahar played for nine seasons, making All-Pro from 1937 to 1940, returned from the war to lead the Bears to the 1946 title, coached the Rams to the 1950 title, and rejoined Halas as an assistant with the 1963 champions. He gained induction to the Pro Football Hall of Fame in 1967.

On the last round, because Halas liked the sound of his name, he took Colgate guard Danny Fortmann, a 6', 210-pounder and Phi Beta Kappa premed scholar. Unlike 1925 when he snatched Grange off the campus of the University of Illinois, never to finish college, Halas took special care with Fortmann. It certainly was not through salary, as he paid him just $1,700, but Halas worked with University of Chicago Medical School dean Dr. B. C. H. Harvey so Fortmann could play football as he earned his medical degree. At age 20, Fortmann was the youngest player in the league in 1936, and one of its elites. From 1936 to '43, he made All-Pro every season. In that time, the Bears won three league championships among five Western Division titles, finished second twice, and finished third once. Dr. Fortmann served the Los Angeles Rams for many years as team physician and was inducted into the Hall of Fame in 1965.

Then there was Jay Berwanger. According to Frank Litsky in the *New York Times*, after the draft, Bert Bell offered the first Heisman Award winner up to $150 a game to play in Philadelphia. Berwanger declined, saying he believed he could better use his education than his football skills. So, Bell traded his rights to the Bears.

Berwanger told the *Chicago Tribune*'s Don Pierson that he talked to Halas just once about a deal and that came in a chance meeting when he was downtown on a date. "I wanted $25,000 for two years with a no-cut contract," Berwanger said. "He just wished me and my date a *bon* farewell." According to Litsky, Berwanger said Halas never made a counteroffer, but they developed an enduring friendship.

The '36 Bears opened the season with six straight victories. The streak began with a 30–3 win over the Packers at Green Bay. It ended in the rematch at Wrigley Field when Clark Hinkle powered for 109 yards on 13 carries and a 59-yard touchdown run to lead the Pack to a 21–10 victory. The Bears still held the reins until they lost to the Lions and Cardinals in the last two games, to finish 9-and-3. Those lapses let the Packers, with one loss and a tie, slip into the title game against the Boston Redskins.

Sick and tired of playing to empty seats in Boston, George Preston Marshall moved the title game to a neutral site, the Polo Grounds, in New York. Reflecting the lack of rooting interest, just 29,545 fans showed up for the game. The Packers won their fourth title for Curly Lambeau, 21–6. Within days following the game, Marshall announced he was moving the Redskins to his hometown, Washington, D.C., to play at Griffith Stadium, home of the American League Senators.

After Halas made Nebraska end Les McDonald his first choice in the 1937 draft, Marshall used the next pick to grab Texas Christian passing ace Sammy Baugh and beat out Lambeau. All he got was the greatest pure passer until the '50s, a man still regarded with Nagurski, Hutson, and perhaps Bulldog Turner of that era as able-bodied enough to stand out in the 21st-century NFL.

Bill Hewitt made All-Pro for a third time in 1936, but with a wife and small child at home and needing more than $130 a game to support them, the great end told Halas he would not return. Halas in turn sent him to Bell, who promptly raised Hewitt's pay to $200 a game and placed him in an off-season job. Hewitt responded with his fourth All-Pro season. He retired after the 1939 season, only to come back at age 34 in 1943 for one final wartime season. He was killed outside Philadelphia in a single-car accident on January 14, 1947. When he heard the tragic news, a shocked Halas immediately called Hewitt "one of the great ends of all time." The coach told *Tribune* sportswriter Ed Prell that Hewitt had just written him to say he planned to attend the team's 1947 reunion. "He had a flaming spirit," the Papa Bear said of one of his abiding favorites.

In 1937, Halas drafted end Dick Plasman from Vanderbilt in the third round. Like Hewitt, Plasman refused to wear a helmet. He was the last of his kind in the NFL.

Halas had a better team in '37 than the year before. Now in his eighth season, Nagurski was back at full strength. He gained 373 yards to complement the quick Nolting, who led the team with 427 yards as the Bears won the Western Division at 9–1–1 to set up the title showdown on December 12 at Wrigley Field with the Redskins, who were winding up a superb 8-and-3 year, their first in the nation's capital.

The weather was cold, and Baugh was red hot. Only 15,870 fans came out in the 15-degree weather to watch the rookie whom Halas had passed over pick apart the Bears defense in the finest passing performance in league history to that date. It would set the championship standard for years. Baugh threw 33 passes and hit on 18, for 354 yards. All three of his touchdown passes came on third-quarter bombs. The Bears were up 14–7 when Baugh hit Wayne Milner on a 55-yard scoring play. After Masterson's touchdown pass to Eggs Manske put Chicago back on top, Baugh returned with a blockbuster. From his own 23, he fired a perfect pass to Milner again at the Bears 48. Milner took off and simply outsprinted Nagurski and Manders to the end zone for the tying touchdown. The winner came at the end of the third quarter when Baugh drew the Chicago secondary to Charlie Malone on a magnificent pump fake and hit a wide-open Ed Justice for a 35-yard touchdown to take the championship trophy home to Washington, 28–21.

Halas lost more than a title that year; he also lost the services of his greatest star, Bronko Nagurski, who'd had enough of Halas's miserliness. When Nagurski asked Halas to give him his first-ever raise to $6,000 from the $5,000 he had drawn from the start of his career, Halas refused to budge. So, the Bronk stayed home in International Falls and opened a Pure Oil service station. When he needed money, especially in winter when nobody came within hundreds of miles of his icy outpost on the Canadian border, he hit the wrestling circuit.

The 1938 season was the worst for Halas and the Bears since the 1929 debacle. The Bears never got on track, going 6-and-5, but, to his credit, Halas blamed nobody but himself for the situation. After suffering through Baugh's bravura championship-game performance, Halas knew he'd better get with the program and get a quarterback if he ever was going to win big again.

As in the past and would happen throughout his life, Halas found the man he could and would count on to make the difference. His name was Clark Daniel Shaughnessy, a head coach with not much to do in a job that used to mean a lot at a school, the University of Chicago, that had done as much as any to popularize the sport of football and now was being swallowed up in an athletic black hole.

If the University of Kansas is the fountainhead of basketball, with the game's founder, James A. Naismith, and his coaching progeny Forrest C. "Phog" Allen, Adolph Rupp, and Dean Smith, and his heirs Larry Brown, Roy Williams, and Bill Self, then much the same can be said about the city of Chicago when it comes to football coaching.

It is the University of Chicago that became the home base in 1892 to a young Yale alumnus named Amos Alonzo Stagg, who started football on John D. Rockefeller's newly minted campus in Hyde Park, on the South Side. At this charter member of the Big Ten, Stagg created the first Monsters of the Midway. Soon everyone copied Stagg in just about every manner, from the huddle to uniform numbers to formations and plays.

In 1910, a North Sider named Knute Rockne moved across the state line to South Bend, Indiana, to attend the University of Notre Dame, where, in 1918, he became even more acclaimed than the U of C's Grand Old Man. When asked where he got his plays, Knute Rockne said, "I took them from Stagg, and he got them from God."

Another Chicagoan who learned his football ABC's from Stagg was Bob Zuppke, who left west suburban Oak Park for the University of Illinois in 1913 to start his own regime of renown. Zuppke coached Walter and George Halas. Walter assisted Rockne at Notre

Dame, and George adopted the T formation from Zuppke, who got it, again, from the source, Stagg.

Enter Clark Shaughnessy. After the 1932 season, Robert Maynard Hutchins, the young, brilliant, and sports-hating U of C president, decreed that Stagg, at age 70, was too old to continue coaching the Maroons. So, he forced the Grand Old Man to retire. The irate and ever youthful Stagg stormed out of Hutchins's office and, at age 71, became head coach at the College of the Pacific.

Hutchins turned to Shaughnessy, a University of Minnesota alum who had made his reputation building winning teams in New Orleans as coach at Tulane before he transferred his loyalties a few blocks away to Loyola University.

Shaughnessy had no sooner settled into Stagg's old office when Hutchins dropped the first shoe. He raised academic standards for athletes and curtly informed his new coach that the academic head would wag the sports tail, not the reverse. The resultant talent drain led to defeat after defeat. Fortunately for Shaughnessy, one of Stagg's final recruits was Jay Berwanger. After Berwanger came the deluge, especially when Hutchins fired another shot across Shaughnessy's bow when he announced that he was deemphasizing all sports, football in particular.

With no more Berwangers in his future, Shaughnessy had time to ponder that future. Now in his mid-40s, he held tenure at the U of C, and the job market was tight. So, he did the next best thing and started attending Bears games on Sundays, where he made notes and also struck up a friendship with George Halas. Halas had been receiving glowing reports from New York about a bright prospect, the athletic tailback from Columbia, Sid Luckman. After seeing film of Luckman easily dodging onrushing defenders and displaying astounding passing accuracy, Halas knew he must have him.

When Shaughnessy watched those same films with Halas, he saw in Luckman the ideal athlete to execute schemes he had in mind to make the T formation football's ultimate weapon. Forget the single wing, Shaughnessy told Halas. The T is the thing.

Shaughnessy was a student of warfare and the movement of troops and units. He was a theorist, seeking ways to transfer warfare to football, and he kept his eye on Europe for possible ways to make his concepts fit to a T. Shaughnessy began to draft plays for the T and a new system of signal calling with Luckman in mind that covered everything from position and play numbering to the snap count itself.

While Shaughnessy, the theorist, devised, Halas, the pragmatist, set the gears in motion. He knew the Bears' constant high finishes would hurt their draft positions, but he also knew the way around the rule. Trade up. So, in 1938, he worked up a deal with Art Rooney in Pittsburgh, who, in turn, chose Luckman for Halas. Halas also worked out another deal after the 1939 season with another weak sister, sending Les McDonald and two other seldom-used players to Bert Bell's Philadelphia Eagles for their top draft choice, who would be George "One Play" McAfee, the brilliant Duke halfback who would rank with Grange and Gale Sayers in the Papa Bear's esteem.

Down on the Midway, the other shoe fell at the end of the 1939 season when Hutchins announced that he was dropping football. Now out of work in his career field, Shaughnessy caught a train to Los Angeles to a coaches convention to look for a job. Stanford needed a replacement for just-fired Tiny Thornhill, liked what Shaughnessy had to offer, and hired him to shape up what had become a moribund program. He went to work immediately, spending hour upon hour studying and analyzing Stanford's films.

Within a few days of his arrival, Shaughnessy called in the press. "Stanford will use the T formation," he announced. He didn't stop there, precisely explaining why he junked the single wing for the "radical" formation that its many doubters were certain only a pro team like George Halas's Chicago Bears could understand and execute. "Our approach will be different," Shaughnessy explained. "We'll coil up the defense in as small an area as possible, then run around it or throw over it. It will make old offenses obsolete!"

Better yet for the dean of Halas U., he now had his own Professor Shaughnessy at Stanford testing their newly devised T-formation theory with its array of pulling linemen, traps, fakes, and drop-back and play-action passes peppered among quick openers and sweeps. This exercise in practical application would benefit both coaches and change football forever. Who could ask for anything more?

NINE

A SON LIKE
NO OTHER

"*G*enerally speaking, you won't find players talking about Halas like they talked about Vince Lombardi. Vince was an equally tough guy, but he did expose his heart now and then," said Jeannie Morris, who knew both men: first as the young wife of Bears receiver Johnny Morris and later as a newspaper writer and television sports reporter.

Regarding the flinty Halas, just two exceptions to his aloofness come to mind, she said. "Sid Luckman helped make Halas famous. Luckman was one of his few football players who felt affection for him. The other was Gale Sayers."

Pro football is rich with stories about legendary coaches who saw special qualities in young quarterbacks and molded them into first-magnitude stars. Bill Walsh and Joe Montana in San Francisco come to mind, as do Lombardi and Bart Starr in Green Bay and Weeb Ewbank and Johnny Unitas in Baltimore. In the case of discovering and fashioning the game's first-ever quarterback, Halas had to do more than create a player. He had to cast the mold as well. He and Clark Shaughnessy had determined that the offense would not work without the correct operative.

When their prototype emerged on paper, the two coaches had retooled their improved model of Ralph Jones's original "modern T formation" into a "boxing" type of offense. The quick openers were the left jabs. The man in motion and backfield faking were the feints. The fullback played to the real "punch," the hooks. The pass plays were the unexpected "sock."

Those weapons operated behind a quick, mobile front, the line, that subordinated strength-against-strength for mental and physical agility. Each individual had to carry out his own exacting assignment within a coordinated unit that broke sharply off the snap, delivered fast-hitting brush blocks or cross-body blocks, opened holes for the quick-starting backs, or protected the passer. On running plays, the linemen had to make their initial blocks and then head downfield to execute second, sometimes third and even fourth, blocks. Ends were split away from the five interior linemen to establish the threat of the pass. Each play was designed to go all the way from any spot on the field.

The "new" quarterback was the most difficult job description Halas ever tried to fill. The reigning premise of single-platoon football was that the best defense is a good offense. The two men would adapt that concept to the T. The quarterback of the Halas-Shaughnessy vision was "not only the brains, but also the heart of the 'T' offense."

Physically, he had to possess a ballet dancer's footwork in designed pivots, step-overs, and spins and the ability to throw with accuracy and precision from a drop-back set or on the run, and he had to be able to withstand punishment from onrushing linemen. Since the rules at that time forbade the coach from shuttling in plays, the quarterback in Shaughnessy's system had to be a "field general."

In Chicago, the national search for the dream quarterback intensified in 1938. Halas had received good reports about a Jewish youth from Columbia University, via the streets of Brooklyn, named Sidney Luckman. Luckman, Halas was told, owned all the athletic gifts and an extremely bright, agile mind.

Sid learned the three Rs at Erasmus Hall, a remarkable high school that would turn out such notables as Luckman's contemporary and author Bernard Malamud, entertainment superstar Barbra Streisand, basketball Hall of Famer Billy Cunningham, real estate and sports mogul Jerry Reinsdorf, and Luckman's co-Master of the Football Universe, Al Davis. To Halas, Sid's background underscored his own positive school experience honed in the tough inner-city environment at Crane Tech in Chicago.

On a rainy afternoon at Columbia's Baker Field, Halas saw how well Luckman ran and passed and, more to the point, how he led the Lions as he executed spins, pivots, and fakes from the tailback position. Halas knew that Luckman could outrun Sammy Baugh and, in handling a wet ball on a sloppy field, was nearly as fine a passer as the Texan. Moreover, in that single-platoon, limited-substitution era, Luckman demonstrated A+ skills as a sure tackler, an outstanding pass defender, and a punter.

When Sid's coach, the legendary Lou Little, assured Halas of Luckman's intelligence, Halas was certain the prospect could make the transition to the Bears' T (for Total Offense) system.

He worked out the deal with Art Rooney, shipping end Edgar "Eggs" Manske to Pittsburgh in return for the second overall draft slot on December 8, 1939—Luckman. Better yet to Halas's way of thinking, Manske was only on loan to Rooney, who returned him to Chicago once the regular season was safely under way so nobody could complain that Halas had rigged the draft.

As important as Luckman was, the Bears' own top choice, Holy Cross fullback Bill Osmanski, became an instant Halas favorite as well, as did a strong, tough guard from Western Michigan named Ray Bray, who came in round seven and stayed through 1951.

The trick for Halas was talking Luckman into signing. He was newly married, had landed an excellent job in Manhattan, and wasn't sure he could handle pro football. Halas traveled to New York to dine with Sid and his bride, Estelle, at their apartment.

After dinner, he made the offer, a $5,000 salary. The young graduate decided to cast his lot in far-off Chicago with the Bears instead of taking a white-collar job in New York. "It was the most money he'd paid to anybody except Red Grange," said Luckman to Richard Whittingham, as recorded in *Bears in Their Own Words*.

Halas did not tell Luckman that Bronko Nagurski got the same sum in 1930. "You and Jesus Christ are the only two people I'd pay this to," Luckman recalled Halas saying. "Thank you, Coach," Luckman said. "You put me in great company."

Halas loved Luckman from the start, and so did his teammates who knew what a winner he was. Johnny Lujack, the Heisman winner from Notre Dame, was drafted in 1947 to replace the master, and for a time he did, until his own brilliant career ended abruptly in early 1952 in a dispute with Halas after just four seasons and two straight Pro Bowl appearances. "I thought Sid was a really fine guy, and I really enjoyed being his teammate," Lujack said. "Boy, he knew how to maneuver Halas. I mean he really did."

In 1939, because Halas loved Luckman and his tremendous upside, he would not throw him to the wolves. The young man came to training camp at St. John's with his brain chock-full of plays but lacking the mind-muscle memory that makes the many spins, pivots, and ball-handling techniques second nature.

Camp proceeded, and Luckman faltered as he tried to master the quarterback position. When Halas saw he was pressing, he moved Luckman to the familiar left halfback position where he could gain game experience in relief of starter Ray Nolting and his backup Bobby Swisher and learn from veteran quarterback Bernie Masterson. Luckman's fellow rookie Osmanski started at fullback and led the league in rushing, with 699 yards.

For years, Halas had established a policy of honoring a player's family by starting him when the Bears visited his hometown. When the Bears hit New York for 1939's sixth game, Halas gave Sid the start in the Polo Grounds at left half in front of the home folk, who had taken the subway up from Brooklyn to Manhattan.

The Bears were trailing 16–0 in the third quarter, and Luckman was back on the sideline, when the coach walked over to him and asked if he felt ready to play. When Luckman answered in the affirmative, Halas said "All right, son. I want you to go back in." He paused. "At quarterback."

The nervous youngster got a lift when fellow rookie Bob MacLeod, a Dartmouth all-American from the western Chicago suburb of Glen Ellyn, told him before they huddled that he could get open for a long pass. Sid agreed to try it. MacLeod went in motion, made a stop-and-go move, and broke free. Luckman's downfield pass fell short, but MacLeod came back, caught it, pivoted, and broke free for a touchdown. A few minutes later, Luckman threw a screen to Swisher, who sprinted 65 yards for the touchdown. It was too late to prevent a 16–13 defeat but the caterpillar had left the cocoon. However, he was not quite ready to float like a butterfly. That would come in two weeks.

Ed Sprinkle was reputed as the Meanest Man in Football in the late '40s, when they still went both ways. That continued in unlimited substitution in the early '50s, when he was the toughest defensive end in the league at 207 pounds. In his dozen years, Sprinkle caught passes from Luckman, Lujack, Bobby Layne, and George Blanda. "Sid probably was one of the worst [looking] passers in the league because he threw sidearm. Sammy Baugh was the most precise passer I ever played against," Sprinkle admitted, "but Sid got the job done. He could play."

On November 5 before 40,537 at Wrigley Field, Halas tapped the rookie to start at quarterback against the Bears' biggest rival, Green Bay, and Hutson, Herber, and Hinkle. The Packers would go on to win the 1939 title, but Luckman demonstrated that a changing of the guard was imminent. He had thrown an early touchdown pass to Osmanski. The Packers held a 27–24 lead late in the game, when the Bears got the ball back. Luckman opened with an 18-yard dart to his home-again trade partner Manske and then hit MacLeod on a 45-yarder to the 10. That set up Osmanski's 10-yard sweep for the winner, 30–27.

Luckman's performance against Green Bay confirmed everything Halas envisioned, especially his greatest and most enduring attribute. Leadership. Each week, the '39 Bears improved behind their fast-emerging rookie who now was playing with a veteran's confidence. They drew more than 42,000 to Briggs Stadium in Detroit a week later, many to see him. Luckman didn't let them down, launching a 50-yard bomb downfield to Swisher, who caught it in stride to complete an 85-yard scoring play as the Bears beat the Lions 23–13.

From the beginning, Luckman was a lightning rod, both positive and negative. No one could fault his performance. But carpers always nibbled at the edges. Many hated Luckman because they hated Halas. Others hated him simply out of bigotry, because he was a Jew, either spitting out the word as they uttered it or letting it slip from a corner of their mouths behind a cupped hand. Out of his "Jewishness" sprang rumors that Luckman had "mob connections" that led from Brooklyn directly into Chicago, rumors that lingered for decades in various city newsrooms.

Bill Gleason heard such talk from his *Herald-American* mentor, sports columnist Warren Brown, who offered his own brand of logic on a topic he never would discuss in print. According to Gleason, "Brown wouldn't go to pro football games. He strongly believed that Halas and Luckman rigged them. He'd say, 'I go down to Notre Dame. Luckman's down there teaching the quarterbacks. And Bill, that son of a bitch could throw a pass through a swinging tire from 50 yards away. At Wrigley Field and they're on the 10-yard line, he throws the ball into the bleachers. Think that was an accident?' "

Such talk even swirled through the pro-Halas *Tribune*. Cooper Rollow heard the stories years after Luckman's retirement. "There was speculation [in those days] that Luckman needed one more touchdown for gambling reasons; that was never proven, but it was speculated. Sid would come into the huddle, clap his hands, and say, 'OK, you guys, one more touchdown.' The team really didn't need it. Then he'd say, 'Even though it may seem we don't need it, I'm gonna take everybody out for a steak tonight.' That story was going around all the time," Rollow said. "I don't think that many people took it seriously because back in those days, there wasn't an awful lot of attention being paid to that type of thing. It was just like a bunch of kids together on the sandlot saying, 'Let's go get another one.' "

Gambling talk always swirled about the game in that pretelevision era. Halas, for one, strongly felt that some things were better left unsaid, whether he knew the truth or not. That held for all his boys, doubly so for Sid. For the coach, no one was more reliable than his boy. When he and his assistants wrapped up the game plan, Halas would call Luckman at home around 11:00 P.M. with the play list. When they met the next morning, Luckman always recited the list in full detail, covering any and all situations and potential weather conditions in the process.

Only 21,398 came out to Wrigley Field on a chilly November 19 afternoon to see the Bears go for three in a row against Bert Bell's Philadelphia Eagles. The Luckman-engineered offense rolled up 246 yards on the ground and 285 in the air, for 531 total yards, as the Bears overcame Davey O'Brien's record-setting 21 completions in 35 attempts to beat the Eagles 27–14. That moved them into second place in the Western Division behind the Packers. The Halas-Shaughnessy plan had shifted into high gear.

They wrapped up '39 with their fourth straight Luckman-led victory, a 48–7 rout at Comiskey Park over the Cardinals. The Bears gained 412 yards as Luckman passed for a pair of touchdowns, 5 yards to MacLeod and a 33-yarder to John Siegal, and ran back an interception 33 yards for another score. They finished second in the Western Division behind the Packers and were now favored to win it all in 1940.

The 23-year-old boy who had never traveled west of Philadelphia before 1939 became, by season's end, king of Chicago. As big a hit as he was on the field, off the field, he was on his way to a fabulous business career. He was a Midas in the flesh. Sprinkle watched Luckman the businessman in action from the time he arrived in Chicago in 1944. "He enjoyed a better lifestyle than most of the other pro football players of that time," Sprinkle said. Luckman started his own business, Cellucraft, a firm that specialized in printing cellophane wrappers. When he was playing, his major client was Brach's Candy. "He made a $100,000 commission off the Brach account," Sprinkle said.

After the war, when new cars were scarce and in hot demand, $500 under the table got a potential customer head-of-the-line privileges. Chrysler set Luckman up as third partner in a dealership on the still heavily Jewish West Side. Sid Luckman Motors doubled its factory deliveries from 100 to 200 a month. "After four or five years, he got out and made a lot of money," Sprinkle said. "Then he got the exclusive Dumont TV distributorship."

In other dealings, though, Luckman was a charlatan, bordering, his detractors say, on absolute fraud. In 1959, Luckman pressured Kraft Foods to capture the lucrative caramel-candy cellophane-wrapper printing contract. That account had been the backbone of Skokie-based Johnsos-Coppock Printers for years. The owners, the Bears' longtime offensive assistant Luke Johnsos and the team's single largest season ticket holder, Charles Coppock, thought they would be renewed, until Luckman so undercut them in his offer that they had no choice but to fold their bid. Losing the account broke up the partnership, caused financial difficulty for both men, and significantly strained their friendship.

Johnsos, who was forced to deal with Sid in coaches meetings, suffered in silence in the same room for the rest of his career, as did their silent partner who had supplied the start-up money in Johnsos-Coppock years before. His name: George Halas.

Charlie Coppock was long dead when his son Chet, who had pared the season ticket list down to 76, returned to Chicago from Indianapolis in 1981 as a sportscaster at NBC's WMAQ-TV. One of the first people to call Chet for seats was a middle-aged, but ever desirous, Luckman, who worked his charms again. "He was unfailingly kind. And he did call us first when Halas died," Chet recalled in 2003. "I've often thought that Sid may have been atoning for what he did to my dad and Luke."

Irv Kupcinet was covering the Bears for the *Chicago Times* and had developed his own close and certainly not objective friendship with Halas when Luckman arrived in 1939. The two young men became such close and enduring friends that when Luckman's two children finished high school in north suburban Highland Park, Sid and Estelle moved back to the city into a showplace apartment in the same Lake Shore Drive building where Irv and Essee Kupcinet lived.

Kup not only covered his pal through the years but also provided cover for him in his gossip column that began in 1943. It was an open secret in Chicago long after his football days were over that Luckman was a womanizer before and after Estelle's death. (It is said that he demanded that his women be blondes, with help from the salon or with wigs, if need be. For years, Luckman himself wore an ill-fitting toupee.) Thanks to Kup and others, such dirt was never dished up in print.

The Luckmans, one former Highland Park neighbor said, lived parallel lives for many years. Estelle retreated to their place near Miami and left Sid alone for long stretches. When she took ill with terminal cancer and underwent treatment at Sloan-Kettering in New York, George Halas stepped forward, ordered his boy Sid to put down his checkbook, and covered every expense of her final illness.

After he retired with four championships to his credit, Luckman rejoined the Bears in 1954 as quarterback coach. He stepped aside the following year but returned in 1956 at Halas's urgent request. Within the team and organization, however, it became apparent that Luckman's presence was not only a mistake but was detrimental to the team and coaching staff because he did virtually no work and made few positive contributions. Many felt that either the Old Man could not see the problem or, if he did, he felt it would be a betrayal of his boy to remove him.

After years of festering undercurrent, it burst into the open in 1969's 1–13 debacle in a midseason story by *Chicago American* football writer Ed Stone, who gnawed at Halas and the Bears almost every day. "During the controversy over the quarterbacks—Bobby Douglass, Jack Concannon, and all those others—Sid was the token quarterback coach," Stone said decades later. "He'd show up maybe once a week in training camp and during the season. He'd do it for nothing. I wrote a piece that they needed a full-time quarterback coach. Anyway, I got a lot of flak from his friends."

Stone sighed as he recalled the supreme irony. Several irate members from the predominately Jewish Standard Club called the reporter. "They accused me of being anti-Semitic, not knowing I'm Jewish," Stone recalled. "To me, it was really funny, and from that point on,

I was on the outs with him of sorts. It's too bad, because when I was growing up, Sid Luckman was my idol, like any Jewish kid growing up on the North Side."

Perhaps Luckman took Stone's pointed public hint, for he quit coaching for good after the 1970 season. After that, he became George Halas's head cheerleader. Cooper Rollow watched him operate at many a banquet through the later years and attested, "Halas got more standing ovations than anybody you'll ever see. Luckman practically made a career by saying, 'And now let's all stand and voice our admiration for the greatest coach of all, Papa Bear!'"

Luckman reappeared from time to time, usually to talk about his beloved coach in television interviews and for NFL Films. His business successes, meanwhile, continued. He even enlisted the backing of a close friend, the financier and multibillionaire Jay Pritzker, and his family to make a run at buying the Bears. Luckman told Halas that the Pritzkers would put it in writing that he remain as CEO in full control of all team matters as long as he lived. Luckman beat a hasty retreat when Halas reminded him that the team would remain in the family's hands.

In the last years before his death on July 5, 1998, just short of his 82nd birthday, Luckman spent more time in Florida. When he was home in Chicago, he loved to entertain friends and visitors. To be invited to Sid Luckman's tastefully luxurious apartment overlooking Oak Street Beach on Lake Michigan for business or pleasure was to receive the royal treatment.

The visit was always special. At the finish of business, more often than not an interview under bright television lights, he invited everyone there to join him for the appropriate meal of the day, breakfast or lunch. Upon his guests' eventual departure, he handed each one a personal gift as a token of appreciation for the time well spent, a sweater, necktie, golf shirt, or similar item.

Over the meal during those visits, leisurely, informed conversation invariably turned to George Halas and the Chicago Bears. Pictures of Luckman and Halas were everywhere. An exquisite bronze statue of the two of them on the sidelines during a game occupied a place of honor. Most prominent among the memorabilia was a framed letter

dated May 24, 1983, five months and one week before the Papa
Bear's passing:

> *My dear Sid,*
>
> *"I love you with all my heart."*
> *When I said this to you last night as I kissed you, I*
> *realized 44 wonderful years of knowing you were summed*
> *up by seven words.*
> *My boy, my pride in you has no bounds. Remember our*
> *word "now!" Every time I said it to you, you brought me*
> *another championship.*
> *You added a luster to my life that can never tarnish. My*
> *devoted friend, you have a spot in my heart that NO ONE*
> *else can claim.*
> *God bless you and keep you, my son. "I love you with all*
> *my heart."*
>
> *Sincerely yours,*
>
> *George*

TE N

"THE GREATEST
TEAM OF ALL TIME"

*A*rthur Daley's lead in the December 9, 1940, *New York Times* stands alone as the most famous in pro football history. "The weather was perfect. And so were the Bears."

Indeed, on the day before, December 8, George Halas's Chicago Bears had executed their T formation with man in motion to precision as they beat the Washington Redskins in as elemental an assault of power, speed, total offense, and swarming defense as ever has been displayed in championship competition. The final, astonishing figure, 73–0, is one of the most famous outcomes in any sport. That single result in a championship game trumps all others.

Daley also transferred another legacy in his opening paragraph when he called the Bears the "Monsters of the Midway." Formerly the property of the Stagg-coached U of C Maroons when they were the scourge of the Western Conference, the nickname stuck and, when the Bears are rolling, ranks in awesome athletic might with the New York Yankees' alter ego, the "Bronx Bombers."

These new Monsters were the product of Halas and Shaughnessy's facile schemes on the one hand and a series of splendid talent judgments on the other. Halas based most of his manpower selections, in that precomputerized era, on the evaluation of coaching peers, cronies, players who knew worthy candidates for Beardom, or friends of a friend and the like. No modern personnel wizard except the late Jack Vainisi at Green Bay in the late '50s and Chuck Noll with his Pittsburgh Steelers dynasty of the '70s has amassed the talent pool that Halas garnered from 1939 through 1942 before he departed for World War II. Like Lombardi and Noll, who coached those players, Halas was at his coaching peak, not only as a motivator, an attribute he never lost, but also as a superb Xs-and-Os man.

His '39 class started with Sid Luckman, Bill Osmanski, backup quarterback Bob Snyder, end John Siegal, and tackle Aldo Forte and ended with the superb guard Ray Bray. "Bray was the strongest man I ever saw," recalled Hall of Fame tackle-linebacker George Connor. "He could do 50 one-armed push-ups, switch hands, and knock off 50 more with ease."

Halas's 1940 class produced a bumper crop at the top equaled only by George Allen's 1965 Gale Sayers–Dick Butkus parlay. It began with Philadelphia's choice from the Les McDonald trade when Bert Bell presented Halas with Duke right halfback George McAfee. McAfee was an all-around demon of a Blue Devil on a football field, a superior runner, the best kick returner in the game, an airtight pass defender, and a sure tackler who happened to be the fastest collegiate dash man in America.

George Vass related Halas's first training-camp impression of McAfee. When the Old Man saw the scrawny 165-pounder with slightly bowed legs line up for the first time in a full-contact scrimmage, he feared for McAfee's life when Luckman called his number on the quick opener. As a linebacker closed in, Papa Bear thought, "The kid's gonna get killed." At that instant, McAfee shifted a hip, spun, and took off, leaving the tackler to grasp at air. "I think we've got something there," Halas mused.

After he broke a 75-yard touchdown run in an early exhibition game, someone gave McAfee a nickname for the ages, "One Play." "That meant I could score at any time on one play. It isn't true," the ever modest McAfee said from his Durham, North Carolina, retirement home in 2002. Qualified observers who saw McAfee break loose from scrimmage, take a pass all the way, turn a spectacular interception into six points, or sprint for the distance with a kickoff or punt in hand said otherwise.

Red Grange called him "the most dangerous man with a football in the game." Hunk Anderson said McAfee was better than both Grange and his high school and college teammate George Gipp. When Gale Sayers was running wild as no other back had ever done, Halas said that the highest compliment anyone could pay any back was to compare him to McAfee.

Bill Gleason recalled a similar conversation with the Papa Bear at May and Halas long after the Old Man had retired McAfee's number 5 jersey. "Halas said, 'Bill, I played McAfee a quarter and a half because if I played him more, he would have ruined the league.' And he meant that," Gleason exclaimed. "He was sincere about it. George Halas was not going to ruin the league. McAfee was that good."

The footage of McAfee in action from the 1941 season highlights, salvaged intact from a 1961 fire, bears him out. One Play McAfee was the most exciting runner of his time, every bit as elusive and speedy as Baltimore's Lenny Moore of the '50s and early '60s, or the nonpareil Sayers.

The fates definitely had to be smiling down on Halas when he landed Bulldog Turner on the seventh overall pick. Halas's sworn enemy, Detroit Lions owner George A. "Dick" Richards, had advanced Turner $200 to "get his teeth fixed"—in other words, to keep his mouth shut and tell anyone who asked that he wasn't interested in playing pro football. The five teams ahead of Detroit passed on Turner.

Then, Lions coach Gloomy Gus Henderson stunned Richards and everyone else present when he chose USC tailback Doyle Nave. Halas jumped up and shouted, "Clyde Turner of Hardin-Simmons" before Henderson could reconsider.

A furious Richards fired Henderson on the spot. Henderson retaliated like few disgruntled employees ever have when he produced letters that cited Richards's wooing of Turner. That bit of chicanery cost Richards a $5,000 fine on February 2, 1940, for tampering. When Richards kept dogging Henderson, his former coach fired the second poisoned arrow in his quiver when he let NFL powers know that he possessed letters from Richards admitting the owner had bet on his own team.

Halas moved quickly to call a cease-fire and to make it stick. Aware that Henderson's betting revelations against Richards could kill his two-decade-old league if they were made public, the Papa Bear took charge. He convinced his fellow owners to keep the Richards betting accusations a secret. Then he enlisted Chicago State Street merchant Fred Mandel to buy out Richards. Eight days later, on February 10, aided by Charlie Bidwill's silent investment, Mandel announced that he would buy the Lions for $165,000. That ensured Richards a 700 percent profit on the $21,500 he paid for the team in 1934 when he moved the franchise from Portsmouth, Ohio, to Detroit. Again, Halas had applied his admonition that some things are better left unsaid, as he would in 1963 when the alleged betting habits of then Baltimore Colts owner Carroll Rosenbloom were bantered about during the Paul Hornung–Alex Karras contretemps.

As for Turner, Halas gained himself a Hall of Famer who vindicated that faith many times over in performance. "Bulldog Turner was the best football player and smartest player I ever knew in my whole life," said George Connor. "He knew everybody's position on every play. He could play halfback. He could play center. He could do everything." In fact, in one game in 1944, Luke Johnsos sent the Bulldog in at halfback. He proceeded to run 48 yards for a touchdown on the only carry of his career.

On the second round, Halas selected LSU's tall, fast, and talented end Ken Kavanaugh. "Clark Shaughnessy's the reason I got to the Bears," Kavanaugh said. "They drafted me on his recommendation after Bulldog. Bulldog was as great at his position as any player who ever lived."

Halas was only beginning his talent sweep. After taking Kavanaugh on the second round, he grabbed tackle Ed Kolman from Temple in round three and followed with four more men who moved right in to play important roles: end Hampton Pool, tackle Lee Artoe, running back Harry Clark, and his third-string quarterback, Young Bussey—like Kavanaugh, an LSU Tiger. Eight men from that draft played significant minutes on that 1940 team, which was three deep with All-Pro–caliber players at every position.

The battle to land Bulldog Turner was child's play for Halas. To land Kavanaugh, the Papa Bear had to go toe-to-toe with a man who was every bit his equal as both a judge of talent and a negotiator, baseball's mahatma. "Branch Rickey signed me to a Cardinals contract, and I joined the Houston team out of LSU. I was a right-handed first baseman," Kavanaugh recalled from his Sarasota retirement home down the street from Otto Graham's place.

"Rickey sent me to Houston in the East Texas League. One day in early July, I was taking infield practice when the clubhouse guy came out and said I had a long-distance call. 'This is George Halas,' the caller said."

" 'Who are you?' I asked. Halas ignored that and said, 'You have to play in the [College] All-Star game before I can sign you.' I told him I had to take infield and hung up," Kavanaugh said with a chuckle."Arch Ward called back the next night. 'You have to play in the All-Star game,' Ward barked. I said, 'I'm not interested. I'm playing baseball with the Cardinals.' "

Ward called again two nights later and passed the phone to Halas. "Get out of baseball," the coach roared, aware he was speaking to the pass catcher Luckman needed to stretch defenses. The young man called Rickey, who let him join the All-Stars on the Northwestern campus in Evanston.

"Green Bay won the game, 45–28. We couldn't cover Hutson," said Kavanaugh realistically. Nobody else could either. Then came time to join the Bears.

"Halas wanted to sign me for $50 a game. I walked out on him. He came back and offered $100. 'Look,' I said, 'I make $300 a month from the Cardinals.' Then he started: '$150.'

" 'No! $300 a game or I go back to baseball.' He agreed to my terms.

" 'You're getting paid better than anyone else in the league,' Halas 'confessed' after I signed." Kavanaugh's "league-high" contract was $3,300 for that season.

Kavanaugh was a Bear to the core, but he knew being one meant you had to pay the price. Literally. "Halas was a fine man. Smart. Tough. He knew the game. He'd fine you for missing a tackle above the belt. He'd fine you $5 if he caught you out on Saturday night."

Shaughnessy, who had been drawing up plays for his new charges at Stanford while they were away for the summer, left for Palo Alto shortly after Kavanaugh reported to training camp. Halas brought back Carl Brumbaugh to work with the backs. With a new baby, Luke Johnsos had to work another job to feed his growing family, so he was available only on Sundays. Halas installed Johnsos in the press box, where, as the game's first eye-in-the-sky, he could see and report what was happening on the field. At first, he wrote down suggestions as he saw openings and sent them down to the field via messenger. Johnsos soon realized that dispatching a messenger through a crowd was too time consuming. He told Halas they needed to communicate instantaneously. "Why not a telephone setup?" Halas said.

It was magic. One afternoon, with Halas's approval, Johnsos demonstrated their new toy to the owner of a visiting team. "Watch this," he alerted the owner as he picked up the phone. "Run 71!" The Bears scored a touchdown. He conducted the same demo the next series, calling another play, with the same result. Soon, to the Papa Bear's delight, everyone adopted the Bears' latest gimmick, another device to advance the game.

To tutor the linemen, Halas called on his longtime friend Heartley "Hunk" Anderson, a former Bear and Knute Rockne's replacement as coach at Notre Dame after the fatal 1931 plane crash. Ed Sprinkle, who joined the club in 1944, was a favorite pupil of the gravel-voiced screamer, a tough guy in the Halas mold. "Old Hunk. Everybody liked him. His favorite expression was 'You b-yass-tards! You b-yass-tards!' He'd get out there and aggressively show you how to block. He told us how he ran around Duke Slater, of Iowa, in college. He was 165 pounds. Duke was 240," said Sprinkle. "Hunk was a pretty shrewd guy. He handled the defense pretty well."

"Anderson was the smartest defensive coach I ever knew," Hall of Famer George Connor said. "Hunk never put us in a bad position. Heartley 'Hunk' Anderson made me a linebacker."

The Bears served notice on the rest of the league in the 1940 opener against the Packers at Green Bay, thoroughly routing the defending champions 41–10. McAfee earned his "One Play" moniker when he ran back a kickoff for a 93-yard touchdown, and Ray Nolting ran another one back 97 yards. Three days later at Comiskey Park, the Cardinals punctured the Bears' bubble with a 21–7 victory.

On Saturday, September 28, 1940, Clark Shaughnessy led his Stanford Indians onto the field at Kezar Stadium in the season opener to unleash his T-formation man-in-motion attack against the heavily favored University of San Francisco Dons. Everything they had tried in practice clicked as they routed USF 27–0. Quarterback Frankie Albert remarked, "This stuff really works!" As it would in the National Football League for Shauaghnessy's colleague, George Halas.

The Bears bounced back from their surprise at Comiskey Park to beat the Rams at Cleveland, 21–14. On October 13, they edged the Lions 7–0 in the home opener at Wrigley Field and then barely eked past the Brooklyn Dodgers the next week, 16–7. Without Shaughnessy's presence, his offense seemed stale.

The Bears got rolling on October 20 in New York as Luckman led the way to an impressive 37–21 win over the Giants. The Packers tightened it up in the rematch the following week, but the Bears' defense stopped them three times inside the 20 in the fourth quarter, allowing Chicago to escape with a 14–7 win. The Bears then flattened out again, losing 17–14 at Detroit, a week before a November 17 visit to the nation's capital. Kavanaugh recalled the frustrating finish: "We ran up and down the field and got only a field goal out of that. Halas kept going for it on fourth down instead of kicking. Baugh got a touchdown, and Washington led 7-to-3."

Luckman led a late drive as McAfee carried to the 1-yard line and faked an injury to stop the clock. Out of time-outs, the Bears took a five-yard penalty to the 6-yard line with time for a final play. "Sid threw a certain touchdown pass to Bill Osmanski in the end zone. The Washington defender wrapped his arms around Bill. No call. We all screamed, but we lost 7-to-3," Kavanaugh said.

When they got home, Halas tacked derogatory newspaper clippings from Washington on the locker room wall each day. With two regular-season games left at Wrigley Field, the Bears took out their anger on their unfortunate victims. They mauled the Rams 47–25 and then took revenge on the Cardinals on December 1 with a 31–23 victory to win the Western Division and set up their grudge match with the Redskins.

Shaughnessy was emerging from the Rocky Mountains at that hour. He was riding the eastbound train to Chicago that he'd boarded the night before in Oakland, still buzzing from the euphoria of Stanford's 13–7 victory over California in the Big Game. That win completed an unbeaten, untied, 9-and-0 season for the right to represent the Pacific Coast Conference as host team on New Year's Day in the Rose Bowl against Nebraska.

Despite Stanford's revolutionary accomplishment, most so-called experts viewed the team's success with skepticism, many dismissing it as a freaky product cranked out by a quirky eccentric. Since practice for the Rose Bowl would not start until mid-December, the "quirky eccentric" decided to leave the California sun to answer an SOS from the chilled Midwest. As he prepared to board the train in California, Shaughnessy told reporters he was off to see some friends in Chicago and then head up to Minnesota to celebrate a combination late Thanksgiving–early Christmas with his family. He did not tell them the Chicago friends were a group of large men named George Halas, Sid Luckman, and the Chicago Bears.

For years, Shaughnessy had studied the tactics of one of his favorite military men, German panzer general Heinz Guderian. On the Chicago-bound train, he pored over Guderian's latest triumph, the Nazis' astounding sweep through France.

In a 1986 article for *Smithsonian* magazine, the late William Barry Furlong wrote that Shaughnessy considered football of the 1920s and '30s a "strategic reprise of World War I. That is to say, the offense was slow, ponderous, mindless, and usually ineffectual." In 1937, when Shaughnessy had friends on the University of Chicago faculty translate Guderian's first book on panzer tactics, he had found his football soulmate. Guderian's ideas, in brief, called for using movement to spread the defense thin and then attack swiftly at a weak point.

Bill Furlong was a brilliant reporter, as much at home discussing engineering or modern art as he was in the press box. He could have been an ace city hall or crime reporter, he was that dogged. As his former *Chicago Daily News* colleague Bill Jauss disclosed, when Furlong was on the prowl, he was known to eavesdrop on conversations in an adjacent room through a stethoscope. Like his competitor Ed Stone on the *American*, he nearly drove Halas nuts, deprecating him as a man who "speaks to players and press in a voice like breaking bones." By contrast, Furlong was crazy about the "mad scientist" Clark Shaughnessy, especially in his application of military science to football.

Germany launched its attack against France on May 10, 1940. "The Allied armies went north," as Furlong reminds us. Guderian's tanks punched a hole through the French defenses in the middle at Sedan and poured through, waiting for neither the infantry nor supplies as they outflanked them. "On May 15, Winston Churchill, prime minister of England for less than a week, received a despairing call from Paul Reynaud, premier of France. 'We have lost the battle!' cried Reynaud."

What Guderian had done was send a 29-division army group to the right (man in motion), thereby drawing the allies to their left toward the North Sea (the sideline) to defend against the German power. Guderian dispatched a tank thrust (quick opener), and as the French line collapsed to cover, the German general swept left around the French flank and broke out on a dead run to Paris. Shaughnessy had a name for it: the fullback counter. That play and other misdirection calls were the finishing touches that had been missing from Halas's attack throughout the 1940 season.

As soon as his train arrived on Monday, Shaughnessy hurried to the Bears' offices on the east end of the Loop at 37 South Wabash to watch film with Halas. They rehashed every play of the defeat in Washington in fine detail. Shaughnessy noticed that the Redskins' defense set up in a five-man front, covered the man in motion, and shut down the quick openers. They brought in Luckman and showed him what the Redskins had done. Then Shaughnessy handed both men a series of plays based on his latest studies, to test the defense.

And beat it. As Furlong wrote, Shaughnessy warned them, "You might score a touchdown instead."

Shaughnessy told Luckman to use the test plays to check if Washington employed the same defense it used in November. While Shaughnessy and Luckman concentrated on the nuts and bolts, Halas fired up the troops. "The gamblers favored us by 21 points for the title game," Kavanaugh said. "That week, George Preston Marshall called us front runners, whiners, and crybabies. Halas plastered all the stories on the locker room bulletin board."

The Bears left on Friday for Washington. It's been reported many times through the years that it was the quietest ride any member of that usually boisterous bunch ever took. No card games, no jokes, no laughter. They had their noses in their playbooks. "When we got to Washington, we were ready to play," McAfee said.

At Griffith Stadium that Sunday, Sid Luckman and his teammates came in from the warm-up and gathered around the coach. All his players through the years say Halas did not deliver stem-winding pep talks. Usually he'd say something in the nature of "Go get 'em." But on this day, as Luckman recalled in 1991, he was as ready as they were, and he fired them up with a final reminder. "He said, 'I want you to go out there and play the kind of football you can play. Let the nation know, and the Washington Redskins' owner know, that we're not crybabies!" Then Halas stepped aside and unleashed his hungry Monsters in quest of a title and an early Christmas bonus, the winner's share, $873.

The only good thing that happened to Washington that day was the marching band's brilliant pregame rendition of "Hail to the Redskins." The 'Skins even lost the coin toss. If ever a championship was won on the flip, the Bears' opportunity to receive and get first crack definitely was it. The venerable footage transferred to videotape provides clear-cut evidence of Shaughnessy's brilliant adjustments and Halas's inspiration that wrought havoc in the wintry sunshine on the Griffith Stadium gridiron.

Ray Nolting took the opening kickoff at the Chicago 3, cut to the right sideline, and broke upfield, where a Redskin knocked the ball out of bounds at the 25. Luckman then called the first of Shaughnessy's three designed plays.

He sent Nolting in motion to his right. At the snap, as fullback Bill Osmanski and right half McAfee made coordinated jab-step fakes to their right, Luckman executed a crossover step and handed off to McAfee with his left hand. McAfee burst through for seven yards on the quick opener to the 32. As McAfee ran, Luckman scanned the field as instructed. The Redskins had not changed that defense! He returned to the huddle and called Shaughnessy's second scripted play: Guderian's counter.

From his right-halfback set, McAfee went in motion to his left across the formation. At the snap, Nolting and Osmanski feinted right. Like Guderian's panzers, Nolting led Osmanski toward left tackle. To avoid a Washington tackler, Bullet Bill dipped to the outside, and off he went around the flank and down the near sideline, tearing past head linesman Irv Kupcinet, who was earning double wages that day as he also covered the game for the *Chicago Times*, an obvious conflict of interest. Nobody cared because most of the game officials owed their jobs to owners. Halas, it seemed, held sway over more men in striped shirts than anyone else. Kup was not a factor in this game.

After the snap, while the backs were performing their ballet, the line was executing its own intricate assignments. George Wilson tore across the field from his right-end position. Just across the midfield stripe, Osmanski must have seen the sprinting Wilson out of the corner of his right eye as he tried to run past the Washington secondary. Ed Justice, who cut off the angle to hit Osmanski, never saw Wilson coming. The big end slammed into Justice like a runaway truck, blasting him into fellow back Jimmy Johnston like one bowling pin splattering another. Osmanski poured it on to the goal line, a 68-yard scoring run on the counter that counted for 6 points. Halas called Wilson's parlay the greatest block he ever saw. Automatic Jack Manders kicked the extra point for a 7–0 Chicago lead. The game was 56 seconds old.

The 36,034 fans thought they were in for a shootout when Max Krause returned the ensuing kickoff 62 yards to the Bears' 32. But they groaned as wide-open Charlie Malone, facing the sun, dropped Sammy Baugh's perfect pass in stride in the end zone. Bob Masterson's field goal fell short, and the Redskins were finished.

Luckman guided a 17-play, 80-yard drive, scoring on a quarterback sneak to make it 14–0. Washington failed to make a first down, and Baugh shanked a punt to his own 42. On the first play, Luckman called Shaughnessy's bread-and-butter fullback sweep to the left, similar to Osmanski's game-opening score. He made a reverse pivot and handed to Joe Maniaci, who scored untouched. It was 21–0 with three quarters to go.

The only score of the second quarter came after a Nolting interception. Luckman delivered a 30-yard pinpoint pass to Kavanaugh, who beat the double coverage of Frank Filchock and Andy Farkas near the end line. It was 28–0 at the half. "He just wanted us to keep it going," said Luckman, who took a seat on the bench at the coach's orders as Halas let his hungry team enjoy the feast.

The third quarter was barely under way when Baugh floated a swing pass that Hampton Pool picked off and ran in for the touchdown. When the Redskins gambled on fourth down and failed from their own 33, Nolting went 10 yards and then broke free for 23 more on a quick opener to make it 41–0. The Bears finally misfired, failing on the conversion.

Soon thereafter, McAfee intercepted third-stringer Roy Zimmerman's pass and took it 35 yards for the touchdown. Turner followed moments later with a 30-yard interception return to make it 54–0 after three quarters. Up in the press box, the writers took bets on whether the Bears would get more touchdowns on offense or defense, and they howled when Marshall's PA announcer drew a resounding chorus of boos when he reminded the fans to order their season tickets for 1941.

The fourth quarter was fun time for the reserves. Harry Clark scored on a 44-yard reverse for the ninth touchdown. Two short plunges finished the scoring, one by Gary Famiglietti, the last by Clark, the only man to score more than once on this wild afternoon. The Bears rolled up 501 total yards—382 of them on the ground, 119 more in the air—completed six of eight passes, and picked off eight passes, scoring on three. The 73 points amassed and equally wide margin of victory set a playoff record that stands to this day.

In many ways, the story was so huge that its observers could not give it justice in their accounts. The *Chicago Tribune*'s George Strickler offered a pedestrian lead: "Greatness came to the Chicago Bears today." In his secondary front-page story, Strickler's colleague Wilfrid Smith heaped due credit on Luckman: "This is the story of the man who this afternoon directed the greatest team professional football ever has produced."

Luckman's pal Irv Kupcinet earned his officiating pay chasing after touchdown-bound Bears all afternoon. At the final gun, Kup charged into the Chicago locker room in his officiating clothes to get postgame quotes. Then he beat a hasty retreat to his hotel room to pound out a story and dictate it to the desk back in Chicago. He stressed the way the Bears, for the first time, put everything together. "Today the Bears unleashed the fury that had been pent up."

The *New York Times*' Arthur Daley summed it up best. "At this moment, the Bears are the greatest football team of all time."

ELEVEN

THE TEAM
OF DESTINY

*T*he 1940 triumph was mere pre-
lude to the still-unprecedented reign of terror that George Halas
unleashed on the National Football League in 1941. No team, not
the '62 Packers, '72 Dolphins, '75 Steelers, '89 49ers, nor '85 Bears,
has approached the '41 Bears in their comprehensive dominance.
"Had the war not come when it did, there's no telling how many
championships we might have won," said George McAfee in 1991.
Ken Kavanaugh agreed emphatically. "We could have beaten anyone
for the next six years had we been able to stay together. Everybody
in the league was afraid of us!" Sid Luckman's eyes glistened when
he talked about '41. "George Halas said it was the best team he ever
saw. We were a team of destiny, really."

Pearl Harbor did break up that dynasty, but Halas had assembled
so many outstanding players that his machine was able to roll on
through World War II without all its components, win titles in 1943
and '46, and still reel off the best overall record from 1947 through
1950 without winning a championship. As it was, from 1940 through
1950, they won four championships, lost one title game and another
divisional playoff, and finished second in the Western Division every
other year except 1945.

Obviously, neither Halas nor anyone else foresaw that 1941 would be the last season before America went to war in Europe and the Pacific. As always, he sought the edge, even as he basked in the glory of the 73–0 rout. While the team slept off the victory party in a Washington hotel, he was hard at work Monday morning, December 9, 1940, at the league draft meeting, also in the nation's capital. He owned 3 of the top 10 picks in round one, including the first overall, from Philadelphia.

Halas was so well positioned that he could employ Mae West's adage that "too much of a good thing is a good thing." He had the luxury of wasting a pick or two, so he led off with a Chicago-area native, Michigan's Tommy Harmon.

"Old Number 98," as the Gary, Indiana, native preferred to be called, immediately announced from New York that he wouldn't play for Halas and was entering radio instead. It didn't bother the Papa Bear in the least. He had satisfied Bears supporters and the press with the gesture, but that rebuff meant he wouldn't have to meet Harmon's anticipated huge salary demands. Furthermore, the 1940 Heisman Trophy winner might not have been able to make the team.

Halas's second choice came in a deal with Pittsburgh. He picked a sure thing this time with Clark Shaughnessy's grizzlylike fullback, Norm Standlee, billed as the next Bronko Nagurski. Signing him would be a snap.

The third first-round choice, the Bears' own, was Ohio State tailback Don Scott. Scott was not available, since he already had enlisted for flight training with the Army Air Corps and would never play. When Scott was killed in action over Europe in 1943, Ohio State immediately renamed its airfield in his honor.

Papa Bear pressed on, grabbing Standlee's Stanford running mate Hugh Gallarneau in the fourth round. Nearly as dangerous a running threat as McAfee, Gallarneau, an Oak Park native who did not play high school football but swam instead, became a Halas favorite. He would enjoy a brilliant postfootball business career as a senior executive with Marshall Field's.

With three weeks left before Stanford's January 1, 1941, Rose Bowl date with Nebraska, Standlee and Gallarneau had no time to think about the Bears. Shaughnessy got an extra edge when he imported Luke Johnsos to apply his "eye-in-the-sky" expertise on the press box phones on New Year's Day.

After Stanford surrendered an opening touchdown drive to the Cornhuskers, Shaughnessy adjusted his defense on Johnsos's advice, and Stanford's Wow Boys got their attack moving. They were trailing 13–7 late in the first half, when Frankie Albert teamed up with Gallarneau for a 40-yard scoring pass. They never looked back, to win 21–13, and every coach in America took notice. Stanford controlled the ball for two-thirds of the time, reeling off 374 yards, to 128 for Nebraska.

From that moment on, everything else in football was obsolete. In the space of three weeks, George Halas and the Chicago Bears and Clark Shaughnessy at Stanford launched a football revolution with their T-formation attack. Coaches flooded both men with letters and phone calls seeking guidance in the T. Both willingly shared their advice at clinics and shipped thousands of copies of their book *The Modern T-Formation with Man in Motion* to colleges and high schools across America. "I still have that book," former Bears assistant Chuck Mather said. "I started in high school football using it."

Another convert was the Philadelphia Eagles' new coach fresh off the Yale campus, Earle "Greasy" Neale, who would turn the former doormat into a league power after the war. One by one, the others joined the "T" revolution. When Curly Lambeau switched over in 1947 in Green Bay, the only single-wing holdout was Art Rooney's Pittsburgh Steelers team. The Steelers clung to the single wing until 1952, when the loyal Rooney reluctantly fired the late Jock Sutherland's successor-disciple, John Michelosen. Rooney rehired former coach Joe Bach, who installed future Bears general manager Jim Finks at quarterback.

The colleges immediately joined the T-party as Notre Dame's Frank Leahy led the way. Leahy arrived in South Bend just before spring practice in 1941. It was too late to junk Knute Rockne's antiquated Notre Dame box, but Leahy opened an immediate dialogue with Halas. After the 1941 season, Halas sent Luckman and his backup, Bob Snyder, to South Bend to conduct a spring-practice crash course in the T. Snyder stayed on to assist Leahy the entire 1942 season before returning to Chicago in '43. Snyder's prize pupil, Angelo Bertelli, became the first T-quarterback to win the Heisman Trophy for the national champion Fighting Irish, which he did with considerable help from another future Bear, sophomore Johnny Lujack.

Bob Snyder had maintained a special relationship with Halas dating from his rookie season in 1939. As the coach's grandson Pat McCaskey related the story, a call came to the Bears' dressing room at Wrigley Field on November 4, 1939, just before the team took the field against the Packers. Snyder's wife told Snyder their eight-day-old son, Bobby Jr., had died unexpectedly in his crib. She urged Bob to stay and play.

The only person Snyder told about the tragedy was his roommate, Ray Nolting. Snyder kicked a field goal that afternoon that turned out to be the edge in the Bears' 30–27 victory.

When Snyder visited the team offices at 37 South Wabash in late December to sign his 1940 contract, Halas handed him an envelope. Snyder was waiting for an elevator when he opened it to find a personal check from Halas for $1,000. He returned to see Halas. "Coach, I don't have a bonus in my contract," he said. "That's to help bury your son, Bob," Halas replied. Both men choked back a tear and hugged. Then Snyder left.

The T formation swept the nation, and by war's end virtually everyone was using it, high school, college, and pro. When Woody Hayes took over at Ohio State in 1951 and told the alumni he was switching the Buckeyes to the T, like it or not, they opened their mouths, closed their eyes, and swallowed their medicine without a peep. After USC kicked Jess Hill upstairs in the late '50s, the last single-wing holdouts were Tennessee and UCLA. By 1960, they too had given up the T. rex for the T.

The 1941 Bears reveled in the collective time of their young lives. Success had never come so easy. To celebrate it, Halas brought out a new anthem by songwriter Jerry Downs (a pseudonym for Al Hoffman) in honor of the team's winning the 1940 title. "Bear Down, Chicago Bears" reminded the fans, "We'll never forget the way you thrilled the nation with your T-formation."

America's attention was focused on the doings of two superb young baseball players in the summer of '41. In early summer, the New York Yankees' Joe DiMaggio rang up a 56-consecutive-game hitting streak, a still-standing record. Down the stretch, Boston Red Sox left fielder Ted Williams just kept connecting and finished the season at .406 as the last man to attain the iconic .400 milestone.

While DiMaggio and Williams hogged the headlines, the Bears breezed through the exhibition warm-ups, barely breaking a sweat as they won all five games. Halas treated each one as practice for the opener at Green Bay's City Stadium against the Bears' biggest rival in the Western Division, Lambeau's Packers.

"The old stadium was built in 1925," recalled Packers public relations director Lee Remmel, who's seen every game in the series since 1944. "Curly Lambeau's father, Marcel, was a foreman on that crew. When it was built, it seated 24,800."

The Bears stayed at the Northland Hotel, midway between the Chicago and North Western train station and City Stadium, the wooden structure situated behind East High. "The hotel didn't always cooperate with the Bears," recalled Charles Brizzolara, who joined his father, Ralph, in the Bears' official traveling party for many a trip to Green Bay. "One year, they had the Wisconsin State Police annual ball at the Northland. The ballroom was on the second floor. And they gave all the Bears rooms on the third floor."

If the noise filtering upstairs from a polka band playing into the wee hours wasn't enough, the crowds outside did the rest. "They would make noise around the hotel all night long, pounding on garbage cans and things like that to keep the players awake," Brizzolara said. "The team had to dress at the hotel. There was no dressing room at the stadium. We took buses there. One year, I believe it was 1942, they stopped the bus and tried to tip it over and almost succeeded. Lambeau was not one of my father's favorite people."

As Gary D'Amato and Cliff Christl wrote in *Mudbaths and Bloodbaths*, City Stadium had no restrooms. The crowds there were fueled by the three *B*s: hatred for the Bears, beer, and booze. Men urinated on the fence. Women had to go below the stands. When they did, the men above peeked down through the bleachers. Green Bay was known as a church-going, pleasant place, but when Chicago came to town, fans near the Bears' bench cursed volumes at Halas, who gave it back and more with some of the foulest language ever spoken or heard in any God-fearing community.

In 1941, every seat was occupied, as usual, and the sidelines behind the low rope-and-wooden-post fence in front of the cinder track that ringed the gridiron were crammed with standees. They booed in unison when Halas led his champions onto the field in brand-new uniforms, the ones that became the symbol of the Monsters of the Midway and continue to this day: naval officer's blue helmets, navy blue jerseys with three orange stripes on the sleeves and white numerals, white pants with vertical navy blue and orange stripes, navy blue stockings trimmed in orange stripes, and black football shoes. They looked big and mean, and they played that way with the semicontrolled fury Halas loved to call "mental heat."

The Packers came out in their bright yellow helmets over deep blue jerseys trimmed in yellow and contrasting yellow pants. That look lasted until Vince Lombardi designed the present uniform, changing the jersey color to forest green.

Chicago was up 15–10 in the fourth quarter, when Clark Hinkle punched in the go-ahead touchdown for a 17–15 Green Bay lead. After a Ray Nolting kickoff return to midfield, Halas inserted the rookie Standlee at fullback, and Luckman cut him loose. As advertised, the 6'2" 240-pounder in Nagurski's image knocked aside everyone in his path like a wrecking ball, smashing for 24 yards on his first carry. Luckman called Standlee's number again, and he drove for another 15 yards to the Green Bay 13. With the Packers stacked up to stop Standlee, Luckman faked to him and handed to McAfee, who swept to his left, showed a Packers defender the limp leg, and cut to the outside to score. Snyder added a field goal to ice the 25–17 victory.

For the next four weeks, the Bears' scores resembled high school scrimmages as they embarrassed Cleveland, 48–21, the Cardinals, 53–7, Detroit, 49–0, and the Steelers, 34–7, in a merciless onslaught. "Halas would fine us $50 if we picked up a guy you knocked down," recalled Ken Kavanaugh. "He'd also fine you $50 if you retaliated when someone knocked you one. If you didn't swing back, he promised to pay you $50 out of his own pocket. He knew what happened, because he had everything on film." He made good on the promise, Kavanaugh added: "One day, Sid got nailed and ran off the field over to Halas. 'That guy just hit me and I didn't swing back. You owe me $50, Coach.' Halas paid up after the game."

When the Packers came into Wrigley Field before a Midwest-record crowd of 46,484, they took a 16–0 lead into the fourth quarter as Lambeau used a seven-man front to hold the Monsters' attack to 183 total yards. The Bears came within 2 points but failed to get in field goal range on their last possession, to fall for the first and only time all season, 16–14. "Nobody was lost into service yet," observed retired *Green Bay Press-Gazette* sports editor Art Daley. "We had a helluva team, too."

The Bears rebounded with four more victories to take a 9–1 record into the finale at Comiskey Park against the Cardinals on Sunday, December 7, 1941. Beyond those in attendance, thousands more fans were listening on the radio in Chicago and up in Wisconsin. Newly-wed Daley had just moved to Green Bay with his wife, Lorraine, to begin his long career at the paper. "The second Sunday we were here, we were listening to the Bears play the Cardinals on the radio. The Packers had the day off. It turned out to be Pearl Harbor Day."

"I used to sit in the middle of our living room on Sunday when we got home from church and listen to all the games," recalled future NFL executive director Don Weiss, then a 15-year-old sophomore at East Aurora High School, 40 miles west of Chicago. "We were listening to the Bears game when they announced the attack."

Weiss, who died in 2003, heard similar stories from old New York hands in the early '50s when he was a young reporter with the Associated Press. "They made announcements all afternoon at the Polo Grounds: 'All servicemen, return to your bases immediately.' "

The Cardinals were giving the Bears fits when the news broke. "They announced it over the loudspeaker," Luckman said. "It was a tremendous shock to everybody in the stadium. The teams just didn't have the same emotions knowing our country had just been attacked."

The Cardinals were up 24–20 when McAfee erupted in the fourth quarter. At midfield, McAfee went in motion to his right, headed downfield, caught a Luckman pass in stride, and ran it in to give the Bears a 28–24 lead. On the Bears' next possession, on second-and-5 from their own 30, Luckman handed to McAfee on a quick opener. Pinned in at the 35, he broke two tackles, slipped free, and sprinted all the way to complete a 34–24 victory. With matching 10-and-1 records, the Bears and Packers would meet the following Sunday in Wrigley Field in the NFL's first-ever divisional playoff for the right to face the Eastern champion Giants.

The following day, the sports editor at the *Press-Gazette* gave Art Daley, the new kid in town, the dream assignment—covering next week's Packers game against the Bears. "I was really quite excited," he said. "I got down to Chicago and sat next to [venerable reporter] Arthur Daley of the *New York Times*." The Chicago weather at 16 biting degrees on December 14, 1941, wasn't perfect, but the Bears came close to that standard before 43,425 fans, who needed an escape after the week's dire news from Pearl Harbor and Europe. Their only lapse came when rookie Hugh Gallarneau fumbled the opening kickoff to set up a Hinkle touchdown. "I just about died, because Halas was unforgiving if you did that in a Packer game," Gallarneau said.

Gallarneau redeemed himself late in the first quarter with an 81-yard punt return for a touchdown that turned the game around. When the Bears finally went on the attack, Luckman saw that the Packers were still employing that seven-man front. His line opened huge holes for Standlee, who had the greatest day of his career as the Bears rolled up 267 yards on the ground. Standlee smashed over twice, and Bobby Swisher finished the scoring in the decisive 33–14 victory to spoil young Art Daley's sportswriting debut.

Despite an unseasonably warm 47-degree day, only 13,000 showed up at Wrigley Field for the title game. Perhaps it was war fears, perhaps not. But huge blocks of seats were empty, especially in the end-zone upper deck at the first-base side of the ballpark. The Bears easily defeated their longtime rivals from New York. Standlee scored two more touchdowns, and McAfee ended it late in the game on a quick opener. Ray McLean iced the 37–9 final with the last drop-kicked extra point in NFL history.

The Bears completed their brilliant run, beating the NFL All-Stars 34–24 at the Polo Grounds. It was the last time this team would ever be together, as many players left for the service. For the record, they won 17 games, against that single loss to Green Bay. That total includes five exhibition victories, among them a 37–13 romp over the College All-Stars. They won 10 and lost 1 in the regular season, scoring 396 points against 147.

Their regular-season scoring average, 36 points a game, prorates to 576 in the current 16-game schedule, against the Minnesota Vikings' 1998 record of 556. The 1961 Houston Oilers scored 513 points in 14 games, for an average of 36.6 a game. The '41 postseason point totals, 70 points against 23 allowed, compare favorably as well.

McAfee, Kavanaugh, and Standlee were the most prominent wartime departures in 1942, but Luckman, Turner, Gallarneau, Fortmann, Bray, and Osmanski remained, as did Halas for the first five games. The 1942 team was almost as strong on offense and stingier on the defensive side of the ball. Yet, this team is all but forgotten. These Bears had the misfortune to lose just once. The championship game in Washington.

After Pearl Harbor, Halas knew the Navy would recall him at some time. Reserve officers with an engineering background were at a premium. This time, though, Halas wanted to go to sea and join the fight for real, unlike in World War I, when he passed his time playing football at Great Lakes. He drove up to Great Lakes and made a personal appeal to a friend, the base commander, Captain T. Dewitt Carr, to pull strings and get him into action. The name Lieutenant Commander George S. Halas, USNR, finally popped up in early autumn. He was ordered to leave on November 2 for the Naval Air Technical Training Center at Norman, Oklahoma, to turn out aircraft mechanics.

Halas roamed the sidelines as usual through the first five games as the Bears roared through the schedule. After they beat the Philadelphia Eagles 45–14 in game five, the Papa Bear turned over the reins to Hunk Anderson and Luke Johnsos, who would run the team as co-coaches, with Paddy Driscoll assisting. Shaughnessy returned in an advisory capacity, leaving Stanford after a 6-and-3 season in 1941.

Lieutenant Commander Halas entrusted the team to his best friend, Ralph Brizzolara, for the duration. The dynamic Brizzolara had served as team secretary since Halas bought out Ed Sternaman in 1931 and kept a watchful eye on team finances as he invested in many of Halas's outside business interests. Since 1919, he had worked for American Steel Foundry, a railroad supply firm that made wheels and undercarriages, where he was vice president and chief engineer. "During the war, I hardly saw my father at all, with George in the navy and my dad running two businesses. He left home at 6:00 A.M. and went to the Bears office at 5:00 and worked until 10:30 or 11:00 and then came home," Charles Brizzolara recalled. When Ralph wasn't spending time in American Steel Foundry's offices in the Wrigley Building, or in the three Chicago-area foundries, he was on the road checking production at locations in Illinois, Ohio, Pennsylvania, and New Jersey.

By comparison, the Bears were a mom-and-pop operation, even with Papa Bear gone to war. "For the Bears, he didn't have a real big staff. The two women, Frances Osborne and Lucille Blessendorf, ran the office. Frances was the secretary–office manager. Lucille handled the tickets. Max Swiatek was there; he also handled the May and Halas store," Charles Brizzolara said.

"Luke Johnsos and Hunk Anderson were the co-coaches, and Paddy Driscoll the assistant. They were there quite a bit because they had what they called the Burgundy Room behind the business office, which is where they kept all the films, showed them, and went over them. There were no facilities at Wrigley Field."

Halas was in uniform on November 1 when he was presented his naval officer's sword at halftime of the Lions-Bears game at Wrigley Field. He then inducted Mugs, a June graduate of Loyola Academy, into the Navy. After watching the Bears finish off the Lions 16–0, he headed downtown to catch a train to Oklahoma City.

The Anderson-Johnsos team carried on as coordinators with a common mission. Hard-nosed Hunk ran the defense while cerebral

Luke ran the offense. The rematch with the Packers at Wrigley Field came two weeks after the Papa Bear left for service.

The night before the game, new Bear Connie Mack Berry, a long-time former Packer, called Anderson after visiting his former teammates at the Edgewater Beach Hotel. He had learned from Green Bay guard Buckets Goldenberg that Sid Luckman was tipping his plays. When Luckman bent his knees as he called signals, Goldenberg knew that was his key to drop back into pass coverage. Conversely, when Luckman did not raise his knees, Goldenberg would stay in to stuff the run. Anderson found the solution. "I came up with what we called '31-late.' It was a fullback delay over Goldenberg's position," Anderson wrote in *Notre Dame, Chicago Bears, and Hunk*. He took Luckman aside and let him know what he had been doing and how to upend Buckets.

Early in the game, the now aware Luckman faded to pass. When Goldenberg dropped back into coverage, Luckman handed off to the fullback, who charged through the vacated hole for a long gain. Then, when Luckman stood behind center as though a running play were on, Goldenberg charged, and Sid shot a slant pass to an end over the middle for another long gain. Finally, after talking it over with Lambeau, the thoroughly muddled Goldenberg played for the run. Luckman trapped him, and the Bears runners sprinted by on his inside. If he stayed in place, they double-teamed him. It turned into one of the longest afternoons for Green Bay in the history of the series as the Bears won 38–7 to continue on their run toward the unbeaten season.

The Bears allowed just two touchdowns among four shutouts in the final 6 games of the 1942 regular campaign. They scored 376 points and allowed just 84 in a perfect 11-and-0 season to run their unbeaten streak to 18 games. The title game was next.

All of Washington had been waiting two years and five days for the rematch. Halas wangled a leave and hitched a military flight to Washington's Bolling Field in time for the December 13 game at Griffith Stadium. Years later, Luckman told Halas's collaborators Gwen Morgan and Arthur Vesey that the team picked the wrong time to get fat-headed. "We were beginning to think of ourselves as unbeatable," Luckman said. "We did not work as before. The inevitable happened."

The Redskins shut down the Bears from the outset, gaining confidence with every possession. Midway through the second quarter, Washington's Dick Todd intercepted a Luckman pass and returned it 10 yards to midfield. On the next play, Todd fumbled. Bears tackle Lee Artoe scooped up the loose ball and ran it 50 yards for the touchdown and a 6–0 lead. The euphoria turned to dismay when Artoe's conversion attempt sailed wide to the left.

The Bears never threatened again until it was too late. The Redskins took the lead late in the second quarter on a 39-yard strike from Sammy Baugh to Wilbur Moore, who got behind Luckman to make the catch and score. Bob Masterson's point after made it 7–6 at the half. Andy Farkas added an insurance touchdown in the first drive of the second half, and the Redskins held on to end the Bears' title run at two, 14–6.

When the angry Halas attended the owners meeting the next day, George Preston Marshall jabbed a needle deep into his bruised ego. "Why don't you take off the uniform and let a younger guy do the job?" Marshall quipped. "I went through the roof," Halas wrote. Art Rooney, who saw the blowup, told a writer, "I thought Halas would kill Marshall."

Actually, Halas's anger at Marshall was a mild rant compared with the troubles he was having on the home front with his daughter, Virginia. Man troubles.

TWELVE

CRISIS ON THE HOME FRONT

*T*he sanctification of Ed McCaskey began on November 1, 1983. It might have started a day earlier, but, out of respect for the memory of the founding father, George S. Halas, who had died the evening of October 31, the McCaskey family allowed the clock to tick past midnight to begin All Saints' Day before they began a process that would take nearly 20 years—or two-fifths of the time it takes for a soul, albeit in this case a living one, to endure purgatory.

Actually, the individual who underwent purgatory every day of her married life, living on pins and needles in fear of what bit of nonsense her husband would say or do next, was the founding father's daughter, Ed's wife and the mother of the 11 children he sired, Virginia Halas McCaskey.

In public, beginning that first day of November 1983, the Chicago Bears family underwent the requisite funeral ritual, replete with wake, flower sprays, requiem mass, and interment in the family mausoleum. Of course, that was the appropriate thing to do.

In fact, the Old Man's body was still warm when the McCaskey family swept in and took charge of the charter franchise the morning after his Halloween passage into the netherworld. When NBC's Chet Coppock had finished an interview with Ann Gleboff, secretary to Bears business manager Rudy Custer, Halas's handpicked general manager Jerry Vainisi rushed in and pulled the sportscaster aside. He told Coppock that Ed had informed him that Ann would be fired by the end of that day. "For your own good, don't run that interview, Chet," Vainisi said.

They couldn't ax all of the Old Man's minions, though. The plan was to let them linger for a number of years until the blessed son-in-law's own heirs got a feel for the inner workings of the operation and learned how to wield power.

The heirs never acquired either quality. Unfortunately, they were too clueless to realize it until they had cleared out the founding father's capable caretakers one at a time. By then, the good ship Halas was foundering in a sea of mediocrity that would consign the NFL's proudest franchise to laughingstock status.

To the McCaskeys, none of that mattered when chairman emeritus Ed later passed away during a nap on April 8, 2003, after a long, often painful illness. By then, despite a few glitches along the way, marked by the utter failure of the number one son as chief executive, the McCaskey family had rewritten team history in their favor despite the odium in which they were held in the old hometown.

The intramural stories concerning the daily critiques Halas delivered when Ed was the team's titular treasurer no longer circulated through the offices to the titters of the secretarial pool, whose members knew them all by heart. The fact of the matter was simple then. George Halas would not permit his son-in-law to see the team's financial statements, nor did Ed ask to see them.

The Old Man did permit Ed's presence at the beginning of morning meetings among himself, Mugs, and then-controller Vainisi. When they were ready to conduct real business, Halas would tell Ed it was time to go, and as the other two men watched, he would dutifully take his leave. As soon as the door closed behind him, Halas, without fail, would exclaim, "There goes the stupidest son of a bitch I've ever seen in my life."

On the day he died, Chicago Bears Chairman Emeritus Edward W. McCaskey, the man who had the good fortune to marry into a fortune when he wed the only daughter of the founder of the Bears and the National Football League, was lauded as the glue of the family business and even a great leader in no less a journal than the *Chicago Tribune*.

It was an amazing tribute to a man who had spent as many waking hours as possible taking the plunge at the racetrack, where he lost a great deal of money through the years. His wife's money. It was appropriate that in his only significant football moment, he lost the coin flip—to his father-in-law's close friend Art Rooney—that would have given Terry Bradshaw to the Bears instead of to Pittsburgh.

By his death on April 8, 2003, only canonization remained for Ed. All else was in order, right down to making his assigned parking space behind the secure gates at the Halas Hall campus in North Shore Lake Forest a sacred plot, never again to be stained by any inert vehicle's seeping its crankcase drippings. Virginia and the second-generation McCaskeys who cared had finally, at least in their eyes, redeemed their father's reputation, which their grandpa had so ruthlessly trampled in private almost daily.

Ed McCaskey was a marvelous raconteur and an enthusiastic, if not quite up to Frank Sinatra standards, crooner of popular music back in early 1941. When he was a student at the University of Pennsylvania, young McCaskey had high hopes of replacing Harry James's singer, that selfsame kid from Hoboken named Sinatra, who'd left for greener pastures with Tommy Dorsey. The singing career didn't pan out.

Back in Chicago, George Halas saw how dreamy-eyed his 18-year-old daughter, Gin, as he fondly called her, looked whenever she gazed at his great young fullback, the future dentist Bill Osmanski. Now, there was a prospective son-in-law who would make him happy! Gin's infatuation was unrequited, however. Bullet Bill wasn't interested. Especially not in a naive girl who had led a sheltered life under the scrutiny of the nuns at St. Scholastica Academy for Girls.

As he prepared for the 1941 season, George Halas was certain that his Gin would be secure when he put her on the train to Philadelphia to matriculate at Drexel Institute. After all, his older brother Walter was Drexel's football coach and long had been keeper of the Halas family flame.

When Virginia met Penn senior Ed McCaskey the following February, she fell madly and irrevocably in love. By early summer, he was working in the Baltimore and Ohio freight yard in Philly for $43 a week and saving up for an engagement ring. In midsummer, Virginia invited him to visit Chicago to meet her parents. Ed brought the ring but wouldn't let her see it until he spoke to her father.

As Ed and Virginia's son Patrick relates in his self-published memoir *George Halas*, on the afternoon of Ed's arrival at the Edgewater Beach Apartments, Halas charged into the flat. "You wanted to see me?" he roared.

When Gin's young suitor acknowledged that he did, Halas growled, "Come on in the bedroom!" Ed followed him into the room. Halas, who owned one of the first window air conditioners, turned it on, stripped to his underwear, and plopped down on one of the twin beds. "Aren't you going to have a nap?" snapped the Papa Bear. Ed dutifully took off his clothes in compliance.

After a brief interlude, Halas snarled, "What's on your mind?"

"I want your permission to consider myself engaged to Virginia," McCaskey said. "I brought a ring."

Halas looked it over. "How much you pay for this?"

"$155."

"Don't you know I have a jewelry store?" he snarled. "You'd have done much better than this." Halas clenched his jutting jaw and glowered for a moment. "OK. We'll go to the Edgewater Beach [Hotel] and you can give her the ring." The young man was relieved. For an instant. "But you can't get married."

The three Halases—George, Min, and Gin—and McCaskey went to dinner. "I've got some work to do," the senior Halas announced after dessert. Young McCaskey rose and proffered his hand. When Halas extended his normal viselike grip and then withdrew it, McCaskey found a $10 bill in his palm. George picked up the dinner tab, and he and Min excused themselves. Ed and Virginia went to the ballroom to hear Shep Fields and his orchestra and take a few turns on the dance floor.

Later, they went for a stroll on the beach walk, where he gave her the ring. Because Ed knew his draft number was coming up, the young couple set a December 18 wedding date, but Halas still had not given them permission to marry.

By December, Halas was on active duty with the Navy in Norman, Oklahoma, and Ed was still awaiting his call-up. When they knew the Bears would meet the Redskins in Washington for the 1942 title, Min bought a round-trip train ticket to Philly to keep tabs on Virginia, now a sophomore at Drexel Institute, and her beau, Ed. Halas arranged his flight from Norman.

At the game on December 11, as it became obvious the Bears would lose, Virginia began to cry. When Ed told her it was just a football game, she replied, "You don't think Dad will let us get married if the Bears lose, do you?"

At first Halas consented, but then he changed his mind, saying he had to get back to Norman after the league meeting and couldn't take another leave the following week. Behind closed doors, he told Virginia he knew a sharp young junior officer in Norman whom she should date. For the first time in her life, Gin said no to her father. Ed was it! And that was that!

According to Pat McCaskey, a priest at the Newman Club at Penn told Walter Halas that Ed had stolen the class treasury at the university. Ed denied it, saying the priest had lied. He told Pat years later that the priest had tried to make a pass at him.

As Ed told his son years later, two men in camel hair overcoats and fedoras paid him a pre-Christmas 1941 visit. One was smoking a cigar. The other took out his upper plate and introduced himself as Bert Bell and his cigar-smoking friend as Art Rooney. Both, they said, were with the Pittsburgh Steelers. "Halas sent us here to investigate you," Bell said. "Bill Lennox says you're OK." Lennox was ticket manager at Bell's alma mater, Penn. "If Lennox says you're OK, you're OK with me."

"If you're OK with Bert, you're OK with me," Rooney said. "Whoever said Halas was an angel?" They walked out.

While McCaskey tried to undo the damage the priest reputedly had caused him, Halas refused to grant his permission for their marriage. Now Gin refused to disobey her father, and the wedding date passed. Finally, in late January, Virginia summoned her courage, took the bit, and rode the B&O from Philadelphia to Baltimore to elope. Ed's father was working there as a construction foreman in a shipyard. They took out a marriage license and found lodging in a rooming house where the senior McCaskey was staying.

On the morning of February 2, they attended mass at Baltimore Cathedral, took communion, and then caught a bus to nearby Bel Air, where they went to a small church. As Ed told Patrick McCaskey, the local priest, Father Reed, married them in the presence of his cook, who acted as maid of honor, and her nephew, a midget, who acted as best man.

Ed had $11 in his pocket. After paying the priest $10, Ed and Virginia McCaskey walked across the street for a breakfast of ham with raisin sauce and mashed potatoes. The bill was $1.20, and Virginia slipped a half-dollar under the table to Ed, who gave everything to the waitress. "Keep the change," said the last of the big-time spenders.

There were many reasons why the McCaskeys could never forget that Groundhog Day of 1943. Not only was it Virgina and Ed's wedding day, but it also was her father's 48th birthday. No one knew the irony of that date better than the young woman who was more her father's daughter than her brother ever could be his son. After he got home from the war, Halas always observed his birthdays with close friends but never honored his daughter's anniversary.

Ed went to war with the army, and Virginia moved to his family's home in Lancaster, Pennsylvania, where she lived for the duration. By the time their first child, Michael, was born, on December 11, 1943, Ed was in England training for the Normandy invasion. He was decorated for valor in France and later received a battlefield commission. He left service as an army captain nagged by a lingering case of hepatitis that dogged him periodically the rest of his life.

When they came home after the war, McCaskey from Europe and Halas from the Pacific, the Papa Bear found a spot for Ed as a salesman for May and Halas. He worked for the organization 25 years.

Back in 1942, after Bell and Rooney had paid their visit to McCaskey, Halas asked Rooney to have a detective tail Ed and check him out. What the detective found infuriated Halas the rest of his life. The detective reported that not only was Ed a saloon singer, but worse, he was also a gambler, a plunger at the racetrack. One of the reasons the Old Man brought him into the club a quarter century later was to keep an eye on him. And he put Gin on an allowance so Ed couldn't blow it all on the ponies.

Ed McCaskey won, though, merely by outliving both Min and George Halas. Virginia gave Ed such privileges as the chairmanship, his parking space, the freedom to gnaw on the cigars he no longer could smoke but still had to chew, and the opportunity to stand beside her and stay mute as she presented the George S. Halas Trophy to the winning coach in the NFC title game, and she gave him more money to wager on the horses. The McCaskeys outmaneuvered Mugs Halas's children in a nasty estate battle fomented by their mother, Terry, and bought them out at what proved to be a bargain price.

In the final irony, Ed's coffin lies next to that of George Stanley Halas Jr., Mugs, in the mausoleum spaces Virginia purchased at All Saints' Cemetery in suburban Des Plaines after her brother's death. It turned out that Ed McCaskey, the son-in-law George Halas loathed from the moment they met in 1942, had the last laugh on the Old Man.

THIRTEEN

WAR, WAR, WAR

*B*y 1943, sports had caught up with world reality. The games, too, were immersed in total war. President Franklin D. Roosevelt had published the "Green Light" letter that kept baseball going for general morale. Many elite college football players entered officers' training programs and now were taking classes and playing football at campuses other than the ones they chose after high school. And after the '43 season, many would be off to fight in Europe or the Pacific.

Michigan coach Fritz Crisler, for instance, conveniently snared a built-in all-America backfield tandem in Wisconsin halfback Elroy "Crazylegs" Hirsch and Minnesota fullback Bill Daley. Hirsch and Daley led the Wolverines to a third-place finish in the polls behind Navy-bound Frank Leahy and his Fighting Irish of Notre Dame and number two Iowa Pre-Flight, coached by Don Faurot and top aides Bud Wilkinson and Jim Tatum.

One able-bodied athlete who somehow never was tagged for active duty was a rawboned kid from tiny Tuscola, in west Texas, named Ed Sprinkle. Eddie's first football experience came in his senior year in high school when a coach at nearby Abilene Christian introduced six-man football to Tuscola. Sprinkle's play earned a football scholarship to Hardin-Simmons, in Abilene, where coach Frank Kimbrough introduced him to the school's favorite son. "He looks like you did when you came here, Bulldog," the coach said to George Halas's great All-Pro center Clyde "Bulldog" Turner. Sprinkle and Turner became friends for life.

"I was 16 years old," Sprinkle said. "So, I worked out there at center. I was left-handed, and when I snapped the ball back, it had a reverse spin, and it caused the backs to fumble, they said. I played that year as a center, and then they switched me to tackle."

The top 20 in 1943 featured almost that many service teams, boasting rosters stocked with top college players, some pros, and football nomads like Sprinkle. "I got an appointment to the Naval Academy and went there for one year," Sprinkle said. "I was the starting right tackle on the Navy team that lost one game, to Notre Dame and [Heisman Trophy quarterback] Angelo Bertelli. We beat Army 13-to-0." Navy finished fourth in the polls.

So many able-bodied pro football players were gone to war by 1943 that Art Rooney and Bert Bell combined their Pittsburgh Steelers roster with Alexis Thompson's Philadelphia Eagles, a concoction that wags called the Steagles. Ironically, in late 1940, Rooney had sold his Pittsburgh Pirates to Thompson and then joined up with Bell in Philly. The following April, Thompson switched franchises with Rooney and Bell. That put Rooney back in business at home in Pittsburgh, where he renamed his team the Steelers.

In 1944, the Rooney-Bell combine merged with Charlie Bidwill in a Chicago Cardinals–Pittsburgh team called Card-Pitts. Because they lost every game, this bunch gained infamy as the Carpets, the league doormat. The Cleveland Rams did not play at all in 1943 and loaned out their players to the rest of the league. The best of what was left were the Bears in the Western Division and the Redskins in the East.

Co-coaches Hunk Anderson and Luke Johnsos would have to accomplish it alone. Their peacetime boss, Lieutenant Commander George Halas, was out of instant communication, halfway around the world with the Navy in the South Pacific. Halas spent a tedious winter training aviation mechanics in landlocked Norman, Oklahoma, until his orders finally came in the spring. His friend from Great Lakes, Captain Dewitt Carr, had pulled strings in Washington; the

Papa Bear would join Carr on the staff of Admiral Thomas Kincaid to serve as welfare and recreation officer for the Seventh Fleet, the huge naval force in support of General Douglas MacArthur's island-hopping campaign in the Western Pacific.

When the 48-year-old Halas arrived down under after nearly a month at sea, one of the first men he met was the friendly faced Commander Gene Tunney, the former heavyweight champion, who had trained at that long-ago Halas property on Petite Lake for the Jack Dempsey rematch in 1927. A young reserve officer, Lieutenant Junior Grade Rudy Custer, was assigned to Halas as his administrative assistant.

Among the first islands MacArthur's soldiers captured was Manus, in the Admiralty Islands. No sooner was the island secured than Halas went to work. Using his considerable requisitioning and recruiting skills, the Papa Bear quickly scrounged whatever movies he could get from army units and engaged a battalion of Seabees to build baseball diamonds, volleyball courts, beer gardens, and rec halls and to set up stages for live entertainment.

At the behest of General MacArthur, Commander Halas escorted Bob Hope and his USO troupe of Jerry Colonna and singer-actress Frances Langford. He gallantly carried Ms. Langford piggyback on roads through the New Guinea jungle. During that tour, he developed an enduring friendship with comedian Joe E. Brown, who became a devout Bears fan and good luck charm. "We never lost a game when he sat on our bench," Halas wrote in his memoir. He continued on his way with MacArthur and Kincaid toward Manila.

Back home in Chicago, Ralph Brizzolara found another way to enhance the tight revenue stream. He made the Bears the first pro football team to offer a regular radio broadcast. The faces of middle-aged Chicagoans still brighten when conversation turns to the ever entertaining, if not 100 percent accurate, WGN presentation from 1953 to 1976 with Jack Brickhouse doing play-by-play and Irv Kupcinet on color.

Every bit as colorful in the beginning were Bert Wilson's calls on the original home for Bears football, WIND, owned by Halas's landlord, Philip K. Wrigley. Wilson, who would start calling Cubs games in 1944, was an unabashed partisan, over-the-top before the term existed. Fondly called "Babbling Bert," Wilson substituted the word *Bears* for *Cubs* as appropriate in his hoary catchphrases, such as "I don't care who wins, as long as it's the Cubs!" and "Remember, fans, the game is never over until the last man is out" or "The game is never over until the final gun."

Chicagoans heard Wilson describe every thrilling play as the Bears ran up the best record in the league under Johnsos and Anderson. Sid Luckman enjoyed the best season of his career, passing for 2,194 yards and 28 touchdowns in the 10-game slate. He had outstanding support with Harry Clark, a third-string halfback in 1940–41, earning All-NFL honors. Johnsos and Anderson added two Rams loanouts, halfback Dante Magnani and end Jim Benton.

After a disappointing season-opening 21–21 tie at Green Bay, Anderson placed an urgent call to 35-year-old Bronko Nagurski in International Falls, Minnesota. According to his biographer Jim Dent, the Bronk agreed to return under one stipulation: "You tell George Halas this is my last season. Period." Nagurski agreed to play for the same $5,000 he was making when he retired after the 1937 season. He made his way to the Twin Cities to catch the first available train to Chicago, where he was handed his number 3 jersey and installed at right tackle, where he would play about half a game.

It continued that way until the fourth quarter of game 10, the regular-season wrap-up at Comiskey Park on November 28. The Cardinals were leading 24–14 at the start of the fourth quarter when Nagurski approached Anderson and asked to go in at fullback to see if he could make things happen.

When the small gathering of 17,000 fans saw Nagurski don his helmet, head into the game, and line up in the backfield, they stood and made as much noise as a sellout in the big ballpark. Everybody, from the Cardinals to the fans, knew what was coming. Nagurski may have been old, slow, and ponderous, but the Big Red could not stop him. Luckman gave him the ball, and he delivered in chunks of brute power and irresistible desire as he smashed, fought, and crawled for every inch. When he carried in for the touchdown to cut the deficit to 3 points, it was over for the Cardinals. The Bears scored twice more to win 35–24 and earn their fourth straight title-game appearance.

Nagurski was "retired" when Sid Luckman joined the Bears in 1939. To call the legend's number in 1943 was an experience Luckman never forgot: "He was devastating, the biggest man I've ever seen. He broke more collarbones than any fullback in history. Nagurski was all muscle, an outstanding football player, the kind you dream about."

The other memorable regular-season performance came two weeks earlier at the Polo Grounds. Luckman celebrated his New York homecoming with the greatest individual game of his career. He shredded the Giants' secondary for 433 passing yards and a National Football League–record seven touchdowns as the Bears romped 56–7. Luckman's seven scoring passes surpassed Redskin Sammy Baugh's three-week-old mark by one. "That game and the '43 championship game against Washington were the personal highlights of my career," Luckman remarked decades later.

The Bears had not played for a month when the Redskins visited Wrigley Field on December 26 before 34,320 fans, including Commander George Halas, home for Christmas leave to see his Bears. Before the game, he entered the Bears' dressing room, where players were involved in card games and loud talk. He walked up to Nagurski and joked that he expected him back for an encore in '44. The Bronk was not biting.

A half hour or so before the kickoff, Anderson walked to the front of the room and ordered all visitors out. "We got a football game to play today," Anderson roared. "That means you, too, George." Halas laughed and retreated, happy to comply.

Baugh was kicked in the head trying to tackle Luckman on a punt and was knocked out of the game. His backup George Cafego engineered a touchdown drive, and Andy Farkas went the final yard to give Washington the lead.

Luckman led the Bears back in another magnificent display of running, passing, defense, and leadership. He tied the game on a 31-yard strike to Clark, the first of Clark's two touchdown catches. With the scored tied 7–7, Luckman called on Nagurski three straight times for

19 yards and completed three straight passes to the 3. He then handed to Nagurski, who smashed over for the final touchdown of his career to put the Bears up for good, 14–7, moments before halftime. Just before Nagurski scored, Washington's irrepressible owner, George Preston Marshall, raised a ruckus. Charles Brizzolara saw it all from the family seats behind the Bears' bench.

"Marshall was dressed in a raccoon overcoat down to his ankles, and he wore a large hat. He came around from the Redskins' bench about seven minutes before the half. At that time, there were seats on the field in front of the wall on the third-base side. He just walked over there and ended up sitting on the edge of the Bears' bench," Brizzolara recalled. Then end George Wilson, the same man who threw that famous double block in the 73–0 rout in 1940, walked over to Ralph Brizzolara. " 'I think that's Marshall sitting on the bench,' Wilson told my father. Father looked, got up, and told him to get off the bench. Marshall refused to move. So, he had the police get him and walk him into the stands. Marshall took an empty seat."

That's when the fun really began. "I don't know who prompted him, but pretty soon an usher came by and asked to see his ticket. And Marshall didn't have one. So, they threw him out. And it was quite a scene. I mean, the Bears were all looking on the sideline and here's my father jumping up and down telling Marshall to get out. Marshall was screaming." Halas was upstairs watching from the press box, presumably laughing.

Luckman took over the game in the second half. He threw four more touchdown passes, two to Magnani, one to Dante's Cleveland chum Jim Benton, and a final to Clark again. Luckman led all rushers with 64 yards and set a playoff record with three interceptions as the Bears won their third title in four years, 41–21, to the delight of Halas, whose only regret was Nagurski's absolute final retirement. He went home for good.

After the smoke cleared from the victory, commissioner Elmer Layden read the riot act to Ralph Brizzolara and Marshall. According to Charles Brizzolara, "They both got fined $500 for conduct unbecoming officials of the National Football League. Then Father said, 'Good Lord! Where will we get $500?' That was a lot of money then.

The specific order from Elmer Layden was they must pay out of their own pockets. The teams were not to pay for the individuals. It was quite a show!"

The Bears lost 19 of the 28 men on the championship roster to the service. Dr. Danny Fortmann traded in his football gear for a naval officer's uniform to serve on a hospital ship in the Pacific, never to play again. Dr. Bill Osmanski joined the Navy Dental Corps and served with the marines in the Pacific. Luckman joined the merchant marine and participated in the Normandy invasion. His ship carried fuel to England for the invasion. From there, it ferried troops across the English Channel to the beaches in France. After the D-day landings, Luckman's ship returned to stateside. He served in Washington during the 1944 season, joining the team on weekends when possible.

Eddie Sprinkle left the Naval Academy after the 1943 football season, joined the Naval Air Corps Reserve, and waited at home for a call-up. The big call came in late July from an unexpected but welcomed source. "Bulldog asked if I wanted to come up and try out for the Bears." Ralph Brizzolara signed Sprinkle for $200 a game for the 10-game season and $400 for the exhibitions. "So, I signed a contract for 24-hundred dollars!" And off he went to the Bears' new training camp at St. Joseph's College in Rensselaer, Indiana, their summer home for the next 31 years.

"My first game with the Bears in 1944 was the All-Star game in Dyche Stadium, in Evanston," Sprinkle recalled. "All the guys were gone. I went there as a tackle, but I was too small at 205. Luke Johnsos and Hunk Anderson were going to cut me because of my weight. Bulldog went down there and said, 'You don't cut the best football player here. If you cut Ed, I'm going with him.' They decided maybe they could switch me to guard." The recollection made him chuckle. In a scrimmage, veteran star halfback Ray Nolting settled under a high punt as Sprinkle charged downfield with two other men. "I came across and hit him. I must have knocked him six feet into the air. That caught the coaches' attention. I played guard for two years!" It was a tough league for tough, mean men. Sprinkle would gain the reputation at defensive right end as the Meanest Man in Football over the next dozen years.

The Bears finished second in the Western Division in 1944, going 6–3–1. By 1945, everyone was ready to come home. In May, after the Seventh Fleet and MacArthur secured the Philippines, Pacific Commander Admiral Chester Nimitz brought Halas aboard as his welfare and recreation officer, and Rudy Custer came along.

Custer was a Wisconsin man all the way: Madison native, University of Wisconsin class of '35, Milwaukee ad man, and, along with his twin brother, a dyed-in-the-wool Green Bay Packers backer. That loyalty ended abruptly when he met his extremely persuasive superior officer in early 1943, Commander G. S. Halas, USNR.

"He took me out to dinner at the end of his tour in '45. At about 12:00, we went into a private room, and he handed me an envelope. It had $500 cash in it. I said, 'George, you didn't have to do this.' Halas replied, 'You don't know how much you've helped me. I'd like you to go to work for me.' Just like that! He offered me $5,000," Custer said. "I got hold of my boss in Milwaukee, who said, 'We'll call you back in about three weeks.' He called a few days later and said I'd better take the job. Five-thousand dollars felt like a million bucks to me," Custer said. He and his wife, Evie, moved to Chicago, and he reported for duty at 37 South Wabash as business manager and all-around troubleshooter, where he remained until 1984.

Many of the great championship veterans returned one by one during the 1945 season. George McAfee made it back for the final three games, as did Joe Stydahar. Luckman led the league in passing and was able to team with his favorite big-play receiver, Ken Kavanaugh, who left for the Army Air Force to train as a bomber pilot after the Bears beat the NFL All-Stars in early 1942.

With three months' terminal leave and mustering out pay in his pocket, Kavanaugh got mustered out in September 1945 in Greensboro, North Carolina. He called Halas, who told him to meet the team in Philadelphia, where the Bears were getting ready for an exhibition in Allentown that Saturday night against the Eagles. Hoping to miss the exhibition, he arrived in Philly at 8:15 Saturday night and ran into Sid Luckman at the hotel. "What are you doing here, Sid?" Kenny asked.

"It's raining," Sid said.

"We always play in the rain," Ken said.

"Not tonight. We play tomorrow night," Sid said.

Kavanaugh tracked down Luke Johnsos, who gave him the plays. "I ended up scoring our three touchdowns that night," Kavanaugh said. But the Bears lost 38–21.

In 1945, they fell to 3-and-7, their first losing season since 1929. What would 1946 bring? The Bears of old? Or the old Bears? As he took back the conn, George Halas realized that question had just one solution.

THIRD QUARTER

1946-1965

FOURTEEN

MONEY THAT BURNS—THE POSTWAR WAR

*W*hen Captain George S. Halas, USNR, packed away his service dress blues and brought his business suits and fedoras out of mothballs in late 1945, he hoped to resume where he left off in 1942 at full speed as he ran a dynasty, made money faster than it could be printed, and kept the league on an even keel as first among his ownership peers.

By the start of 1946, a more realistic Halas, now 51, knew his Bears would struggle as they went for their seventh league title. He would be forced to pay his stars far more than he ever imagined as he navigated his Bears and NFL through the shoals and snags of a costly war of a different kind. The enemy was his onetime ally, powerful *Tribune* sports editor Arch Ward, and Ward's new All-America Football Conference. This for Halas was purgatory and hell rolled into one money-draining bundle of terror and peril.

Papa Bear's troubles with Ward had started at the league meeting in late 1942 the Monday morning after he'd suffered in the Griffith Stadium stands as George Preston Marshall's Redskins denied his Bears an unprecedented third consecutive championship. For Washington, the 14–6 score was sweet vindication for 73–0. How George Halas hated to lose. And no man could be worse to face at that moment than that insufferable Marshall with his incessant gloating and ragging.

At that moment of despair the morning after, in had walked Ward. Ever the promoter, Ward wanted the NFL to award a proposed Buffalo expansion franchise to his best friend, the Chicago horse-racing baron Benjamin Lindheimer, and his partner, another good friend of Ward's, the actor Don Ameche. "Sounds good," Halas replied warily. Then Ward threw in the clincher. Lindheimer and Ameche would move that franchise to Los Angeles and open the West Coast to professional sports.

Halas stunned Ward as he threw a fit. None of the flying fur that ensued made sense to Halas's longtime friend, who reacted in kind. "Arch was furious," the Papa Bear wrote years later in his memoir. "His fury was to prove costly."

Truth be told, George Halas carried a secret whose revelation would have smashed all ambitions and everything he had built. It went back to 1941, before Pearl Harbor and Halas's rejoining the Navy. Halas had promised Los Angeles to Charlie Bidwill. Bidwill, in turn, would move the Cardinals west, give Halas back his stock, forgive the 1931 debt, and leave Chicago alone to his friend. These were secrets Halas could never divulge to anyone, especially Arch Ward, as he headed off to a war that would last God knew how long.

Back in Chicago, Ward plotted his revenge. On June 4, 1944, in St. Louis, he held the first of two meetings to organize a new league. This league, Ward said, would provide a postwar outlet for the many excellent players who never got a chance to play pro ball. He said there were plenty of players to go around to fill both leagues.

The news hit Halas like a bomb. Deathly afraid a vengeful Ward would have his sports copyeditors hack away at his well-earned "special" coverage in favor of the new league and place the Bears in back of the section with the tire ads, Halas also knew he could not seek special favor from his close friend Don Maxwell, for when Maxwell was promoted to city editor in 1930, he selected Ward to replace him. Ward and his promotions made sports the biggest moneymaker on the powerful paper.

Yet, Halas knew that he must tell Maxwell about the Bidwill-to-L.A. promise. He couldn't let his friend hear about it from a third party. They discussed the situation over a drink, and Maxwell calmed his friend's fury. He told Halas that his stature as first among equals at the paper would remain unquestioned. *Tribune* sports coverage of the Bears, Maxwell assured, would continue as before. Totally favorable.

However, Maxwell could not guarantee that the rest of the NFL would fare so well in *Trib* coverage. Ward, after all, had his own forum, the venerable column made famous by Ring Lardner, "In the Wake of the News." Maxwell would never interfere with the creator of the All-Star baseball and football games, Golden Gloves, and Silver Skates, nor could he as long as Colonel McCormick was in charge of his World's Greatest Newspaper. And Robert Rutherford McCormick was alive, quite well, and absolute monarch.

At the second meeting, on September 3, 1944, in Chicago, Ward unveiled the league's new name, All-America Football Conference, or AAFC. Then he trotted out his well-heeled risk takers, who were willing and able to match Halas, Marshall, Mara, and the rest of the National Football League establishment dollar for dollar.

The AAFC announced it had approved a resolution similar to the longtime NFL bylaws enacted after the Grange imbroglio. No AAFC club could sign a player or coach under contract to any NFL team, nor could the league sign any player with remaining college eligibility. Once the niceties had been dispensed with, Ward revealed a promotion more than two decades ahead of its time. Instead of "Super Bowl," he would call a championship game between the two leagues a "World Series" of pro football.

Ward knew exactly how that would play elsewhere in downtown Chicago in the office of his fellow Notre Damer, the former member of the Four Horsemen and rather dull NFL commissioner Elmer Layden. "Let them get a ball, draw a schedule, and play a game. Then I will talk to them," Layden declared.

On November 22, 1944, Ward countered with his AAFC commissioner, one of Layden's fellow Horsemen, Sleepy Jim Crowley. The contrast was obvious. Unlike the insipid Layden, Crowley was glib, witty, often sarcastic, and always good copy.

Ameche and Lindheimer in Los Angeles took the initiative when they broke the long-standing antipro embargo at 100,000-seat Memorial Coliseum when they obtained a lease for their Dons. That same embargo had kept Bidwill in Chicago before Pearl Harbor, and the war had tabled all western expansion notions.

Ward's man in Cleveland was Arthur "Mickey" McBride, who made his fortune in real estate and ownership of Cleveland's Yellow Cab fleet. Notre Dame refused to let McBride talk to his first coaching choice, Frank Leahy. So, McBride turned to a man who would change the professional game. He was Paul Brown, the coach of Ohio State's 1942 national champions, who was on duty with the Navy as coach at Great Lakes. McBride lured Brown with a $25,000 salary—outstanding executive pay in that era—and gave him 15 percent of the team's stock, adding a $1,000 monthly stipend until he was mustered out of service. Then came the icing, the vanity appeal. McBride would name the team in the coach's honor. Thus were born the Cleveland Browns.

Brown recruited a ready-to-go team from his top sailor-athletes and former Ohio State players, adding an opponent from rival Northwestern named Otto Graham, a single-wing tailback in college, who would impress Brown to the end of his life as the best passer he ever saw. Brown was certain Graham would equal, if not surpass, both Sid Luckman and Sammy Baugh as the best T-formation quarterback in pro football.

The other major owners were the Morabito brothers, Tony and Vic, in San Francisco. With San Francisco and L.A. in his pocket, Ward was sitting pretty. The old league was confined to Chicago and points east and still traveled mostly by train. To make his move all the more imposing, Ward called on his hometown friend W. A. "Pat" Patterson at United Airlines. They struck the most lucrative charter deal to that time to make United the exclusive carrier of the AAFC as the first league to travel by air. Suddenly, cross-country travel—especially, fluid movement to the West Coast—was viable.

After gaining the Coliseum lease, Ameche and Lindheimer started signing players. They conducted a bold raid inside the Bears' den. The first NFLer to jump was Halas's nasty and talented tackle-placekicker

Lee Artoe, who accepted $15,000 for the privilege. The Dons also landed 1943 All-Pro halfback Harry Clark, followed by Sid Luckman's backup Charlie O'Rourke. When Halas tried to stop O'Rourke from jumping to L.A. with Artoe and Clark, the brash Bostonian told the old Bohemian to read the contract. As Halas digested the fine print, he cut loose with a string of his choicest curses. The standard NFL contract language stated that a player who entered military service was a free agent. Period. O'Rourke, indeed, was a free agent.

Tony Morabito joined the raiding party, asking Ameche to rope in the rookie star of the 1941 Bears, fullback Norm Standlee. "Ameche got Standlee drunk and signed him to a contract with the new 49ers," Charles Brizzolara said. "Standlee wanted to return to the Bears, but he had signed that contract and couldn't get out of it." As before, Halas was stuck with the service free-agency clause in the prewar boilerplate.

The 49ers also bagged another Halas prospect, 1942's top draft choice, quarterback Frankie Albert, Standlee's backfield mate with Shaughnessy's 1940 Wow Boys, who also had been away in the service. The 49ers, with Albert, Standlee, and guard Bruno Banducci, became the AAFC's number two team after the Browns.

Before getting that football and starting play, the AAFC kept it going, grabbing several more key Bears including ends Bob Nowaskey and Hampton Pool. Halfback Edgar "Special Delivery" Jones came home from the war in 1945 to play one game for Johnsos and Anderson. Then Brown hauled him off to Cleveland for '46.

The coup de grâce came when the upstarts stole an entire team. Brooklyn owner Dan Topping merged his NFL Dodgers with the Boston Yanks and announced he was joining Ward's AAFC. Topping then gave the NFL the back of his other hand when he moved the team into Yankee Stadium, which he held as co-owner of the Bronx Bombers, and declared war on Mara's Giants.

That was the last straw for Halas. Fed up with the bumbling Layden, Halas called a meeting after the 1946 New Year and sent the horseman to the open range. Then he put the word out that Art Rooney's partner Bert Bell was the right man for the job. Some owners thought Bell was a clown, a football version of baseball's Casey

Stengel before he donned the Yankees pinstripes. Halas knew Bell as the man who dreamed up the draft and as smart, honorable, and an able negotiator. With Rooney's endorsement and Marshall's help, Halas and his supporters stood fast for Bell and persuaded everyone else to step into line. It was a move the National Football League never regretted.

Halas then turned to his hometown situation. His AAFC opposite with the Chicago Rockets was transportation tycoon John Keeshin. Thanks to Ward, Keeshin worked out a lease with the Chicago Park District on a lakefront white elephant, Soldier Field, where Ward's Chicago Tribune Charities staged the annual College All-Star game.

To outsiders, Keeshin's maneuver sounded impressive, but Halas knew the reality of 1946-vintage Soldier Field. Although the *Tribune* could fill most of the 100,000 seats for the company's annual charity All-Star game, that was a once-a-year event. Also, the place was unfit for watching a football game.

A half-mile track built for chariot racing in the '20s ringed the field. The best seats in the shallow-angled stadium were too distant to enjoy a game. Coal mines were better lit at night. The press box was the size of a chicken coop. Restrooms were few, and the ones that did exist were a step up from privies.

Keeshin still made waves, proving it when he signed the likes of Big Ten stars Elroy "Crazylegs" Hirsch, of Wisconsin and Michigan, and Indiana's Bobby Hoernschmeyer. When Keeshin offered Luckman $25,000 to jump, Halas drew the line. Halas knew his boy Sid would be torn, so he appealed to his sense of loyalty.

Halas did not match Keeshin, of course. Had he given in, that would have been perceived as weakness and might have led to a wholesale run on his roster. Halas offered Luckman a solid raise in the $20,000 range, well above the $12,000 he was making. Luckman graciously accepted in a well-covered show of public support.

"While Halas developed his skinflint reputation, he also engendered a fierce loyalty," sportswriter Bill Jauss recalled. "He imposed a dress code, and that impressed players. When he died, I was out getting responses, reactions from players. One was Bill Osmanski, our family dentist. When Osmanski was discharged after World War II, Slip

Madigan had an AAFC team and offered Osmanski $40,000 a season to play, which was enormous bucks in those days. Osmanski went to Halas and told him of this offer."

" 'Kid,' Halas said to Osmanski, 'how much did I pay you the last year before you went into the service?'

" 'Twelve-thousand dollars, Coach.'

" 'I'll give you 15!' Halas said. Osmanski signed on the spot," Jauss said. "Osmanski was not a stupid man, but he saw something in this patriarch of the business that was worth sticking with him when he'd been offered three times the money to go elsewhere."

Halas then implemented a plan to kill two birds with one stone by making his natural rival, the Cardinals, his ally. First, he persuaded Bidwill to stay in Chicago and fight instead of wasting his money in an L.A. arms race against Lindheimer's millions. When Halas told Bidwill that two strong Chicago NFL teams would benefit not only them but also the league as a whole, Bidwill signed on, feeling perhaps he might have a chance to win in the long run.

To make the Cardinals strong, Halas urged Bidwill to bring back his long-ago teammate, the Cardinals' clever prewar coach Jimmy Conzelman. Bidwill hired Conzelman, who built a team around a "dream backfield" of Paul Christman, Elmer Angsman, Pat Harder, and Marshall Goldberg running behind linemen such as Stan Mauldin, Buster Ramsey, and Vince Banonis. Now the South Siders were a factor.

The other "bird" in Halas's scheme was Cleveland. The Rams' 34-year-old owner, Dan Reeves, was desperate to move his newly crowned NFL champions to Los Angeles and go head-to-head with Lindheimer. That suited Halas, who knew that the league needed to get to L.A. fast to win the war and, with Bidwill staying in Chicago, Reeves had both the means and know-how to hang tough against the Ameche-Lindheimer AAFC Dons.

Reeves was just 28 in early 1940 when he walked away with $11 million after selling the family's New York–based grocery chain to A&P. With plenty of walking-around money burning a hole in his pocket, and itchy to buy a sports franchise, Reeves plunked down $100,000 and picked up the moribund Cleveland Rams.

By 1945, Reeves was working with his fourth head coach, Adam Walsh, one of the seven mules of 1924 who blocked for Knute Rockne's Four Horsemen, which included the two league commissioners, Layden and Crowley. Walsh turned loose his brilliant young quarterback Bob Waterfield from UCLA and let him pass the Rams to the 1945 title game against the Washington Redskins on December 16. In an icy wind off Lake Erie, the Rams edged the Redskins 15–14. The margin of victory was a safety that resulted when a gust of wind blew a Baugh touchdown from his end zone into the goalpost upright (the posts were still on the goal line, courtesy of Halas and Washington owner Marshall's rules change of 1933). That safety rule was changed the next year, too late to help Washington.

At the next league meeting, Reeves made his move. This time, the once steadfast opposition melted as if by magic. Once he had Bidwill's endorsement, Halas was able to engineer a show of hands, and the National Football League had the lucrative film capital in hand. Reeves then went to the Coliseum Commission, which suggested the Rams give UCLA's first all-American, Kenny Washington, from 1939, a tryout. In other words, you get the lease if you integrate.

Reeves signed Washington, the league's first black player since Fritz Pollard and the Cardinals' Duke Slater, and added his former Bruins teammate Woodrow Strode. Except for Marshall, all opposition to integration around the league retreated. Reeves added glamour in the person of World War II hero Tom Harmon, of Michigan, the man Halas could not sign. As fast as you could say the name of Waterfield's glamorous movie-star wife, Jane Russell, the home of the Rams no longer was Cleveland, but Los Angeles.

Halas benefited immensely from Ralph Brizzolara's managerial skills. The team, already in excellent financial condition, was the best-positioned franchise in the league, and Halas was able to devote full attention to the team itself while his new business manager, Rudy Custer, handled all administrative details from the steno pool to press credentials and every item in between.

Thanks to Wrigley Field groundskeepers Bobby Dorr and later Pete Marcantonio, Halas had the best playing field in pro football in an era when every team but Los Angeles, Green Bay, and San Francisco was a co-tenant in a major-league ballpark.

"The Bears were the only ones who sodded the infield and scaled down the pitcher's mound and the bullpen mounds. The grass took; the sod always was firm," Charles Brizzolara recalled. "Most people talked about Halas not spending much money," former Bears backfield coach Chuck Mather remarked in 2002. "You can't imagine the amount he spent keeping that field dry. From the minute the Cubs quit playing, no drop of rain fell on that field. He wanted the field covered constantly. They put the tarp back down as soon as we finished practice."

In bad weather, Halas and his staff moved practice to Wilson Park, a mile north of the ballpark. Mather said Halas reveled in those practices. "There's a hill there, and he wanted them to run up and down it. The players hated that."

Money always won out, though, and no man showed more ingenuity when it came to squeezing out a buck, even to literally putting the squeeze on his ticket holders in the lower boxes. "The Bears had different box seats from the Cubs," said Charles Brizzolara. "The Bears' seats were a couple of inches narrower, giving them 10 in a box, versus 8 for the Cubs."

It was a vendor's nightmare. Vendors couldn't navigate the jammed aisles. As if Halas minded. In the original lease terms in 1921, the Cubs got all the profits from concessions. Halas felt they got enough of the gate receipts anyway. In the off-season, Halas stored his thousands of box-seat folding chairs—green wooden slats on metal frames—below the Wrigley Field stands.

Halas felt he needed every edge in order to compete yet turn a handsome profit. Perhaps that angst came from the realization that he had to pay up or lose his men. If too many left, he would lose far more than a title possibility; he would lose the fans. The dollars that AAFC teams were offering his players nearly made the thrifty, if not miserly, Bohemian physically ill. Going in, he knew the days of $5,000 contracts for the likes of Luckman and far less for his supporting cast were history. Also, the NFL had raised the player limit to the prewar 33 from 28. That meant five more salaries he had to put on the books.

When it came to coaching, Halas separated his fiscal fears from the task at hand. In his first meeting with the 1946 squad, he set everyone at ease. "Relax," he said. "Nobody will be cut because he's a little rusty." He told the players they would win or lose as a team. "You've probably had enough discipline and regimentation to last a lifetime— I know I have," Halas said. "All rules are off. No curfews. No bed checks. You're on your own," the coach told his grateful men. He did not have to add the next statement, as he now owned their complete loyalty. "It's up to you individually to get in shape and play football."

Getting his players ready for the 1946 season turned out to be the easiest task Halas would tackle for the rest of the decade. Ed Sprinkle, beginning his third year but his first under the returning coach, was seeing the Papa Bear in action for the first time. "George Halas was an intimidating guy for a little country boy like me. He said, 'You all-Americans have an equal chance to make the team.' He was trying to put them down ahead of time, I guess. He and I got along real fine." They did because Sprinkle played the game the way the coach loved it. Hard, all-out, and nasty.

"In '46, they switched me over to end. I played both ways," Sprinkle said. The end on the other side of the defensive line was 10-year veteran George Wilson, who later coached the Lions. "During the season, they tried to switch me to left [defensive] end. I'm left-handed, and I didn't feel comfortable there," Sprinkle added.

Sprinkle's reputation as the Meanest Man in Football began that season as the master of a long-since outlawed tactic in a league in which anything went. "Back then, you could clothesline them guys." Sprinkle laughed out loud and his eyes twinkled. "They never called any penalties then. It wasn't illegal. They'd swing a halfback out, you know? I'd swing out and clothesline 'em. It was just part of things." Sprinkle, nearly 79 when he was interviewed, roared at the memory. "Coaches never taught you how to play defensive end. I did it on my own."

George Connor insisted that Sprinkle belonged in the Hall of Fame. "Eddie went 120 percent, 100 percent of the time," Connor said. "They called Eddie dirty. He wasn't. Just tough. He never hit a guy from behind." He never had to. Going nose-to-nose with Sprinkle was a nightmarish prospect for any unfortunate opponent.

Halas and the Bears won in 1946, as much with the relentless Sprinkle desire as with the prewar Monsters of the Midway image. Luckman staked the Bears to a 17–0 halftime lead in the traditional opener at Green Bay on touchdown passes to Scooter McLean and Ken Kavanaugh and a field goal, to coast to a 30–7 win. They then beat Conzelman's Cardinals 34–17 at Comiskey Park but flattened out in the Wrigley Field opener, escaping with a 20–20 tie against Adam Walsh's defending champion Los Angeles Rams.

On the lakefront at Soldier Field, the Rockets fizzled from the beginning. Hard-nosed coach Dick Hanley tried the same approach he used with his marine service teams. He lost control of the team three games into the season. Keeshin tried to land Luckman again, this time as coach. No deal.

The sorry situation turned comedic when Keeshin had to appoint three players, Bob Dove, Ned Mathews, and Willie Wilkin, as tri-coaches. Five disastrous games ended that experiment in football democracy. Hanley's former assistant Pat Boland finished the season in the coaching role as the crowds trickled down to near invisibility scattered throughout the cavernous stadium.

In an attempt to maintain daily interest, the AAFC scheduled games every night during the week. After that failure, the new league confined play to weekends in 1947. In Chicago, Halas's scheme with Bidwill to double-team the Rockets worked to perfection. The fans flocked to the NFL games each Sunday and rarely bothered to look in at Soldier Field whenever the hapless Rockets played, day or night.

On top of the Western Division and apparently headed for the title game, the Giants shut out the Bears 14–0 in the Polo Grounds in late October. The Bears came back to lock up the division at Wrigley Field on November 24 when they routed Detroit 42–6.

The rematch with the Cardinals on December 1 at Wrigley meant nothing to the Bears but everything to the Big Red. Before 47,511 screaming fans, the Bears took a 7–0 lead into the second quarter, when Paul Christman led the Cardinals to three quick touchdowns.

The Bears came back and tied the game 28–28 when Joe Osmanski, Bill's brother, scored with 55 seconds left.

Not content with a tie, Halas went for broke, trying an onside kick, which the Cardinals recovered at midfield after a huge pileup. The pushing, shoving, and swinging continued after the whistle, and the officials marched off 15 yards against the Bears as an irate Halas cut loose with every invective in his deep and seasoned vocabulary. Paul Christman followed with a 30-yard pass to Mal Kutner and, with time growing short, hit Kutner for the Cardinals' winning touchdown with 14 seconds to go.

The 35–28 victory so thrilled Bidwill that he went to Halas and told him he no longer was a Bears fan. He said he was ready to sell the stock he bought for $5,000 back in 1931 to save the team from Ed Sternaman. Bidwill asked Halas to appraise the team to establish a fair market value for his shares of stock in 1947 dollars.

Before Halas could do that, he had to prepare for a title game with the Giants. Despite the earlier loss to the Giants, the Bears entered the December 15, 1946, championship game in New York as favorites.

Gambling reverts to the caves, and so does the crooked game. People have been willing to bet on just about anything, even when they know that anything can be and has been fixed, from presidential elections to shell games on street corners—and at least one World Series. Halas, of course, was well aware of gamblers and gambling. He'd hated the activity from childhood when his father tanned his hide for shooting craps, and he was furious that his son-in-law was a racetrack plunger. Yet, under the guise of team unity on that long-ago train ride between Chicago and the Twin Cities, Halas did roll the bones. He also was not averse to a lively game of gin rummy for a buck or two. In cities such as Chicago and New York, gambling talk was as plentiful as it was cheap. Halas was too aware not to hear the rumors. Otherwise, he would not have spent so much money on private eyes to keep tabs on his boys.

Nobody can say with any degree of authority who devised the point-spread system, but it goes back at least to World War II. Any big-time bettor and a lot of small-timers agree with the anonymous gambler who told Nevada operator Peter Ruchman, "The invention of the point spread is the single greatest creation since the zipper!"

Pro football has been an "action" game since its beginning. Newspapers have been publishing the point spreads in recent years with little comment, but back in 1946, the spread passed by word of mouth. Bookies knew, and so did any interested bettor, let alone reporters, whose job it is to learn such things. Of the upcoming title game, Robert W. Peterson wrote in *Pigskin* that "there was a buzz on the streets of New York because of the point spread favoring the Bears." The spread fell anywhere from 10 to 14 points.

All hell broke loose on the eve of the game, when New York mayor William O'Dwyer called Tim Mara from city hall and spoke the authoritative words that can strike fear into the strongest individual. "You better come over here."

The elder Mara dispatched his sons Jack and Wellington and coach Steve Owen. O'Dwyer and NYPD commissioner Arthur Wallender greeted Owen and the Maras and led them inside, where they saw detectives grilling their fullback Merle Hapes and quarterback Frank Filchock. Someone had seen them with a small-time but notorious gambler named Alvin Paris and turned them in. Commissioner Wallender's sources said Paris offered Hapes and Filchock $2,500 each to throw the game to ensure that the Bears won by at least 10 points. The detectives learned that Paris also agreed to bet $1,000 for each player for the Giants to lose by that margin.

Hapes admitted Paris's offer but said he refused it. Filchock denied everything. Neither man was charged with a criminal offense. Coach Owen wanted to enter the interrogation room where the police were holding Paris and beat a confession out of him. "I'm, sorry, Steve," Wallender said. "You know I can't do that."

The story splashed across Sunday-morning front pages around the country. New NFL commissioner Bert Bell suspended Hapes, but he gave Filchock the benefit of the doubt and let him play.

In his pregame prayer in the Giants clubhouse, team chaplain Reverend Benedict Dudley reminded them that the game had sunk into the shadows of doubt. "It's up to you to restore the faith of the fans in pro football," Father Dudley pleaded. The somber Giants filed out of the clubhouse to face the Bears before a then championship-game record crowd, 58,346, at the Polo Grounds.

On the other side of the field, Hunk Anderson told Halas he was flip-flopping his ends on defense. "They played Wilson at left end, and I started at right end," recalled Sprinkle. "I got around my blocker and hit Filchock from the blind side as he was just throwing a pass. Dante Magnani was playing defense, and the ball went up in the air; he caught it and practically walked in, but Filchock stayed in the game."

With blood pouring from his Sprinkle-administered broken nose, a vindication-seeking Filchock played the game of his life. He threw two touchdown passes to send the game into the fourth quarter tied 14–14. Luckman led the Bears to the New York 19. That situation and field location, expressly stated in the game plan, called for a special play. Luckman called time and ran to the sideline to visit the coach. Before Sid could utter their code word "now," Halas looked him in the eye. "Now!" he said firmly.

Because Halas feared possible injury and had a marginal backup, Luckman had not carried the ball a single time all season. Now was the time. "That was the play, Bingo Keep It," Luckman recalled in 1991. "I faked to George McAfee on a run around left end. They feared that play and overshifted to the left side of our offensive line."

"Everybody pulled and went to the left, and Sid did a bootleg," Sprinkle agreed. "Everyone chased McAfee," said Luckman. Sprinkle was now jumping up and down on his seat as he spoke: "I was playing offensive right end, and I was alone blocking for Sid. It was pretty open, and he ran it in. He was a good runner."

"I ran the easiest 19 yards of my life," Luckman said. The bootleg gave the Bears a 21–14 lead. Frank Maznicki's late field goal to make it 24–14 iced the Bears' seventh championship and fifth for Coach Halas. The 10-point margin, for those who cared, was not enough for the Bears to cover the spread. Bettors who wagered on the Bears to collect needed them to win by at least 11 points, which they did not.

Bell learned at Paris's trial that Filchock had lied about his ignorance of Paris's offer. But he was saved from a lifetime ban when he testified that he did not accept it. Accordingly, using the absolute powers he possessed at a time when authority went unchallenged in such matters, the commissioner barred Hapes for life and suspended Filchock indefinitely. Hapes played several more years in Canada. Filchock also played and coached in Canada for more than a decade before he returned to the United States in 1960 as the first coach of the Denver Broncos in the American Football League. He lasted for two losing seasons, was fired, and died in 1984.

In Chicago in early 1947, John Keeshin gave up the ghost and returned the Rockets to the league. Ward found new owners and moved Crowley into the Rockets' managerial team and installed him as coach. Ward's new commissioner was retired admiral Jonas Ingram, the wartime Atlantic commander. Admiral Ingram moved the commissioner's offices from Chicago to the Empire State Building, in New York.

With Frances Osborne managing the move, the Bears transferred headquarters to their own building at 233 West Madison, between the Loop and the Chicago River, from their longtime home at Wabash and Monroe. The new structure housed the Papa Bear's holdings, the team, and May and Halas catalog and retail operations. It would be their home until January 30, 1961, when everything went up in smoke.

FIFTEEN

BEST RECORD, NO TITLES

*F*rom 1947 through '51, the Bears fashioned the best record in the National Football League. Yet, they never won a title in any of those years. In 1947 and '48, they weren't even the best team in Chicago.

Charlie Bidwill grabbed the headlines for his Cardinals after the 1947 New Year with his night-and-day wooing of Georgia's triple threat Charley Trippi, that year's equivalent to Red Grange. The buildup began in 1945 when Trippi was on active duty with the Army Air Force and Bidwill and his capable general manager Ray Benningsen drafted him first as a "future," as his original college class had already graduated.

The stakes rose dramatically when Trippi marched back to Georgia after his discharge that fall and led Wally Butts's Bulldogs to six victories, including a 33–0 rout of hated rival Georgia Tech and a 20–7 win over Tulsa on New Year's Day in the Oil Bowl at Houston. Trippi kicked into high gear in 1946. He came off an all-America baseball season to run and pass Georgia to an unbeaten, 11-and-0 football season and win the Maxwell Award, second in prestige only to the Heisman Trophy, for which Trippi finished second behind Army's Glenn Davis.

After Georgia beat North Carolina 20–10 in the Sugar Bowl, Bidwill scared off Dan Topping's AAFC football Yankees. Topping turned over the Trippi courtship to his baseball people, and Charley wavered between football and baseball for days. When the Cubs outbid the Yankees, Bidwill said, "Enough." On January 14, 1947, he introduced Trippi as the dream player in the dream backfield as well as the game's highest-paid player. His four-year deal was worth an unprecedented $100,000, at $25,000 a year. As lucrative as the deal was for Trippi, it meant far more to Bidwill, who finally stepped out of Halas's sizable shadow in the football world.

"Nobody could compete against Bidwill if he wanted something," said Bill Gleason, then a 25-year-old reporter with the *Herald-American* and, as a lifelong South Sider, an avid Cardinals partisan. "He had the money. He had the charm and personality. He was a legendary figure." And he was not a man to trifle with. Bidwill, as Gleason noted, had connections through his horse-racing interests, legitimate and otherwise. And Halas knew it.

"Congratulations on a great victory for our league," wrote Curly Lambeau in a telegram to Bidwill. Halas himself predicted the Trippi addition would make the Cardinals the Bears' strongest rival. How right he was.

Charley Trippi was the dream player for sure, but the man who wooed and won him with such ardor never ever saw him play. On April 15, Bidwill entered St. George's Hospital in Chicago for treatment of a persistent heavy cold. By nightfall, the doctors diagnosed it as bronchial pneumonia complicated by heart disease. Four days later, at age 51, Charles Bidwill was dead.

Condolences flooded the Cardinals' offices on Plymouth Court and at his various businesses: Bentley, Murray, which printed most of the country's pari-mutuel tickets and racing programs as well as the Bears' game tickets; and his Chicago racetrack interests, Sportsman's Park, where he was majority stockholder, and Hawthorne, next door, which he personally operated.

More than the Cardinals, which, until the serious Trippi courtship, he had considered as fun rather than business, Hawthorne was his pride and joy. Bidwill and his wife, Violet, lived on one side of a converted barn at Hawthorne during meetings. Stables in the middle of the barn housed his 51 horses. His office, on the other end of the barn, featured a huge picture window, which cost him $100,000, so he could look up from his desk to watch workouts and races.

Mourners at the long funeral procession north to Calvary Cemetery, on Evanston's border with Chicago, included NFL commissioner Bert Bell, former Chicago mayor Edward Kelly, and former heavyweight boxing champion Jack Dempsey. Halas served as a pallbearer for his close friend.

As Bidwill's body was lowered into the grave, the era of good feeling between the Bears and Cardinals was buried with him. Violet now not only owned the Cardinals but also held Charlie's one-sixteenth share of the Bears, which he was in the process of selling back to Halas when he died. That matter would have to be settled when the substantial estate went into probate.

Halas's immediate concern by summer was not Bidwill, but winning football games. The Bears represented the National Football League once again at Soldier Field against a College All-Star team coached by one of Halas's friends, Notre Dame's Frank Leahy.

In Indiana, Halas drove his defending champions ultra-hard at their St. Joseph's College training camp. The Bears arrived in Chicago on Thursday, August 21, the day before the game, to a veritable steambath with temperatures in the 90s and the air thick with humidity. Halas decided to reward the team, so he called Ralph Brizzolara to make it happen. Air-conditioning was in its infancy, and Brizzolara scoured the city until he found a big blower unit at Midway Airport. He got it installed and operating in the Bears' dressing room by Friday afternoon. That evening, the players walked out of near 100-degree heat and into a dressing room that Halas called "a delightful 72 degrees."

When they charged onto the sweltering field for the kickoff, the huge men wilted like long-stemmed roses out of water. Leahy's sweating rookies beat them to the punch all night long. They stymied the Bears in a 16–0 shellacking thanks, in large part, to the running of Trippi, Illinois's hometown hero Buddy Young, and the sharp passes of Notre Dame quarterback George Ratterman.

Nobody whooped it up more than Arch Ward. As if beating Halas and the NFL weren't enough, most of the All-Stars, including game stars Young and Ratterman, were AAFC bound, as in 1946, when 44 of the 60 players were property of Ward's new league.

The Bears' malaise continued into the regular-season opener at Green Bay. Curly Lambeau had reluctantly junked the single wing for the T. "He got Jack Jacobs, Indian Jack Jacobs, up here as quarterback," Green Bay sage Art Daley recalled. "Until then, the quarterback was a blocking back."

The veteran Jacobs passed for a pair of touchdowns, ran for another, and made two of the Packers' five interceptions in a 29–20 victory. The next week at Comiskey Park, Jimmy Conzelman's Cardinals drummed the defending champions 31–7.

The naysayers were clearing their throats a week later when the Bears roared out of hibernation at Wrigley Field to rout the Philadelphia Eagles 40–7 in the home opener. Luckman went 14-for-25 for 314 yards to start an eight-game winning streak. A week later, Luckman drummed Detroit with 18 completions in 26 attempts for 342 yards.

Luckman passed his way to his eighth All-NFL season, but he began to show wear around the edges. Although he gained a career-high 2,712 passing yards and completed 24 touchdown passes, he also threw a dreadful 31 interceptions, leaving his quarterback rating at a so-so 67.5 despite the presence of the virtually unstoppable Ken Kavanaugh. "Luckman was a great player and smart. But he never threw me the ball enough," Kavanaugh said. "In 1947, I averaged 22.4 yards a catch. I scored 13 touchdowns on just 32 catches."

Bulldog Turner enjoyed another All-NFL season as well. He turned in one of the great individual efforts in team history in a 56–20 rout at Washington. The Redskins were driving, when Turner dropped back into coverage, picked off a Sammy Baugh pass at the Bears' 4, cut to the sideline, and sped upfield like George McAfee, carrying Baugh into the end zone for a touchdown. Turner's 96-yard interception run held up as a team record until 1962 when Rich Petitbon returned a pickoff 101 yards against the Rams.

The Bears needed just one victory in their final two games—against the Los Angeles Rams and Chicago Cardinals, both at Wrigley Field—to clinch the Western Division title. On December 7, they blew a two-touchdown lead and lost 17–14 to the Rams on a late Bob Waterfield field goal. The rematch with the Cardinals no longer was a mere grudge battle. Everything was on the line.

Conzelman long believed that a touchdown strike to open a game might be such a stunner that his team would win easily. When they drew up the game plan, his top aide, Buddy Parker, and line coach Phil Handler assured Conzelman that the Bears would double-team the Cardinals' outstanding right end Mal Kutner. So, Conzelman drew up a play-action pass keyed to Kutner. He was to run 10 yards upfield and raise his hands to call for the ball to draw double coverage. That would isolate the speedy Babe Dimancheff breaking from right half on the Bears' slower linebacker, Mike Holovak. Paul Christman, Conzelman said, would airmail the package, special delivery, six points due on receipt.

There was only one snag. Dimancheff sat in a hospital all week waiting for his wife to deliver their baby. He missed the practice when Conzelman introduced his special play. Moreover, when he came to Wrigley Field on the morning of the game, Dimancheff had yet to see a diagram of the play.

In those days, the officials held the pregame toss during the warm-up before the teams returned to the dressing rooms for their final instructions. The Cardinals won it and chose to receive. Bobby Dorr's grounds crew had cleared an overnight snowfall off the gridiron, the sun was out, and the footing was adequate. Before they took the field, Conzelman, Parker, Handler, and Christman patiently gave Dimancheff his assignment.

Many of the late-arriving 48,000 fans still were heading for their seats when the kickoff sailed into the north end zone for a touchback. What ensued was one of those rare instances when every element of a play evolves precisely as diagrammed. From the 20, Kutner lined up split 5 yards from the right tackle. He broke 10 yards upfield and raised his hands. From his right halfback spot directly behind Kutner and screened off from the defenders, Dimancheff broke behind the end. In that split second when Holovak took a step toward Kutner into double coverage, Dimancheff took off, looked up near midfield, caught Christman's perfect pass in stride, and kicked into high gear. He sprinted toward the goal line, where he was brought down from behind at the 2 and skidded into the end zone. According to the Halas-Marshall catch-as-catch-can rules of that era, a ball carrier could crawl, bounce, slip, or slide for extra yards. An official could not blow the play-ending whistle until the ball carrier was brought to a dead stop. There was no dispute. It was a touchdown, a rule that was changed in 1956 to stop late hits on ball carriers.

Luckman countered with a TD pass to Kavanaugh, but the defending champions had run out of growls. With a 27–7 halftime lead, the Cardinals stymied Luckman, intercepted four of his passes to win 30–21, and advanced to the championship game.

The Big Red faced the Eagles a week later at Comiskey Park before just over 30,000 fans. Trippi opened the scoring on a 44-yard run and ran back a punt 72 yards for another score. Elmer Angsman clinched the 28–21 victory on a 70-yard sprint to the end zone in the fourth quarter. The team dedicated the championship to the memory of their beloved boss Charlie Bidwill. For Halas, the late-season failure put a coffin nail on an accursed season that included Bidwill's death and the air-conditioning fiasco and flop in front of Ward at the All-Star game.

Halas's woes had actually begun at the draft on December 16, 1946, the day after his team beat the Giants for the title. To counter the AAFC and create public interest, the NFL instituted a so-called bonus pick, complete with popping flashbulbs and champagne toasts, before the start of formal selections. The league would continue this yearly sideshow until each team got its single shot.

The owners drew lots, and, lo and behold, the champion Chicago Bears won the draw. With a chance to redeem himself after Tom Harmon's 1941 rejection, Halas chose the decidedly obscure Oklahoma A&M halfback Bob Fenimore. The euphoria, if there was any, wore off that summer at camp when Halas and his staff quickly ascertained that Fenimore could not play. He got into just 10 games, gained only

189 yards, scored three touchdowns, fumbled four times, and did not return for a second year in 1948.

Fenimore was a blatant example of poor personnel decisions that eroded the base Halas so diligently constructed in the late '30s and with his 1940 bonanza. By 1948, his cupboard was running bare. Both Norm Standlee and Hugh Gallarneau from the 1941 draft were gone, Standlee to the AAFC 49ers and Gallarneau to retirement. Even Tommy Harmon, who turned down Halas after he was chosen first in '41, returned after surviving two plane crashes to play two mediocre years with the Los Angeles Rams before starting a successful broadcasting career.

Had Bulldog Turner not persuaded Hunk Anderson to sign Eddie Sprinkle in 1944, the Bears would have had no players at all from the draft classes of '41, '42, '43, and '44. The only '45 survivor was the excellent end Jim Keane, a 16th-round pick from Iowa, whose 64 catches in 1947 led the league.

Yet, at the start of 1948, Halas was all grins. With three swift strokes, he knew he had added the championship ingredients: two exceptional quarterbacks and an athlete who may have been the single greatest player in Notre Dame history. Their names were Johnny Lujack, George Connor, and Bobby Layne. By 1952, only Connor would remain, and the Bears would be awash in defeat.

Lieutenant Junior Grade John Lujack served on a destroyer chasing U-boats for nearly three years before he returned to the Notre Dame campus in 1946. Sid Luckman had scouted the sophomore Lujack at Notre Dame's 1943 spring practice sessions while he helped coach Frank Leahy refine the T formation he had installed the previous year. "Maybe Luckman said something. Maybe they had scouts down to the games that year. But I was drafted number one," Lujack said.

With Luckman still at his peak in '46, Halas figured he could wait the two years for Lujack to complete his eligibility in Leahy's veteran-dominated finishing school. Lujack justified Halas's confidence as he led Notre Dame to back-to-back national championships in 1946 and '47, his Heisman season. He was thoroughly schooled and pro-ready in all aspects of the game.

Lujack came into Chicago in early 1948 to meet with both the Bears and the Chicago Rockets of the AAFC, who also had drafted him. "I didn't know how you did this stuff," Lujack said more than a half century later in 2002. "They didn't have agents at that time. I really wish I would have gotten some advice."

Lujack had a brief chat with Halas and then went to the Rockets, where he talked with a man named Slim Garn, who was nearly as naive about negotiating as the young player. "Am I supposed to ask you what you want, or am I supposed to tell you what we'll pay?" Garn asked him. "Slim, I don't know," replied Lujack. "Well, how about if we start at $30,000?" Garn asked. "What about that?"

"Well, that's a pretty nice figure," Lujack said. "Can I let you know?" Garn told him that was fine. Lujack recalls, "I was really anxious to play for the Chicago Bears. I didn't know Halas from the man in the moon, anything about him, but we got to know him pretty quick."

Thanks to the interleague war, John Lujack was in line to make more money than earlier rookie whizzes. "I agreed to a four-year contract with Halas for 17, 18.5, 20, and 20. I thought maybe that other league might fold and their money wouldn't be any good," Lujack said regarding his ignoring the Rockets' $30,000 offer.

The well-connected George Connor had wanted to play for the Bears since his childhood on Chicago's South Side. That he could play football at all, let alone as well as he did, was a miracle. George weighed less than three pounds when he was born two months prematurely on January 21, 1925. A physician told his parents, Esther and Dr. Charles Connor, to feed the baby boiled cabbage juice through an eyedropper to supplement his mother's milk. Esther lived in the baby's room for a year until he was able to carry on normally. George grew into a 6''3", 240-pound big foot with a 15-and-a-half EEEE shoe size. "Good for tripping ends," he loved to say in later years in his many appearances as an extraordinarily witty after-dinner speaker.

After Connor's graduation from De La Salle High School, fellow alum Ed "Moose" Krause recruited Connor, known as "young Moose," to Holy Cross. By the time Connor arrived at Holy Cross in

1942, Krause was coaching Leahy's lines at Notre Dame. With 10 underclassmen in the lineup, 3 of them freshmen, including Connor, Holy Cross lost its first four games. "We won our last four and tied one," Connor said. "Then we played the number one team in the nation, Boston College. Nobody gave us a chance. So, we dug in. We beat 'em 55-to-2."

The BC team had reservations at the Coconut Grove nightclub in Boston that night to accept a bid to the Sugar Bowl, but because they were routed in the biggest college football upset since World War I, BC's players missed the horrific fire that killed 492 persons, including the cowboy actor Buck Jones. "We saved their lives and beat the hell out of 'em too," a wistful Connor recalled.

Connor served with the Navy as a junior officer for the rest of the war and then transferred to Notre Dame to play for Leahy and his line coach, Moose Krause. After the war, teams could draft players who had been in service and wait for them to finish their college eligibility.

"I was drafted number one by the New York Giants after 1946," Connor said. The Moose told the Giants he didn't want to play in the East and then informed the AAFC 49ers, who also selected him, that he did not want to go west. The Niners dealt his AAFC rights to the Browns, but Connor turned down Paul Brown and returned to Notre Dame, where he earned all-America honors twice, was named captain, and won the first Outland Trophy in 1947 as the nation's best lineman. "If there was anybody better than him, I'd like to meet him," said Lujack. "He was one terrific ballplayer." "He came to us very mature, very fit, very experienced, most determined," Halas wrote in *Halas by Halas*.

"Halas was a helluva guy. I liked him," said Connor, who put his body and soul on the line for the Papa Bear from the years 1948 through '55, five of them All-NFL seasons at tackle and linebacker. "I played both ways," he said. "So did Lujack." Connor paid the price after he quit, undergoing 32 surgeries, from body part replacements (artificial toes, knees, a spinal disk) to beating colon cancer in 1974. One can infer that when he died at age 78 on March 31, 2003, after 14 months in a Chicago rehabilitation facility, he finally wore out.

Lujack could speak for all of Connor's teammates through the years at Notre Dame and with the Bears: "He loved to play, and I'll tell you, he put 150 percent into every play."

Connor graduated in 1948 and returned home to Chicago. He said, "I went to Halas and told him I wanted to play with the Bears. 'Stick to your guns. I'll get you,' Halas said."

For his part, Connor had to step lively through a virtual NFL minefield to get there. He drove up to the Cardinals' camp in Waukesha, Wisconsin, outside Milwaukee. "I told Conzelman I was property of the Giants, but I wasn't going to play there, so they could get me if they wanted me. 'We don't need any tackles,' Conzelman snapped."

That was fine with George, who next had to deal with the Boston Yanks when their owner, singer Kate Smith's manager and partner, Ted Collins, obtained his rights from the Giants. When the Moose turned him down, Collins threatened to call Notre Dame president Father John Cavanaugh. "Go ahead," countered Connor. "My mother dated Father John when she was a nurse at Notre Dame during the 1918 flu epidemic before he entered the priesthood."

Halas shipped tackle Mike Jarmoulak, a veteran of the 1946 champions, to Collins for the rights to Connor. Then came Connor's talks with Halas. "He was a helluva businessman. All you needed was a handshake. That was it. In order to get to that, it was tough," Connor said, as he grinned at the memory of negotiations in the inner sanctum.

"When you went to his office, the chair you would be sitting on had the legs sawed off. You'd look up, and when something got feisty, I swear to God, he had a button there that rang his phone. He'd pick it up. Then he'd talk to nothing. He'd come back and say, 'Where were we?' and you'd lose your train of thought."

When Connor returned a day or two later, Halas slapped down a pen and contract. "I want my lawyer to look at it," the young man said without looking at the document. This was the first time since C. C. Pyle represented Red Grange that any player had dared to try using an agent in dealing with the Papa Bear. "Who's your lawyer?" Halas snapped. "Judge Cornelius Harrington," Connor replied firmly. Judge Harrington was a patient of George's father. Harrington would reemerge in 1966 as the trial judge in Halas's breach-of-contract suit against George Allen when he left to become head coach of the Rams.

"I left the Bears office and went to the circuit court at 26th and California. The judge ruled out certain things and then came back with me. I didn't know there was a press conference. Lujack was signing that day, and I would have gotten a lot more money," Connor said. "That's when Halas got to know Harrington."

"George and I signed the same day," Lujack said. "Thank goodness he played for the Bears. I didn't want to play against him."

"Lujack and I joined the team in time to hear Halas lecture us about the 'Cardinal cunts' and 'Packer pricks,'" said Connor.

"I know this," said Lujack: "When I was in the service, I never heard such words. He had a way of expressing himself that was quite unique and so totally different from Frank Leahy. Leahy never used a swear word. Swearing was Halas's cup of tea."

"We played an exhibition with the Eagles, and Bucko Kilroy kneed Ray Bray in the groin," Connor recalled. "Fred Davis and a couple of others stomped Kilroy in retaliation. 'Now, that's the way you cacksuckers should look out for your teammates,' exhorted Halas at halftime."

Lujack insisted that Halas's crudities did not bother him. "I didn't know anything about pro ball, and I thought, 'This is the way they do things.'"

The third 1948 rookie became arguably one of the top five quarterbacks in NFL history, but not with the Bears. Bobby Layne made his name with one of Chicago's hated rivals, the Detroit Lions, and finished his Hall of Fame career in 1962 with the Pittsburgh Steelers. Halas told anybody who ever listened that getting rid of the tough, colorful, Texas towhead was his absolute worst mistake, one that cost him titles galore.

Halas accompanied assistant Luke Johnsos to personally scout Layne at the Sugar Bowl in New Orleans on New Year's Day 1948. When Halas saw Layne pass and push fifth-ranked Texas to a 27–7 rout of number six Alabama, he knew he had to sign him, no matter the offer from the AAFC Baltimore Colts. By the start of training camp, Halas had the three most expensive quarterbacks in football.

Luckman was getting $20,000. Lujack drew $17,000. Layne inked a three-year deal at $22,000 a year plus a $10,000 bonus.

Layne was a single-wing tailback at Texas until 1947, when Blair Cherry took over in Austin and installed the T. Layne fit right in from the beginning, especially with his rookie rival Lujack. "After every practice, he and I used to throw to each other. Bobby and I were very close friends," said Lujack. "After the season was over, he came here to Davenport, Iowa, and stayed at my in-laws' house. The next day, he left for Las Vegas."

When he finished his daily throwing sessions with Lujack, Layne hurried down Clark Street to a team hangout, the Cottage, where the Bears slaked their thirsts far into the night. "It ruined more guys," Connor recalled. "Bulldog Turner had his own crew of Texans. They'd get drunk and yell out, 'Hiya, kid! Hiya, kid!' The booze didn't bother Layne. He ran right through it. He was great. And a party animal."

Ed Sprinkle was Turner's best friend on the team. Ed delighted in the company of Layne, their fellow Texan, of whom he said, "He loved to party." To Layne, a game the next day was no reason to miss out on the fun. "He'd go out drinking the night before and get in the huddle and smell of booze, but he'd play the game," Sprinkle recalled. "He was good."

Like Shakespeare, George Halas always understood that the play is the thing. Also like the Bard, Halas did everything to make his Globe Theatre, Wrigley Field, the best possible venue in which to make his play, a football game, a memorable show.

It started with the warm-up. Chicago had a Sunday blue law that forbade liquor sales before noon. Fans left home in time to get in place in front of the neighborhood saloons such as the Cubby Bear Lounge, the Sports Corner, or Ray's Bleachers when the doors opened. The moment those doors were unlocked at noon, the streets emptied like unplugged bathtubs. In surged the fans, dressed in appropriate football wear: sport jackets over sweaters, ties, wool slacks, and hats, for the men; wool suits for the women; weather-dictated outer garments for both. They grabbed quick hot lunches, and the adults knocked down a drink or two, before they left for the ballpark across the street. Bears fans arrived at the last minute, never late. They might not make the national anthem, but no one missed the kickoff.

As the fans headed to their seats, the green field was empty, with the players inside their dressing rooms. For most spectators, the routine never varied: get to the seats, spread the blankets, uncap the flasks, and start taking nips. This crowd liked its liquor, liked to yell, and loved its Bears even as the considerable amount of cynics among them griped about the owner-coach and his ways.

While they settled in, Halas gave his fans the trimmings. The sideshow featured the house group, Colonel Armin Hand's Board of Trade Band. During the game, the colonel's crew would pound out "Bear Down, Chicago Bears" after every home-team score and blare out a whining trombone chorus after an opponent's conversion. Once a year, Halas imported his alma mater's huge band, the Marching Illini. When Green Bay visited, Halas let the Packers bring along their Packer Lumberjack Band clad in their plaid woolen jackets and matching hunting caps. Otherwise, he staged halftime peewee football games between Chicago Park District teams.

The real show began the instant the locker room door opened, when his Monsters took the field. Then, out stepped the Papa Bear himself, impeccably dressed in a well-tailored dark suit, tugging at the brim of his fedora, and, soon, racing up and down the sidelines as he taunted officials and opponents alike. Halas was the star of his rollicking crew of tough mugs. What a show!

In 1948, Halas reconfigured Wrigley Field for football to bring the fans as close to the action as possible. "George conceived the idea of the temporary bleachers," Charles Brizzolara recalled. "He certainly talked Phil Wrigley into doing it. My father designed them and supervised the construction. They blocked out a large part of the permanent bleachers, from the right-field corner to the center-field wall, but they weren't good seats for football anyway." Ralph's wooden and steel-framed bleachers extended 70 rows high and seated about 13,000 fans, increasing Wrigley Field's seating capacity from a baseball 35,000 to 48,000 for football. "That made it more like a football stadium."

By selling standing room, Halas and Ralph Brizzolara could jam more than 50,000 fans into the ballpark, which they did on many occasions. When the action was hot and much of the crowd was liquored up, as happened especially on cold days, the noise from the bleachers combined with the noise from the high grandstand along the western sidelines and south end zones to make Wrigley Field the loudest stadium in pro football.

"The view from the upper deck was outstanding," said Brizzolara, who sat behind the boisterous Mugs Halas. Downstairs, Ralph and Florence Brizzolara sat in box 33, tier 2, next over from Minnie and Virginia, by the third-base dugout. "Minnie would yell at George," Charles remembers. "When her yelling got to be too much, he'd slip over by the dugout during a break and tell her to calm down."

Fans liked the proximity so much that they started asking for the same seats every week. Soon they asked to buy the whole year in advance. Knowing a good thing, Halas and Brizzolara rewarded that loyalty, allowing season ticket holders to pass along their seats in their estates.

Only two caveats applied: no scalping, and all the money had to be in by a stated cutoff date, May 1. In either case, a violator would forfeit the ticket rights. Halas and Brizzolara, of course, banked that season ticket money and the short-term interest that accrued. By the mid-'50s, most every seat was occupied by a season ticket holder. They began a waiting list that, in time, grew into the thousands. The rest of the league teams soon followed Halas's lead with their own season ticket packages. In time, NFL tickets became the most prestigious commodity in business, let alone for private individuals.

Fans and writers began to compare the 1948 Bears to the '41 Monsters. The world knew the transition from Luckman was under way when Halas started rookie Lujack in the opener at Green Bay. Through the first 11 games, the change seemed almost seamless. The plan called for Lujack to probe the defense as Luckman observed the first quarter by Halas's side. In the second quarter, Luckman took over on offense. Lujack, as talented a defensive back as a quarterback, stayed in on defense under the league's limited-substitution rules. Once the game was iced, Layne came in to gain game experience.

At Green Bay, as Luckman watched, Lujack, the heir apparent, made Halas look like a genius. He marched the team downfield after the opening kickoff and scored the season's first touchdown on a three-yard run. Luckman took over in the second quarter and picked the Packers apart while Lujack was making a team-record three interceptions. "After our first three touchdowns, Halas called me over," Lujack said.

"Did you ever kick any extra points in college?" the coach asked.

"Yeah. I tried one," Lujack said.

"Did you make it?"

"No, I missed it."

"Well," Halas said, "go in and kick this one."

"So, I kicked three in a row," Lujack recalled. "We came back to Chicago, and, to save money, he fired our extra-point and field-goal kicker, Fred Venturelli. I played quarterback and defense, kicked extra points and field goals, and went down on kickoffs."

Sprinkle caught two scoring passes, a 1-yarder from Luckman and Layne's first of 196 touchdown passes, which covered 34 yards, in the fourth quarter. The Bears' 45–7 victory was the largest margin to that time in the Packers rivalry.

Eight days later on Monday night, October 4, at Comiskey Park before 52,765 fans, the Cardinals were playing their first game since the shocking death of their great tackle Stan Mauldin, who suffered a fatal brain hemorrhage in the dressing room shortly after their victory in the opener against the Eagles. The defending champions were leading 17–14 in the third quarter, when Frank Minini returned Pat Harder's kickoff 95 yards to give the Bears the lead for good as they won 28–17.

Lujack, Luckman, and, when he played, Layne were virtually interchangeable as they led a potent attack that ran up 375 points, 31.3 a game, second only to the Cardinals' 395. Their only misfire through the first 11 games was a 12–7 loss at Wrigley Field to the Eagles on October 24.

Lujack, however, was lost for a month when he was kicked in the kidney in Los Angeles while making a tackle in the third quarter as the Bears beat the Rams 21–6. Luckman reclaimed his starting role, with Layne as his backup, and the machine kept rolling. A healed Lujack came back to start the final tune-up with the Lions on December 5 before the showdown rematch at Wrigley Field with the Cardinals. Luckman took over to complete 18 of 26 passes for 185 yards and three touchdowns in a 42–14 romp.

Both the Bears and the Cardinals entered the December 12 finale with 10-and-1 records after enduring the biggest pregame hype since Red Grange's professional debut in 1925. So many fans clamored to see it that Halas granted telecast rights to two new stations, *Tribune*-owned WGN-TV and ABC's WENR-TV.

Since few households had sets, most of the viewers packed corner taverns or gathered outside department stores to watch the telecasts through picture windows. To Halas's delight, a team-record 51,285 fans came out on the unseasonably warm afternoon, TV or not. Everyone watching, live or on the tube, saw a game worthy of the buildup.

An extra-sharp Lujack completed his first seven passes, one a 15-yard touchdown to Ken Kavanaugh to open the scoring. Pat Harder's field goal cut the margin to 7–3. Luckman took ill after throwing one pass and left the game. "I was having a good day and so forth, so I just kept playing," Lujack recalled.

Lujack stayed on the field as the Bears took a 14–3 lead into halftime on the first of two George Gulyanics touchdowns. The Cardinals' dressing room was calm. "I told my boys, if they'd go out and score a touchdown, the Bears would fold," Conzelman said after the game to *New York Times* writer Roscoe McGowan.

In the Bears' dressing room, an unwitting Halas played into Conzelman's hands when he ordered kickoff man Thurman Garrett, a reserve center, to open the second half with an onside kick. "We never practiced an onside kick. We had a kicker that didn't know how to do an onside kick. I don't know what Halas was trying to do," Lujack said, still puzzled a half century later. "It surprised us more than the Cardinals."

The ball went just 6 yards. From the Bears' 46, Christman struck in three plays—a 28-yard strike to Kutner, a handoff to Trippi, who carried for 14 more yards to the 2, and a pitchout to Harder, who scored untouched to cut the lead to 14–10.

Lujack revived the Bears. On the last play of the third quarter, he threw a rope to halfback Don Kindt, who ran 34 yards to the Cardinals' 4. Gulyanics opened the fourth quarter with his second touchdown, and Lujack nailed the point after to make it 21–10.

Noting that Lujack had played all the way on offense, defense, and kicks without a rest, Cardinals coach Conzelman told backup quarterback Ray Mallouf to attack the rookie. It paid off when an exhausted Lujack tackled Billy Dewell on an overthrown pass for an interference call at the 10. Trippi followed with a touchdown to shrink the margin to 21–17.

On third-and-long after the kickoff, Lujack threw a slant to his left for Kavanaugh. The Cardinals' alert linebacker Vince Banonis intercepted and carried to the Bears' 19. Two plays later, Elmer Angsman sprinted in from the 12 to give the Cardinals a 24–21 lead with eight minutes to go.

Halas sent in the rested Luckman, who brought the screaming crowd to their feet with a series of crisp completions. On second-and-5 from his own 42, Luckman hit halfback J. R. Boone on a bomb along the shaded western sideline to the Cardinals' 14. But two plays later, the season ended when Red Cochran intercepted Luckman's poorly thrown pass in the end zone.

The Cardinals went to Philadelphia, where, a week later, they lost their title to the Eagles 7–0 in a blizzard. Back in Chicago, a confident Halas looked ahead to a championship in 1949, despite a rules change he fought in vain. Free substitution.

After the New Year, he made the most inexplicable move of his career, one he publicly regretted to the end of his life. He traded Bobby Layne to the troubled New York Bulldogs for two draft choices and $50,000. Halas claimed he did it as a favor to Ted Collins, the team's beleaguered owner. When the Bulldogs folded after the '49 season, Layne ended up in a dispersal pool, and the Detroit Lions grabbed him, to Halas's eternal dismay.

Layne was no sooner gone than the other shoe dropped. Luckman felt listless for months, even before the Cardinals rematch. Finally, he visited a doctor, who ordered immediate surgery. "Luckman had a thyroid operation in 1949 and was never the same," Connor recalled.

Despite a slow recuperation, Halas kept Luckman on the active roster, where he saw spot action. The third-string quarterback was an unready 12th-round pick from Kentucky named George Blanda. "He was inexperienced, but you could tell George was going to be a good player," said Lujack.

Yet, all was not lost, as Connor noted: "Lujack led the league in passing. He had a helluva year. Played defense." Said Lujack, "It was the best season of my career. I had 23 touchdown passes. In the last game against the Cardinals, I threw 468 yards, which is still a Bears record, and six touchdown passes. Two more were downed on the one-yard line."

That 52–21 victory over the Cardinals ended a frustrating 9-and-3 season for the Bears as the Los Angeles Rams won the Western Division by a half game with 8 wins, 2 losses, and 2 ties. In their home-and-away set, Clark Shaughnessy, who had taken over the Rams' head coaching job in 1948, outfoxed Halas when he introduced a three-receiver wide set. Bob Waterfield and rookie Norm Van Brocklin filled the air with footballs to the likes of Tom Fears, Elroy Hirsch, and Vitamin T. Smith. The "pass-crazy" tactics paid off with two Rams victories over the Bears, the second a week after the Bears lost in New York.

That playoff-killing third loss came from a curiously sentimental, and untimely, Halas decision. For years, the Old Man would showcase a favored player in his hometown. It paid off in 1939 when he gave rookie Luckman his first action at quarterback at the Polo Grounds and he nearly led the Bears to victory against the Giants. Now a decade later, the Bears were 3–1 when they walked into the Polo Grounds. Lujack had run the show all season, but the Old Man decided to call on "his boy" once more.

"Halas gave Luckman the green light," Connor said. "I mean someone literally hung a green lightbulb in his locker the week before the game." It was a debacle. "Luckman started and did nothing, and the Giants took a 28–0 lead." Lujack took over and led a comeback to tie the game. "They beat us with a screen pass to win 35–28. That cost us the championship," Connor said. "We won the rest of our games."

The All-America Football Conference started the 1949 season with just seven teams, its third commissioner, O. O. Kessing, and a fourth ownership group in Chicago, which changed the team name to Hornets. In a desperate last-ditch attempt to save his AAFC, Arch Ward tried to break the College All-Star contract with the NFL that he had negotiated years before the interleague war erupted. Bert Bell, with Halas's help, went over Ward's head to his boss, Don Maxwell, at the *Tribune* and quashed the attempt. When that failed, Ward tried to throw in the towel.

The NFL's Bears and Redskins and the AAFC Browns were the only pro teams making money at the time. The hard-nosed Halas and Washington's Marshall were in a take-no-prisoners mood and blocked all settlement moves. Despite the money Dan Reeves bled in his battle for Los Angeles with the Dons, Marshall demanded that the Rams owner pay the Redskins' expenses for their West Coast trip. Halas, it was reported, was equally hard-nosed when he dumped spare Bears on sorry Ted Collins and his pathetic Boston Yanks/New York Bulldogs.

Halas's favorite foe, the Green Bay Packers, were also on the ropes. The Packers won just three games in 1948. In '49, they finished last at 2-and-10. Reporter Art Daley of the *Green Bay Press-Gazette* was a daily eyewitness to the total disintegration, from Curly Lambeau on down. Lambeau was so hated in town that he had to coach from the press box. According to Daley, "They almost ran out of money in '49. They held a Thanksgiving Day intrasquad game in '49 to get money to pay off their bills." After the season, the Packers' board of directors ran a stock drive and raised $70,000 to save the team.

Bell at last lined up enough league support to vote down Halas and Marshall and end the war. The carnage ceased on December 9, 1949, with the announcement that the Cleveland Browns, San Francisco 49ers, and Baltimore Colts would join the NFL. Collins folded his New York Bulldogs and was awarded control of yet another New York franchise, which he named the Yanks. The league now had 13 teams and new conference names, American for the East and National for the West.

Alignment was the next issue. The bartering, trade-offs, and back-stabbings were as duplicitous as the World War I peace conference at Versailles in 1919. George Halas dictated the terms for the NFL against the vanquished AAFC majordomo Arch Ward. Halas forced his former friend and *Tribune* ally to sacrifice the Ameche-Lindheimer Los Angeles Dons for the NFL's established Rams. Ward in turn saved the San Francisco 49ers to give the NFL two West Coast franchises, the powerful Cleveland Browns, and, surprisingly, the weak Baltimore Colts, not the stronger Buffalo Bills. Buffalo's owner, Jim Breuil, gained a consoling 25 percent share of the Browns.

Nobody benefited more than Paul Brown. "Brown extracted his pick of the Buffalo roster, Charles Brizzolara said. "That gave him Abe Gibron, Hal Herring, Rex Baumgardner, and John Kissell." Each would be a major contributor. Brown already owned the outstanding receiver Dub Jones, who came from Brooklyn in 1948, and would land George Ratterman in 1952 from the New York Yanks to back up Otto Graham.

The rest of the players were scattered throughout the league. No one took more hits than Halas. He'd lost the most men to the AAFC during the war, but under the settlement, he could reclaim only three of his former players. Most important, he could not reacquire the one he wanted above all others, Bobby Layne. The Detroit Lions snatched the great quarterback from the dispersal pool on the advice of new backfield coach Buddy Parker, fresh from the Chicago Cardinals. Parker had urged Violet Bidwill to get Layne from Halas after the 1948 season.

Halas may have lost the skirmish over reclaiming former players, but he won the main event. Because the league had 13 teams, he persuaded his fellow owners to fill his own National Conference in the West with three new teams: the 49ers, the Colts, and, to give the Giants breathing room, Collins's New York Yanks, for a total of seven. Then came the spiteful move that would trigger the Cardinals' decade-long decline in Chicago and their 1960 move to St. Louis. Halas exiled them to the eastern American Conference, geography be damned, which is how the league operated until its 2002 realignment divided 32 teams into two 16-team, four-division conferences. The Arizona Cardinals landed in the NFC West with St. Louis, San Francisco, and Seattle.

After Charlie Bidwill's death, the accommodation between Halas and the Cardinals erupted into rancor when the widow Violet Bidwill married St. Louis businessman Walter Wolfner. Since her young sons, Charles II "Stormy" and Bill, were too young to run the club, she entrusted it to her new husband, who alienated everybody. "He just wrecked that franchise," Bill Gleason said. "Ray Benningsen, the general manager, quit, as did coach Buddy Parker. It unraveled, and the players were dispersed."

Then, on February 1, 1950, Earl "Curly" Lambeau, the man who founded the Green Bay Packers and led his team to six NFL titles in a 29-year reign, resigned in bitterness to announce he had taken the Cardinals job. Lambeau and Wolfner would part company after 7 wins and 15 losses in just one year plus 10 games. To replace Lambeau, the Packers' executive committee went south and returned with Halas assistant and former star Gene Ronzani. It would take two more coaching failures after Ronzani before the Pack finally came back with its savior—a man from New York named Vince Lombardi.

Up in Detroit, brewery executive Edward Anderson drove out his partners to take control of the Lions. One of his first hires was the capable former Cardinals coach Raymond "Buddy" Parker as offensive assistant. Anderson told Parker to stand by for the inevitable failure of head coach Alvin "Bo" McMillin. He also gave Parker carte blanche to build an offense around Layne, rookie halfback Doak Walker, and Notre Dame's 1949 Heisman winner, end Leon Hart. Walker, the 1948 Heisman winner from SMU, led the NFL in scoring in 1950 with 126 points. Walker's high school teammate and best friend from Highland Park, Texas, Layne, passed for 2,323 yards and 18 touchdowns. Parker replaced McMillin four days before Christmas 1950 and added two of his best Cardinals, center Vince Banonis and fullback Marlin "Pat" Harder. The Lions were on the prowl.

The Bears still had the growl in 1950, though. An aging Sid Luckman was on hand for one final season, but strictly as emergency relief for the already established Johnny Lujack. "Lujack looked like a worthy successor, but he got his shoulder knocked out playing defense," said George Connor.

Lujack, who may have been the best all-around player in the league as one of the last two-way players, paid the price for Halas's cheapness. "They didn't operate on shoulders in those years," Connor said. "He spent half the season not throwing during the week. Lujack was a tough guy." But this was a tough guy whose effectiveness suffered as the season wore on.

Halas brought in Steve Romanik as third-string quarterback. Late in training camp, he dealt Blanda to the Colts for all-league guard Dick Barwegan. When the Colts waived Blanda the day after the opening game, the Packers picked him up. When Blanda arrived in Green Bay, Coach Ronzani told him that Halas had gone to the league, complaining that he had the right of first refusal. The league awarded Blanda to the Bears, where he spent the rest of the 1951 season at outside linebacker as he started his Hall of Fame career as a placekicker. He kicked 6 field goals in 18 attempts for 18 points and also handled kickoffs.

The reconstituted league enjoyed two races to the wire, resulting in playoffs for both conferences. The New York Giants relied on defense to force the Cleveland Browns to a playoff in the American Conference. On a brutally cold afternoon in Cleveland, reminiscent of that 1945 Rams-Redskins playoff, the Browns outlasted the Giants 8-to-3 on two Lou Groza field goals and a late safety when Charlie Conerly was tackled in the end zone.

As for the National Conference, just over 83,000 fans jammed the Coliseum to see the battle between the teacher and his pupil. It was the 9-and-3 Bears of George Halas versus the 9-and-3 Rams of Jumbo Joe Stydahar. The mutual respect that would continue as long as both men lived was set aside that afternoon as Stydahar, the rookie head coach, opposed the man who made him his first-ever draft choice in 1936. Lujack could barely throw, but he could think, as he marched the Bears to 7–3 lead on a 25-yard Al Campana touchdown run.

The game turned in the second quarter when Waterfield, who had been ailing with the flu, came off the bench in relief of Norm Van

Brocklin. He connected with Tom Fears on three long touchdown passes to seal a 24–14 Rams victory and trip back to Cleveland for the first time since the move.

The championship the following week was the first televised title game, at least in the East, as the coaxial coast-to-coast connection was still under construction. In a back-and-forth game, the Rams were 28 seconds away from their second title, when Lou Groza hit a 16-yard field goal to give the Browns their first NFL championship, 30–28, and fifth straight title, counting the four they won in the late AAFC.

Lujack still went both ways in 1951, but Halas was tinkering with the quarterback position. Lujack's production dropped from 21 touchdown passes to 8, but he also gave up the fewest interceptions in the league, also 8. Halas gave substantial playing time to backups Romanik and first choice Bob Williams of Notre Dame, but neither showed enough to push Lujack. Blanda, again, played on defense and placekicked.

The Rams won the National Conference with an 8-and-4 record, a half game ahead of Layne's fast-moving Lions and the exciting San Francisco 49ers. The Bears dropped to fourth at 7-and-5 after they blew two chances in December to tie or beat out the Rams. They had their chance.

Wrigley Field was bathed in 60-degree sunshine on a balmy December 2 afternoon. Many of the 50,286 there wore windbreakers or sweaters as the fired-up Bears took a 14–0 lead barely eight minutes into the game. Connor, Sprinkle, and Co. had the Rams pinned within nine yards of the north end zone, when Waterfield changed the dynamics of the game and season in 10 seconds. When the charging Bears linemen bit on Waterfield's play-action fake to Paul "Tank" Younger, Waterfield threw down the right side toward midfield. Elroy Hirsch made a leaping catch, spun, and took off to complete a 91-yard touchdown play. That opened the floodgates as the Rams rolled to a 42–17 victory.

Two weeks later, only 15,000 fans braved near-zero weather to root on the Bears against the Cardinals. The Cardinals knocked them out of any playoff dreams early that afternoon and went on to take a 24–14 lead with seconds left. Time was nearly out, and Ed Sprinkle was getting up slowly after being knocked to his knees, when Charley Trippi walked over and measured him.

From the moment he entered the league, Sprinkle had terrorized opponents, especially running backs, with his devilish assortment of trips, elbows, and clotheslines. Trippi had taken more than his fair share of Sprinkle shots through the years. With time expiring on this arctic afternoon, Trippi planted his feet and leveled his tormentor with a perfect right cross. Lights out. Revenge. After that, the two adversaries became close friends. "Eddie was a prince off the field. On the field, he did what he thought Halas wanted," was all Trippi would say a half century later concerning the incident. Sprinkle would not talk about it.

Seven Bears played in the 1952 Pro Bowl in Los Angeles. Other than rookie fullback John "Kayo" Dottley, the other six were repeaters from the inaugural 1951 Western Conference squad: Connor, Sprinkle, Turner, guards Ray Bray and Dick Barwegan, and Lujack.

Late in the game, the National Conference scored when Detroit's Bobby Layne pitched out to teammate Doak Walker, who threw a seven-yard touchdown pass to L.A.'s Hirsch to make it 29–13. Coach Stydahar sent Lujack in to kick the extra point, which he drilled to make it 30–13.

After John Lujack walked off the Coliseum field that January day, he never suited up for another game of football. The loss of that supreme player began the woes that have bedeviled the Chicago Bears ever since. The Monsters of the Midway were no more.

SIXTEEN

THE LUCKMAN CURSE, OR WAS IT LUJACK, LAYNE, OR BLANDA?

*L*ong before the Old Man died, he decreed that when it comes to quarterbacks, Sid Luckman was it. He stands alone. Certainly, no other Bear has approached his 137 career touchdown passes. If you follow the party line, the Chicago Bears have not had a great quarterback since Luckman retired in 1950.

Wrong! Two Bears named Bobby Layne and George Blanda were championship quarterbacks, and both are in the Pro Football Hall of Fame. But neither man won a title until he left the Bears.

Neither Layne nor Blanda could beat out another signal caller who won all-league honors three times and played in the first two Pro Bowls, in 1951 and '52. Johnny Lujack certainly had Hall of Fame ability. Had Lujack stayed, he might have become the greatest quarterback the Bears ever had, but he left George Halas and the Bears at age 27 after just four seasons. And contrary to the Halas Hall party line, he did not quit because he was hurt. He left because he couldn't stand to play anymore for the founder.

Other meritorious signal callers in the long navy blue and orange line include Ed Brown, Zeke Bratkowski, Bill Wade, Rudy Bukich, and Jim McMahon. Wade and McMahon are the only quarterbacks since 1946 who won titles for Halas U.

Green Bay Packers Hall of Famer Paul Hornung, who learned a thing or two about championship quarterbacking in the same backfield with Bart Starr, is well aware of what Halas squandered: "He had the four best quarterbacks. He had Luckman, Lujack, Layne, and Blanda! On one team! Incredible!" And they were there from 1948 through 1951.

The saga began in 1948. No football team has ever landed a better parlay than did the Bears that year when Halas signed both Lujack and Layne with the express purpose that either one, or maybe both of the kids, would replace the great Luckman. In 1948, John Lujack was the crown prince in waiting, the people's choice. Only, the public never knew that of the three, the one who never kowtowed to Halas, and never would, was the polite, squared-away World Ward II naval officer from Connellsville, Pennsylvania, and the University of Notre Dame, John Christopher Lujack Jr.

Lujack's trouble with Halas started the way it did with so many players. Over money. Unlike so many others, though, Lujack did not let Halas flummox him. Each time the Old Man dipped into his reservoir of negotiating tricks, the young man called him on it.

Before he went to see the Papa Bear to talk turkey, Lujack cut a $5,000 endorsement deal elsewhere in Chicago with Wilson Sporting Goods. While he was at the Wilson offices, someone there told Lujack he should expect Halas to give him a $5,000 signing bonus. Then he headed to 233 West Madison Street.

"Now we were talking," Lujack recalled, "and he said, 'I'll give you a $2,000 bonus for signing.' 'No! I understand I'm supposed to get $5,000.' Halas replied with an expletive."

They met the next day. "Here's your [expletive] $5,000!" Halas said, as he set the cash on the table in two piles. "Here's my two and here's three from Wilson Sporting Goods." Lujack acknowledged, "I didn't know anything about pro ball, and I thought, 'This is the way they did things.'"

Lujack justified his worth in a brilliant rookie season that saw him start every game at quarterback except the three he had to miss because of a kidney injury, play full time as a defensive back, and kick extra points and short field goals.

The next surprise came within days of the shocking 1948 season-ending 24–21 loss to the Cardinals that knocked the Bears out of a title shot. "I found out at the end of the year that the $3,000 from Wilson was an advance on my royalties. So, he ended up giving me $2,000, and I feel he cheated me out of $3,000." Lujack paused to find the correct words to avoid sounding bitter. "I'm his number one draft choice, I'm going to take over for Luckman, and the first thing I know is he cheats me."

The rookie bonus fiasco was the second time Halas tried to chisel Lujack thin 1948. The first was with the contract itself. "I signed for $17,000 my first year when I could have gotten $30,000 from the other side. The $17,000 then bumped up to $18,500, $20,000, and $20,000 for 1951, the last year. "So, I turned the pages before I signed it to see all those numbers because I thought I was stealing, you know? And he had in there, $17,000, $18,000, $19,000, and $20,000."

Lujack told him, "That isn't what we agreed on."

"What did we agree on?" Halas asked.

"I told him, and he changed it in two seconds. He was going to cheat me out of another $1,500, and again, I'm the number one draft choice. That would indicate our relationship kind of quicklike." For Lujack, the acrid aftertaste of his dealings with Halas has lingered through the years. "I don't mind anybody being a hard negotiator. I just don't want to be cheated because of my inexperience."

By 1949, Layne was gone, and Luckman was ill and, at age 33, an old athlete. So, Lujack had the job to himself. He responded with a league-leading 23 touchdown passes and 2,658 passing yards. He was the best quarterback in football.

By the next season, 1950, reporters and fans could see that Lujack's passes lacked the zing he showed in that brilliant '49 campaign. "I got a separated left shoulder in an exhibition game with the New York Giants. I was supposed to be out for four or five weeks.

Hell, at the end of 10 days, I'm taking novocaine shots to practice with my arm in a sling. I'm under center with my left arm in a sling. And I took novocaine shots every day," Lujack said. "Then I got a partial separation on my right shoulder playing defense." When the Bears played the Rams for the right to meet Cleveland for the title, Lujack could barely comb his hair or grip a football, let alone throw one.

"I didn't know how badly he was hurt. I think there probably was a lot of foolishness there," said Bill Gleason, who covered Halas and the Bears for more than three decades. "The thing I loved about Halas: Say a guy had a sprained right ankle. George would tell the press that it was his *left* ankle. He really believed that this worked. 'George,' I said, 'these guys watch the game. Which ankle are you looking at?' 'Ah, bullshit, Gleason,' Halas would say. The stuff that he did!"

"I had a lot of respect for Johnny Lujack," Ed Sprinkle said. "He got *both* shoulders knocked out. And they were still trying to play him out there."

"The second week after I hurt my right shoulder, I started and played the whole game on defense and half the game on offense," Lujack said.

"Nowadays when somebody has a separated shoulder, you wait until it heals up. Back then, they didn't do that," Sprinkle said. "He had to go out there on Sunday and throw. That didn't make good sense."

As the 1950 season wore on, Lujack's performance naturally suffered. The writers and fans did not understand why. The secretive Halas revealed the injuries only after the playoff loss to the Rams, in a corrupted twist of justification: "You don't tell the enemy of a weakness. It's like wartime!"

Halas claimed the doctor who treated Lujack found torn fibers in the shoulder. Halas stressed that the doctor assured everyone that rest would cure the condition and young Lujack could throw on Sundays without risking permanent injury. With Layne gone, Luckman virtually useless, and Blanda playing out of position as a linebacker, Halas had to keep Lujack in there.

"People demeaned Lujack, but they can't demean him in the record book," said Gleason. "He gave them four damn-good years, and he did everything. He played defense. He kicked extra points. He just was special."

Lujack's special qualities extended far past the record book to intangibles such as leadership and loyalty. "I saw one of my good friends on the team come off after a pass was completed in his territory, and Halas kicked him in the shins. They almost had a fight," Lujack said. That teammate whose name Lujack did not reveal was Don Kindt. The kicking incident happened in a Packers game. Years later, Kindt said Halas apologized and claimed he was trying to kick the grass when he accidentally got him.

Lujack, however, did not feel as kindly disposed to the Old Man. Unlike such men as George Connor, who insisted that Halas's word was his bond, John Lujack experienced the flip side, if indeed there was one. "I signed a four-year contract," he said, "and when it was done, I wanted to be traded!" To Lujack, a contract was a contract, no matter how odious. He honored it with another All-Pro performance and second straight Pro Bowl appearance at the L.A. Coliseum in January 1952.

Lujack's National Conference coach was former Halas star Joe Stydahar, just off leading his Rams to the 1951 title over the Browns. "I was throwing really well out there," Lujack said. Stydahar watched Lujack work with his receivers for a while and then walked over. "I heard you had a bad arm," Jumbo Joe said. He knew Lujack played in spots the last part of the '51 season and had seen for himself that he did not throw that well in a 42–17 loss to the Rams in December. "This was the first chance I had to rest it," Lujack replied as he continued to hit his receivers in stride on downfield diagonal patterns, the hardest passes to throw.

When Lujack got home after the Pro Bowl, Frank Leahy called from Notre Dame and offered him a job as assistant backfield coach. "When I told Halas I had a Notre Dame offer and had to give them an answer before spring practice, he said he was taking a month off in Arizona and could not talk until he got back. So, I went into coaching at Notre Dame." Lujack had moved to South Bend by the time

Halas returned from the Valley of the Sun. In early spring, Lujack took a call from Los Angeles in his office near Leahy's. "When Stydahar found out I wasn't going to get together with Halas, he tried to make a deal for me. Halas wanted four first-team Rams! Silly! So, that didn't come about."

For the next two seasons, Lujack developed the top Fighting Irish backfield quartet since the Four Horsemen: quarterback Ralph Guglielmi, fullback Neil Worden, and two halfbacks, Joe Heap and Heisman and two-time Maxwell winner Johnny Lattner. In 1953, he also worked with a freshman from Louisville named Paul Hornung. The Golden Boy is football's only triple crown winner: 1956 Heisman Trophy; 1957 bonus pick, by the Packers; and election to the Pro Football Hall of Fame in 1986.

Each of those five men became a first-round NFL choice. Lujack was positioned to succeed the master. After his first coaching season, 1952, at least one pro coach remained interested in Lujack as a player. "Stydahar became head coach with the Cardinals. He still wanted to make a trade for me," Lujack said. Unfortunately for Lujack, the reserve clause made him Halas's indentured servant in perpetuity as property of the Chicago Bears. "Halas told Stydahar he wanted three first-team Cardinals. You see, that was his way of keeping me out of the league."

In early 1954, Leahy resigned as head coach at Notre Dame. University president Reverend Theodore Hesburgh hired 1953 freshman coach Terry Brennan instead of Leahy's choice, Lujack. So, John, his wife, Pat, and their children moved to Davenport, Iowa, Pat's hometown. He started with one of the family's auto dealerships and eventually ran the whole business as he enjoyed the good, albeit quiet, life in the Quad Cities.

In recent years, Lujack endowed a $200,000 scholarship at Notre Dame. He and his friends stayed close, and he came to Chicago several times each year to participate in various golf outings with such former Bears teammates as Connor, Kindt, and Sprinkle. "I liked him," Sprinkle said. "I figure he would have been the best of all of them had he stayed."

For the record, the Bears still parrot official dogma that injuries ended Lujack's career. Halas, in his memoir, did not acknowledge Lujack's departure. Instead he wrote, "My worst problem was at quarterback. It became intense when Lujack injured his throwing arm. I went from feast to famine overnight." If George Halas had hoped Lujack would return and kiss the ring, he never divulged it. For his part, John Lujack steered a steady course. Not once did he attend any official Bears function, alumni or otherwise.

For pro football fans in early television's black-and-white era, the game's most colorful star was a swaggering cowboy of a quarterback with the Detroit Lions and, later, the Pittsburgh Steelers. Bobby Layne, number 22 on his jersey and number 1 in the hearts of his fans, wore a boy's tiny shoulder pads under his jersey. With a pot-belly slopping over his belt and a beefy butt, Layne didn't need any other protection. He said face masks were for sissies, so he was the last position player in the league who didn't have one attached to his helmet. The helmet itself looked two sizes too small and barely fit over his shock of blond hair.

Directors took constant close-ups of Layne's pudgy, squinty-eyed face to see what might happen next. Lip-readers had a field day watching him chew out huge linemen as if he were attacking beef jerky. Lithe ends and swift backs who dropped one of his wobbly, ducklike passes or coughed up the ball paid the price in the huddle as he let them have it uncensored. And the cameras caught every purple syllable.

This was a leader in the flesh. If ever a player fit a coach, a team, and city, that player was Bobby Layne, that coach was George Halas, and that team was the Chicago Bears. Unfortunately for the loyalists, he will always be known as a Hall of Fame Lion or Steeler, not a Bear, on the "NFL Greatest 100" list. He never got the chance in Chicago.

As Lujack was the Bears' first choice in 1946 as a future, both the NFL Bears and AAFC Baltimore Colts drafted Layne number one in 1948. "He always had three guys," said Bill Gleason of Halas. The names through the years were interchangeable. Luckman, Lujack, and Layne, the three *L*s, became Blanda, Bratkowski, and Brown, the three *B*s. Halas even buzzed in with a fourth *B*, Bukich. "They were nullifying each other, and he loved that. He always wanted that quarterback rivalry."

Layne was a single-wing tailback at Texas until his senior year, when the legendary Dana X. Bible turned over the team to his assistant Blair Cherry. In his first act as boss, Cherry installed the T formation. He then gave Layne the reins and let him drive the 'Horns to a number five ranking in the polls. Armed with the Steelers' first pick on draft day, December 12, 1947, as he had been a decade before when he landed Luckman, Halas was certain that, in Layne, he was getting another ace.

In *The Game*, Tex Maule wrote that Baltimore coach Cecil Isbell went to Texas and met with Layne in a hotel room. He laid out 10 $1,000 bills on a bed and told the quarterback that would be his signing bonus. Isbell then handed Layne a three-year, no-cut, no-trade deal starting at $20,000 that escalated to $22,000 and then $25,000. When Layne left the room, Maule wrote, Isbell thought he had him.

Then Halas, whom Maule called a "master salesman when it came to football talent," made his move and roped in his man. There can be no doubt that Halas, who never made any transaction without thoroughly checking out a player's background, knew all about his target. Like the Old Man, Bobby Layne endured a rough upbringing. He was just 7 when his father, a used car salesman, died unexpectedly at age 37.

Bobby's life changed for the better when his uncle Wade and aunt Livinia Hampton adopted him and moved him to the upscale Dallas suburb of Highland Park, where he became fast friends with Doak Walker before enrolling at Texas in 1944. After a year in the merchant marine, Layne returned to Texas, where he made all-America as a senior.

Halas also knew that Layne was a boozer, a party animal. Layne himself once told a reporter he had cut his teeth on Pearl Beer. For Layne, the real chase began after the lights were down low. No football player in history saw more sunrises before he hit the sack. This was a rogue in the Halas tradition who would blaze a trail for future Bears named Casares, Atkins, Hill, and Ditka.

Those who know say he was always the same—in college, as a rookie in Chicago, and as a 15-year league veteran. They also stress that nobody managed a football game better. "Bobby was a helluva guy. Just legendary about drinking. It's all true!" said Rick Casares, no shrinking violet himself on the party circuit in his Bears years from 1955 through '64.

According to Casares, he and Layne got acquainted socially the Monday before the 1957 Pro Bowl in L.A. as they waited to check in at their hotel. "Bobby said, in that whiskey voice, which really was a whiskey voice, 'Rick, when you get to your room, come in the conference room over here.' When I went to the conference room, there were about four or five Detroit guys and Bobby. A giant punch bowl was in the middle of the table, white, with a ladle in it, and they all had cups."

"Have some punch," Layne commanded. "What the hell is that?" Casares asked. "Brandy and milk," Bobby snapped as though any fool would know what the hell *that* was.

"That's what they were drinking the day I checked in." Casares continued, "Of course, I had some. It about gagged me. Christ, we got half pie-eyed before I got to my room."

From that stomach-churning initiation, Casares, Layne, and fellow pub crawler Paul Hornung became close friends off the field. Rick's biggest problem whenever Layne was around, he said, was trying to avoid him on the night before a game, and he cited another example. The Steelers roared into Chicago on Saturday December 5, 1959, for a game the next day at Wrigley Field. "Before the kickoff, I ran by Bobby in the warm-up, and he said, 'Hey, Rick! Where were you, man? I tried to reach you all night.' I knew he was trying to reach me. I was staying at a hotel, and I told the people who answered to say, 'Mr. Casares is out.'

" 'I was at the Playboy Club, Rick,' Layne said, as he peered at the overcast sky and shook out the cobwebs. Layne loved to say he slept fast, four or five hours' worth, and got up movin'.

" 'Jeez, I must have just missed you, Bobby.' "

With the passage of 43 years, a mellower Casares admitted where he really was. "Christ! I was in bed. I wouldn't go out on the night before a game with anybody. I don't know how he did it. He'd be hung over. That night, he was at the Playboy Club until three in the morning. He played the whole game, kicking guys in the can if they missed blocks! And he threw three touchdowns against us!" Casares scored three touchdowns himself.

Layne just missed a fourth and winning touchdown that would have further enhanced his legend. Trailing 27–21, Layne marched the Steelers to a first down at the Bears' 10 with 11 seconds left. He was able to get off four passes, all incomplete, in that span! It was a rare failure. Layne's lifelong best friend, teammate, and fellow Hall of Famer Walker put it best. "Bobby never lost a game in his life," Doak said. "Time just ran out on him."

Ed Sprinkle verifies the man's grace under pressure. "Layne was a clutch player." Was he better than Johnny Lujack? "It would have been a toss-up," said Sprinkle, a close friend to both.

"I loved Bobby. He was a leader," said George Connor, whose best friend at Notre Dame and with the Bears was John Lujack. "Lujack and Layne! We would have been unbelievable," Connor mused. "Layne would have taken over if Lujack had been hurt." Lujack agreed: "Bobby Layne and I could have played for a hundred years."

When he traded him, Halas himself said he believed that Layne "may develop into another Luckman or Baugh." Such praise was unknown from a man not given to kindly rhetoric about any player, let alone one he cut loose. "Layne is an excellent competitor and wishes to play regularly, not sit on the bench," the Papa Bear said on that day of the deal in 1949.

Typically, George Halas clung to his stars who asked to be traded, especially a player like Layne. That's why that deal ran so against Halas's traits. When Lujack was sidelined for the 1948 rematch with Green Bay at Wrigley Field and Luckman couldn't move the team, Halas called on Layne. It was scoreless when he entered in the third quarter with the ball at Green Bay's 46. On the third play from the Packers' 34, Layne hit George McAfee at the 15, and McAfee ran in for the lone touchdown as the Bears won 7–6.

Halas started Layne a week later in Boston on November 20 in an unintentional showcase for Yanks owner Ted Collins. Layne hit his first three passes, the last a 17-yard touchdown to Neal "Moon" Mullins to open the scoring. For the afternoon, he completed 10 of 17 for 110 yards and ran 5 yards for another touchdown as the Bears romped 51–17 before only 18,048 fans.

Those late-season displays of poise, nerve, and accuracy under pressure make Halas's decision to trade Layne, a player he loved, for two draft choices and $50,000 cash incomprehensible. In reality, the draft choices Halas acquired for Layne were incidental. He traded Layne for the money, because he desperately needed it.

As George Vass reported, Halas claimed in early 1949 that he wanted to help Ted Collins. Better known as the partner and manager of the singer Kate Smith, Collins lost so much money in Boston in 1948 with the Yanks that he got league permission and the Giants' blessing to move into the Polo Grounds as a co-tenant to save the franchise. The show-business-savvy Collins was well aware that no one can make it in New York without a star.

Collins saw that star the previous November when charismatic Bobby Layne picked apart his Yanks. Best of all, Layne was third banana in Chicago, most likely to be available, and any fool could plainly see he was already every bit as good as either Luckman or Lujack. Collins burned up the lines to Chicago, regaling Halas with story after story—showbiz gossip, who was sleeping with whom, the works. Every time he brought up Layne's name though, Halas changed the subject.

Now, Ted Collins was a man who had dealt with the toughest nuts in the business. The word *no* had never stopped him before, nor would it now. He kept calling, and George kept saying no. One day, Collins just knew, George Halas would say yes.

When Bill Gleason was a young sportswriter for the *Chicago Herald-American*, he learned that Halas owed Charlie Bidwill $50,000. "He helped George through some tough times," is the way Gleason put it. "Sometime after Charlie's death, his widow, Violet, went to Halas. It was 1949. 'George,' she said, 'I'll cancel the debt if you let me have Bobby Layne.'" Halas knew that Layne in Cardinals' red and white could have tilted the balance of influence in Chicago to his detriment. Also, it would rekindle the animosities from 1926

when Halas stole Paddy Driscoll away from the South Side. As Gleason said, "Layne would have won for the Cardinals! It was so wonderful." Halas, Gleason said, excused himself. "He went out and
borrowed the money and paid her off rather than give her Layne."

Gleason was close to that story but not fully informed as to Halas's
reason for sending Layne away. And Halas did not borrow a dime.

We now know that Halas did not owe Charlie Bidwill for a debt,
per se. Rather, it was that stock deal from 1931 when Bidwill, Ralph
Brizzolara, Barbara Halas, Jim McMillen, and George Trafton's
mother gave Halas the money to buy out his partner Ed Sternaman.
In lieu of loan paybacks, they took stock in return. Mrs. Trafton,
who'd invested $20,000, got the most, just over 25 percent. The oth-
ers—Bidwill, Brizzolara, Barbara Halas, and McMillen—had each
kicked in $5,000, which, as we learned from Jim McMillen's account
book, bought each of those four investors nine and five-eighths shares
of stock, the core of the transaction that Halas held in absolute
secrecy all his life.

By 1949, Charlie had been dead more than a year, and Violet Bidwill was ready to marry Walter Wolfner. First, Violet had to clear up
several outstanding matters in her late husband's estate. One of those
obligations was "the debt" Halas owed Bidwill, which led to that
query about Layne.

In a July 2003 conversation, a source close to that situation mentioned that in 1946, Charles Bidwill, the sole owner of the Cardinals,
still held the Bears stock he bought in 1931. The source said Bidwill
had remained an avid Bears fan until he saw the way his emerging
Cardinals beat the Bears late in the '46 season. After the game, Bidwill declared to Halas his undying allegiance to his own team.
Accordingly, it was time for Charlie to sell back his stock. That forced
Halas to put an appraised value on the club for the first time since
1931. Back then, Halas and Sternaman agreed on a $38,000 price for
the Dutchman's 50 percent share, making the club worth $76,000.
Sometime in early 1947, Bidwill and Halas came to terms and agreed
on a $50,000 price. Before the money changed hands, Bidwill died.
That put his substantial estate into probate, freezing its assets and
leaving unfinished business on hold. When Violet Bidwill went to
Halas for the $50,000 he owed for his stock, Halas had to act.

Player-coach George Halas, 1921, when the Staleys moved from Decatur to a permanent home in Chicago. The team was renamed the Bears in 1922. His #7 was retired. Charter member Hall of Fame, 1963.
Courtesy of the CHICAGO BEARS.

George Halas as a New York Yankees right fielder in 1919. Halas could not hit the curve and turned to football. A man named Babe Ruth joined the Yankees in 1920 and more than adequately replaced Halas in the lineup.   Courtesy of the CHICAGO BEARS.

Red Grange, 1925. The signing of the Galloping Ghost of Illinois made pro football. Grange played from 1925 to '34. His #77 was retired in 1949. Charter member Hall of Fame, 1963. Courtesy of the CHICAGO BEARS.

Bronko Nagurski, 1932, fullback and tackle from Minnesota. Considered the greatest player of the leather-helmet era of the '20s and '30s. Played from 1930 to '37 and came out of retirement in 1943 to help the Bears win their sixth title. His #3 was retired in 1949 with Red Grange's #77 and Bill Hewitt's #56. Charter member Hall of Fame, 1963.   Courtesy of the CHICAGO BEARS.

Luke Johnsos in 1941 calling in strategy from the press box on the telephone as football's first "eye-in-the-sky."
Courtesy of the CHICAGO BEARS.

Twenty-year-old Virginia Halas and her soldier, Ed McCaskey. They eloped on February 2, 1943, against her parents' wishes.
Courtesy of the CHICAGO BEARS.

U.S. Coast Guard bosun's mate second class, the actor Cesar Romero sits on the Bears' bench with Ralph Brizzolara in 1944. Ed Sprinkle is to the right.
From the CHARLES BRIZZOLARA COLLECTION.

Min Halas (seated, left) with team wives, including Estelle Luckman (standing, third from left), 1959.   From the CHUCK MATHER COLLECTION.

"The Three *L*s"—1948 quarterbacks. The greatest three quarterbacks ever
assembled on one team in NFL history: Notre Dame 1947 Heisman Trophy
winner Johnny Lujack (#32) started that year and stayed in on defense. Lujack
quit in 1952 after three All-NFL seasons in his four-year career in a bitter
dispute with Halas. A college Hall of Famer, veteran Sid Luckman (#42) from
Columbia took over in the second quarters and, at age 32, was still a Hall of
Fame performer. He was inducted in 1964. Rookie Bobby Layne (#22) from
Texas got traded after the season in a deal Halas called his biggest mistake.
Layne led the Detroit Lions to three NFL titles and finished with Pittsburgh.
He made the Hall of Fame in 1967.   Courtesy of the CHICAGO BEARS.

"The Three *B*s"—1958 quarterbacks George Blanda (#16), Zeke Bratkowski (#12), and Ed Brown (#15). After 10 seasons, Blanda, in Halas's doghouse as a third-stringer, left the Bears as the leading scorer in team history; he resumed his career in 1960 in the AFL for 16 more seasons and a 1981 induction into the Hall of Fame as an Oakland Raider.   Courtesy of the CHICAGO BEARS.

Harlon Hill, end from Florence State
Teachers College (now University of
Northern Alabama). Rookie of the Year
in 1954. NFL MVP in 1955. All-NFL in
1954, '55, and '56. Most dangerous
player in the game until injured in 1957.
Left after 1961 to finish with Pittsburgh
and Detroit in 1962.
Courtesy of the CHICAGO BEARS.

Rick Casares, fullback from
Florida, 1955–64. All-NFL five
seasons. Respected for his
ability and toughness. Led the
league in rushing in 1956 with
then team-record 1,126 yards.
Courtesy of the CHICAGO BEARS.

1962 coaching staff. (From left) George Halas with offensive coach Luke Johnsos, technical adviser and defensive coach Clark Shaughnessy, defensive assistant George Allen, line coach Phil Handler, offensive backfield coach Chuck Mather, and special projects assistant Paddy Driscoll, who served as head coach during 1956–57.   Courtesy of ETTY ALLEN.

Coach Halas and Gale Sayers at the north end of Wrigley Field in 1965. Sayers, the NFL's all-time-great open-field runner, was elected to the Hall of Fame in 1977 after playing just 68 games.
From the CHARLES BRIZZOLARA COLLECTION.

Brian Piccolo, running back, 1965–69. Died from cancer. Remembered for the made-for-television film *Brian's Song*, which depicted his life and struggle with the disease. His #41 was retired after his death in 1970.
Courtesy of the CHICAGO BEARS.

1963 title play. Bill Wade (#9) follows the lead of center Mike Pyle (#50) for the winning touchdown, his second scoring quarterback sneak, in the Bears' 14–10 title victory over the New York Giants at Wrigley Field on December 29, 1963. From the CHUCK MATHER COLLECTION.

A grinning George Halas turns
over coaching duty to Jim Dooley
on May 28, 1968.
Courtesy of JIM DOOLEY.

(From left) Ed McCaskey with wife Virginia Halas McCaskey and brother-
in-law Mugs, George Jr., in 1971. Mugs was the designated heir until his
unexpected death in 1979 at age 53.   Courtesy of the CHICAGO BEARS.

Dick Butkus, middle linebacker from Illinois, 1965–73. All-NFL seven times. Runner-up to teammate Gale Sayers as 1965 NFL Rookie of the Year. His #51 was retired in 1994 with Sayers's #40. Considered the greatest linebacker in NFL history, if not its greatest defensive player. Butkus sued the team doctor for medical malpractice and won a $600,000 settlement. Inducted into Hall of Fame in 1979.
Courtesy of the CHICAGO BEARS.

Mike Ditka, 1986, tight end from Pitt. 1961 Rookie of the Year, All-NFL five seasons, cocaptain 1963 champions. Traded to Philadelphia in 1967 and to Dallas in 1969. George Halas brought him back to Chicago as head coach in 1982. The 1985 Bears went 18–1 and won Super Bowl XX. His Bears teams won 112 games.
Courtesy of the CHICAGO BEARS.

Jerry Vainisi, 1986. Hired by George Halas Sr. and Jr. in 1972 as comptroller and in-house counsel. Became vice president, general manager, and treasurer by 1983. Fired after 1986 in a power struggle with team president Michael McCaskey. The Bears have never been the same since his departure.
Courtesy of the CHICAGO BEARS.

Walter Payton, 1975–87, retired
as the NFL's all-time ground
gainer. Contracted a rare form of
liver cancer and died in 1999 at
age 45. Many consider Payton the
greatest all-around player in NFL
history. Hall of Fame, 1993.
Courtesy of the CHICAGO BEARS.

Halas's grandson and team president Michael McCaskey brandishes the Super
Bowl XX trophy on January 26, 1986, after the Bears' 46–10 win over New
England. At right is his father, Ed.   Courtesy of the CHICAGO BEARS.

Team photograph of the 1963 NFL champions. Hall of Famers include head coach George Halas (3rd row, right); assistant coaches Sid Luckman, Paddy Driscoll, George Allen (3rd row, from left), and Joe Stydahar (4th row, left); and players Mike Ditka (#89), Doug Atkins (#81), Bill George (#61, top row, third from right), and Stan Jones (#78). This was the Bears' eighth title and the sixth for Coach Halas, tying him with Green Bay's Curly Lambeau for most championships as coach. (Lombardi won five in seven years.) The Bears went 11–1–2 plus the title-game win.   Courtesy of the CHICAGO BEARS.

Team photograph of the 18–1 1985 Bears, who won Super Bowl XX on January 26, 1986, in New Orleans. Many regard this Mike Ditka–coached club as the best-ever one-season team in NFL history. Hall of Famers include Ditka (6th row, left), Walter Payton (#34), Mike Singletary (#50), and Dan Hampton (#99). Courtesy of the CHICAGO BEARS.

Since Bidwill and McMillen each owned a one-sixteenth share, the value of the club at 16 times $50,000 was $800,000. Given that Halas took out loans every off-season at American National Bank to keep the club solvent until ticket money arrived, it is unlikely that the team had $50,000 stashed away for a rainy day. Instead, he held assets, players whom he could sell to raise money. The only individuals who could bring that chunk of cash were the quarterbacks: Luckman, Lujack, and Layne. They were his living, breathing rainy-day funds. He would never sell Luckman; he was his boy. Lujack was the local hero. Violet Bidwill thus made Layne the only viable option.

Halas knew she did not possess the football savvy to drop that name. Jimmy Conzelman and Violet had turned over coaching duties to Conzelman's two bright top assistants, both Texans, Buddy Parker and Phil Handler. Both men would have known all about Layne and would have told her to go after him.

So, Halas made his move on Collins. He told the impresario he could have Layne for two number one draft choices. The deal maker or breaker, he told Collins, was the $50,000. No cash, no deal. Like Halas, Collins was cash poor himself, but he needed that star, so he agreed to Halas's exorbitant terms. Halas took the money and ran back to Chicago, where he immediately transferred it to Violet Bidwill. Better to sacrifice Bobby Layne and a championship or two than his beloved Bears, reasoned Halas.

Afterward, he went to the local writers and delivered his own version, as George Vass reported years later. "I don't think I would have done it for anybody else, but I enjoyed him so much because he was one of the funniest fellows I have ever known," Halas said. "Ted was such a pleasant man. I happily passed hours listening to his stories. I agreed reluctantly."

Halas, a spinmeister decades before the term was coined, offered a tidy make-sense version to Ken Kavanaugh. As he told it, "When Halas traded Layne after the 1948 season, I went to him. 'George, why did you trade Bobby Layne?'" The brief conversation proceeded as follows:

"Where's Layne from?" Halas asked.

"Texas," Kavanaugh replied.

"Where's Lujack from?"

"Notre Dame."

"But, George," Kavanaugh, a Layne fan, said, "if you win, they will fill the stadium no matter where you come from."

After the Halas payoff, Violet Bidwill married Wolfner and let him run the team. Parker resigned after the season and joined the Detroit Lions. Ted Collins's transplanted Boston Yanks died in New York in 1949. Collins almost went broke, while Layne barely survived one of the worst poundings since London endured the Nazi blitz. The league, likely at Halas's urging, granted Collins another chance after the interleague settlement, this time with a reorganized New York Yanks. To make it go, Collins had to find a team willing to take on Layne's $22,000 salary. That team was the Detroit Lions with coach-in-waiting Buddy Parker.

Layne ran the show from the outset. With Parker as his ally, and his lifelong buddy Walker in close support, the Lions quickly became the elite team in the renamed Western Conference. They beat the Browns in 1952 and again in '53 for back-to-back titles and were going for three in '54 until Otto Graham and the Browns destroyed them 56–10 in a bravura performance.

In that '53 game, Layne literally invented the two-minute drill on the fly. Trailing 16–10, with the ball on Detroit's 20, Layne took command. He fired sideline passes to stop the clock, drew up plays in the dirt, kept throwing, and finally called time at the Browns' 33 with seconds remaining. Ignoring Parker's orders to go short, he fired long to Jim Doran, who scored. Layne held as the Doaker drilled the extra point for a 17–16 Detroit victory and second straight title. The Layne legend had begun.

Parker was gone in 1957 when Layne broke a leg and, on crutches, had to watch his backup Tobin Rote pass the Lions to a 59–14 rout over the Browns again, for the title. Then, hours after the second game in 1958, they shipped Layne to Pittsburgh, where he was reunited with Buddy Parker, now coaching the Steelers.

Until now, only a few people have known why the Lions dumped their greatest and most popular star. Paul Hornung was in his second year at Green Bay, the season before the coming of Vince Lombardi. "The score was tied 13–13," Hornung said, recalling a sunny October 5 afternoon at City Stadium. As Hornung watched from the Packers' sideline, Layne was marching the Lions toward another of his patented late victories. "It was fourth-and-3 on the 11. Naturally, here comes the field goal team. Only 40 seconds were left. Jim Martin was going to kick a field goal, which was like an extra point," Hornung said, concerning the chip shot–like 17 yards Martin's kick would have to travel.

"Layne waved them off," a still-disbelieving Hornung said four and a half decades later. "They went for a touchdown! He went back, and it fell incomplete in the end zone. We took over the ball and ran out the clock, a 13–13 tie." This was a moral victory for a 1958 Packers team that won just once, lost 10, and tied this one.

"On Monday, he got traded to Pittsburgh! The very next fuckin' Monday, he was gone!" Hornung exclaimed. "Do you know, there was not a thing written about it!"

"I remember they say he was drunk," I said.

"Drunk? Bullshit, he was drunk! He was betting 15 or 20 thousand. He told me! He gave four or five points, and he had to cover. He didn't give a shit. When Bobby made a bet, it made the rest of the guys who bet look like paupers."

"He was the biggest hitter in the league, wasn't he?"

"Sure," Hornung replied.

"When it came to throwing money around?"

"Absolutely!"

"That's another guy Halas loved."

"He had to," Hornung said. "He was a winner."

"George admitted a year or two before he died that the worst trade he ever made was sending Layne away," Ken Kavanaugh said. Retired *Chicago Tribune* sports editor Cooper Rollow agreed, "Halas made that admission hundreds of times through the years."

Money was never a problem for Layne. Not only did he make more than any other player in his time, but also he married well. In 1947, he wed the understanding Carol Ann Krueger, the daughter of a prominent surgeon from Lubbock. The Laynes had two sons. Layne coached the Steelers' quarterbacks in 1963 and '64, did the same for the St. Louis Cardinals in '65, and scouted for the Dallas Cowboys in '66 and '67, the year he was elected to the Pro Football Hall of Fame. He then left football for good, trying business ventures in oil and sporting goods.

Layne survived three head-on collisions and two throat cancer operations and went blind in one eye. He died on December 1, 1986, two days after undergoing surgery to stop hemorrhaging in the lower esophagus. He was 18 days short of turning 60.

Bobby Layne was leaving through one door as George Blanda was entering another in the spring of 1949. The total opposite of the disciplined and poised Lujack, and Layne, the two-fisted-drinking firebrand, Blanda was a cantankerous, ornery, scrappy fighter. In the words of his college coach at Kentucky, Paul "Bear" Bryant, he was a "fanatic competitor." Blanda was also bigger and taller than both Lujack and Layne. He weighed 215 pounds and stood 6'2" to their 6' even.

For his first four years in Chicago, he wore Layne's number 22, a daily reminder to Halas of who he was not and never would be. George Blanda was his own man, and everyone else could go shit in his hat as far as he was concerned. That went double for the man in the fedora who prowled the sidelines.

In the autumn of his years, the George Blanda of yesteryear underwent a total transformation regarding Halas. At least for publication. "I enjoyed playing for the Bears, and it was a thrill to play for the founder of pro football. I had 10 great years there and love and respect George Halas," said Blanda in October 2002. "The run-ins we had were over negotiating contracts. In hindsight, I understand what he had to do at that time in the NFL and in the economic conditions of the times for the league. In those early days, 1949–50, Halas was getting $5 a seat. Now I realize how tight money was."

This stands in marked contrast to the authorized biography, *Blanda, Alive and Kicking*, that Bay Area writer Wells Twombly wrote in 1972. The trouble started when Blanda, the 12th-round draft choice, took the train from Lexington, Kentucky, to Chicago to negotiate with the founder of the National Football League, if slapping down a contract and telling someone to sign it or else is negotiation.

The coal miner's son from Youngwood, Pennsylvania, quickly agreed to Halas's deal that called for $6,000, twice as much money as Blanda had expected to earn as a teacher. When Blanda mentioned the Los Angeles Dons were interested before he signed, Halas convinced him he would be joining a "Mickey Mouse" league. He then added a $600 bonus to get his signature.

Blanda signed the contract and a piece of paper that accompanied the bonus check. As he left the office, he turned over the check to read "Advance on 1949." If that didn't raise the hackles on the back of his neck, the slip of paper did the rest: he learned he had agreed to repay the club at 1 percent interest if he was cut. A seething Blanda rode back to Lexington to rejoin his wife, Betty, vowing that Halas would have to chase him into the Pennsylvania coalfields to get back his money if he didn't make the team. Most of all, he knew he'd been screwed. And he didn't like it. "He told me he never got a raise for seven years with the Bears," Ed Sprinkle said.

That was the first exchange in a decade-long pitched battle between Blanda and Halas, the confident player his teammates loved and the coach who made strong men bend to his will. Blanda moved right into the veterans' circle, joining men such as Turner, Sprinkle, and Sid Luckman.

"Luckman tied a tin can to Blanda's tail," George Connor said. Blanda hung around the great quarterback like a puppy, driving Sid's Chrysler Imperial convertible to the Luckman summer home while the great quarterback sunned himself in the backseat. "Luckman thought Blanda didn't look like a quarterback, with his big butt and thick legs," said Connor. But something about the determined kid, perhaps the set of his square jaw, the hard, all-seeing eyes, the huge hands, and the lively arm convinced Luckman the kid was worthwhile. He gave Blanda the playbooks and ordered him to study the 1,000 running plays and like number of pass plays and all their variations, which he did.

The Halas playbook had grown like Topsy since Halas and Clark Shaughnessy wrote the first draft in the late '30s. Each book was five inches thick, with color coding and the like. Only the quarterbacks knew them in their entirety with all the subtleties. The other players had to learn only their own assignments. In the huddle, the quarterbacks had to call the plays in complex jargon, plus call the blocking combinations.

Men such as Luckman, Lujack, Layne, and Blanda were smart enough to get it. Others tried and failed. Either they could not remember all the plays, plus the requisite footwork, handoffs, and pitches, or they could not execute them. "The thing destroys quarterbacks," Blanda told Twombly. "How many championships has Halas won with this system since my rookie year? Just one [1963]. Professional football passed him by in 1954."

In 1950, after he returned from his brief Baltimore exile, and again in '51, Blanda was not allowed near the quarterbacks. He played linebacker and defensive back, and he kicked. Lujack still handled extra points in 1950 and field goals up to 20 yards. Halas wanted Blanda to take the longer field-goal attempts and to kick off. Blanda, a straight-ahead kicker, as every kicker was then, went to Halas and told him he needed a kicking shoe. As Twombly related, that simple request only aggravated the situation. "Kid, if you want special equipment, you have to buy it yourself," Halas said. "The Bears are happy to supply you with regulation equipment. But a kicking shoe doesn't come under that heading." Blanda took $32.51 out of his own $6,600 salary and bought a kicking shoe. Years later, he discovered that every other team in the league supplied square-toed kicking shoes as regulation equipment.

George Blanda's inner strength rubbed Halas the wrong way. Blanda knew he was better than the others, and so did his peers. But, whether out of spite or plain stubbornness, the coach would not play him. When the team was sinking in 1952 and Halas had run through the other quarterbacks, he finally turned to Blanda.

Lujack's replacement in 1952 was his fellow Notre Damer and 1951's top draft choice, Bob Williams. Halas consigned Blanda to third string behind Steve Romanik. Williams played so poorly that Halas forbade the Bears to draft another quarterback on the first round until 1982, when Mike Ditka chose Brigham Young's Jim McMahon.

Blanda's first mercy mission came on November 2 in San Francisco against the 49ers at Kezar Stadium with five minutes left in the game. "It was tied 17–17, and Luke Johnsos wanted to go for a touchdown on fourth down. I went to Halas and urged him to let George kick a field goal to win it," Sprinkle said. "Halas, who wanted to win above all else, listened." Blanda kicked a 48-yarder to give the Bears a 20–17 victory. That was miracle number one.

Two weeks later, the Rams were whipping the Bears 40–7, when Halas sent Blanda in to mop up. He proceeded to complete 10 passes, 2 good for touchdowns, to bring respectability to a 40–24 defeat. The following Wednesday, the founder announced that Blanda would start against the title-bound Detroit Lions.

In his Monday-morning wrap-up after the Lions game, the *Tribune*'s Ed Prell observed that Blanda made his first start since college. "He stayed in the big league only because of his skill in kicking off, booting points, and his desire to play, which earned him a chance as a linebacker."

Blanda came out leading and throwing that afternoon. He connected four times with another first-time starter, Billy Stone, for 149 yards and two touchdowns. With time running out, the Bears were up 17–16 when Detroit's Jack Christiansen pulled in Curly Morrison's low punt at his 21 and ran it back for the go-ahead touchdown and a 23–17 lead with 1:31 left.

Blanda brought the team up at the Bears 32, faded, and fired long to Stone, who was tackled at the Detroit 25. Blanda then looked long again and threw short to Morrison, who carried to the 1. He tried a quarterback sneak, lost a yard, and called time-out with nine seconds left and ran over to the bench to ask Halas what he should do. Twombly picked up the account: " 'Shit. You're the quarterback,' the Great Innovator said. 'You keep telling me what a great quarterback you are. You call the play.' " Turner, in his first of five years as an assistant and last as a player, told Halas to put Sprinkle and himself in the game.

Blanda returned to the huddle, where they made up their own play. Turner told Blanda to send Stone on a dive, fake the handoff, and pass to Sprinkle, which he did for the winning touchdown. He kicked the point after to give the Bears a 24–23 victory, and the Age of Blanda Miracles was born. Blanda had thrown for 218 yards and three touchdowns.

"You son of a bitch, where did you get that play?" Halas roared as the team came over to the sideline. "We made it up," Blanda replied. In the clubhouse, Halas told the press, "Blanda called the play himself. Give the kid credit. It was a great play. It worked."

In the dressing room, Prell's *Tribune* colleague George Strickler faithfully chronicled Halas's moment of triumph in a disastrous season, noting that he "shook hands, slapped backs, and brushed away an occasional tear." In the press box, the astute Prell bestowed due praise on a new star: "Blanda had it all over Layne, a quarterback the Bears sent away four years ago when they had quarterbacks to spare." After the scribes left, the coach took his quarterback aside for a final message, "Don't you ever pull that shit again."

In 2002, Blanda said the way the Bears handled him after he suffered a shoulder separation against Cleveland in 1954 prolonged his career. After he came back in 1955, he played as backup to Ed Brown for the next two years, backed up both Brown and Bratkowski in 1957 and '58, and placekicked all the way through the rest of his career. "I was not beaten up," Blanda said. "I got cut in 1959, but I had a job."

Rick Casares and his teammates loved it when Blanda came onto the field. "Blanda knew his stuff," Casares said. "He knew our offense cold. He was confident and was one of the greatest field generals. He came into the huddle after Halas put him in a game at our 15-yard line. He says, 'OK! Tough Mo! 32 on 2! Red! Bang!' He used to run to the line of scrimmage, and I'd grab him and say, 'George-o, you gotta slow down.' His adrenaline was flowing. He'd be at the line of scrimmage starting the call before we were set. He was such a competitor. No indecisions. He knew his stuff. He took us down the field, five plays, touchdown. Boom. And he never played another play that game."

A man takes his team down the field, scores fast, and never returns. Why?

"We were on the 10-yard line, when Halas sent in a play," Casares said. " 'Christ, I'm not calling that!' Blanda said. And he called a little swing to me. He completed it for a touchdown. Halas was on the sideline and looking like he's standing on the edge of a cliff, waiting for Blanda to come off the field. His face was all red. He was screaming at him, 'Why didn't you call the play I sent in?' 'I knew it wouldn't work,' Blanda said. He sat his ass down, and he didn't play another play," Casares said.

"That was Blanda's last year with the team," he continued. "He was just great. The field goals. Forget about it. He was just automatic. He never thought he'd miss one. We had the greatest sense of security. All we had to do was get past the 50, and we had three with George."

"When Halas decided a person was through, he would convince him not to come back," said Sprinkle. "It was a player's decision. If he did that, then Halas could put him on the reserve list, and he'd still be the property of the Bears. Blanda said, 'Give me my contract.' 'No,' Halas said. 'I'm not quitting,' Blanda said." If Halas wanted to let Blanda go, he had to give him his release. Halas didn't give Blanda his release, so George had to lay out a year. Halas had to pay him. Blanda went to commissioner Bert Bell, and he got paid for that year.

"I think it's more than that," said Cooper Rollow. "When people think of Blanda, they think of him as getting into spats with Halas. It's his opinion that he wasn't really appreciated here." Rollow attended the 1959 Bears' alumni party as a guest of Halas, who always invited the media. He spent a few minutes with Blanda, who was sitting out that year.

"What are you going to do with the rest of your life?" Rollow asked.

"Oh, don't worry. I'm gonna play some football."

"Where?"

"Can't tell you."

"What do you mean, you can't tell me?"

"There's something going on that you don't know about."

"That's all he would say," Rollow said in 2002. "That 'something' was the formation of the American Football League. That would have been a great story for me if I'd been smart enough to get it."

"The thing is, Halas cut Blanda," a still-angry Casares said 43 years later. "We went into the 1959 season without a kicker. We had the best!" Blanda hung around with his now former teammates all season, meeting them for lunch near Wrigley Field. "Blanda would be there at least once or twice a week. He missed playing so. He couldn't go to another team. Halas cut him and forced him into retirement. That's what Blanda said."

"He [Halas] didn't realize at all that Blanda was a great player," Gleason mused. "Had he let Blanda open up the field in the NFL, the way he did in the AFL—" He paused to shake his head. "Whew!"

"The next year, he told us he made more money with Houston than all the years with the Bears," said Casares. "We had a line—'Poor George.' And here he was winning championships and making all the money and success, which we Bears were so happy about. Halas did him the greatest favor, but losing him was terrible."

Jeannie Morris is certain Halas believed that Blanda and others like him—young Mike Ditka, George Allen, and, later, Jim Finks—were threats. "There are different kinds of threats, but they're threats," Morris said, "not threats to his power, but to his control—the sense of control over the Bears. The team itself was what he was in love with, nothing else. He felt like everybody should be subservient to the team."

After Blanda quarterbacked and kicked the Houston Oilers to back-to-back AFL titles in 1960 and '61, he joined the Oakland Raiders in 1966, where he kicked for another decade, to retire as pro football's all-time leading scorer. In 1970, at age 43, Blanda thrilled the nation when he led the Raiders to a series of comeback victories as a backup quarterback in relief of Daryle Lamonica, along with making clutch placekicks. Halas, according to Jerry Vainisi, admitted over a glass of wine in the late '70s that getting ride of Blanda was a "major mistake."

By his mid-70s, in 2003, a more mellow George Blanda sang a different tune: "I have the utmost respect for George Halas as the founder of the National Football League. He was a great, great man." The truly great man in Blanda's life, though, is the "genius" who runs the Raiders. "Al Davis is the greatest owner in sports," Blanda said. "And he is closest to George Halas in the way both were great coaches, great football men, shrewd businessmen, managers, and outstanding judges of talent."

Blanda said the McCaskey family has treated him wonderfully and he is proud to be a former Bear. He entered the Hall of Fame, though, as a Raider. Blanda also said former Bears such as Connor, Sprinkle, Hill, and Casares would have nothing bad to say about Halas.

How little he knew.

SEVENTEEN

TUBE OR CONSEQUENCES

*O*n Monday morning, November 24, 1952, the *Chicago Tribune*'s George Strickler likely irritated many of his local readers when he wrote, "37,508 hysterical fans and millions of video witnesses lived a lifetime of thrills as the Chicago Bears snatched victory from the Detroit Lions, heavy favorites, in Wrigley Field yesterday, 24–23."

Millions of video witnesses? Not in Chicago, where the last time anyone had seen the Bears on television was a rainy December afternoon in 1949. "Strickler," Bill Jauss noted, "always had a reason for inserting a word like *video* into a story." He was writing for the readers in that great "Chicagoland" circulation area who had seen the game on television.

"When it came to television, nobody saw it the way Halas did. George was a visionary," Charles Brizzolara said.

The fear of giving away the product the way his landlord, Cubs' owner Phil Wrigley, did with televised baseball games was the precise reason Halas had his business manager and, in television parlance, operations producer, Rudy Custer, draw a radius 75 miles away from

State and Madison, and declare anything inside the arc a "blackout area." That is why Halas told Bert Bell to draw similar boundaries around every other league city when home games were being televised. The blackout remained league policy until Congress changed the law in 1973.

Outside the arc, millions of fans enjoyed televised access to every home game that the Bears and Cardinals carried on their own network, the largest independent television grid in America. The owner, operator, and, in effect, executive producer was none other than George Halas himself. In fact, Halas had been at this television thing since 1947. George Halas was Roone Arledge before Roone Arledge was Roone Arledge!

George Halas certainly did not invent television, but he was far ahead of the pack in his understanding of the medium's incredible potential and long-term value. Conversely, the astute Halas feared that television was "this time bomb" that could destroy everything he and his league partners so carefully constructed.

Thanks to the labors of Custer and moonlighting producer Bill Fay, whose day job was sports editor of *Collier's* magazine, Halas, in 1951, fashioned the first network to carry pro football to the masses. His Falstaff Beer–Standard Oil Network became the prototype for the way CBS, NBC, ABC, and, later, Fox would blanket the country with NFL telecasts from August through January.

The marriage of television and pro football that Halas brokered literally changed the American way of life. Thanksgiving became a meal eaten between football telecasts, and the world stopped on Super Bowl Sunday.

In early 1947, Halas still believed that gate receipts drove success. The Bears led the league in profits. The Bears and his May and Halas operations had just moved into larger digs at 233 West Madison, between the west end of the Loop and the Civic Opera House, and Halas needed to find new revenue sources. Ralph Brizzolara's temporary bleachers would be ready for the 1948 season, but that wasn't enough.

In late spring, Halas was hard at work, when the phone rang. As was his lifelong wont, whether at home or in the office, Halas picked it up. He kept Frances Osborne and her steno pool busy enough without wasting their time screening his calls. Besides, he felt the public needed to know that he was accessible. "Hey, George, you doing anything later in the day?" asked the caller. It was Don Maxwell, still city editor at the *Tribune* but soon to be appointed to the top job, editor. "I've got something you should see."

Shortly after 4:30, Halas strode into the Gothic structure that houses the daily that its eccentric publisher, Robert Rutherford McCormick, boldly called the World's Greatest Newspaper. The colonel so loved that motto that he plastered it across the masthead. From the *Trib*'s entry into radio in 1924, McCormick used those initials, *WGN*, as the station's call letters.

The reporters and copyboys in the immense city room stayed their distance as Halas entered Maxwell's office, where his friend motioned to him to lay down his hat and overcoat on a corner chair. "Hey, Don," the coach said, a grin splitting his lantern jaw, "just what is this damn thing you want me to see so bad?"

Maxwell rose from his chair and pointed to a little rectangular box placed on a nearby end table. It was about two feet square in front, framing an opaque window perhaps nine inches across on the diagonal. From the front, it stretched back three feet.

"Just watch, George," Maxwell said as he walked to the set. Maxwell fingered the on-off switch that also controlled the volume and deftly rotated it to the right. The screen turned white and started to split like a curtain as a high-pitched whine followed by strange gurgling emanated from its insides. "It'll take a few minutes to warm up," the editor said.

After what seemed an eternity to Halas, an odd-looking line drawing sharpened into focus on the screen while a steady, ear-splitting high-pitched tone shrieked from the speaker below the picture tube. Quickly, Maxwell lowered the volume. The drawing of a derricklike tower with waves radiating from the top appeared at the top of the screen. Below that tower stood an Indian warrior in full headdress. "WBKB, Channel 4, Chicago" was printed inside a set of concentric circles.

"That's a test pattern," Maxwell said as he checked his watch. It was 4:45, time for the first program of the day. "Here she goes." They saw the test pattern dissolve into an American flag that rippled in the wind as a marching band played the national anthem. When the music finished, the station logo appeared on the screen. "You are tuned to WBKB, property of Paramount Pictures and Balaban and Katz Broadcasting, Incorporated, in Chicago," an off-camera announcer said.

"There it is, George," a pleased Maxwell said as he gestured toward the box. "Television." They watched the images for a few minutes. "What do you think?"

"Shit, Don, the screen is so small," Halas said. "You can't see much of a football game on that. The picture's so fuzzy."

"For now," Maxwell said, nodding. "Soon the picture tubes will get much larger and clearer. They're working on it right now. Hell, they're already testing color."

"How soon?" the impatient Halas asked.

Maxwell ignored the question. "This is the fastest-growing thing ever. Look, George, they've already got sound and pictures. It took the movies a good 15 years to go from silents to talkies. This thing won't be a toy for grown-ups, either."

Maxwell told Halas that any image a camera can capture can be seen that instant on a set miles away from the transmitter. "In time, you'll be able to deliver that picture into every home in America," Maxwell said. "They already have it going in the East. That little box will change the American way of life."

"How about your business, Don?"

"We don't know what it'll do to newspapers. But the colonel's all for it, and that's good enough for me." Halas was well aware that McCormick was an early backer of radio and that WGN had made millions for the Tribune Company through the years. "The colonel had vision then," Maxwell said. "Publishers who took the other tack regretted it. He's ordered WGN to gear up for pictures."

"I can't see a football field shrunk to that size," Halas said as he pointed to the set. Maxwell again ignored the comment and looked back with a mocking smile that Halas recognized as a challenge. "What are *you* going to do about television, George?"

When Halas shrugged, Maxwell fired another salvo. "Television is coming fast. We'd both better treat it as a friend rather than an enemy or rival," Maxwell said. "Remember, George, you can squeeze just so many people into Wrigley Field. Television's audience will be huge. The potential is unlimited."

Television was strictly experimental in 1939 when NBC televised the Brooklyn Dodgers and Cincinnati Reds doubleheader opener from Ebbets Field on August 26, 1939, as an adjunct to the RCA exhibit at the New York World's Fair. The network tried pro football on a cloudy Sunday, October 22, 1939. NBC telecast the first pro football game, again from Ebbets Field. Allen Walz called the action as Potsy Clark's Brooklyn Dodgers beat Bert Bell's Philadelphia Eagles 24–13 before 13,051 fans in attendance. The telecast was not acknowledged in the Monday-morning newspapers.

Out in Chicago in 1940, while RCA and Zenith raced to develop television, another experimental station was on the move. The fledgling's call sign was W9XBK, an initialism derived from the owners of Chicago's far-flung Balaban and Katz movie theater chain. The Balabans operated the largest chain of movie houses in the greater Chicago area, if not the country, with ornate palaces in the Loop, Chicago' vast neighborhoods, far-flung suburbs, and smaller Midwestern cities as far away as South Bend. Going to a B&K "show" was as much an experience for moviegoers as the films themselves.

The movie business, which underwent heavy retooling costs as talkies supplanted silents, hit the skids in the Depression. Barney Balaban moved to Hollywood and reinvigorated Paramount financially and artistically. In Chicago, brother John raked in the money as the theaters, mirroring the New Deal economy, revived and prospered.

In 1940, the Balabans applied to the government for a license to W9XBK. They hired the best man available to run it in the person of retired Navy captain Bill Eddy, an electronics wizard who helped develop radar. The Balabans assigned Eddy space in the State-Lake Building at 190 North State, gave him an ample budget, and issued a simple directive: build the station and get it on the air. Captain Eddy hired every bright young electronics engineer he could find. Eighty-hour weeks were the standard as Eddy's engineers conducted test after test.

Everything stopped in place on Sunday, December 7, 1941, when the Japanese bombed the sleeping Pacific Fleet battleships into scrap metal at Pearl Harbor. All television development ceased and would stay that way for the duration as the economy went on a war footing. Captain Eddy and most of his W9XBK technicians worked on radar over at Navy Pier. When the war news improved in 1943, the Balabans successfully petitioned the government to convert W9XBK into commercial station WBKB, and they aired a signal of sorts on the channel 4 frequency to the 50 or so sets in the Chicago area.

The peacetime economy took off in early 1946 when shipload after shipload of soldiers, sailors, airmen, and marines landed daily for discharge and demobilization. Home again, with money burning holes in their pockets to spend on everything from denied necessities like cars to luxury items, the vets were prime candidates for something new and wonderful. Something like television.

Back at RCA headquarters in New York, General Sarnoff put out the word to his factories in Camden and Indianapolis: turn out television sets. Now. And put an RCA set in every American home, and sell America on the idea of watching NBC programs.

Returning veteran William S. Paley came home, gathered his troops, and told them that CBS also was going to dive into television. Paley said they would make some sets but would concentrate their effort on entertainment product, not hardware, to kick NBC around the block. He then wooed NBC's biggest stars and best producers and writers.

In another part of New York, an enthusiastic scientist-operator named Allen Dumont was building his own sets with their distinctive circular picture tube. Operating on a lower budget, Dumont knew that his best route to the victory stand with larger NBC and CBS was to knock off NBC's weak court-mandated spin-off, ABC. Dumont knew that the way to win on his limited bankroll was to air sports as a staple in his live programming.

In early 1947, those 50 sets in the Chicago area a year earlier had grown to nearly 500, and WBKB, now a newly minted CBS affiliate, was in full operation on channel 4. As fast they could be assembled and boxed, sets moved out of the factories and onto the trains, where they rolled into Chicago's huge freight yards. Many were trucked directly to department stores, appliance outlets, and radio shops.

Other receivers landed in downtown showrooms, where passersby gathered each night in front of huge sidewalk picture windows to gawk at the new marvel. Bars and hotels snapped up most of the early sets, but the word was out that television was the rage, perhaps the biggest thing ever, and sets could be had. Prices fell as production kept up with demand. The demand only intensified, and aerials sprang up on rooftop after rooftop in town and country.

By Labor Day 1947, the Chicago area had 7,000 sets. Captain Eddy decided to televise sports—not just the scripted stuff, like wrestling, but also baseball, hockey, and the singular game that best suited television, football. In late summer, the captain's crew ran a test from Notre Dame Stadium in South Bend, Indiana. Unlike the subway World Series that would be played in New York in October, in which NBC merely had to beam a direct microwave signal from the ballparks to the Empire State Building, South Bend presented distinct problems.

Television transmissions follow the curvature of the earth. At a distance of 71 miles from Chicago as the crow flies, South Bend was too far to deliver a line-of-sight direct signal to the big city. Why not set up a microwave relay, one of his engineers figured. To boost the signal, the crew erected a 144-foot tall tower in New Carlisle, Indiana, a midway point between Notre Dame Stadium and another tower in Michigan City, 34 miles away. From Michigan City, they had a clear shot 37 miles across the lake to Lincoln Tower, a Chicago skyscraper just north of the Loop, where the signal could be relayed into home plate three blocks away at the WBKB studios. The test worked.

With great fanfare, WBKB announced it would broadcast the home games of Frank Leahy's soon-to-be national champion Fighting Irish, led by Heisman-winning quarterback Johnny Lujack, whom Halas already made his top pick as a future. Notre Dame's rabid Chicago following and Halas's equally frenzied Bear maniacs were in heaven.

As defending National Football League champions, the Bears had become a "tough" ticket, nearly selling out Wrigley Field each week. Eddy knew their popularity would sell more television sets as it helped him sell advertising time. Assured that his crew could send a sophisticated microwave relay signal across the lake from South Bend, Eddy reckoned a five-mile hop from Wrigley Field would be a lead-pipe cinch. And he still was the only game in town.

When Halas called on Eddy, he fully expected to pay to get his games televised. Before Halas could speak, the captain launched a preemptive strike: "I will pay you $900 a game for your six home dates." A few minutes later, the delighted Papa Bear left 190 State Street with a $5,400 guarantee. Don Maxwell had been right on the money.

By 1948, Eddy's WBKB was the leader in sports television. The station aired Cubs baseball from Wrigley Field, two periods of Blackhawks hockey from Chicago Stadium on Sunday nights (to hold viewer interest, with just one between-periods intermission), Notre Dame football, and the wrestling matches. Eddy needed a renewal from Halas and the Bears to complete his roster, but the suddenly guarded Papa Bear decided to sit tight. He knew what was coming.

By late autumn 1948, Eddy and WBKB were battling two tough competitors, and a third was on the way. The *Tribune*'s WGN-TV on channel 9 and ABC's WENR-TV on channel 7 had come on line that year. In New York, Sarnoff was hounding his managers at the NBC-owned-and-operated WNBQ-TV to complete their tests and get that station up and running. They waited until January 5, 1949, when the networks finally connected the coaxial cable from Chicago and the Midwest to the East Coast.

Until the network linkups, WGN-TV and WENR-TV copied Eddy, filling their limited programming slates with announcers who read news scripts, some over still pictures; B movies; old Saturday-matinee shoot-'em-ups; puppet shows; and a heavy diet of wrestling.

The *Tribune*'s WGN plunged into television in a big way. The area now had 16,000 sets, a good quarter of them at corner saloons and downtown hotel bars. WGN-TV established a sports presence even before its official April 4 launch. It aired Arch Ward's Golden Gloves in a March trial run. Jack Brickhouse, already a 14-year broadcasting veteran at age 32, called the blow-by-blows. Brickhouse, in those days, announced everything from baseball to football to wrestling and election coverage, running from job to job, be it radio or Topsy-like television.

Before the 1948 season, Maxwell told Halas that WGN-TV wanted to televise the Bears, with Brickhouse calling the action. WENR-TV, the fledgling ABC station, put its bid on the table as well. Halas still would not budge. Playing before sellouts every week at home and away, Halas let people believe that the 1947 telecasts were a one-shot deal and that he no longer needed television. The old Papa Bear was sitting pretty with the television ace up his sleeve, ready to pounce.

Desperately needing something besides its regular "Wrestling from Rainbo" show, WENR-TV granted Halas airtime to run a filmed highlights show. Custer sold it to Standard Oil of Indiana, and Bill Fay edited the highlights. The "Bears Quarterback Club" aired each Tuesday night on Channel 7 at 8:30. The host was football's greatest hero, Harold "Red" Grange of Illinois, still revered in Chicago as the man who carried pro football into the big time.

Introduced as "Old number 77, the Galloping Ghost himself," Grange, at age 45, delivered a play-by-play of sorts. The cohost, Bears assistant coach Luke Johnsos, grateful that his boss had given him this chance to make extra money and gain exposure for his packaging business, chipped in with the "inside" commentary. For the next half hour, they showed clips of the previous game and talked up the team.

"There's that old split buck, Luke. Look at that big guy go!" gushed the Redhead when one of the Bears ripped off a big gain. "The kid's really coming around, Red," chimed in Luke, the partisan expert. Among the game action, Grange and Johnsos weaved in reminiscences about noted former teammates, men of their era such as Bronko Nagurski and Jim McMillen, or current stars, such as Sid Luckman, Sid's heir apparent Johnny Lujack, and colorful end Eddie Sprinkle.

Without fail, the two buttered up the off-screen presence who loomed over every facet of his team, owner-coach George Halas. "George is a great guy," Grange would say on a weekly basis. "And still the smartest in the business," Johnsos would chime in. Viewership grew by the week as the show created new fans for pro football and the Bears. Grange made it possible for Halas, who was uncomfortable on camera, to avoid a medium he never chose to master, let alone the broiling klieg lights in the ice-cold studio.

The more the Bears and Cardinals kept winning, and the more the viewers saw programs like "Bears Quarterback Club," the more they wanted to see the real thing on the screen. Live. Late in the season, the station managers called on Halas again, hats in hand. He held firm.

Down on the South Side, the Cardinals badly wanted to get on television. As good as, if not better than, the Bears, the defending league champions remained mired in the low ground in Chicago's all-important publicity and exposure war. The Big Red finally found an unlikely ally at Tribune Tower with Halas's friends. In mid-November, Cardinals general manager Ray Benningsen cut a deal with WGN-TV through his friend Brickhouse. As a result, Brickhouse and his baseball color man Harry Creighton handled the "exclusive telecast of the Cards-Lions game from Detroit on Thanksgiving Day."

The Cardinals won at Detroit, and both the Bears and Big Red easily won their December 5 tune-ups to go 10-and-1 and set the stage for the Western Division showdown. Longtime *Tribune* writer Wilfrid Smith sensed the charged atmosphere. "No Cardinal-Bear game has caught the complete attention of the sports public as this since Harold (Red) Grange joined the Bears in 1925," Smith wrote. With all tickets sold, and expecting a record standing-room-only crowd, the crafty Halas relented and let the game go on local television. For his price.

Partisans with access to a set had a choice of two telecasts. Cardinals fans could dial in WGN-TV on channel 9 and get Brickhouse. Bears fans who wanted their own slant could choose WENR on channel 7 and hear the Galloping Ghost root openly along with them. All who watched saw one of the best contests of the postwar era as the Cardinals came from behind in the fourth quarter to beat the Bears 24–21 before a record Wrigley Field crowd of 51,283.

The Pabst Brewing Company paid Halas $5,000 to carry the WENR-TV telecast, enough to cover the salary for a decent lineman and almost as much as Captain Eddy paid for all of 1947. Halas pocketed an undisclosed sum from WGN-TV as well. While Halas had mixed feelings, nobody was happier about the game than the managers at WGN-TV and WENR-TV. Those viewers who saw either station's telecast had witnessed the future, but they would see no more televised games in 1948, and few others in coming seasons.

Throughout 1949, Bears fans clamored for more. Halas, the power broker, again stood fast until the season-ender with the Cardinals at Wrigley Field. A cold December rain drenched Chicago all day, and the field quickly turned to mud. Over WENR-TV, Grange described Lujack's greatest professional game as he passed for a then-NFL-record 468 yards and six touchdowns in a 52–21 Bears victory. The Bears, who had sold out the game, announced a gate at just over 50,000, but no more than 15,000 fans braved the conditions and bothered to show up at Wrigley Field. Halas did not like it one bit and was quick to blame television.

Heading into 1950, sport was facing its first serious dilemma with the new medium. Cubs owner Phillip K. Wrigley had embraced television in 1948. Convinced by initial returns that television would soar, Wrigley let WGN-TV and WBKB air competing telecasts of Cubs home games from 1948 through 1950. WENR-TV had made it a threesome for select weekend games in 1949 but never returned. WBKB barely lasted through the 1950 season, as WGN-TV with Brickhouse at the mike and the power of the *Tribune* locked up an exclusive deal with the Cubs and also aired White Sox day games from Chicago.

All this exposure, Wrigley reasoned, would create new fans and, most important, lure the curious to the ballpark. Even with a lousy product, P. K. Wrigley sold it hard. On WGN-TV, a promo featuring announcer Paul Fogarty wearing a Hawaiian shirt invited the viewers to visit Wrigley Field and enjoy a picnic. "Oh, yes," Fogarty added, "you also can see a major-league ball game." (One wag noted that any resemblance between the Cubs of that era and major-league baseball was pure coincidence.)

Despite some of the worst baseball ever displayed in any major-league setting, the Cubs' attendance held fast. Averaging close to a million fans, Wrigley gave full credit to television. Thousands of

Chicago-area youngsters, who raced home after school in the '50s to catch the last couple of innings of WGN-TV's telecasts, became Cubs fans for life. Years later, hardly anybody blinked at the obvious conflict of interest when Brickhouse, the pied piper who created that rabid following, was invited to sit on the Cubs' board of directors.

Before the 1950 football season, Halas viewed the future through darkened lenses. He had seen how unlimited telecasts consumed baseball's minor leagues like a raging prairie fire. He vowed that would not happen to his National Football League. His steel-trap mind always reverted to that 1949 finale. He just couldn't expunge the nightmarish sight of all those empty seats despite a sellout. The Papa Bear's heart only hardened the more when his spies confirmed that a large number of the no-shows, not willing to brave that miserable December afternoon, either stayed home or packed corner taverns to watch on television. Once you lose the gate for any reason, Halas believed, people would opt for convenience every time. The old easy chair.

That lone game and the experience of the 1950 Los Angeles Rams provided all the ammunition Halas would need. In 1949, the Rams drew 205,000 fans in six games—in a two-team city. A year later, with the AAFC now dead but with all their home games on television, regular-season attendance for six games dropped to 110,000, barely more than stadium capacity for a single contest at the vast Los Angeles Memorial Coliseum. Admiral, which had bought the television rights from Rams owner Dan Reeves, had to refund $307,000 in lost game-day revenues.

Halas carried the television issue to his crony, commissioner Bert Bell. Bell was caught in a bind. He could read other gate numbers as well as Halas, but he was equally aware how powerful television would be for his league. Bell had seen what happened in his hometown, Philadelphia. The Eagles, two-time defending NFL champions, quickly sold out their 1950 opener against the Cleveland Browns, the defunct AAFC's perennial champions. Interest was so high that the Eagles moved the game to outsized Municipal Stadium, where they more than doubled sales for their regular home venue, Shibe Park. The buildup captured the national fancy, so the Eagles let Dumont carry the game to the outposts of the coaxial cable, as far west as Omaha.

The pro-Eagle stadium crowd of 71,237 and huge television audience that anticipated a Philadelphia rout before the kickoff watched in amazement as Paul Brown's well-drilled units, led by quarterback Otto Graham on offense and end Lenny Ford on defense, demolished the defending champions 35–10.

Bell read the ratings report and saw what a valuable ally television could be. It was clear that pro football could thrive on television. Yet, Bell had to honor Halas. He consulted with the NFL's other influential owners, most prominently, Washington Redskins owner George Preston Marshall and the Maras, Jack and Wellington, sons of New York Giants founder Tim Mara. The commissioner then announced a new Halas-directed policy. Starting in 1951, Bell imposed a local blackout rule on home telecasts. To preserve the economic health of the league, Bell decreed that no game could be televised within a 75-mile radius of the home city. The arc Halas and Custer created.

The Justice Department then filed a brief charging that the NFL and its 12 teams illegally restricted television coverage of games. Giants president Jack Mara countered with a well-documented brief that showed a direct correlation between steadily declining attendance and the proliferation of sets in metropolitan New York. Mara noted that 91.5 percent of the Giants' reserved seats at the Polo Grounds were sold in the Eastern Division championship season of 1946; 1950 attendance fell to 62.5 percent of capacity, a year when the Giants forced a divisional playoff with the Browns.

After nearly two years of litigation, Judge Allan K. Grimm issued a ruling in 1952 that the league would live by for the next 21. Grimm ruled that the 75-mile television blackout within a team's home area was legal but added that the league could not prevent road-game telecasts nor stop radio broadcasts of any kind.

The league was ecstatic. Road telecasts were exactly what Bell and the owners sought all along to create fans for pro football. Also, by late 1951, the coaxial cable was completed, and the NFL now could tap the lucrative California and West Coast market as well.

For Chicagoans, the TV coin came up tails on both sides. Because the city had two teams, one would play at home each week while the other was on the road. Thus, Chicago was always blacked out, with two exceptions—both of which were Bears losses. Grange and CBS carried the September 29, 1957, opener at Green Bay to dedicate the new City Stadium. The Packers scored a late touchdown to win 21–17. The other telecast came on Saturday night, October 4, 1958, when young Johnny Unitas passed the Bears dizzy in a 51–38 Baltimore Colts victory televised on WGN-TV.

Halas never forgot Don Maxwell's admonition. "Get Chicagoland," the *Tribune*'s home-delivery area: Illinois, Wisconsin, Indiana, and Iowa. To build a Chicagoland network, Halas needed a transmission system. Maxwell suggested he contact Dumont, now existing on *Tribune*-funded life support.

In 1949, Dumont established a "fourth network" led by a nightly adventure serial, "Captain Video," and low-budget prime-time shows. The Dumont lineup included "Rocky King, Detective," starring former B-movie actor Roscoe Karns; Brickhouse's "Wrestling from Marigold" twice a week; and a weekly Friday-night show, the "Cavalcade of Stars." John Crosby, the *New York Herald Tribune*'s influential TV critic, flipped over "Cavalcade" star Jackie Gleason and second banana Art Carney, paying special notice to their "Honeymooners" sketches. Paley started watching, knew they could do for CBS what Milton Berle had done for NBC, and signed them to long-term contracts as soon as they gained their freedom.

Dumont entered sports immediately. With Maxwell as intermediary, the network contacted Halas, who, early in 1951, told the Cardinals all they had to do was come aboard and hang on for the ride. Cardinals boss Walter Wolfner signed on the spot.

Custer ran the network. WGN-TV picked up the production. Grange called the play-by-play and, when games got out of hand, spun yarns about his playing days. Fay filled with color. Both teams, Custer hoped, would net a profit. That first season, the Halas network aired Bears and Cardinals home games on eight Sundays to Minneapolis; Rock Island, Illinois; Omaha; Indianapolis and Bloomington, Indiana; Columbus and Dayton, Ohio; Louisville; and Nashville.

Local stations sold advertising to pick up line costs. The TV network lost $1,750 that season, but the broadcast operation ran well in the black thanks to the "Bears Quarterback Club" show and the radio rights on WIND in Chicago.

Custer upped the total to 15 stations in 1952. Standard Oil bought half the commercial breaks at $30,000 for the entire season. The network even was able to telecast a Monday-night game between the Cardinals and Redskins from Comiskey Park. Custer's efforts paid off. "The second season, we made $8,500," Custer said.

By 1953, Dumont was in a fast fade as Gleason jumped to CBS. The network carried a Saturday-night package shown in Chicago built around the Steelers, Eagles, and reconstituted Baltimore Colts, with guest appearances from the Cleveland Browns. Dumont's stable of fine young announcers included Pittsburgher Ray Scott, New York–based Chris Schenkel, and Chuck Thompson, of Baltimore. Dumont no longer could afford Halas, who wanted more stations for his network than they could drum up.

Although the Halas-engineered rules prevented NFL telecasts in Chicago's number two television market because the Bears or Cardinals were always at home, ABC, now infused with Paramount Pictures money, approached Halas with an offer for two years at $50,000 a season. In Halas's case, ABC was letting him use its lines to transmit his games, because it knew football would build viewer loyalty and network recognition in the hinterlands.

In 1953, WBKB, now in business as the ABC-Paramount–owned station in Chicago on channel 7, handled the production with a three-camera pickup, shooting from each 20-yard line and midfield. Custer was extremely active that winter and spring. He expanded the network throughout Illinois, including Rockford, Springfield, and Champaign, southward through to St. Louis, and even over to Madison, Wisconsin, in Packers territory.

In another quick strike, Custer, who already had the Midwest south of Michigan and west of Ohio in his pocket, aced out Marshall and the Redskins as the Bears' network tied up leasing rights to the cable in the Deep South. On one link, he grabbed Nashville, Birmingham, Tampa, and Miami. On the other link, he cut through the Mississippi Valley, moving through Memphis and Jackson to New Orleans and west into Dallas and Fort Worth and on to Los Angeles.

"By the end, our network was the largest independent sports network in the country, at a profit of $153,000," Custer said. The shrewd Halas knew it was time to fold. The Bears were a football team, he reasoned, not a broadcasting company. Line charges gobbled up profits. Worst, the network had become impossible to manage for just two men, Custer and Fay, both of whom were moonlighting from their regular duties. "I also did advertising, public relations, travel arrangements, the stadium, box office, credentials, halftime entertainment, and personnel records," Custer said. "Just about everything but coaching and scouting."

When ABC offered to pay $100,000 to extend the deal for the 1955 season, Papa Bear reluctantly agreed to hang on for one more season. While Halas and his coaching staff put their charges through training camp in Rensselaer, Indiana, a one-time-only horse race back in Chicago altered the sports broadcasting landscape forever. It was the most-discussed single event since the War Admiral–Seabiscuit match race of 1938, and again, it involved two champion Thoroughbreds.

The actor Don Ameche and a group of his Hollywood friends, among them Jimmy Durante and Desi Arnaz, approached Arch Ward's old AAFC ally, Chicago horse-racing impresario Benjamin Lindheimer. They persuaded him to promote a winner-take-all match race to pair Swaps, the California-bred Kentucky Derby champion, and Nashua, the Churchill Downs also-ran who won the Preakness and Belmont Stakes after Swaps was shipped west.

When Lindheimer proposed the idea to the owners, Rex Ellsworth for Swaps and William Woodward Jr. for Nashua, both men accepted with a handshake. The race was set for Lindheimer's Washington Park on August 31. Never before had a sporting event of this magnitude been telecast. Interest ran so high that Lindheimer sold—more correctly, gave away—television rights to CBS-TV, which signed a single sponsor, Tums, to pick up production costs for a song, perhaps $10,000.

The telecast from Lindheimer's Washington Park, in Homewood, 25 miles south of Chicago's Loop, signed on at 5:00 P.M. CDT on Wednesday, August 31, 1955. In less than a half hour, Nashua and jockey Eddie Arcaro routed Swaps and rider Bill Shoemaker in the breakout event for television sports. America had slightly more than 100 million TV sets then. A. C. Nielsen reported that more than half of them were tuned to CBS on that Wednesday afternoon, giving CBS

a phenomenal 50+ rating. In New York, the salespeople and accountants took note and sprang into action, as did the NFL.

The Dumont Saturday-night package was simply too limited to
give the league the requisite muscle to attack and supplant baseball
as the national sport. Before 1956, autumn Sundays in America were
family-oriented days of rest: church, the big early-afternoon dinner,
perhaps a drive in the country, family gatherings, reading, and conversation. Only those city dwellers who had tickets attended pro football. For the networks, Sunday-afternoon television was a wasteland
of mostly commercial-free or, when sponsored, low-rated, cultural
programs.

The NFL didn't know that for a good two years, the networks had
tracked ratings on the Bears', Giants', and Redskins' networks. They
saw how those games scored in places such as Rock Island, Utica,
and Richmond. Factor in the Swaps-Nashua match race numbers, and
the networks had proof positive that sports would sell and sell big.

Bell visited CBS that fall and left with a $1 million annual regular-
season package, to start in 1956. Every team except Cleveland and
Baltimore, which retained NBC tie-ins in their hometowns, and Pittsburgh, through KDKA-Westinghouse, would dip into the CBS package. Bell then walked over to 30 Rockefeller Plaza and sold
championship-game rights to NBC. The league never looked back as
Bell's successor Pete Rozelle ran the rights fees to the billion-dollar
level, and Rozelle's successor Paul Tagliabue kept driving it onward
and upward.

"One of the first things Rozelle did was go for a single league contract, the CBS contract in 1961," said Don Weiss, executive director
of the NFL during much of the Rozelle era. The key was revenue
sharing, each team an equal partner. And the rights fees made it possible for Halas and his partners to emerge into the permanent black
with plenty of cushion. That meant he no longer had to take out off-
season loans at American National Bank.

When Rozelle told Halas and the Maras in New York what he was
doing, they fanned out and buttonholed Art Rooney and George Preston Marshall, who then spread the word. Everyone signed up, and
the single act that made the National Football League the most pow-

erful entity in sport, with no fiscally weak partners, was fact. A federal judge struck down the deal, but the astute Rozelle went directly to Congress that September. By the end of the month, President Kennedy signed the bill that gave the NFL its right to negotiate comprehensive single-network contracts.

Halas immediately claimed telecast rights to his former network cities. Late in life, he admitted he did it to keep any other teams from airing their games in Chicago. That worked until merger with the AFL altered the landscape again and the league began to air doubleheaders to cover the increased rights fees.

Many changes would occur. When the NFL signed its first contract with CBS in 1956, Grange and his new sidekick, future Bears Hall of Famer George Connor, called both Bears and Cardinals home games as before through 1959. When the Cardinals moved to St. Louis, Grange and Connor traveled with the Bears, and Chicago fans got to see their Monsters of the Midway, at least on the road, for the first time until Congress lifted the home-city blackout in 1974. Grange retired after 1963, and CBS assigned non-Chicagoans to the play-by-play mike: Jack Buck and then, in 1966, Lindsay Nelson.

Through 1967, each telecast offered a single video production and split, highly partisan audio packages geared to each hometown. For instance, when the Bears played the Packers, Chicago fans would hear Grange and Connor while Green Bay got Ray Scott and Tony Canadeo.

When the league signed a new deal in 1968 that considerably raised the rights fee, the networks scaled back to single, neutral announcing teams. Productions had become multicamera, multi-slow-motion-replay extravaganzas. For George Halas, the television time bomb would tick on for his heirs and their contemporaries. He and the National Football League had arrived, and he could take it to the bank.

EIGHTEEN

BEARS DOWN

"I used to try to pull his leg," George Connor said on a warm spring afternoon in 2002. "Every year about a month before practice started, the coach sent everybody a letter. He'd write, 'I want you to go out and run a mile; get toughened up. By the way, a lot of valuable time is lost with dental problems. Make sure you have your teeth checked and your spare set of dentures fixed.' So, I wrote him a letter back. I said I had everything checked and my extra set of dentures was ready, and I finished by saying, 'Let's hope we can put the bite on our opponents.'"

From 1951 through 1953, Connor's All-Pro play on both sides of the ball, and the nonstop fiery competitiveness of Sprinkle and Blanda, were about all the bite the Bears had. The Bears put on a false front the first two-thirds of the 1951 season. A fandom that had known nothing but winning since 1930 had every reason to believe they were contenders.

After two years as Rams head coach, Clark Shaughnessy was back with Halas, armed with the highfalutin title technical adviser, a super assistant of sorts who freely dispensed his expertise to anyone willing to listen, others who didn't, and at least one top staffer who thought he was a 24-karat fraud. Hunk Anderson, whom Halas called the greatest line coach who ever lived, had long despised the guru of

the modern T formation. Anderson noted in his book *Notre Dame,
Chicago Bears, and Hunk* that Shaughnessy dropped in during the
1942 season when he and Luke Johnsos were running the show in
Halas's absence. Anderson asked for Shaughnessy's advice on a play.
"Call an end run," Shaughnessy declared. "Which one do you want
me to run, and what blocking do you want me to use?" Anderson
asked, noting that the Bears had 28 end-run plays, using all four
backs, with many blocking variations for each play.

" 'Any one. Any end run,' was Clark's *expert* reply," Anderson
wrote. He invited Shaughnessy to sit down and stay out of the way.

In the week before the 1943 championship game with the Redskins, Anderson ordered the Wrigley Field groundskeeper to lock all
the gates except one. He stationed trainer Andy Lotshaw there to
block any attempt by Shaughnessy to gain entry. He did not get inside
until game day, when he walked in with Halas, who was in uniform
and back home on Christmas leave to see the game.

Connor swore by Anderson, the man who installed him at linebacker. "Anderson was the smartest defensive coach I ever knew. Like
[tackle] Fred Davis said, 'Hunk never put us in a bad position.' "

In this reincarnation, Shaughnessy had been mandated by Halas to
devote most of his time to analyzing what had been Anderson's exclusive turf, the defense. Connor, as a player, did not like the designated
technical adviser. "Shaughnessy didn't know diddly-shit about
defense!" Connor said. Moose truly despised him when he served as
an assistant in 1956 and '57: "He was a phony all the way."

Halas may not have invented the concept of creative tension, but
he took it to the breaking point, pitting unit against unit, and coach
versus coach. "Anderson and Johnsos didn't get along. There was
always friction there," said Ed Stone, a young beat man in the '50s
with the *Chicago American*. "Shaughnessy was his own man. He
went his own way." As much as Halas liked and appreciated Anderson for his many years of service, in 1951, he turned up the heat. He
wanted Anderson out. "Hunk was a very colorful guy. He had a great
vocabulary. Profane. One of the most profane of any guy I ever
knew," said Rudy Custer, Halas's trusted aide and business manager.

"Shaughnessy didn't get along with the other coaches. He was smarter than they were. They were jealous of him."

At the end of the season, realizing he couldn't work with Shaughnessy, whom Halas had just brought aboard, let alone beat him, Anderson resigned to devote full time to his executive position with Production Steel, of Detroit. Halas replaced him with longtime Cardinals line coach Phil Handler, who stayed until his death in 1968.

By the time of the switch, the season was a disaster, the 6-and-2 start long since forgotten. The slide had begun when the Bears went to Cleveland on November 25 for the clash of the titans, George Halas for the NFL establishment against Paul Brown, the master organizer who dismantled the old AAFC and continued rolling through the NFL by winning the title in 1950, the Browns' first year in the league. "Paul Brown told me that the first time the Bears came to Cleveland, he went down to Terminal Tower to meet Papa Bear," recalled former NFL executive Don Weiss. "Halas got off the train with Bill Downes. They'd been playing cards all the way from Chicago, and Downes was going to referee the game."

Not even Downes could pull Halas through this wringer, though. Brown unleashed Waukegan native and childhood Bears fan Otto Graham, who proceeded to pick on Johnny Lujack, trying to cover Dub Jones in single coverage. By the end of the day, Jones tied Ernie Nevers's record six-touchdown performance, scoring every Cleveland point except Lou Groza's conversions, as the Browns won 42–21 to send the Bears into a tailspin that ended in a 7-and-5 season.

The only good thing that came out of 1952, besides Blanda's late-season emergence, was the draft. Seven of the first eight players became immediate, enduring starters and major contributors to the eventual 1956 Western Division champions. The top pick, Jim Dooley, of Miami, played until 1961, joined the coaching staff, and then succeeded Halas as head coach when he retired in 1968. The second choice, Eddie Macon, a back from College of the Pacific, was the first black player in team history. Used mostly as a kick returner, Macon was gone after the 1953 season. The third choice, the tall end Bill McColl, of Stanford, played slot back and studied medicine at the

University of Chicago, where he became an orthopedic surgeon and, after football, a medical missionary. Guard Herman Clark, from Oregon, played through 1956.

The fifth round produced two strong defensive linemen. Xavier left end Jack Hoffman started as a rookie and held the spot until he broke an arm in 1958. Fred Williams, a steady, solid, and witty tackle from Arkansas, drank with and entertained Doug Atkins and their teammates until he got hurt in the fifth game of the 1963 season. He spent the last two years of his career in Washington.

In the sixth round, Halas picked the gifted quarterback of the famed unbeaten 1951 San Francisco Dons, Ed Brown. Though Brown would be in the service until 1954, he became arguably the best long passer in pro football through 1963. Halas's seventh-round choice, Joe Fortunato, of Mississippi State, started at outside linebacker after he got discharged from the army in 1955 and starred until his retirement after the 1966 season.

Eighth-round choice Bill Bishop, of North Texas State, partnered alongside Fred Williams at defensive tackle through 1960. Two other players worth mentioning in that draft were 1951 Heisman Trophy winner Dick Kazmaier, of Princeton, who did not play pro ball, and the 18th-round choice, Illinois's 1951 Rose Bowl quarterback, Tommy O'Connell, a future selection scheduled for delivery the next year.

The "future," not to be confused with a future draft choice from a trade, was a feature of the draft process from 1949 until the NFL-AFL merger in 1967. Under that rule, a team could pick a player whose original college class would graduate by the next season and hold his rights in perpetuity. Halas landed such players as Brown, Fortunato, Zeke Bratkowski, Bill George, and Rick Casares under that rule.

In 1953, Halas infuriated Blanda when he gave O'Connell a $14,000 contract and the starting position, a situation that lasted for a handful of games. It turned out to be the worst season to date in the team's history. The Bears won three games, lost eight, and tied the Packers 21–21. People talked, and it was not pleasant.

The angry Blanda wasn't the only one who thought the game had passed Halas by. More than a few observers, experts, and Bears fans were certain that Halas no longer had it, and the proof was the losing record and utter failure to either hold on to or develop a replacement for Sid Luckman.

Deep in his den, though, the Old Man had plotted and planned his resurgence. His 1952 rookie bumper crop gained valuable game experience. The best newcomer was 1951 future, middle guard Bill George, from Wake Forest, who reminded him of young Bulldog Turner in skill and smarts.

Like Turner, the 6'2", 240-pound George was a natural leader and, to George Connor, every bit as fun off the field as Bulldog. "Bill was a champion college wrestler, strong and quick," Connor recalled. "We kidded George about being Greek, and he'd get furious. 'I'm no goddamned Greek,'" he'd scream. Early in the exhibition season, we were playing in Little Rock. I took Bill out to dinner to the best Greek restaurant in town. When we got there, I took the owner aside and told him Bill's nickname was the 'Golden Greek.' I said he was sort of shy, but he sure was one helluva guy." Connor chuckled at the thought of the ridiculously wonderful moment. "The owner came out during dinner and poured us a glass of wine: 'Opaa! To my countryman, the Golden Greek.' Everyone in the restaurant stood up and cheered. Then the owner turned to Bill: 'This one is on me, my friends. You don't pay for a thing.' After that, when we went on the road, Bill and I always went to the best Greek place in town. Never paid a nickel for anything when I was with the Golden Greek."

Halas and Shaughnessy also saw how well George recognized offenses. They let him call the defensive sets and audibles. Noting how well he dropped back into pass coverage, Shaughnessy offered a suggestion to Halas that, like the T formation, would define the key position on the defense. In 1954, Bill George would become the game's first defensive quarterback, taking his position off the line as the middle linebacker. He would ride it all the way to the Hall of Fame and start the Bears' remarkable tradition of Hall of Fame middle linebackers that passed from George to Dick Butkus and then Mike Singletary, to the current All-Pro, Brian Urlacher.

Halas also held a couple of hole cards for 1954. He quickly learned that O'Connell, his fellow Illini, couldn't play in his system, but he discovered that Blanda could. And he had two rookies to push his whipping boy. They were Ed Brown, the 1952 future, and a future choice for 1953, Georgia's All-America quarterback from downstate Danville, Illinois, a boy named Zeke Bratkowski.

He also landed college football's top offensive lineman, Maryland strongman Stan Jones. Jones, the first weight lifter of note in pro football, moved in at right guard. Prior to the draft, Shaughnessy showed Halas a film of a tall, rangy athlete from obscure Florence State Teachers College, in northern Alabama. When Halas saw a clip of the kid making a spectacular catch and then leaving the defenders in his wake, the Papa Bear spoke the words that would terrorize the National Football League. "Let's give this kid a look, Clark."

On the 15th round of the 1954 draft, the Bears selected Harlon Hill, who, for the next three years, blazed across the NFL as its brightest star like a meteor, only to disappear almost as quickly.

NINETEEN

THE KIDS WHO CAME TO PLAY

*P*at Summerall acquired broadcasting fame and fortune on CBS and, later, Fox telecasts of National Football League games over 42 seasons. He worked his way to the top of his profession, starting as an analyst and then, for most of his time, doing play-by-play in a spare, distinctive, direct style that matched his no-nonsense broadcast personality.

Before his broadcasting career, Summerall made his name as a heroic placekicker with the New York Giants in their 1958 run to the first sudden-death title game, the epic 23–17 loss to the Baltimore Colts in overtime. That was the apex of a pro career that began in 1952 in Detroit and continued from 1953 to '57 in Chicago as a defensive end and placekicker with the team from the South Side, the Cardinals. That's where he faced George Halas every season, and where he learned the true meaning of rivalry.

"It was not a very happy existence at that time," Summerall said. "We had good guys who became good friends, but we always played second fiddle. The Cubs and Bears and Wrigley Field got all the attention. The White Sox and us fought for a bigger slice of the pie."

Pat's first coach with the Big Red in 1953 was a legendary former Bear, Jumbo Joe Stydahar. "Joe came in after a loss the week before the Bear game carrying all our paychecks with a rubber band wrapped around them. He threw the packet across the room at Comiskey Park and said, 'All right, you gutless sons of bitches, if you don't beat the Bears, you don't get paid.' That's about as severe a fine as you can get," Summerall said with a realistc sigh. "Some players wanted to go to the owners to complain, but nothing ever happened. We beat the Bears anyway. So, we got paid."

That 24–17 Cardinals victory ended a 3–8–1 1953 season for the Bears, the worst to that time for George Halas and the team. Many people in town and around the league thought the Old Man's time had come. Summerall saw it otherwise. "I never heard it said about Halas that the game passed him by. Never did," Summerall said. "Halas never forgot the small details and kept up with every aspect of the game. I think his total involvement with the team, as owner-coach, with enthusiasm kept him going, and it kept him young."

Indeed, Halas thought young as he prepared for 1954. The team was led at the top by two future Hall of Famers: Halas, the head coach, and his assistant Paddy Driscoll. He built his 33-man roster around the leadership of 4 other men who would gain enshrinement in Canton: quarterback George Blanda; his defensive cocaptains and star linebackers, George Connor and Bill George; and rookie guard Stan Jones, who would anchor the offensive line for eight years and then cross over to solidify the championship defensive line in 1963. They were young and hungry.

The unquestioned star of that team, though, was a hick from a small Alabama college who burst out of obscurity that summer to become the most talked-about player in the NFL. Nobody in major college football in 1953 had ever heard of Harlon Hill or anyone else from Florence State Teachers College. That December, Clark Shaughnessy was scouting the Blue-Gray game in Montgomery when he talked to a couple of coaches from nearby Jacksonville State University. "Those boys were saying that the best player was not playing in the game," an ever modest Harlon Hill said in 2002. "He asked why, and they said he, meaning me, was from a small college like them."

When Shaughnessy told Halas about Hill, they sent away for a film. When they saw the rangy, 6'3" 198-pounder get free, snatch the ball with his huge hands, and sprint away from defenders like a gazelle, their eyes popped. The draft ran 30 rounds then, and they figured they could take the risk. So, they waited until round 15, called Hill's name, and sent him a train ticket. "I didn't really know what George Halas or anybody else in the pros was like," Hill said. "You know, coming from the sticks in Alabama. No TV back then."

When Harlon got off the train in Chicago, he had never seen anything like this huge city—the pace, the noise, the tall buildings, and the sheer numbers of people. The bright lights would come later. With a vengeance. On this day, he followed orders and dutifully made his way to 233 West Madison Street. "I found out he was a tough negotiator *after* my first year. The first year wasn't any negotiatin' at all. I was happy to sign anything," Hill said. "He gave me a $3,000 bonus. I signed for $5,000. After that, he was pretty tough. My top was 14.5, I believe."

"Harlon Hill was the best piece of rawboned talent I ever saw walk into a training camp," George Connor said. "I came home from camp one weekend and told my brother, 'You should see this kid we got from Alabama. He can run all day and all night and never break a sweat, never drop a football.' I swear he had three speeds. He was great."

Running was as natural as breathing for Hill, part Cherokee from his mother's side. "I gained speed running through cotton pastures. I ran with friends. I just loved to run," Harlon said. He was always the fastest boy at every level through college. He reported to camp at St. Joseph's College, in Rensselaer, Indiana, ready to go. "I enjoyed it there. A lot of running, catching passes, two-a-days, and three meetings a day," the wide-eyed Hill said. "The rookies got there a week early, and then the veterans came in. It was exciting."

As exciting as it was for Harlon Hill, it was sheer delight for the veterans, who wanted to see what he had to offer. One of them issued the challenge. "We went out to run some sprints to see who would win. I guess they timed them, but I never heard the results," Hill's rookie-year roommate and future Hall of Famer Stan Jones said. "The veterans said, 'Watch this kid Bill Anderson.'"

Billy Anderson was the Bears' top choice in the 1953 draft as Halas made one of the most head-scratching selections in the history of pro football. Perhaps the Old Man was inspired by the zany Fido Murphy, a self-styled super-scout and full-time con artist, who, for some bizarre reason, had the Old Man's ear. Maybe not. The kindest way to describe Billy Anderson's being chosen is to call it a major mistake. Billy was no football player, but he was a world-class sprinter who happened to have a famous father, Jack Benny's hilarious comedic foil Eddie "Rochester" Anderson.

"Billy lined up in a track stance. He took a couple of practice starts," Jones said. "Then here came Harlon. He lined up in a three-point stance, and he beat Anderson!" Billy Anderson was gone and forgotten after the seventh game of the season.

Then Hill showed his teammates why Halas and Shaughnessy chose him. "I started learning the offensive schemes, and I caught on pretty fast. I had a good camp, and everything kept going good. They spread me out at left end from the start, most of the time."

"Boy, he was fast," said Jones. "Harlon was ahead of his time, running deep patterns. Without too many moves, he could run right past people."

"George Blanda was the quarterback, and Ed Brown and Zeke Bratkowski were rookies with me," Hill said. "I learned more about running routes from George than anybody. If I didn't run it right, he let me know right quick."

Hill's education away from training camp began in the six-game preseason. The Bears, and most of the 11 other teams, could not move into their home stadiums until baseball season ended. So, they hit the road in August, selling pro football to the hinterlands. One early stop against the hated crosstown Cardinals in Chattanooga, Tennessee, left a lasting impression on Stan Jones. "I didn't know anything about the rivalry between Trippi and Ed Sprinkle. We played that game for Reverend Stoney Jackson's Milk Fund. Reverend Stoney Jackson gave us a little talk before the game on sportsmanship and what it means."

Halas rested the veterans most of the night and gave the bulk of the playing time to rookies and free-agent hopefuls. The Cardinals were winning 10–0 late in the fourth quarter, when the fun began. "Trippi and Sprinkle got into it, and both benches cleared. We never finished the game," Jones said. "Afterward, I talked to Frank Halas, our traveling secretary, George's older brother. 'At least we gave some money to the charities,' I said. 'Hey, did you hear what happened?' Frank Halas said. 'Reverend Stone Jackson absconded with the money.' I couldn't believe it," Jones said, still astonished by it all a half century later. "That was my introduction to pro football."

A month later, Halas decided to pull a surprise against the defending champion Lions in the opener at Detroit. Aware the Lions prepared for Blanda's passes, Halas told the rookie Bratkowski the morning of the game that he would start. Blanda, so mad that he was "burning up inside," watched from the bench as the Lions' veterans overwhelmed the rookie. After Blanda had come in to lead the Bears back to within a point at 24–23, Halas reinserted Bratkowski, who threw an interception to key a 48–23 Detroit rout.

Blanda regained his starting job the following week as the Bears eked out a 10–3 victory at Green Bay, followed by a win over the Baltimore Colts, 28–9, in a daylong downpour in the Wrigley Field opener. A week later, on October 17, the unbeaten San Francisco 49ers came to Chicago on a sunny, 50-degree afternoon with their Hall of Fame backfield: quarterback Y. A. Tittle and fullback Joe "the Jet" Perry, flanked by John Henry Johnson and the league's leading rusher, Hugh "the King" McElhenny.

The Bears had no ground game, but they had Blanda, who peppered the Niners' secondary throwing to receivers Hill, steady Jim Dooley, and slotback Bill McColl. "Blanda was a great quarterback. He could throw a beautiful short pass and had the arm to throw long," said Dooley. In 2003, Dooley pinpointed a major reason for the friction between the tough quarterback and Coach Halas. "George had a little way of kidding with the players more than Halas liked. Getting rid of him was probably one of the worst decisions Halas ever made, because you see what Blanda did. For George, kidding was his tension release."

Blanda opened the game with a 43-yard strike to the wide-open Dooley, who fell down at the 49ers' 30 with nobody between himself and the goal line. On the next play, Niners safety Joe Arenas halted the drive with an interception.

It was one wild afternoon of back-and-forth crowd-pleasing action. McElhenny gained 110 of San Francisco's 294 rushing yards and scored twice, once off a quick pitch and 46-yard end run down the right sideline to daylight, and again on an off-tackle slant from the 7. Blanda had staked the Bears to a 17–14 lead in the third quarter with a field goal and touchdown passes to Dooley and Hill, when Sprinkle shot around 49er left tackle Doug Hogland. Once free, he hung out Tittle on his left-armed clothesline to finish him for the day.

Niners coach Buck Shaw replaced Tittle with seldom-used rookie backup Maury Duncan and issued simple instructions: hand off and stay clear of Sprinkle. Duncan followed Shaw's order to a T as he sent Perry, Johnson, and McElhenny on a 17-point surge, running through gaping holes opened by Hogland, Clay Matthews, Tiger Bill Johnson, Bruno Banducci, and Bob St. Clair.

Blanda countered with a scoring pass to McColl, to cut the final margin to 31–24. Blanda and Brown, the rookie, had passed for 347 yards, but they also gave up six interceptions. Two more lost fumbles, eight turnovers in all, told the tale.

Two weeks later, on October 31, after losing at Los Angeles to fall to 2-and-3, the Bears saw their promising season tilt on the brink as they prepared for a Halloween rematch at San Francisco's Kezar Stadium. Halas and his coaches observed the methodical pregame routine they had practiced since the beginning of the franchise. "They went over personnel, plays, and things we were gonna do," Ed Sprinkle said. "You'd know your job and what you were gonna do."

Pep talks? "Halas never was big on that high school or college stuff. Not like Knute Rockne," said Sprinkle. "He'd say, 'Let's go!' and everybody jumped. I don't ever remember any memorable speeches Halas gave."

"We caught 'em with a crippled-up defensive secondary," Harlon Hill said. When the teams took the field, Blanda noticed that 49ers safety Arenas was hurt, and he knew Billy Jessup could not keep up with Hill. "I was having a pretty good day, and he kept throwing me passes," Hill said. He had scored three touchdowns on catches that covered 47, 21, and 11 yards. The game was tied 24–24 late in the fourth quarter when Tittle took charge.

With McElhenny out of the game and headed for surgery after he suffered a season-ending shoulder separation, Tittle marched the 49ers downfield. As darkness closed in, Gordie Soltau knocked in a short field goal with 45 seconds left to give San Francisco a 27–24 lead. The Niners kicked off into a stiff wind blowing off the Pacific Ocean across Golden Gate Park.

Sprinkle caught Soltau's short kick by the sideline and stepped out of bounds at the Bears' 34 to stop the clock. In near-total darkness, 49ers coach Buck Shaw inserted his fastest man, John Henry Johnson, to play deep and guard against the home run to Hill. Halas sneaked Ed Brown into the game behind a couple of linemen and had him line up at right half in the pro set. "We faked an end-run option," Hill said. "I went down the field, broke inside, then cut across toward the corner."

As Hill broke, Blanda handed to Brown, who rolled left, planted, and cut loose with the wind at his back. Hill got behind Johnson and caught Brown's bomb in stride. "He threw the ball 60-something yards. I ran it in for the touchdown," Brown said. Blanda added the extra point to make it 31–27 Bears. The old scoreboard clock with its mechanical hands showed enough time for a kickoff and one play.

Connor batted down Tittle's final pass at the gun to end the remarkable comeback, and Halas tossed his fedora in the air. In the dressing room, he called Hill's seven-catch, 214-yard, four-touchdown performance "the greatest pass-catching exhibition I've ever seen."

The team awarded the game ball to Blanda, whom, two days later in Chicago, Halas called "the best quarterback in football." Until he got nailed late in the game when he tried to crawl for an extra yard, McElhenny, the best runner in football, was on his way to a record-setting season. In just six games, he ran for 515 yards and averaged 8.0 yards a carry, second only to Beattie Feathers's still-standing 1934 record, 8.4. Without Hurryin' Hugh, the 49ers won just two more games, finishing at 7–4–1 behind the 8-and-4 Bears in the West. After the season, 49ers owner Tony Morabito fired Shaw, who had been the only coach in franchise history, and replaced him with veteran journeyman Norman "Red" Strader, who would last a year.

That big victory was the lift the Bears needed. They beat the Packers with two minutes to go, 28–23, on a Blanda touchdown pass to John Hoffman. Blanda's heroics had become so commonplace that George Strickler in the *Trib* called it a "regular miracle." After seven games, Blanda was chasing the NFL record book with 16 scoring passes and 2,200 passing yards.

The Age of Blanda Miracles in Chicago ended abruptly the following week when area native Otto Graham, in his only Wrigley Field appearance, passed the Browns to a 39–10 rout. Cleveland's huge end Lenny Ford and tackle Don Colo added injury to insult when they squeezed Blanda in a sandwich and brought him to earth on his right shoulder. He got up and trotted off the field with a complete shoulder separation. Dr. Ted Fox repaired the damage that night at nearby Illinois Masonic Hospital.

With the season two-thirds over and the team treading water at 4-and-4, Halas gathered his Bears the next Tuesday, told them Zeke Bratkowski, the rookie, would start at quarterback, and issued a challenge. Although incentive contracts in today's big-money NFL are commonplace, in 1954, Halas had to tell his players he could not pay them a bonus to win an individual game. That was a league bylaw to prevent gambling. But the rules Halas made allowed equal incentives for all. "I'll give you guys a $250 bonus for every game that you win. But if we lose a game, I'll deduct $250," Halas said.

"If you won three out of four, you'd win $500. If you won four out of four, you got a $1,000," Sprinkle said. "We won all four of those games and got a $1,000 bonus. That fired us up. Then I heard that some of the guys never got that thousand—I mean guys that weren't starters—that Halas didn't pay 'em. I didn't believe it then. I'm not sure I do now. I don't know how he could not pay you. It's the squad; you pay 'em all."

Just as Bratkowski was emerging, off he went to the army until 1957. Bob Williams's service obligation was completed, and he would return in 1955, but he would play third string behind Blanda and

Brown. Halas dusted off his 1948 game plan that saw Lujack probe the opposing defense as starter while Luckman finished up in style.

He had two capable quarterbacks, so he would employ Blanda, still recovering from the shoulder operation, as the starter and, as usual, the placekicker. A fresh Brown would take over in the second quarter to utilize his many gifts as a superior long passer, excellent runner, and excellent play caller and leader. In Hill, the 1954 NFL Rookie of the Year with 45 catches for 1,124 yards and 12 touchdowns, Halas owned football's most dangerous threat. Also, for the first time since 1941, Halas had an excellent, run-blocking offensive line plus three fine running backs, one a gifted fullback with sprinter's speed. His name was Rick Casares.

Rick Casares was a renowned high school athlete in Tampa, starring in football and basketball. Many thought that his best sport was boxing and that he might become heavyweight champion. He was called up for army service in the fall of 1953, halfway into his senior season at Florida. The Korean War had ended, so he was assigned to Special Services. To play ball. "I made All-Service at Fort Jackson, in Columbia, South Carolina, and really developed in the army," he said. "Then the Bears drafted me."

Halas took Casares as a future on the second round in the deep 1954 draft that produced Hill on the 15th round and another future lineman, tackle Herman Lee, from Florida A&M, on the 23rd. With another year to go on his hitch, Casares passed the time starring on the Fort Jackson basketball team. During his hitch, the Argonauts of the Canadian League flew Casares to Toronto on a weekend pass. "They wanted to give me $20,000!" Casares said. "A $20,000 contract! I almost passed out. It was good money for 1955."

On his way back to South Carolina, Casares stopped in New Jersey to visit his mother, a widow who had moved back north to be near her family after Rick joined the army. "I'm in my mom's house for a half hour when the phone rings. It's George Halas: 'Rick, I understand you went to Canada.' I mean, I wasn't back in the States a half hour!"

Earlier that year, Halas had offered Casares $10,000 shortly before he met with Toronto, which doubled it. "For Christ sake!" Halas roared from his office in Chicago. "Those 'cacksuckers' won't pay you! They promise everything, but they won't pay you!"

"I really want to play for the Bears, but they want to give me twice as much money," the naive Casares said to Halas.

"Oh, bullshit!" Halas said. "They won't give you the money. That league will never last."

"Sir, I always wanted to play for the Bears," Casares replied. "The difference is I want to help my mother."

Halas persisted. "Look, I'm gonna send you a ticket. I want you on the plane tomorrow to Chicago."

"My leave is up," Casares said.

"Don't worry about that," Halas said. "I'll take care of it."

Halas wired Casares a ticket. With the help of Fleet Admiral Chester Nimitz, who introduced him to then army chief of staff, General of the Army Dwight Eisenhower, Halas had sponsored the annual Armed Forces game charity exhibition at Soldier Field since 1946. "His contacts went right to the top in Washington," Casares recalled. "They went right to the president. He could do anything he wanted to do. Halas was really powerful."

Once the Papa Bear lured an innocent into his den, it was all over. "He was relentless and shrewd. You sure didn't want to be across the table from him doing business if you were an inexperienced football player," Casares said.

Halas knew Casares wanted to play for the Bears, a team that at that time was as admired in football across America as the Yankees were in baseball. "Nobody's gonna see you up in Canada. You'll be buried," Halas again told Casares, who had to agree with the founding father's wisdom. "I can't raise your contract, but I'll give you a $2,000 bonus," Halas said, closing fast.

"Good," Casares said, happy to get what he believed was something of value as he signed the contract. "I want you to know I'm not about money."

Halas gave the young man a quizzical look over the top of his glasses. "Most things are about money, kid. That's what we're doing here."

In the winter of 1955, Paul Brown phoned Halas from Cleveland and said he had a problem he wanted to get off his hands, a 6′8″, 260-pound problem in the person of a defensive end named Doug Atkins. Halas told Brown he'd think about it and get back to him. Halas immediately called Frank Korch, the WGN sports editor who moonlighted as his personnel director, to get a read on Atkins. Korch told him basically the same thing Bill Gleason said nearly a half century later.

"The Browns' fullback before Jim Brown was Maurice Bassett," Gleason said. "Somebody asked, 'Who's gonna block the kid?' Bassett piped up, 'I'll block him. I'm the biggest fullback in the league.' Bassett got into a pass-blocking stance to demonstrate what happened," Gleason recalled. " 'I looked up, and that son of a bitch jumped over my head,' Bassett said. I saw Atkins do that many times," Gleason said.

Korch would have told Halas that Atkins was a world-class college high jumper and All–Southeastern Conference in basketball as well. Then Halas would have asked Korch why Brown would want to get rid of an athlete like that. The word came back that Atkins had let out a roaring belch in one of Brown's classroom sessions. "Makes sense," Bill Jauss said, barely able to stifle a guffaw. "It probably shook the rafters and made the whole room smell of gin."

Halas, who had long been a zookeeper with his assortment of raucous night crawlers, knew this was a man he had to get. He'd figure out how to handle him once he got him. Halas got his deal when Brown tossed in safety Ken Gorgal. In return, Halas gave Cleveland the Bears' third and sixth picks in the 1956 draft. Gorgal had a fine year, intercepting six passes in 1955. Atkins, of course, was the prize.

"In those days, we'd fly out of Midway," Gleason said. "So, I'd get on the bus. Halas being Halas, the bus was a yellow school bus. Two or three yellow school buses from Midway, and we'd ride to St. Joe." Gleason continued, "I was sitting on a side seat, and Atkins was right there across from me. I'd been a big fan of Tennessee and Major Robert Neyland, who got promoted to general during the big war. 'Doug,' I said, 'it must have been a big thrill for a boy like you to come down from the hills and play for the great Major Neyland.' "

"Mr. Gleason, I want to tell you that old major was a pain in the ass. It was all football and not much bull. I played for Paul Brown, and it was much of the same thing." Atkins, who played a dozen seasons for the Bears, said Halas's controlling personality neutralized his great players. "He kept his old coaches years and years until they passed away. So, football passed them by."

Before the 1955 training camp, Halas announced he would step down as coach after the season. With everything in place for a title run, the Bears fell flat in the opener at Baltimore. On the first play from scrimmage, Wisconsin's 1954 Heisman Trophy winner, Alan Ameche, burst through a huge hole and went all the way, 79 yards. After a Bears defensive lineman left with an injury on the play, rookie Stan Jones was pressed into double duty. "I did a great job that day," said a sardonic Jones. "Ameche ran for 175 yards." The Colts held on to win 23–17.

The irony wasn't lost on Halas when someone told him after the game that Alan the Horse was a cousin of his old AAFC nemesis Don Ameche. A week later, the Packers ran all over the Bears 24–3 in Green Bay. The 49ers were next for the October 9 home opener at Wrigley Field.

Halas started two big backs behind Blanda, Chick Jagade at fullback and John Hoffman at halfback. Hoffman, a seven-year veteran, came up as a fullback in 1949 and was making his first backfield start since 1950 when Halas moved him to end. On the first play from scrimmage, Blanda tossed to Hoffman, who took off behind pulling left tackle Bill Wightkin. Wightkin's cross-body block on Hardy Brown sprang Hoffman for 31 yards to open a big 135-yard afternoon. The Bears were trailing late in the second quarter and driving for the go-ahead touchdown when the hands on the center-field scoreboard clock stopped in place. The public-address announcer relayed the official time to the crowd between plays. When Blanda drove the Bears to just inside the 1, Halas sent word to Blanda to pull a then-legal maneuver.

"I was supposed to fake this injury, see, to get an extra time-out," Jones said. "I gave my great Academy Award–winning performance. I rolled over on the ground." Blanda lined up the rest of the team as

Jones writhed. " 'Get up, Stan, get up. We got plenty of time,' George said.' So, I got up, and by God, the gun went off!" Blanda had scored, but the referee waved it off. "Halas met me halfway off the field going to the dugout. He kicked me the whole way through the dugout to the clubhouse," Jones said. "Goddamn George almost got me fired." That play was the difference as the Bears lost 20–19. They were winless and dead last after three games.

The season turned on a single play the next week against the Colts. Baltimore was up 3–0 after Bert Rechichar's first-quarter field goal. Halas sent his big rookie Casares onto the field. "I substituted for Chick Jagade, the regular fullback," Casares said. "We were on our 19, and it was third-and-5. Bobby Watkins, the halfback, really got dinged on the previous carry. George Blanda called a toss to the halfback. We broke the huddle and Watkins said, 'Rick, I'm dizzy. Can you take it?' 'Absolutely,' I told Bobby. I hadn't carried the ball any, and I was dying to." As they lined up, the alert Casares realized the Bears' playbook did not include a toss to the fullback. "So, we switched positions. We were interchangeable. I knew all of his plays. I don't know if he knew mine, all my blocking assignments, but I knew all the ball carries. So, we just switched."

Blanda took the snap from center Larry Strickland and turned left to make the toss. "When George came out from underneath the center, he didn't know that we had switched. He looked over to toss that ball, and I could sense it in his eyes, on his face: 'What the hell are you doing there?' But he went ahead and tossed it to me, and I went 81 yards with it."

Getting there for Casares, however, was no Sunday-afternoon romp to glory down the sideline. After nearly 50 years, he recalled every detail of a run that was more like hitting the Normandy beaches on D-day under heavy enemy fire: "I'm just about to make a cut. Bill McColl throws a block on the outside linebacker that knocks him out, so I cut back. Which is the key to it, instead of extending it. As I cut back, Larry Strickland went through and circled around behind Don Joyce, who had the angle on me. Larry knocked off Joyce." The only Baltimore defender who had a chance at Casares was linebacker Bill Pellington. "He wore a cast on his arm and used to knock out guys left and right when he extended his arm. Chick Jagade told me before the opening game, 'Listen, when you swing upfield, on a pass play, give Pellington a wide berth. Swing wide. Don't cut your swing short, because Pellington's gonna take your head off.' "

In that opener, Casares saw Pellington knock out Watkins and club Henry Moseley so hard that he never played another game. So, he knew what he had to do to finish his superb run. "I put up my left arm, 'cause he was the outside linebacker to my right. So, when I swung, my left side was facing him, and I caught him comimg across. I blocked Pellington's shot. He's the guy I stiff-armed to go the last 10 yards."

Casares's run ignited the Bears, who stomped the Colts 38–10. That started a six-game winning streak that included home and away victories over the first-place Rams. The fourth game in the streak, played at Wrigley Field, was one of the wildest in the long history of the Bears-Packers series. "They didn't belong on the same field with us, but they beat us up there 24–3," George Connor said. "I knew this was my last year. My mom and dad came to the game with my brother Jack, who was home on leave from the marines. I wanted to show them something."

The Bears opened with a rush, literally, as Casares and Watkins each gained 115 yards. "We were out for blood," Connor said. "We came out and ran it down their throats. Sweeps, traps, counters, sheer power, passes to Hill and McColl, the works. On defense, we poured all over Tobin Rote, their great quarterback. We took a 21–3 lead in the second quarter and lined up for the kickoff. I took my spot, fourth in from the right. Blanda sent one deep to their safetyman, Veryl Switzer, near the goal line. I was flying. I don't know what happened to their up men except I was all alone."

Casares watched it happen from the Bears' sideline. "The Packers' wedge men saw Moose coming and got out of the way, leaving Switzer wide open." Connor continued, "The last guy was Al Carmichael, the other returner, from USC. Those guys from SC never block, you know, and Carmichael got out of my way. I led with my right shoulder and ran right through Switzer."

"You can't believe the collision," Casares said. "I don't think either man saw the other. I'm sure Moose shut his eyes, bracing for the collision with the wedge. Instead, he smashed into Switzer, whose helmet went flying. The ball went the other way, both about five feet in the air."

"I kept running right back to the bench," Connor said. "The crowd went silent. I knew he was hurt, but so was I. I sat on the bench to get my bearings." Casares noted, "It took several minutes to revive Switzer and help him off the field."

Connor said, "About five minutes later, a huge cheer rose. I asked Bill George if they were cheering me. 'Hell no,' Bill said. They're cheering Switzer. He just got up and walked off under his own power.' I said, 'That does it, Bill. I guess I'm losing my touch.'"

"It's the greatest hit I ever saw," Casares said.

"Several Packers told me the next year that Switzer couldn't put on the uniform again," Connor said. "Every time he tried, he got the shakes. He never played again."

After the hit, the Bears ran the score to 45–3, and then Halas took out as many starters as possible. The Packers ran up 28 points in the fourth quarter to close the margin to 52–31. In reality, the game ended with Connor's defining hit on Switzer.

And, in many ways so did the season. The Bears took a 6-and-3 record into the 10th game at Comiskey Park, the Sunday after Thanksgiving, a half game ahead of the Rams. Had they won the three remaining games, they would have played host to the Browns at Wrigley Field for the title the day after Christmas.

Ed Stone in 1955 was a 23-year-old copyeditor and spare writer for the *Chicago American*. Like his older colleague Bill Gleason, Stone was crazy about pro football. Unlike Gleason, who grew up a Cardinals fan, Stone cut his eyeteeth on the Bears. But when it came to journalism, he played it the only way he knew: right down the middle, directly from what he saw and heard, let the chips fall where they may. "Everybody romanticizes the Packers as the great rivalry. It's nothing like the Cardinals were when they were in Chicago. That was a matter of hatred, especially after Charlie Bidwill died," Stone said.

"Halas hated Walter Wolfner and did everything until 1959 to chase them out of town. Those were wars. The Cards were lousy, and the Bears usually were good, but the record never counted."

Wolfner fired Joe Stydahar after losing to the Bears in 1954. Now his replacement, another former Bears tackle, Ray Richards, was playing head games with the Papa Bear. Halas had not been this edgy before a Cardinals game since the Western Division showdowns in 1947 and '48. On the Wednesday before Thanksgiving, Halas griped at the Bears' alumni luncheon that a scout, likely Fido Murphy, reported that the field was "a disgrace" and apparently had not been covered during a Tuesday-night rain.

Richards countered that he had not planned to cover the field. Halas groused that the Cardinals intended to bog down his Bears in the mud. The Cardinals returned the fire, saying their backs, Ollie Matson and Dave Mann, both faster than the Bears' Watkins and Casares, ran better on a dry track. So it went. The field, as Halas feared, was a muddy mess. The tight Bears played to the poor conditions, the Cardinals played loose as they enjoyed a lark in the park. They took the opening kickoff and plowed downfield toward touchdown territory. "I was covering the Cardinals, and Mac the Bears," Bill Gleason said, fondly recalling his late colleague at the *Chicago American*, Harry MacNamara. "We did a column side-by-side, and I picked the Cardinals. So, I couldn't help but laugh. Was Mac furious. He wanted to punch me."

"I remember it well," Pat Summerall said of that game. "A lot of guys were running loose. We never rushed the passer like we did that day. We had weapons, some pretty good players: Ollie Matson, of course, Dave Mann, two good receivers in Don Stonesifer and Gern Nagler. Lamar McHan, the quarterback, had a hot day."

The game was barely under way when it began to snow—big flakes, steady, sticking. "I always think of Don Stonesifer," Gleason said. "Stoney made the most remarkable catch. Stoney went to Schurz and Northwestern, played with the Cardinals. Hated Notre Dame. Hated the Bears. McHan threw a downfield pass, and he slipped and went down on one shoulder with his legs in the air and caught the pass." "I was lying on my back in the end zone when the ball landed on me and stuck," Stonesifer said in 2003. "It was our day."

"I turned to Mac and said, 'It's all over for the Bears, now,' " recalled Gleason.

"The Cardinals took an early lead, then it started to snow. Everything they tried worked, and they poured it on as the snow covered the field," Ed Stone said.

"It was long into the game, and we were just killing the Bears," a sympathetic Summerall said. "Doug Atkins was standing in dismay, and a guy jumped over the first-base wall behind the dugout and ran out on the field, jumped up and slugged Atkins, and kept running. After the game, Doug said, 'I don't mind when one of you guys hit me, but when one of those guys comes out of the stands, I do mind.' Doug chased him back to the stands. Didn't catch him. He would have killed the guy had he hit him."

"It was one of those kind of games that will live in infamy," Stan Jones said, still smarting from that long-ago loss. "After that, Halas always read out the players who played in that game. We owed it to him to redeem ourselves because we were part of a game that was infamous. A disgrace. You couldn't feel good about losing the city championship."

"I was there with two friends who were Cardinal fans," Stone said, "and they gave it to me as the Cardinals ran it up—Ollie Matson, Dave Mann. They won 53–14, and the party began in the snow." The Cardinals carried Richards, their victorious coach, off the field on the ironic night, for Bears fans, that Chicago—at least on the old North Side—died.

"We went back to Comiskey Park the next day, and the chef who cooked for the White Sox and us, Ernie Carroll, prepared that special meal, the lamb roast. There weren't a lot of those," Summerall recalled.

Stone drew the assignment to cover the feast in the clubhouse, earning one of his first bylines in the *American*. "Dave Mann grabbed a leg as easily as taking a Lamar McHan pitchout," Stone wrote. "He disappeared into a corner and a few minutes later, came back for more." Equipment manager Phil Bouzeous, the feast organizer, observed, "I bet the Bears aren't feasting."

"That loss knocked the Bears out of a title-game shot with the Browns. Probably a good thing they didn't have to face Otto Graham in his final game," Stone recalled.

On Sunday, December 11, 1955, 34,783 fans turned out to see the Bears beat the Philadelphia Eagles 17–10 and bid Papa Bear farewell after 30 seasons and 248 victories as coach of the Chicago Bears. At age 60, he had acceded to Minnie's wishes to retire and run the team from the front office. It was presumed that he would turn over coaching duties to a younger man.

TWENTY

PADDY CAKE, PADDY CAKE, PAPA'S MAN

*T*he news broke early on the morning of February 2, 1956, that George Halas was going to introduce his successor as coach of the Chicago Bears later that day.

"Mac had the story," Bill Gleason said as he discussed the historic scoop that his colleague and mentor, the late Harry MacNamara, had bagged on that long-ago Groundhog Day. MacNamara, who played high school football for Bob Zuppke in Oak Park with another writer of note named Ernest Hemingway, had covered Halas since the beginning. In fact, MacNamara joined the *Chicago American*'s predecessor, the *Herald-Examiner*, on June 14, 1920, before the Decatur Staleys played their first game!

Television was decades away from the 24-7 news cycle. Newspapers were the latest source for breaking events, printing several editions, and, when warranted, extras. "We went to press real early for an afternoon paper," Gleason said of his *American*. "The early issue would be on the street for people getting off the train going to work."

MacNamara wrote that the new coach to be named at a 1:00 P.M. press conference that day, ironically on George Halas's 60th birthday, was a former Bears player, current assistant coach, and Halas's off-field friend. "We had a front-page head, over the masthead, Gleason said. "Luke Johnsos was going to be the coach." In his story in the four-star edition that rolled off the presses at 7:00 A.M., the blunt MacNamara observed that nothing really would change. "Johnsos, his assistants, and the Bears themselves will be Halas's marionettes."

"When Halas heard about that, he changed it. The *Tribune* was supposed to have the beat," Gleason said.

How did Halas know about "that," and when did he know about it, are questions that may never get satisfactorily answered. As Rick Casares had realized the year before, Halas had his ways of learning something before anybody else did. And he had his sources—or, to be more correct, his spies. More than a few of them worked for local papers other than the *Tribune*, in focal points of the operation such as the pressroom or in circulation. They were the ones at newspapers who knew everyone's business, and knew it first. And they were always willing to keep the Old Man informed.

At some point overnight, an *American* insider ("no one in our sports department," Gleason insisted) called Halas at home in the Edgewater Beach Apartments to report that the paper was going with Johnsos. All hands from that era agree that Halas dealt with a matter that serious by calling his confidant, Don Maxwell, at home in Evanston. Maxwell, the *Tribune*'s editor, then called his sports editor, Wilfrid Smith. Arch Ward, Smith's predecessor and the only media power in town who ever dared to stand up to Halas, had died on the eve of the 1955 All-Star baseball game, and Smith did exactly as Maxwell told him. In this case, Maxwell ordered Smith to stand by for an important call and prepare to stop the presses.

"Halas leaked the story to Smith in the *Trib* that it would be Paddy Driscoll," said Ed Stone, Gleason and MacNamara's young colleague. "That made the home edition on February 2 as the *American* went with Johnsos."

In the Halas-dictated story, the *Tribune*'s Smith referred to Driscoll, Halas's friend and colleague since their Navy days in 1918, as the "logical" choice from the staff. This despite Johnsos's success as co-coach, with Hunk Anderson, of the 1943 champions.

In the press conference that day, Halas, of course, said the correct things. He called Driscoll a man who would keep the Bears in the title run and stated, "I know of no man who has made a greater contribution to football." "This is a great honor," the taciturn Driscoll declared.

"We replated immediately," Stone said. By replating, Stone meant that the editors ordered the immediate scrapping of the front page with the Johnsos headline and MacNamara's exclusive. That called for a rewrite followed by an immediate press run, for circulation to get the updated edition on the streets posthaste and retrieve the unsold papers wherever possible.

"To his credit," Stone said, "*American* sports editor Leo Fischer, who never supported his reporters, raised hell with Halas's public relations man, Dan Desmond, over making us look foolish. This was the worst imaginable embarrassment we ever suffered."

Chet Coppock, whose father, Charles, was Johnsos's partner in a printing business that Halas supported as a silent partner, said Johnsos never recovered from what he called a "betrayal."

Johnsos loyalists had to wince when Wilfrid Smith called Driscoll the "logical choice." Johnsos had proved his worth at all levels. He was a dedicated player for Halas from the time he joined the club in 1929 out of Northwestern and a loyal liege as an assistant from 1941 on. While the Old Man served with the Navy in the Pacific, Johnsos and Anderson guided the Bears to the 1943 title. He passed his tests with flying colors.

Driscoll had much thinner coaching credentials. True, he had been player-coach for the Cardinals from 1920 through '22. But that was 34 years before in the single-wing era. In Driscoll's four-year stint as Marquette coach, his Hilltoppers won 9 games, lost 24, and tied 1. He had served as Halas's backfield coach since 1941 and was not known as a tactician, let alone a strategist.

What happened? Because Johnsos was so adamant with his use of the word *betrayal* to family and close friends, in hindsight it became apparent that he was MacNamara's source for the scoop. When Halas's source or spy told him what MacNamara was doing, a furious Halas cut off his nose to spite his face. Halas, in fact, likely had told Johnsos the job was his, but he would have considered such a leak, especially to the "wrong" paper, far worse than insubordination. This, to Halas, was an act of "betrayal."

After the formalities, the Bears staff celebrated the founder's birthday. He was 61, 22 days younger than his successor. Johnsos had to swallow his pride and go along. He could not afford to lose his Bears' salary.

Minnie may have wanted George to slow down in his "retirement," but he did not intend to sit around the office clipping coupons. Soon after he awarded Driscoll the title as head coach, he hit the road for a 200-mile trip north to Green Bay. He had to save a franchise—and, to his way of thinking, the league—from making a fatal error.

When George Halas left Decatur for Chicago in 1921, he made it possible for the league to clear out of the tank towns of the Midwest and set up shop in the big cities. Yet, Halas was always grateful to the small towns for supporting the game, especially the one little community that became his most enduring and beloved opponent—Green Bay, Wisconsin, and its Packers.

"Go back to Halas and Curly Lambeau, for sure: Green Bay was a smaller Chicago," Bill Jauss said. "It was a bustling packing town, everybody a meat packer. That was Chicago; everybody was a packer. Hog butcher of the world. Green Bay was hog butcher of Wisconsin. It's a perfect match: Halas versus Lambeau. Chicago and Green Bay are similar cities."

To Halas, Green Bay's presence and excellence set the National Football League apart from Major League Baseball and from pro basketball, which, by the mid-'50s, was cutting its ties to places like Syracuse, Fort Wayne, and Rochester. By 1934, the same year that George Richards moved from Portsmouth in order for Detroit to become the Lions, the Bears-Packers rivalry—Halas versus Lambeau—was the best show around.

On two Sundays a year, Halas might exhort his men to knock the starch out of those "Packer pricks," but the rest of the time, he loved that little town. As the lightning rod in the rivalry, the hated enemy from the town Billy Sunday couldn't shut down, he was Green Bay's best out-of-town friend. Now, in the winter of 1956, he stood up to be counted.

The wooden City Stadium with its 24,000 capacity was too small and run-down for a league on the verge of overtaking baseball. It had to go. If Green Bay could not raise the money to build a new stadium, the league threatened to move the franchise. Halas knew Green Bay's success was everybody's success. "Halas came up here to speak in '56, said Art Daley, who covered the event for the *Green Bay Press-Gazette*. "It was on all the radio stations and in all the papers, which was a hell of a thing. He was a real friend."

In 1956, Lee Remmel, for decades the Packers' executive director of public relations, also covered Halas's appearance for the *Press-Gazette*. "Halas had a fund-raising rally at a place called the Columbus Club, which is right downtown," Remmel said. "Halas made another personal appearance explaining the Packers' importance to the Bears. He said it was very important for the Packers to continue in the league. I don't think anybody who was around at the time has ever forgotten that. It was a great thing for him to do."

Thanks to the efforts of men such as Jack Vainisi, Fred Miller, Tony Canadeo, and Dominick Olejniczak, along with Halas's outside push, the stadium referendum passed in April 1956. The new 32,000-seat stadium on Green Bay's west side would open for business on September 29, 1957. The opponent, naturally, would be the Chicago Bears. "For sure, Halas did not want that franchise moving to Milwaukee or anywhere else," Jauss said.

As for the Bears and their new coach, when they gathered in Rensselaer, Indiana, for training camp, the players immediately realized that the diminutive Driscoll was coach in name only. "Halas didn't really step down anyhow. He was behind the scenes," Harlon Hill recalled. "He was at camp, and he was calling the shots. Old Paddy was just out there standing on the sidelines and didn't know what was going on. Nothing ever changed when it came to Halas."

That's not quite true. Halas may not have actively resisted the coming of the black athlete, but until 1952, he did not buck his buddy George Preston Marshall, who refused to integrate his Washington Redskins. The National Football League had been lily white since the early years when Fritz Pollard, black Chicagoan and College Football Hall of Famer from Brown, coached and starred for the Akron Pros in the early years.

Change came to the NFL in 1946. To gain their L.A. Coliseum lease for 1946, the Rams broke Marshall's mandate when they signed UCLA's great prewar star Kenny Washington and his Bruins team-mate Woodrow Strode. That story made a small stir compared with the splash their fellow Bruin Jackie Robinson would generate the fol-lowing spring when he broke big-league baseball's color line in Brooklyn.

Most, but not all, of the early black players were backs. The Rams moved ahead, adding Paul "Tank" Younger from Grambling in 1949. Deacon Dan Towler arrived from Washington Jefferson the next year along with end Bob Boyd from Compton JC. The San Francisco 49ers built their offense around fullback Joe Perry in 1949. John Henry Johnson joined in 1954. The New York Giants added Iowa's Emlen Tunnell in 1948, and he became the top defensive back in the league throughout the '50s.

After watching Cleveland's talented, quick middle guard Bill Willis dart around Bulldog Turner, fullback Marion Motley smash through his defense, and Horace Gillom pin back the Bears near their own goal line with his high, deep punts in 1951, Halas reacted the only way he ever did: he joined the party. He didn't succeed at first because he placed too much reliance on a character named Fido.

"Fido Murphy had undue influence on the draft, for one thing. And that was what Halas had him around for," Ed Stone said. "I don't recall where his relationship with Halas began, but it was some-thing people in the organization couldn't comprehend." Stone was a young reporter when he first met the irrepressible Murphy. "Fido would try to court the media. He got a ride with me back from Rens-selaer. He wore a pretty heavy cologne. Yuck!"

Why would Halas place so much trust in someone like Murphy? "In the beginning, he probably uncovered some sleeper somewhere for Halas, 'cause the Bears in the early drafts got a Bulldog Turner from Hardin-Simmons," Stone observed. "That time quickly passed. But he kept Fido around."

On Fido's advice, Halas's first black player was 1952's second-round choice Eddie Macon, from the small College of the Pacific. Macon was extremely fast, but he couldn't hang on to the ball. He fumbled eight times in '52 and lasted just one more year. Macon was the prelude to Fido's all-time disaster, 1953's first choice, the unfortunate Billy Anderson, who couldn't escape the shadow of his famous actor father, Rochester, nor play football.

Halas signed Michigan State quarterback Willie Thrower as a free agent in 1953. Smallish at 5'11", Thrower relieved George Blanda on October 13, 1953, in a 35–28 loss to the 49ers. He completed three of eight passes for 27 yards and his last play in the NFL, an interception. He went to Canada in 1954, lasted for three seasons, and went home to New Kensington, Pennsylvania, near Pittsburgh. He lived in virtual anonymity for 48 years as a social worker until he was featured in an ABC Black History Month documentary in 2001. Until then, whenever he told neighbors he had been the first black quarterback in the NFL, many called him a liar. After that program, until his death a year later on February 20, 2002, at age 71, he was a hero in his community.

Halas got out from under Murphy's thumb in 1955 when he landed Ohio State halfback Bobby Watkins in the second round and made him a starter alongside Rick Casares, and he stuck. Then, in 1956, he struck it rich. In the fifth round, he chose Florida A&M's Willie Galimore as a future for delivery in 1957. In the seventh round, he grabbed a fellow Illini who had played for a year in Canada.

James C. Caroline grew up in the Jim Crow environment of Columbia, South Carolina, where he starred in football at Booker T. Washington High School. He came north to enroll at the University of Illinois in 1952 and burst onto the national scene the following autumn, the year when college football returned to limited-substitution, single-platoon football. It changed the game dramatically, forcing coaches to play athletes who could go both ways. Notre Dame's legendary Ara Parseghian explained, "We put our best players on defense and built from there. We had no other choice."

Caroline, superb on both sides of the ball, led the nation in rushing with 1,256 yards in 9 games as Illinois went 7–1–1 to tie Michigan State for the Big Ten championship. In 1954, the team flopped, going 1-and-8. In Illinois's only victory that year, a 34–6 win over Syracuse at Champaign, Caroline got hurt tackling Jim Brown. "I knocked Brown out of bounds on about the three and lost the feeling in my left shoulder," Caroline said. The injury destroyed the nerve, he said, and never healed correctly. "I can raise my left arm over my head, not much else. It has atrophied."

Caroline was elected captain of a 1955 Illinois team that included a pair of future Hall of Famers in the backfield, fullback and linebacker Ray Nitschke and halfback Bobby Mitchell. However, a professor who didn't want Illinois to have a black captain gave him a failing grade. The Illinois Athletic Association investigated and found that Caroline had been mistreated. "By the time he changed the grade, I already was [playing] in Canada," Caroline said. "I grew up in the South, so I was used to discrimination. It was no big deal."

Halas ordered Driscoll to put Caroline on defense. "They needed a cornerback," he said. "I ended up playing both ways anyway." When Watkins got hurt late in the 1956 season, Caroline played 60 minutes. He did it again in '57 after Galimore got hurt.

"J. C. Caroline was one of the greatest players I ever saw. He could play anything," Rick Casares said. "He ran wild when they put him on offense. On my 68-yard run against the Lions, I cut back in the open field, and he threw the block that sprung me. On defense, he played the tightest coverage in the league. He thought he could beat anybody. He always took the best receiver."

"I was able to play in the Pro Bowl after the season. It was kind of nice to play with the big boys," Caroline said.

After an opening-day 28–21 loss in Baltimore at the hands of the 1955 bonus pick, quarterback George Shaw, the Bears headed for Green Bay and their final appearance at ramshackle City Stadium, behind East High School.

For the first time, fans in Wisconsin could watch a televised Bears-Packers game from Green Bay. CBS had the network contract, and the Packers' new play-by-play man was a Pittsburgh native named Ray Scott. By the end of the game, people around the state would be talking about his direct, terse, dramatic calls—most of them, on that day, dominated by the Bears. "Brown . . . Casares . . . touchdown . . . Chicago!" Quarterback Ed Brown played without relief and ran for a touchdown, passed for two more, and turned loose Casares, who scored twice and ran for 139 of the Bears' 278 rushing yards in a 37–21 romp. The only Packers highlight was Al Carmichael's league-record 106-yard kickoff return in the first quarter, a foretelling of coverage woes that would bedevil the Bears in the title game.

The Bears kicked into high gear, routing the San Francisco 49ers 31–7. The rematch with the Colts at Wrigley Field turned into a shoot-out. The Colts were leading 20–14 in the second quarter, and George Shaw was having another brilliant afternoon, when he got blindsided near midfield under a heavy pass rush and was carried off the field with a season-ending knee injury.

By necessity, Baltimore coach Weeb Ewbank made what became perhaps the most prescient substitution in the history of football. He sent in a guy whom Colts general manager Don Kellett had acquired that spring for 90 cents, the cost of a long-distance phone call to Pittsburgh. John Unitas made the team that summer as Shaw's backup and had not thrown a pass in a league game. No time like the present, the young man figured. Johnny U. faded back in that crossover shuttle-step series that millions of boys emulated for the next decade and a half and fired. "I figured he was going for Lenny Moore, his top receiver," said J. C. Caroline. "I got myself in position where I was ready to roll."

Roll, Caroline did, as he made the interception and turned on the speed that had made him an all-American at Illinois. The 59-yard scoring play triggered a 44-point explosion, the only flaw coming when Blanda missed the first extra point of his career after 156 consecutive conversions. Time was running out when Unitas threw the first touchdown pass of his career, starting a string of 47 consecutive games in which he would throw at least 1 scoring pass. It is pro football's equivalent of Joe DiMaggio's 56-game hitting streak. After the Bears notched the 58–27 victory, they were the league's most potent offense.

By Thanksgiving Day 1956, the Western Conference race was deadlocked between the Bears and Lions, each with a single loss. At Detroit that afternoon, safety Ken Gorgal intercepted a Bobby Layne pass to preserve a 24–20 upset win for the Green Bay Packers. It's ironic that Gorgal was wearing a Packers uniform that day. For the first seven games of the season, he was a valued member of the Bears. What happened to Gorgal was a disgrace to the National Football League and its founder. Ken Gorgal's football career was destroyed by wrongheadedness, innuendo, and deceit to the extent that he refused to be interviewed for this book. Others have filled in details of his searing ordeal.

Like most of his high school friends in downstate LaSalle, Illinois, during World War II, Ken Gorgal was a Bears fan. At Purdue, Gorgal played quarterback and defensive back for Stu Holcomb, who recommended him to Paul Brown in Cleveland. Gorgal made six interceptions for the 1950 champions. Then he entered service for two years.

He returned to Cleveland in 1953, where he started in the Browns' 17–16 loss at Detroit for the 1953 title. He won a second championship ring in 1954 when the Browns routed the Lions 56–10.

In that off-season, Paul Brown dealt future Hall of Famer Doug Atkins and, at Halas's insistence, Gorgal to the Bears for two 1956 draft choices. Gorgal enjoyed another six interceptions for Halas in 1955 and was Paddy Driscoll's starting safety to open the 1956 season on a team that most news organizations in America picked to win it all.

Nineteen fifty-six was the summer of discontent in every NFL training camp but the Bears' in Rensselaer. Unlike Halas, who always gave every player $400 at the end of camp—whether or not he made the team—not just a bus ticket home for those he cut, the other owners gave their athletes room and food. Nothing else. No money.

Several players, led by Los Angeles Rams quarterback Norm Van Brocklin, hired a Cleveland lawyer, Creighton Miller, to see what they could do about forming a union. Miller, an all-American at Notre Dame in 1943 and Johnny Lujack's best friend, had been an assistant general manager for the Browns.

By the time the Browns came to Chicago for the Armed Forces game on September 21, Miller had several players recruiting other teams for members. Before the game, Browns backup quarterback George Ratterman buttonholed Gorgal, his former teammate, and asked if Miller could send him materials regarding the fledgling union. Gorgal told him it was fine. "Just circulate them," Ratterman said. "That's all you have to do." Before they parted, Ratterman warned Gorgal to stay quiet around George Connor and ex-Brown Chick Jagade. Both men had retired after the '55 season and were assisting Driscoll. "They're Halas men," Ratterman warned. Gorgal paid heed.

In a colossal faux pas, a month later, someone in Miller's office mailed a huge envelope to Gorgal at the Bears' offices at 233 West Madison Street. It is reasonable to believe that Frances Osborne, Halas's loyal personal secretary, intercepted it, steamed it open, and took it to Halas. It contained organizing material that included an appeal and pledge cards.

Gorgal got the resealed envelope just before the team left for the annual West Coast trip in October. He played in the fifth game in San Francisco, which the Bears won 38–21. In Los Angeles, Halas went to Gorgal the day before the game. "You're not gonna suit up," he said. The team then announced that John Helwig was being activated off injured reserve.

When they returned to Chicago after the Bears' 35–24 victory, Halas told Gorgal to see him at the office on Tuesday. When he arrived, the Old Man told the safety he was on waivers. Then Halas called the papers and gave them two items to chew on. He announced that 1954's top draft choice, Stan Wallace, was back from service and would replace rarely used rookie fullback J. D. Smith on the active roster. Smith was picked up by the 49ers, with whom he starred for the next decade. Then Halas announced that another returning GI, McNeil Moore, was replacing Gorgal on the roster.

Green Bay was the next opponent at Wrigley Field. Packers assistant Lou Rymkus called Gorgal and said coach Lisle "Liz" Blackbourn, who replaced ex-Bear Gene Ronzani in 1954, wanted him. Gorgal did not accept the Green Bay offer and stayed home as the Bears beat the Packers 38–14. The following week, he went up north to Wisconsin.

Blackbourn asked him about the envelope and nothing else. Bert Bell had told Blackbourn that Gorgal was a ringleader in the nascent players' union movement. Ken denied it and joined the Packers to finish the season.

On Friday, November 16, the *Tribune*'s David Condon praised Gorgal for refusing to join the Packers before they played the Bears. Calling it an example of "the great Bears spirit," Condon quoted Gorgal: "I have too many good friends on the Bears. I didn't want to get up to Green Bay and be pumped by the coaches." Sources close to Gorgal reported that he did not speak to Condon, let alone give him that quote.

Gorgal never was offered another NFL contract after 1956, blackballed at age 27. Years later, Gorgal started attending the Bears' alumni reunions. Without fail, he would see Halas and introduce himself, and Halas would say, "I know you, Ken. Nice to see you." When Gorgal and the Old Man finished the perfunctory pleasantries, Ken would join his former teammates for more comfortable rounds of fellowship. He settled into a career as an insurance broker in Chicago that continued into his 70s, but the hurt always lingered.

TWENTY-ONE

DÉJÀ VU AND A DOSE OF HALAS HUBRIS

*O*n Sunday, November 25, 1956, the New York Giants pulled back a veneer of invulnerability and exposed the Chicago Bears as fraudulent pretenders to the National Football League throne.

When they lined up for the opening kickoff at 2:05 P.M. EST, the Bears, resplendent in their menacing dark uniforms, looked like champions. The way they'd torn through the first eight games of the schedule suggested no less. They answered an opening-game upset at Baltimore with seven straight routs. This team was the closest thing to a sure thing since George Halas's mighty prewar Monsters of the Midway teams. The notion of defeat this afternoon was so remote that heated buses waited outside Yankee Stadium, ready to whisk the team to the NBC studios in midtown Manhattan after the game for a well-advertised appearance that night on the "Steve Allen Show." Originally, Rick Casares, that year's marquee player in the NFL, was the only invited guest, but when Allen's producer called Halas for permission to let Casares appear, the Old Man refused to grant it unless the whole team was invited.

With the Bears' offense scoring 36 points a game on the record-chasing running of Rick Casares and the league-leading passing of Ed Brown and his ultimate weapon, end Harlon Hill, plus an immovable defense led by Bill George, this game, the experts reasoned, was virtually in the bag. It looked to be a mere dress rehearsal for the championship game in New York on December 30 against these same Giants.

When it came to common opponents, both teams beat the San Francisco 49ers at Kezar Stadium by identical 38–21 scores, and the Bears had cuffed the Niners around in Chicago as well, 31–7. The Giants had won six and lost twice, both times on the road, 35–27 in the second game of the season, against the Cardinals at Comiskey Park, and 33–7 on November 18 at Washington, perhaps looking ahead to the Bears instead of staying focused.

Giants head coach Jim Lee Howell, the delegator supreme, had turned over the detail work on Monday, as always, to his capable coordinators, Vince Lombardi for the offense and defensive boss Tom Landry. Then he went to his desk, lit a cigar, and relaxed for the next two days until they brought in their plans.

Lombardi, the career assistant with Army and now the Giants, was fostering an intellectual image in the New York press. As opposed to a raging volcano, as he would be remembered in Green Bay, Lombardi was described by David Maraniss in *When Pride Still Mattered* as "the bespectacled chart-toting teacher of a thinking man's game."

"Lombardi got his power sweep at a clinic I conducted in 1950. It was the same one we used at Massillon," said longtime Halas assistant coach Chuck Mather decades later. "We used it to spread the field." After repeatedly viewing film of the 1954 Rams as they ran their power sweep, Lombardi broke that version down into components and rebuilt it as the staple of his attack. The "Giants' power sweep" was the same one Lombardi would run in Green Bay. Instead of Paul Hornung and Jim Taylor, his New York ballcarriers were halfbacks Frank Gifford and Alex Webster or fullback Mel Triplett. They ran behind ex-Bear Ed Kolman's superb line, anchored by center Ray Weitecha, guards Bill Austin and Jack Stroud, and tackles Roosevelt

Brown and Dick Yelvington. Don Heinrich, a fine ball handler and smart passer, would open the game at quarterback to probe the defense as graying veteran Charlie Conerly watched and studied. Conerly then finished the job from the second quarter on. Lombardi's end coach Kenny Kavanaugh knew the Bears hadn't changed Halas's smash-and-destroy tactics since his rookie year. He fed Lombardi all he needed. Lombardi kept the playbook simple. "It was six passes, six runs," Mather said. "Make 'em go," Lombardi said.

Tom Landry, the cerebral defensive wizard, believed he had found the keys to shut down Casares. While his front four of Andy Robustelli, Rosey Grier, Dick Modzelewski, and Jim Katkavage fought off the Bears' offensive line, rookie middle linebacker Sam Huff would dog Casares's every footstep. The problem for Emlen Tunnell and Jimmy Patton and their secondary mates, Dick Nolan and Henry Moore, was how to handle Hill.

No defense had come close to a solution since Harlon blazed through the league in 1954. As well as Hill played in his MVP season, 1955, he played even better in '56. Hill was the Bears' ultimate weapon, running at full speed on every play, without letup, until the defense was about to burst waiting for Ed Brown to throw his way. When Brown did, Hill made big things happen, averaging 24 yards on every catch and scoring a touchdown every fourth time he got his hands on the ball.

The only problem the Bears could not solve was how to keep Halas from meddling. The team was his baby, of course, but everything, with the exception of the Gorgal affair, was running smoothly. "We led the league in offense in '56," Casares said. "Paddy Driscoll was one of the sweetest guys who ever lived. But Paddy was just a figurehead. He didn't say 10 words."

For the record, Luke Johnsos ran the offense, calling the shots from the press box. Clark Shaughnessy offered his suggestions from time to time, but Johnsos told him to mind his own business and stick to the defense. Then there was the looming presence of The Coach. Now that he had solved the Green Bay stadium issue and nipped Ken Gorgal's player uprising in the bud, he had time on his hands. George

Halas did not want to hurt his beloved friend Driscoll. It never entered his mind. He just wanted to win, and certainly, when it came to the game of football, Papa Bear knew best!

The first crack in the hull of the good ship Halas came in David Condon's "In the Wake of the News" column in the October 13 *Tribune*. A never-fail New York source told Condon at the World Series that he had it on solid authority that the Papa Bear was issuing orders during games. Condon, a Don Maxwell loyalist, which meant he was a Halas man as well, called the Old Man, who assured his Chicagoland readership that all was well. "I haven't said a word during a game yet," declared Halas to Condon. "I think it's just as well—the Bears right now are 100 percent better than at this same time last season."

The Bears arrived in New York with only one significant injury, left over from the second Packers game. Doug Atkins, who had begun to terrorize quarterbacks as he would until 1969, got hurt on a freakish play in a rare appearance on special teams, in replace of Goose McColl. "Bill McColl didn't want to be on the receiving team, and I got on it," Atkins said. "It was a short kick. I caught the ball, and they hit me right on that shoulder and broke my collarbone. I got out and cussed Goose out." Although Atkins was sidelined, Halas still held a trump card and didn't even need the ace in his sleeve.

Eddie Sprinkle retired after the 1955 season, his 12th, but he was only 33. "I could still maneuver. I would have played another year if they had brought me back," Sprinkle said. "Halas wouldn't do it. They went to a four-man line, and he figured I was so small at 210 that I couldn't play inside."

Size was Halas's declared reason, but the real issue, as it always was with Halas, was the size of Sprinkle's salary, not his barbed-wire-tough frame. In their 1955 deal, Halas paid Sprinkle $14,800 and refused to budge when his longtime star asked for $15,000 straight up. " 'Coach,' I said then, 'I'm not asking for a lot of money. Why don't you give me the $200, and for once as a Bear I can say I got what I asked for?' 'Can't do it, my boy. Can't do it,' he said. He wouldn't give me the $200 then—he knew I'd have the upper hand in '56." Halas instead ordered Driscoll to replace the injured Atkins with Ed "Country" Meadows, a decision that nearly destroyed the team at the end of the season.

In the game itself, the Giants took control on both sides of the line of scrimmage and treated the Bears like baby bruins. Landry's defense, led by Huff, stymied Casares, holding him to 13 yards in as many carries. Lombardi's offense dispatched the Bears' defense like a farmer clearing away brush on the back 40.

They were leading 3–0 after a Ben Agajanian field goal, when Huff intercepted a Brown pass near midfield and returned 27 yards to the Chicago 28. Heinrich then sent a 17-yard scoring pass to end Kyle Rote for a 10–0 lead at the half. The Giants made it 17–0 early in the third on Alex Webster's 12-yard touchdown run.

The Giants still had the game in hand after Blanda hit a 21-yard field goal to cut the lead to 17–3. Then Lombardi inserted Conerly in the fourth quarter. He ordered him to play it safe, keep running, and bleed time off the clock. It worked until the final five minutes, when the Bears took over after a punt.

Upstairs, offensive coach Johnsos recalled a similar situation in the 1933 opener at Green Bay when the Bears were in danger. In that one, Bill Hewitt took an end-around handoff and hit Luke on a long pass for the tying touchdown. This time, Johnsos sent McColl in motion from the left slot to his right to take a pitchout from Brown. Bill set his feet and threw as far as he could. Hill broke across the middle on a deep slant, got behind Jimmy Patton, pulled it in 65 yards downfield, and sprinted in with Patton grabbing at the back of his pants. The play covered 79 yards and cut the Giants' lead to 17–10.

The Bears recovered a fumble after the ensuing kickoff, but Huff intercepted Brown's pass to apparently salt it away. Instead, the Bears forced a Don Chandler punt and took over at their own 20 at the two-minute warning. Passes to Hill and McColl moved the ball to the Chicago 44 with a minute to play.

Brown faded to his left and fired down the left sideline for Hill at the goal line. As Patton clung to his back, Hill lunged, got his hands on the ball, juggled it twice, and landed in the end zone with the ball clutched to his chest. "Even a blind squirrel finds an occasional acorn," the modest Hill said decades later. That acorn brought the Bears a 17–17 tie that saved their season.

After the game, the Bears, as Halas had arranged, went to NBC to appear with Steve Allen, but the whole thing seemed anticlimactic. They had escaped with their lives, and they knew it. On the other side of Yankee Stadium, Vince Lombardi vowed that never again would he sit on a lead. Nor would he ever settle for a tie.

The Lions were loaded for Bear when the teams met a week later in Detroit. Bobby Layne put on brilliant show as Detroit slashed through the Bears' defense for 481 yards, 267 in the air. It was a disaster at all levels for Chicago. As the *Tribune*'s George Strickler put it, "George Halas, who gave up coaching with the declaration that he would never step back on the field again, had picked this day to make his first appearance on the Bear bench since last season." Halas grabbed the headset connected to Johnsos in the press box and relayed messages to Driscoll.

The Old Man got a close-up and personal view of his former protégé's performance as Layne passed for two touchdowns, ran for another, and kicked all six extra points to help the Lions kick the stuffing out of the suddenly tamed Bears 42–10 and take a half-game lead in the Western Conference.

Halas had the good sense to remain upstairs in the press box the following week with both the Cardinals and Bears in must-win situations. Already-heated passions were further inflamed in near-zero weather by two disputed calls that wiped out a pair of long touchdown runs by the Cardinals' great Ollie Matson. Those calls were so controversial that, for the only time to that point in decades of pro football coverage, the Bears' editorial partisans at the *Tribune* did not identify the officials in either the box-score summary or stories. The *Trib* resumed that practice the next week and also for the title game in New York.

The game was scoreless in the first quarter, when Matson took a Lamar McHan pitchout, bolted through the split defense, and streaked 65 yards to the south end zone. "Matson was the only guy who was so fast, you could hear him go by, the wind he created was so strong," Pat Summerall said of his Hall of Fame teammate. Back on the Big Red 30, the referee picked up his white handkerchief and gave the palm-down reverse wave from his chest to signal illegal motion. No score.

Placekicking in the extreme cold was nearly impossible for both George Blanda and the Cardinals' Summerall. Somehow, Blanda gave the Bears a 3–0 lead on a 36-yard field goal in the second quarter, his only success in four tries. Summerall tied it at the half with a 42-yarder. He missed four other attempts.

The Cardinals thought victory was in sight in the third quarter. The Bears clearly jumped offside as Matson ran to his right, cut upfield, broke free in the secondary, held his balance when Ray Gene Smith tried to shove him out of bounds, and sprinted all the way, 83 yards. Again the officials conferenced back near the south end zone.

Everyone in Wrigley Field and those watching on television saw the Bears jump offside. Virtually nobody, though, saw the call that nullified the touchdown. When the referee signaled holding, the Cardinals' sideline erupted. "They called holding against Joe Childress, our fullback," Summerall said. "Joe not only never held anybody in his life, he never blocked anybody in his life. So, I knew that was a bad call." Instead of gaining 174 yards on 11 carries, Matson was credited with 26 on 9 trips.

The Bears were able to spring Casares for 111 yards on 24 carries. He missed a chance at the go-ahead touchdown when he fumbled into the end zone and the Cardinals recovered. The next time was the charm. Brown, who completed just 3 of 15 passes, set up the score with a 21-yard strike to Hill. Then J. C. Caroline, who carried 18 times for 68 yards, scored on a second-effort burst from the 3. The Bears led 10–3.

The constant skirmishes and pushing and shoving finally erupted into a full-scale brawl late in the game. "I got into a fight with Harlon Hill along the sideline, I think," Summerall said. "I do remember we were by the Bear bench, and there wasn't a lot of help for me." "Hill started the one with the Cardinals, and Blanda was right there, too," Casares said. "Harlon and Pat Summerall went toe-to-toe the longest."

Harry McNamara, who had covered the Bears for the Hearst papers since 1921, doubled as the *American*'s boxing expert. "Harry and the guys from the *Front Page* era lived wildly," Bill Gleason said. "They would go cover an event, like a fight, write their stories, then gather at a speakeasy afterwards and drink all night until dawn." McNamara displayed his acquaintance with the sweet science in his description of the Hill-Summerall set-to: "Hill raised Summerall's helmet and smashed him in the face with two rights and a left hook."

Bill George, according to the *Tribune*'s Strickler, nailed Carl Brettschneider with "the best punch since Floyd Patterson upset Archie Moore." That knockout blow had come at Chicago Stadium the previous November 30 and brought Patterson the heavyweight title.

After the officials, with help from the police, cleared the field of brawling players and some trouble-seeking spectators, there was time for one last play. As in a pickup game on the prairie when the defense drops back against the anticipated desperation pass, each side went with its best. Cardinals coach Ray Richards set Dick "Night Train" Lane to the right side and Matson to the left and sent them downfield. Shaughnessy put his best man, Caroline, as deep as possible.

"For some reason, I was shifted over from the left corner to the safety," Caroline recalled. "You had Ollie Matson and Night Train Lane both flanked out, and maybe they felt I could be more helpful in the middle of the field, able to go both ways [directions]."

Lamar McHan dropped back near the goal line and fired toward Lane, who made the catch near midfield, with Caroline in close pursuit from the middle of the field, where he had the angle. "When Lane caught the ball, I had to go get him," Caroline said.

Caroline finally wrestled Lane to earth at the 9 near the south end zone after a 75-yard gain. The ball squirted loose, and McNeil Moore picked it up and ran to the Bears' 29, where he landed in concert with the report of the final gun.

Condon devoted his Monday "In the Wake of the News" column to the postgame glee in the Bears' dressing room, where the happy Halas was greeted by his 11-year-old grandson, Tim McCaskey. "Tim kissed Halas and said, 'That was pretty good, Grandpa, and I'm real proud of you.' " Tim, Condon wrote, then introduced a friend named Dick Kautz to his famous grandfather by saying, "Dick, this is my grandpa, and the Bears belong to him."

After the Bears smashed, mugged, and all but mutilated Bobby Layne and his Detroit teammates the following week in a 38–21 rout to win the Western Conference title, Lions owner Edwin Anderson and his coach Buddy Parker wrote a three-page letter to commissioner Bert Bell urging him to ban Meadows for life for knocking Layne out of the game on a late hit. "Halas is a pillar of this league," Bell said when he was interviewed after receiving the Detroit letter.

Parker said he was dismayed at the way Halas and George Preston Marshall were running the game and threatened to quit. "If that is so," Bell replied, "then how come neither of them has won a championship in 10 years or more?" He also defended Meadows. The Lions, Bell said, "have no right to crucify this kid."

Meadows even threatened a countersuit. Referee Ronald Gibbs said he did not call a penalty because the hit was legal. The *American*'s picture on page one, however, makes a liar of Gibbs. In the shot, he obviously is looking ahead at Detroit ballcarrier Gene Gedman while Meadows, to Gibbs's right, is behind Layne, his arms wrapped around the quarterback's middle prior to a hard takedown. Meadows excused his actions by saying, "He could have been hiding the ball in his stomach, for all I know."

Layne fell hard to the ground, sustaining a concussion, and was helped off the field. "I never saw anything. I never heard anything. All I know is the lights went out," he said.

The Bears themselves detested Country Ed Meadows. "Meadows was no good—not a good football player, not a good person," said George Connor, a defensive assistant in 1956. But Connor said the Lions were off base in their charge. "Halas never ordered anybody to get anybody."

"What do they want those tacklers to do?" Bell asked. "Just watch those quarterbacks?"

The clamor about Meadows overshadowed the fact that the Bears took it to the Lions all day. "I took a stinger late in the game," Casares said. When he left the field, Casares was 25 yards shy of Steve

Van Buren's game-record 215 yards and, at 1,126 yards, a mere 20 short of Van Buren's season-record 1,146. "I didn't know I was that close to the record, or anything else, not like today. Everything is current." He put on a new jersey and was ready to go, but he was never put back into the game.

"Casares was an all-around tough guy. He asked no favor, and he wasn't going to return any," said J. C. Caroline, who scored another touchdown that afternoon and played superb defense in another week of double duty. He added, "Rick's knock-down, drag-out attitude, as far as I'm concerned, made him a great football player. He might not have gotten all the publicity, but one-on-one, he could handle himself with any of those fullbacks they have nowadays."

With the title game in New York two weeks off, Halas ordered Driscoll to put the team to work and follow the usual routine, to eliminate distractions: morning meetings, lunch break, on the field in the afternoon for two and a half hours. "We were there all day from 9 in the morning until 6 o'clock at night," Casares said. "I know I didn't go anywhere for the holidays. Halas did that. Practices were as extreme as anybody's in the league. We wore pads, but it wasn't like full contact. You could bang with dummies, and defensive guys held shields. We didn't have pads on Saturday. Every other day, we were in pads."

The Meadows brouhaha was reborn on December 22 when Cardinals managing director Walter Wolfner accused the end of having got away with roughing his quarterback McHan in that now two-week-old battle at Wrigley Field, the week before the Layne fracas. Wolfner just couldn't let that December 9 game go.

It came to a head when he accused the league commissioner of maintaining two sets of rules, a double standard that favored Halas and the Bears. He said the Cardinals suffered nine penalties that cost them Matson's two overturned touchdowns while the Bears got away with 25 uncalled rules infractions. Wolfner said Cardinals assistant coach Chuck Drulis, himself a former Bear, pointed out the discrepancies when he showed the film to Bell at his home in suburban Philadelphia.

When Wolfner announced he would show the film to the television audience and stop play with each infraction, Bell threatened him with a fine and suspension if he did. Bell allowed that Wolfner could show the film without stoppage and could use no stills, and his announcer could not name officials and players involved. Wolfner canceled his plans to show the film and charged, "Commissioner Bell and George Halas of the Bears do not want the public to know the truth."

Halas blasted back, "Mr. Wolfner has never been more wrong." He said the movies showed conclusively that the Bears did not commit the violations Wolfner alleged. Then Halas reminded Violet Bidwill Wolfner's husband that he was in violation of Article VIII of the league constitution, which forbade any official of a team to publicly criticize any league official.

Back in New York, Jim Lee Howell gave his men three days off to spend Christmas at home with their families. In Chicago, Halas's defensive staff was pulling apart and not speaking. "Driscoll and Halas put me in charge of charting the Giants' offense," George Connor said in 2002. "I had films of six games, including the one we played against them. Within a few days, I could see down and formation and call the play they would run every time—without exception. I went to Shaughnessy and showed him what I had. He said, 'That's not what they do.' He refused to listen, and finally I stormed out of practice and went home."

Bill Jauss joined the *Chicago Daily News* sports staff in 1956. His wife, Kenmar, was ready to deliver at any time, but Bill, a lifelong Bears fan, could not pass up the trip to New York. "I wasn't covering the game," Jauss said. "I paid my own money. Our first son didn't arrive until a couple of weeks into January, but that was the kind of nut I was, that I went to Yankee Stadium to see that game when our child was due. Halas must have learned of that, so that when David was born, he sent a contract predated 22 years from the date of the kid's birth, which is when he would graduate from college. It was for $10,000. I knew what the players were making, and that was pretty good money, $10,000. So, one day I asked Halas, 'How come you're so generous?' And he said, 'I was allowing for the natural inflation of the times.'" Gleason laughed, adding, "You see, he was thinking all the time."

When the Bears arrived at their New York hotel, Halas called a meeting. Decades later, defensive tackle Bill Bishop told Chet Coppock the players left that meeting positive the Old Man had lost his mind. He had ordered them to change everything he ever taught about the way the Bears play football. "All right, you 'cacksuckers'!" Halas exclaimed. "We're going on national television tomorrow. I don't want the usual penalties! Especially, *no* holding, and, goddamit, *no* slugging!"

"Halas was here and there. Halas kept us in at night," Doug Atkins recalled. "He should have let us relax and play the game. He choked." The players were not ready to play the biggest game of their lives.

Nor were they represented at the Waldorf-Astoria on the Friday and Saturday before the title game when every other team participated in the first meeting of the once and future NFL Players' Association. Norm Van Brocklin, representing the Rams, presided over a meeting that included future Hall of Famers Joe Schmidt, of Detroit, and Y. A. Tittle, of San Francisco.

They sought (1) league recognition; (2) training camp pay and meal money expenses; (3) injury compensation; and (4) a pension. The 10 men there plus the Steelers' Lynn Chadnois, who could not attend, appointed Creighton Miller as legal counsel. Bert Bell agreed to meet with Van Brocklin and Miller in Philadelphia on January 28, 1957, prior to the owners meeting.

Baltimore Colts representative Bill Pellington told those attending the New York meeting that owner Carroll Rosenbloom favored a players' association, as did coach Weeb Ewbank and his staff.

In a postmeeting memo to the player reps, Van Brocklin stated that while the Bears did not send anybody, he had learned that Halas paid his players from $100 to $500 a game in the preseason. This was the hammer Halas held over his club, that he was giving them far more than union bargainers could get them. Thus, he reasoned, they were better off staying where they were.

Until this moment, Halas had set league policy, made the rules, and stumped for the major improvements—most recently, television money for all. Now he and his Bears were the renegades—the villains in fact, not just in name.

They also had this little matter of a championship game to attend to on Sunday afternoon. "We flew out of Chicago the day before, and one thing Coach Halas always did was keep up with the forecast," Harlon Hill said. "The weather was going to be rainy and cold. No weather report said it would stop raining completely and turn cold." They prepared for a muddy field and brought the requisite footwear. For mud.

Before he came to practice on Saturday morning, Giants defensive end Andy Robustelli stopped by his sporting goods store in Stamford, Connecticut, and picked up 48 pairs of basketball shoes, enough to outfit the team—just in case the field should freeze.

"It turned real cold, dropped down to 13 above. That field froze, and it was iced over," Hill said. Connor recalled, "We had poor sneakers with little rubber cleats. I know they were old: one pair had Bronko Nagurski's number 3 painted on the heel. I guess they were the same ones Halas ordered after the 1934 sneakers game, when the Giants beat us for the title in the Polo Grounds. The rubber was starting to crack, they were so old."

"I was coming back off the broken collarbone. I really wasn't well, but I was gonna play anyway," Atkins said. "I think Meadows started."

In an effort to give its readers the most comprehensive coverage, the *Chicago Tribune* hired a courier-messenger to run unprocessed film shot by its photographers to LaGuardia Airport, from where it was flown to Chicago in time to make the early editions. One of the first action pictures was a graphic shot of Giants tackle Roosevelt Brown taking Meadows out of a running play on a vicious two-fisted block under his chin. "I played just about as much as Meadows, maybe a little more," Atkins said. "After we lost, I think he wanted to get out of there anyway."

"It was the second time in Halas's career that happened," Hill said. "They came out in basketball shoes. They had good traction. That was a psychological thing. They were slipping some, too, but when we saw that—we were slipping and sliding around—we saw that and I think that just knocked us for a psychological loop."

The Bears were three-point favorites as Blanda came out for the kickoff the same as he would for any game in early autumn—with his sleeves pulled up to the elbows and joking with referee Bill

Downes as Downes handed him the ball. Blanda gave it a squeeze at both ends with his huge hands, marked it just below the middle with a stub of chalk as a target for his toe, and set it on the tee. He waved downfield, ran up, and kicked it toward the checkered end zone in front of the left-field bleachers.

Gene Filipski, of Villanova, and previously a Lombardi favorite at West Point before his expulsion in the 1951 cribbing scandal, caught the ball at the New York 8 and took off on sure feet. As the unsteady Bears skittered and slipped like novice skaters in their ancient sneaker-cleats, Filipski followed his blocking and kept going until they downed him at their own 39. The Giants had the comfort of knowing what to do and the confidence that they could do it.

Heinrich rocked Shaughnessy's defense with a fail-safe fade pattern over Caroline into Gifford's hands at the 17. The game was barely under way and the Bears were in a state of panic. Heinrich next called Mel Triplett's number, and it was 7–0 Giants. "We ran a trap in the middle," Sam Huff said in the *New York Times*, "and with his head down, he went straight over an official and into the end zone for our first touchdown."

"From that first play on, it was all Giants," Hill said. "We'd get something going and then mess it up. It was awful. I still think about it, and it was nearly 50 years ago."

"On game day when they were killing us, I went to Shaughnessy again, and he told me to get lost," Connor said. "So, I stood on the sideline and called all the plays in advance. They ran them just as I knew they would, and they kept scoring." Watching the Bears get clobbered 47–7 was a reality check for Connor's coaching ambitions. He gave it one more year, but when he realized that Shaughnessy had Halas's ear, he quit and applied his considerable energy and talent to the packaging business he started in 1949. "Everybody knew Shaughnessy didn't know anything. Just a bag of hot air," Connor said. "I don't know what Shaughnessy had on Halas. Nobody could figure it out."

When CBS was looking for an ex-player to join Red Grange on the Bears telecasts in 1958, Halas came through with the recommendation, and the Moose moved seamlessly into the booth, ending a personal nightmare. Until his dying day, March 31, 2003, Connor called coaching the "worst two years of my life."

Hill was never the same after the 1956 season. "I got hit on that icy field. Knocked the vertebrae in my lumbar region out of line. I had trouble with that back the rest of my career," Hill said. "The back injury came on a little pinch over the middle. I think it was a crossing pattern. The ball was thrown a little behind me; I had to slow down a little bit, and I got hit on the back. When I got out on the West Coast for the Pro Bowl game, the trainer thought it might be a sciatic nerve problem. It was worse than that. I never did run like I did before."

Despite the totality of the defeat, most of the players left New York believing they would bounce back. Casares was certain they would, until he had a brief conversation that gave him pause. "At our postgame meeting with Halas after we lost the '56 championship game to the Giants, he asked me how I felt about 1957," Casares said. His answer: "We'll be even better, Coach," to which Halas responded, "You're right, kid. We'll have Zeke back." Dismayed at the implication that Halas wanted Bratkowski, not Brown, at quarterback, Casares replied, "Ed's the best in the league, Coach," but he knew it was futile. "He was going to play Zeke, and we suffered," Casares said. "When we were in college—I at Florida, Zeke at Georgia—we always knew we could rush him, and he'd put it up in the air [for interceptions]. Ed Brown was our man, and we loved him."

Sport magazine featured Casares, Bill George, and Stan Jones on the cover of its pro football preview issue. Like the "Steve Allen Show," *Sport* had wanted to spotlight Casares for a profile. Again Halas refused permission, forcing the magazine to run a team story instead.

The 1957 season opened in Green Bay with the first game at New City Stadium. Paul Hornung, the Packers' bonus pick after his 1956 Heisman season at Notre Dame, watched most of the way from the bench as Babe Parilli quarterbacked the Packers to an upset victory over their great rival. "I can't complain. We won the game, 21–17. I know the stadium seated 32,000. Richard Nixon dedicated the stadium, vice president at the time," Hornung said. Halas sat beside

Nixon. James Arness, of "Gunsmoke," Matt Dillon himself, rode in the gala parade and came to the game. After that bright day, the gloom descended on Green Bay.

Matters weren't much better in Bears country. After the defeat, the *American*'s Bill Gleason paid a visit to coach Paddy Driscoll's room at the Northland Hotel. "Paddy was lying on his bed, and I kept thinking how tiny he was," Gleason said. "I just couldn't get over how this kindly old man had been such a great football player in the league's beginning. Now here he was. Then he said, 'Gee, Bill, wasn't that a great game?' I knew this was the beginning of the end."

The Bears lost four of their first five games. The crusher came in San Francisco. They were leading 17–7 when the news broke that 49ers owner Tony Morabito had died in the press box from a heart attack. The grief-stricken 49ers rallied behind quarterback Y. A. Tittle, who unleashed pro football's latest ultimate weapon, the "alley-oop," a high lob to his tall end R. C. "Overdrive" Owens. Owens, a former college basketball star, seemingly could jump over the moon and had great hands to boot. The Bears lost 21–17, and the season slipped away to a 5-and-7 finish.

By the start of 1958, Halas realized he was the only man who could clean up the mess he'd created in the first place when he appointed Driscoll. As Cooper Rollow reported in his *Bears Football Book* for 1977, Halas confided that he'd told Driscoll before the 1956 announcement that the appointment would last for two seasons only, and then he would resume coaching. He repeated that story in *Halas by Halas*. The Old Man went further, telling those who would listen that he'd wanted his dear friend Driscoll to have the same chance as head coach that trusted lieutenants Johnsos and Anderson received in 1942.

If he did nothing else, the old Papa Bear always covered his tracks.

TWENTY-TWO

CHANGING TIMES

"*P*ro football has changed so much, I thought it would be a good idea to step in the picture with the things I've learned." With those words, on February 16, 1958, owner George Halas, now 63, grabbed the traces for the fourth time as head coach of his Chicago Bears. He said he would coach for only one season, with this catch: "I don't know what will happen after the year."

Paddy Driscoll disappeared into a makeshift sound-good title that only someone like Halas could have contrived, administrative vice president. "He'll be busier than ever," Halas promised. Driscoll would "help with the coaches and work with methods and organization." In other words, he would be paid to watch game films and do nothing else.

In the two years he had been off the sidelines, Halas also learned something that everyone else in the league knew about his Bears: he realized he needed new coaching blood with fresh ideas. In 1957, *Collier's* sports editor Bill Fay, who moonlighted as Halas's television producer, visited Kansas University coach Chuck Mather in Lawrence to discuss his innovative use of modern electronics as coaching tools. Mather was the first coach to use computers and closed-circuit television so coaches on the sideline could see formations and plays from the press-box view.

He also was the hottest high school coach in America in the early '50s at Washington High School in Massillon, Ohio, where Paul Brown made his name. One day, a fan from rival Canton McKinley who worked for IBM approached Mather. "He saw that we graded by hand," Mather said. " 'Why don't you grade on IBM cards?' he asked. 'They will sort it out to save you all that calculating.' "

Kansas recruited Mather after he built a 57-and-3 record at Massillon. The Jayhawks lost all 10 games in 1954, his first year, and won only 3 in both '55 and '56. They opened the '57 season at 1–4–1, and following a 48–6 loss to the Miami Hurricanes, Mather announced that he would resign after the season. With the heat off, Kansas won Mather's last four games, beating Nebraska, Kansas State, Oklahoma State, and archrival Missouri in the finale to finish 5–4–1. Mather was named Big Eight Coach of the Year, but the die was cast. He was moving on.

"Bill Fay got Halas to interview me, and he hired me," Mather said. When Mather and his wife, Mildred, and their two children, George and Nancy, arrived in Chicago, they discovered that everything cost twice as much. "Our salary was only $13,000. Fortunately, I had in my contract I could sell insurance."

Mather built a thriving insurance business that he still operated in 2004 at age 90. In the beginning, though, Halas gave him little free time to prospect for clients. His first task: square away the playbook. "In 1958, I had to stand in front of the offense and hold up plays for the men to copy into spiral notebooks," Mather recounted. "Halas used to give a reward, $100 or $200, for the best notebook. Johnny Morris and Merrill Douglas kept the best ones."

In the next off-season, Mather convinced the coach they would gain valuable practice time if he issued the team loose-leaf binders. He mimeographed the plays and handed them out on individual sheets to be inserted at the proper spots. By July, it was time to make the 90-mile drive to the training camp at St. Joseph's College, in Rensselaer, Indiana. Coach Halas asked the younger man to accompany him in his car.

Mather's first experience with the Old Man at the wheel was nearly his last. "Halas always drove a big Lincoln. He was the worst driver

I ever saw. I've never been so frightened in my life," Mather said. "Instead of waiting, he challenged trucks and everything on this two-lane highway. When we were ready to come back, I said, 'Coach, if you don't mind, I'll drive.' He said, 'OK.' From that time on, I always drove when we traveled together."

At the training camp, when Mather asked Halas for the day's practice schedule, the coach showed him a wrinkled envelope with a few notes scrawled on it. "I told him we needed to organize it. 'You do it,' Halas said. So, I did, and Jean Doyle typed up the daily schedule from that day on."

On the field, Halas embroiled himself in yet another episode of what had become an ongoing soap opera, a quarterback controversy. "Ed Brown was our boy, and Bratkowski was there. Blanda was third string at that point," Mather said. "We all had reservations about Zeke."

Compared with 1957, all was calm. "Halas screwed up our offense," Rick Casares said about that lost season of '57. "He wanted Zeke Bratkowski at quarterback. Zeke had just got out of the army and was not ready. Ed Brown had led the league in passing, but Halas didn't like Ed personally. He was the owner-coach, and that's a terrible situation, the owner being coach. And so, we went from being favored to win the championship in '57 to finishing next to last. Halfway through the season, he was alternating the quarterbacks. It didn't work."

For a while, the Bears had a fourth quarterback on the roster, the talented but peripatetic Ronnie Knox. The boy's publicity-hungry father, Harvey, led him by the nose through three Los Angeles–area high schools; enrolled him at California, where he never played; transferred him to UCLA in 1955, where he helped lead the Bruins to the 1956 Rose Bowl; and then sent him up to Canada. Halas chose Knox in the third round of the 1957 draft and signed him to a three-year contract.

After cameo appearances in four exhibition games and the opening loss at Green Bay on September 29, 1957, Ronnie blew off practice. Then Harvey confronted Halas, charging that the Old Man had breached the contract by paying his son just $75, not the promised

$500, for the exhibition period. Halas tried to explain that $500 was coming and that the $75 was meal money. When Harvey Knox announced that Ron planned to join the players' union, the NFLPA, Halas threw up his hands, suspended the boy, let him twist slowly in the wind, and then cut him loose.

Halas still wanted another quarterback and finally landed him late in the 1958 season, when he announced that the team had purchased the contract of veteran backup quarterback Rudy Bukich from the Washington Redskins. "As the American Football League was formed, Halas collected quarterbacks," Ed Stone said. "He figured it would be the most valuable commodity the new league would want. He had the four Bs—Brown, Bratkowski, Blanda, and now Bukich." Once again, four quarterbacks.

The four Bs buzzed in discordant harmony at the end of a 1958 season that saw the arrival of the coach who, years later, not only should have replaced Halas but also might have won multiple Super Bowls had he done so. After the war, George Allen started working his way up through football's backwaters, the small colleges. He fashioned good, but not spectacular, records in head coaching jobs at Morningside, in Sioux City, Iowa, and then Whittier, in suburban Los Angeles. In 1957, Rams coach Sid Gillman hired him to coach ends. "Sid fired Allen after the 1957 season," Mather said.

"He got fired four times by the Rams," Allen's widow, Etty, said. "He was naive. He believed in Santa Claus. He did. He trusted them." In the summer of 1958, the car wash he'd opened in Los Angeles was sinking in a sea of red ink, and he needed a job.

"Allen came to Rensselaer in 1958 selling weighted footballs by Voit," Mather said. "He asked me to get Halas to see him. Halas didn't want any part of them." Allen went home to L.A. with no idea where he would land in or out of football. "When he got home, Allen wrote me a letter telling me how lucky I was to coach pro football," Mather said. "I felt sorry for George on that basis."

George Halas was too busy getting reoriented to coaching and getting a team ready to take pity on a kid named George Allen or on anyone else who wanted a job that did not exist with the Chicago Bears. His operation was in full order the way he wanted it as training camp moved into the preseason games and preparation for the regular season.

Thanks to the efforts of his longtime personnel director Frank Korch, Halas felt he had the players to make a run at the defending champion Detroit Lions and the emerging Baltimore Colts to get back into the title game. He especially liked a trio of promising defenders: linebacker Chuck Howley, his top choice, from West Virginia; pass-catching end Willard Dewveall, from SMU, a likely replacement for Bill McColl; and Erich Barnes, a head-hunting defensive back from Purdue.

Frank Korch had been the hardest grinder on the Chicago sports scene for a quarter century. Korch was a nonstop, do-all guy who wore two hats seven days a week in serving two demanding masters: Jack Brickhouse at WGN and Halas, for whom he filled two slots. At WGN, Korch was the indispensable man behind the scenes who fed Brickhouse the facts, figures, and anecdotes that enlivened his television and radio broadcasts. Korch had been around so long that it was hard to believe he was only 45 in 1958.

Korch started with Halas in 1933, handling publicity, as he cranked out countless articles for the football programs along with "Bearographies" and other pertinent publicity for the annual guides that Standard Oil dealers gave out to customers throughout middle America. Korch also devoted hour upon hour as personnel director, working his network of college sports information directors to find future Bears. "Frank never visited anyone," Chuck Mather said. "But press agents aren't the worst guys to know. They have a realistic view, while a head coach might be attached to a guy."

Korch was on duty as usual in the press box on Friday night, September 5, 1958, in Dallas, producing the WGN radio broadcast from the Cotton Bowl for Brickhouse and Irv Kupcinet. The game may have been a meaningless exhibition, but not to Detroit, who wanted blood and revenge against Halas in his first coaching appearance against the Lions since the Layne-Meadows fiasco of 1956. The Bears emerged with a 24–17 victory in a game marred by excessive penalties and cheap shots. They spent the night in Big D and took a bus to Love Field to catch a morning flight home.

"Frank was running for the plane, carrying two suitcases," Mather said. "I said, 'Frank! Frank! Slow down, Frank!' He sat down and had this snort, and went white."

"George Connor and I were kids together. I would often ride the plane home after a game," Bill Gleason said. "Frank Korch was sitting in the seat in front of us. People came running over. He was slumped over. He appeared to be asleep—he was tired all the time. George's father was a doctor. George looked over the seat and said, 'Bill, he's dead.' They had to get him off the plane." Bill McColl, a resident at the University of Chicago Medical School, tried everything but could not revive Korch.

"We had to leave Frank in Texas until the coroner would release his body," Mather recalled. " 'Chuck, you stay with Frank,' Halas said. I had to answer the questions. I had to buy a casket. You can't get a body out of Texas without one. I spent a day and half there; that wasn't too pleasant."

Mather accompanied the body to Chicago on a Sunday flight. "Frank had four young children. He had a wonderful, beautiful wife named Virginia. He did all the shopping, everything. Virginia was left in a position of not knowing how to care for herself. Halas devoted a lot of effort to take care of her." It was not the first time, nor would it be the last time, the coach would take the extra step for someone in need.

Halas resumed his routine and began his regular-season comeback with a 34–20 victory at Green Bay over a dispirited Packers team coached by former Bear and Halas favorite Ray "Scooter" McLean.

Johnny Unitas conducted a precision-passing clinic at Halas and Shaughnessy's expense the following Saturday night in front of 60,000 screaming Baltimore fans and a couple of million disappointed Bears fans watching on WGN-TV. Now the unquestioned top quarterback in football—and to many observers, already the best they had ever seen—Unitas continually hit targets such as Raymond Berry, Jim Mutscheller, and Lenny Moore on short and long patterns, and stirred in Alan Ameche's tough runs, to lead the Colts to a 51–38 romp.

For the next month, the Bears would play the 49ers and Rams, two weeks in Chicago followed by a fortnight on the West Coast. Mather went to Halas and asked him to bring George Allen to Chicago to debrief him on the Rams. "He can tell us about Sid Gillman's audibles," he told the coach. "Good idea, kid," Halas said.

"We brought George in, and he helped us win when we got an interception off an audible," Mather said. The Bears routed the Rams 38–10. "Halas didn't want anyone to know we had Allen here, so he said, 'Get him the hell out of here.' So, I had to tell George I was sorry—that's all there was."

Allen again returned home to Southern California, but Mather kept working on Halas. He urged him to get a personnel man to replace Korch, and he pushed hard for his friend, reminding Halas how Allen helped the Bears beat the Rams. "George knows a lot of college guys," Mather persisted. "He'd be a good personnel guy."

"The Bears flew George back to Chicago, and he got the job," Etty Allen recalled. "We had just moved from Whittier to Encino, where I built my second house. Everybody used to ask me, 'How can you build houses when your husband is a coach?'"

It wasn't easy. She had to watch her pennies and cope with three young sons—and, three years later, a daughter, Jennifer. A real estate broker told Etty that selling a house is easier if people are living in it. So, she said, "I stayed in the house in Encino for nine months while George lived at the Y and in Chicago. He would send me the paycheck," Etty Allen recalled. "I don't know how he survived."

Just being around George Halas was all the encouragement Allen needed. "George always wanted to coach. The first two years, '58 and '59, Halas didn't let George do any coaching," Mather said. Like a theatrical understudy, Allen watched the master's every move, learned and absorbed his lessons, and finally was assigned to Clark Shaughnessy to help with the defense, where he learned what and what not to do.

He became an astute judge of professional talent, bringing players to the Bears who would make major contributions. "George really should have the credit for bringing in the players who made it possible for us to win in '63," Mather said. Allen picked up Rams Joe Marconi, Jon Arnett, and Larry Morris; a Minnesota castoff, guard Mike Rabold; and cornerback Davey Whitsell, from the Lions. All would play important roles.

In 1959, the "37-year-old" Allen was ensconced in his role with Halas as personnel director and aspiring assistant. One night, he came home after work and, after pouring himself his usual glass of milk while Etty lit a cigarette and poured herself a glass of water, he sat her down at the kitchen table. "He told me that he was 41, 4 years older than he said when we met," Etty said. "I could tell he was so embarrassed. It took him time to get through college. He served in the Navy and went to Marquette, Alma College, and finally Michigan."

Jennifer Allen later explained that before her father finished at Michigan, he had to drop out of both Marquette and Alma to work and earn tuition, plus help his sister support their parents after his father was permanently disabled in an auto factory accident. Because Allen did not want to appear what he was in 1945, a 27-year-old undergraduate, he lopped 4 years off his age.

George Halas may or may not have known those details, but, for certain, he would have had somebody check out Allen thoroughly. It was his way. Most important, in Allen, he had found a younger version of himself, a kinsman at heart, a dedicated, loyal, hard-working protégé who learned every trick of the trade. George Allen was his boy.

"George told me that when everyone else left the office, he and Mr. Halas still would be there," Etty recalled. "He said Halas would always turn off the lights when he left a room. 'I'm the one paying the bill,' he'd say. It became a ritual at our home. A lesson in frugality, but it's correct."

Since the league's founding in 1920, Halas was the driving force who made the rules, whether to fit his own needs or for the betterment of the league. When it came to the officials, he wanted his favorite referees—Bill Downes or Ron Gibbs—and their crews to handle the big games and most of the little ones in between. And woe betide the official who worked a game the Bears lost. Dan Tehan, a veteran head linesman from Cincinnati, took Mather aside after he joined the club and told him how his boss really treated the men in black and white stripes.

"They would go into a room after the game to get their money," Mather explained. "Halas would put the money into piles for the three officials there; the referee got more than the umpire, who got more than the head linesman." One day after the Bears lost a close one, Tehan and the two other officials were changing before heading downtown to catch trains for home, when Halas came in, late, as they were ready to leave. He arranged the cash in its appropriate piles. "Then," Mather said, "he ran his hand through the money and swept it to the floor. 'There, you bastards. There's your money,' Halas said as he left the room. Tehan said he and the others had to get on the floor to pick up their cash and sort it out."

Halas could get away with such stunts as long as his man Bert Bell served as commissioner. That all changed on October 11, 1959. Bell was sitting among the fans in the end zone at Franklin Field in Philadelphia, watching the Eagles-Steelers game, when he was stricken by a massive heart attack. He was pronounced dead a short while later. League treasurer Austin Gunsel was named interim head and would be in charge until the league meeting in January 1960.

Bell's death came at a difficult turn for the NFL. The summer before, Lamar Hunt, of Dallas, and K. S. "Bud" Adams Jr., of Houston—sons of two of America's wealthiest oil barons—decided to start their own pro football teams. They and Bob Howsam, of Denver, met with Halas at 233 West Madison Street early in the second week of August 1959. Halas told the three that the NFL was not thinking of expanding but would consider Houston and Dallas and, perhaps, their applications. He told Howsam he had no interest in Denver.

By then, George Blanda was off the active roster but still on the payroll, trying to get his release. Halas also knew that Tex Schramm, former general manager of the Rams, was finishing his business with CBS Sports and already was at work with another Texas oilman, Clint Murchison Jr. Murchison and Schramm wanted the Dallas franchise, and they had Halas's blessing.

That single meeting with the Papa Bear in his den convinced Hunt and Adams that they were wasting their time. Undaunted by Halas's aloofness, they held a news conference in Chicago on Friday, August 14, to announce they were forming a six-team American Football League. The AFL would operate with franchises in Houston, Dallas, Minneapolis, Denver, Los Angeles, and New York.

Intrigue and Machiavellian tactics were as natural to Halas as breathing. He undercut the AFL with several urgent calls to persuade Max Winter's Minnesota group to join the established National Football League instead of casting their lot with a bunch of renegades. Bell then announced that the Murchison-Schramm Dallas Cowboys would start play in 1960, and Winter's Minnesota Vikings would begin in 1961.

Aware that Southern Methodist's popular hometown quarterback Don Meredith was the key to Dallas supremacy, Schramm signed him to a personal services contract. Then, Halas drafted Meredith in the third round and immediately announced he had traded him to the new Cowboys franchise. Schramm also signed another cornerstone of the franchise to a personal services deal, fullback Don Perkins, from New Mexico.

With the new league a reality, Halas had no choice but to grant Blanda his release. The last thing he and the NFL wanted or needed was a restraint-of-trade suit, and Blanda had built a strong case by refusing to retire. Houston's new general manager, John Breen, who had just left the Cardinals and was aware they were ready to move to St. Louis, knew all about Blanda's troubles. He signed him for $18,000 for 1960, twice what Halas ever paid, and then went after Heisman Trophy winner Billy Cannon, of LSU, who also signed.

By then, Halas had discovered that not only was Allen an exceptionally skilled handler of men, but also he was smart and, like himself, a planner and a detail man. Allen saw how Halas chose sides on the field to keep the sun out of his receivers' eyes at the crucial point of a game. Years later, Allen had an assistant check the sun angles every day before his Washington Redskins faced Miami in the 1973 Super Bowl. If no detail was too small for George Halas, it held double for George Allen.

Sun angles begat spying and diverting potential spies, which begat the art of drafting and the even finer arts of combing the waiver wires for help and, the biggest of all, trading. In his first draft, 1959, Allen missed on the top pick, Ohio State halfback Don Clark, who went to Canada for more pay. He recouped on the second round, landing the team's superb strong safety for a decade, Rich Petitbon. Petitbon would follow Allen to Los Angeles and then to Washington, where he would become defensive coordinator and, for a short term, serve as the Redskins' head coach, succeeding Joe Gibbs.

By 1958, Harlon Hill was a falling star. By 1959, Hill was on his last legs. "I had the ability to be a Hall of Famer until my back injury," Hill said. "It restricted my speed and led to the ruptured tendon." The back injury in the 1956 title game coincided with the onset of his heavy drinking. "Booze hurt me some," he conceded, "but if I had not hurt my back and my tendon, I believe I would have had four or five more great years. I really do."

Hill was in denial in his battle with the bottle. Even the fans could see that something was missing. He still had the moves, if not the speed, but he began to drop wide-open passes. "I tried to stay away from him when he started drinking," said Doug Atkins. "Harlon just couldn't control it."

The injuries followed. He suffered a season-ending shoulder separation in 1957. The next year, in a 17–0 loss to the Colts at Wrigley Field, the Bears' first shutout loss since 1946 to the Giants, Hill was running a pass pattern early in the fourth quarter, when his left Achilles tendon snapped.

"I couldn't walk," Hill said 45 years later. At nearby Illinois Masonic Hospital, Dr. Ted Fox performed the surgery that night, with his resident, Harlon's teammate Bill McColl, assisting. "Dr. Fox says I was the first one that he knew of in the history of athletics, any sport, to ever recover from a complete rupture. He did a good job. I played again, but it wasn't the same," Hill said.

Hill came back to play in 1959, but his behavior off the field only worsened. "Halas called me and tried to help me out. He helped a lot of people, and he was rude to a lot of people," Hill said. "He wasn't straddlin' no fence." Halas showed Hill the thick dossier that the

Burns Detective Agency had amassed concerning his drinking bouts and freewheeling bar brawls. Hill couldn't change. He left after the 1961 season and finished his NFL career the next year in stops at Pittsburgh and Detroit.

"Harlon Hill should have been a Hall of Famer, but you don't get in on four years," George Connor said. "Raymond Berry and I talked about Hill. He had more moves, more speed, than Berry." In the three years before he got hurt, Hill caught 134 passes for 3,041 yards and 32 touchdowns. He averaged 22.7 yards a catch, and he averaged a touchdown for every 4 receptions, both unprecedented and unequaled marks. Even more telling is his overall record including his injury-filled years: Hill still averaged 20.2 yards per catch.

In all, he scored 40 touchdowns on 233 receptions, a touchdown for every 5.8 catches. Only Paul Warfield, who also averaged 20.2 yards a catch, has a better TD-per-catch ratio: 1 for every 5.02 receptions. Hill's prorated career numbers beat the marks of Jerry Rice and Don Hutson in average yardage and TD-per-catch ratio. Does he belong in the Hall of Fame? Stan Jones thinks so. On merit. "Since 1986, they've given an award for the top player in Division II. The Harlon Hill Award."

In 1966, four years after he left football, Harlon Hill moved back home to Killen, Alabama. He earned his master's degree and, in 1969, began a teaching career at Brooks High School. "Smartest thing I ever did," Hill said. One morning in 1974, he got out of bed and decided he'd had it with hangovers and constant guilt. "I never liked the taste of alcohol. People ask, 'How did you stop?' I quit cold turkey." And he never took another drink. His teaching career prospered. "I became a principal in January 1980 at Brooks High School and retired in 1992," Hill said. He ended his teaching days as president of the Alabama principals association.

With the possible exception of George Blanda, the player who had the most run-ins with George Halas, until the arrival of young Mike Ditka, was fullback Rick Casares. No individual on the team drew more respect from teammates and opponents alike. "He's 70 years old. He's the strongest son of a bitch you ever saw. You grab a hold of his arm and it's like a piece of steel!" exclaimed Packers legend Paul Hornung, Casares's close friend, in late 2002.

Casares was the toughest man on a team of hardened pros. He took injections to enable him to play with cracked ribs and even a broken ankle. "Dr. Fox told Halas when he shot me for my ribs, I would stretch, and he'd stick the needle in there. That's really something to see—that long needle going in your rib. You wonder how it's not going to puncture something inside there."

One time, after the injection, as he was getting ready for the game, Casares said to Fox, "Wait a minute, I can still feel something here. Over here." He bent over for another shot. "Rick, I've given you enough," Fox said, but Casares was insistent. "I can still feel this here," he said. "I've never given anybody that much novocaine," the doctor said, but he finally yielded.

"He did it," Casares said. "I dressed next to Joe Fortunato. I was putting on my shoes and putting on my stuff, when I got dizzy as hell, and I slumped over." He told his friend Joe that he felt "funny." "What the hell? Rick," Fortunato responded. "Look at your shoes."

"I had put my shoes on my wrong feet," Casares said. "Then I started getting dizzy again, and they took my stuff off and packed me in ice while the team went out for the warm-up. I reacted to all that novocaine." Casares waited until he stabilized and then got dressed and went out to play football.

Then there was a memorable confrontation with Halas as the team prepared to leave for an overnight road trip. Casares, a clotheshorse, hated to wear the same outfit after taking a trip. "Most people carried just a toothbrush in a soft handbag. Halas would stay in the same suit for three days," Casares said. But Casares, a stylish dresser who would not wear the same clothes two days in a row, had other ideas. He boarded the team bus toting a garment bag over his shoulder. "I had a jacket, another pair of pants, and a shirt inside. I was gonna change."

"What the hell is that?" Halas yelled.

"A change of clothes," Casares answered.

"You 'cacksucker'! You're always thinking of pussy. You're up to no good. That's gonna cost you a hundred dollars!"

"What?"

"You're thinking about cabareting! We're gonna play a football game."

"For Christ's sake!" Casares said. "Just because I like to change my clothes? You can go to dinner with me."

"It'll still cost you a hundred!" Halas roared.

After the Bears' 1960 game in Los Angeles, Bill Gleason called the Bears the "most overcoached and undertaught team in the NFL." That comment came after an incident involving Casares on the Saturday before the game.

"I have nightmares to this day about it," Casares said. The team was taking a bus to the Coliseum for a workout, when Halas saw a park and ordered the driver to stop and open the door. "He put in a whole new series of 'bastard plays,' " Casares said.

"We're gonna do this here, because they'll be watching us at the field," Halas said, ever the paranoiac about spies.

According to Casares, "He put in a whole new goal-line series! He reversed the player and hole numbers. Instead of even being to the right, he put even to the left."

Late in the game the next day, Ed Brown marched the Bears to first-and-goal to set up the winning touchdown. Back in Chicago, fans watching on CBS saw them come up empty in a bizarre sequence of mishaps that looked as though the Bears were fixing the game. In reality, it was the result of the confusion Halas initiated the day before.

"We got in the huddle," Casares said, "and Brownie called this new shift, and I didn't have a handle on it. 'Brownie, which side do I go to? Which side?' I wasn't sure. I had to head up to the middle, and I didn't know which way he was going to turn to make the handoff." The confused Casares forgot whether he was supposed to clear out of the way of the halfback on a fake, or take the handoff. If only he could remember the new signal sequence. "He called a fake to me and a handoff to the halfback. So, I wanted to get the hell out of the way, and I didn't know which side of him I had to go." In desperation, Casares jumped—and the flags flew. "That's the only time in my entire career I went in illegal motion," he said. Things didn't improve. "I went in motion on the next play." A false start. "On the next play, Brownie called a similar play, and I ran into him. So, we came off the field. It was one of the worst experiences of my life." The game ended in a 24–24 tie.

The 1960 season was also notable as the first in which Bears fans were able to see the team's road games on the tube. For the first time since the founding of the National Football League, they had Chicago to themselves. After that memorable 1956 brawl-filled game at Wrigley Field, the Cardinals series was never the same. Walter Wolfner got rid of his best players.

He traded Pat Summerall to the Giants in 1958. In New York, Summerall kicked the Giants into championship contention and began his successful and enduring television career. The trade that ended any strong feeling in Chicago for the Cardinals came between the 1958 and '59 seasons when Wolfner shipped Ollie Matson to the Los Angeles Rams for nine players. In 1959, the Cardinals moved to Soldier Field, where they played to small crowds in a dismal 2-and-10 season that had ended for all practical purposes in their 10th game when the Bears routed them 31–7 before 46,000 fans—well below capacity in the huge stadium.

"The league wanted the Cardinals out, plus the fact that Wolfner wanted the team in St. Louis. That was how it worked out," said Bill Gleason. To Gleason, the quintessential South Sider, the Cardinals' departure always rankled.

On September 29, 1957, Harry MacNamara covered the Bears' opener and the City Stadium dedication at Green Bay for the *American*. It was his last assignment. "He had cancer, and they gave me the Bears," Gleason said. "I astonished the sports editor at the time when I told him, 'I don't want the Bears. I want to stay with the Cardinals.'" The editor, Leo Fischer, prevailed, and Gleason started his long and often contentious relationship with Halas. McNamara died in 1958, heralded by his peers in their obituaries as the first pro football writer.

Thanks to fast finishes, the Bears were second in the Western Conference with 8-and-4 records in both 1958 and '59. Instead of taking the next step, though, they continued to run in place—initially behind Baltimore and then, by 1960, behind Vince Lombardi's resuscitated and reborn Green Bay Packers.

The 1960 team might have broken through, but leadership at the top, namely Halas, was a drag on performance. A week after the 24–24 tie in L.A., the Bears flopped in a 25–7 loss at San Francisco.

They headed into the seventh game at three wins, two losses, and a tie, trailing the Colts and Packers. The Colts were next at Wrigley Field on November 13. Halas put everything on one roll of the football dice, an all-out, make-or-break-the-season effort.

The Colts had humiliated the Bears 42–7 at Memorial Stadium in the second game of the season. So, getting the Bears ready was no problem. Those who saw the rematch called it the hardest-hitting regular-season game they ever saw. Both teams traded shots all day. Casares scored both Chicago touchdowns. Alan Ameche plunged for one Baltimore score, and Unitas and Lenny Moore teamed up on a 36-yard scoring pass for the other. Otherwise, the Bears contained and often overwhelmed Unitas with an all-out blitz. They took a 20–17 lead with two minutes to go on John Aveni's 37-yard field goal.

Aveni followed with two out-of-bounds kickoffs and a short third one that left Unitas just 60 yards away. He pushed the Colts to the 33, where Doug Atkins drew blood from his forehead, nose, and mouth on a shot to the face mask with no penalty. Unitas shook off the hit, but Bill George roared in and sacked him for a 10-yard loss at the Bears' 39. Seventeen seconds remained as Unitas shot the works. He lofted a pass toward Moore, who was going one-on-one against the Bears' best cover man, J. C. Caroline. Chuck Mather, who saw the play develop from the Bears' sideline on the west side of the field, reported, "Moore went into the north end zone by the east stands."

"We had a little collision," said Caroline. "I was knocked off stride and off balance. It was the last play of the game, and Moore caught the ball for the touchdown."

"Everyone there stood up, and when they did, the entire bleachers shifted about three feet. It was a miracle the entire stand didn't go down," Mather said. "Had it collapsed, thousands would have been injured, many killed. Halas had Ralph Brizzolara make certain the stands were strengthened."

The Unitas-to-Moore miracle gave the Colts a 24–20 victory. The Bears, especially Halas, screamed foul in the dressing room, claiming Moore had pushed off Caroline. The story, under dark headlines, led every sports section in Chicago's four newspapers on Monday. It continued to rage after Halas called the papers Monday morning and told them to send writers and photographers to the team offices at 233 West Madison.

"Howie Roberts, who usually covered the Bears for us, was on another assignment, so John P. Carmichael told me to go down to Madison Street to the Bears' briefing," Bill Jauss recalls. Jauss was in his fifth year at the *Daily News*. "Halas was still irate over the call, and he showed us movies of the controversial play, which you weren't supposed to do at that time. But Halas, since he wrote all the rules anyway, could break them, I guess."

"See, gentlemen," Halas said, "this proves conclusively that it was incorrect and there was a mistake on the play. I'd appreciate it if you would run the sequence of photos in your papers tomorrow. Are there any questions?" "Yes, sir," Jauss said. "Would you mind replaying that? I just want to be sure."

"Well!" Halas responded. "Do you know the rules of football?"

"Sure," Jauss said. "Not as well as you, but I do think I know pass interference. I've had a couple called against me."

"I admire your thoroughness," Halas said. "You can look at the film as many times as you want."

Jauss relates, "I said I would take the pictures back and let my photo editor take it from there." He told Halas, "I'm not going to write it as clear-cut as you say it is. I'll quote you as saying it's clear-cut. Besides, people don't want to know what I think about it. I'm just a punk."

With a final chuckle, Jauss concluded, "I guess that impressed him, because from that day on, we always had a respectful—ah—I always respected him, and I guess he respected me for that."

The last word came 43 years later in a conversation with Caroline from the Urbana, Illinois, middle school where he has taught so long that his students' grandparents may be the only ones old enough to have seen him play at Illinois or with the Bears. "It was unintentional," Caroline stressed. "Moore was going for the ball. I might have tackled him and gotten a penalty. I was in position when the ball was coming; then I hit the back of his legs and felt the contact and fell off to the side. He caught it. There was a little contact, but that was part of the game."

Both the Bears and Colts left everything on the battlefield. The Colts drew a bye the week after the Bears' victory. They would not win again. The Bears regrouped with two straight wins—over the Detroit Lions, 28–7, and the winless Dallas Cowboys, 17–7. Green Bay was next. The Bears held a half-game lead over the Packers, whom they beat in the opener, 17–14.

The Colts dropped their last four, including an unbelievable 20–15 loss to the Lions at home. Unitas and Moore had teamed up for the apparent winning touchdown with 14 seconds to play. After the giddy fans had been cleared off the field, the Colts kicked off. With time for one play, the Colts dropped back eight men. Earl Morrall hit wide-open tight end Jim Gibbons over the middle, and he went all the way, 65 yards, untouched, for the improbable victory.

The Bears still had a chance in Chicago that same day against Green Bay. Halas was not about to let that smart New York guy named Lombardi run his power sweep around his flanks all day. No way!

TWENTY-THREE

BUILDING FOR ANOTHER TITLE

*O*n Sunday afternoon, December 4, 1960, a seismic event shifted National Football League influence from its longtime Chicago base 200 miles northward to Green Bay, Wisconsin. Smart, aggressive Vincent T. Lombardi blew into Wrigley Field that day from sport's smallest city and, in two and a half hours, boldly snatched the scepter and mace from the clutches of league founder George S. Halas to carry it home in triumph.

"Halas used to roam up and down the sidelines," Paul Hornung recalled. "He went down near the end zone, the five-yard line. Coaches weren't supposed to be down there, and he would cuss like a sailor. I loved it. It was an absolute honor to have him cuss me out during a ball game. 'Get that son of a bitch!' he'd yell."

Lombardi's Packers answered Halas's rants with a resounding, irresistible display of crisp, clean, hard-nosed football. They blocked, tackled, ran, and passed their way to a 41–13 trouncing of the Bears. Clark Shaughnessy's defense could not stop Lombardi's basic, thoroughly schooled, and precisely executed plays. "They played like champions," Halas admitted after the game. He would not beat Lombardi again for nearly three years.

"They started out as adversaries," said former *Tribune* sports editor Cooper Rollow. "They wound up with a wonderful relationship." In the '60s, Rollow spent almost as much time in Green Bay with Lombardi as he did in Chicago covering Halas. "You gotta remember," he said, "that this was Halas's territory when Lombardi came into this area. Lombardi was an almost immediate sensation." The Packers won the Western Conference title in 1960, and in his third year, they won the first of five titles they would accumulate over the next seven years. "People began saying Lombardi was the greatest coach in history, which didn't go over very well, of course. After all, Halas had been in business for 40 years or so."

Before it got too one-sided, Lombardi made certain to get Halas lined up on his side. So, he took him out to dinner. "They had a wonderful meal and wonderful evening," Rollow said. "Lombardi did everything, I'm told, down to pouring Halas's wine. By the end of the evening, Lombardi kept repeating to Halas, 'You are the greatest coach in history! Never mind what I've done. I haven't been here very long. You're the greatest! The greatest of all time.'

"The two became inseparable," Rollow said. "After that, you would never hear Halas say a word about Lombardi. They became real good friends. Now, that's not to say they didn't have competitive urges, of course. Naturally, they did. Halas really wanted to clean his ass every time, and, I suppose, vice versa."

Vince Lombardi had paid his dues in a lifetime of living, studying, playing, and coaching in and around New York. His hero was his boss at West Point, Earl Blaik. At Army, Lombardi carved out the reputation that got him hired in 1954 as the Giants' offensive coordinator. Then, in 1959, when he was 45, the Green Bay Packers called.

The postwar Packers had been on the ropes. After Lambeau, the founder, was run out of town in 1950, the three men who followed him—Gene Ronzani, Lisle Blackbourn, and Ray "Scooter" McLean—failed miserably. Jerry Vainisi, who served the Bears as controller and Halas's last general manager, grew up observing the Packers through the eyes of his brother, Jack, 14 years his senior. "Jack was the only guy who survived for 10 years through a Packer organization that underwent four regime changes," Jerry said.

Jack Vainisi, who was born in 1927, was just behind Mugs Halas at St. Hilary's School, at Bryn Mawr and California. Gene Ronzani, a Halas favorite, became a family friend when he shopped at the elder Vainisi's grocery, in Uptown, a mile or so north of Wrigley Field. When Ronzani returned from service in 1944, he mentored Jack while he starred at St. George's High School, in Evanston. "Jack played right tackle in 1945 at Notre Dame for Hugh Devore," Jerry Vainisi said. "After the season, he was drafted for the mop-up campaign in Japan, where he took ill with strep throat."

In a move to prevent malingering, the army had enacted a regulation that a soldier could not go on sick call unless his fever reached 103. Though ill, Private Vainisi had to stay on duty. When the fever surpassed 103, the medics finally admitted Jack. "The strep became rheumatic fever and damaged his heart," Jerry said.

Forbidden to play sports, Jack Vainisi returned to Notre Dame, earning his degree in 1950. When Green Bay hired Ronzani to replace Lambeau, he asked Jack to handle personnel. "He was always on the road," Jerry said. "He established a network of college coaches who sent him reports on their own players and opponents as well."

One of Jack's campus scouts in 1956 was Jim Finks, who had left the Steelers to assist Terry Brennan at Notre Dame. "Finks told me Jack paid him $25 a game to file a report on Notre Dame's last opponent," Jerry said. "He'd supply a breakdown so Jack wouldn't have to sift through all the players. The word of a guy like Finks and the coaches he knew was valued."

The Packers were a league doormat, but Jack Vainisi was drafting for the future. In 1956, he landed the two championship-era tackles Forrest Gregg and Bob Skoronski and, in the 17th round, Alabama quarterback Bart Starr, considered a backup at best. He struck gold in 1957 when he chose Hornung with the bonus pick and, with the next pick, his own, took Michigan's all-time great end Ron Kramer. The bonanza came in 1958 when, in the first four rounds, he bagged linebacker Dan Currie, of Michigan State; fullback Jim Taylor, of LSU; Illinois linebacker Ray Nitschke; and Idaho guard Jerry Kramer. But the team was green, wet behind the ears, and still losing. "I was ready to give it up," Hornung admitted in 2002.

"Jack was named interim GM," Jerry Vainisi said. "His first job was to hire the coach. Jack was really the guy who brought in Lombardi." As David Maraniss explained in *When Pride Still Mattered*, Jack Vainisi had to convince the Packers' executive committee that Lombardi was chairman Dominic Olejniczak's idea. "Vince told them he wouldn't go there unless he had Jack with him."

Lombardi told the executive committee he must hold the general manager title. Not only did it put him on equal footing with Halas in Chicago and Brown in Cleveland, but also, it made him the last link in the chain of responsibility for personnel decisions. As soon as he was hired, he met with Jack and explained his new duties and his importance to the organization. "You'll be general manager for all intents and purposes, except I'll have the title. That way, I won't have to go anywhere where someone's going to say I must keep a player due to financial commitments or whatever. Other than that," Lombardi said, "you're the general manager."

"Jack's title was business manager," Jerry said. "He was scout, traveling secretary, everything. He was absolutely in charge of player personnel, but he didn't make the ultimate decisions."

While new coach and GM Lombardi was turning Hornung into another Frank Gifford, Jack Vainisi brought in the heart of the Green Bay defense in a series of trades with Cleveland through Paul Brown. "Paul Brown was such a great man," Jerry Vainisi said. "When I got the GM job with the Bears, he called from Cincinnati and told me that when he was at Cleveland, he never wanted to trade within the Eastern Conference. He found a trading partner with my brother at Green Bay. It turned out great for Jack. From Brown, he landed such great Packers as Bill Quinlan, Willie Davis, and Henry Jordan, essentially the heart of Lombardi's great defense."

Lombardi won the Packers Backers over in his debut, a 9–6 victory over Halas and the Bears on September 27, 1959, on Jim Taylor's fourth-quarter touchdown and a safety. Halas evened the score at Wrigley Field on November 8 when the Bears capitalized on two Hornung fumbles to win 28–17. Then Halas took a lead in his personal duel with Lombardi for the last time, with a 17–14 win in the 1960 season opener. The Western Conference was up for grabs the entire season, as neither the favored Bears nor defending champion Colts could establish dominance.

On Sunday, November 27, 1960, three days after Thanksgiving, Jack Vainisi was shaving when his wife heard a thud in the bathroom. "The fire department had to break down the door," Jerry said. "He was wedged in there. Dead." Jack Vainisi's rheumatic heart had burst at age 33. After the funeral, the team dedicated the game against the Bears the following Sunday to his memory.

Lombardi had his offense primed, and defensive coordinator Phil Bengtson and his squad were just as pumped. The Packers ran their game plan to perfection, especially the power sweep, with Hornung or Taylor running behind guards Jerry Kramer and Fred "Fuzzy" Thurston, a onetime castoff from the Bears' training camp and another Jack Vainisi gem. Starr hit on 17 of 23 passes for 227 yards and touchdowns to Hornung and Max McGee as the Packers blasted their biggest rival 41–13.

Hornung, who would shatter the one-season NFL scoring record with 176 points, scored 23 points on two touchdowns, a pair of field goals, and five conversions. This was his breakthrough game, and he punctuated it on a 10-yard touchdown run that iced it at the start of the fourth quarter. One fan asked Hornung for a souvenir. "Somebody down the left-field bleachers hollered, 'Hornung! Throw me the ball!' I flipped it up. It was a reflex motion for me," Hornung said. "Halas really got mad: 'Son of a bitch! You prick!' That was the first one—the first end-zone antic. If I had known what I had started, I would have shot myself."

Horning added, "Casares and I went out that night, and he told me what Halas screamed on the sideline to anyone within earshot and no one in particular: 'That son of a bitch will pay for that ball!' So, I told Lombardi that. He laughed and said, 'Don't worry. I'll pay for it!' "

Lombardi also paid penance over the death of Jack Vainisi. As his brother Jerry recalled, while Lombardi certainly loved Jack for the way he built the championship team, the coach also pushed Jack harder than anyone else in the Packers organization. Lombardi took Jack's widow, Jackie, out to dinner and asked her if she thought he had killed him. "Absolutely not," she answered, to his relief. Jackie Vainisi never remarried. She died in 2002.

After their triumph over the Bears, the Packers flew to the West Coast, where they defeated the Rams and 49ers. They then went to Philadelphia and played the Eagles at Franklin Field on Monday, December 26, for the title. They fell 17–13, just nine yards short of the winning touchdown at the final gun. No Lombardi team would ever again lose a game for a championship, and the Eagles have not won a title since.

The Packers had left their Chicago rivals for dead at Wrigley Field. The Bears traveled to Cleveland, where the Browns humiliated them 42–0. The Lions then administered the coup de grâce to 1960's disappointing collapse in a 36–0 rout at Tiger Stadium.

Halas vowed that changes would be made. He knew he no longer had his way on the field, and earlier that year, he was reduced to being the league's elder statesman, no longer its monarch.

That happened at the end of January 1960. The first order of business before the league formally admitted the Dallas Cowboys and Minnesota Vikings was the election of a new commissioner. Bert Bell had operated out of Philadelphia. In his later years, he moved the operation (no more than four or five people, according to former NFL executive director Don Weiss) to a small office in a bank on City Line Avenue close to his suburban home in Narberth, on the Main Line. The league by now had grown too big to be run like a ma-and-pa grocery. "Bert didn't like to travel," Weiss said. "How he ever ran that league by staying in Philly boggles the mind."

Bell's death prompted changes on several fronts. "The logical successor was an attorney named Marshall Leahy, from San Francisco," Weiss said. Leahy insisted he would not leave the Bay Area. "The owners did not want the office on the West Coast, especially when television was really just taking off. Madison Avenue was getting interested. I don't think there was ever any doubt, among the people that ran the networks, that pro football was the best game."

Leahy needed eight votes, a two-thirds majority of the league, to gain election. He was stuck on seven with the backing of Halas and Art Rooney. The voting continued without a majority. After 20 ballots, one of the owners offered to break the deadlock in the personage of a virtually unknown compromise candidate named Pete Rozelle.

The Los Angeles Rams' 33-year-old general manager, Alvin "Pete" Rozelle, had caught Bell's eye when he soothed hard feelings and a feud among the Rams' partners and was able to keep Dan Reeves in control of the operation. Before he got to the Rams, Rozelle had attracted notice as the publicity man for the unbeaten 1951 University of San Francisco team, which sent such stars as Ollie Matson, Gino Marchetti, Ed Brown, Dick Stanfel, Red Stephens, and head coach Joe Kuharich into the pros.

"The guys who really championed Pete were Paul Brown and Carroll Rosenbloom, of Baltimore," Weiss said. "When they were finally going to vote, Rozelle went to the washroom to be out of the way. When one of the owners came in, Pete would wash his hands just to have something to do while he was standing in there. When he finally was elected on the 23rd ballot, he said, 'At least I come to this job with clean hands.'"

Halas, for the first time in his career, was out of the mainstream. "His influence was diminished somewhat when that occurred," Weiss said. Instead of pouting, the Papa Bear hitched a ride aboard the Rozelle bandwagon. "You couldn't have found a more supportive person of Rozelle than George," Weiss said. "He was tremendous. That doesn't mean that they were constantly voting the same way, necessarily, but he had great admiration and respect for Pete."

Within six months, Rozelle moved the office to New York, where he began work on a new television deal. It would bring the National Football League regular season under the CBS umbrella and raise NBC's rights fee for the championship game. Halas and the Maras swung the agreement when they consented to share television revenue equally, regardless of wealth or market size. When President Kennedy signed the NFL antitrust exemption into law in 1961, George Halas knew he would never have to take out another loan to keep the club afloat in the off-season. Thanks to Pete Rozelle, all the owners truly were rich.

Rozelle then seized the opportunity to challenge Halas's longtime control over the officials, under which he had his favorite referees game after game, men such as Bill Downes and Ron Gibbs. "Pete created an officials department, a well-developed one, in New York, where the assignments were made on merit," Weiss said.

That move followed the big showdown that ensued when Halas sharply criticized the officiating after the Bears' only loss in 1963, at San Francisco. Later the next week, Rozelle called Chicago. "He told George that he wanted him to visit New York and have a chat," Weiss said. "George said he would meet him at O'Hare. 'No,' Pete said, 'get on a plane and come to New York. I want you in my office.' "They left that meeting with a great deal of mutual respect," Weiss said. "George realized there was a guy who was going to be fair and firm as well. Rozelle didn't settle for something less, but he made you feel you got part of what you wanted. That's persuasion."

Ironically for George Halas, Rozelle's assumptions of so many of his longtime league duties gave him more freedom to do the single thing he loved best, coach his Bears and plan ways to counter Lombardi in Green Bay. Halas came to work early, shut down in midafternoon for a 60- to 90-minute nap, woke up refreshed, and worked until near midnight.

The office operation at 233 West Madison was a cross between a ma-and-pa store and the marvelous, three-ring-circus–like confusion of Kaufman and Hart's *You Can't Take It with You*. The Old Man's loyal secretary, Frances Osborne, ran the day-to-day business with Jean Doyle. Rudy Custer handled the various external business dealings with broadcasting, media credentials, programs, and advertising, while Lucille Blessendorf, an eccentric who wore what appeared to be a housecoat and house slippers, handled the tickets. *Handled* is the right word.

Six-game season ticket packages in 1960 cost $30 for boxes and $24 for the grandstand. Wrigley Field was not sold out as of 1960, and the club was still taking applications. Charles Brizzolara, who worked in the ticket office in the '40s during the summer when he was in college, described the system. "Lucille took a paper clip and attached the cash to the application when she got it," he said. "That included coins as well." She would set the applications aside until the end of the day, when she somehow noted the applicant and assigned seat locations. *Somehow* is the operative word here. Blessendorf had a "system" that only she could understand. Yet, she never lost a single application, nor the money. The record keeping was, by any account, nonexistent because she committed every seat location and its holder throughout the ballpark to memory!

On Monday, January 30, 1961, Halas was plotting out ways to utilize newly acquired quarterback Bill Wade, whom he had picked up earlier that week in a trade with the Rams for Zeke Bratkowski. While he toiled at his desk, a fire smoldered in the basement of his three-story building, which now housed only the Bears, since he had closed down the mail-order and jewelry operations. In late afternoon, the fire flared up and roared through the structure. Halas, Frances Osborne, and Max Swiatek, the only ones still there, escaped without injury. Damage estimates ranged anywhere from the fire department's $75,000 to Halas's $200,000.

No sooner did Chuck Mather arrive at home than he saw the fire story on television. "I went back downtown and saw Halas standing across the street watching the fire," he said. "I had all this IBM stuff and notebooks from the guy who put it together. Flames were coming out of the windows."

"Isn't this awful?" Mather said to Halas.

"The hell with it. Let's go get a drink," Halas said.

"So, we went over to a nearby place and got a drink," Mather recalled. "The thing that's so unusual and remarkable about him is he never said, 'We lost something in the fire.' He said, 'We lost *everything*.' He had everything, every piece of paper he'd ever saved, in the basement. Everything. After he finished his drink, he set down the glass, put everything behind him, and moved forward."

The fire consumed most, but not all, of the files, the records, and many historic films, including the one of the 1933 championship game. "They moved temporarily into the basement at the American National Bank," Charles Brizzolara said. A short time later, they set up shop at 173 West Madison, at the west end of the Loop, above Maurice's Restaurant.

The fire became a story again during the Soldier Field renovation in 2002-03. Ticket manager George McCaskey, one of the grandsons, justified his many controversial decisions regarding reallocation of the tickets and removal of many Halas-era seat holders from the list to "lost records from the fire," a blaze McCaskey said occurred in 1972.

George McCaskey was either misinformed or misinforming, but in either case, he was off by 11. And the records were not lost, per se, because the keeper of the records, Lucille Blessendorf, returned to her post to straighten out the mess and put her memory to work. "Lucille," according to Brizzolara, "reconstructed the seating chart from memory."

In 1966, Charlie Coppock stopped by the office at 173 West Madison to pick up some seats. Lucille's office, he told his son Chet, "looked like a tornado hit it. Tickets were everywhere on the floor in no apparent order." But, Lucille, dressed in her customary housecoat and slippers, walked to a spot somewhere in the chaos, reached down, and picked up the tickets Charlie Coppock needed. "Not a one was wrong," Chet said. "She never missed a beat," contrary to the 2003 word from George McCaskey at Halas Hall.

On December 28, 1960, a month before the fire, George Allen called the name of a player as his first draft choice. This player would invent a position, become a Hall of Famer as well as the team's Super Bowl–winning coach, and serve as the team's living link to George Halas decades after his death. Mike Ditka, a 21-year-old end from the University of Pittsburgh, strode into Chicago like a crown prince. The only thing that kept him from assuming the throne was the king himself. They were made for each other.

"I never imagined he was 65," Ditka said. "He had such a vigor about him. He was so enthusiastic about everything. His whole life was the Bears and the National Football League. He was special."

The AFL-NFL war was raging, and more money was flying around pro football than ever before. "I could have made more in the AFL. No question about it. Houston drafted me," Ditka said. "But I wanted to play with the best. I wanted to play in the NFL."

In early January 1961, Ditka was returning to school from the Hula Bowl in Honolulu via San Francisco. Instead of flying straight through to Pittsburgh, the plane stopped in Chicago. "George Allen got on the plane with me, and we flew on to Pittsburgh," Ditka said. "He came right to our house, and we did the contract."

Unlike the many others before him, Ditka had Halas's number: "He said I was getting the highest contract ever paid a rookie, but he probably forgot about Red Grange and those guys. There were other guys, too." The big television contracts had not kicked in yet, and money was measured in thousands and hundreds of dollars, not millions. "He cut it pretty close," Ditka noted. "He paid me $12,000 with a $6,000 signing bonus."

Halas had seen few players as fundamentally sound as Ditka. He blocked like a tackle, ran well, and had the sure hands of a young Harlon Hill, the killer instinct of a Bronko Nagurski in the secondary, and the burning desire of an Eddie Sprinkle to excel and win. Moreover, he was smart, he was an attacker, and he was born to play offense.

"If I had been drafted by anybody else," Ditka said, "I was going to play linebacker. Washington, Pittsburgh, and San Francisco already told me so. He brought me in and said, 'You're going to be a tight end.' I said, 'Fine. It's OK with me.'"

Bill Wade joined the team in 1961 and worked with Ditka and fellow rookie Bill Brown at Soldier Field, under the supervision of Sid Luckman, every morning for weeks before they headed to the All-Star camp in Evanston. "I had to learn how to be a receiver. I led Pitt with 12 catches in 1960. That's ridiculous," Ditka said.

"Sid was one the most gracious men I've ever been around," Ditka added. Luckman, he said, taught him to reach up and snatch the ball out of the air. "Sid told me to catch the ball and look at the number. He wrote numbers on the ball. I had to catch it and call out the number. I had to look at it all the way in and put it away before I started to run with it. Bill Wade was the greatest. He stood out there for 10 weeks and threw me ball after ball."

That extra work paid off in a Rookie of the Year season for the steelworker's son from Aliquippa, who was grateful to Halas for making it possible. "He revolutionized the position," Ditka said. "We split the tight end open more than any other people had done. We didn't move him across the formation or anything like that. He had as much to do with my success as anybody, because he made a conscious effort to get me the football."

"My favorite, a great guy," said Chuck Mather of Ditka. "Mike was just as gung ho in practice as he was in a game. Mike was my guy on the basis of hustling all the time. Mike was also critical of anybody who wasn't playing as hard as he should. He was like a coach on the field as a player."

Halas felt so strongly about his prized rookie that he let capable Willard Dewveall take the AFL money and run off to Houston. With Iron Mike there, he didn't need to pay starter's wages to a backup, especially when he knew that the backup, Dewveall, was diabetic. Diabetes would manifest itself again, a few years later, in another Halas star, cocaptain Mike Pyle.

Ditka caught 56 passes for 1,076 yards and 12 touchdowns to earn Rookie of the Year and All-Pro honors. His biggest afternoon came in the rematch against Green Bay at Wrigley Field. The Packers were rolling 31–7, when Ditka took over the game. He ended up with nine catches for 190 yards and three touchdowns as the Bears ran out of time in a 31–28 loss to Lombardi's first title team.

Not only did George Allen land the Rookie of the Year and a future Hall of Famer in Ditka, but also, he came up with four other NFL stars. Unfortunately, only one of those four, Mike Pyle, played for the Bears. The second-round pick was fullback Bill Brown, from Illinois, who went to Minnesota in 1962 and became an enduring star. Ernie Ladd, the 6'9", 290-pound mountain of a defensive tackle from Grambling, chosen fourth, signed with and starred for the AFL San Diego Chargers, as did the fifth pick, Washington State running back Keith Lincoln.

The Bears desperately needed a center and found their man in the seventh round. Instead of choosing the son of a steelworker or coal miner, George Allen called on a hometown boy from nearby Winnetka who grew up watching the Bears play at Wrigley Field. W. Palmer "Pinney" Pyle, the father, was the influential general manager of one of Chicago's most prominent corporations, Kraft Foods. The Pyles had three sons: Palmer, the oldest, Mike, and Harlen, younger by 11 years than Mike.

Palmer starred at tackle on Duffy Daugherty's great Michigan State teams of the late '50s and went on to play pro ball with Baltimore, Minnesota, and Oakland. Mike was the top-rated high school player in Illinois in 1956, with undefeated New Trier. He also won the state heavyweight wrestling title and set records in shot put and discus that lasted for years. He turned down Daugherty in favor of Yale. The 6'3", 250-pound Pyle was clearly the top lineman not only at Yale but also in the East—Ivy League and otherwise. He captained the Elis' unbeaten 1960 Ivy League champions and, for the good of the team, played out of position at tackle instead of his natural spot, center.

"I was drafted on the 17th round by the New York Titans. That's when I started to think about it," Pyle said. The Giants also checked him out. Then George Allen called his name in the seventh round. "Someone told me, 'Mike, for God's sake, don't tell the Titans you're not interested in playing, or you won't get any money.' So, I met with the Titans, and they offered me about five grand more than Halas did."

Pyle went home over Christmas break and went in to see Halas, as did every draftee. "He overwhelmed me," Pyle said, "and I agreed on a contract." They had to skirt the NCAA rules so he could finish the track season in the spring of 1961. "I signed for $9,500 and a thousand-dollar bonus, which Halas paid to my dad. Dad then lent me the money for the rest of the school year so I wouldn't lose my eligibility." Pyle laughed at the hypocrisy of major college athletics, even Ivy League style. "There're ways to skin a cat. I didn't try to break any rules. I wanted to have some fun the spring of my senior year."

The *Tribune* invited three future Bears—Pyle, Ditka, and Bill Brown—to play in the College All-Star game. "At All-Star camp at Northwestern, E. J. Holub was my roommate. He chewed tobacco when he was sleeping," Pyle said.

Before the game itself, the College All-Stars got their first taste of pro football in an annual scrimmage against the Bears at Rensselaer. "I caught a couple of passes and ran over a guy or something," Ditka recalled. "The Old Man was screaming, 'Who the hell is that guy?' 'That's your first-round draft pick, Coach,' one of the assistants said.

He wasn't sure who it was, I guess. 'That's OK,' Coach Halas said."
A tight smile curled at the ends of Halas's mouth. He knew.

In addition to gaining the approval of the NFL founder, Ditka
learned his first lesson in NFL life. "You're scrimmaging a guy like
Atkins, and he's going half speed, maybe three quarters. You'd hate
to see what it would be like when he was going full speed."

Back in Chicago a few days later, the Philadelphia Eagles, led by
Norm Van Brocklin's more-than-capable replacement, Sonny Jur-
gensen, beat the All-Stars 28–14. Since the Bears were playing in
Montreal the night after the All-Star game, Halas ordered Ditka, Pyle,
and Brown to report to camp on Sunday.

"I was supposed to pick up Ditka and drive to camp that Sunday
morning, but my dad passed away that Saturday night," Pyle said.
"Dad had an old-fashioned sudden heart attack. There was no indi-
cation at all. I had to call Ditka and say, 'Mike, I, uh, Mike, I know
you want to leave your car home with Marge and the baby, but I
won't be able to go with you.' So, I went to camp the following
Thursday and two weeks later started the fourth exhibition game and
played every play until I got hurt in '64."

Training camp provided an instant postgrad education for all the
rookies. "Halas was 66, retirement age, when I started playing," Pyle
said. "What an amazing guy. He had this fabulous reputation as the
founder of pro football. Pro football had been around for 40-plus
years, and here's one of the founders as head coach. You can bet I listened to everything he said. He mostly let his assistant coaches do the
coaching, but he had an amazing ability to make sure you heard what
he said, and you did. It was like being a private in the army and having Dwight Eisenhower tell you what to do. He was it."

The 1961 Bears were the only team in the NFL that did not belong
to the NFLPA. "Halas was the only coach who paid his players anything for the preseason games," Pyle, a future NFLPA president,
recalled. "We got paid $100 a game for the preseason over and above
the regular season. There was a per diem for several of the teams.
Yeah, they fed 'em; that's all. Halas was ahead in that way and in
other ways. Yet, we never came home for the first seven weeks, and

we were just two hours away. I was still single, but it's not much fun to take a bus from Rensselaer, Indiana, to South Bend, fly to a game, fly back Saturday night after the game, take a bus back to Rensselaer, and get back at three or four in the morning. That only lasted for a couple of years; then it loosened up."

About the pay, Pyle explained, "The $100 a game was Halas's way of keeping the Bears out of the association. He did it for four or five years through his captains: at the time, Stan Jones and Bill George. I never knew what Halas offered the captains to tell the team, but there was a real effort to stay independent. He was that kind of guy. He thought he knew how to do things better than anybody else; and in a lot of ways, he did."

Two of the best free safeties in league history had come up a year apart. As much as Vince Lombardi loved the play of Hall of Famer Willie Wood, George Halas loved watching Roosevelt Taylor, an undrafted free agent from Grambling.

Because their All-Stars did not make the trip to Montreal, Halas and the coaches got a good look at other rookies and undrafted signees. Billy Wade, for one, made his first appearance with the Bears that day. "Harlon Hill was the best receiver I ever saw, and he still had the moves," Wade said. Hill caught four passes and scored a touchdown in a 34–16 Chicago victory. That was Hill's last game on offense for the Bears. He played defensive back the next week.

The real competition that night in Montreal was the battle for a roster slot, based not on position, but on race. "Halas had a meeting," Mather recalled. "He wanted seven blacks. It came between a white guy from Mississippi State, Bobby Bethune, and Roosevelt Taylor. George Allen and I wanted Rosey."

Taylor would have been the eighth black on the roster. It was Allen and Mather against whomever Luke Johnsos and line coach Phil Handler wanted. "They would go whichever way Halas did, three against two," Mather said. "Halas voted to keep Bethune, the [white] quota man, but it all depended on how they performed in the exhibition."

"Rosey, make sure you field all the punts. You're on the bubble," Mather told Taylor.

"We played Canadian rules in the first half and NFL rules in the second half," Mather explained. "I ordered both Bethune and Rosey to field all punts." Canadian rules called for three downs, not four, and a receiver had to run every punt back, especially out of the end zone, or else the kicking team got a point, the rouge. They did not allow fair catches. "They played double safety on the punt return then. This one punt soared, and Rosey cut across the field, cut in front of Bethune, and made a long runback," Mather said. "He covered so much ground. He put on such a show. There was no way we could not keep a player with that much speed."

In 1963, Taylor hurt a knee four or five games into the season, and Dr. Ted Fox wanted to operate. Mather reminded Halas that no one else was available. He vetoed the surgery, and Taylor was healed by the time the championship game rolled around. "Rosey made seven unassisted tackles that day from the safety position. When Hugh McElhenny was young, he was the greatest back I've ever seen. Rosey caught him just as he was breaking away. That saved our championship," Mather said. "Thank God Rosey wasn't operated on."

Harlon Hill's move to the defense, his last stop before his departure, opened the way for Johnny Morris. Morris joined the Bears in 1958 as a utility halfback and kick returner with small but sure hands, superior moves, and the heart of a champion. He excelled in everything he did, from pitching pennies to on-camera reporting in his postfootball career as the highest-rated sportscaster on Chicago television.

"Johnny had special intensity," Pyle asserted. "He was a player. He didn't play small. The great smaller players use their quickness and ability. Johnny held the world record for the 50-yard dash, and that's what you need on a football field. You don't run a hundred, you run 30, 40, or 50. Johnny Morris was our punt returner, and I can't tell you how many times I'd come onto the football field and there'd be four of five guys on top of him. I just knew he'd pop up as soon as they were off. That's tough. He was tempered steel."

On September 2, 1961, the Bears walloped the expansion Minnesota Vikings 31–7 in a preseason game in which they could have scored 50. In the opener on September 17, Minnesota starting quarterback George Shaw got hurt early, and rookie coach Van Brocklin inserted rookie Fran Tarkenton. "Fran was angry that Otto Graham didn't play him in the All-Star game," Pyle said. "He played a great game, and they just whupped us." Tarkenton earned his nickname, "the Scrambler," as he wore out the defense and passed the Vikings to a 37–13 win.

Pyle's other lasting memory from that game is the blast-furnace intensity of Mike Ditka. "Ditka came into the huddle after a punt and screamed at everybody, 'Get your head and heart into this game. We aren't gonna let this happen.' Every veteran in the huddle looked up as if to say, 'Who is this guy?' No one had seen this behavior. Ditka missed almost every training camp because he worked so hard, pulled muscles, but he was always ready to go at the start of the regular season. They stared at this guy and said, 'Oh, Oh!' I'll never forget that. We didn't take that loss well."

Everyone in the Bears' family was furious—Papa and son. "We came in, and Mugsy Halas was swearing, and you could hear a pin drop in the locker room," Stan Jones said. "Then it was, 'Bam! Aah!' Mugsy had kicked the wall and broke his big toe."

"I can tell you that Mr. Halas didn't say very much after the game," Ditka recalled. "On the plane coming back, he got on the intercom and used one of his favorite words. 'I want to say just one thing to you guys. You're nothing but a bunch of cunts!' That was it. The final word."

The Bears rebounded with a 24–10 win over the Rams the next week in Los Angeles. They lurched through the league's new 14-game schedule until the final month, when they won 3 of the last 4. The season ended on an upbeat note as Halas beat Cleveland and Paul Brown for the only time, 17–14. The next week, Wade passed for 355 yards, and the Bears beat the Vikings 52–35 to close the season.

"I had a great year and went in to get a raise," Ditka said. "He had everything written down that I'd done the whole year: if you had missed curfew, or you were out in a bar, or whatever. He had it all written down."

"You've had a good year," Halas told him. "We'll give you 14."

"Wait a second," Ditka said. "Last year, I got 18."

"You got 12."

"No. No. You gave me 12 and a $6,000 bonus," Ditka retorted. "That adds up to 18. I won't sign for a penny less than 18!"

He didn't have to. "He pulled out another contract for 18, and I signed the damn thing. That's the way it was," Ditka said. "He was devious, but it was in a good way, really. People today, athletes, will never experience what we did—you go face-to-face with the owner and coach. That doesn't happen anymore. I mean, everybody is separated by agents, and they have other people."

George Halas turned 67 on February 2, 1962. He desperately wanted another title. To get there, he knew he had to cast aside the man whose ideas made the Monsters of the Midway. "I visited Lombardi," Bill Gleason said, "and he talked about Shaughnessy's defenses, which were so complicated and glorified by the press. 'Red,' Lombardi said, 'we put Shaughnessy's defenses on the board, and some of them are humanly *impossible* to execute.'"

George Halas was thinking the same thing.

TWENTY-FOUR

PRIMED FOR THE PUSH

*T*he Bears started their drive toward the 1963 championship the season before. As the football world rightly focused on Vince Lombardi's championship success in Green Bay, George Halas stirred his brew in Chicago, a potion with money as the main ingredient. The Bears players and their wives saw Lombardi reward his champions and their women with gifts ranging from color television sets to rings and furs.

Jeannie Morris endured that tension while handling three young children and her big kid, flanker Johnny. "Before 1963, Halas used material wealth as a motivator," she said. "If they won a championship for him, he was going to reward them. They all believed that. Nobody on that team that won the title had family money or anything like that. Nobody had well-paying jobs in the off-season. Their whole lives were dependent on the Bears, and Halas promised to reward them."

In the 1962 off-season, Halas cast adrift two key members of the mid-'50s teams that might have won at least two titles but came up empty. No longer willing to cope with Harlon Hill's drinking and sick of hearing reports about Ed Brown's escapades, and feeling secure at quarterback with Bill Wade, he sent Hill and Brown to Pittsburgh for a number two draft choice. That man, tackle Clyde Brock, played for Dallas in '62 after Halas cut him in camp.

"Halas ran a silent conspiracy," Ed Stone said. Stone was covering the Bears for the *Chicago American* in 1961 and beginning to get under Halas's skin. "When it came to the operation of the team, its maneuvers and personnel, he did everything in secrecy."

A prime example is backup quarterback Rudy Bukich, who came to the Bears in late 1958 from Washington as the fourth *B* in Halas's string of quarterbacks: Brown, Bratkowski, Blanda, and Bukich. Rudy the Rifle—the acknowledged long-distance champion of the league, who could throw a football from end zone to end zone flat-footed—stayed as a backup in Chicago in '59 after Blanda left and then was shipped to the Steelers for seasoning in 1960. Two seasons later, he bounced back to the Bears in one of those curious lend-lease arrangements between Halas and Art Rooney.

"We went to a league meeting in early 1962," Stone said. "I joked to Pittsburgh PR man Ed Kiely, 'Hey, Ed, when's Bukich coming back to Chicago?' Kiely was floored. 'Who told you?' Kiely asked. Now, this was winter. The deal wasn't announced until July, six months later."

The Bears were filled with intrigue and machination. Defense was the team's most vital—and, under Shaughnessy, most volatile—element. He had great players but erratic schemes. In 1961, the San Francisco 49ers turned the NFL topsy-turvy when coach Red Hickey unleashed the most dynamic attack the league had seen in years: the shotgun. He alternated three quarterbacks one play at a time. Billy Kilmer was the best runner of the three, John Brodie was the best passer, and Bob Waters was a combination of both. The 49ers came into Wrigley Field on an incredible run after destroying Detroit 49–0, the Rams 35–0, and Minnesota 38–24. Chicago fans feared the worst.

"Bill George told me Clark Shaughnessy wanted to install a three-man front with five linebackers. George thought he was crazy, and so did I," said George Connor. "When I prepared for the telecast with Red Grange, I saw on film that 49ers center Frank Morze couldn't stand pressure. He had to look down to make the direct snap. I told

George to play a four-three but go on Morze's nose. So, they played a five-three or five-two. Morze would go one way, and George ran the other way so fast that he tackled the quarterback as he took the snap. The Bears won 31–0. Shaughnessy of course took credit for what George had done."

Hall of Fame tackle Stan Jones took the opposite view of Shaughnessy. "He was, how do you use the word, guru, a genius. It was like having Albert Einstein work with first-year algebra students. He went to the board with his back to everyone. He never used an eraser, just the back of his arm. He'd be up there breaking chalk and writing up all those things," Jones said. "Bill George was the one who interpreted what he was doing."

The quirky Shaughnessy owned a tin suitcase that George Allen carried for him in the manner of a military aide-de-camp tending to his general. A usually reliable source told Bill Jauss's *Chicago Daily News* colleague Bob Smith that the suitcase contained the great coach's secrets. "Then, one time, the strap to the valise broke, and all that fell out was a mackinaw," said Jauss. "Smitty told that story and there were almost tears in his eyes. When the suitcase opened, he expected to see reams of plays and playbooks and stuff, not a rainjacket!"

Some might call it creative tension. Or was it anarchy? Stories about Halas pitting unit against unit, coach versus coach, abound from those years. "Shaughnessy and Johnsos never got along," Chuck Mather said.

According to Bill Gleason, Halas could not control the brilliant designer of the Modern T Formation with Man in Motion turned blitz master. "Shaughnessy wouldn't let Halas near the defense. 'Get away from me. Get away from my players,' he'd say. That imbued the defense with a total lack of respect for the head coach."

Unfortunately for Shaughnessy, Coach Halas could see that his defenses didn't always work. Worse, the Bears were lagging behind both Green Bay and Detroit in the Western Conference. By1962, George Halas, who would put up with anybody as long as the team was winning, had enough of Shaughnessy's noise. "I constantly kept after Halas to use the Green Bay and Dallas–New York defense,"

Mather said. "Shaughnessy would practice one defense all week; then, on the plane, I could hear him change the scheme. He'd tell someone, we're gonna do this and do that."

Mather finally persuaded Halas to do something. Sid Luckman's protégé, end Jim Dooley, had just gone on the injured list. Halas recalled Dooley's saying he wanted to coach for him when he quit playing. So, the coach called him in and asked him to create a new defense. "Dooley," Halas said, "we have great material, but they seem to be playing '50s defenses. I want them to play in the '60s and further on. I want you to come up with the system Green Bay is using."

"He loved that because he didn't have to pay me that much," Dooley said. Ever the good soldier, Dooley, the analytical wizard, went to work. "I took the Giants' and Packers' defenses off film and found the connection between their systems." In the course of his research, Dooley saw that all 11 Packers or Giants defenders executed coordinated, but specific, assignments within a set. "If it was a run, you had seven gaps filled by seven men every which way. If it was a pass, or play action, they all fell back, and only the front attacked."

He briefed the boss on his findings. "Halas was so elated that he called in the entire coaching staff," Dooley recalled. He gave it to them in book form, flipping 8-by-10 sheets one over another. "I did it with film too. I clipped every one of these plays that I drew up and had it on film: the passes, flares, with drops." That enabled the coaches to match diagrams to the clips. Dooley literally was teaching visualization.

"George Allen took it and designed his defenses afterwards that way," Dooley said. "Halas called it 'RUB'—rush men, or 'BUZ'— backers drop back. That's how it all started." Dooley then delivered his visual presentation to the entire team. "Everybody applauded. All the players realized their eyes had been opened." They could see that the system Landry installed with the Giants and now taught in Dallas was the same that Lombardi adapted and modified in Green Bay. Both were far ahead of the league.

Allen added his own touches to the Dooley discovery when he created zone coverages, which Halas accepted. "Shaughnessy was against that, of course," Cooper Rollow said. "Shaughnessy was strictly a traditional guy. He liked the old man-to-man."

Being a student of military tactics, Shaughnessy also disguised his calls in indecipherable terminology. "We had terms you couldn't believe," Jones said. "We'd have a hossy-gee-shuffleback mini-blast. All those words."

"Shaughnessy had one scheme where I lined up at defensive end; then I had five different places to go," recalled Hall of Fame defensive end Doug Atkins. "It was slam, slide, slue, smooch, and all that. You were supposed to react. You just can't do that. We were struggling all the time."

Shaughnessy still held the technical adviser title at the start of the 1962 season, but at Halas's direction, the charismatic Allen ran the defense in all but the title. "Allen simplified it. He made everybody understand what was going on," said Jones.

Rollow was covering practice one day for the *Tribune* and ended up being called on the carpet. "George Allen was down at one end of the field, and Shaughnessy was at the other end of the field. They separated themselves because they couldn't stand each other," Rollow said. "I talked to George for a while about the new zone he was putting in with a nickel, dime, and stuff like that. That since has become the way to play over the years. Then I went down to Shaughnessy and asked, 'What do you think of all this?' 'Well, you won't win by setting up a silly little bunch of zones all over the field. I'll tell you that,' Clark said. So, I wrote that story, and I got called in the next day by Wilfrid Smith, the sports editor, and George Strickler, his number two man, and really got chewed out."

"Do you realize what's going on here?" Smith asked.

"No. What do you mean? What is going on here?"

"Why, when you write a thing like that, it's so embarrassing to Halas!" Smith said.

"Why is it embarrassing to Halas?"

"Because Allen and Shaughnessy don't get along," Strickler, the assistant sports editor said, gnashing his teeth. "Shaughnessy isn't going to stay very long. He's probably going to be out of there, and that's very, very dangerous. It really hurts Halas for you to write stuff like that!"

"I don't know if there's anything hurtful about it, and I wasn't aware of it until this minute," Rollow said, mindful of Halas's close relationship with Smith and Strickler's big boss, *Trib* editor Don Maxwell.

"Somebody in New York thought it was pretty good," Rollow said in 2002. "The league picked the story up and put in their publicity release the next week. Not only did it get into the *Tribune* with the embarrassment it might or might not have caused Papa Bear; it also got sent around the country."

To the relief of many, Shaughnessy walked out in midseason and went home to Santa Monica. Four months later, he called Halas, and they patched it up. Knowing he could not discard his longtime collaborator like yesterday's mashed potatoes, the Old Man kept him on the payroll. He paid him $1,000 a game to scout pro contests close to home in L.A.

With Allen's defense in place, the Bears went on a tear, winning five of their last six games. On November 25, they devastated the Colts in a 57–0 rout at Baltimore. The only loss in that stretch came a week later at home, 26–24 to the Eastern champion Giants.

One player who thrived under George Allen was the massive and mobile Hall of Fame defensive end Doug Atkins. "When George Allen got [control], we went to basic defenses, and he turned us loose," Atkins said. "The coverages were simple." The Bears finished at 9-and-5 and by season's end had proved they could play with the best in the East. Dealing with the best in the West, Green Bay, who had creamed the Bears 49–0 and 38–7 in 1962, was another matter, one Halas would attack all winter and spring.

As for the team itself, Halas had amassed the most colorful, rollicking wild bunch in football, men who let it all hang out with reckless abandon on and off the field. In those days, the Bears gave the players and coaches, Halas included, a bottle of Coca-Cola at halftime. Atkins was one of the few players who had anything to do with trainer Ed Rozy. Most of the team despised Rozy and were certain he was a Halas spy. "Rozy told me Halas would always have him put some good bourbon in his Coke bottle, where nobody could see it," Atkins said. On one unseasonably warm day, Rick Casares was seated by his locker during the break, waiting for Halas to appear, when Rozy came into the room carrying a Coke. "Rick grabbed the bottle out of Rozy's hands and took a pull on it," Atkins said. "He just spit it out. 'That's whiskey!' That was George Halas's whiskey inside a Coke bottle!"

Casares and Halas had not gotten along for several seasons. An already tense relationship that had soured after that goal-line incident in Los Angeles in 1960 reached the breaking point in 1962. It began the previous fall with an innocuous item in Kup's column in the *Sun-Times*: "New twosome in town. Rick Casares and Susie Smith, the niece of Eddie Barrett." Edward J. Barrett, a politically powerful friend of Halas, was a Democratic-machine fixture for decades, mostly as county clerk, the office that runs elections. Barrett's career crashed in the '70s when he was convicted of accepting kickbacks from a firm that made voting machines.

"Kup put me in there all the time when I'd be seen at Mr. Kelly's or the London House. He didn't know he was really hurting me with Halas," Casares said. "Yet, I was always at those places within curfew, especially after games."

One day at practice, Halas walked over to his star fullback and said, "Hey, kid, I see you're finally dating a nice girl. You're finally getting away from those racetrack floozies."

The Bears were scheduled to play the Rams on November 26 at Wrigley Field. Halas held a short practice Thanksgiving morning and gave the team the afternoon off. "Susie invited me to dinner with her parents and her sister. It lasted four or five hours. We had a nice time," Casares said. Rick had agreed to meet Ed Brown at a neighborhood bar owned by a friend named Don Wright, who invited them to help his mother celebrate her birthday.

"I can't do any drinking, Don," Rick said when he spoke to his friend.

"Nah, just come in and have a glass of champagne and sing 'Happy Birthday' to Mom," Wright said. "She loves you."

Doug Atkins happened to be having a drink at a side table when Rick and Susie entered the bar. "The detectives who were waiting for them outside her parents' apartment followed Rick and the girl to this bar," Atkins said. "They didn't know who she was or the friendship her uncle had with Halas."

While they waited for the cake, Casares noticed a funny expression on Ed Brown's face. "What the hell?" Brown said.

"I turned around," Casares said. "There with the hat and black coat with the collar turned up was George Halas himself. Holy Christ, I thought. 'Hello, Coach.'"

A scowling Halas motioned Casares aside. "I'm so disappointed in you, Rick. We have a big ballgame on Sunday, and here you are. You been shacked up all afternoon." Susie looked at him, not sure what to think, Casares said. "Now you're down here drinking. I counted on you. I'm so disappointed in you," the coach said.

Casares realized he had nailed his nemesis. "For your information, Coach," he said, "this is Susie Smith. Susie, this is Mr. Halas." At the mention of her name, a stunned Halas recoiled. "Susie," Casares continued, "tell Mr. Halas where I was all afternoon."

"Mr. Halas, Rick was at my parents' this afternoon having Thanksgiving dinner. We just left there," Susie said. "We just came down here, and we haven't had anything to drink all day." Newly poured glasses of champagne sat untouched on the bar. "He's been with me all afternoon. He hasn't been anywhere else."

"Halas was choked up," Casares recalled, "at a loss. Then he spoke up: 'You're breaking training by being in a saloon. I'll see you tomorrow.' Then he got up and left."

By 1962, Chicago's Press Row had been reduced to just two holding groups. *Sun-Times* owner Marshall Field IV paid John S. Knight a record $24 million for the *Daily News* and its skyscraper on the west bank of the Chicago River at Madison. He then sold the building and moved the *News* around the river bend to his new Sun-Times Building at 401 North Wabash. The *Tribune* bought the *American* from the Hearsts in 1956 for $14 million, placing total control of both papers in the hands of Don Maxwell.

Before 1962, no inside story detailing George Halas's relationship with his players ever made print. Then, Ed Stone, of the *American*, fell into a scoop after the New Year when he made a routine call to Casares at his bowling alley to check on his recovery from a late-season ankle sprain. Halas recently had traded Casares's close friend

Ed Brown to Pittsburgh. Stone asked for a comment. "Rick went into a tirade about how Halas had manipulated the quarterbacks, destroyed their confidence by not letting them know from week to week whether they were starting, and all this," Stone said.

"I was so frustrated with what he had done with our team, our great teams of '56, '57," Casares admitted in 2002, explaining why he spoke with Eddie Stone that day.

"Rick, this wasn't the story I called you about," Stone said that long-ago afternoon, "but I'll tell you right now I'm going to write it." Casares's response was, "Go ahead!"

"So, I wrote this story, and it was late in the afternoon, so the editors were gone," Stone said. "I left it for our nightside guys, who always supported anything I did." The night editor called Stone at home to confirm his story. "This is absolutely true," the reporter told him. The night man cleared it with managing editor Luke Carroll and ran it the next day in the *American* under a front-page headline that read "Casares Rips Papa Bear."

"Halas called me down to the office," Casares said. "He had the paper spread out in front of him, the whole page. He had it underlined in red. I felt like a dummy. One of the few compliments Halas paid me, before this, was, 'Kid, I gotta tell you this: you're honest.' With this one, when he asked me, 'Did you say this?' I said, 'Yeah.' If I had it to do over again, I would have told him I was misquoted. But that just wasn't me," Casares said. "Then he lit into me: 'Nobody can talk about me like that!' He cussed me out."

When Halas's tirade ended, Casares told him, "Listen, I apologize to you for one thing: for being a stool pigeon. I should never have talked to a newspaper guy, but I didn't realize what would happen."

Ed Stone, meanwhile, knew he had a scoop of major proportions. "All the other papers came back and talked to Casares the next day," Stone said. "All he said was, 'Yeah, I said those things, but I also said some real nice things about Halas, and he didn't print that.' That's as strong a confirmation as you can get from a player criticizing Halas."

That story was one of the grievances Halas would invoke in 1963 to Don Maxwell in his successful mission to get Ed Stone pulled off the Bears beat. "I did a reporter's job," Stone said. "If you fell into a story like that covering the Bears, you felt like you were going to win the Pulitzer Prize, because no employee ever said anything out of line about the organization. Never."

"After the story, Halas benched me, and Marconi became the starting fullback in 1962. He was using Marconi instead of me," Casares said. "Joe was a beautiful guy. Joe came to me and was apologizing for starting ahead of me. 'I know I shouldn't be playing in front of you,' Marconi said."

Casares responded simply, "Joe, what are you going to do?" He felt horrible over the predicament and sensed that Halas hated him.

One day, Casares was in the office and struck up a conversation regarding Halas with the woman he called "Mother Cabrini," Halas's executive secretary, Frances Osborne. "He loves you, Rick," she told him, to which Casares replied, "Frances, he doesn't know the meaning of love!"

If it was love the Old Man felt for the prodigal player, their relationship received its sternest test when the Bears came back late to edge the underdog Dallas Cowboys 34–33 at the Cotton Bowl on November 18, 1962. A major reason the Bears failed to cover the point spread was a misplay involving Casares deep in Cowboys' territory.

For most of 1962, rumors raced through the football universe that a player in the Midwest was consorting with gamblers. "Casares was the suspected guy because he hung around Rush Street and knew a lot of people and such," Stone said. "I used to go to Vegas," Casares said. "I loved to go to the casinos, which of course was documented. There was no problem; half the NFL went to Vegas after the Pro Bowl game."

The accountants at the *American* had told the sports department that Stone would have to cover the Bears-Cowboys game at home via television because there was no room in the budget for the trip. That changed suddenly, Stone said. "On the morning the team was going to leave, Luke Carroll, the managing editor, called. 'Get on that flight.'" The *American*'s crime reporter had passed along information to Carroll that the league had suspicions about Casares.

"I have informed Halas," Carroll said. "We want you there. Forget about the game; you just watch Casares's every move."

"So, I rushed to pack, got a flight, and covered the game," Stone said four decades later.

"I hadn't played in a couple of games. He put me in, and I was really rolling. I still had the goods," Casares said. "There was nothing suspicious except a play at the goal line," Stone said. "It was supposed to be a handoff. Casares never touched the ball; Wade fumbled before he got the ball to Casares. Shortly after that, Halas took Casares out and put in Marconi."

"You gotta put me back in," Casares pleaded. "I can't trust you." Halas replied.

Stone recalled, "On the plane, I asked Halas about the suspicions. He praised Luke Carroll, saying, 'What a wonderful man, that he considers the welfare of our league, but I had no suspicions [about Casares].' So, I had nothing really hard to go by. I couldn't just write or drop any hints that something was wrong."

After he landed at O'Hare, Stone made a beeline for the *American* newsroom, now operating out of Tribune Tower. He later learned that Luke Carroll, at Maxwell's direction, went to the airport to pick up Halas. Stone was working on his story when the phone rang. It was Carroll, the managing editor.

"What did you talk to Halas for?"

"You told me to report on this thing," Stone answered. "So, now I have to question one of the principals involved in this thing."

"Hey, listen, if this thing breaks and is a big story, you're not gonna get it! Our city desk people will cover! You're not gonna be any tinhorn hero!" the irate Carroll exclaimed.

"So, I just wrote a routine game story and let it go at that," Stone said.

Casares was still steaming on the Monday after the game when he went to see Halas in his office behind the dressing room at Wrigley Field. He told the coach, "I insist on taking a lie detector test." "No problem," Halas replied.

"I never had bet on a football game in my life at that time," Casares said.

"What I didn't know till later is that Carroll had a copy in his desk of a league lie detector test that had been given to Casares, clearing him," Stone said. "After the league was satisfied Casares was clear,

Carroll still led us to believe that there were suspicious reasons to pursue the story."

Halas reinstated Rick Casares as starter in the 1963 training camp. That camp also would be the first as offensive cocaptains for Mike Ditka and Mike Pyle, with Joe Fortunato for the defense. Longtime captains and Halas loyalists Bill George and Stan Jones lost their stripes late in 1962.

The NFL Players' Association was nearly six years old and had gained neither league recognition nor affiliation with a larger AFL-CIO union. Unions were starting to turn on the heat to join up—most prominently, the Teamsters, still under the thumb of Jimmy Hoffa. The Bears had stood apart when they refused to attend the charter meeting in New York before the 1956 title game.

Midway through the 1962 season, NFLPA president Pete Retzlaff, of the Eagles, called Stan Jones from Philadelphia. Idled with a broken leg, and able to conduct business, Retzlaff asked Jones if the team had voted recently on the association. The Bears players had always voted no because Halas threatened that he would strictly honor the few crumbs the other teams conceded to the association. "They [the union] asked for $50 a preseason game. Halas paid us $100!," Jones exclaimed. "We'd be taking a 50 percent cut!"

"If you don't join, we'll lose the ability to take care of this thing," Retzlaff said, telling Jones that other unions, like AFTRA, the broadcast performers union, and the Teamsters, who had no connection with football at all, were doing their best to organize the league. "If I come out, can I talk to the team?" Retzlaff asked Jones.

"Let me talk to Halas," Jones said.

"No friggin' way!" Halas responded when his captain came in hat in hand.

"Hey, Coach," Jones replied, "we'd better do something. If we vote it down again, we might get a union you'll regret."

Halas yielded. "So, Retzlaff came in and gave one hellacious presentation to the players," recalled Jones in 2003. "To make a long story short, we had a few dissenting votes, but we agreed to make it unanimous. I had to go take the result of the meeting up to Halas. I came and that jaw went out. He took me into the bathroom section of the locker room."

"What was the result of your fucking vote?"

"It wasn't my fucking vote! It was the team's vote."

"You're fired!" Halas screamed. "That reflects on the leadership of this team!"

"Are you firing me as the captain or player, or what?" Jones asked.

"In time it passed, and he never held that against me. I think," Jones said. "It might have been the most courageous thing I ever did in my life to face that man. I was shaking; I guarantee that. I know he liked me, but he would never say anything like that, you know?"

By then, the coach was planning to knock over Lombardi.

TWENTY-FIVE

HOORAY FOR GEORGE!

"I give Halas credit for our '63 win," Chuck Mather said. "He went to Lombardi's party in December '62 up in Green Bay. All the New York writers were in, priests, Lombardi friends, Halas. He came back and said, 'We're going to beat that son of a bitch.'"

The decade of tumult and shouting had begun in earnest that year, 1963. Civil rights marches intensified in their fervor and boldness, but violence lay in wait as President John F. Kennedy sent more advisers to South Vietnam to help the Ngo Dinh Diem government deal with the pesky Vietcong guerrillas. At home, many other Americans embarked on bunion-busting 50-mile hikes in homage to the president's fitness campaign. An old-line New York law firm named Mudge, Guthrie and Alexander brought the former vice president aboard as headline partner after he lost the California governorship in a rout so huge that he declared to reporters, "You won't have Nixon to kick around anymore."

In March, Loyola University coach George Ireland started four black players who pressed, ran, and shot the lights out to beat twice-defending-champion Cincinnati in overtime to win Chicago's only NCAA basketball championship.

At 173 West Madison that spring, George S. Halas turned over the Bears presidency to Loyola alum George S. Halas Jr. That title gave Mugs, the club treasurer since 1953, the prestige to handle league business on an equal footing with the other NFL owners. His father had a football team to coach.

Then, on April 17, the country woke up to banner headlines and lead stories on every radio and television newscast screaming one of sports' most dreaded words: *Gambling*! National Football League commissioner Pete Rozelle issued indefinite suspensions to two of the game's most prominent stars. They were Paul Hornung, the Golden Boy of the National Football League and leader of the twice-defending-champion Green Bay Packers; and the Detroit Lions' superb defensive tackle Alex Karras, the Glib Greek of Gary, Indiana, and younger brother of Bears guard Teddy Karras.

"Here's what happened in the deal," Horning said in December 2002. "First of all, Karras should never have been suspended. He got on a TV show and thought he was trying to be a smart-ass, I guess. He admitted that he bet on parlay cards. Rozelle was about to suspend me. So, when Karras said that, Rozelle had to include him. Karras bet those cards like all the other players did. They bet. They all bet. Shit. I told Rozelle, 'I'm not answering any questions about anybody else, but me. That's it. I want to tell you the truth.' " Hornung added a warning to the commissioner: " 'If they have a Senate hearing in Washington, and I gotta raise my hand, this league's in dead trouble. I'm not gonna lie. You just better keep me out of Washington,' which he did, of course."

Asked if he knew of any fixed games then or at any other time since, Hornung replied, "There weren't any that were fixed." Not named then, nor ever implicated, was Bears star fullback Rick Casares, whom many thought was the unnamed Midwest player cited in news reports and rampant rumors concerning NFL gambling that circulated for nearly a year.

Three weeks after Rozelle imposed the Hornung and Karras suspensions, news from Baltimore broke late in the night of May 10 that Gene Lipscomb, the fearsome 6'7", 290-pound tackle known as "Big Daddy," was dead. An autopsy revealed that Lipscomb, who played for the Steelers in 1961 and '62 after he terrorized opposing linemen and quarterbacks for years with the Colts, died from a massive overdose of heroin. Foul play was suspected, since he was known to have a pathological fear of needles and never allowed trainers to give him shots. The case was never solved.

In the aftermath of the Hornung-Karras brouhaha and Lipscomb death, George Halas knew two things: the Packers were nearer to the world of mere mortals than they had been since Lombardi arrived from New York, and he had the goods to take the title.

Chuck Mather recalled, "He said to me in January, 'I want you to get the plays you think will work against Green Bay. We're going to use them once a week in summer practice and not use them in games until the regular season.' "

Mather then pleaded, "Coach, that's a waste of time. We got all these teams to think about." Unmoved, Halas exclaimed, "Listen! I want you to get these together, and we're going to do what I said. Don't argue."

Mather didn't argue. "During preseason, we practiced Green Bay plays once a week. I can see now that it put into the players' minds that we have something here they don't know about," Mather said. "It's the mental thing, and Halas knew that. In the pros, motivation is 80 percent of the game. The motivation he generated for our two games against Green Bay resulted in their only two losses."

"We played the Giants in early preseason up at Cornell," Mike Ditka recalled. "Halas called me afterward and said, 'I'm going to make you one of the captains. What do you think about this?' 'Coach, I think we're close,' I said. 'I think we can win it this year. I do.' "

Speaking of the talent on that team, Ditka emphasized, "People forget how good Willie Galimore was. Had he lived and stayed healthy, there's no telling how good he could have become. He could fly. We had John Farrington. We had a lot of guys. Our defense in '63 was probably as good as the defense we had in '85. It was awfully good."

What Halas understood from a lifetime of working with driven young athletes is their need for reinforcement. Mike Pyle's parents gave him all the financial and emotional support he ever wanted.

Mike Ditka, the son of a steelworker in Aliquippa, Pennsylvania, or street-smart Johnny Morris, from industrial Long Beach, California, had to battle with fathers who took them to the woodshed and then asked questions. In 1963, Halas had their trust.

"Halas was like the ultimate stern father figure," said veteran journalist Jeannie Morris, who saw the fear he instilled in her husband, Johnny, and his teammates. "They called him 'Mr. Halas,' " she said. "They never called George Halas 'George.' "

One of the rising young defensive stars did not go to camp. "They took an EKG, and I couldn't pass the physical," Ed O'Bradovich said. At the time, he had just turned 23. "Dr. Brown, who was the head internist, wouldn't let me play. I told him I had an irregular cardiogram all my life."

O'Bradovich grew up in west suburban Hillside and went to the huge Proviso High School, in neighboring Maywood. Ed's older sister Jane took him to Proviso games to watch quarterback Ray Nitschke, her classmate. Proviso belonged to arguably America's best high school conference, the Suburban League. Each school had between 3,000 and 5,000 students and turned out scores of pros and Olympic champions. Famed Suburban League athletes include Otto Graham, of Waukegan; Paddy Driscoll and the third Heisman Trophy winner, Clint Frank, both of Evanston; Oak Park coach Bob Zuppke; and New Trier's Pyle brothers, Palmer and Mike.

O'Bradovich, a halfback in high school and rugged rebounder on the basketball team, enrolled at Illinois, where he filled out and was moved to end. He hung on for three years under the gun of academic probation. He did not flunk out, per se, but the bursar's office said his grades were too low for him to stay. He played in Canada for a year until he was eligible for the NFL draft.

"For me, there's like, family and God; the Bears; then Halas," O'Bradovich stated with pride. "George Allen brought me down to talk before they drafted me. Then he introduced me to Coach Halas. I guess it was like some kid aspiring to be a politician meeting the president of the United States."

O.B. made two 1962 All-Rookie teams; was *Pro Football Illustrated*'s co–defensive rookie of the year—with Merlin Olsen, of the

Rams; and led the league with six enemy fumble recoveries. As his teammates prepared for Green Bay, he took his medication and improved day by day, week by week. He returned in the ninth game, against the Rams at Wrigley Field. While he was out, though, the secretive Halas operation left O.B.'s condition open to speculation by saying nothing. He was ordered not to speak then, and he did not discuss it until 2002.

"We always opened in Green Bay," said Mike Pyle, Ditka's offensive cocaptain. "Halas always stressed its importance in the last two or three weeks of training camp: 'You win this game, you got a chance to win it all.'"

"We were anxious to break camp from Rensselaer," Stan Jones said. "It got on your nerves, a remote place like that, on top of each other for the whole two months."

While the team flew to New Orleans for the last preseason game with the Colts, Halas traveled to Canton, Ohio, to lead the 17 inductees in the charter class into the Pro Football Hall of Fame on Saturday morning, September 7, 1963. He was the founder, accompanied by his greatest early Bears stars, Red Grange and Bronko Nagurski. Other charter inductees included the first NFL president, Joe Carr; postwar commissioner Bert Bell; New York Giants founder Tim Mara and his star center Mel Hein; Halas's close friend and crony George Preston Marshall, of the Washington Redskins; and Marshall's supreme quarterback, Sammy Baugh. The pioneer star players Jim Thorpe and Wilbur "Pete" Henry came in with the Papa Bear's rival, Green Bay Packers founder-coach Curly Lambeau and his threesome of Johnny "Blood" McNally, Cal Hubbard, and Halas nemesis Don Hutson. The Cardinals' Ernie Nevers and the Detroit Lions' Earl "Dutch" Clark completed the first class. Halas left immediately after the ceremony to catch a flight to New Orleans. In that final preseason tune-up that night, he coached the Bears to a 14–7 win over the Colts.

Halas arranged for the pilot of his slow, cramped DC6 charter to fly to Chicago immediately after the game. Yellow school buses picked up the team at the tarmac for the two-and-a-half-hour drive to camp. Before they jumped into their cars and headed north, Halas delivered the news that the homesick players feared the most. They weren't going home. Instead: "When you get to Route 30, turn left and head west to DeKalb to the Holiday Inn, where we will have a brief meeting and the rest of the day off."

"Unfortunately, we barely beat Baltimore," Jones recalled with a chuckle. "This called for a little extra from Halas in his prebreakfast remarks to the team. He ended it up with, 'Are there any fucking questions?' J. C. Caroline raised his hand, and Halas was irritated. 'What is it, J.C.?' 'When are we going to eat, Coach?'

" 'J.C.,' Halas replied, 'Mahatma Gandhi went 40 days and nights without any bread and water. The least you can do is wait five more minutes for breakfast.'

"With that," Jones recalled, "J.C. turned to the guy next to him and said loudly, 'What team did Mahatma Gandhi play for?' I think Halas probably secretly laughed somewhere, but he sure didn't laugh at that moment!" Jones said.

"Halas loved that rivalry," Ditka said. "He wanted that rivalry to be what it was. He drilled it into us: 'You gotta beat the Packers.' Before Lombardi got there, Green Bay's mission was to beat the Bears. Period. That's all there was to it. Then the rivalry got more intense as the competition got more even. We started climbing the ladder to get even with them. Then it became a truly great rivalry."

The regular season opened on September 15 at Green Bay. Like Dr. Martin Luther King Jr., who thrilled the nation with his "I Have a Dream" speech at the Lincoln Memorial two and a half weeks earlier, the Bears had their own dream.

"Before the first game, Bill Gleason wrote that the Bears looked solid, except for the left side of the defensive line manned by a schoolteacher and an artist," Jones said. "Bob Kilcullen, the artist, was at left end in Ed O'Bradovich's place, and I was the schoolteacher taking Earl Leggett's place on the defense. The night before the ball game, we were in this restaurant in Green Bay, and Kilcullen saw Gleason sitting at another table. 'Hey, Gleason! I just want you know that Stan Jones and I are going to show up for the game!' Kilcullen roared.

"Thanks a lot, Bob. That's really great," whispered the disapproving Jones to Kilcullen.

"God damn! The next day I think they ran every play at us. Forrest Gregg and Jerry Kramer were right across from us. They didn't get a touchdown. We beat them 10–3. It was the greatest thrill of my entire life. We shut down the world champions."

George Allen's gang intercepted Bart Starr five times and held the Packers to 150 total yards, never letting them closer than the 33. Halas had a game ball made up that remains on display in the Halas Hall trophy case. Under the date and 10–3 score are the words "Greatest team effort."

"It was," Jones said. "We came back on the train, and it was a great feeling of accomplishment. When it came time for my induction into the Hall of Fame, I had Bob Kilcullen be my presenter, because he gave me one of the greatest thrills of my life. We played the whole year like that."

The defense so dominated play at Green Bay, as well as for the rest of the season, that the offense suffered by comparison. Much of the problem, according to Pyle, was the odious presence of Halas's boy Sid Luckman as the dollar-a-year quarterback coach. Pyle and his teammates quickly realized that Luckman had not stayed current and was not a hands-on coach.

"He didn't sit in on coaches meetings," Pyle said. "He wasn't a part of building offensive strategy." Wednesday was the only day of the week devoted to the offense and practicing the game plan. "Luckman would come an hour before practice and run the skilled position players," Pyle said. "I snapped and watched those guys run themselves ragged."

Every offensive player hated those sessions, convinced they were an absolute waste of time, let alone demoralizing. As they strutted their stuff for Luckman's benefit, Pyle related, they would look up to see him engrossed in conversation with Halas or his own business friends and cronies. Moreover, Halas forbade the other coaches to speak while Luckman was on hand during that extra hour ahead of the two-hour practice session. Pyle never forgot. "Their legs are going to be tired. But that's OK; that comes back. But it's when you're working 11 on 11—all of a sudden, half the team is fresh, the other half is tired. It never helped the team one iota."

Halas devised a bare-bones attack that played to his strength. "We needed to control the football and keep our defense off the field," Pyle said. "Thus, our defense was fresh and able to make plays."

"I thought George Allen was the reason we won the '63 championship," Doug Atkins said.

"Allen came along and rewrote the rules of how to play defense, like breaking down opponents four and five ways," said O'Bradovich. It was defense this, defense that, and—in a late-season write-up in *Time* magazine in praise of Allen and the men who would go through fire for him in his attack—a fill-the-gap scheme.

"We all knew he was the man," O'Bradovich said. "He had the youth. He had the knowledge. And he treated us like men, not like some retarded escapees from an institution who gotta be guarded and watched. He threw all that stuff out the window."

"We knew exactly what we were gonna do in '63," Atkins said. "We'd line up and just tee off and play football."

The Bears opened the 1963 season with five straight wins, and Ed Stone was covering for the *American*, in the press box, at practice, on the phones, at home, or at the office, as he had been since he replaced Bill Gleason. Gleason, the South Sider and lifelong Cardinals fan, thrilled to the battle with Halas. "I criticized him. I once wrote a column that appeared on December 23 or Christmas Eve that inspired him to write a long letter. I said the best Christmas present he could give the fans of Chicago was his resignation as head coach. That really got to him."

Rather than lose Gleason over his set-tos with Halas, the *American*'s editors pulled him off the Bears beat and bumped him over to columnist before the 1961 football season. "And they gave Eddie Stone the job," Gleason said with amusement. "Halas thought, 'Well, this kid is a Bears fan from childhood.'"

"Yeah, I've always been a Bear fan. So, when I got the beat after Gleason became a columnist, you had to get rid of the fan," Stone said. "I was influenced by Gleason's relationship with him, which was very strained. And so, I didn't come into it with a worshipful attitude toward the Bears, even though I was a big fan. I knew the things that were wrong with the organization, so I had a critical eye."

Broadcast journalism was virtually nonexistent then, so the writers were the public's conduit to the clubs for information and knowledge. Most everyone else who covered the Bears was friendly with the team. Too friendly. Not Ed Stone. "You always had this adversarial relationship with the Bears because Halas created that atmosphere," Stone said. "He said it to me explicitly, 'You should be cheerleaders. You should be pulling for my team. You're the home writers, and you should be pulling for us.' 'That's not the way it works, Coach.' Halas actually knew that, but he wanted people on his side."

Stone had been scheduled to travel with the Bears on their 1963 West Coast swing, but he had to stay home and cover off the television broadcast in a management-dictated cost-cutting move. At Los Angeles, Ditka had the biggest game of his career, with four touchdown catches, to lead the Bears to a 52–14 rout.

San Francisco and the 49ers were next, and they were the worst team in the league. With the Bears trailing 13–0 at halftime, Halas pulled Billy Wade in favor of Rudy Bukich. The Bears staged a comeback, but Bukich threw three interceptions, and the Niners held on to win 20–14. "I wrote that Halas choked by not staying with Wade, the established quarterback," Stone said.

"After the Bears came home from the trip," Stone said, "I was working at my desk when I saw Leo Fischer rush into Luke Carroll's office at the other end of the city room. When he returned, he called me in and said, 'You've been taken off the beat.' I was reassigned to the copy desk.

"I never blamed Fischer for removing me from the beat. I do blame the editor of our parent paper, Don Maxwell at the *Tribune*, for not standing up for an employee. I never really met Maxwell. Again, this was another Halas thing," Stone said. "The year before, 1962, he brought Maxwell to Rensselaer to watch a practice. They sat in Halas's golf cart. Halas knew the *Trib* owned our paper. He made a point of introducing me to him. This was almost subtle intimidation. 'Geez, kid, I'd like you to meet the man who owns your paper. He runs the *Tribune.*'"

Regarding his demotion, Stone reiterated, "I'm sure Maxwell did it for Halas, but I never heard directly from anyone."

The season telescoped into the rematch with Green Bay at Wrigley Field on November 17. Interest was never greater for a regular-season game in Chicago, before or since. On Thursday of game week, ticket brokers told the *Tribune*'s Cooper Rollow they hadn't seen any tickets for months. Those who did have the precious pasteboards were getting $50 to $65 for seats with $4 or $5 face value. Those prices, many say, were a low estimate.

The *Trib* described in detail where fans who wanted to see the game on television could go outside the blackout area. Nearest outlets were in Rockford, over the Wisconsin border in Milwaukee or Madison, or in South Bend, Indiana. CBS announced that 116 stations across the country would carry the game.

Leaving no stone unturned, the *Tribune* soberly reported that Andy Frain Sr., founder of the nation's leading ushering service, was hospitalized and could not attend a Bears game for the first time since 1938. But, the paper noted, "the Frain team has a good bench." Sons Andy Jr., Mike, Pete, Francis, and Pat would step up and direct the crowd-management force "while Dad rests up."

Another invitee who would not make it was the nation's number one football fan, President John F. Kennedy. He had endured a troubled month in foreign affairs with the coup and assassinations of Ngo Dinh Diem and his brother Ngo Dinh Nhu on November 2 in Saigon. It would take years before the revelation that the coup was orchestrated by the CIA and had been green-lighted by the Oval Office. The president was about to embark on an important trip. To Texas.

One fan who attended that game called the crowd the loudest he'd ever heard in a half century of seeing virtually every Bears game in person. The players were sky high as well. "I've never been more up for a game than I was getting ready for that Green Bay game," Pyle acknowledged.

The roar of the crowd was deafening on the opening kickoff. Bob Jencks kicked off to Green Bay's Herb Adderley three yards deep in the left corner of the north end zone. "We were good friends," said J. C. Caroline, who shot downfield to make what Johnny Morris and other Bears teammates called the greatest special-teams play they ever saw. "A mutual friend told me that Herb said he was going to run back a kickoff against me for a touchdown," Caroline said. "So, I just sent a message back. It wasn't going to be against me."

"When J. C. came down and nailed Herb Adderley at the 20-yard line, it just went from there," Pyle said. Bart Starr was injured and did not play, and the Bears took after his replacement, John Roach, as if he were covered with honey. They stopped ballcarriers Jim Taylor and Tom Moore in their tracks. The scoring opened with a pair of Roger LeClerc field goals. Then Adderley took off on his second kick return of the quarter, only to lose the ball when John Farrington stripped it away and LeClerc recovered.

Three plays later, Wade handed to Willie Galimore. Galimore, in his first extended action after off-season double-knee surgery, slashed toward the outside, cut back and hurdled Ditka on the ground as he made a block, and flashed Jesse Whittenton a hip dip. "No linebacker could cover him downfield," Wade said. "Galimore had the ability of a Jerry Rice to turn on the afterburner." He sped for a 27-yard touchdown run, a play so electric that it was featured on the cover of *Sports Illustrated*.

The issue was never in doubt after that. The Bears rolled up 248 yards on the ground, intercepted five passes, and recovered two fumbles. Casares complemented Galimore with 48 yards before he had to leave. "I was roaring. I was having a great day. And I got high-lowed. Nitschke cleaned up on me," Casares said.

"Nitschke dove off to the side and grabbed his ankle and broke it. It was really a dirty tackle," Paul Hornung said. "Rick didn't say a word. Didn't say a goddamn word. Rick tried to play the next year, but the ankle wouldn't hold up."

"After the season, Ditka and I were at an appearance," O'Bradovich said, "when some guy asked, 'What happened with the demise—collapse—of the Green Bay Packers?' 'Demise? Collapse? What the hell are you talking about?' Ditka yelled. 'They lost only two games. And it was to us!' "

In no way was this season over, though. The Bears still had four games to go, starting in Pittsburgh with the Steelers. As they finished their Friday workout, someone came into the dressing room at Wrigley Field with the news that anyone who was alive and aware at that moment still cannot comprehend. Somebody shot President Kennedy in Dallas. Within minutes, word came that the youthful, vital leader was dead. "We were so shocked," Mike Ditka said. "We didn't know if there would be a game or not. Everything was put on hold."

AFL commissioner Joe Foss canceled his league's Sunday schedule, and virtually every college in America had followed suit by Saturday morning. Only NFL commissioner Pete Rozelle did not. The games would be played, but not telecast. "They said, 'You're traveling on Saturday,' and, boom, that's basically what happened," Ditka said.

Ward Quall, the vice president and general manager at *Tribune*-owned WGN, the Bears' flagship radio station, called his staff together on Friday afternoon to discuss plans during the emergency. "He asked me if we had a contract with the Big Ten to broadcast the Illinois–Michigan State game for the conference title that Saturday on our 'Game of the Week package,' " retired WGN sports editor Jack Rosenberg said. When Rosenberg said they did, Quall dispatched the crew as previously planned to East Lansing. A violent rainstorm had forced cancellation of flights to Lansing, so Rosenberg booked train passage to the capital city for announcers Jack Brickhouse and Jack Quinlan and himself.

"It was so quiet on that train; it was eerie," Rosenberg recalled. "Nobody spoke a word anywhere in our car." The next morning, Big Ten commissioner Bill Reed called Rosenberg and informed him the game would be postponed until Thanksgiving. The storm front, meanwhile, had moved east, allowing the three WGN men to catch the 45-minute flight back to Chicago in time to board the Bears' charter to Pittsburgh. When they landed, Rosenberg called Quall. "We won't broadcast," the general manager said. "This is no time for a football game."

"It's the only time in all those years that we did not air a scheduled Bears broadcast," Rosenberg said.

It was a throwback to the pioneer days of the league. No radio. No television. But the NFL games went forward. "I wanted to play that day," cocaptain Mike Pyle recalled. "I didn't feel the world had come to a stop. For a period of time on Friday, yes. But sitting home all weekend, I wouldn't have been as happy as doing what I felt my job was."

"Our job as football players was to do what they told us," Ditka said in agreement. "Rozelle made the decision, and to this day some people say he regretted it. I don't know if he did or not, and I don't know if he should have." "I know there was tremendous pressure on the commissioner," Pyle added. "I was glad, believe me, that he decided to play."

"I don't know what Jack Kennedy would have said, but he probably would have said, 'Go ahead and play,'" Ditka said emphatically. "That's what I felt."

"Coach Halas came to us on Sunday morning," Bill Wade recalled. "He said, 'We're going to play this game to get people's minds off the assassination.' That was a very difficult game to play. It didn't wear off after one game. Our nation was hurt, and it lingered. It will never be forgotten."

"It was my first trip back to Pittsburgh since I graduated," Ditka said. "It was very eerie. It was one hell of a game. They really should have beat us, but they didn't."

"I was an awestruck rookie, starting, and trying to survive against Mike Ditka," said the Steelers' all-time-great outside linebacker Andy Russell.

"We were playing conservatively. I think the defense was playing well," Pyle said. The Steelers overcame a two-touchdown deficit to take a 17–14 lead in a dramatic fourth quarter. Other than the NFL personnel, only the 36,465 fans and newsmen on hand could bear witness.

"Halas loved Wade," Chuck Mather said, "but Bill was a hard guy to coach. In those days, teams used certain defenses by down. Bill would say, 'Maybe.' Here I was trying to help him, and he'd say, 'Maybe.' 'Don't bother him,' Halas interjected."

"Bill threw a pass out in the flat," Ditka said. "It hit John Reger right in the stomach. He could have intercepted and walked right into the end zone." Wade would not say who missed his assignment, but others said Ditka ran the wrong pattern. "Halas was so mad, he pulled Wade out of the game," Mather recalled.

Where Mather saw the near miss, Pyle and his teammates saw a "leaner," the luck of the horseshoe. "I still think George Halas should have given a championship ring to John Reger because he dropped it," Pyle said.

Ditka had given his all in front of his family and friends. He was running on empty and trying to catch his breath when Wade returned to the huddle after one play on the sidelines. "It was about third-and-20 at our own 20," Mather recalled.

"Bill came back to me and said, 'We gotta get a first down.' I was dead tired," Ditka said. Looking around the huddle at his equally spent teammates, he blurted to Wade that he couldn't run a deep pattern. The season was on the line. So, he stepped up and accepted a captain's responsibility. He told Wade, "Throw me a hook about 10 yards out and I'll try to get free to get the first down."

Ditka lined up outside left tackle Herman Lee and made his cut at the 30. Wade hit him on the break. He caught it as he always did— hands up, snatching the football from the air—and tucked it away. "I started running. Guys started missing." Nearly every defender took a shot as Ditka kept churning and bouncing ahead. "Finally, when Clendon Thomas, the last guy, got me, I went down. I was exhausted."

Ditka lay spread-eagle on his back for a good minute and then was helped off the field. "Mike Ditka's play in that game was just the greatest inspiration you will have. I have never seen a play so great," Pyle said.

"We never would have won the championship had it not been for Mike's great run," Mather said. But in the passage of time, the old coach forgot what happened next. Ditka remembered: "I was on the sideline. On the next play, Bill threw a pass to John Farrington, and he dropped it in the end zone. Roger LeClerc kicked a field goal. We would have won the game."

They tied the Steelers 17–17, but in the euphoria of the great escape, Ditka forgot the last tightrope act of the afternoon. The memory stayed with Andy Russell for four decades. "Forbes Field was set up so both teams were on the same sideline. The Bears were just a few feet away from us," Russell said. "Our running back Dick Hoak broke loose for what should have been the winning touchdown, but the officials ruled the ball dead. Our tough old guys Ernie Stautner; Joe Krupa, a Chicagoan; Myron Pottios; and John Henry Johnson swore at Halas. They charged that he paid off the officials to rig the game."

"After the game, some stuff happened in the locker room," Ditka said. "Guys started calling out when a Pittsburgh writer came in. I do know the writer chased Halas and yelled, 'You paid the officials!' A couple of us grabbed that guy and ran his ass out of there."

They learned after the game that most of America witnessed the murder of President Kennedy's accused assassin Lee Harvey Oswald on live television, an event repeated countless times on video replays. Dallas County sheriff's deputies were leading Oswald to a car to take him to their jail when a man named Jack Ruby emerged from off camera and shot Oswald point-blank. In short order, it was disclosed that Ruby ran a sleazy Dallas strip joint, the Carousel, and was a native Chicago West Sider with mob ties whose given name was Jack Rubenstein. Football definitely was not America's game on Sunday, November 24, 1963.

Football returned on Thanksgiving Day with a wild one at Detroit's Tiger Stadium, where the Lions stung the Packers with a 13–13 tie. So, both the leaders hit the stall button at the same time. The Bears' great escape became a sequel three days later at Wrigley Field when Chicago overcame a 17–0 deficit to tie the Minnesota Vikings 17–17 and hold that razor-thin half-game lead over Green Bay with two games left.

Both teams took care of business on December 8. The Bears clobbered the 49ers 27–7 in icy Wrigley Field. Knowing the Bears had won, Green Bay came through against the Rams 31–14 at the L.A. Coliseum to set up the final week's showdown. The Packers dialed up the pressure on Saturday when they polished off the 49ers 21–17 in half-filled Kezar Stadium.

In Chicago, a biting cold snap in the wake of a heavy snowfall was forecast for Sunday's game between the upset-thinking Detroit Lions and the Bears at Wrigley Field. Chicagoans woke up to screaming banner headlines that Northwestern's brilliant football coach Ara Parseghian had accepted college football's most prestigious coaching assignment, to stir the echoes at Notre Dame.

Parseghian's appointment ended days of speculation that at one time had Vince Lombardi all but packing up his snowshoes and electric blankets to forsake Green Bay for South Bend. Ara was the final choice deemed fit to join the legendary Knute Rockne and Frank Leahy at the head table of distinguished Irish coaches, which he did in style and dignity for the next 11 seasons.

Another event would prove far more important to the outcome of the day's game. The renowned jazz and blues singer Dinah Washington had died overnight in her Detroit home. Shortly before 5:00 A.M., her husband, Lions cornerback Dick "Night Train" Lane, had leaned over to kiss her good-bye before he left to catch the team's charter to Chicago. When she didn't stir, he called the fire department, whose emergency crews could not revive her. She was 39. Night Train Lane, a longtime Chicago favorite from his days with the Cardinals, went into seclusion.

Johnny Morris had a field day against Lane's replacement, Tom Hall, as he caught eight Billy Wade passes for 171 yards. The flanker's big play came in the third quarter when he and Wade teamed up on a play called South Len Pass 27 Full Sponge. "Sponge and Steel," Wade recalled. "Against a zone defense, Ditka [Steel] would go to his right, then shoot between the corner and safety, and I threw it over the linebacker's head."

On this play, Ditka's cover men chased him downfield to clear the side for Morris (Sponge). Morris broke from the right flanker and made a sharp cut 12 yards upfield to his left to catch Wade's pass on the break. He spun back and sprinted to the end zone, completing a 47-yard touchdown play to give the Bears a 10–7 lead.

Three minutes later Wade connected with Ditka on a "Steel" call, a 22-yarder, to make it 17–7. The Lions battled back and were trailing 17–14 in the closing minute with the ball. Earl Morrall threw a quick out to Terry Barr, who turned in to the clutches of Bennie McRae, who picked him up and slammed him to the frozen ground like an enraged stevedore breaking a crate of eggs.

Jack Brickhouse's call of the next play over WGN radio is still replayed on Chicago stations more than four decades later. "The clock continues to move . . . 38 seconds to go . . . 36 seconds to go . . . back goes Morrall . . . he throws to the sidelines . . . it's intercepted by Whitsell! He's gonna go! *He's gonna go! Touchdown! Hey, hey! Oh, buddy! Davey Whitsell!*" The engineer increased the volume as the crowd screamed.

"That was the biggest play of the year," Ditka said. "I could just see Davey running. That was the happiest I've ever been in my life for one guy, for Davey. I knew that meant we were going to the championship game. People don't realize it's only one or two plays in a whole season that can make the difference. That one made the biggest difference."

The 24–14 victory put the Bears in the title game for the first time since 1956. Allen's defense had allowed just 144 points, 10.3 a game. They would face the New York Giants at Wrigley Field on December 29, the sixth and last time the two ancient rivals from the nation's two greatest cities would square off for the league championship. Announcers on the NBC telecast were Chicago's Brickhouse and New York's Chris Schenkel.

When Red Grange signed off the CBS telecast at the conclusion of the Detroit game, he joined Halas and the Bears for the annual alumni blowout. The next morning, he flew to Florida to start a pleasant retirement that would last until he died in 1991 at age 87.

On Thursday, December 19, Bill Gleason devoted his column to the death of Ruth Jones, who had come home to Chicago's South Side for her funeral and burial. Known to the world as Dinah Washington, she had been married to Dick Lane for barely five months. Gleason wrote that "the league saw fit to play on the Sunday after the assassination of President Kennedy, but Dick Lane did not play on the Sunday after the death of his wife." Mahalia Jackson sang the final hymn as the mourners filed out of St. Luke's Baptist Church in silence.

Gleason still was upset by what happened to Ed Stone in midseason. Stone had to put in his hours downtown editing and rewriting the copy of others who covered the Bears in their only championship season between 1946 and '85. So, the day before the title game, Gleason took Stone along to meet Boston's earlier equivalent of a Mike Royko, the *Herald*'s star columnist George Frazier, at the Sheraton-Chicago Hotel, near Tribune Tower. After they visited, Frazier wrote a 1,400-word front-page column printed the morning of the championship game. "He dictated his story to his office off the top of his head. No notes," Gleason said. "His was a rather well organized mind."

The column, which he called "A Monster of the Midway," focused on Halas as the founder of the hottest sport around and on the interest the game with the Giants had generated. "The Bears are blessed," Frazier wrote, "the most beatified is Papa Bear, George Halas himself, who at the age of 68 has grasped all the bygone glory, all the hurrahs that were his when his team was known as the Monsters of the Midway."

Frazier wrote that the legendary Halas just might have had another side, a mean side that would pull strings with friends in high places to undercut the career of a young sportswriter who dared to report the truth about his Bears. Noting that Ed Stone had dared to challenge Halas on many personnel, not personal, fronts, Frazier wrote, "Somewhere along the line, Mr. Halas could not have been too pleased with Mr. Stone's prose."

For his eastern readers, Frazier delineated the coziness between the Papa Bear and the *Trib*'s Don Maxwell as overseer of Stone's raffish *American*. "There's one Monster on the Midway and whoever he is, whether George Halas, or someone else, he is an enemy of Freedom of the Press," Frazier wrote.

It had been a hectic 57 days since the coup in South Vietnam started the misshapen run of tragedy. Sunday morning, December 29, was brutally cold. Kickoff was bumped up to noon in case of a tie, so the teams could play an overtime period, if needed, before darkness descended shortly after 4:00 P.M. The grounds crew ran blowers under the tarp in a futile attempt to keep the field from freezing.

It was no day for the faint of heart, but 45,000 Chicago fans came out anyway in the eight-degree cold for the first title game at home since 1943. Unlike in 1934 and '56, both teams came out for this one in appropriate footwear, sneakers or similar shoes. Nearly 26,000 more fans jammed into three heated venues—McCormick Place, International Amphitheatre, and Chicago Coliseum—to a watch the game on closed-circuit television.

"Yeah, it was bitter cold," Ditka recalled. "Once the game started, I don't remember being cold. I knew I was cold against Detroit the game before. I think we were wrapped up in the game and it didn't matter."

The Bears fumbled three times in the first quarter, two of which led to scores—one for New York, one for them. They escaped trouble when Billy Martin recovered his bobble on the opening kickoff. Moments later, Wade lost the ball at the New York 41 at the end of a 12-yard run. "Dooley discovered that [Sam] Huff, the middle linebacker, would go to his right on a passing situation," Wade said. "That's why I called a quarterback draw. Some guy came from behind and knocked the ball out of my arms. That put us in a bad situation early in the game."

After ex-Bear Erich Barnes recovered, Y. A. Tittle dumped a screen to Joe Morrison that netted 11 yards. From the Chicago 14, Tittle found Frank Gifford alone in the end zone, and the Giants had a quick 7–0 lead that evoked memories of the 1956 rout when they scored early, often, and all day.

Chuck Mather believed the Bears would have lost had Tittle continued to throw to Gifford. "Gifford beat Bennie McRae easily," Mather said. "But Del Shofner was Tittle's favorite target, and Gifford never saw the ball again."

Still in the first quarter, Willie Galimore coughed it up. Giants safety Dick Pesonen recovered, and New York was ready for the kill. "The Giants believed Davey Whitsell was the weak link as weakside corner," Mather said. Tittle attacked Whitsell with a bomb that the wide-open Shofner dropped in the end zone. "There was ice on the field in certain places. Shofner had several guys around him," Wade said.

Ditka saw that play from a coach's perspective. "Hey, listen! When you're running into that end zone and it's part ice and part hard dirt, it's very hard to keep your balance. It was a pretty tough play even though the ball bounced off him."

"I remembered what Lombardi said about the Giants two years before when the Packers won the championship," Jim Dooley said: " 'I know their keys. We're going to beat them with their own keys.' And he did it. That's what we tried to do, and we did."

Weakside linebacker Larry Morris was about to make the biggest play of his career, one of several that day that would give him the *Sport* magazine Corvette as Most Valuable Player. He knew the keys Allen and Dooley had drilled into his head. "I didn't know the screen was coming until Tittle sent a guy in motion. His key was to look right and give the left tackle and end time to slip over to the left." Morris was already moving ahead as he intercepted at the 34 and took off for the New York end zone. "One guy said it took me five minutes to get 5 yards," Morris said as he recalled a wild, weaving run toward the left-field bleachers that nearly went the distance. "I started to overstride, and I finally got brought down at the 6."

Wade took it the rest of the way, as he followed the wedge blocking of center Pyle and left guard Karras on the quarterback sneak for a 7–7 tie. "Someone can be moved. It's a matter of leverage," Mather said of a play he first saw at a 1937 coaching clinic conducted by Pitt's legendary Jock Sutherland. "We often used the silent count. Watching the ball gives you an edge over your opponents."

In the second quarter, Tittle faded to pass under pressure from Morris. "I tackled him, and he couldn't walk when he rose. I think I hit him just as he planted his foot," Morris said. "We were good friends, and I certainly did not intend to hurt him."

Tittle was helped to the Giants' dressing room, where he received two novocaine shots in the knee. He came out for the second half with the Giants up 10–7 on a Don Chandler field goal.

The Giants nearly put the game away on the second-half kickoff. Hugh McElhenny took the ball and burst upfield. "When McElhenny was young, he was the greatest back I've ever seen," Mather said. "Rosey Taylor caught him just as he was breaking away. I felt Rosey saved our championship." Instead of a touchdown, the Bears forced one of six Giants turnovers, five on interceptions. "Taylor made about seven unassisted tackles from the safety position."

The sequence that decided the outcome came in the third quarter. "If you get a team that screens and you take that away from them, they're in trouble," Dooley noted. "George Allen took away the screen, setting up O.B.'s interception."

"We were looking for tendencies," Mather said. "Most quarterbacks got to call their own plays in those days. Most successful quarterbacks had a tendency to call the same thing all the time. Allen got Tittle's tendencies. That made Larry Morris and O'Bradovich's interceptions possible. We would never have scored on that frozen field. Those two interceptions took us to the goal lines."

Tittle always went for the screen on third down. "Joe Fortunato called our defenses," O'Bradovich, the left end, said. "He told me to look for the screen. When the late Jack Stroud, at right tackle, dropped back without a push back, I sensed it was coming. I stuck out my left hand, and it stuck! A one-handed catch!" O.B. took off for the south end zone with Stroud giving chase. Stroud brought him down at the sideline at the 14.

The Giants' defense reluctantly allowed a single yard in two tries, to set up a third-and-9 situation. "Luke Johnsos was foremost in his day at calling plays from the press box," said Mather, who was manning the phone on the sideline. "He called down a quick pass to Ditka. We had not practiced it for some time. Besides, when you are near the 10-yard line, it's an ironclad defensive rule to never let the tight end out. So, I said, 'Luke! No! No! It'll never work.' Luke persisted. I sent it in. Ditka was smart enough to move out 3 yards from the right tackle. He caught the pass to the 1-yard line."

"I should have scored," Ditka said. "I really should have, but the safety made a really good tackle on me. He kind of caught me before I could get my shoulder down and stood me up, so I didn't have any momentum. If I could have gotten my shoulder down, I could have scored, but it was fitting. That's the kind of team we were."

"Wade used my very favorite play, the quarterback sneak," Mather said. The Bears had a 14–10 lead with 15 minutes to go. They killed time on short, effective runs by 1962 Rookie of the Year Ronnie Bull. It finally ended when Tittle lofted a prayer to the south end zone that Richie Petitbon clutched to his chest, leaving time for Wade to fall on the ball, which he did.

On the Bears' sideline, George Halas shouted in triumph as he raised his hands in the touchdown signal, before Phil Handler gripped him in a bear hug. As he left the field, Tittle, with blood streaming down from his bald pate, dashed his helmet to the frozen ground and cracked it. Across the way by the left-field corner, the Bears' final hero of the day, Ed O'Bradovich, joyously pitched his helmet into the left-field bleachers. The fan who caught it returned it 20 years later to the now retired Bear, who proudly displayed his championship "hat" in his den.

In the Bears' dressing room, as George Connor, working the room for the NBC telecast, tried his best to interview the whooping champions, Bill George made an announcement awarding the game ball to their hero, defensive coordinator George Allen. Then came a little ditty that either shocked or delighted millions of Americans, who'd never heard the likes of such before over the air, as Allen shyly grinned somewhere between embarrassment and gratification. "Hooray for George! Hooray, at last! Hooray, for George! He's a horse's ass!" In his book, Halas lamely made a case that they were singing for him. He knew better.

Ed O'Bradovich set the record straight for every man who played on the Bears' eighth championship team, Halas's last. "George Allen called us 'men.' Men. And call you by your first name and always give you respect. Instead of cussing at you constantly and doing everything to bring you down, his philosophy was just the opposite. And what greater time for Halas to step out, when we won the world championship, on December 29, 1963?

"What greater time for him to step down and go out and to this day still be remembered for doing that?" O'Bradovich said, ever emotional, but this time, almost wistful. "We had George Allen. I remember Paul Hornung telling me, 'With the talent you had, you should have won three or four or five of them.' When Allen left, that was the demise."

"I still had my season tickets," Ed Stone said. "After the championship game, I went to the dressing room. I congratulated Halas, and Gleason was upset that I did." Stone paused. "Gleason thought Halas was sinister."

For the first time in his long career, George Halas was named Coach of the Year. For the Chicago Bears, as it had been for the Kennedys until November 22, 1963, this was their Camelot, a brief, shining moment.

In the early hours of 1964, the team would begin a journey into hell.

TWENTY-SIX

TROUBLE COMES IN MANY PACKAGES

*L*ike George Halas himself, the post-victory tributes reflected the partisan viewpoint. "Right after they won the championship, friends of Halas—people like George Strickler, all kinds of Halas's old cronies—really assumed he would retire, but he just didn't do it," Cooper Rollow said. "He refused to give up. He wanted to come back for another year. That's the way he was; he just hated to quit." The man himself scotched such talk: "Where else could a 68-year-old find another job?"

The euphoria barely lasted into the next morning. "Everyone expected something," cocaptain Mike Pyle recalled. The players wanted raises and felt they deserved rewards similar to those Vince Lombardi had bestowed on his champion Packers. After all, the Bears reasoned, they took away Lombardi's title. They sought bonuses like those Carroll Rosenbloom awarded his 1958–59 champion Colts. "Now, we didn't know what was going to happen," Pyle said. "We still were happy enough to win the championship."

The first order of business the morning after the triumph was a visit to a special Monday meeting of the Chicago city council. "Everyone was invited," Pyle noted. That only Halas, Billy Wade, and J. C.

Caroline appeared in person to receive Chicago's highest civilian award, the Medal of Honor, from Mayor Richard J. Daley was a clear-cut sign that all was not well within the Bears family. The city mailed the medals to the other players.

With the exception of Pyle, the hometown boy who knew the significance of the award, and the three who did attend, the medals meant nothing to most everyone else on the team. Small-time stuff, they figured. They just knew that the things that really counted, the gifts and national endorsements, would flow their way after the holidays. "We all waited to see what would happen," Pyle said.

"Auld Lang Syne" was next. Several team members and their wives or ladies prepared to ring in the New Year at a west suburban bowling alley in which their captain held an ownership stake. In return for use of his name on Mike Ditka's Willowbrook Lanes in southern DuPage County, Ditka got 12.5 percent of the net profits without putting up a nickel. Not a bad deal, even when Iron Mike and his big Bears brethren poured in after games and figuratively drank up the profits.

The revelers in the Bears group were Ditka, the host; his wife, Margie; the Ditkas' Downers Grove neighbors fullback Joe Marconi and his wife, Janet; Ed O'Bradovich and Arlene Gala, his fiancée; and Tony and Nancy Parrilli. "I had planned to be there, but I couldn't make it," Pyle said.

Parrilli and O'Bradovich first met in high school at Proviso, where Ed played halfback and Tony played guard and linebacker. They became best friends and were teammates at Illinois, where Parrilli was elected Most Valuable Player in 1961. Unlike the many footballers who leave school after they use up their eligibility, Parrilli stayed to earn his degree. "He had the sense that Butkus did that there is life after football," Bill Jauss said.

Parrilli might have tried coaching years ahead. He gave the pros a whirl in 1962. The 49ers cut him that summer, but he tried again in '63 with the Redskins, only to get axed again. Both times after he was cut, he joined the Bears' taxi squad. That was not unusual in a business in which Packers all-time-great Fuzzy Thurston kicked around with the Bears and Baltimore before he found a home and fame with Lombardi in Green Bay.

While he was not one of the 40 members of the active championship squad, the 6′, 225-pound Parrilli was accepted as a full-fledged teammate, a dedicated worker who partied just as hard. "Tony was a wonderful guy," Pyle recalled. "We were on the same All-State team—he at Proviso, me at New Trier."

Shortly after 1:00 A.M., Parilli excused himself from the revelries at Ditka's Willowbrook Lanes to visit the men's room. "We were minding our own business," O'Bradovich said. In the men's room, Parrilli and a 32-year-old clothing salesman named Ray Messmaker exchanged words that led to punches. Two off-duty cops from the tiny police force in unincorporated Willowbrook, Chief Frank Winthers and Deputy Stanley Yorka, worked that night as plainclothes security. The two men and alley restaurant owner Thomas Giles barged headlong into the cramped room to break up the fight. None could cope with the situation.

Deputy Yorka was a plumber by trade. Chief Winthers, a full-time carpenter and part-time cop, packed a Smith and Wesson .38 target pistol but was virtually untrained in handling firearms. Yorka and Winthers would testify that they had just separated Parrilli and Messmaker when Joe Marconi entered the room to do his part. After that, the story, to this day, remains confused.

Marconi testified that he took a sharp blow to the head just as he nearly had Parrilli pulled to safety. Winthers admitted that he drew his gun with his finger pulled back on the trigger and smashed Marconi's head. "Marconi stood between Parrilli and this guy," Pyle said. "The gun went off. Why would a guy at this time have his gun ready to go off? It was a stupid mistake, and the guy probably to this day fully regrets it."

The single shot hit just over Parrilli's left eye and killed him instantly. "You get these morons who want to prove how tough they are, and lo and behold, you get the unfortunate accident and your buddy's gone. Sheer stupidity," O'Bradovich said. "That's something that never should have happened. Never."

Marconi took eight stitches to close the scalp wound. Marconi, Ditka, and O'Bradovich served as pallbearers for Parilli on January 4. "Tony happened to be in the wrong place at the wrong time," Jauss said.

Halas got the story off the front pages within a day of the shooting. Winthers pleaded guilty to charges of second-degree manslaughter. He was sentenced to probation. Nancy France Parrilli filed a civil suit seeking damages for the loss of her husband. The largest award under the Illinois wrongful death law at that time was $30,000. The wheels of justice move at a glacial pace in local Illinois courts. "O.B. spent an awful lot of time with Nancy after Tony's death," Pyle recalled. "They fell in love and married, happily so ever since." In 1967, Nancy settled for $14,000.

The episode faded in the crush of so many events in that era, in football and away from sports, but, for the Chicago Bears, it was nonetheless a precursor of trouble. By mid-January, the players were edgy, anxious to hear from the Old Man. Anything. They waited, and waited, and waited. "We were all hyped up, because Green Bay got the wives mink coats and, the next year, color TV sets," Stan Jones said. "My wife knew about the stoles because we were out at the Pro Bowl and we went out with Jim Ringo and Forrest Gregg and their wives. Darliss was wearing a little sweater, and they were wearing mink stoles."

Jones was home in Maryland teaching school when Joe Fortunato called from the Pro Bowl. "Joe was taking a poll of the team, asking everybody what they wanted so he could talk to Halas about it," Jones said. Halas conveniently was coaching the Western Conference team as winner of the league title.

"Here's our choices, Stan," Fortunato said: "Would you want your wife to have a mink coat, color TV, or silver service?" "I think my wife would like the mink coat," Jones said. "I'll put you down for the mink," Fortunato said. Joe did not call back right away, but Jones did not suspect anything was amiss.

"After we finished," Jones recalled, "I turned to Darliss: 'Listen, when that present comes, I want to be here. No matter where I am. Even at school.' She called me one day: 'Come on!'"

Jones asked, "What's it look like?"

"It's a small package," Darliss answered.

"Big things. Small package," he said.

"So, I came home. The package was insured, wrapped tight. I took a knife and cut through the paper. And this chunk of metal fell out, hit the top of the coffee table, and broke it. It fell clean through the glass," Jones said, laughing. "It was a medal from the City of Chicago!" Jones roared. "That's what we got for winning the championship. Everybody still laughs at me for what happened. I still have the medal too. The coffee table? We got rid of it. Isn't that something?"

Already dispirited by the Parrilli shooting and the well-intended but, to many, backhanded compliment from the Chicago city council, the players still thought Halas would come through. Finally, as summer rolled around, they knew the score. "We didn't receive a thing," Doug Atkins lamented four decades later. "All he did was give us a cheap little old ring and give the wife the top of that ring and a charm bracelet. It was the worst I've ever seen. A lot of them didn't even want to play."

Larry Morris, the title-game MVP, expressed the sentiments of many players. "We went to New York and got that little red Corvette as MVP. I really thought I was somebody." Halas brought Larry and his wife, Kay, and the others back to Earth by doing nothing. "He was more interested in money than in the players," Morris said.

When it came to rings, though, beauty was in the eye of the beholder. "I think the ring is beautiful," Mike Pyle said. "Yes, it's not of the caliber the Packers got. Some guys got pretty upset about that. Several players changed the ring. I don't look at that as a critical thing that George did. He was like that. He was tight with the dollar. I think the design on the ring is magnificent. The top of the ring has a gold carve-out of Wrigley Field, which is really neat. There's a diamond in the middle."

Some players, who thought it was a cheap trinket, had their rings appraised. The chip was a .30-carat flat-cut diamond. "I still have it the same way it was made, and I love it," Pyle said. "I want to remember him for the way he was. That was him. He made the top of that ring a beautiful pendant and gave it to all the wives. This is what made me angry: the single players didn't get one. And all of us had mothers; some of us, fiancées."

As offensive cocaptain and now the player rep as well, Pyle took the case for the single men, himself included, to Mugs Halas, the titular team president. "Evidently, we didn't contribute as much to the championship as the other guys," he said. Mugs scratched his head and asked, "What are you talking about?" Pyle explained, "We didn't get the pendants you gave to the players' wives." "We don't want to see any of those pendants on any Rush Street floozies or Playboy Bunnies," the younger Halas cracked, echoing his father's earlier admonition to Rick Casares.

Stan Jones made more in his final year with Washington at the end of his career than he ever got from Halas. "When we talked contract, he always started with the same question, 'Stan, what can you ask for that I won't have to say no to?' I'd say whatever it was, and he'd say, 'I can't justify that to the board of directors.' There was no board of directors," Jones said. "Halas was the board of directors. I could never get any more money out of him."

"When he didn't reward them and, in fact, treated them with contempt over the whole union thing that came up at the same time, they collapsed as a team and lost respect for him," Jeannie Morris said. "That team never again was going to play for him."

Bill Jauss offered an outsider's appraisal in a different light. "On the night of Halas's death, Abe Gibron [a Halas loyalist as player and coach] said, 'He's accused of being cheap, which he was, but if you needed something, he'd be first in line to provide it for you.'"

Thus, the dilemma. As Jauss noted, "How could someone be cheap when he's there with a check when you hit tough times? Regarding the fur coats, they weren't in tough times. They were well paid. They had just gotten the championship-game bonus. And a ring. Maybe that is greed." Jauss, whom nobody would ever call a management toady, offered the players' perspective as well: "If the Packers got it, and the Packers were not a richer team than the Chicago Bears, Halas could have done it if he wanted. I don't know."

So, they gathered again at Rensselaer to defend their title. For most of that summer session, it was fun and after-hours games as usual, and opportunity for the new blood. One newcomer was Evanston native and lifelong Bears fan Jim Purnell. Purnell starred at linebacker on Wisconsin's 1962 Rose Bowl team, but, at 197 pounds, he was considered too small for the pros and left undrafted. Purnell's father had a friend who had a friend named George Allen, who never ever turned down a potential diamond in the rough. "We might want you to try out as a free agent," Allen said. "By July, when rookies report, you're going to weigh 225."

"How?" Purnell asked innocently. "You're going to lift weights and eat a lot of food," Allen said.

"All I did was lift and eat," Purnell recalled in the spring of 2003, a few months before his death from rheumatoid arthritis. During spring term of his senior year in Madison, Purnell lifted weights like a Hercules wannabe and chowed down constantly, especially on dairy products. "Three malts or milk shakes a day. You could put a knife in the middle of it and it wouldn't move," he said.

"I reported to Rensselaer at 225 and gained a 10th of a second in the 40. I was in tremendous shape," Purnell said. He joined the linebackers, tight ends, and fullbacks for the tortuous Halas Mile, which the veterans despised. "I set the record," Purnell said. "As I passed Ditka on my last lap, he said, 'Slow down, rookie, you make us all look bad.'"

No veteran hated the Halas Mile more than Doug Atkins, who was proud to be a football player, not a trackman. "I tried that mile run the first day. None of us made the time. I was so tired, I told Halas I wouldn't ever run that damn thing again. 'You'll run it tomorrow,' he said. So, I figured that would be a good time to break in my helmet," Atkins said, seeing an opening to torment Halas as he had done over so many years in so many ways, day and night (including phone calls after midnight in which he shouted after being overserved). Wearing shorts, a T-shirt, cleats, and his helmet, he moved at a snail's pace. "I just took my time, didn't work up a sweat, and jogged back. Somebody asked me what I was doing. 'Just breaking in my headgear.' They had me do it again, and I did the same thing. I wore 'em out. There was never a dull moment around Halas."

As camp wore on in its monotonous way, disillusionment enveloped the team. Unlike the Giants, who capitalized on New York's many lucrative opportunities, individual players for the Bears were not permitted to accept endorsements or have television shows. "You guys get paid to play football," Halas said. Several players, Atkins and Davey Whitsell among them, did participate in a national TV ad for Mennen's Speed Stick deodorant that ran during the 1964 season. Also, thanks to Yale alum Chet LaRoche, who owned a New York ad agency, Pyle landed a Chap Stick print ad, in which he appeared on a ski slope. The stricture also didn't quite apply for Johnny Morris, who started at the bottom in the off-seasons with WBBM-TV, the CBS-owned station that carried the Bears. After retiring in 1968, he made a seamless transition into a career as the most popular sportscaster in Chicago for decades.

Captain Pyle and many others sensed the drift during camp. "There was a feeling that Coach Halas didn't appreciate the championship team coming back. We just didn't feel we were any different from the way we were in the summer of '63."

In the coach's quarters at Rensselaer, football-consumed George Allen endured the ultimate distraction. Two of his sons, 8-year-old Bruce and 10-year-old Gregory, joined him at camp while Etty cared for 2-year-old Jennifer back home in Deerfield. Their eldest son, 12-year-old George, the future politician, spent the summer in Paris with Etty's parents, who'd raised her in Morocco before she came to America after the war and met George Allen, the handsome, young coach at Morningside College, in 1949.

Bruce, whom the family always called "Little Bear Bruce," was the unknowing terror of training camp. One day, he crashed Halas's golf cart. Then, as Jennifer recalled from hearing it many times through the years, he decided to do something constructive. "Mr. Halas would gather the men and have them take off their helmets and set them down so he could look them in their eyes," she said. "When they took off their headgear, Bruce saw all the helmets lying in piles." Bruce, now general manager of the Tampa Bay Buccaneers, explained, "In the spirit of my meticulous father, I had a thought, 'I'm gonna organize them.'"

"He lined them up in straight lines in the end zone," Jennifer said. "This was before they had names and numbers on the helmets," Bruce pointed out. "They came back and were trying on the helmets."

"Halas shook his head," Jennifer said. "It was very funny. Bruce was just trying to help."

Then, in mid-July, George Allen was called off the field to take a telephone call from Etty at home in Deerfield. Her parents had taken young George on a trip to Etienne, near the Swiss border. As they walked down the stairs of their hotel for dinner, a gunshot went off. Her father was hit. It was an accident. "It was the bell captain, who was cleaning a gun, and it went off," Etty Allen said. She had to leave for Paris immediately to join her father and mother. "Mr. Halas told George, 'If Etty needs any money to go, I'd be happy to loan her whatever she needs for the trip.' We didn't have very much money at all. That touched me so much. Mr. Halas held masses every day for my father. It was so wonderful of him to do that. I always had a lot of respect for him, and George did too. We really loved the Bears."

"Coach Halas gave my mom the money to fly there, and we were gone a couple of months, all summer," Jennifer said. "After a couple of weeks at training camp, the boys were driving my dad crazy. He shipped them to Vern Buhl [an Allen family friend] and his wife, in Deerfield."

Among the training camp rites through the years were the gatherings at the nearby country club for a couple of beers after the evening meetings, before Halas went on his bed-check rounds after the 11:00 P.M. curfew. "I saw [Willie] Galimore and [John] Farrington earlier in the day after practice. I wasn't out at the club," Doug Atkins said. "We had a weigh-in the next day, so nobody drank much, 'cause everybody would have had a problem reaching the weight. He'd fine you." Later that night, Galimore was driving back to camp from the country club in his Volkswagen Beetle, with Farrington in the right seat. "They were coming down the back road," Atkins recalled. It was dark and moonless, and neither man wore a seat belt. The sunroof was open to circulate what air there was on the muggy Indiana night. The players, who drove it hundreds of times, knew that the back road was paved with blacktop mixed in with gravel three or four inches deep. It had a sharp unmarked curve that doglegged to the left before it crossed a bridge. A three-foot-wide gravel shoulder separated the blacktop from a ditch.

"Somebody there later said they drank just two beers and said, 'We gotta go. Weigh-in tomorrow.'" Atkins said. "I know they weren't going fast, 'cause Galimore didn't drive fast. The house ahead usually had a light on. That was the marker that the curve was coming. It wasn't on that night. They got there and all of a sudden had to make that turn. That car went off the road."

The VW jumped the ditch and rolled. As it tumbled, Farrington sailed through the sunroof and landed on his head. He was killed. Galimore died from a broken neck. "I was in my room right across from trainer Ed Rozy when he got a phone call," Atkins recalled. "He came into my room shaking. 'We had a little trouble with some of the boys,' Rozy told me. I thought we might have had a fight between some of the whites and blacks, but Rozy kept talking. 'Something awful happened. It wasn't a fight. You gotta go with me. I'm so nervous.' Then he blurted it out: 'Galimore and Farrington got killed!'"

Rozy and Atkins drove into town to identify the bodies. "They lay on tables in the doctor's office. Didn't have a bruise on them," Atkins said. "That was a sad thing. Then they put a sheet over them. Galimore was a good friend of mine. I didn't know Farrington as well. Had they worn seat belts, I don't think it would have hurt them. We went and saw the car. It didn't have a bump on it." In case of rolls, the four wheels on VW Beetles were designed to splay as they landed and then spring back to normal position when the car came to a rest—similar to a cat landing on all fours from a vertical drop.

Both men were just 28. Without publicity, which was the way he insisted such things be handled, George Halas did right by the Galimores, who discussed it years later with Jauss when Willie's son Ron became a world-class gymnast. "The family admitted that Halas agreed to pay the educations for Ronnie and any other siblings. He helped out a lot of people. He helped newspapermen who were tapped out. Ex-players. Officials. Referees. All understood that they would not talk about it. This," Jauss said, "was the Christian way to do it, I guess."

Willie Galimore had swooshed through football like his nickname, Will-o'-the-Wisp. He remained the classic what-might-have-been, dead before he reached his peak. "The Bears could have had Galimore and Sayers in the same backfield. They would have been unstoppable," Bill Gleason said, noting that as shifty as Gale Sayers was, Galimore was faster. "Once Galimore got out beyond the line of scrimmage, the linebackers and secondary were helpless. Nothing they could do. Here he comes and there he goes!" said Gleason with a whistle.

Cooper Rollow, who represented the Chicago writers on the Pro Football Hall of Fame selection committee for 15 years, lamented that Galimore's candidacy was never taken seriously. "I don't know why. I tried to get Willie in there as an old-timer, and it didn't work."

Ed McCaskey urged the *Boston Globe*'s late pro writer Will McDonough to help pull Galimore through the process. "So, we put him up," Rollow said. "We voted him in, our old-timers committee. Then Will kind of deserted us when the name came up before the big group." People on the committee offered such reasons as Galimore's seven-year career was too short, or he could not compare to Sayers. "Sayers just happened to be the most exciting running back in the history of the game," Rollow countered. The voters, though, turned collective deaf ears to Coop's pleas on behalf of the Will-o'-the-Wisp.

The team wore black mourning bands on the left sleeve of their uniform jerseys that season for Galimore and Farrington. Experience was their ally as they beat the College All-Stars 28–17 to kick off the season. Little else went their way. But, for Jim Purnell, the rookie who grew up a block away from Don Maxwell's Evanston home, the great thrill of his young life came the night before the annual Armed Forces game at Soldier Field, that year against the Dallas Cowboys.

"Halas had us come to the Edgewater Beach Hotel to take the bus to Soldier Field," Purnell remembered. "I was sitting alone on a couch in the lobby when he walked my way: 'Jim, we're going to put you on the team this year. What do you think of that?' I was stunned! It was my dream since I was a little kid. Out of the inside pocket of his sports jacket, he pulled an envelope. It had the name of a guy he'd cut and crossed out—Gus Kasapis, of Iowa, a tackle. He started to write on the envelope. 'The Chicago Bears agree to pay Jim—er, ah—'; Halas stopped," Purnell said. "He looked up at me and had forgotten my last name. My dad had this envelope framed. It reads 'Jim (blank) agrees to be on the Chicago Bears 1964 squad for $8,000.00.' And he signed it 'George S. Halas.' " Purnell laughed at the memory. "To my knowledge, that is the only piece of evidence that contractually obligated me to the Bears that season."

It was that sort of year. Out of kilter. Out of sync. Paul Hornung returned from his suspension for the opener at Green Bay. With eight seconds left in the first half, a Packers kick returner made a fair catch on a punt at the Green Bay 48. Vince Lombardi invoked an obscure rule that a team that made a fair catch is entitled to a free kick on the subsequent play. The teams lined up as they would on the kickoff, except the ball was held on the ground, and the defense could not rush. Lombardi sent in Hornung, who booted the 52-yard field goal out of Bart Starr's hold to give the Packers the halftime lead on their way to a 23–12 victory.

In a touch of irony, Jim Dooley would turn the tables on Lombardi's successor Phil Bengtson four years later in his first game as Bears head coach at Green Bay. In that one, Cecil Turner made a fair catch at the Packers' 43 with 32 seconds left. In 1964, Rich Petitbon stood by helplessly when Hornung made his free kick. This time, Richie held for Mac Percival, who drilled it with plenty to spare to give the Bears a 13–10 win on a day when Gale Sayers ran for a career-high 205 yards.

The season lurched ahead as the defending champions won only two of their first nine games, the worst defeat being a 52–0 drubbing from the Colts in Baltimore for Don Shula's first win over the man whose record he would surpass nearly three decades later. The only good thing about the season was the record-setting play of receivers Johnny Morris and Mike Ditka.

Late that season, the two Bears appeared at a local Monday business luncheon. Neither Morris nor Ditka recognized the *Chicago Daily News*'s recently-named football beat writer Ray Sons in the audience. Sons was looking for a quote—anything—to fill a slow day about a team going nowhere. "I got them in deep trouble," the affable Sons admitted in the fall of 2002.

The most popular player on a losing team is the backup quarterback. Not only was Rudy Bukich liked, he had outplayed starter Billy

Wade the day before in the second half of a big loss. The crowd, getting worked up after a few rounds, shouted at Morris and Ditka to support Bukich, the "people's choice," especially because everyone in town knew Halas loved Wade.

"Morris and Ditka did admit that if it were their choice, they'd start Bukich," Sons recalled. "I even talked to them after the luncheon. I wrote the story, and I got a call the next morning from Morris, and he asked, 'Did we really say that?'"

"Sure you did," Sons answered.

"I've just spent all night on the carpet at Halas's office," Morris admitted. "He called me at 2 o'clock this morning and got me up. He called Ditka and me down there. 'You dirty cacksuckers!' screamed the Old Man. He chewed us out for hours. I just got out of there."

"Ditka, a very honest man," Sons recalled, "admitted his transgression. 'Yeah, I said it!' Iron Mike said.'"

"'Ditka's still at the office,' Morris told me," Sons said. "'He's still on the carpet.' This had been a seven-hour interlude for Ditka, at any rate. I believe both of them were fined."

"I'm afraid he's gonna trade me tomorrow," Morris told Sons. "Can't you call him up and tell him the circumstances under which this happened? We had a bunch of drunken guys in there badgering us on that for an answer. Finally we gave them what they wanted."

Fear of being traded was the ultimate weapon Halas held over his men. Morris had carefully planned to enter television when he retired. (He networked his way into a business future in Chicago after football.) "Johnny was scared," Jeannie Morris recalled. "Halas scared them both. He ruled by fear." In the era before Viet Nam drastically changed societal mores, she noted, people got married younger, and players reflected the culture.

"A guy comes to the NFL; he's 22, 23 years old. He has a wife and children already, which they don't now so much," Jeannie noted. "All of a sudden, he has a daddy again who has complete control over him. He can't change jobs. He can't go play for another team. He doesn't want to do anything else. He's a football player. He's completely under the control of the grown-up, and he's a kid again. They have curfews. They're told all kinds of rules. It's not natural."

Today's wealth has empowered the players to a much greater extent. "Yet," Jeannie Morris said, "they are sort of psychologically imprisoned."

As angry as Halas was with his two star receivers, he heeded their pleas and turned to Bukich. "We lost seven of our first nine games, and I started playing," Bukich said. "We won every game until I suffered a left shoulder separation against Green Bay in Chicago." Bukich returned home to the West Coast for an operation that prepared him for a banner 1965 season.

Johnny Morris set an NFL record with 93 catches, and Ditka was close behind at 75. In those days, statistics like that meant two things. Both bad. The team had no running game in a league that traveled on the ground. Consequently, the team that could not run would not win. The 1964 Bears opened the new year with the Parrilli shooting and, with three Bukich-led victories, finished with five wins and nine losses.

For George Halas, 1963's Coach of the Year, the sixth-place finish was a hard landing that left a sour outlook, and grumbling in the sanctum of the locker room. "Sure, things were said in the locker room about the Old Man," Jim Purnell acknowledged. "Deep down we all loved him. He was a classic."

And he still was the man in charge who paid the bills and negotiated all the contracts, an experience Purnell could not forget nearly 40 years later. "I went in to do my second year's deal in a place that resembled Scrooge's office. He had a brass spittoon sitting three or four feet from his desk. I had written down all the tackles I made, all my stats on special teams, on an index card. I spewed off all this. 'I think I should get $11,000.' He looked at me like I was trying to bankrupt the Bears. 'What are you trying to do? Put us out of business?' He made a throaty sound, cocked his head back, and spit a hocker into the middle of that spittoon. Dead center," Purnell said. "I got more nervous before contracts than any game I ever played."

By no means was Jim Purnell alone. He settled for less and was happy to get it.

TWENTY-SEVEN

THE GREATEST STARS, THE GREATEST LOSS

*I*n 1965, the Green Bay Packers began a string of three straight National Football League titles. To George Halas's eternal dismay, that run indelibly forged Vince Lombardi's stature as pro football's greatest coach.

The events of the next decade further battered his pride and standing when he made a series of wrongheaded, puzzling, and utterly sad decisions, to make a joke of the NFL's once-dominant charter franchise. He could have avoided all that had he quit on top when he was named Coach of the Year for 1965 at age 70, the second time in three years that he won that honor.

The 1965 Bears were the best team in the league, but they woke up too late to win. After they wiped out the Packers 31–10, Vince Lombardi himself said they were better than the '63 champions, with as equally superb a defense and easily the league's best offense. "I did the passing game," Jim Dooley recalled. "Abe Gibron and Chuck Mather did the runs, and I called all the plays from the sidelines. Everybody does it now. I called it according to down and field position, which I prepared. It was a great time, and we had a hell of a team." Certain they were the best, the Bears never quit, but they operated under the handicap of three losses off the top.

The War Between the Leagues went nuclear in late 1964. NBC paid $36 million over five years for the AFL television contract. Then CBS upped its NFL ante to $28 million for just two years. The arms race was on full main, and even Halas had to loosen the purse strings.

With the stakes so high, both leagues employed so-called babysitters, men who were assigned to players the moment they were drafted. These babysitters would stash away the draftees, often at out-of-the way locations and often incommunicado, to keep them out of contact with teams from the other league that also had drafted them. Players who had agents to handle their negotiating could avoid the babysitter game. But even those few players were tailed and watched as in a spy thriller. It was the sort of intrigue atmosphere that supercharged men like Halas and Al Davis.

George Allen had learned from the master, and by 1964, he was considered the crown prince. Etty Allen confirmed that in 2003: "Mr. Halas told George, 'When I retire, I want you to be the head coach.'" For certain, Allen attacked that '65 draft like a man whose future belonged to the Chicago Bears. Both leagues chose the same day, November 28, 1964, the earliest-ever draft. Nobody did better than Halas's man, Allen.

With the third and fourth overall picks, Allen presented the coach with the two biggest prizes of that or any other draft. The New York Giants and San Francisco 49ers kicked off the process and played into Allen's hands when they picked plodding fullbacks Tucker Frederickson and Ken Willard. Allen licked his thumbs and went for the kill, grabbing Illinois middle linebacker Dick Butkus and, arguably the greatest-ever game breaker, Gale Sayers.

Allen also bagged Tennessee tackle Steve DeLong with the sixth pick and filled out his card with pile-driving Syracuse fullback Jim Nance; Michigan State's jet-quick pass catcher Dick Gordon; tackle Frank Cornish, of Grambling; and, on the 20th and final round, Wisconsin fullback Ralph Kurek, who would star on special teams for the next six years. For good measure, Allen signed undrafted free agent Brian Piccolo, the nation's leading ground gainer, from Wake Forest. "Donny Anderson and Jim Grabowski were the Gold Dust Twins in Green Bay," Piccolo's pal Kurek recalled. "Pic and I called ourselves the Poopsie Dust Twins, 'cause we didn't sign for shit!"

For George Allen, this was a shopping spree to equal Halas's prewar bonanzas. "He may have been the greatest general manager ever," said Dooley, Allen's coaching colleague through 1965. "As a coach and general manager, a personnel man, he was like Al Davis. He didn't have ownership, but he acted in the same way. He knew how to use it. Sometimes it was legal. Sometimes it was not. But he knew how to do it."

The Old Man, who negotiated the contracts as always, signed everybody but DeLong and Nance. Gaining the two stars, Sayers and Butkus, was no cinch. American Football League founder Lamar Hunt badly wanted local favorite Sayers for his Kansas City Chiefs. The Denver Broncos took Butkus in the second round to hedge their bets in the unlikely case that Halas would fail to sign him. Denver's owners, the Phipps brothers, waved plenty of NBC's cash at Butkus, a $400,000 package.

"Butkus is the best player I ever saw," Bill Jauss said. "He could play all the linebacker slots, line, offense and defense, and fullback." Butkus was so feared at Chicago Vocational High School that his coach Bernie O'Brien did not let him scrimmage lest he destroy his own team.

At Illinois, he played linebacker and offensive center in shortyardage situations for Pete Elliott as he earned all-America honors in 1963 and '64, won the Silver Football as Big Ten Most Valuable Player, and finished third in the 1964 Heisman Trophy balloting behind quarterbacks John Huarte, of Notre Dame, and Jerry Rhome, of Tulsa. Most important, as a matter of personal honor and pride, he walked across the stage at commencement in 1965 to accept his degree on time.

Halas had a hard-and-fast rule about agents. He would not draft players who had them except when the need was absolute. Red

Grange, of Illinois, was the first exception, in 1925. George Connor, of Notre Dame, was the second exception, in 1948. Grange's fellow Illini Dick Butkus was next.

Butkus did not employ an agent per se but was represented by a La Salle Street lawyer named Arthur Morse, who kept the same company with Halas. Morse was a Chicago athletic power broker, a wheeler-dealer who dealt on equal terms with men like Halas and hockey, basketball, real estate, and liquor magnate Arthur Wirtz. Morse served Wirtz for decades as his promoter for college basketball doubleheaders at Chicago Stadium. In that role, he doubled as associate athletic director for Loyola University, official stadium doubleheader host.

In light of what happened, Halas's mating dance with Morse sounded orchestrated. Allen had his close friend Vern Buhl babysit Butkus, and the two men developed a friendship. Denver's $400,000 bid for Butkus was peppered with such clauses as deferred pay, shelters, and the like. Morse walked away from the meeting and told Butkus it was phony. "We have a few ideas of our own on how we can set up an investment for him," Morse informed the Phippses.

Jauss's former *Daily News* colleague, the late Bob Billings, ghosted a Butkus biography in 1972, *Stop-Action*. According to Jauss, "Butkus describes a meeting among Halas, Allen, Morse, and himself. After the light talk, Halas said, 'Well, Dick,' always addressing the question somewhere, 'why don't you give me a figure how much you're looking at?' Butkus knew he was not to talk. Then, Billings wrote, 'Arthur Morse came out with a figure well over a couple of hundred thousand dollars that made me gulp.'" Jauss stifled a laughed and continued, "As Butkus-Billings wrote, 'Halas smacked his lips and said he and Allen had to talk about it.'"

Morse asked Halas to move quickly because Dick had to catch a flight to New York to appear on the Kodak All-American show, hosted by Johnny Carson. "Morse's cheek always amazed me," Butkus wrote. While his client visited New York, Morse finished the deal. When Butkus returned to Champaign, Morse told him he negotiated a $6,000 signing bonus within a five-year contract that started at $18,000 and escalated to $60,000 in the last year. The deal paid the great linebacker more than $200,000. Unlike Joe Namath's $427,000 from the Jets, which was filled with qualifiers that he did earn, Butkus's money was "solid."

Sayers was a different story. Buddy Young, the flea-on-a-hot-griddle scatback from Illinois in the '40s, who lasted nine years in the pros and eventually joined the commissioner's staff, was his designated babysitter. "I chose the NFL, because I had to play against the best," Sayers said. "On TV, I saw Jim Brown. I saw Lenny Moore. I saw Raymond Berry. I didn't see AFL players that good."

Halas, Chuck Mather insisted, outfoxed Lamar Hunt to land Sayers. "In the 1964 KU-Missouri game, Gale walked off the field when he got hurt. They accused him of quitting. Gomer Jones, of Oklahoma, disagreed. Gomer told me Sayers was tremendous and not a quitter," Mather recalled. "I called Don Pierce, the KU publicity man, who sent me a film of Gale. Most all his great runs came as a sophomore. I think he was thinking of a pro career and protected himself after that. I showed Halas the movie of Gale in the Oklahoma game running a punt back when he made the defender drop to his knees. Halas said, 'Hey, we have to get him,'" Mather said.

"Coach," Mather replied, "Lamar Hunt has drafted him too and has Sayers in Kansas City. He'll be hard to beat."

Mather continued, "When Sayers came in to Chicago, Halas said, 'Gale, we'd like to have you play for the Bears. Now, I don't like to negotiate around. I'd like you to go to Mr. Hunt. Tell him you want your very best offer, because you are going back to the Bears.' So, Gale went to Hunt, got his offer, and came back. I can't believe Lamar was so naive," Mathers said. "Sayers said, 'This is Mr. Hunt's best offer.' 'OK,' Halas said, 'we'll beat it.'"

Halas actually did not beat Hunt's offer, nor did he even have to match it. As in the case of Lujack in 1948, he sensed that the player cared about more than mere money. He persuaded Sayers to accept his price and the inherent advantages he would gain from living in Chicago and playing for the famed Bears.

For decades, it was written that Halas paid Sayers $100,000. He did, but not in a lump sum. And there were no bonuses. "I signed a four-year contract with the Bears for $25,000 a year," Sayers said in late 2002. "Lamar Hunt offered me 27.5. Had he offered me $50,000 a year, maybe I would have signed there," Sayers said, admitting he took a chance with Halas. "It wasn't guaranteed. If I played, I got it, $25,000. Next year, if I played, I got $25,000, and so forth. It was good, and I'm glad I played for a man like George Halas."

That summer, at the practice sessions for the College All-Star game, Sayers crossed swords with the only person he would ever meet in football who didn't like him, his coach, the legendary quarterback Otto Graham. "I tweaked my knee a little bit," Sayers recalled. "It wasn't bad, but it hurt, and I took a couple of days off. Graham charged I was faking, and he didn't play me in the game. 'Gale Sayers will never make it in pro football, because he's not tough,' " Sayers recalled Graham's saying. Graham did not let Sayers go against Jim Brown, his idol.

"When I went in to see Mr. Halas, he said, 'Gale, I know you had a problem at the All-Star game. Forget that. I'll judge you by what you do from this day on.' That's all I needed to know."

"Going into 1965, we didn't know what to expect," Mike Pyle admitted. "There was no question how good Butkus would be. We didn't know how good Gale Sayers was." They learned in a hurry.

Bill George was aging and injured, but Halas started him ahead of Butkus in the exhibitions. The same with Jon Arnett over Sayers. And Halas returned to Bill Wade as his starting quarterback. Palmer Pyle came home that summer to start at left guard next to his brother Mike. "In the Armed Forces game in Soldier Field, the last preseason game, Palmer blew out his knee," Mike said.

Halas picked up the disgruntled but talented George Seals from the Redskins. While Seals sought to find his way, veteran Mike Rabold, who later was killed in an auto accident in 1970, took over. "We lost the first three games," Pyle recalled. "Sayers wasn't starting. Butkus wasn't starting. We had real problems early on."

"Ditka, Fortunato, and Pyle called a team meeting at Notre Dame High School, in Niles, where we practiced before we could move into Wrigley Field," Kurek recalled. "No coaches were allowed, no equipment managers. The message was simple: We have the personnel and team unity. We can win games despite the Old Man."

They went to Green Bay desperate for a victory. "George Halas would never tell you who was starting," recalled Sayers. "After we came back in from the warm-up, he named the starters. He called, 'Gale Sayers.' That was my first start with the Bears." Sayers and Dick Butkus in their initial starts could not overcome a disastrous first half as the Packers built a 23–0 lead. At the break, Halas turned to Rudy Bukich. "Rudy was a risk taker who got rid of the ball and believed the running game complemented their passing game, unlike Wade, who lived to pass," Kurek recalled.

"The season turned 180 degrees at halftime," Pyle said. "Sayers started running wild. We scored 14 points on his two touchdowns. Seals did the right thing. Butkus was on the field. We lost but beat the hell out of them."

"It all jelled at Green Bay," Bukich recalled. "We damn near caught them in the second half. We could hear Lombardi scream at them after the game through the locker room wall."

Life began at 33 for Bukich, until then a career backup and vagabond. Rudy's father worked for US Steel in Gary, Indiana, and then took a supervisory job at Granite City Steel on the Illinois side of the Mississippi River across from St. Louis. Bukich played quarterback at Roosevelt High School, in St. Louis, and enrolled at Iowa in 1950. When Dr. Eddie Anderson, the coach who recruited him, left Iowa for Holy Cross, Jeff Cravath induced him to transfer to Southern California. He'd barely arrived at USC when Cravath got axed and track coach Jess Hill, a single-wing proponent, took over the football team as well.

"Only four schools in the country were still playing the single wing, and two were in L.A.," Bukich said, "UCLA and us, USC." He was forced to play backup tailback to Jim Sears as USC made it to the 1953 Rose Bowl against Wisconsin. When Sears had to leave with an early injury, Hill inserted Bukich, who delivered with the game's only score, a 22-yard touchdown pass to Al Carmichael, in a 7–0 USC victory.

The Rams drafted the Rifle to understudy Norm Van Brocklin and 1952 bonus pick Billy Wade. He seldom played. Few men have been as blessed with such a quick release and ability to scan the field and hit receivers at any range. From L.A., Bukich landed in Washington in 1957. A year later, the Rifle wanted out.

"I refused to sign a contract with the Redskins," Bukich said. "They put me on waivers, and I flew up to Toronto to talk to my ex-coach with the Rams, Hamp Pool. While I was there, Halas called me. He said if I came to Chicago, he would give me a three-year, no-cut contract at a big raise over what I was making with the Rams. I didn't have a no-trade in my contract, so [Halas] sent me over to Pittsburgh. I played quite a bit behind Bobby Layne and came back to Chicago for another seven years. Ted Karras, Bobby Joe Greene, Herman Lee, and I played for Rooney and went back and forth between there and Chicago."

Everything coalesced in 1965. "Rudy had the best year of his life," Dooley said. He led the league in passing. The Bears lost the second game, in Los Angeles, 30–28 when they blew a 28–9 lead after Sayers broke free on the first of his 22 touchdowns that season, a fake pass, and a 22-yard dash to the end zone. In the rematch two weeks later, they put up their first win with a resounding 31–6 rout over the Rams. A trip to the Twin Cities followed, and they came home from Minnesota with a 45–37 victory in a game Sayers insists was his best performance. "I scored four touchdowns. The last was a kickoff return to win it. Every time I scored, Fran Tarkenton would bring them back to score. We needed every one of those touchdowns."

The Bears had become the scourge of the league. On October 24, they smashed the Detroit Lions 38–10. The rematch with the Packers at Wrigley Field was next, and the Bears were ready.

It was no contest as Allen's stunting defense baffled Bart Starr while Sayers, his running mate Andy Livingston, and Bukich's pinpoint passing keyed a 31–10 rout. "I knew we could beat them in the second game, which we did," Bukich said. He was leading the league in passing. It was Lombardi's worst defeat and the last time a Halas-coached Bears team beat the Packers.

Baltimore came to Wrigley Field on November 7 for another classic. Before the game, Don Shula's Colts complained to the officiating crew that Wrigley Field's end zones were dangerous and unsafe.

The Bears dominated the statistics as Butkus made one interception and a strip. They lost, though, when Johnny Unitas threw a pass to Raymond Berry in the end zone that he dropped almost as quickly as he got his hands on it. The crowd screamed when the official, who had listened to Baltimore's pregame complaint, raised his arms to signal a catch, possession, and score. The Colts won 26–21, to leave the Bears at 4-and-4. "If we had beaten Baltimore at home, we would have tied them and maybe won a championship," Bukich noted.

They regrouped and continued the chase, determined to catch the leaders, Green Bay and Baltimore. They beat the St. Louis Cardinals 34–13, roared into Detroit and came back with a 17–13 win over the Lions, and then headed into New York for the most heralded opponent's visit since Grange's 1925 tour. Gale Sayers gave Gotham an eyeful as he made two spectacular touchdown runs and threw for another on a halfback option pass to lead a 35–14 Bears rout. Halas's two rookies, Sayers and Butkus, were the talk of pro football.

The rematch with the Colts at Baltimore Memorial Stadium was a classic grudge match. On the first series, Bukich made a reverse pivot and sent a quick pitch to Sayers, who burst around the right end and took off on an untouched 63-yard dash to the end zone. Earl Leggett and Atkins took down Unitas before he could set up to throw. He was finished for the season with a torn knee ligament. Chicago added two field goals and went home with a 13–0 victory at 8-and-4 for the season's final two games.

On Sunday, December 12, 1965, Gale Sayers delivered one of the most spectacular performances in history against the San Francisco 49ers. He became the third NFL player to score six touchdowns in a game, as the Bears romped 61–20. Incidentally, all three six-TD games involved the Bears. Ernie Nevers was first, scoring all the points—six touchdowns and four extra points—in a 40–6 Chicago Cardinals victory on Thanksgiving Day 1929. Dub Jones scored his six touchdowns in 1951 when the Browns beat the Bears 42–21 in Cleveland. Sayers's magnificent performance came under impossible conditions in the mud during a daylong downpour driven by 20-mile-an-hour winds off Lake Michigan.

Sayers opened the scoring with an 80-yard screen pass from Bukich. He ran for touchdowns from the 21, 7, 50, and 1. Then, he caught a Tommy Davis punt at the 15 and took off on an 85-yard return. He accounted for 336 yards: 113 rushing, 89 on receptions, and 134 on punt returns. "Was it the best football game I ever played? I don't think so. We won 61–20. Was it a great game? It was," said Sayers.

That bravura effort climaxed a rookie season that saw Sayers amass 2,272 yards rushing, receiving, and returning kickoffs and punts. He was Offensive Rookie of the Year and All-Pro. Dick Butkus was Defensive Rookie of the Year and All-Pro as well.

Unfortunately, they did not win. "We were the best team in the league. We killed the Packers in the second game and, in the last game, let the Vikings tie us and beat us," Mike Pyle said. The 24–17 loss to Minnesota in a meaningless finale left them at 9-and-5 and filled with hope for 1966. They rehashed the might-have-beens at home as the Packers edged the Colts 13–10 in a memorable playoff at Green Bay a week before they beat the Browns 23–12 to win the title on sloppy Lambeau Field. "Halas treated me well," Bukich said. "He paid me well with increases. I was happy being in Chicago and playing. I liked the guys. It was a great team."

George Allen's key defenders, Atkins and Fortunato, were aging. Bill George was all but finished. And Stan Jones was ready to hang it up after a dozen Hall of Fame–caliber seasons. The season-ending loss to Minnesota on frozen Wrigley Field did it. "We were chasing Tarkenton when that son of a gun reversed his field. Some guy blind-sided me and hit me to that frozen tundra. I hit that field and said, 'I've had it!' "

Jones told his wife, Darliss, to get the kids ready while he checked out with Halas, as he had done after every season. "I turned in my books and all my stuff. He was reading a newspaper," Jones recalled.

"Well, Coach, this has been a great opportunity, and I certainly appreciate it. It's been a great experience," Jones told the Old Man.

"He rattled the paper, looked up, and said, 'Well, kid, keep in touch.' That was my last visit with George Halas," said Jones, perhaps the most loyal and dedicated player the Old Man ever coached.

George Allen had been Halas's loyal liege since his arrival in 1958 after Frank Korch's death. He watched, listened, and absorbed Halas's lessons. He kept up with the trends and advanced a few himself when it came to zone defenses and attacking principles. He drafted smartly and aggressively. He developed greenhorns and turned them into shrewd, hard-nosed veterans. He even learned how to spy and how to avoid opponents' sleuths. George Allen had proved to one and all that he was a winner all the way. And there was that nagging matter of succession.

Allen was not as young as he appeared and as he had stated since college. Now in 1965, he was actually 47, not the claimed 43, and would turn 48 on April 29, 1966. He knew that Vince Lombardi was considered old when the Packers gave him his chance at 45 going on 46. His mind said, "Get your own team now; the window of opportunity is closing." His heart said, "Stay with the team you love in the city you love with the players you love for the boss you love."

"George Halas told my dad that he would succeed him as coach," said Jennifer Allen. "Sid Luckman told Dad to 'get it in writing.' Sid was a great businessman, and my dad was not. Dad never read his contracts and the fine print. He wasn't business savvy; he just wanted to coach."

"George asked Luckman what he should do," Etty Allen said. "He had the opportunity to become a head coach. He just got a raise to make $19,000 a year. 'George,' Sid said, 'you have to think about your family.'"

"But we love the Bears," Allen told Luckman.

"When Luckman told him to get it in writing," Jennifer said, "Dad asked Halas, and he replied, 'My word is good.' He did not put it in writing. Sometime that year, Halas asked my dad what the team needed to do to improve, and my dad wrote a 28-page outline—perfect order, Roman numerals, capitals, et cetera; totally scholarly, with footnotes—on how the team needed to improve."

The outline contained concepts that Allen later would incorporate into his Redskins operation, including the isolated and secure training facility with running track, pool, and weight-training quarters, plus organized and cataloged films and files. Computers were new then, but had Allen been more familiar with electronics, he would have included them as well. Unfortunately, the sole copy of that memo was lost in a flood in the Allens' Palos Verdes Estates home. Halas, Jennifer Allen said, never replied to the original.

Etty Allen lived with her husband's anguish as Christmas approached. "George told me this later: 'Sid told me you have to love yourself first.' We were shocked Sid would say this, because Sid loved the Bears, and so did George. Mr. Halas kept on coaching the Bears. We left for the opportunity. George never looked back."

That opportunity came when Allen and Los Angeles Rams owner Dan Reeves agreed on a coaching deal and waged a bitter court battle with Halas that included tampering charges and violations of his Bears contract. Halas initially claimed Allen's presence was vital to the Bears' 1966 title hopes.

Allen, like everyone else in his profession, worked under a contract, but like all the others, the boss called all the shots. It was a renewable arrangement, year by year. In case of a guarantee, and few deals were then, the owner would have had to pay his coach after he was fired. It's been a long-standing tradition that, in most cases, a boss—be it an owner, athletic director, or the like—does not stand in the way of an employee who has the opportunity to improve his career with better money as well as title.

Allen had been ready, willing, and eager to run the whole show and, by Christmas 1965, was frustrated by Halas's refusal to step aside and let him have the Bears. So, on Christmas Day, Allen called Rams general manager Johnny Sanders in Los Angeles to say he was interested in the open job there. Rams owner Dan Reeves was more than interested. Allen was the NFL's "hot" assistant, and Reeves wanted him as he had wanted no other coach, even a Clark Shaughnessy or Sid Gillman. Reeves called Allen and told him to ask Halas for permission to talk. Halas granted Allen his permission to talk with Reeves. Allen testified under oath that Halas told him eight or nine men were being considered and "you won't get the job."

When Reeves got serious, Halas snapped back and denied permission to Reeves, saying Allen violated his contract by failing to ask permission in writing and by not telling Reeves he was supposed to say he was unavailable. Halas invoked Article XI of the NFL bylaws concerning "prohibited contact," regarding tampering with players or coaches under contract to or property of another club. Halas was even more furious when he called Reeves on December 29 and learned that Allen had made the first call to the Rams.

Had Allen, who never read contracts, checked his own deal with Halas, he would have seen that his deal lasted to March 31, 1968. Reeves and Allen came to terms on January 4, 1966. "With the Rams, he earned $44,000," Jennifer Allen said. Reeves gave him control over coaching and personnel and a dedicated facility in Long Beach to run the operation.

George Halas was not about to let his boy get away. He filed suit, charging Allen with breach of contract. The case landed in the Chicago circuit court in the hands of a man who long ago played a different role in the Bears' history. "The judge was Cornelius J. Harrington, my father's patient, the lawyer who represented me when I signed my contract in 1948," said George Connor. "Any kind of ruling Judge Harrington made would be monumental. It could have changed the whole league."

As Bill Furlong wrote in *Sports Illustrated*, Halas claimed Allen wanted to return to Chicago in three or four years to succeed him after he retired. Halas claimed Allen told him he would stay with the Bears if Halas gave him an option to buy 5 percent of the Bears' stock and matched his salary offer with the Rams.

"I'm sure that Halas backdoored the judge," Connor said, amused. "Judge Harrington said, 'Based on the prima facie evidence, the contract is binding.' Halas jumped up and said, 'Your honor, that's all I wanted to prove. I withdraw my case.' Bud Short, Halas's attorney, didn't even know what the hell was going on," Connor said.

When George Allen went over to shake his former coach's hand, the Old Man replied, "Young man, I can assure you that you will never coach this football team."

"Halas also told Allen, 'Be sure to turn in your playbook,' Bill Jauss said. "That was a bone of contention in the case that Allen would steal those mighty secrets from the Chicago Bears, as though nobody else knew these plays, these secrets."

The Allen family has adamantly denied that George Allen asked Halas for stock in the team. At that time, Paul Brown, who was no longer with the Cleveland Browns, was the only other coach besides

Halas with equity in his team. That was a major reason Lombardi
left Green Bay. Because the Packers are publicly held, no such deals
are possible. The Washington Redskins gave him stock as part of his
deal when he joined them in 1969. Redskins' owner Edward Bennett
Williams gave Allen a stock option, but he never exercised it because
he could not afford it. Had Allen received proper advice, he could
have taken out a loan and bought the stock, which would have been
worth millions.

"After the lawsuit, we were invited by Governor Kerner to a ball,"
Etty said. "We went and saw Mr. and Mrs. Halas and Virginia and
Ed McCaskey there. The press was beside themselves. They had just
been at the courtroom two days before. They asked for a picture.
George Halas said, 'OK.' My George wasn't going to say no. So, I
fixed Mr. Halas's tie like it was my father's tie. They said, 'Smile.' I
told him, 'I love you all my life.' Mr. Halas said, 'Me too.' I still love
him today."

It took less than six months for fissures to develop in George
Allen's relationship with the erratic Reeves.

1966-2003

TWENTY-EIGHT

THE MESS

$\mathcal{G}$eorge Allen did leave behind his playbook and films. He took his ideas, vision, and ability to build winning football teams west to Los Angeles. His mentor may have had the NFL's two best players in Gale Sayers at his marvelous peak as the league's rushing champion and Dick Butkus as football's most ferocious defender, but without Allen to stir the potion, the Old Man was lost.

Halas neither hired a new personnel man nor bothered with strategic planning. He did not act on Allen's futuristic memo, if he even read it. Such was the price George Halas had paid in early 1966 to win a rigged case in a Chicago courtroom, that he then backed away from the overwhelming weight of pro-Allen public opinion and let him escape.

Halas also lost Chuck Mather, who left at age 52 rather than wait any longer for his chance at the top. "Halas said I could stay, but it was time to make a move," Mather said. He interviewed for head coach openings with Pittsburgh, St. Louis, Washington, and expansion Atlanta. "Had Halas helped me with Rooney," he said, "I would have gotten the Pittsburgh job. I didn't want to be an assistant the rest of my life. My insurance business was making twice as much money as my Bears salary. I scouted college talent for 10 years until Jim Finks came."

"When Allen left, I was really at the top as the offensive coach," Jim Dooley recalled, "but we had so much bickering among the staff that I went to Halas. 'Coach, I want to move over to Allen's spot,' I said. 'I know the defense, and I can do the job.' I wanted to get away from all that bitching."

When Doug Buffone retired in 1979, he held the distinction of being the final Bear drafted by George Allen. "Hey, you gotta come to Chicago," Allen pleaded when he reached Buffone at the University of Louisville after the 1966 draft. "We really need you."

Buffone, a middle linebacker in college, did not understand why Allen wanted him when the Bears had second-year-man Dick Butkus, already the best in the league, plus All-Pro outside linebacker Joe Fortunato. "Times are changing," Allen warned. "Joe's gonna be moving on." To Buffone, Allen's words were not those of a man about to take a powder.

As Allen predicted, times were changing. Fast. Allen "was gone before I signed," Buffone said. Buffone would play special teams and backup in 1966 and take over the strongside spot the next year, where he stayed for the next 13 years, well after Butkus had retired and settled his medical malpractice suit against the team.

In April 1966, the American Football League scrapped its first commissioner, World War II air ace Joe Foss, in favor of hard-charging Oakland Raiders chieftain Al Davis. The minute that soccer-style placekicker Pete Gogolak played out his option and jumped from the AFL Buffalo Bills to the NFL New York Giants, Davis declared an all-out spring offensive. He aimed to land as many top NFL stars as he could by enticing them to play out their options and sign personal services deals with his AFL clubs. It started with quarterbacks, as Houston Oilers owner Bud Adams signed John Brodie, of the 49ers, and the Raiders inked Roman Gabriel from the Rams.

Houston handed Mike Ditka a $50,000 bonus check behind Halas's back to come over in 1967 after his option season. "All I had to do was kiss the ring, but I didn't do it," Ditka said. "I never understood why he never saw my value for the way I played for him. I played hard for him. I'm not even saying I played good for him; I played hard. Every down, I played hard. If somebody could come to me who never had me play for him and offer me that much more money, as Houston did, then I really couldn't understand that. It wasn't that I was greedy about the money; money was money. What the hell—we didn't make enough in those days to worry about it. We all had jobs in the off-season."

Ditka's deal with Adams came to light as everything changed on June 8, 1966, when Pete Rozelle announced the NFL-AFL merger, which nullified all Davis-inspired deals. Ditka pocketed the bonus. When he did, the furious Halas cut Iron Mike's salary by 10 percent. Late that fall, Ditka assured his departure when he accused the parsimonious boss of "nursing nickels like manhole covers."

By then, the team was foundering on the field as well. The Bears ran aground in an opening-day 14–3 loss at Detroit. The showdown with Allen at the Coliseum was next, and Halas, now 71, was full of the old vinegar. No one could accuse him of going soft in his dotage. "He had a meeting before we left for Los Angeles," Buffone recalled. "He called L.A. the 'cesspool of sex.' He was worried about the guys' getting out there and getting into trouble."

No other coach in Buffone's football experience had ever spoken this way to a team, and Halas was just warming up. "Now, I can talk to you like you're gentlemen," Halas cooed at the front of the room. Then he snarled, "Or I can talk to you like you're coal miners. You 'cacksuckers'!"

"He was on those referees from the time we got on the field until the time we got off. He gave no leeway," Buffone said. He could also size up opponents in one sentence. According to Buffone, "As a tactician, he was simple: 'They're either gonna knock you down, or you're gonna knock them down.'"

On Friday night, September 16, 1966, George Allen's Rams did most of the knocking down, as they whipped the Bears 31–17. The enduring moment of that game came when a drunken fan staggered toward the Bears' huddle, and Ditka leveled him with a wallop. "I talked to Ditka after that game," the *Tribune*'s Cooper Rollow recalled. He asked Ditka, "Why did you punch out that guy?"

"That guy's got no fucking right to be on the field! The field's for players!" Ditka roared. "And that's all there is to it!" Halas exiled

Ditka to Philadelphia on April 26, 1967, for quarterback Jack Concannon and a draft choice. Two years later, Ditka landed in Dallas,
where he revived his career with Tom Landry and the Cowboys.

The Bears would somewhat settle the score with the Rams later in
the year, 17–10, but the die was cast on a 5–7–2 season as Allen's
Rams, a Western Conference bottom-feeder throughout the '60s,
rebounded from a 4-and-10 season in 1965 to 8-and-6 in '66. "Our
veterans got old very quickly," Gale Sayers said. "We were predicted
to win the division, but we just didn't have it."

Without Allen's shrewd talent judgment as personnel boss, the
Bears could not replace the worn-out parts. "They had terrible drafts
after Allen left," Ed Stone said, "guys like Loyd Phillips in '67 and
Mike Hull in '68. Hull was a handsome guy from USC, a fullback,
who could not play football." Halas drafted Hull as a tight end.
"When you saw him in camp trying to catch a football, he showed
no natural coordination," Stone recalled. In more irony, when the
Bears cut Hull in 1971, Allen, in his first year at Washington, picked
him up and plugged him in as special-teams captain, where he thrived
through 1974.

From the smooth Allen-run organization that pumped blue-chip
draftees and superb veteran free agents into the Bears came chaos.
"Halas was out of the mainstream and had no organization, no scouting operation," Stone stated. "In many drafts, the identity of the
player agents dictated who the Bears selected."

"We didn't have a general manager nor a personnel man after Allen
left," Dooley said. "He always had sensational players, the best
money can buy. I thought to myself, 'How nice it must be.' "

New Orleans joined the league in 1967, to force the second expansion draft in as many years, after Atlanta's in 1966. Rozelle then
broke the league down into four C divisions: Capital and Century in
the Eastern Conference; Coastal and Central in the Western Conference. The Central, or "Black and Blue," cold-climate clubs were Chicago, Detroit, Green Bay, and Minnesota. In the expansion draft, the
Saints reeled in aging Davey Whitsell and Halas foil Doug Atkins.

The Saints paid Atkins $50,000, twice as much as he ever made
with the Bears, and he responded with an All-Pro season in 1967.
"The most I ever made from Halas was $25,000 and a $5,000 bonus

that we agreed to have tied in with $30,000 we had negotiated instead of $25,000," Atkins said. "If you didn't set the woods on fire, he'd take that bonus away from you. The next year, you'd be playing for $5,000 less from what he paid you the year before. After a year, you got smart and you counted your bonus as part of your contract."

Out in Los Angeles, George Allen traded draft choices for veterans he knew were winners and could still play. He offered the Saints a number one choice for Atkins. They said no. Then Atkins retired after he broke a leg in late 1969. When Allen landed in Washington in 1971 and started building his "over-the-hill gang" under the slogan "The Future Is Now," he called Atkins and asked him to come back for just one more year. "Allen offered me $100,000 to play on third downs only, but I had to tell him, 'Buddy, it's just so good to get out of it and those training camps.' I sure would have liked to have the money, though. He was going to guarantee me the $100,000."

By 1967, Mugs was handling the team's affairs in a league now run by the Rozelle–Tex Schramm axis with strong support from Art Modell and Carroll Rosenbloom. Mike Pyle served as the Bears' player rep and would succeed Detroit's John Gordy as NFLPA president. In those meetings, Halas sat at the table as the league's elder statesman, its sage, the godfather. "He had an ability to lead that was incredible," Pyle said, as one who watched the Old Man operate in those owner-player sessions. "He had interesting disciplines. He always took notes."

Pyle got much of his information about the way Halas worked inside closed-door meetings from an owner who kept his comments in deep background. "We'd argue for two days, each owner representing his own interests," the owner said. "At the end of two days, Halas, who took notes all that time, would stand up and say, 'Gentlemen, this is what I think we should do.' He would refer to his notes and state his feelings about each item. When he finished his remarks, he'd say, 'Can we just move forward from there?' Everybody would agree, and that's how the meetings would end," Pyle's source said. "Up to 1968, he was in charge."

As for the Bears, Halas in 1967 was a cranky 72-year-old for good reason. Despite the All-Pro presences of Sayers and Butkus, the team reeked, which became apparent when the Bears traveled to Kansas

City for an exhibition six months after the Packers, laughing all the way, had cuffed the Chiefs around 35–10 in Super Bowl I.

This time, the determined Hank Stram, who grew up a Bears fan in nearby Gary, poured it on with a vengeance on a steamy summer night. Stram unleashed his "offense of the '70s" arsenal—moving pockets, traps, slants, bombs, blitzes, the works—for touchdown after touchdown. It got so bad that players feared that the Chiefs' white stallion had circled the field so many times in a hard gallop after Kansas City scores that he would he keel over in the heat.

Covering that night for the *American* for the first time since the championship year was none other than Ed Stone. Almost out of the blue, the paper's sports editor had tapped Ed Stone on the shoulder one evening at the copy desk in 1967 to deliver the news: the shackles were off; he had served his confinement in a journalistic gulag. "I was restored to the beat. Halas greeted me warmly," Stone said. "It was always that way with him. He acted like nothing had happened, although we both knew the truth."

The coach's gimpy right hip, which had annoyed him for decades since his 1919 baseball injury with the Yankees, hurt constantly, making movement difficult and uninterrupted sleep impossible. Then, Mike Royko, star columnist of the *Chicago Daily News*, slashed the Old Man in a spiteful October 23 diatribe. Calling Halas a "tight-fisted, stubborn, willful, mean old man," Royko noted that "there isn't a famous Chicagoan in or out of jail who generates such intense dislike." He twisted the figurative knife when he wrote, "George Allen has taken a rabble in L.A. and built it into a possible champion, and since Allen has left, Halas has taken a champion and turned it into a rabble."

But the unkindest cut of all came when Royko described his single meeting with Halas, which took place in the Bears' dressing room after a loss. "He was sitting in his long underwear, on a bench in front of his locker sipping from a pint of whiskey."

"Halas was furious," said Royko's then colleague Bill Jauss three and a half decades later. "He never forgave Royko for writing that he was drinking whiskey from a pint bottle, because that fact literally was untrue. Actually, the trainer would pour off a considerable amount of a Coca-Cola bottle and refill it with whiskey." So it went in Halas's never-ending battle for truth and accuracy in media, sentence by parsed sentence.

Still, civil rights advocates would have taken immense pleasure in the way Halas stood tall to integrate his team in 1966 when it traveled to southern locales that frowned on such things. His first black and white roommate combination was Sayers and Brian Piccolo.

"We went to Memphis to play an exhibition," Ralph Kurek remembered. "At the hotel, Frank Halas was arguing with the desk manager. They held us in the lobby. Then the Old Man went up to him: 'If my team doesn't stay together, black and white, in this hotel, we are out of here. I don't want my black players staying in some other hotel down the road. The Chicago Bears as a team stay in the same hotel.' He held his ground."

"I see it as a story where two football players, one black, one white, roomed together and had a good time together," Sayers said. "There wasn't any race involved. Yeah, we told jokes and things like that. Then Brian died. I think before that movie came out, people thought all athletes cared about [was] knocking somebody on their butts. When one of my teammates got hurt, we cared about him. He was part of our team; he helped us in victory and helped us in defeat. That's what the movie brought out."

The award-winning 1970 television film *Brian's Song* brought instant stardom to James Caan as Piccolo and Billy Dee Williams as Sayers and was punctuated by Jack Warden's powerful portrayal of Halas. The film was based on Sayers's autobiography, *I Am Third*, ghostwritten by Al Silverman, and another bestseller, *Brian Piccolo: A Short Season*, by Jeannie Morris.

In the spring of 1968, 48 years after founding his team and his league, George Halas was a worn-down 73-year-old man. He had the satisfaction of knowing his game, pro football, was now the biggest, richest, and most powerful sport of all.

Fewer familiar faces were answering the roll call. Curly Lambeau suffered a fatal heart attack on June 1, 1965, while mowing the lawn at his home in Sturgeon Bay, near Green Bay. "Halas came up and was one of the pallbearers. I rode with him out to the cemetery," former *Green Bay Press-Gazette* sports editor Art Daley said. Daley recalled that Vince Lombardi was miffed when the Packers' executive committee renamed Green Bay's stadium Lambeau Field. "If there hadn't been a Lambeau, there wouldn't have been a Lombardi," Daley snorted. "I wonder what would have happened to him. Holy Christ!"

Green Bay did honor its greatest coach when it named the street that leads to Lambeau Field from the US 41 freeway Lombardi Avenue. Lombardi died on September 3, 1970, nine weeks after doctors in Washington diagnosed a fast-moving abdominal cancer. Just before the 2003 season, the Packers again honored both Lambeau and Lombardi with 14-foot-tall statues at renovated and modernized Lambeau Field.

Within six weeks of Allen's leave-taking, the senior and junior George Halases were attending the league meeting in Miami when word came of Min's unexpected death at home on February 14, 1966. By late spring 1968, Paddy Driscoll also was ill. He died on June 29 that year. Halas's trusted secretary Frances Osborne suffered a stroke in 1968 and would never be the same. She jumped out a window to her death in 1969. On top of that sorrow, Halas's bad hip finally forced the issue.

Bill Wade, an assistant in 1967, was haunted by the thought that he might have been the heir. "Coach Halas gave me his overcoat before I went home to Nashville. At our postseason meeting, he said, 'If you come back, something nice will happen to you. You think about it. Call me May 1. If you come back, something nice will happen to you.'"

Wade was torn, but he had problems at home. He made a tearful call to Halas on May 1 to inform the coach he would not return. "In 1970, I mentioned to somebody that I was honored to have Halas's overcoat," a wistful Wade said in 2003. "The man thought for a second, then asked if Halas was Bohemian. The tradition in Bohemia, he explained, was, if a man gives away his overcoat, the one who gets it will get his job." Halas, Wade stressed, never told him, "The job is yours." Whether Wade had that opportunity is problematical. Halas admired Jim Dooley for several years, letting everyone know that "he handed Allen the '63 defense on a platter." These were concepts that Dooley's patron Sid Luckman was all too glad to reinforce. "Sid was in my corner on this. Sid was always in my corner. And he had Halas's ear," Dooley said.

Dooley, though, was never able to operate in a football and business sense around the Old Man the way Allen did. Halas invited Dooley to his apartment on May 26 and told the young assistant he had to deal with his worsening hip. "Then, he handed me the contract. You always got the sad story before he handed you the goods," Dooley recalled. Halas presented Dooley a take-it-or-leave-it, no-questions-asked offer. "You take what's there," Dooley reasoned. "I had to take five years at $35,000 a year. No bonus. Then he gave me a 25-item sheet of things I could not do!"

Halas had never quashed George Allen's outside activities. In return for his coaching work and personnel chores, Allen enjoyed the same perk Luke Johnsos claimed in television's infancy when he cohosted the "Bears Quarterback Club" with Red Grange and, later, Jack Brickhouse. By 1963, Allen was cohost of his own Saturday-night television show on CBS with his sportscaster friend Bruce Roberts. After the show, Roberts would drop in at the Allen house in Deerfield to share a bowl of Jell-O with the coach, not drinks.

"Halas said I couldn't have a TV show," Dooley said. "He didn't want anybody to have anything that would take away from being in that room studying films and getting ready for the season, whatever." That meant no signed newspaper stories and no commercials. No outside income.

Halas was able to keep the lid on his retirement until the morning of the announcement itself, May 27, 1968. "Dan Desmond wanted to pass the story to his buddy Harry Sheer," Bill Jauss said. Desmond and Sheer had been colleagues in the *American* sports department before Desmond became Halas's publicity director. "Brent Musburger overheard Sheer at his end of the phone, jumped in there and intercepted it, so to speak, wrote fast, and got that banner on the front page of the *American*." Jauss chortled as he remembered the delicious details of perhaps the last *Front Page*–style coup ever pulled off at the newspaper MacArthur and Hecht depicted in their famed play and its film incarnations. "I see nothing wrong with that. That's enterprising, even if you're stealing from your own colleague on your own paper!"

Jauss continued, "I got to the Bears' offices about 20 minutes after Musburger's story hit the street. "There was Halas. He had checked out his dictionary and had all those words to describe it. If there were any tears to be shed, it didn't happen in public. He was all business-as-usual. 'I haven't lost my alacrity,' the Papa Bear said. Physically, he didn't think he was up to the chase. He told us that he was going after a ref in his last season, to curse the guy, and he couldn't gain on him. That gave him ideas that maybe it was time to quit. It was a bomb-shell," Jauss said.

"We had begun to believe Halas was going to coach until the day he died," Jauss added. "I think all of Chicago, maybe all of professional football, thought that, because he didn't retire when they won it in '63. Halas was still vigorous. He thought he was as good a coach as ever. When he told his boy Sid Luckman he was stepping out, Sid said he was totally flabbergasted. Luckman said, 'I thought that Halas would retire from coaching, but I didn't think this was the time.'"

Halas formally introduced Dooley as his successor the next day and then flew to Europe for treatments that never took. Afterward, he flew to the Mayo Clinic, whose doctors recommended surgery. He heard of an English doctor named John Charnley who performed total replacements. Three weeks after the procedure, he went home to Chicago. He returned for a second operation the following May.

Before Halas left for the first operation in England, Gale Sayers was at his dashing best. He gained 205 yards as the Bears won 13–10 at Green Bay. After the game, Lombardi told Ed McCaskey that Sayers had put on the greatest exhibition he ever saw.

A week later, Halas watched from the press box when Sayers's teammates carried him off the field after his right knee collided with the helmet of submarining 49ers defender Kermit Alexander. The hit tore all the ligaments, and Dr. Ted Fox operated that day. "If they had arthroscopic back then, I could have played three or four more years," Sayers said. "I was in a cast for 10 weeks. When my leg came out of there, it looked like a pencil. I was crying like a baby, 'How am I going to get back in shape?' "

Sayers's devastating injury gave his roommate his starting chance. "He was a tremendous ballplayer," Ralph Kurek said of Piccolo. "He had a tremendous amount of confidence, rightly so. He wasn't fast or flashy, but he was smooth and could pick a hole and slice through— more like a Paul Hornung runner, not elusive like Sayers."

Led by the slashing inside runs of Piccolo and Ronnie Bull, the Bears squeaked out a 17–16 win at Los Angeles. In the final minute, the officials penalized the Rams on first down for holding, which moved the ball back to midfield, out of field goal range. After the game, when the downs marker operator told Rams executive Elroy Hirsch that head linesman Burl Toler told him to change the marker to second down, Hirsch went to the league. The game was over by then, the damage done. Without the correct replayed down, the Rams' Roman Gabriel threw incomplete passes on the next three plays, and the Bears took over to win.

In the past, the league would have said nothing. For this lapse, though, commissioner Pete Rozelle suspended the entire officiating crew, one of the NFL's most respected, informing them and the fans that each official is responsible for the rules, not just one. Referee Norm Schacter, umpire Joe Connell, head linesman Toler, line judge Jack Fette, back judge Adrian Burk, and field judge George Ellis got no assignments for the rest of the season and the playoffs.

Such a lapse is highly unlikely in the 21st-century NFL, as every play is closely monitored by the official scoring team and instant-replay officials. Even if one somehow evaded detection, the victimized coach would toss a red flag to stop play, and the situation would be reviewed until it was corrected.

The Bears entered the finale with a statistical edge over Minnesota to win the Central Division. All they had to do was beat Green Bay at Wrigley Field. Instead, they lost 28–27 and would not return to the playoffs for a decade.

Sayers labored night and day to overcome his knee injury and rehabilitation from Fox's surgery. "I wanted to prove that you could come back within one year from a knee injury, and I had one of the worst ever. It was bad," Sayers said, but he added, "It worked out for me. It worked out." Unable to make his full-speed 90-degree cuts, Sayers reinvented his game so well that he came back to lead the NFL in rushing in 1969, with 1,032 yards. In 1970, he stretched the ligament in the left knee during a kick return. He gave it a brief, futile try in 1971 and then quit.

Despite Sayers's successful return and the spectacular play of Butkus, the 1969 Bears finished with the worst record in team history, a single win against 13 defeats. The club was in disarray, starting with the draft, Dooley's first as head coach. "In the history of the league, there had never been a team that passed on the first-round draft choice," the star-crossed Dooley said. "We passed on our first-round choice. The Giants jumped on a defensive end right away: Fred Dryer."

The Bears' 1969 draft was anarchic. Halas decreed that everyone in the selection process was equal and they should exercise democratic procedures to make their choices. "They had to give the Bears two rooms because they had all these people. It was like a Keystone Kops comedy," Ed Stone recalled. "We took 15 minutes for that decision, and we said, 'Pass,'" Dooley related. "Then we took another 15 minutes before we took tackle Rufus Mayes." In my four years as head coach—I hate to say it—overall, our drafts were generally horrendous. We had no scouts. Halas listened to everybody. We had nobody in authority to take over."

The Bears opened the 1969 season with seven straight defeats, peppered with improbable plays that included an intercepted snap in St. Louis that was returned for a touchdown, and an onside kickoff in Atlanta that Harmon Wages ran back for a touchdown. Stone's editors at the tabloid *Chicago Today*, as the remodeled *American* now was called, ordered him to write a three-part "What's wrong with the Bears" series.

"I wrote that Dooley had great technical knowledge but he lacked a head coach's leadership skills," Stone said. The next day at practice, Dooley grabbed the reporter by the shirt in front of the players. He told them not to talk to this "leech." The players, especially the jocular Brian Piccolo, thought Dooley's display was hilarious.

The following Sunday, the Bears beat the Steelers 38–7 for their only victory that season, and Dick Butkus was named Player of the Week. Stone's editors dispatched him to Wrigley Field to interview the great star. "Dooley had barred me from the dressing room," Stone recalled. "It was a cold November day, and I told one of the assistants I had to talk to Butkus; it was the league rule. Someone called Dick out, and he came out in the left-field corner by the entrance to the dressing room. He was barefooted, in his football pants and T-shirt. 'What the hell do you want?'"

Stone told him, "I gotta talk to you. I gotta do a story, but I can't come into the dressing room."

With that, Stone said, "Butkus, on his own, got a towel, and we stood in that storage area just before the main dressing room, on dirt, to do the interview. Dooley looked out the door to the dressing room. Here he had just barred me and was upset with me. In a quiet voice, he said, 'It's pretty cold out there. You can come in tomorrow.'"

Stone continued, "After I wrote the story with Butkus, I went back to the paper and told the office what happened. 'You gotta tell the artist,' they said. The artist drew up a cartoon of this undersized reporter talking to this Neanderthal guy and ran a big cartoon. I saw Butkus the next week at a game when they were on the road, and he growled, 'What the hell did you do that for?' Remember those early stories in *Sports Illustrated* that made Butkus out to be an ape? He always resented that. I explained to him that I didn't have anything to do with the cartoon; my office saw the story, and they just wanted to depict it."

Stone noted, "Dooley was too decent a guy to remain a hard-liner. After that, we were on friendly terms, and he never held any grudges against me. I always felt sorry for him. He's remembered in such a bad light, but he had a very brilliant football mind. He just wasn't meant to be a head football coach."

In that Bears victory over the Steelers, an elated Brian Piccolo scored a touchdown and tossed the ball high into the air. He was coughing as he returned to the bench. "Everything happened so fast," Kurek said. "In October, he had a flulike cough."

"No one ever bothered to diagnose the persistent cough he had," said Jeannie Morris. That included the team physician, Dr. Ted Fox.

However, she stressed, the much-maligned Fox did not cause Brian's malady. "It wouldn't have mattered. It turns out he would have died no matter when they diagnosed the illness."

George Halas stepped up and paid Brian Piccolo's large medical bills. "The Old Man knew that Brian had such a huge respect for the institution of pro football," Morris said. "He knew that George Halas had created this thing that he loved and wanted to be a part of. It didn't matter what else George Halas did; he was a great man to Brian." She added, "Brian was the kind of man who wouldn't hear anything bad about someone he felt loyal to. The Halas family remained very close to the Piccolo family and was very supportive. They helped them through that and through the decades afterward."

"By June, he was gone," Kurek said. "He was my youngest daughter's godfather. He was something else." Brian Piccolo, just 26, was survived by his widow, Joy, and three daughters. Joy later married Richard O'Connell, who cared for the girls as they grew into adulthood. The team retired Brian's number 41. From 1970 on, the Bears have honored a rookie and, since 1992, also a veteran who exemplifies the player's courage, loyalty, teamwork, dedication, and sense of humor with the Brian Piccolo Award.

At the end of the 1969 season, the league held a coin flip to decide whether the Bears or Steelers, both with 1-and-13 records, would choose first in the draft. The Steelers won the toss and took the player Dooley desperately wanted, the acclaimed Louisiana Tech quarterback Terry Bradshaw. Bradshaw became a Hall of Famer for Chuck Noll as he led the Steelers to four Super Bowl titles.

The Dooley era ended after 1971, but not without a few memorable moments. In the sixth game, at Detroit, Dooley was forced to start his only uninjured quarterback, the erratic and colorful blond southpaw Bobby Douglass.

To tutor the free-spirited, Li'l Abner–like Douglass in the fine points of executing a game plan, Dooley had moved in with him. "That was one hell of a week," Dooley recalled. He did his best to pound the playbook into his pupil's head as they studied until they dropped. "You'd put him in the house and he'd sneak out at night. So, I had to go and get him on Rush Street and bring him back."

They went out to dinner and came back for role-reversal drills. "He understood everything," Dooley said. "He could remember it all, but usually, he didn't want to spend the time putting it in the right category. He did it that time and had his best game."

Douglass drove the Bears to a 28–23 lead and apparent victory, as the Lions came back. Greg Landry threw a pass over the middle to receiver Chuck Hughes. "Hughes had a strange look on his face as he walked toward me," Butkus recalled. An instant later, Hughes lay motionless on the field. "I can still see Dick Butkus hovering over him calling for a doctor," Ed Stone said. Not a sound was heard in Tiger Stadium as the doctors worked over Hughes for several minutes before they placed him on a stretcher and moved him to an ambulance. Chuck Hughes had died on the field from a massive heart attack.

They finished the game and the Bears won. "The morning papers had to write about Hughes," Stone said. "The afternoon papers wrote more about Douglass."

The Bears went on to beat the Dallas Cowboys, the eventual Super Bowl champions, and knocked off Allen's first Washington team two weeks later when Butkus caught a Douglass pass in the end zone for a conversion to win 16–15. Then, they lost their last five games.

As the season hit the downslope, word circulated that Dooley had many personal problems, especially gambling. "I enjoyed the races. I shouldn't have done it, but I enjoyed it," Dooley freely admitted. People in the know say Dooley kept thorough charts, as dedicated horseplayers do. "I never bet on football, baseball, anything else. I never bet through a bookie. I didn't drink or smoke. Unfortunately, I should not have done the gambling. I enjoyed it."

Everybody with the Bears knew for years how Halas maintained a climate of fear with his spies and private detectives. People dreaded the information he locked away in huge file cabinets. By late 1971, Halas had amassed a detailed dossier on Dooley regarding his gambling as well as womanizing, often in the company of Luckman.

Dooley received a death threat late in the 1971 season, and Halas notified the FBI. One night when Dooley left the office after working until midnight, per Halas custom, he was reaching for his car keys when he noticed two men in fedoras and overcoats sitting in a car parked down the street. As Dooley started his car, he heard the engine from the other car rev up. "This is it," Dooley thought as he dug out and headed for the northbound entrance ramp to the Kennedy Expressway five blocks up Madison Street.

The other car kept pace about 300 feet behind, changing lanes in concert with Dooley. He sped to the junction five miles away, took the Edens Expressway fork, and exited at Lawrence Avenue. He stopped at an open gas station and went inside. "I'm Jim Dooley," he said to the attendant, who recognized him. "I need to call the police. Some guys are trying to kill me."

Dooley placed the call and stayed inside as the other car stopped at a gas pump. In quick order, two police cars pulled up, hauled the two men out of the car, disarmed them, and hustled them inside one of the squad cars. Soon after, one of the cops came inside to see the coach. "Mr. Dooley," the officer said, "you won't believe this. Those two guys showed us their badges and IDs. They're with the Burns Detective Agency and they say they work for George Halas."

Dooley knew what was coming when Halas summoned him to his office the day after the Minnesota Vikings beat the Bears 27–10 to end the season. "It's over, kid. I am so disappointed," the Papa Bear said as he withdrew a stuffed file folder from a drawer and set it on the desktop. "Coach," Dooley pleaded as he looked into the hard, all-knowing eyes, "I have another year left on my contract. I have five kids and my wife. I'm broke. I need that money."

The Old Man sighed and then started speaking in that deliberate way that made grown men quiver. "Very well, kid." He pulled out a piece of paper and read aloud details of a waiver Dooley had to sign, or else. "You will sign this . . . ah . . . and I will pay you." Halas looked into the frightened eyes of his now former coach. "You will not write a book or any article about the Chicago Bears for 10 years. You will not submit to any interview with any writer or reporter for 10 years. If you do, you understand that you will pay everything back. Understand?" Dooley signed it. "Now, go out through the back way. Nobody will see you leave."

Within minutes, Halas introduced his new head coach Abe Gibron. Sid Luckman hired Dooley and carried him through a personal bankruptcy that Luckman helped cause with poor advice. "After five years, he gave me severance pay, $50,000," Dooley said. "I had never seen anything like that. 'Jim, I can't leave any kind of a will for you,' Luckman said. 'This is for the job you have done and from me to you, should anything happen to you.'"

Thanks to Luckman's endorsement, Halas rehired Dooley late in the 1981 season to work in quality control and to report—or more correctly, to inform him—on the way then coach Neill Armstrong handled the team. That mission accomplished, Dooley became an invaluable aide to Mike Ditka during his coaching term, with his ability to break down game films as he'd done for Halas and Allen in the glorious championship days of 1963. By 2004, he spent most of his waking hours in a wheelchair, a victim of amyotrophic lateral sclerosis—Lou Gehrig's disease.

One by one, the Halas veterans departed, either to other teams or through retirement. Butkus was just 30 in 1973, but his right knee was so crippled that he could barely walk, let alone play football. He did not practice and took the field only on game day. The trouble began in the off-season between 1970 and '71 when Dr. Ted Fox performed two operations. After the first procedure to tighten loose ligaments, Fox pronounced it a complete success.

When Butkus developed a persistent, horrendous pain in his groin, Fox removed the cast to bare a massive, pus-filled infection. Fox operated again to install drains. Butkus got back on the field and was again voted All-Pro, but he now had constant trouble with his knee. Despite that, he still played on Gibron's special teams, along with most of his defensive mates, including Ed O'Bradovich. "Butkus went to Abe one day and asked him why the benchwarmers weren't manning the special teams," O'Bradovich said. "You know what Abe's answer to Dick was? 'We can't trust them.'"

"What!?" the great linebacker replied. "You can't trust them? Then, what in the fuck are they doing on this team?"

By 1973, Butkus's right leg was bowed like an old cowhand's. He needed help from his wife, Helen, in the simple act of pulling on a pair of pants. With his agent, Ed Keating, who replaced Arthur Morse in 1970, Butkus negotiated a new deal with Halas. Keating came away with five one-year contracts at $115,000 a season, $575,000 in all. Furthermore, Halas did not make Butkus take a physical before he signed the contract, a fact that Butkus, at the time, let pass but did find unusual.

Dr. Fox, better known to the players as "Needles," had been shooting up Bears for years, from Casares to Butkus and plenty in between, each shot administered with the approval of George Halas, be it express or tacit. "I played with separated shoulders. I was shot up week after week," O'Bradovich recalled. "We were coming back on a plane, and Ted Fox called me to the back so I wouldn't have to go in on Monday. We were up 27-, 28,000 feet in the air, and he blasted away with the cortisone and hydrocortisone. We were out there playing: Butkus, Buffone, [defensive tackle] Bill Staley, Doug Atkins, and me. Constantly getting shot up and laying it on the line."

Butkus continued to lay it on the line in 1973 as he had since he played pickup games on the prairies of Roseland, on Chicago's Far South Side. For the $115,000 he earned without taking a physical, he felt he had no choice. But he couldn't move. By the time the Bears went to Kansas City to play the Chiefs on Monday night, November 12, 1973, it was evident to his roommate, Doug Buffone, that the party was over.

"We stayed up all night talking about it," Buffone said. " 'I used to come up the middle,' Butkus told me. 'They'd run the ball, and I'd knock the guy in the numbers. Now I drag my leg, and he runs another five yards.' 'Dick, it's time,' I told him. He'd go out there, and they'd take big hits all day long," Buffone said. "He finished off a lot of guys in their careers, and now it was payback 'You better watch out,' I said, before we started the game. Dick came in at halftime and couldn't go back out. It was hard to watch, awful to see a champion like that get knocked out of the box."

At first, the Bears acted as though Butkus was not seriously injured. When he requested an outside opinion on his knee, Mugs Halas told him that Dr. Fox was the best surgeon in the business and it was Fox or nothing. Butkus knew that Fox had destroyed the ligaments as he removed the cartilage. His right knee joint was bone on bone.

Butkus spoke to Keating, who reaffirmed the contract language stipulating that the Bears were obligated to pay him through the term of the deal. At his own expense, Butkus made the rounds of the best orthopedic practices in America. His last stop was Oklahoma City, where the well-regarded Dr. Dan O'Donoghue told him football was out.

When Halas took personal charge of the matter away from Mugs, he told Butkus he was free to have surgery performed by a doctor of his choice. But, the Papa Bear warned, that would negate the contract. Butkus hired noted personal-injury attorney James Dooley. Dooley would do battle with Halas's influential counsel Don Reuben, who also represented the *Tribune* and its WGN radio and television arms, as well as the Chicago archdiocese, among his many clients.

Dooley and Butkus sued Halas and the Bears for $1.6 million. Halas, on Reuben's advice, based his case on the series of five one-year contracts that Butkus signed, arguing that each year had to be validated in turn to obligate the team.

By 1975, when the case began, the *Tribune* had folded *Chicago Today* and brought Ed Stone over with many other staffers. "Reuben was aware that James Dooley, Butkus's attorney, was having his way with the news media because he was so cooperative and easily understood," Stone said. "He didn't speak in legalese, and he was getting across his point very well."

Reuben's lack of access gave Dooley a wide berth to dominate coverage for Butkus. "Dooley explained to me how the contracts were structured in the NFL," Stone said. "A player had to pass a physical every year. It didn't matter if you signed a 10-year contract; they could void the last 9 years of it if you didn't pass the next physical."

That would have held fast, except Dooley had the escape clause that would turn the case. In 1965, Arthur Morse insisted on an iron-clad clause in Butkus's contract that the linebacker would be paid whether he was physically able to play or not. That guarantee slipped past Halas, Reuben, and the other attorneys the club retained in Butkus's contract negotiations in 1970 and again in 1973.

By 1975, the two lawyers agreed on a judge to try the case. He was longtime political figure Robert Cherry. When Judge Cherry issued a ruling unfavorable to Halas, Reuben tried to get him disqualified on grounds that he had been a partner to Butkus's former attorney, Morse, and therefore was prejudiced. Judge Cherry refused to step aside. His position was secured when Chief Judge John Boyle tossed out Reuben's motion.

Reuben turned to a close friend, WGN commentator Len O'Connor, to apply the pressure as a matter of conflict of interest. Judge Cherry finally did step aside, but his rulings stood the tests in the Illinois supreme court. When Mike Royko took up Butkus's case in the *Daily News*, public opinion swayed toward the plaintiff. Royko slashed at Reuben, O'Connor, and the *Tribune* connection without mentioning Halas. Before it could move further and get ugly, Halas ordered Reuben to settle the case. It ended on September 13, 1976, when Halas agreed to pay Butkus $600,000.

By 1976, with the popular Butkus's endorsement, James Dooley was running what became a successful campaign as the Democratic candidate for a seat on the Illinois supreme court.

The case may have been over, but by no means did it have a clear-cut ending. Three years later, when *Halas by Halas* was published, Dick Butkus attended a book signing. In Butkus's copy, Halas wrote, "To Dick Butkus, the greatest player in the history of the Bears. You had that old zipperoo!"

"Butkus certainly knew what kind of person George Halas appeared to be to a football player, but he also respected what Halas achieved," Jeannie Morris observed. "I'm sure he did not forget the cruelty he endured and the incredible way it happened, but that would not stop him from thinking about George Halas as the great pioneer of the game, which he loved so much."

It is bitterly ironic, existential perhaps, that Dick Butkus and Gale Sayers, the two greatest players Halas would ever have, who also rank at the top echelon of National Football League Hall of Famers, arrived together in Chicago at the end of his career.

Despite their brilliance, the two won no championships, and both saw their careers end from treatable knee injuries aggravated by the maltreatment of one of the sorriest excuses for a surgeon who ever practiced the medical science.

Butkus and Sayers admired George Halas, and both men returned to the fold. In his lifetime, he did not retire their numbers. Had he honored Sayers, who never gave him trouble, and not done the same for Butkus, who did, the fans would have given him more grief than even he was prepared to handle. In his own way, though, he did honor them. No other player ever wore Sayers's sacred number 40. Six players donned number 51 after Butkus. It just did not seem proper when they did.

Finally, to much fanfare, Michael McCaskey, the grandson the founder did not want as his successor, announced before the 1994 season that the long-deferred ceremony at last would be conducted. More than one skeptic observed that McCaskey, by this time the most hated public figure in Chicago, responsible for the Bears' free fall into the abyss from the 1985 Super Bowl season, desperately needed positive public relations. With this gesture, even Michael could not fail. Yet, he could not control fate and Chicago's fickle weather.

The teammates whose entire professional careers and magnificent accomplishments had always been linked, Gale Sayers, number 40, and Dick Butkus, number 51, would stand together again and be honored at halftime of a Monday-night date with the team's ancient rivals from Green Bay.

There has never been a more miserable Halloween in Chicago than October 31, 1994. A record daylong, 2.26-inch downpour that drove in horizontally on 45-mile-per-hour winds off Lake Michigan drenched the city. Bret Favre and the Packers doused the Bears as they sloshed, slid, and pounded their way to an embarrassing 33–6 halftime lead. By then, only a smattering of fans remained in the Soldier Field stands as television sets clicked off by the millions around America. Few fans saw Sayers and Butkus ride around the field in a soaked convertible to receive their long-overdue honor.

It was the 11th anniversary of the death of George Halas. More than one Chicagoan who believes in the afterlife was certain this was his way of expressing himself from the grave.

TWENTY-NINE

MUGS AND JERRY

"*H*iya, Mugs" were the first words the doting George Stanley Halas uttered to his newborn son and namesake on November 4, 1925, at St. Anthony's Hospital, on Chicago's West Side. Mugs it was then. Mugs it was forever.

Mugs was the only son and thus, in Bohemian custom, the heir, who would run the Bears when his dad was gone. If ever that would happen. "The Old Man never made any contingency plans for his death, his mortality," *Chicago Tribune* pro football writer Don Pierson said. "He thought he would live forever."

Mugs's sister, Virginia, outlived both Halas men. Therein lies the tragedy for the family Halas that transmuted into unplanned inheritance for the unready McCaskeys, who got the whole shebang. They readily admit that Mugs was the one. "That was the plan from the beginning, the only plan," said Jerry Vainisi, who, at the end of George Halas Sr.'s life, was his trusted aide and confidant and also was extremely close to Mugs.

Vainisi, in 1972, was a 31-year-old tax accountant with 7 years' experience at Arthur Andersen, the Chicago Bears of a profession that he studied as a business school undergraduate at Georgetown University. At Georgetown, Vainisi happened to develop a friendship with young Paul Tagliabue, the future NFL commissioner. Vainisi got to Andersen in a roundabout way. After graduation, he came home to Chicago to study law at Loyola, quit, took an $85-a-week broadcasting job in sleepy Monmouth, in western Illinois, got married, and then returned to Chicago to join Andersen. And he had a plan. "Because I knew the worth of a contract is the after-tax value, I had to learn and understand the workings of taxes."

By day, Vainisi did his CPA work for Andersen. By night, he attended classes at Chicago's Kent College of Law. A year before his graduation in 1969, he made an appointment in Green Bay with general manager Vince Lombardi, for whom he had served in 1959 as a ball boy, thanks to his late older brother Jack.

Lombardi, 55 in 1968, had just stepped down as coach after five titles in 7 years. Almost immediately, he realized he had too much time on his restless hands. He granted the young accountant and budding attorney a 20-minute audience to discuss his theory that NFL teams needed lawyers to negotiate the ever complex contracts against the new sharpies, player agents.

"We talked about it for two hours," Vainisi recalled. 'Jerry,' Lombardi said, 'what you say has a lot of merit, but if the Green Bay Packers do create that position, there's another former ball boy who's also getting out of law school now who would get it: Vince Jr.' We had been ball boys together in 1959."

Lombardi asked Vainisi to send him his résumé and promised to circulate it with a letter of recommendation. In time, the young man heard from NFL headquarters. He interviewed for two jobs, one as the New York–based assistant to AFC president Lamar Hunt, of the Chiefs, and the other as assistant to George Halas in his role as NFC president. The league decided to keep those jobs in-house. Then another position came up, serving as the league's in-house lawyer for labor affairs. Vainisi told his prospective boss, NFL management council executive director John Thompson, that he had no labor law experience. So, Thompson hired Sarge Karch, but he passed along Jerry's name to Mugs Halas in Chicago as someone to watch.

"The phone rang one day, and I answered. 'This is George Halas Jr.,' said the voice on the other end. You know, you think a friend of yours is pulling your leg, and you want to make a smart-ass comment. Something told me not to do it; I don't know why. I was sure someone had pulled a joke on me, but all I said was, 'Yes.' "

"I understand you're interested in working for the NFL?"

"Yes."

"Would you be interested in working for the Chicago Bears?"

"Yes. Absolutely."

"When would you be available for an interview?"

"My time's rather flexible. I schedule my own appointments. I can meet with you anytime."

"How's later this week?"

"I'm fine."

"What you are doing Thursday?"

"I'm fine."

"What are you doing today? Are you open today?"

"Yes, I am."

"When would you be available?"

"If you're available, I'll see you in 10 minutes."

"Great! Why don't you come over?"

Vainisi said in 2002, as his eyes twinkled in delight, "I don't remember touching ground as I walked over there. Andersen's offices were at 69 West Washington, and the Bears' offices [were] at 173 West Madison, a block or two away. I walked on air going here. I sat down, and in 30 seconds knew I had the job. I wanted it." The Halases needed to replace the woman who had been their controller. "Mugs and I hit it off right off the bat. We laughed a lot and shook hands."

The second interview was barely under way when Halas Sr. entered Mugs's office. "I learned that was his style. He walked into the office with some papers he wanted to give Mugs, and he 'didn't know' Mugs was in a meeting. The whole purpose of that was to give me a visual once-over," Vainisi said.

"Of course, as soon as I saw him walk in, I popped out of the chair and shook his hand. I am naturally that way. My mother is 95 and still going strong. I've always had a rapport because of the Italian family ethnicity, respecting elders and all that. He also wanted to feel the firmness of my handshake," Vainisi recalled. "He was there about two minutes. Was I masculine? Was I respectful? How did I appear? It was an eyeball view."

They wanted Jerry to wear two hats, serving as controller and handling certain legal work that would evolve into estate planning for the Halases and McCaskeys. "Mugs offered the job. We went to the consultant, and I took my psychological tests. I knew I blew him off the charts, because I knew football and would fit. Now, you gotta remember that at this point, I was a Green Bay fan because of my brother. Even had a dog named Packer."

Then came the salary. At Andersen, Vainisi made $24,000. "Mugs was astute enough not to ask me what I made, because that becomes the focal point of the number that you're going after."

"What do you think the job is worth?" Mugs asked.

"I would probably pay somebody $16,000 to $18,000," Vainisi said then. "I think if you were to hire somebody back then, that's probably what you would have made," Jerry said in 2002.

"OK. We'll make it 18," Mugs said.

"He gave me the high number, but my naïveté cost me. I think he probably would have given me $24,000 at that point as well. But money was not the issue. Opportunity was. Before I accepted the job, I said, 'I know you and your father will live forever and the opportunity to become general manager of this team is nonexistent. If this won't train me to become a GM somewhere in the NFL, do you and me a favor and don't offer me the job.' 'Jerry, you'll be involved in everything in the organization,' George Halas Jr. said firmly. 'It will be a great training ground for you.'"

Shortly after Vainisi's arrival, the sad news came on August 3, 1972, that Ralph Brizzolara was dead at 76. No man shared more important personal experiences with the Papa Bear from high school on, nor meant more to the financial underpinnings of the Chicago Bears football club through the decades. Following the funeral service at Assumption Church, behind the Merchandise Mart, Ralph was buried at Calvary Cemetery, in Evanston.

While it was impossible on so many fronts for Jerry Vainisi to ever supplant a Ralph Brizzolara, George Halas Sr. and his son increasingly turned to their young controller and counsel, not only to increase his responsibilities but also for his advice.

"Mugs became a surrogate brother," Vainisi said. "I own a bank today because of him. When a friend approached me in 1974 to become a partner in a bank, I went to Mugs, because he was on the board of a bank, and asked him to evaluate the deal. 'By all means, do it,' Mugs said. I might have done it anyhow, but I felt comfortable with his blessing."

Mugs was 38 when he married 20-ish Therese Martin in 1963. Mugs and Terry had two children, Christine and Stephen, but they were incompatible from almost the beginning, as were Terry and Halas Sr. She particularly angered the Papa Bear when she created a scene during a 1968 game at Wrigley Field. As Chet Coppock recalled, the auxiliary press box was jammed that afternoon. Two visiting-team assistant coaches joined Terry, who sat between the Halas men; along with Joe Kupcinet, Irv's brother, and his wife, Kay; Charlie Coppock; and Chet. Several others stood behind them.

"At the end of the game when the Bears lost, Terry heaved an audible sigh, tore up a flip card, scattered the debris all over the box, and threw her program up in the air," Coppock said. "Out of respect to Mugs, the Old Man said nothing, but if looks could kill, he would have unloaded a howitzer shell into her hide. He was that angry and, most important, that embarrassed."

By 1974, Mugs and Terry were embroiled in a nasty divorce that she made worse when she further aggravated her father-in-law. "George was always wonderful with his grandchildren on both sides, Mugs and Virginia," Charles Brizzolara said. "He was extremely upset that Terry did everything to keep him away from her children. George wanted Steve to be next in line, years down the road after Mugs, of course, to keep the Halas name on the Bears."

The Halas name was the blessing and the bane that drove and tormented Mugs from childhood. Vainisi saw it each day: "He lived all his life being Junior, son of a famous man with high expectations. Plus, his father second-guessed things he did."

Mugs took out his frustrations in many ways through the years, either by drinking or by playing the temperamental tough guy whom people feared to cross because of the Old Man. "He sometimes seemed surly," Don Pierson recalled. "I remember when he knocked the television over on Ed Sainsbury."

Sainsbury, the sports editor at Chicago's United Press International bureau, was covering a game in the early '70s when the Bears pulled a boner. Mugs reacted with a string of profanities punctuated by a solid kick to the flimsy partition that separated his box from the press box. In the shock wave, a TV set installed on a shelf above Sainsbury fell onto his head.

A witness in the press box was aghast when Mugs hurried out and first told Sainsbury he would pay for any damaged clothing rather than inquire into his condition. "He really had a volatile temper," Pearson said. "Anyone would be standoffish from that."

Worse for Mugs was the way his father often acted in public. "He treated him like shit!" Jeannie Morris said. "It was awful for a parent to do to a child of any age. Who knows what it was like in private, but a lot of people saw the public humiliation."

After a dismal 1973 season, the Abe Gibron–led Bears had no stars and no hope. Ed Stone was covering Super Bowl VIII in Houston when he ran into commissioner Pete Rozelle. "What's going on in Chicago?" Rozelle inquired rhetorically.

"Not only were they a laughingstock, they were a mysterious laughingstock," Stone said. "They did everything in secret, and it did them no good. Al Davis did everything in secret, but they won; you don't laugh at a guy like that. You lose, and it really becomes a joke. The league did not want the Chicago franchise to be a joke, not in one of their biggest markets that happened to be the home of the league founder, who was still alive."

"Mugs and Jim Finks had spent time together on a league committee," Mike Pyle said. "When I was president of the players' association, Finks, at Minnesota, was chairman of the player relations committee. Mugsy was on another committee with Jim, and that's how he got to know him."

"When Mugs approached his father in '74 to bring in Finks, he was going through the divorce, the team had been unsuccessful for 10 years, and he, Mugs, was genuinely unhappy," Vainisi said. "The

Old Man saw that and agreed. He agreed because Finks was available and the Old Man knew Jim. He may not have wanted him, but he trusted him. Mugs came into my office on September 12, 1974, and asked, 'Jerry, what do you have going on this afternoon?' 'Whatever you want.' 'Why don't you come over to the Hilton at 2:00 P.M.,' Mugs strongly advised. He wouldn't tell me what it was. 'You'll be happy.'"

"Mugs was the absolute reason that Finks came in here," Pierson said. "He convinced his dad not only to restructure the place, but to turn over the day-to-day operations to Finks. That was entirely Mugs. I'm sure it was over his dad's objections."

Halas, now 79, stood in the back of the hotel suite far off center stage as his son, for the first time since he'd founded the club in Decatur, awarded complete control of his team to an outsider. If he wasn't pleased with the situation, he did not let on to the many reporters crowded into that room.

"I don't know how happy I was when I first heard the announcement, because I was 'fast-tracking,'" Vainisi said. "In retrospect, it was the best thing that ever happened to me as far as football goes, because I worked with probably the best GM in the business for nine years."

"Finks had a plan and confidence in what would work, almost to a fault, and was able to organize and carry out the plan," Pierson said. "Excellent people person. He understood that all business is people oriented, and that was why he was successful with three general managerships, plus the Cubs, and probably should have been running United Airlines. He was a natural businessman. You forget the guy was a player. I can't imagine any player now, any quarterback, with all that money they make, moving that smoothly into an executive role."

"Overall, Mugs and his dad got along great," Vainisi said. "Mugs seldom stood up to him, but when he brought in Finks, they had two-to-one, and it was easier to convince him. The reason the Old Man never wanted Finks was he never wanted anybody. It was going to be a Halas running the team. In the Old Man's mind, Mugs was going

to remain as president. So, he would still oversee Finks and the operating of the team, representing the Old Man. The fact of the matter
was as soon as Jim came in, Mugs relieved himself of all that."

Vainisi noted, "While the three or four of us, or five with Ed
McCaskey, would meet, Mugs backed away and really started to
enjoy life. Mugs met Pat Kerin Navilio again, his classmate in grade
school at St. Hilary's. He should have married her in the first place.
They started seeing each other, and you could see the levity in him."

In a single stroke, Mugs, by hiring Jim Finks and utilizing his bright
young man Jerry Vainisi, transformed a rusting hulk into a sleek,
streamlined operation. It was smartly run, with well-designed fiscal
controls, and had regained leaguewide respect.

The strong, quiet Finks moved swiftly to upgrade facilities. He
resettled the operation from its dreary digs at the western end of the
Loop to the 12th floor of the upscale CNA Building, at 55 East Jackson, on the east side of the Loop. This new office was filled with
roomy, well-lit offices and ample storage space.

Finks then changed the summer training camp to the Cardinals'
old facility at north suburban Lake Forest College. Unlike the suspicious Halas, Finks sought maximum coverage, not only from the
newspapers but also from the most important medium, television, and
its radio cousins. He cut another deal with Lake Forest College to
build a dedicated training facility, with weight room, meeting rooms,
offices, and an adjacent practice field. When the first Halas Hall
opened in 1979, Finks moved the football side of the operation there
and kept the ticket office and administration downtown with the
Halases. Before Halas Hall, the Bears had practiced at the site of the
former private girls' school Ferry Hall, a few blocks from the Lake
Forest College campus.

Finks made two moves that displeased the Papa Bear. He changed
charters from hometown United Airlines to Twin Cities–based Northwest. Then he dumped the team's longtime radio station, WGN, and
its broadcast team of 24 seasons, Jack Brickhouse and Irv Kupcinet,
for CBS-owned WBBM and his former Vikings play-by-play man Joe
McConnell, with sports reporter Brad Palmer handling analysis.

"Finks and I developed a rapport," Vainisi said. "As soon as the season ended, though, Finks isolated himself. I was supposed to report solely to Finks, but the Halases would always come to me directly anyhow to ask what was he going to do."

He did a lot, according to Vainisi. "First, he fired the coaches. Then he fired Dan Desmond, the PR guy," Vainisi said. "He brought in his own people like Bill McGrane, from Minnesota, then Ted Haracz, from Purdue, two professionals. Once their cycles were over, people figured they were history. Sure enough, after the draft, he got rid of Bobby Walston and every scout except Jim Parmer. He kept Parmer because they knew each other from the NFL of the '50s and from Canada."

Vainisi feared he was next after he completed the audit and tax return the following May. "As much as I liked working for Jim, he never let you get comfortable. I didn't know when he was hired that the Halases said, 'Vainisi comes with the franchise.' Finks revealed that much later. I thought that on May 15, 1975, I would be applying to the Green Bay Packers for a job." He stayed.

With the first pick of his first draft, Jim Finks chose Walter Payton, a running back from Jackson State. "I've always said Payton was the best player I've ever seen, but Gale and Brown were the best running backs," Mike Ditka said. The gifted and mysteriously charismatic Payton became the all-time leading ground gainer in league history, a record that lasted for 18 years until Emmitt Smith broke it in 2002.

Finks ordered his scouts to scour the country for quality players, and they found them. He hired young, strong, and smart Jack Pardee to coach them. Pardee had proved his physical toughness at Texas A&M as one of the Junction Boys, the 13 survivors of Bear Bryant's torturous boot camp in 1955. He passed an even more rigorous test, when he came back to play for the Rams after an operation to remove a malignant black mole. Pardee's coaching mentor was George Allen, for whom he played in L.A. before he followed him to Washington. As impressive as was Pardee's résumé, Finks chose him for the way he held together his World Football League Orlando team the whole season without being paid. "They played for the WFL championship and lost," Vainisi recalled, "but keeping that team together, focused and playing, really impressed Finks even though he didn't know Jack all that well."

"Finks came in and, in his first draft, started out with Payton, then Mike Hartenstine, and others," Doug Buffone said. "All of a sudden we became better that quick. Pardee came in, and we were in the playoffs in his third year."

Finks then sent shock waves through the franchise and city of Chicago when he pink-slipped the colorful, Halas-backed quarterback Bobby Douglass the day after the 1975 opening-game 35–7 loss to the Baltimore Colts. A distraught Douglass told a reporter that "Jim Finks was so cold, he could chill a case of beer by placing it next to his heart."

That move got the players' attention. The Bears began to play something that resembled NFL football for the first time since the Old Man prowled the sidelines. By his second year, 1976, Walter Payton was acknowledged as the NFL's top player, and the team had moved up to semirespectability at 7-and-7, .500, the first tier of development.

The Finks plan was working. He had his feet planted in both essential team camps, George Halas Jr. and the McCaskeys. When the Halases hired Finks in 1974, Mugs had Vainisi draft a clause to make Jim president as he bumped himself up to chairman. That clause was withheld from his agreement, but Mugs paid him a yearly bonus in lieu of the title for his running the franchise from top to bottom. Halas Sr. was unaware of the arrangement.

When a member of the press would inquire about his easy way with Ed McCaskey, Finks would take the reporter aside, light one of the 50 Kools he smoked each day, and spin a yarn that may or may not have been apocryphal. McCaskey, Finks said, offered an unsolicited football-related suggestion just once. "Ed," Finks responded, "players play. Coaches coach. Scouts scout. General managers manage. And owners own." He paused. "Now, Ed, go own!"

Keeping an 80-something George Halas busy was never a problem. He continued to follow the diet, exercise, and sleep regimen that had carried him through since childhood in Pilsen, on the West Side. At the office, he went over the financial report with Mugs and Vainisi, answered his mail, conducted interviews, and made appearances—the things a living icon does.

For a brief interlude, from 1970 until 1975, Halas enjoyed a twilight romance. She was Rita Hauk, widow of Roy Hauk, who ran the White Bear laundry for years. "Rita was wonderful. We went out all the time," Vainisi recalled. "The Halases would buy ten-person tables at charitable events. Mugs and Pat, Ed and Virginia McCaskey, Coach and Rita, Judge Marovitz and somebody, my former wife, Doris, and I, would attend. They were like teenagers. They'd be pinching each other and giggling. It was just wonderful," a grinning Vainisi said. "Here was an 80-plus-year-old man, and Rita wasn't far behind him. They were just dynamite together. My wife would turn to me and say, 'Why can't you be like that?' "

After Rita died, Halas seldom dated, but he often brought along his secretary Ruth Hughes, a woman in her 60s whom Vainisi hired after Mugs transferred Frances Osborne's successor, Jean Jensen Doyle, to the ticket office. "When I interviewed somebody, I was to leave them in the vestibule and let him know, so he could walk by and just take a cursory glance to see what she looked like," Vainisi said. "He'd walk back to his office and take a second look and disappear. Then I'd call in the candidate and bring her into my office and interview her. He did the same with Ruth to check her appearance, demeanor, looks, and poise. She had to be someone he could use socially as well. He wanted somebody who had seasoning, somebody that he could take out socially without eyes moving and tongues wagging," Vainisi said.

"Ruth was very good for him in that way," Vainisi acknowledged, "but she became overly protective. She tried to block people from going in to see him. She even tried to block me, and Finks, too. The Old Man said, 'Don't pay any attention to her. Just come on in.' He wanted to know what was going on."

The 1977 Bears were falling off the map in midseason when the Houston Oilers ambushed them 47–0 in the Astrodome, to leave them at 3-and-5. They were a few ticks of the clock away from a sixth defeat to the Kansas City Chiefs, when Bob Avellini threw long to wide-open tight end Greg Latta with :00 on the clock for a 28–27 victory.

That began a 6-game winning streak. Payton ran for a then-league-record 275 yards the following week in a 10–7 win over the Vikings, and Payton went on to lead the league in rushing, with 1,852 yards. The final weekend of the season saw the Bears make a rare visit to New York to experience a game in space-age Giants Stadium. It turned out to resemble the 1934 sneakers game at the Polo Grounds. Falling temperatures quickly transformed steady rain at kickoff into a slushy mess that made footing difficult. Payton had to abandon sweeps and cutbacks to run straight-ahead slashes. Meanwhile, the big fullbacks, Larry Csonka for the Giants and Robin Earl for the Bears, thrived.

In a reversal of sorts out of 1934 when Giants coach Steve Owen dispatched Abe Cohen to Manhattan College to bring back basketball shoes, a Chicago sportswriter took matters into his own hands. The *Chicago Tribune*'s knowledgeable columnist Bob Markus called around, found an open sporting goods store that had an inventory of cleats for grass fields, and told the Bears. The team sent an equipment man to pick up enough shoes to outfit the team to allow for proper footing. They came back to tie it on Earl's late touchdown to make it 9–9 and send the game into overtime.

Up in the owner's box, Mugs Halas; his fiancée, Pat; Virginia and Ed McCaskey; and Michael, who came in from Boston for the game, lived and died with every play, every fumble, and every missed opportunity. Kicker Bob Thomas withstood the ultimate test on the field. He missed an extra point, was wide on one field goal, and lost another when the slippery ball squirted off the holder's hands. With time running out in the overtime period, he was poised again to go for the winner.

"Mugs ducked down to the floor in our booth," said Pat Halas. "After those misses, he couldn't bear to watch." The moment he heard his family roar, he stood up to join the celebration. Bob Thomas had nailed the field goal of his life to give the Bears a 12–9 victory and their first playoff trip since 1963.

Bill Gleason stayed behind in New Jersey to have dinner after the game with quarterback Bob Avellini and his parents, before he caught a later flight to Chicago. He arrived at O'Hare to bedlam in the terminal, where several thousand fans had gathered to greet their returning heroes. "Here came Thomas. They had erected an iron-mesh gate to keep the fans away from the players. The players were walking through. Thomas must have been with us. Thomas was walking with us on the iron-mesh side of the fence. He went up and said, 'I've gotta be with the team.' 'And who the hell are you?' the guard roared. 'I'm one of the B—' The guard cut him off: 'You aren't one of the Bears, you little son of a bitch!'

"I came up and introduced him," Gleason recalled with a loud laugh. 'This is Bob Thomas. He won the game.' The fans saw Bob, picked him up, and threw him over the mesh fence, and someone caught him on the other side." In 2000, Judge Robert R. Thomas was elected to the Illinois supreme court.

The flight home to Chicago was the greatest trip of Mugs Halas's life, his first of any kind in triumph as president. He led the celebration in first class with toast after toast to his dad, to the team, and, especially, to and with Phyllis Pardee for her husband, Jack, the coach. Finks, as was his custom, sat in the last row of coach. To Finks, it was time for the boss to enjoy the privileges and perks of owning.

The Dallas Cowboys clobbered the Bears 37–7 the day after Christmas to start their run to their Super Bowl XI victory. Pardee was off to Washington within two weeks. His opening came when George Allen decided to return to the Rams, a disaster that rebounded against the former Bears heir when Rams owner Carroll Rosenbloom fired him after an exhibition loss the following summer. Like Allen, Pardee sought the say-so in player personnel. "Finks wasn't going to give that up. I think that's the primary reason why Pardee left to go to Washington," Vainisi reasoned.

George Halas, for his part, deemed Pardee a traitor. For his next coach, Finks turned to a football man he had known for years back in Canada and again with the Minnesota Vikings when Finks was general manager. He was Bud Grant's quiet and conservative defensive coordinator, Neill Armstrong.

Pardee left Armstrong a 1978 team favored to win the NFC Central and go far in the postseason. The Bears opened with three wins and then hit the skids, losing eight straight. Now out of it, they rallied with four wins in the last five games, gaining a small bit of pleasure as they finished the season with a 14–10 win over Pardee at Washington.

Finks struck gold in the 1979 draft. "Finks was an 'A' drafter. He never missed on great linemen. Had he been more daring, though, he would have been A+," said Ed Stone. "My only problem with Finks was his conservative quarterback philosophy. He refused to draft a quarterback in the first round. You can't fault who he picked. Payton in 1975 and Dan Hampton in 1979 were brilliant selections. After taking Hampton, though, he passed on Kellen Winslow, who would have given the club their first great tight end since Ditka, in favor of Al Harris," Stone recalled. "Harris was good, but no Winslow. Then he passed on Montana in the second and third rounds."

Stone reasoned, "In a way, though, it was a blessing for both Terry Bradshaw and Montana that they did not come to the Bears. They might have been ruined. Walsh and Montana were a great fit, as were Noll and Bradshaw."

Halas still resisted estate planning until Mugs and Vainisi broke through; the two men persuaded him to take the legal step of freezing the value of the franchise. "We created a subchapter S corporation in 1978," Vainisi said. "We made Halas Sr. a minority owner with 49.35 percent of the stock. That enabled him to receive a 30 percent discount on the valuation for estate purposes, which is done every day."

Halas Sr. then became minority owner when he let Mugs give Finks five shares to fulfill his contractual requirement. At the same time, that move aided the Halas-McCaskey stock transfer. In a percentage breakdown, The Old Man now held 49.88, Mugs and Virginia each held 19.68, the Brizzolaras had 8.33, and Finks had 2.43. Charles Brizzolara, Finks, Virginia Halas McCaskey, Mugs, and Vainisi sat on the board of directors.

The 1979 season, like '77 began, with a 3-and-5 record. Armstrong turned to Mike Phipps, a disappointing quarterback whom

Finks had imported from Cleveland for a first-round choice in 1977. With Payton at his best, the rejuvenated Phipps led the Bears to the verge of the playoffs with six wins in seven starts, setting up an odds-maker's dream for the final Sunday with the NFL's complicated tie-breaking formula.

To gain a wild card berth against the NFC East champion Philadelphia Eagles, the Bears had to beat their former neighbors, the now St. Louis Cardinals, by at least 30 points while the Dallas Cowboys had to beat the favored Washington Redskins.

It had been an especially happy time for Mugs. He married Pat Navilio in 1978, and they moved into a condo in the upper reaches of Water Tower Place, on North Michigan Avenue. Life had never been more beautiful for George Halas Jr. than it was on Saturday night, December 15, 1979. "Mugsy took care of himself," George Connor said. Mugs had quit smoking and taken off weight and was so happy with Pat. "I was in Miller's Pub earlier that evening, and he seemed fine," Connor said. "Then he died early the next morning."

It happened too late to make the Sunday papers, but the family had to get word to the senior Halas before he heard it on the radio. They sent a favored grandson, Tim McCaskey, to tell him the dreaded news, which had been embargoed all night on radio. Rain mixed with sleet was swirling in off Lake Michigan as he left the suburbs to reach Halas's apartment at 5555 North Sheridan before he arose at 8:00 A.M. to the clock radio in his bedroom. Tim arrived within 30 seconds of Halas's physician, who had already entered apartment 1802 with the devastating word. The sight of his weeping 84-year-old grandpa was almost too much to bear for the young man.

The show, of course, would go on, as the cutting snow and sleet blew directly into Soldier Field. This was Doug Buffone's final regular-season game in his 14-year Bears career. "I heard about Mugs that morning. It was a shock, his dying and we needing to do what we needed to do," Buffone said.

"Let's pull out all the tricks," Buffone said to his teammates before they took the field to complete their impossible assignment. "I called a fake punt and ran 35 or 40 yards and almost got killed," Buffone recalled in late 2002. "We pulled a fake field goal. I caught a pass from Bob Parsons. 'Here's the deal,' I said to Parsons when I called the fake. 'Just find me.' I told Bob I would check the guy coming up to block me and take off. I hit the checkoff. Parsons, a former quarterback, led me perfect. I was down the sidelines. Gone. So, we pulled out every stop, did everything, and won the game 42–6."

Instead of leaving, the Bears stayed in the warm dressing room to watch the Washington-Dallas telecast. They saw Roger Staubach beat the Redskins and Pardee to put the Bears back in the playoffs for the second time in three years.

A disconsolate George Halas secluded himself at home. "It set the Old Man back dramatically," Vainisi said. "His whole preordained plan was to live forever. If the unconscionable thing happened that he died, certainly Mugs would run the club and live forever. It was *never* to go through the McCaskey family. Part of it was the Latin primogeniture, that everything goes to the oldest male, plus he was the one running the team. If that had happened, if Mugs had stayed alive, the front office wouldn't have changed really until one of them died, Mugs or Finks. The attitudes and feelings were so strong."

THIRTY

HALAS AND
THE McCASKEYS:
THE LEGACY

"*K*id, this is the tough one," the grieving father said, just above a whisper, to a consoling reporter inside the Birren and Sons funeral home, on Chicago's Far North Side. His eyes were red-rimmed and showed a deep hurt, totally unlike the strident public persona that generations of Chicagoans had known from childhood.

It was Tuesday evening, December 18, 1979, a week before the saddest Christmas the George Halas family would ever experience. Halas Sr. accepted solace as best he could, his gnarled handshake still firm as he remained seated beside the open coffin in which the body of his only son lay.

Former Cardinals co-owner Charles "Stormy" Bidwill commiserated with the father of his own dad's close friend. Bidwill told the *Tribune* that Mugs "was very well respected."

Hall of Famer George Connor was a longtime friend and champion of both Halases. "Jim Finks told me that Mugsy was the smartest owner of any of them," Connor said. Finks's judgment was borne out when the younger Halas solved the arcane scheduling stumper that had baffled fellow owners for decades. "He understood how it connected," Don Pierson recalled. "Fourth place plays fourth place; third place, third; et cetera. All of that." The league quickly adapted Mugs's "parity-plan" and has scheduled its games in that manner ever since. Fans could talk about their favorite team's next-season schedule before the first playoff game from the present season had been played.

Storm clouds already were gathering inside the funeral parlor. The McCaskeys; Pat Halas, Mugs's wife of just over a year; and George Sr. received the callers near the bier. In another part of the room, Mugs's former wife, Terry, set up her own mourning zone. Still displeased with the terms of her divorce settlement, she ordered her lawyer, William Harte, to sue Mugs's estate and charge that Halas Sr. and, later, Virginia maltreated her children.

Terry Halas's constant litigation became the routine. Years later, she asked a court to order the exhumation of Mugs's body when she asserted that he was a victim of foul play. In that suit, she claimed his first autopsy was incorrectly performed because the internal organs were not with the body and could not be tested. The court ruled against her. Physicians say that usual practice is to discard organs after they have been tested in other than suspected-murder cases. The bitter litigations continued into 1990, until Terry depleted her children's inheritance from their father.

The following day, on a cold, sunny morning, many of the league's most powerful figures led the mourners into tiny Assumption Church for the funeral service. Finks held the distraught Halas at the elbow as he gently escorted him inside, where friends and NFL colleagues, from Pittsburgh's Art Rooney to George Allen, and many other owners had gathered.

"I made all the funeral and cemetery arrangements for the family. I seated the NFL people," Vainisi said. "Inadvertently, I placed Pete Rozelle next to Al Davis. "I didn't realize it until it was too late, and I said to myself, 'Oh, Christ!' I really felt bad about it, and I apologized to Pete. 'Don't worry, Jerry,' Rozelle said. 'It's not an issue.' "

Virginia was equally grateful. "Jerry, I don't know what we would have done without you," she said after Mugs was interred in one of four adjoining mausoleum crypts at All Saints' Cemetery, in Des Plaines. Finding and buying the crypts was a hastily executed, but successful, operation, thanks to the work of Vainisi and Mugs's nephew Tim McCaskey.

Vainisi handled the purchase the day after Mugs's death when Virginia told him that neither she nor her brother owned burial plots. Tim went to All Saints', where he found a number of vacant spaces in the mausoleum. After he did, Tim's father, Ed, issued specific instructions. Ed said the crypts must be situated on an eastern wall so they would "face the track," Arlington Park, to the west, where he spent so much time. Tim fulfilled the mission.

The following weekend, Halas Sr. stayed home to watch the Bears-Eagles first-round playoff telecast from Philadelphia. The game turned on a disputed call when umpire Pat Harder, the former Cardinals and Lions fullback, flagged Brian Baschnagel for illegal motion as Walter Payton cut behind him and took off on a 79-yard run to the Eagles' 1. Instead of pushing for the lead and possible win, the Bears could not overcome that penalty. The Super Bowl–bound Eagles advanced to the NFC championship game, 27–17.

"Senior went into an eight-month period of mourning that included his usual two months in Arizona," Vainisi recalled. Before he left for Phoenix, the Old Man told Vainisi to issue an order that under no circumstances was anyone to enter Mugs's office. Everything on his desk was to remain in place as it was when he left the office the last time. That "shrine" edict remained in effect as long as George Halas lived.

"He came back to town, and we tried to keep him informed," Vainisi said. "He would only occasionally come to the office to meet with either Finks or me. I wasn't trying to usurp anything, just trying to get him back in the swing of things. We needed to know who was in charge and how we were going to operate."

Vainisi and the Kirkland and Ellis team of estate lawyers, led by Bill Rowder, carried on without the Old Man to rework his estate.

Halas Sr. most feared Terry Halas, who, as legal guardian of Mugs's underage children, Christine and Stephen, might use them to wrest control of the club.

Vainisi and Rowder fashioned a new estate based on the generational-skipping principle. "When Mugs died, his share was split between his two kids, with Terry as trustee in control of that money," Vainisi explained. "The Old Man's 49.35 percent was divided into 13 trusts among the grandchildren: 11 McCaskeys and 2 Halases. Halas was the trustee in his lifetime, with Virginia his successor."

The values of professional sports teams had not yet left the launching pad as they would a decade later. The Kirkland lawyers and Vainisi established a "frozen base" value for the Bears at $16 million. That made Halas's personal share worth just under $8 million and the 30 percent discounted value of the team, for tax purposes, at $11.2 million.

Because liability would "skip" a generation, the grandchildren would not have to pay taxes on their inheritance. The trustee—in their case, Virginia—was charged with distributing their estate shares at her discretion. As of 2003, all 13 were still alive. The heirs of the McCaskey and Halas children would be tax-liable.

With his affairs in order, Halas returned with a vengeance late in the summer of 1980. With the terse statement that "only a Halas can be president of the team," the 85-year-old George Halas reassumed the team presidency he'd ceded to Mugs in 1963. He did not formally demote Finks, but they now were operating at cross-purposes, if not in actual open warfare. The figurative smell of gunpowder was in the air. "That was an affront to Jim. Unfortunately, Halas started to erode his authority," Vainisi said. "I told Jim he needed to talk to the Old Man. 'Tell him what you have done and intend to do. He's not going to stop you. I guarantee it.' All Halas wanted was to be informed and be treated with the respect that he felt he was due," Vainisi said.

"It's akin to my original hiring interview when I popped out of the chair," Vainisi said. "He and Jim had developed a good relationship, but it always ran through Mugs. The Old Man was never comfortable, I suppose, with Jim having let go of all of his people. Jim always assumed Mugs would tell the Old Man about his moves. There were times Mugs didn't say what Finks had done, and Halas got pissed. For instance, he'd go to the Tavern Club at 7:00 P.M. Mike Notaro, Moose Connor, Judge Marovitz, Luckman, or another of his cronies would tell him, 'I hear you traded for a linebacker today.' When he didn't know about it, he would be embarrassed," Vainisi noted. "Something as simple as covering his bases, or deferring to him, would have changed all that for Jim. Whether it was Jim's pride, or stubbornness on his part—Jim Finks always acted in the Bears' best interests. Therein lay the rub."

The situation grew worse for Finks's handpicked coach, Neill Armstrong, when the Bears fell to 7-and-9 in 1980 and sank even deeper in 1981 at 6-and-10. During the '81 season, Halas usurped Finks when he brought back Jim Dooley as a special assistant.

Many observers believed Halas was using Dooley as a spy. "I was *never* a spy!" Dooley said emphatically in 2003. "But I did answer his questions. Halas was upset with Neill for bringing in his players from a cold day of practice in December. A day or two later, it must have been 20 degrees," Dooley recalled, "Halas came to Lake Forest and went outside in a regular shirt and sat in his golf cart for an hour and a half just to show Neill that you must stay out no matter what."

Halas tightened the screws on Armstrong the moment the regular season ended on December 20. Word circulated that the head coach and his staff were in trouble and that Finks couldn't save them. By midweek, the drumbeat was rolling, and the story was dominating the news like a soap opera run amok.

"Halas had a flair for the dramatic," Ed Stone said. "He had Rudy Custer call a press conference for Christmas Eve." Stone was on duty at the *Tribune* sports desk when that call came. He attended the gathering at 55 East Jackson. "Halas said that the defensive players wrote him a letter asking him to retain Buddy Ryan as coordinator."

Future Hall of Fame defensive tackle Alan Page, it was learned, wrote the letter. Page had announced his retirement and return to the Twin Cities to begin a law career that would eventually take him to the Minnesota supreme court—the second member of that team, with Bob Thomas, to serve at that judicial level. Yet, Page so cared about the future of his teammates that he drafted the letter and got their signatures. That letter may have won a Super Bowl.

"After the news crews left, Senior came up to me and said, 'I'm going to meet with Buddy Ryan, and I would like you to be available,' " Vainisi said. "I didn't know what he was thinking. At this point, Neill Armstrong was still not fired. He was gonna go, but the Old Man wouldn't cut him loose. 'Coach,' I told him, 'Neill Armstrong is a genuinely good person. He doesn't deserve to be held in this state. If you don't want him here, let him go. Just do the right thing for both him and the club.' " Vainisi paused. "He still let him dangle, and he had blocked Finks from hiring a head coach."

Few days on the calendar are slower in the news business than the day after Christmas, especially when that day falls on a Saturday. Not Saturday, December 26, 1981, though. The reporters and crews gathered again to see and hear Halas call Ryan, until then an obscure assistant, the best defensive coach in football. "He announced that Ryan's contract had been extended for three years, through 1985," Vainisi recalled. "It was Halas and Ryan before the media, and Finks wasn't there. I was in the background, not a part of it, doing what he told me to do. Ryan thought he was coming in to be named head coach."

The saavy Halas, now approaching 87, did not believe Ryan had the goods to be head coach. Besides, he was not a longtime Bear as the other headmen before Finks's arrival, namely Jones, Johnsos, Anderson, Driscoll, Dooley, and Gibron, had been.

Halas had seen the effectiveness of Ryan's unique "46" in Armstrong's otherwise drab operation. The "46" was an attacking defense based on the conventional "seven-in-the-box" principle: four linemen and three linebackers, with a wild card who could operate as an eighth man up front or a safety. In this case, the "46" was the number worn by safety Doug Plank, a free-flowing blaster from Ohio State, who could move up and back within the formation. Plank was quick enough to shift tactics and stick to a fast receiver after he had lined up to blitz.

That "46" man put the offense under unique pressure. Finks drafted accordingly to back up and supplant Plank. Another Ohio Stater, Todd Bell, replaced Plank when his career ended with neck and spine injuries. Then, Dave Duerson, of Notre Dame, came in 1983. The defense required a smart, quick-thinking player. Ryan found that leader in tough, yet scholarly, middle linebacker Mike Singletary, who would be named NFL Player of the Year in 1985 and become a Hall of Famer.

"So, he retained his defensive coach while his head coach was still hanging," Stone reflected, smiling slyly. "Only the Bears. Only the Bears could do that. Only Halas."

With Ryan's issue settled and before anyone could speculate about Mike Ditka's or anyone else's taking over as head coach, there was that little matter of the incumbent. "After the Ryan hiring, tension was high in the office," Vainisi said. "I went in again and said, 'Coach, you've gotta let Neill Armstrong go!'"

Vainisi continued, "Finally, he let Armstrong go, but he still wouldn't let Finks hire the new head coach. I was called in to Halas's office again, where he handed me a pair of two- or three-inch-thick files on Mike Ditka. He gave me the files and said, 'Jerry, would you organize these files and tell me what's in them?'"

Vainisi accepted the assignment. "There were all kinds of things," he said in 2003. "First were player contracts and negotiating notes. They also contained different stuff about Mike from his playing career." The "different stuff" included every bit of information Halas ever amassed on Ditka as a player, from cloak-and-dagger investigations into his nighttime activities and adventures to the fatal Parrilli shooting of January 1, 1964.

"Then," Vainisi said, "there was a letter on small, personal stationery, like five by seven. This was written in December before everything went into motion. It basically read: 'Dear Coach, I'm not trying to take Neill Armstrong's job. But word around the league is you might be looking to replace him. If that's the case, then I would like to be considered for the opportunity to fulfill my dream of bringing the Bears back to the days of glory when you were the coach and I was a player.' Once I read that letter, I knew that he was going for Mike," Vainisi said.

That interest began on Thanksgiving Day 1981 when the Dallas Cowboys escaped with a 10–9 win over the Bears despite Payton's acrobatic runs and Buddy Ryan's defense built around Singletary, Dan Hampton, and Gary Fencik. Sid Luckman watched the telecast with Halas at his apartment. "Sid told me afterwards that they had a shot of me on the sideline, and Mr. Halas said, 'He's the next coach,'" Ditka recalled.

George Allen had been out of coaching since 1977. Now, at last, the job he always wanted was once again open. He called Jim Dooley and asked him to please call Halas. "I don't know whether I can," Dooley said, but he offered to give it a try.

"Halas called me over to his home one night," Dooley said. "'I have an idea who I want to be the Bears head coach,' he said. He led me to believe it was Ditka. He said he saw Ditka on television and liked the way he yelled and screamed on the sidelines, his energy." Dooley told Halas that Ditka would be a good coach. "He has everything you had," Dooley told him.

"Allen called several times," Dooley said. "Finally, I went to Halas again about it: 'George Allen has been calling me, and if you decide you don't want Mike, you might talk to George.' Did he get upset!" Dooley recalled. "'I don't want to have anything to do with him!' said Halas in a loud voice. That was it. When they parted, it was bitter—more than Halas ever let on to the public."

By 1981, Bill Gleason was well established at the *Sun-Times* as star columnist. "I advocated Ditka. All the other writers said, 'Ah, he's just a big blowhard! A big pain in the ass.' 'Just wait,' I said. 'The guy can coach. He'll have this team playing football.'"

By January 4, 1982, the Ditka watch was well under way, but Ditka was still occupied with his job on Tom Landry's Dallas staff as special teams and tight ends coach and could not talk to another team. Halas kept it churning, though, when he announced he had resumed operational command to add to the title president.

"I went down to the Bears office and tried to see Halas," Cooper Rollow said. "Ruth Hughes, the secretary, wouldn't let me in. 'You tell Halas I've got to talk to him.' She still wouldn't let me in. 'He'll see me.' Sure enough, he called me in. He refused to say anything other than, 'This is for the good of the team. It's not a reflection on

Jim Finks's ability. I'm simply moving in and taking over the team.' I went back across the office, and Finks beckoned me in. 'What's he saying?' Finks asked. Then he gave me his quotes, which were the same thing: 'I'm going to do things to the best of my ability. I'll respect the terms of my contract.'"

In the *Tribune*, Rollow wrote, "Unlike Woody Allen, Jim Finks has decided to 'Take the Money and Stay!' He might have added, 'even if I have to sweep the floors.' Owner George Halas said in effect, 'Fine. As long as I hold the broom.'"

Don Pierson bagged the quip of the year when he tracked down long-retired Bears great Stan Jones. "It was like Orville Wright coming back to run United Airlines," said the jocular Jones.

On January 10, 1982, Joe Montana hit Dwight Clark in the back of the Dallas end zone with "the catch," for the 27–24 victory to punch San Francisco's ticket to Super Bowl XVI. Mike Ditka now was free at last to open the talks that would bring him back to the team with which he achieved playing greatness, the Bears, in the city he loved, Chicago, with the coach who angrily exiled him a decade and a half before.

"It was like foreign intrigue," Ditka remembered. "Max Swiatek picked me up in the so-called limo, which was a black Lincoln Town Car. He drove me to Mr. Halas's apartment, and we went upstairs and sat down at the kitchen table. The first thing he said, and I always remember this, was, 'Tell me about your coaching philosophy.' 'Coach, what do you want me to do? Bullshit ya? Your coaching philosophy is the same as mine: I want to win. I know how to win.' That was the end of that conversation," Iron Mike said.

Ditka related: "'Here's what I'm going to do,' he said. 'I'm going to give you a three-year contract.' Basically that was all that was said. 'I'm going to pay you $100,000 a year.'"

"I gotta escalate," Ditka said.

"What do you mean?" Halas exclaimed. He was on his home ground, negotiating with the former tight end he loved, a fire-eater at age 42, the prodigal, back from exile. The prodigal responded, "'It has to be more. You have to give me a 15 percent raise.' So, it went to 130, which was nothing, but it was an opportunity. We shook hands, did the contract, and bang—I was the Bear coach. I snuck into town and snuck out."

Ditka said, "I believe that Bears football is Halas football the way he taught us to play." He spoke in the urgent voice that would lead his team to six divisional titles, three NFC championship games, and the team's only Super Bowl title over the next 11 seasons. "It was always within the rules, but it was always to be the toughest guy on the block. That got hard when you went up against guys like Nitschke and those guys in Green Bay, and Marchetti and those guys down in Baltimore. The rivalries we created with those teams were based on respect, 'cause they respected us and we respected them. It wasn't a hatred thing or anything like that."

At the press conference on January 20, 1982, Gleason asked Halas if he had lapsed into senility. "He stood up and said, 'Bill, there's not one senile bone in this body!' Everybody got such a charge out of that." Also at that press conference, Halas stressed that his "game plan" was in place. That game plan involved much more than on-the-field happenings.

In 1980, the team's lease at Soldier Field was about to expire on the eve of the final preseason game, when Mayor Jane Byrne had a messenger drop off a contract renewal at 55 East Jackson after the close of business at city hall. Her cover letter told the Bears they had 24 hours to sign the contract or be evicted from the stadium.

She had a figurative gun pointed at Halas's head. "We were forced to sign a 20-year lease. We did that in Mayor Byrne's offices," Vainisi said. "One of the things we were able to extract was the right to build skyboxes and control them."

The Bears had to pay for construction, with all the risks. Once construction costs were amortized, the Bears would receive 80 percent of the revenues. The Park District would get 20 percent. "In conjunction with the skyboxes, Halas created 13 grandchild trusts: 11 McCaskeys and Mugs Halas's 2 children," Vainisi said of the contract that matched the will drawn up after Mugs's death.

The skybox money could not be realized until all the debt, some $2 million, was paid off, which it was within a few years. Virginia, as trustee after her father died, controlled any distributions, as she would with the estate at large. As the estate trustee, she had paid annual stipends to her children, all of whom are more than 40 years old. As of 2003, seven McCaskey children were either connected with or employed by the team.

The Bears' stadium lease arrangement with the Chicago Park District ran from 1980 through the 2001 season. "It was 12 percent of the gross plus $3,000, a nominal cleanup fee," Vainisi said. "Some teams pay 15 percent, but they get concessions, parking, stadium advertising revenues. We got no breaks. The Bears had the highest rent in the league. In 1985, our Super Bowl year, tickets were only $12.50. So, rent was a couple of million a year. Later, it was $400,000 to $500,000 a game for eight games, less for preseason, roughly $4 million in all."

Once he had redirected the football team, Halas confined himself to a tight circle of friends. "In later years after Ralph Brizzolara died, the guy who became his best friend in the last couple of years was probably Mike Notaro," Vainisi recalled. "He had a very small circle of "good" friends: Judge Marovitz certainly, Connor, Luckman, Kup—that was his group."

It would have been easy for Jim Finks to take his money and do nothing. That was not his way. He still ran the draft and, with personnel director Bill Tobin, set the table for the Super Bowl team. In 1980, he picked linebacker Otis Wilson in round one and fullback Matt Suhey in the second round. He drafted offensive right tackle Keith Van Horne first in 1981 and Singletary in the second round.

Ditka stepped forward in 1982 to take quarterback Jim McMahon in the first round, the first time since Bob Williams in 1951 that the Bears had gone for the glamour spot to lead off their selections. Negotiations got dicey when Halas suggested that the Bears should sign the Brigham Young bad boy at a discount because he was partially blind in one eye from a childhood accident. Vainisi smoothed out the problem. "Had Jim McMahon not gotten hurt in 1984 and again in 1986, I am convinced we would have won three straight Super Bowls. Whenever he played, we won. Period."

Vainisi explained, "I had this grading system regarding Jimmy Mac: If he was hurt but on the sidelines, and could play, the team played to a C level. The players figured he would come in and save the game. If he was hurt and not dressed, we played to a B level. The players knew they had to do it themselves. If he was hale and hearty, we were A. No way could we lose."

On April 26, 1983, and again the next day, Finks, Ditka, and Tobin pulled the greatest draft since Allen landed Butkus and Sayers for 1965. Seven men from that draft started on the 1985 Super Bowl team. In order of selection, they were offensive tackle Jim Covert, receiver Willie Gault, cornerback Mike Richardson, safety Dave Duerson, guard Tom Thayer, defensive end Richard Dent, and guard Mark Bortz. Finks signed everyone but Thayer, who already had signed with the Chicago USFL team. Vainisi brought him aboard in 1985 for the Super Bowl season.

Training camp was well under way when the fastest man in the draft, Willie Gault, of Tennessee, agreed to terms. Finks was unusually happy that afternoon as he cracked one-liners while he watched over the workout, especially his outstanding rookie class.

Just before he signed Gault, Finks still entertained ideas that he might acquire the unfilled presidency that Mugs promised but never executed. Ed and Virginia McCaskey hoped to use their oldest child, son Michael, as the lever.

Michael left for Yale in 1961 and had been gone ever since. He served in Ethiopia with the Peace Corps, earned his doctorate in business from Case Western Reserve University, and taught at UCLA and then Harvard. He maintained no connection to the team, because, until Mugs's death, it was not an issue. In 1982, when Virginia and Ed McCaskey knew the extent of Halas's illness, they told Michael, their eldest, that, as in royalty, he would be the successor.

Sources say that, among the McCaskey children, Halas felt closest to Tim, the second-oldest son, or Patrick, the third son. He definitely did not want Michael. The McCaskeys and Finks went to see Halas in February 1983. At that time, they hoped Halas would bring in Michael as an assistant general manager to learn the ropes. They wanted Finks to succeed Halas as president during a transition year and then elevate Michael to president. Halas rebuffed them.

That August, Virginia, Ed, and Finks made another run at the Old Man. He again rebuffed them but conceded that the club president must be a Halas family member. The Papa Bear let those around him know that he considered Michael an academic and not capable of handling the job. Halas reportedly said, "Anybody but Michael."

On August 24, the day after Finks signed Gault, Vainisi was preparing to leave the Loop for Lake Forest, when Halas called and asked him to stop by his apartment on the way. When he arrived, Halas tossed out a question. "Are you aware there's a press conference this afternoon at Halas Hall?" Vainisi said he heard about it as he was leaving the Loop.

"Do you know what it's about?"

"I know that we need a linebacker. I just figure we made a trade for one and are just announcing it."

"Did we make a trade for a linebacker?" the Old Man asked.

"No," Vainisi acknowledged. "I don't know what the press conference is about at all."

"You're not aware the press conference has been called because Jim is resigning?" Halas asked.

Vainisi was floored. "I had no idea."

"He called last night, and he told me he was resigning," Halas said firmly.

Vainisi recalled, "I had gone to his apartment thinking it was a routine call. He said, 'Prepare a statement from me accepting his resignation.' I wrote some words and read them back. As always, he tinkered with it a little bit. He was satisfied with the statement."

"Now, the next paragraph," Halas said. "Write a statement about the fact that I have named you the general manager to succeed him."

Vainisi was stunned. "I asked him if he talked to Virginia about it. He shook his head and then called Virginia, and he said he told her, 'I have my men in place: Jerry Vainisi and Mike Ditka.' Then we spoke," Vainisi said. His exact words to the founder of the Bears and NFL were, "I will do everything possible to make you proud and show the world that you have made the right decision."

"I know I have," the Old Man said.

"My old college roommate, a fellow named Phil Clark, said, 'I know you didn't know.' I had a blue seersucker suit on that day," Vainisi said. "You wouldn't have been dressed that way if you knew you were going to be doing all kinds of television interviews and stuff," Clark told him.

"I laughed about it, for it had been a routine day. Until then," Vainisi said. "I called Pat McCaskey, who was our PR guy at the time, and read the statement to him. 'Pat,' I said, 'have your father read this at the press conference.' Then I went up there. Even that day, when I met with Halas, I thought he was perfectly lucid."

Vainisi further recalled, "When he appointed me, he said he wanted me to work with Mike Ditka and get us to the Super Bowl. He said he knew we would work hard to accomplish that."

The new Ditka Bears set out to do just that, but they were still baby bruins, not fully matured grizzlies. They felt their way through a 3-and-5 first half of the schedule, beating the Eagles at Philadelphia 7–6 on October 23, the last exhilarating victory George Halas would see and feel to the fiber of his core.

After the explosive, franchise-shaking events of August 24 came the denouement for George Stanley Halas. He continued to issue orders from home until the middle of October. Then he was too ill to continue. The Papa Bear had lapsed into a coma the final weekend of the month and would not regain consciousness. Death came quietly at 8:27 on Monday night, October 31, Halloween. Ever the master of timing and the dramatic, the coach, a modernist to the end, would have been pleased to know that his passing gave the broadcast stations time to put together pieces with sound and pictures. Most vital for this last star of the *Front Page* era, he would get the ink he so greatly deserved in the morning press.

No one was more eloquent on November 1, 1983, than *Sun-Times* columnist Ray Sons, who expressed the mood of a city and football-crazy nation. "George Halas is dead, they say. It can't be. The Old Man is too tough to die." Halas, Sons wrote, not only dwarfed every other Chicago sports figure but also "ranks with Ruth, Thorpe, and Dempsey among the giants of sports in this nation." Finally, as Sons saw it, "He was the creator who breathed life into the sport."

The next morning, Sid Luckman told Sons, "Coach Halas was ahead of everybody else by 10 years. There was never anybody to compare with him." Luckman headed a list that started with Red

Grange, Bronko Nagurski, and George McAfee and ended with his two young operational heirs, Jerry Vainisi and Mike Ditka, who lauded Halas.

"He's been like a father to me," Vainisi told the *Sun-Times*' Kevin Lamb.

"George Halas was the driving force of the NFL," Ditka said to Lamb.

"I thought I was going to end my career with the Bears," George Allen told Brian Hewitt of the *Sun-Times*, regarding his formative years in Chicago with his mentor. "I loved the Bears," Etty Allen said, echoing her husband's sentiments.

After George Halas's death, the Bears began to show marked improvement on the field for the first time since he shocked the football world with his "takeover" of the team to reassert supreme authority. The turnaround came in late 1983 after Vainisi talked to the players for one of the few times in his tenure as general manager.

"Factions had evolved within the team. You had the Halas faction, the McCaskey faction, and the Finks faction," Vainisi said. "I told them, 'There are no factions on this team. You can't play one against the other. No one's ever going to be able to come to me and think they are going to circumvent Mike. And vice versa. What he knows, I'll know. What I know, he'll know. We have only one purpose in mind, and that's to win the Super Bowl and become as good a team as we possibly can be.' We did."

He noted, "Mike Singletary called me after that meeting that same morning and asked me to call his agent to extend his contract. He was going into his option year and wanted to be with us." Vainisi also told Ditka straight ahead to pull himself together and control a temper that was hurting team performance. Ditka listened and responded. It took Mike Ditka just one year after the Papa Bear's death to forge a team in his mentor's mold. By 1984, the name Chicago Bears once again generated respect and fear throughout the National Football League.

In early 1984, Ditka persuaded Vainisi to move the training camp to the Platteville campus of the University of Wisconsin. Seeing his players sail through a comparatively easy camp before family and friends at the home base of Lake Forest had made Iron Mike angry. Ditka wanted to restore the sense of togetherness and toughness the Old Man imparted under the blazing Hoosier sun, where the young Iron Mike and his teammates came back to Chicago hardened and tough, full of constant football, and ready to battle the National Football League.

Ditka loved everything about Platteville. Its remoteness in the moraines of southwestern Wisconsin where the closest towns of any size were tame Galena, Illinois, and Dubuque, Iowa, would allow Iron Mike and his coaches to pound football into their minions night and day. Temptation was little problem in Platteville. The alluring babes were back in Chicago. Yet, a two-block strip of bars five minutes away from campus offered brief escapes from camp confinement for the players to enjoy a couple of cold beers between the evening classroom sessions and the 11:00 curfew.

It worked. The team broke camp with a chip-on-the-shoulder defiance that bred supreme confidence and the swagger that marked every Chicago Bear who endured a Halas training camp. Ditka's bunch carried that "Bear attitude" as far as the throne-room door in a bravado 1984 season.

In October, Walter Payton surpassed Jim Brown as the top ground gainer in league history. The Ditka Bears, in the Halas mold, ran the ball down opponents' throats with the league's top rushing attack. When they didn't run, the exciting and efficient McMahon passed and led them to a 7-and-3 record and leadership in the NFC Central Division.

On November 4, 1984, the Bears staged a bravura performance for a national television audience on NBC and its top announcers, Dick Enberg and Merlin Olsen. The Bears regained what Ditka deemed their rightful place as the league tough guys when they literally beat up and shoved aside the Los Angeles Raiders 17–6. Ditka called it the hardest-played football game in five years. The Raiders, who loved to boast that they took what they wanted, were taken to the woodshed.

The Bears didn't emerge from the combat unscathed, though. They had to finish the season without their leader, quarterback Jim McMahon, who suffered a lacerated kidney when he got sandwiched between Raiders linemen Howie Long and Bill Pickel. Ditka regrouped his Bears as quarterback after quarterback was forced to the sideline. Finally, with a late pickup of USFL refugee and ex-Lion Greg Landry, the wounded Bears battled to the NFL Central title with a 10-and-6 record. Todd Bell's textbook tackle that flattened the Redskins' Joe Washington set the tone for a smashing 23–19 playoff victory as the Bears advanced to their first NFC championship game at San Francisco.

During that week before the playoff, Michael McCaskey called an impromptu press conference after a workout to announce he was extending Mike Ditka's contract. The contract Ditka had signed with George Halas was in its third and last year, and Vainisi had been after the team president for months to do something about it. At $130,000, Ditka was easily the lowest-paid head coach in the league. "He deserved a raise, of course," Vainisi said in a 2004 conversation. "That was a given. I felt the head coach needed that extension as a vote of confidence, and he needed to be positioned as the boss, not, as Buddy Ryan saw himself, as co–head coach."

McCaskey had sat on the Ditka extension throughout the summer and fall of the successful '84 season that saw the Bears rejoin the league elite. "Mike Ditka came to me in midseason and told me he didn't want to talk about it anymore," Vainisi said. "One day, when we were in the Bay Area practicing for the 49ers, Michael announced the extension out of the blue." Ditka went to Vainisi when he heard the news. "Did you know about this?" he asked his friend and contractual boss. "That was the first I heard about it," Vainisi told Ditka.

They had to get ready for a football game. After the season, Ditka signed the extension that "raised his salary up to, or at least close to, the league standard," according to Vainisi.

"I'll never forget Butkus," Jerry Vainisi said. "We were having dinner in San Francisco the night before the NFC championship at a long table that included Ditka and other friends. In time, everybody left except Dick and me. We moved into the bar." Alumni relations had deteriorated in recent years until Ditka and Vainisi made it clear to all the old Halas Bears, Dick Butkus included, how much they were wanted and needed. "Jerry," the man Halas called the greatest Bear of all, said, "thank you for making us proud to be Bears again."

The 49ers shut out the Bears 26–0, but the pride that motivated Butkus and his fellow alumni was back. They vowed to march into that throne room in 1985 and take it all—crown, mace, and scepter—despite the penurious policies of team president Michael McCaskey, who offered previews of coming attractions.

In the off-season, when star safety Bell and linebacker Al Harris refused to accept the team's final offer, Michael McCaskey called their bluffs and let them sit out the 1985 season. "I have no oil wells," McCaskey cracked in a not-too-subtle reference to his grandfather, a man who always kept a sharp eye out for gushers in the ground and on gridirons.

The young team president stood fast, well aware that Vainisi's people had lined up two men of at least equal quality to Bell and Harris in safety Dave Duerson and linebacker Wilber Marshall. In 1985, he pulled it off, but he could not allay an irate Buddy Ryan, who called Bell the key to the "46" and maintained his fury even after the Bears leveled the league with an 18-and-1 record.

The 1985 Bears broke from the blocks and never let up in a magnificent display of all-around excellence, both on offense with McMahon and Payton, and on the most dominant, if not downright scary, defense ever. By midseason, the fear factor took over as Ryan's lethal "46" cut a devastating swath through the league—foremost, a 44–0 shutout of America's Team, the Dallas Cowboys.

They weren't America's Team, but these Bears became the most popular team across the country in merchandise sales—and far-and-away the biggest television attraction. Ditka made a star out of 320-pound rookie defensive tackle William "the Refrigerator" Perry. When he put the Fridge in the backfield in a Monday-night game with the Packers and the Fridge plunged for a touchdown, he became an instant folk hero and an endorsement magnet worth millions. They had the gall to record "The Super Bowl Shuffle" song and video, and make it stand up.

McMahon mocked the NFL fashion police, ignoring the rules when he wore a white headband with "Adidas" embossed across the front. Commissioner Rozelle fined him. In the divisional playoff on January 4, 1986, in near-zero cold that Ditka proudly called "Bear weather," McMahon joshed the commissioner when he hand-printed "Rozelle" on his headband. In the main event, the Bears smashed the Giants 21–0 as Dent threw Phil Simms to the rocklike Soldier Field turf with three and a half sacks.

A week later against the Rams, McMahon sported a headband to promote his support for treatment of juvenile diabetes. The defense was overpowering again. The Bears pitched a 24–0 shutout to earn the Super Bowl trip, with an apt ending as Wilber Marshall grabbed a fumble and sprinted for the final touchdown. At that instant, snow flurries began to fall. Many in the crowd, sober or not, entertained a notion that it was the spirit of Halas.

The McCaskeys almost fumbled an issue during Super Bowl Week in New Orleans, which Vainisi smoothed over. "At the Super Bowl, I wanted to set aside a block of tickets for former Bears players. The McCaskeys wouldn't allow it," Vainisi said. "They said the tickets were so scarce, we couldn't do that." The father and son also did not want to invite the retired players to the team's postgame party. Holding back tickets for his Raiders alumni was standard procedure for Al Davis, as it had been for the Dallas Cowboys and was for Halas in his lifetime.

"Ed," Vainisi said to the elder McCaskey, "how can you do that?" An embarrassed chairman McCaskey relented in the ticket matter. Yet, neither he nor president Michael would open up the postgame party. "You know what's going to happen?" Vainisi said. "Every guy who ever even put on a jersey for a day will walk up to you and say, 'Ed, can you help me get a couple of tickets?' Then he'll ask, 'Can I come to the postgame party?' You won't be able to say, 'No!' Then, what happens? 'Nah, nah, nah,' Ed said, 'it's a private party.'"

Vainisi had been prescient: "Sure enough, two days before the game, Ed and Michael came to me. 'We have a problem,' Michael said.'"

Vainisi answered, "What's that?"

"Former players," Ed said.

"They want to come to the party, and we need to open it up for them," Michael said.

Vainisi said in 2003, "I wanted to take a football and stuff it up his you know what. Then I took a breath and told him, 'Let's figure out what we can do.' It broke down our entire security," Vainisi lamented. "We had a guy the McCaskeys knew forever who recognized all the old players. I think he was a clubhouse guy on game days. So, they stationed him out by the front desk, and he would identify the players. A couple hundred tickets were set aside for the party, and they could get a pair. This guy was supposed to say who could get party tickets and who could not. All they had to do was give them the tickets before they came out, and it would have been all done. Instead, the whole security thing just collapsed."

In Super Bowl XX itself, McMahon was superb and the defense was at its absolute best as 41,490,000 viewers on NBC watched the Bears complete their magnificent season with a 46–10 plastering of New England. The only clinker of a sour note was sounded late, when Ditka inserted William "the Refrigerator" Perry on offense by the goal line and ordered McMahon to give him the ball. Denying a bit of glory to Payton, who had given his all to the franchise for so many years, deeply hurt Payton's pride, as it angered virtually all of his teammates.

Yet, when it was over, the gleeful players carried Ditka and Ryan off the field in triumph. At the postgame party, Alicia Duerson approached Ryan and thanked him for all he had done to make her husband a better player. "He wouldn't have played a minute for me if Todd Bell had been here," Ryan snapped. He turned on his heels and left Alicia shaking her head at his rudeness.

When the team returned to Chicago from New Orleans, Ryan moved on to Philadelphia to become the Eagles' head coach. Ditka said nothing about the departure and afterward was especially testy whenever Ryan's name was mentioned in his presence.

This was no short-term spat. Halas's handpicked leaders barely spoke back in 1985. Some who were there at the time say they exchanged swings that may or may not have connected at halftime of a Monday-nighter in Miami, when Ditka criticized Ryan for assigning linebacker Marshall to cover Miami's outstanding wide receiver Nat Moore. The speedy Moore scorched Marshall all night as Dan

Marino's passes to Moore and the "Marks Brothers," Clayton and Duper, led the Dolphins to a 38–24 victory to end the perfect-season dream. For sure, no tears were shed at Halas Hall when Ryan left town.

Michael McCaskey had not interfered with Vainisi or Ditka in 1984, nor in early 1985. But, late that season, without Jim Finks around to remind him to own, McCaskey began to meddle. He came to the sidelines late in games. Then he started to come down earlier, cheering big plays. The players noticed. They didn't like it then, and they never got over it when he took the victory stand in the Loop in bitter cold, brandished the Vince Lombardi Trophy, and yelled the fans' "Woof, woof" cheer into the microphone.

Rating the Bears strictly on performance, *The Sporting News* named Michael McCaskey Executive of the Year. Someone might have asked the players.

OVERTIME

Not Sudden Death!

*T*he long descent began precisely at the moment of triumph on January 26, 1986, at Super Bowl XX. The first off-season issue that cried for settlement was Ditka's contract, one that also would affect general manager Jerry Vainisi. "I kept asking Michael to extend Ditka's contract," Vainisi said. "I drafted it when Finks was still there. It was specific that Ditka reported to the president [still Halas], not the GM. When I took over, it was written that I would have complete authority over the entire team."

No sooner had the Bears taken their arctic bus ride down LaSalle Street to celebrate their triumph, than Buddy Ryan hustled out of town for his head coaching job in Philadelphia. The night before the Super Bowl, when Ryan told his unit he was leaving for the Eagles, he told them, "You are my heroes." They responded in kind the next day against the overwhelmed Patriots. Fans were just as upset when they heard the "46" mastermind was leaving.

"In fact," Vainisi said in 2004, "Ryan was entering the last year of his contract in 1985, and I was not going to renew him. He caused too much trouble, and Mike Ditka was the man here, not Ryan."

Vainisi, with Ditka's endorsement, had a ready-to-go replacement waiting most of that championship season. "In the fall of 1985, we decided to bring in Bill Tobin's brother Vince the next season." Vain-

493

isi said. "I must stress that Bill did not come to us and urge us to hire his brother." Vince Tobin had been under contract as Jim Mora's defensive coordinator with Philadelphia of the USFL. The league folded after its spring-summer season ended in '85, and Vince was a free agent.

"We brought Vince to Lake Forest in '85 to handle some quality-control matters; actually, that was done to let him look over our defense and personnel," Vainisi admitted. "He wanted to run the three-four he used in the USFL. Then he saw what we had at training camp and stayed with the four-three."

Flashing his large, diamond-studded championship ring, Mike Ditka was the toast of pro football and, with his new contract, absolute boss on the field. The Coach, as he loved to be called with a capital *T* and *C*, reveled in a busy off-season that saw him make millions as he cashed in on the Super Bowl triumph. The week after the victory, he filmed an American Express commercial at Brookfield Zoo by the polar bear exhibit. The sponsor was crazy about Ditka as the endorser, and suddenly, so was Madison Avenue.

Ditka was not close to being the highest-paid coach, but no other coach came close to raking in the endorsement dollars. He bagged endorsement after endorsement, to the extent that a local clothier, Gallagher's outfitted him from head to toe. All he had to do in return was appear in full regalia on the sidelines, making him the first coach in years to work a game dressed to kill, not in polyester.

That fall, he fronted a restaurant, Ditka's, with its companion nightclub City Lights, in the trendy River North area. The restaurant was the hottest place in town until his manager Jimmy Rittenberg ran it into the ground and forced its closure.

When the Bears returned to Platteville in July 1986, the players retained their chip-on-the-shoulder attitude, but much of that was directed toward management—namely Ditka, who grabbed so many endorsements, and McCaskey, whom they perceived as an ungrateful glory hound. The only joyful moment that summer of '86 came when Matt Suhey arrived in Platteville at the wheel of Walter Payton's huge camper. Walter himself arrived late that afternoon aboard a helicopter that landed at the end of one of the practice fields. Dressed in shorts, tight T-shirt, and low-cuts, Payton stepped onto the field and signaled a backup quarterback to grab a ball. "Sweetness" took off at full speed, motioned for a pass, and caught it in stride 50 yards away, *behind* his back. He was ready.

That was one of the few bright moments in camp, especially for Payton. He still burned over Ditka's Super Bowl call that denied him a sure touchdown to end the game when he ordered McMahon to give to Perry instead. The grumbling started in earnest when the players heard that the league wanted to administer a drug test without warning. Many stormed player rep Mike Singletary and demanded he stop it. With Ditka's help, Singletary bought enough time for those who might have taken a recent recreational hit to pass drug traces through their systems. Nobody tested positive for cocaine.

The only two players who truly cleaned up on endorsements were Perry and McMahon. At camp, it was obvious to the naked eye that the Fridge had been raiding his home icebox all winter and spring. He looked closer to 400 than 300 and was extremely touchy about references to his heftiness. Early in camp, when an NBC crew from Chicago photographed Perry after practice as he stood chest-deep in a massive plastic trash can filled with ice water, the angry Fridge tried in vain to squirt the cameraman. That shot was dropped into channel 5 sportscasts throughout the season and for years to come.

McMahon carried an obvious beer gut and was not meshing at all with Ditka. Thanks to his deft collaborator, the *Chicago Tribune*'s witty columnist Bob Verdi, McMahon's name headed an autobiography that peeled the hide off McCaskey and the veneer off the Super Bowl season. Accusing his boss of everything from being the lucky beneficiary of his family name to draining the life from the club, the punky QB cast down the gauntlet: "Michael McCaskey might think we won because of him; he'd be offended to know we won in spite of him."

McMahon's teammates knew he had signed his exit visa. When he would depart was the question. The indecisive McCaskey would keep McMahon around until 1989 when his market value had dropped after he'd suffered multiple injuries. By then, many other of the Super Bowl Bears had hit the road, to be replaced by inferior players.

The party was more than over in 1986. The thrill was gone, and so was the fun that characterized the colorful team. Virginia McCaskey initiated the clunky descent into drabness late in the Super Bowl season when she ordered Michael to disband the Honey Bears, the popular dancing group that had injected life and charm into time-outs and halftimes since 1975.

Reflecting her parochial schooling, Virginia took a prudish view of the peppy young women who waved orange and blue pom-poms and were uniformed in white vests, short white skirts, high white boots, and navy blue long-sleeved shirts. The Honey Bears, each of whom earned every penny of her $15-a-game salary, certainly were tame by comparison with such other NFL units as the famed Dallas Cowboys Cheerleaders, the Rams' Embraceable Ewes, or the Denver Broncos' Pony Express. True to form, Michael ordered Vainisi to deliver the unpleasant tidings.

Similar to her late brother, who would not give pendants to the bachelor players in 1963 in dread that the jewelry would show up on "Rush Street floozies," Virginia thought the Honey Bears looked and acted cheap. And her word was law at Halas Hall.

In due course, she did away with a superfan named Rocky, who cheered along the sidelines, and also axed a man who wore the Bear costume. In 2003, the club introduced a cartoonish bear mascot, "Staley," named for the sponsor that Virginia's father so hurriedly scrapped in 1922 when he took A. E. Staley's money and ran home to Chicago.

The demise of the Honey Bears was the prelude to a 1986 season that became a soap opera in 17 episodes: 16 regular-season games and one miserable playoff defeat that ended with the biggest franchise loss since the departure of George Allen, Halas's trusted administrator, and general manager, Jerry Vainisi.

Operationally, Ditka, now in complete control and with far more important matters to address, could not get Buddy Ryan out of his head. The Coach was determined to erase every trace of his former intramural rival, to the detriment of the team. Under Vince Tobin, the 1986 defense was performing at an even higher level than it did under Ryan. Unlike the flamboyant and bordering-on-reckless Ryan,

Tobin played it close to his vest with a "bend, don't break" style. He employed the fan-pleasing "46" only on a limited basis or when necessary late in the game when the team needed big plays. Ditka backed him all the way.

But, by decree of The Coach, the "46" didn't even exist—in name, at least. In Ditka newspeak, the "46" became the "Bear Defense." He had taken away the pressure-filled attack weapon that had made the Bears the most feared defensive unit the game had ever seen, with the possible exception of Pittsburgh's "Steel Curtain" Super Bowl teams.

In one sense, Ditka was as bullheaded as his mentor. In another sense, he had cut off his nose to spite his face, out of a kidlike case of jealousy toward a man who might have been irascible but whose concepts made him a winner. Since Ryan had doubled as linebackers coach, Ditka had to hire another assistant. He found an excellent one in Dave McGinnis, who would stay with the team for the next 11 seasons. Two other newcomers to Ditka's staff were defensive line coach John Levra and quarterback coach Greg Landry.

Virtually every 1986 game became a high-wire act as the team would muddle through three quarters and then pull out victory in the end over lesser opponents on sheer talent. The only time the Bears resembled the '85 team was at Cincinnati against the AFC-leading Bengals, when McMahon led a 44–7 destruction. "As good as we were, we wouldn't have won without McMahon," Mike Ditka said. "When it came to the game, he played it like a warrior. He didn't give a shit about certain people, but he cared about his offensive linemen. He took them to dinner. He expected his receivers to catch the ball when he threw it to 'em."

McMahon's shoulder ached and got worse with each pass he threw and every hit he absorbed. He had to take painkilling shots, and his availability each week was in doubt. Steve Fuller, the 1985 backup, also was hurting, and Ditka and the third quarterback, Mike Tomczak, had all the rapport of Halas and Blanda.

In mid-October, Ditka convinced Vainisi to go after 1984 Heisman winner Doug Flutie. Flutie had signed an $8 million contract to play for Donald Trump's New Jersey Generals in the winter-spring U.S.

Football League, which folded after the 1986 season. Flutie's NFL rights belonged to the Los Angeles Rams, but he wasn't playing, just collecting Trump's nearly $4 million in guaranteed money.

The appraisal on Flutie drew a split decision among the management and scouts. McCaskey sided with personnel director Bill Tobin, who honored a line of thinking that the 5′9″ Flutie was too short to see over the heads of NFL linemen. Ditka and Vainisi, on the other hand, believed Flutie was a miracle worker, a big winner. Ditka and Vainisi won out, but Vainisi expended much political capital in the process. "It may appear to some that I compromised my position to back Ditka," Vainisi said. "I don't think I ever did. I always felt I did what had to be done at the time to keep us focused and keep the team together."

On October 14, despite the antagonism of his boss and Tobin, Vainisi went ahead and grabbed Flutie. "Doug cost us a conditional sixth-round pick, that would escalate based on playing time and performance," Vainisi said. The trade rocked the fragile egos on the tension-filled team. Flutie seemed even smaller than advertised and, at this midseason juncture, found it impossible to crack the front that the team built around McMahon. Ditka countered by taking Flutie home for Thanksgiving dinner, a point not lost on the team, Jimmy Mac's many allies, and McMahon himself.

McMahon's season ended on November 23 in a 12–10 victory over the Packers when Green Bay's Charles Martin picked him up from behind after he threw a pass and slammed him to the Soldier Field artificial surface. Later that week in Los Angeles, Dr. Frank Jobe repaired a torn rotator cuff in McMahon's right shoulder, enabling him to stay in the league long enough to win a second ring at Green Bay while observing Brett Favre from the bench.

Back from Los Angeles and with his arm in a sling, McMahon stood on the sidelines like a wounded gunslinger back from the showdown on Front Street, in big black (of course) hat, jeans, and leather jacket under the sling. To reporters, he minced no words about his jealousy toward Flutie, who had done nothing more than go to work each day. Ditka started Flutie against Tampa Bay, and he led the Bears to a 48–14 win. The little man again led the Bears to victory over Detroit in the finale.

The final gun had barely sounded when the press and the man who signed the paychecks blamed Flutie for the Bears' 27–13 playoff loss to the Washington Redskins on January 3, 1986. Flutie completed only 11 of 31 passes, for just 134 yards. The Bears were hanging on to a 13–7 lead when Flutie tried to make a big play. Darrell Green stepped in with an interception that set up Jay Schroeder's 23-yard touchdown pass to Art Monk, to put the Redskins up to stay. Hope turned to despair when the Bears went for the tying touchdown and Payton took a whack on a sore shoulder and fumbled away, it turned out, the season.

Vainisi sensed trouble when he reported for work the following Tuesday and was called into Michael McCaskey's office, where Ed sat in witness. "He said he had five counts against me at the time that he fired me," Vainisi said. "He claimed that I lied to him about a fan club, which was untrue. 'Michael, I'll go to my grave telling you I didn't lie to you,' I said. The Flutie trade was supposedly one of my crimes, for a sixth-round pick that bumped up to a third. Ultimately, Pete Rozelle stepped in, and I won on all points." And he got the deferred money due him.

"That should never have happened," Mike Ditka said. "Why did it happen? It's jealousy to the 100th degree. It's a tragic case of small people not understanding what it takes to be a winner, to build an organization and to win. I told McCaskey, 'It's the biggest mistake you ever made when you got rid of Jerry.'"

Vainisi moved to Detroit, where he served as general manager of the Lions until 1990. He ran NFL Europe until 1995 and then returned to Chicago and assumed the presidency of his Forest Park Bank and Trust Company and practiced law. And he saw the team he loved trickle down a drain clogged with pettiness and incompetence.

The Bears opened the 1987 season in a Monday-night game with a resounding statement as they hammered the defending champion Giants 34–19. The players' union walked out two weeks later in a strike that lasted five weeks. The teams carried on with replacement players and continued to play before small crowds and minuscule television audiences.

Ditka took it upon himself to rip the regulars and called his replacements the "real Bears." "He lost the team when they returned," said Vainisi, who wasn't there to counsel his friend when he needed him most. The regulars retaliated with labor's ugliest word, *scabs*. The scars lingered for years.

Payton hoped to gain another Super Bowl ring as a retirement present after the 1987 season. Instead, his 13 years as perhaps football's greatest all-around player ended in a burst of emotion, as he sat in tears alone on the bench at Soldier Field after a 21–14 Bears defeat to the Redskins, the eventual Super Bowl champions. The team was fraying around the edges.

McCaskey became his own general manager without title. Unable to take decisive steps, the 1985 Executive of the Year demonstrated why that award was a hollow tribute to his grandfather. McCaskey graphically displayed his lack of football knowledge. Off the field, he showed his lack of the street smarts required to gain a desperately needed stadium.

He raised the fans' ire when he made no appreciable effort to keep his fastest and most dangerous offensive threat, receiver Willie Gault, and the most electric defender in the league, linebacker Wilber Marshall. Their replacements were adequate but not championship-caliber players. The '85 veterans sensed they'd been had. His make-do approach that compromised talent for budget considerations caught up at home in the bitter cold of so-called Bear weather on January 8, 1989. Bill Walsh's 49ers, led by Joe Montana and Jerry Rice and with better support talent than Ditka could summon, crushed the Bears 28–3.

The growl was gone, and the Bears were sliding slowly out of contention. They fell to 6-and-10 in 1989. They rebounded with a final NFC Central title in 1990 but lost five games in the process, ending in a 31–3 loss to the eventual Super Bowl champion Giants at the Meadowlands. They came back to finish second in the division in 1991, but they lost the playoff opener at home to Jimmy Johnson's rising Dallas Cowboys. While the Cowboys won the first of three

Super Bowls in the next four years, the Bears began the slide into the depths.

By 1992, McCaskey painted a mentally drained Ditka into a corner and, finally, let him go to make way for the "hot" assistant he wanted. He was the Cowboys' Super Bowl defensive coordinator, Dave Wannstedt. McCaskey outbid the Giants for Wannstedt by giving him control over personnel.

"I don't live in the past. I never have," Ditka said late in 2002. "Whether I think it was fair or not that I was let go, that Jerry was let go—it doesn't matter. You just go on and deal with life as best you can."

Ditka returned to coaching for three years with the New Orleans Saints before returning to Chicago to devote time to his restaurant Mike Ditka's Grill, talk football on radio and television, play golf and gin rummy by the hour, and peddle virtually every product known to humankind. The longer he was out of coaching, the more popular Ditka became in Chicago, bigger than ever before, the living symbol of the Halas Bears.

With both Vainisi and Ditka gone, McCaskey was free to operate with his own man, Wannstedt. Unfortunately, he could not exorcise their memories nor accomplishments. Bears fans would not forget them, nor would they forget Halas, despite the McCaskey attempts to eradicate his memory.

Concerning the new coach, the fans immediately realized that, unlike Ditka, who lived and breathed the Bears tradition, Wannstedt, in his first head coaching job, was tone-deaf to the unique nuances of the Bears, Chicago, and the loyal fans who had been raised on Halas football. The faithful nearly crucified Wannstedt when he called the Packers rivalry just another game. In Wannstedt's defense, many of his problems might have been averted had his boss clued him in. But that would have assumed that Michael McCaskey, who lacked a grasp of Bears history and its meaning, not just past scores and records, was not clueless.

The fans cut Wannstedt some slack in 1993 when the Bears beat the Packers 35–30 on December 5, 1993, to go 7-and-5. Then Wannstedt lost them when they finished with 4 straight defeats.

Donning his personnel hat in the off-season, Wannstedt trimmed Super Bowl MVP Dent, Steve McMichael, Keith Van Horne, and McCaskey's former protégé, quarterback Jim Harbaugh. Wannstedt teased the fans with a playoff appearance in 1994 and then dug his own grave before the 1995 season when he proclaimed that "all the pieces are in place."

The Bears led the Central Division at the halfway point in 1995 with a 6-and-2 record. Bill Cowher's young Pittsburgh Steelers, of the AFC, marched into Soldier Field and escaped with a 37–34 win in overtime. The upward-bound Steelers charged all the way to the Super Bowl. The Bears went on to lose 4 of the next 5 games. Wins in the last two weeks provided a cosmetic 9-and-7 record, too late and too little to make the playoffs. In a move he never explained, McCaskey further infuriated the fans when he blithely extended Wannstedt's contract into 2001. Then his coach cut the last Super Bowl Bear, placekicker Kevin Butler.

The 1996 Bears went 7-and-9 and followed with back-to-back 4-and-12 seasons. By the end of 1997, Wannstedt's stay in Chicago was doomed, thanks to the worst trade in team history when he gave Seattle the Bears' top pick for psychologically fragile quarterback Rick Mirer. The hopeless Mirer was cashiered when he threw no touchdown passes in limited work. The team had descended back into the pre-Finks abyss.

On December 28, 1998, McCaskey reluctantly fired Wannstedt. At that moment, the meter started ticking around the league as other teams also launched coaching searches. McCaskey reacted to the crisis by leaving town to go skiing.

Michael McCaskey's cavalier behavior with the coaching situation was only the latest in a series of head-scratching moves, most of which had concerned the stadium difficulties. George Halas was forced to leave Wrigley Field when Pete Rozelle decreed that after 1970, no team could play its home games in a stadium with a capacity below 50,000. That left unhospitable, but larger, Soldier Field. The Bears made a one-game deal in 1970 with the Evanston city council and Northwestern to play at the University's Dyche Stadium. They beat the Eagles 20–16 but lost their lease opportunities forever when stadium neighbors complained loud and long to the university and council about drunken fans urinating on, vomiting on, and otherwise trashing their property.

Until 1971, the Bears had played their final exhibition, the annual Armed Forces game, at Soldier Field. The lakefront arena not only was the worst stadium in the league but also might have been the worst ever used for football. Two-thirds of the seats were situated behind the goal lines. The low-angle sight lines were terrible. What passed for plumbing was primitive in a facility that had virtually no washrooms, especially for women. In the early 1970s, the Chicago Park District, the nominal stadium landlord, had to bring in carpenters to shore up the seating areas, lest they collapse under the weight of a crowd.

To his credit, Michael McCaskey recognized the problem that he inherited from his grandfather. In trying to find a solution, though, he wandered into a political thicket that destroyed his credibility. Unfortunately, he carried an academic trait, annoying his listeners as he conducted public tutorials on the stadium problem. As he thought aloud in public, Michael McCaskey so infuriated Richard M. Daley that the mayor refused to take his calls.

McCaskey then talked about building a stadium in Arlington Heights on a corner of the vast acreage at Arlington Park racetrack, nearly 30 miles from the Loop. Daley chided McCaskey, wondering if he planned to call the team the Arlington Heights Bears.

The chortling turned to outright laughter when McCaskey talked up the virtues of a toxic-waste dump in northwest Indiana. This place lay off the Indiana Toll Road, within nose-shot of the Calumet region's aromatic steel mills and oil refineries. It was a good hour to hour and a half away from his Chicago base.

McCaskey's nadir came when he unveiled a West Side stadium plan that encroached on property owned by William Wirtz, Chicago Stadium's power broker. Shortly after that plan was announced, Jerry Vainisi, long gone from the Bears but always deeply respected throughout the business and sporting community, was passing the time at a hockey game in a Chicago Stadium luxury box when Blackhawks executive vice president Bob Pulford stopped by. Pulford said

Wirtz wanted to see him as soon as possible in his personal room off the main floor for a drink and a chat.

After the first sip, the furious Wirtz unloaded. McCaskey, he complained, had tried to "steal" his land. He'd committed the unpardonable sin of not bothering to inform Wirtz or Jerry Reinsdorf, owner of the Bulls, his Chicago Stadium tenant, of what he hoped to do. In addition, Wirtz said, McCaskey had tried to end-run both them and Mayor Daley by going directly to Illinois governor Jim Edgar. In their meeting, McCaskey asked the governor to have the state condemn that Wirtz-owned vacant land for him.

When Edgar, of course, reported that conversation to Wirtz, one of his major political donors, the mogul went ballistic. Within months, Wirtz and Reinsdorf unveiled their joint plan to build what became the United Center on Wirtz's vacant land across the street from the stadium. The political reality of Chicago and Illinois had crashed on his head with a resounding thud, leaving Michael McCaskey without any choice but Soldier Field. And something had to be done before the dilapidated dump came crashing down. McCaskey sought out architects.

This was the McCaskeys' second encounter with people close to Reinsdorf. When Finks was forced to sell his stock before joining the New Orleans Saints, the McCaskeys balked at his terms. Finks approached Gene Fanning, a prominent luxury auto dealer and major investor with Reinsdorf in the White Sox and Bulls. When Fanning made a bona fide offer for Finks's stock, Vainisi advised the McCaskeys to exercise their right of first refusal and match it, which they did to avoid the presence of a Reinsdorf ally in their midst.

The McCaskeys initially were upset with their old friend Finks, failing to understand that he was making a business arrangement. Time salved any hard feelings, though, and in 1995 when Finks was elected posthumously to the Pro Football Hall of Fame, his presenter was none other than Ed McCaskey.

By 1990, after draining Mugs's inheritance that had been earmarked for her children, Terry Halas was forced to sell her children's stake in the team to pay her considerable legal fees. Had they bought out Terry, the McCaskeys would have had to pay Mugs's estate tax. Fearing that payment of the estate tax plus buying Mugs's stock would cut too deeply into their cash resources, they made a deal with two prominent Chicago businessmen. Insurance baron Pat Ryan bought 19 percent of the team, and sportsman Andy McKenna picked up another unit. Ryan and McKenna paid the tax and gained minority seats on the board of directors—apparently, though, without right of first refusal in case of a McCaskey sale. Jerry Vainisi questioned the McCaskeys' wisdom in selling to Ryan and McKenna. Why they didn't buy it themselves is "mind-boggling," he said.

Mind-boggling is also the only apt description of Michael's slipshod coaching search to replace Wannstedt. By the time he returned from his skiing vacation in January 1999, McCaskey had squandered any opportunity to tap the A-list of available candidates. By then, 169 of the best and brightest coaching minds in the National Football League already had been hired for head coaching and assistant positions.

McCaskey had to settle for a reduced pool of candidates, which he quickly cut to a short list of five names, all current NFL assistants. That meant his new coach would be forced to dip into the dregs for his own staff. One of McCaskey's targets was Jacksonville defensive coordinator Dick Jauron. Another was Wannstedt's former offensive backfield coach, Joe Pendry. Had Michael forgone his skiing trip, at the worst, he could have interviewed Mike Holmgren's talented top assistant in Green Bay, Andy Reid. The Eagles hired Reid as coach and executive vice president on January 11, 1999. He twice has won Coach of the Year honors.

McCaskey thought he was still carrying a four-leaf clover in his back pocket with his preferred candidate. That man was the popular linebackers coach for Ditka and Wannstedt, Dave McGinnis. McGinnis, a solid football man who was media savvy as well as a McCaskey family favorite during his 11 years at Halas Hall, bridged all camps. He had left the Bears in 1997 to become defensive coordinator for the Arizona Cardinals under his old boss in Chicago, Vince Tobin.

When McGinnis interviewed with McCaskey on Thursday, January 21, he told the president that he would hire the most innovative offensive mind in the league, Mike Martz, then at Washington. When McCaskey made an offer that evening, McGinnis asked if he could take a night to consider it. McCaskey then alerted his public relations department to call a 1:00 Friday news conference to announce the hiring. Unfortunately, he repeated that 1984 maneuver when he then announced Ditka's extension without first informing him. Again, this time, he did not bother to tell the subject what he had done, all the worse given that the prospective coach had not agreed to a contract. When McGinnis heard what was up, he exploded. McGinnis, who had publicly called the Bears position his dream job, was a man of integrity. He considered this McCaskey maneuver an attempt to low-ball him on money.

The news conference was pushed back all that day and then rescheduled for Saturday. McGinnis then told the McCaskeys he would not work for anyone who treated him the way Michael did. Even a pleading Ed could not make him reconsider.

By the time McGinnis and his wife arrived at O'Hare on Saturday to board a Phoenix-bound plane, McCaskey was introducing his second choice, fellow Yale alum Dick Jauron, as the 12th coach in Chicago Bears history.

McGinnis replaced Vince Tobin as Arizona head coach in 2000 and stayed until he was fired after the 2003 campaign. Martz, his would-be offensive coordinator, took the same job with Dick Vermeil in 1999 in St. Louis, where he unleashed the most explosive attack since Halas and Shaughnessy unveiled the modern T, as onetime grocery bagger Kurt Warner passed the Rams to the NFL title. When Vermeil quit after that Super Bowl, Martz replaced him. In 2001, Martz hired Lovie Smith from Tampa Bay as defensive coordinator. Martz's wide-open attack and Smith's attacking defense led the Rams to Super Bowl XXXVI, where they lost 20–17 to the New England Patriots on a game-ending Adam Vinatieri field goal.

After the McGinnis fiasco, the Bears and the McCaskeys, especially Michael, a glib individual who, in the words of one source, "tried to intimidate us with his knowledge, which underscored the fact that he could not communicate with people," again became the laughing-stock of football. The laughter ceased on February 2 when Walter Payton revealed he was suffering from a rare autoimmune disease called primary scolerosing cholangitis. The disease had so aggressively attacked his liver that he needed an immediate transplant to survive. It advanced so fast that, by midspring, all Payton could do was wait for the end. He died peacefully at home on November 1. The NFL's all-time rushing leader before Emmitt Smith surpassed him in 2002 was just 45.

A few days after the shock cleared, the McCaskeys again took center stage. On February 10, Virginia Halas McCaskey stepped to the Halas Hall podium before a mob of reporters and clusters of television and radio microphones. She made the difficult announcement that she had fired her son Michael as president and demoted him to the ceremonial title of chairman. To make room for Michael, she placed her husband, Ed, on emeritus status.

As Michael stood behind her, his mother introduced his replacement as president and designated leader in the effort to make a stadium deal. He was longtime family loyalist and vice president of administration Ted Phillips. Phillips was the first non–family member to hold the presidency. From the standpoint of a stadium deal, she stressed that only Phillips would conduct business with Mayor Daley. Michael's new duties, some wags suggested, meant he was chief gardener and groundskeeper at the team's sumptuous new Halas Hall II facility in west Lake Forest. No other move was possible because the mayor refused to talk to Michael McCaskey. The team desperately needed that stadium deal.

Michael was forced to take a major salary hit, from the $800,000 he made as president to $300,000 as chairman. As an incentive, the board of directors, namely his mother and father, awarded Michael a $200,000 bonus before Christmas 2000.

The team also had to convince the taxpayers and politicians of the urgency of passing the legislation before the NFL's $100 million loan offer ended. This was a ruse. They imposed an artificial deadline. In fact, the league wanted to get the Bears into a new stadium, and the money was there in 1999, as it would have been in 2002 or even later.

Once Phillips brought Mayor Daley aboard, the key man to gaining legislative approval was former governor James Thompson. Thompson was a veteran of stadium maneuvers, having pulled Jerry Reinsdorf's new Comiskey Park deal through the Springfield minefield in 1988. Phillips executed flawlessly. The agreeable state legislature cinched the deal in 2000. The Bears agreed to put up $200 million of the necessary $606 million (before the $49 million overrun, which they agreed in 2003 to pay). That burden was considerably eased when the league came through with a $100 million "forgiven" loan covering 15 years.

If the McCaskeys maintained control of the franchise for that amount of time, through 2018, they would not have to pay back a cent of that loan. If they sold, however, the buyers would be forced to repay the entire loan amount to the league. The feeling persisted that if they decide to sell, a buyer would willingly pick up the extra $100 million for the privilege of gaining control of a franchise that, with its new stadium, ranked in value at the top with New York and Washington.

"The Chicago franchise is the most valuable in the league," Vainisi insisted. "New York's market is shared between the Giants and Jets. L.A.'s problem is its climate. The most attractive teams there are USC and UCLA. The climate and the beaches are distractions from football interest."

When the Bears tried to sell naming rights, the mayor got his city council to rise in righteous indignation to prevent what would be considered a desecration of the war memorial. A "Doughboy" statue to honor the original intent of the stadium—to commemorate the fallen of World War I—was commissioned and unveiled before the rededication game with the Packers on September 29, 2003.

To ensure municipal operational control, Daley appointed the experienced and politically connected Tim LeFevour as stadium manager. The appointment particularly irked the McCaskeys, who had fired LeFevour from a similar position several years before.

The biggest break for the McCaskeys came in 2001 when the Bears turned around after a decade of disrepute on the field, with a team that not only went 13-and-3 and made the playoffs but also earned Coach of the Year honors for Jauron. That success enabled Phillips and George McCaskey, the family's designated ticket manager, to put the arm on season ticket holders in 2002 and the first nine months of 2003 while the stadium was undergoing construction.

The Detroit Lions did not force their ticket holders to buy personal seat licenses when they opened Ford Field in 2002. The Bears, however, followed the lead of the Dallas Cowboys, who started the PSL scheme when they opened Texas Stadium in 1971. Phillips and

George McCaskey charged upward of $10,000 for the PSL privilege, highest in the league, just to buy tickets at $315 per game in new Soldier Field. In their zealous drive to sell PSLs, they pushed around many long-standing ticket holders, taking some seats away altogether. One who lost her seats was Nancie Gallarneau, widow of 1940s-era star Hugh Gallarneau.

They were relentless, if not ruthless. They reminded their PSL holders that failure to buy season tickets would result in forfeiture of the licence and the money they paid for it. They also pushed them into buying before a deadline or face loss of potential season ticket rights. After all that pushing, prodding, bullying, and goading, they sold almost every designated PSL and other non-PSL tickets as season packages.

The Bears were fortunate they had made the major ticket push in 2002 before the team flopped back into its uncomfortable post-Ditka losing ways. They went 4-and-12, and cries for Jauron's ouster rose anew as the Bears opened the 2003 season with a trio of losses.

Besides tripping over the tickets, the McCaskeys stepped into another public relations mess that they had all the power in the world to avoid. Instead of honoring George Halas with a statue, as the Packers had done for Lambeau and Lombardi when they remodeled their stadium, the Bears did nothing for their patron.

For $655 million, Chicago got a massive facility replete with underground garages, berms, tiers that stretched up and away 151 feet to the structure's top on the west side, and luxury boxes behind green-tinted glass on the east side. The whole thing was squeezed inside the now puny-looking colonnades that lent the old stadium its classic look. The *New York Times* applauded, while the hometown *Chicago Tribune* bestowed raspberries by the barrelful.

Writing in the September 30, 2003, *New York Times*, Herbert Muschamp, an unfettered modernist, awarded high marks to architects Ben Wood, of Chicago, and Carlos Zapata, of Boston, for a major breakthrough, proclaiming that "their liberation of sports advanced architecture from sports architects" and calling their creation "easily a match for the most advanced stadium design in the world."

Pulitzer Prize–winning *Chicago Tribune* architecture critic Blair Kamin was at his caustic best when he wrote in the September 21,

2003, Sunday edition, "The bulbous West Grandstand weighed down as heavily on the 'once proud' columns as if Bear Super Bowl hero William 'Refrigerator' Perry had plunked down his ample haunches on a picket fence." Further, Kamin wrote, "compared with the old Soldier Field, which was long on tradition and short on amenities, the new field was a pigskin palace, a big poke in the eye," and its placement on the lakefront "inexcusable."

Coincidental with the reopening were the first public appearances of Michael McCaskey after his five years of exile. He consented to a general interview with the *Tribune*'s Don Pierson and was spotted in nonspeaking roles at alumni events and on the field before the game, a 38–23 loss to the Packers and Bret Favre. That defeat, the 19th in the last 22 games against Green Bay, pared the Bears' longtime series dominance to just eight wins, the smallest margin since 1944. In an informal conversation at the alumni dinner, Michael McCaskey said he was extremely pleased with the stadium, but he acknowledged, "We need victories."

At the end of the season, Virginia McCaskey announced a new, lucrative deal for Ted Phillips. She was pleased with the way he was running the team. Michael would not be coming back to resume command, contrary to what had been rumored for months. Phillips, in turn, awarded Jerry Angelo a new title, vice president and general manager, and absolute control over coaching and player personnel.

Angelo immediately fired McCaskey family favorite Jauron, signaling the beginning of a new regime. His first stop in a coaching search was Baton Rouge, Louisiana, where he tried to lure his longtime friend Nick Saban to Chicago and back to the pros. Saban, who sat in the catbird seat as coach of LSU's national cochampion football team, wanted control over player personnel. Angelo was not about to give that up. So, they shook hands and parted amicably.

Angelo talked to three other college coaches and then turned to the pros. He brought two NFL assistants to Lake Forest for interviews: Pittsburgh Steelers line coach Russ Grimm and St. Louis Rams defensive coordinator Lovie Smith, a hot candidate around the league since his 2001 success with the Rams.

On January 14, 2004, Angelo introduced Lovie Smith as the 13th head coach in the 85-year history of the Chicago Bears and the first

African American to follow in the legend and tradition of George Halas. Angelo had known Smith since they worked at Tampa Bay—Angelo in personnel and Smith with the defense.

Smith promised a brand of football that Chicago fans had not seen since Mike Ditka's departure in 1992. He would employ an attacking, aggressive defense and, to run it, one of Ditka's favorite players, Ron Rivera, most recently linebackers coach with the Eagles. He entrusted the offense to Terry O'Shea, Dick Vermeil's quarterbacks coach in Kansas City. O'Shea would build the attack around second-year quarterback Rex Grossman, who watched and waited through 13 games during his rookie season before Jauron cut him loose at Soldier Field, where he led the Bears to wins over the Vikings and Redskins. In those late-season appearances, Grossman reminded many old-timers of Halas's iconic Sid Luckman.

Smith ordered his players, especially overweight linemen, to take off weight. He wanted speed and toughness. Lean, mean players being another Halas trait, the Old Man might have liked the way Smith approached matters of football.

Halas's McCaskey heirs still had not seen fit to evoke his name, but his legacy was everywhere, not just in the stadium on the lakefront. Thanks to the television deals George Halas advocated and his sound fiscal practices, the league he founded in 1920 along with his team had become so vigorous that *Business Week* called it in a January 28, 2003, cover story "the NFL Machine."

Halas had no way of knowing that his league would take in $4.8 *billion* in 2002 and be able to share 63 percent of that money equally with the league's 32 franchises. Accordingly, the Bears were able to spend as much as $83 million on player salaries, and they had to spend *at least* $72.5 million.

The trick was, as it always had been, knowing *how* to spend that money effectively. The Bears had done a poor job of talent evaluation since McCaskey fired the superb Vainisi, who combined studied football knowledge with acute business sense.

As much as George Halas loved money, and let there be no doubt that he did, his legacy was his team and his league and the secular religion of pro football. But he could not control the future—only hope for the best. His heirs after Mugs demonstrated an unfitness to own and operate the club in his image, and the same held true for the rest of the league.

Both team and league had become soulless money machines, down to selling a sponsorship for the national anthem, as the McCaskey Bears did with Boeing to reopen Soldier Field. Too many people choose to ignore that the games are played by large men to entertain other people. Halas knew that football stadiums are supposed to be like Lambeau Field, in the city of the rival he loved so much, where everything is built around a game and the success of Green Bay's beloved Packers. To Halas, the playground was not meant to be a gladiatorial arena for the wealthy where the average guy who built and supported the league was priced out of existence, and gigantic telescreens with bells and whistles and slick graphics were more important than the product on the field.

Rather, it was the common touch that Halas had and retained to the end. Reporter Ed Stone, like so many other men who crossed swords with George Halas, saw many unique qualities that made him stand apart from the crowd. Unlike an icy Paul Brown or forbidding Vince Lombardi, Halas was totally approachable.

"When you called the Bear office, maybe 5:00 in the afternoon, he answered the phone. Like Old Man Wrigley or Bill Veeck," Stone said. "He had a lot of the common man in him, which he was. Here was a neighborhood guy. So, there was no pretension about him."

Despite all he endured with George Halas ("Sometimes I loved him. Sometimes I hated him"), Harlon Hill never could break the bond: "Like the old saying, 'Once a Bear, always a Bear.' I'm a Bear to this day. The Monsters of the Midway get in your blood. The reflection of the Bears starting with Coach Halas is still there. It was initiated by him, and it was so forceful that it's never gotten away."

BIBLIOGRAPHY

Interview Subjects

Bruce Allen Tampa Bay Buccaneers general manager, youngest son of George Allen

Etty Allen Widow of George Allen

Jennifer Allen Daughter of George Allen

Doug Atkins Hall of Fame defensive end 1955–66

George Blanda Hall of Fame quarterback/kicker 1949–58

Charles Brizzolara Son of Ralph Brizzolara

Doug Buffone Outside linebacker 1966–79

Rick Casares Fullback 1955–63

George Connor Hall of Fame tackle/linebacker 1948–55

Chet Coppock Sportscaster and largest Bears season ticket holder

Rudy Custer Bears business manager 1947–83

Art Daley *Green Bay Press-Gazette* sports editor, retired

Mike Ditka Hall of Fame tight end 1961–72, head coach 1982–93

Jim Dooley End 1952–59, head coach 1968–72

Peter Gent Dallas Cowboys end 1964–68, author

Mark Giangreco ABC-TV Chicago, sportscaster

Bill Gleason *Chicago American* and *Sun-Times* sportswriter, retired

Patricia Halas Widow of Mugs Halas

Harlon Hill Wide receiver 1954–62

Paul Hornung Green Bay Packers Hall of Fame halfback
    1957–66

Joe Horrigan Pro Football Hall of Fame curator, Canton, Ohio

Lamar Hunt Kansas City Chiefs owner

Bill Jauss *Chicago Daily News, American,* and *Tribune*
    sportswriter

Stan Jones Hall of Fame guard/defensive tackle 1954–65

Ann Kakasek Daughter of Jim McMillen

Ken Kavanaugh End 1940–50

Ralph Kurek Fullback/special teams 1965–70

George Langford *Chicago Tribune* sports editor, retired

Wayne Larrivee Bears announcer 1985–98, Green Bay Packers
    announcer since 1999

John Lujack Quarterback 1948–51

Chuck Mather Assistant coach 1958–65

George McAfee Hall of Fame halfback 1940–50

Jocelynne McCall Daughter of Phyllis McCall, secretary to
    Mugs Halas

Patrick McCaskey Grandson of George Halas

Jeannie Morris Former wife of Johnny Morris, author,
    sportscaster

Johnny Morris Wide receiver 1958–67, NBC/CBS TV
    sportscaster 1968–95

Larry Morris Outside linebacker 1959–65

Lester Munson *Sports Illustrated* associate editor/legal reporter

Ed O'Bradovich Defensive end 1962–71

Bill Orr Target Marketing president, Wayne, Pennsylvania

Betty Osmanski Widow of Bill Osmanski, Halas neighbor

Don Pierson *Chicago Tribune* pro football writer

Jim Purnell Linebacker 1964–68

Mike Pyle Center 1961–70, NFLPA president 1967–68

Lee Remmel Sportswriter and Green Bay Packers executive since
    1944

Andy Robustelli Los Angeles Rams/New York Giants Hall of
Fame defensive end 1951–64
Cooper Rollow *Chicago Tribune* sports editor, retired
Daniel M. Rooney Pittsburgh Steelers owner
Barry Rozner Arlington Heights *Daily Herald* sportswriter
Andy Russell Pittsburgh Steelers linebacker 1963–76
Gale Sayers Hall of Fame running back 1965–71
Ray Sons *Chicago Sun-Times* sportswriter, retired
Ed Sprinkle Defensive end 1944–55
Ed Stone *Chicago American* and *Tribune* reporter, retired
Pat Summerall CBS-TV and Fox sportscaster, retired
Jerry Vainisi Controller, general manager 1983–87
Bill Wade Quarterback 1961–66
Tom Ward Son of Arch Ward, *Chicago Tribune* sports editor
1930–55
Don Weiss Former NFL executive director
Joanna Williams Widow of Fred Williams

Books

Allen, George, with Ben Olan. *Pro and College Football's 50
Greatest Games*. New York: Bobbs-Merrill, 1983.

Allen, Jennifer. *Fifth Quarter*. New York: Random House, 2000.

Anderson, Heartley, with Emil Klosinski. *Notre Dame, Chicago
Bears, and Hunk*. Oviedo, FL: Sun-Gator Publishing, 1976.

Asinof, Eliot. *Eight Men Out*. New York: Holt and Rhinehart,
1963.

Barber, Red. *The Broadcasters*. New York: Dial Press, 1970.

Butkus, Dick, and Pat Smith. *Butkus: Flesh and Blood*. New York:
Doubleday, 1997.

Butkus, Dick, and Robert W. Billings. *Stop Action*. New York: E. P.
Dutton, 1972.

Carroll, Bob, Michael Gershman, David Neft, John Thorn, eds. *Total Football II: The Official Encyclopedia of the National Football League.* New York: HarperCollins, 1999.

Carroll, John M. *Red Grange and the Rise of Modern American Football.* Champaign, IL: University of Illinois Press, 1999.

Cope, Myron. *The Game That Was.* New York: The World Co., 1970.

Daley, Arthur. *Pro Football's Hall of Fame.* Chicago: Quadrangle Books, 1963.

D'Amato, Gary, and Cliff Christl. *Mudbaths and Bloodbaths: The Inside Story of the Bears-Packers Rivalry.* Madison, WI: Prairie Oak Press, 1997.

Danzig, Allison. *Oh, How They Played That Game.* New York: MacMillan, 1971.

Dent, Jim. *Monster of the Midway: Bronko Nagurski, the 1943 Chicago Bears, and the Greatest Comeback Ever.* Dallas: Thomas Dunne Books, 2003.

Ditka, Mike, with Don Pierson. *Ditka: An Autobiography.* Chicago: Bonus Books, 1986.

Fink, John, and Francis Coughlin. *WGN: A Pictoral History.* Chicago: WGN, 1961.

Grange, Red, and Ira Morton. *The Galloping Ghost: The Autobiography of Red Grange.* Wheaton, IL: Crossroads Communications, 1953.

Griffin, Woodson Jack. *Grif.* Matteson, IL: Great Lakes Living Press, 1977.

Halas, George S., with Gwen Morgan and Arthur Vesey. *Halas by Halas: The Autobiography of George Halas.* New York: McGraw-Hill, 1979.

Hamlin, Rick. *Tournament of Roses: A 100-Year Celebration.* New York: McGraw-Hill, 1988.

Harris, David. *The League: Rise and Decline of the NFL*. New York: Bantam Books, 1986.

Hayner, Don, and Thom McNamee. *The Chicago Almanac*. Chicago: Bonus Books, 1991.

Howard, Robert P. *Illinois: A History of the Prairie State*. Grand Rapids, MI: William B. Erdmans Publishing, 1972.

Izenberg, Jerry. *Championship: The Complete NFL Title Story*. New York: Scholastic Book Services, 1968.

Keteyian, Armen. *Ditka: Monster of the Midway*. New York: Pocket Books, 1992.

Maraniss, David. *When Pride Still Mattered: A Life of Vince Lombardi*. New York: Simon & Schuster, 1999.

Maule, Hamilton B. *The Game: Official History of the National Football League (revised ed)*. New York: Random House, 1964.

McCallum, John D. *Big Ten Football Since 1895*. Radnor, PA: Chilton Book Company, 1976.

McCaskey, Michael B. *Executive Challenge, Managing Change and Ambiguity*. Mansfield, MA: Pitman Publishing, 1982.

McCaskey, Patrick. *George Halas*. Lake Forest, IL: Author, 2003.

McMahon, Jim, with Bob Verdi. *McMahon!* New York: Warner Books, 1986.

McPhaul, John J. *Deadlines & Monkeyshines: The Fabled World of Chicago Journalism*. Englewood Cliffs, NJ: Prentice-Hall, 1962.

Miller, Jeff. *Going Long: The Wild, 10-Year Saga of the Renegade American Football League in the Words of Those Who Lived It*. New York: McGraw-Hill, 2003.

Mullen, Peter. *Chicago Bears Trivia*. Boston: Quinlan Press, 1987.

National Football League. *75 Seasons: The Complete Story of the National Football League, 1920–1995*. Atlanta: Turner Publishing, 1994.

Peterson, Robert W. *Pigskin: The Early Years of Pro Football*. New York: Oxford University Press, 1997.

Pope, Edwin. *Football's Greatest Coaches*. Atlanta: Tupper and Love, 1955.

Rice, Grantland. *Tumult and the Shouting*. A. S. Barnes & Company, 1954.

Richards, Gregory B., and Melissa H. Larson. *Big-10 Football*. Greenwich, CT: Bison Books, 1987.

Rollow, Cooper. *Cooper Rollow's Bears Football Book*. Ottawa, IL: Jameson Books, 1985.

Shaughnessy, Clark, Ralph Jones, and George Halas. *The Modern T-Formation with Man in Motion*. Chicago: Author, 1941.

Twombly, Wells. *Blanda: Alive and Kicking*. Los Angeles: Nash Publishing, 1972.

Vass, George. *George Halas and the Chicago Bears*. Chicago: Henry Regnery, 1971.

Ward, Arch. *Frank Leahy and the Fighting Irish: The Story of Notre Dame Football*. New York: G. P. Putnam's Sons, 1944.

Whittingham, Richard. *Bears in Their Own Words: Chicago Bear Greats Talk About the Team, the Game, The Coaches, and the Times of Their Lives*. New York: McGraw-Hill, 1992.

———. *The Bears: 75-Year Celebration*. Dallas: Taylor Publishing, 1994.

———. *The Chicago Bears: An Illustrated History*. Chicago: Rand McNally, 1979.

———. *What a Game They Played*. New York: Harper & Row, 1984.

Ziemba, Joe. *When Football Was Football: The History of the Chicago Cardinals.* Chicago: Triumph Books, 2000.

Articles

Borden, Jeff. "A Bear Market for McCaskey's Stadium Play." *Crain's Chicago Business*, April 17, 1995.

Boss, Bill. "Leahy Gives Lowdown on T-Formation Plans." *Notre Dame Scholastic*, March 27, 1942.

———. "Meet the Notre Dame Coaching Staff." *Notre Dame Scholastic*, Sept. 18, 1942.

———. "Sparkling Material Fitted to a 'T.'" *Notre Dame Scholastic*, March 6, 1942.

Brown, Paul, with Bill Fay. "I Watch the Quarterback." *Collier's*, Oct. 28, 1955.

Cahill, Joseph B. "Financing for Gary Stadium Not a Snap." *Crain's Chicago Business*, Nov. 29, 1995.

Deford, Frank. "I Don't Date Any Woman Under 48." *Sports Illustrated*, Dec. 5, 1977.

Eig, Jonathan. "Sacked!" *Chicago Magazine*, Sep. 1999.

Fay, Bill. "Meanest Man in Football." *Collier's*, Nov. 25, 1950.

———. "Touchdown Target." *Collier's*, Nov. 25, 1955.

Frazier, George. "A Monster of the Midway." *Boston Herald*, Dec. 29, 1963.

Furlong, William Barry. "How the War in France Changed Football Forever." *Smithsonian Magazine*, Feb. 1986.

———. "The Last Puritan." *Sports Illustrated*, Jan. 31, 1966.

Hewitt, Bill, as told to Red Smith. "Don't Send My Boy to Halas." *Saturday Evening Post*, Oct. 1944.

McCloy, Robert. "Fear and Loathing in Papa Bear's Den." *Chicago Magazine*, June 1987.

"The NFL Machine." *Business Week*, Jan. 27, 2003.

Snyder, David. "Time for Ryan, McKenna to Bear Down on the McCaskeys." *Crain's Chicago Business*, Feb. 1, 1999.

Strahler, Steven R. "Political Pressure Will Revive McDome." *Crain's Chicago Business*, April 17, 1995.

Internet

Grosshandler, Stan. "All-America Football Conference." Professional Football Researchers Association (PFRA), footballresearch.com.

Newspapers, Periodicals, Research Sources

Boston Herald (Courtesy Boston Public Library)

Chicago American

Chicago Daily News

Chicago Herald-American

Chicago Public Library

Chicago Sun

Chicago Sun-Times

Chicago Times

Chicago Today

Chicago Tribune

Evanston, Illinois, Public Library

New York Times

Northwestern University Library

Pro Football Hall of Fame; Joe Horgan, Director of Public
Relations

University of Notre Dame, Hesburgh Library; Charles Lamb,
Curator

INDEX